The Conduct of
Soviet Foreign Policy

The Conduct of
Soviet Foreign Policy

edited by

Erik P. Hoffmann
State University of New York at Albany

Frederic J. Fleron, Jr.
State University of New York at Buffalo

Aldine·Atherton   *Chicago·New York*

ABOUT THE EDITORS

ERIK P. HOFFMANN teaches at the Graduate School of Public Affairs, State University of New York at Albany. He has contributed numerous articles to scholarly journals and books.

FREDERIC J. FLERON, JR. teaches at the State University of New York at Buffalo. He is the editor of *Communist Studies and the Social Sciences: Essays on Methodology and Empirical Theory* and has contributed numerous articles to scholarly journals and books.

First published 1971 by
Aldine · Atherton, Inc.
529 South Wabash Avenue
Chicago, Illinois 60605

Library of Congress Catalog Card Number 70-140008

ISBN 202-24024-X, cloth; 202-24025-8, paper

Printed in the United States of America

To Our Students

Contents

Contents

Introduction

More and more American college students are studying Soviet foreign policy. Courses in this field are plentiful, and student interest is high. But teachers of these courses must cope with several problems: (1) primary source materials are relatively scarce; (2) accessible documents are not easily interpreted by expert and novice alike; (3) Western scholars have produced relatively few monographs and analytical essays in the field; (4) the best of these essays are widely scattered throughout many scholarly journals; and (5) almost none of this literature is closely linked to the broader field of international relations.

The first of these problems is particularly difficult to cope with. Some very basic facts about Soviet intentions and activities are not known. Memoir literature is virtually nonexistent, and candid interviews with Soviet foreign affairs officials are not common. New information about Soviet behavior is sometimes gleaned from Western archives, from the statements and actions of foreign officials (Communist and non-Communist) who have dealt with their Russian counterparts, and from the observable activities of Soviet representatives abroad. But the college student, even if he reads Russian, does not have access to key sources of information that facilitate the study of Soviet domestic politics. Central Committee decrees, for example, almost never deal with the USSR's international affairs. Not surprisingly, there is much more public communication between Communist Party leaders and domestic audiences than between Party leaders and Soviet personnel abroad.

The second problem is more serious than commonly recognized. Through the *World Marxist Review, International Affairs*, or *The Current Digest of the Soviet Press*, the college student gains access to selected "primary" source materials. Many of these are purposeful attempts to influence individuals and groups in other Communist and non-Communist countries. But what do these documents reveal: Official Soviet policy? Policy alternatives under consideration? Actual Soviet behavior? Desired events? Moreover, how does one distinguish among these and other possibilities? How does one determine the purposes, or "propaganda goals," of statements in the Soviet press? How does one ascertain "to *what extent*, and in *what manner, which* statements emanating from *which* sources are credibly representative of the international relations perspectives of *which* persons or identifiable groups"?[1] These are just a few of the methodological questions confronting the student of Soviet foreign policy. Valuable Soviet documents have been compiled, but problems of interpretation persist.

The small number of detailed studies on Soviet foreign policy is more understandable in this light. Fortunately, Western and Soviet scholars are devoting more attention to this subject, and several major textbooks and monographs have appeared in recent years. But many excellent interpretative essays have not reached the wide audience they deserve. In fact, of the two distinguished anthologies on Soviet foreign policy, one (Alexander Dallin, ed., *Soviet Conduct in World Affairs*, New York, Columbia University Press, 1960) is now out of print; and the other (Ivo Lederer, ed., *Russian Foreign Policy: Essays in Historical Perspective*, New Haven, Yale University Press, 1962) compares Tsarist policies with Soviet behavior prior to 1960.

The essays in the present collection focus on contemporary Soviet foreign policy. Like the Dallin and Lederer anthologies, this collection is intended primarily for classroom use. Our main purpose is to stimulate discussion and thought, not to defend a particular position or point of view. Indeed, we have carefully selected studies that present alternative viewpoints and that have stimulated lively, often heated, discussion in our own classes. In the past, we have had to rely on the unsatisfactory arrangement of library reserve shelves to make these valuable articles available to our students. A few relevant articles are readily accessible in the Bobbs-Merrill Reprint Series and hence have been omitted from our collection.[2] By reprinting the articles below in a single volume, we hope to disseminate more widely some key literature on Soviet international behavior. We feel these are some of the most thought-provoking

1. William Zimmerman, *Soviet Perspectives on International Relations, 1956–1967* (Princeton: Princeton University Press, 1969), p. 12 (italics in original).
2. For example, Daniel Bell, "Ten Theories in Search of Reality," *World Politics*, X, 3 (April, 1958), pp. 327–365; Historicus (George Morgan), "Stalin on Revolution," *Foreign Affairs*, XXVII, 2 (January, 1949), pp. 175–213; X (George F. Kennan), "The Sources of Soviet Conduct," *Foreign Affairs*, XXV, 4 (July, 1947), pp. 566–582.

and informative essays on Soviet foreign policy to have appeared in recent years.

The structure of this anthology and the introductions to each section are a modest effort to link the study of Soviet foreign policy with the broader field of international relations. Our main purpose is to examine the internal and external factors that shape Soviet policy and behavior. After a brief section on methodology, each section focuses on the effect of a single factor (or set of similar factors) on Soviet actions. Soviet policy and behavior are the dependent variables in every chapter. The independent variables — domestic Soviet politics, ideology, Western diplomacy, developments in the Third World — vary from section to section. In other words, each section examines the influence of a different set of factors on Soviet decisions and behavior. Above all, we are interested in analyzing the forces that shape Soviet international behavior; we are not directly concerned with the effects of Soviet foreign policy on Soviet domestic politics or on the behavior of other Communist and non-Communist countries.

Our set of factors is by no means complete. We could easily have included a chapter on the impact of geography, economics, or changing weapons tech nology on Soviet policy. And we could certainly have included a chapter on developments in the international Communist movement — particularly the changing role of Communist China and its important effects on Soviet behavior. (One important article on world Communism is included in this volume — see Joseph R. Starobin, "Origins of the Cold War: The Communist Dimension," Chapter 16 below.)

Given limitations of space, we have chosen to examine some factors and relationships in detail, rather than attempt to be exhaustive and spread ourselves too thin. What we sacrifice in scope, we gain in depth. The space limitation was dictated by price considerations. We are well aware that part of the increasing financial burden on students is the skyrocketing cost of textbooks. Therefore, we felt obliged to keep the price a reasonable one for a supplementary text, while not compromising the intellectual integrity and pedagogical utility of the anthology.

Our decision concerning which factors to emphasize and which to ignore was considerably influenced by the nature of the available textbooks on Soviet foreign policy that this anthology would most likely be used to supplement. We tried to take into consideration the strengths and weaknesses of recent textbooks, especially the two which we use in our own courses: *Expansion and Coexistence: The History of Soviet Foreign Policy, 1917-67* by Adam B. Ulam and *Soviet Foreign Policy* by Jan Triska and David Finley. In order to avoid repetition and fill gaps, we de-emphasized subjects they emphasize (for example, international Communism, international law, international organization, foreign policy elites, policy-making institutions) and stressed subjects they do not (for example, ideology, the origins of the Cold War, and competitive coexistence).

Articles in the same section present several different viewpoints. In Part III, "Communist Ideology, Belief Systems, and Soviet Foreign Policy," for example, some writers argue that Soviet ideology has a great impact on foreign policy behavior, while others contend that this factor has little influence under most conditions. By juxtaposing different arguments on the same subject, many of them classic statements of their respective positions, one can more easily compare and evaluate the logical and empirical evidence presented and the conclusions reached. It is precisely this kind of critical analysis we hope to encourage.

PART I

The Study of
Soviet Foreign Policy

Soviet foreign policy is a field in which "theories" abound. A survey of the literature in 1956 identified at least eight prevalent theories, each purporting to have found the main factor that influences and "explains" Soviet foreign policy behavior (for example, Marxist political philosophy, Great Russian imperialism, bureaucratic tyranny, Byzantine traditions, national defense, Eurasian environmental characteristics, the urge to the sea, Russian national character).[1] A recent review of the literature again reveals many diverse theories that focus on four major themes: the impact of ideology, "Soviet nationhood," history, and geography on the foreign policy of the USSR.[2]

Most of these theories contend that one or more factors are especially important determinants of Soviet behavior in all or most situations. Implicit are generalizations to the effect that certain factors consistently influence Russian actions more than others. Reference to these factors, it is claimed, will always or usually provide the best possible explanation of Soviet policies and performance. Critics reply that there is little empirical evidence to support the

1. William Glaser, "Theories of Soviet Foreign Policy: A Classification of the Literature," *World Affairs Quarterly*, XXVII, 2 (July, 1956), pp. 128-152. See also Daniel Bell, "Ten Theories in Search of Reality," *World Politics*, X, 3 (April, 1958), pp. 327-365.
2. Richard Brody and John Vesecky, "Soviet Openness to Changing Situations: A Critical Evaluation of Certain Hypotheses About Soviet Foreign Policy Behavior," in Jan Triska (ed.), *Communist Party-States: Comparative and International Studies* (Indianapolis: Bobbs-Merrill, 1969), pp. 353–385. See also William Welch, *American Images of Soviet Foreign Policy* (New Haven: Yale University Press, 1970). This important analysis of numerous American theories of

sweeping generalizations contained in most existing theories, that certain Russian political, economic, and environmental characteristics may or may not influence Soviet behavior generally or in specific cases, and that factors may vary in relative importance in different situations. Yet broad generalizations — verified, unverified, and unverifiable — are integral parts of past and present theories of Soviet foreign policy.

Different theories affect not only one's perception of the *facts,* but also one's assumptions about which *facts* are *factors* (i. e., relevant variables). One's theoretical orientation, whether consciously or unconsciously held, significantly affects the form, nature, and quality of one's explanations. Indeed, some philosophers argue that "One theory cannot be understood literally as fitting *the facts* better than another because each, in a significant sense, carries with it its own facts and observation reports. . . . To adopt a theory is ultimately to change one's observational framework, and this means more than one's perspective on a basically unchanging reality; it means, in one degree or another, to accept a new reality."[3]

A recent discussion of conceptual models and the study of foreign policy illuminates these ideas. A "rational policy" model, an "organizational process" model, and a "bureaucratic politics" model are outlined.[4] Each has its own basic unit of analysis, organizing concepts, dominant inference patterns, and general and specific propositions.

The "rational policy" model is the most widely used by students of international relations and Soviet foreign policy.[5] It assumes that national governments act purposefully and respond in a calculating manner to perceived problems. However, if one accepts the view that conceptual models do not order "reality" but create it, one must seriously consider alternative paradigms. Students of Soviet foreign policy may find the "organizational process" and "bureaucratic politics" models particularly appealing, because they directly challenge the view that the USSR is a "totalitarian" or "monolithic" state.[6] They also focus attention on the implementation of policy, not merely

Soviet foreign policy came to hand after the present work went to press, and hence the views presented therein unfortunately could not be incorporated into our discussion.

3. John G. Gunnell, "The Idea of the Conceptual Framework: A Philosophical Critique," *Journal of Comparative Administration,* I, 2 (August, 1969), p. 165. On the controversial subject of the nature and functions of theories and models, see, for example, Abraham Kaplan, *The Conduct of Inquiry* (San Francisco: Chandler, 1964).

4. Graham Allison, "Conceptual Models and the Cuban Missile Crisis," *American Political Science Review,* LXIII, 3 (September, 1969), pp. 689-718. See also James Rosenau, "Foreign Policy as Adaptive Behavior: Some Preliminary Notes for a Theoretical Model," *Comparative Politics,* II, 3 (April, 1970), pp. 365-387; and K. J. Holsti, "National Role Conceptions in the Study of Foreign Policy," *International Studies Quarterly,* XIV, 3 (September, 1970), pp. 233-309.

5. For example, see Hans Morgenthau, *Politics Among Nations* (4th ed.; New York: Knopf, 1967); Joseph Frankel, *The Making of Foreign Policy* (London: Oxford University Press, 1963); and Arnold Horelick and Myron Rush, *Strategic Power and Soviet Foreign Policy* (Chicago: University of Chicago Press, 1966).

6. See Carl Linden, *Khrushchev and the Soviet Leadership, 1957–1964* (Baltimore: The Johns Hopkins Press, 1966); and Michel Tatu, *Power in the Kremlin from Khrushchev to Kosygin*

on the decisions made by Soviet leaders. In short, alternative modes of analysis contain different assumptions and often produce very different explanations (for example, of the Cuban missile crisis).

An important question to ask is, "Which theories and models best help one to explain and understand what one wants to know about Soviet foreign policy behavior?" One's approach to the subject will shape both the questions one asks and the answers one finds. The "rational policy" model, for example, relies heavily on the "motive-belief" pattern of explanation. Explanation of this kind "consists of showing what goal the government was pursuing in committing the act and how this action was a reasonable choice, given the nation's objectives."[7] However, it is very difficult to ascertain the motives and beliefs of Soviet decision-makers in general and in specific instances. Perhaps the easiest task is to document the views of an individual Party leader on a single issue at a given moment in time. But even this may require considerable "Kremlinological" insight and skillful use of content analysis.[8] Furthermore, the relationships between beliefs and behavior pose formidable research problems in all of the social sciences. They present especially great problems in the study of international relations, where much available data are contained in highly manipulative communications and reliable and significant information are often lacking.

Knowledge of many factors that *may* influence Soviet behavior is important to the student of Soviet foreign policy. The conceptual framework depicted in Figure 1 suggests numerous possible influences. "All foreign policy systems," it is argued, "comprise a set of components which can be classified in three general categories, inputs, process, and outputs. The notion of flow and dynamic movement in a system which is constantly absorbing demands and channelling them into a policy machine which transforms these inputs into decisions and outputs is portrayed [below]."[9]

The creators of this framework emphasize that foreign policy decision-makers act in accordance with their perceptions of reality. "Underlying this research design is the view that the operational environment affects the results or outcomes of decisions directly but influences the choice among policy

(New York: Viking Press, 1969).

7. Allison, *op. cit.,* p. 693.

8. See Frederic J. Fleron, Jr., "Introduction," and Erik P. Hoffmann, "Methodological Problems of Kremlinology," in Frederic J. Fleron, Jr. (ed.), *Communist Studies and the Social Sciences: Essays on Methodology and Empirical Theory* (Chicago: Rand McNally, 1969), pp. 1 – 33, 129 – 149. Also see Alexander George, *Propaganda Analysis* (Evanston, Illinois: Row, Peterson & Company, 1959).

9. For elaboration of this research design and statement with some preliminary findings supported by quantitative data, see Michael Brecher, Blema Steinberg, and Janice Stein, "A Framework for Research on Foreign Policy Behavior," *The Journal of Conflict Resolution,* XIII, 1 (March, 1969), p. 80. On the nature of "issue areas," see James Rosenau, "Foreign Policy as an Issue-Area," in James Rosenau (ed.), *Domestic Sources of Foreign Policy* (New York: Free Press, 1967), pp. 11 – 50; and James Rosenau, "Pre-theories and Theories of Foreign Policy," in R. Barry Farrell (ed.), *Approaches to Comparative and International Politics* (Evanston, Illinois: Northwestern University Press, 1966), pp. 27 – 92.

INPUTS

OPERATIONAL ENVIRONMENT

External:	Global	(G)
	Subordinate	(S)
	Subordinate Other	(SO)
	Bilateral	(B)
	Dominant Bilateral	(DB)
Internal:	Military Capability	(M)
	Economic Capability	(E)
	Political Structure	(PS)
	Interest Groups	(IG)
	Competing Elites	(CE)

COMMUNICATION—The transmission of data about the operational environment by mass media and face-to-face contacts

PSYCHOLOGICAL ENVIRONMENT

Attitudinal Prism: Ideology, historical legacy, personality predispositions

Elite Images: of the operational environment, including competing elites' advocacy and pressure potential

PROCESS

FORMULATION of strategic and tactical decisions in four <u>issue areas:</u>

Military-Security	(M-S)
Political-Diplomatic	(P-D)
Economic-Developm'l	(E-D)
Cultural-Status	(C-S)

IMPLEMENTATION of decisions by various structures: head of state, head of government, foreign office, etc.

OUTPUTS—the substance of acts or decisions

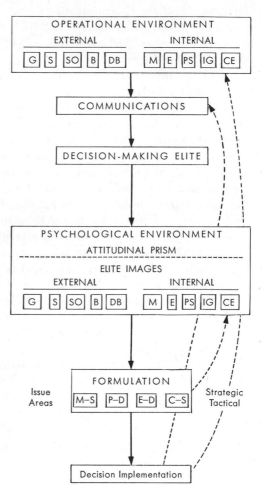

options, that is, the decisions themselves, only as it is filtered through the images of decision-makers."[10] An important but difficult task of the analyst is to identify and suggest relationships among factors that may link elite images with decisions, policies, and behavior. Whether certain factors do indeed influence Soviet actions in general or in specific cases are, of course, empirical questions.

It must be emphasized that this "systems" model is not the only or necessarily the best method of studying foreign policy behavior.[11] Like any theory, model, or conceptual framework, it contains numerous explicit and implicit assumptions and is not "value-free." Recalling our earlier discussion, one might reject out of hand the authors' assertions that "All data regarding foreign policy can be classified in one of these categories," and that "All foreign policy issues may be allocated to four issue areas."[11] To be sure, other conceptual frameworks may generate different data and produce better explanations. But this framework does identify numerous potentially relevant sets of factors that may influence the external behavior of the Soviet Union, and it also suggests some possible general relationships among these factors. For both these reasons the framework merits careful study.

Considering the difficulties involved in using the "motive-belief" pattern of explanation and in studying the "psychological environment" of foreign policy-makers, it is perhaps unfortunate that many analysts assume that certain factors significantly influence Soviet behavior in all or most situations. It is probably more fruitful simply to look at specific situations and ask, "Why were these decisions reached and why were these actions taken?" (Why did the USSR sign the Nazi-Soviet pact? Why were satellite regimes created in Eastern Europe after World War II? Why does the Soviet Union pursue its present policies in Eastern Europe, the Middle East, Southeast Asia, Latin America, Africa? Why do Soviet leaders compete and cooperate with the United States in various fields?) Careful study of individual events, policies, and policy changes has made it possible and will continue to make it possible to evaluate the relative importance of factors — external and internal — that influence individual Soviet decisions and types of activities. From this less shaky empirical base, with its emphasis on discovering and describing the actual behavior of Soviet officials at home and abroad, one can gradually verify, refine, or reformulate one's generalizations so that, employed with caution, they may help to explain Soviet behavior in other contexts.

Professors Zimmerman and Gati, in their essays below, examine the state of contemporary research on Soviet foreign policy. Zimmerman notes that some theorists emphasize the importance of external factors ("macro-anal-

---

10. Brecher, Steinberg, and Stein, *op. cit.,* p. 81.
11. For an analysis of many of these same questions that does not utilitze systems theory, see Harold and Margaret Sprout, *The Ecological Perspective on Human Affairs with Special Reference to International Politics* (Princeton: Princeton University Press, 1965).
12. Brecher, Steinberg, and Stein, *op. cit.,* pp. 80, 87.

ysis") on Soviet international behavior, while others stress the impact of domestic factors ("micro-analysis"). He contends that both are essential components of adequate explanations, and that both derive their importance from their effect on elite attitudes, which in turn shape the purposes and policies of Soviet leaders. (Compare these views with the conceptual framework above.)

Zimmerman maintains that changes in the international environment have significantly altered the attitudes and perspectives of many leading Soviet officials, and that this has increased their propensity and capacity to respond to external influences in a flexible manner. He concludes that the increasing "reactive" or responsive capabilities of Soviet leaders greatly enchance the potential influence of external factors (for example, the actions of other important nations) on Soviet international behavior.

But to describe changes in elite perspectives is merely the first step toward understanding the effects these changes have on Soviet performance under various circumstances. And to observe divergences in the perspectives of Soviet officials is not to explain their impact on or their relationship to other factors that influence behavior. Fully aware of these problems, Zimmerman bemoans the paucity of tested and testable hypotheses in the theory of international relations and its subfield, Soviet foreign policy.

Zimmerman urges greater analysis of external influences and the ways in which Soviet policy-makers, individually and collectively, react to these influences. Stressing the complexity of the entire field, he identifies many key questions and relationships that must be examined. But crucial questions remain. What kinds of explanation should be sought? What kinds of data should be collected? How can these data be acquired? For what purposes should they be used?

Some of these questions are discussed in the essay by Professor Gati. His analysis focuses on two major textbooks in the field of Soviet foreign policy and their strikingly different methodological approaches. Ulam's *Expansion and Coexistence* is a "traditional history"; Triska and Finley's *Soviet Foreign Policy* is primarily "social science" research. Each seeks to provide different kinds of insights into Soviet international behavior. The reader must decide for himself which is more successful and why. Perhaps he will conclude that both books and the two following essays raise more questions than they resolve.[13]

13. The Ulam and Triska and Finley books "reflect the present state of flux in Soviet studies. Both are important efforts to explain Soviet foreign policy behavior. But they are based on fundamentally different concepts of explanation. Ulam's analysis is essentially eliminative — that is, he seeks to demonstrate that other possible explanations of events do not logically and empirically 'fit' as well as his. Triska and Finley, employing various deductive and inductive research strategies, seek to generate and verify probabilistic generalizations to be used in explaining different aspects of Soviet behavior. The strength of the former approach is that it helps us to understand complex nonrecurring events about which information is difficult to obtain; the strength of the latter is that it helps to uncover trends and behavioral patterns through more rigorous analysis of available data." Erik P. Hoffmann, a book review, *The Journal of Politics*, XXXI, 3 (August, 1969), pp. 828 – 829.

ONE

CHARLES GATI

History, Social Science, and the Study of Soviet Foreign Policy*

1.

The nearly simultaneous appearance of two significant works on Soviet behavior in world politics provides an opportunity to consider and contrast divergent approaches to the study of Soviet foreign policy. *Expansion and Coexistence and Soviet Foreign Policy* make a methodological inquiry particularly interesting and apposite because of the authors' fundamentally different modes of analysis.

A professor of government, Ulam has nevertheless written an interpretive history, one in which the emphasis is on specific events, trends, external and internal circumstances, and the leaders who have made policy. Largely chronological in its basic organization, the book exhibits the hallmarks of historical scholarship in its thoroughness and judicious presentation of available information. Avoiding jargon, Ulam attempts to explain the past and present significance of historical events and influences. His book is a comprehensive and often brilliant *tour de force* that surpasses any other previous effort in making the history of Soviet foreign policy intelligible.

*Reprinted from *Slavic Review: American Quarterly of Soviet and East European Studies,* XXIX, 4 (December, 1970), pp. 682 – 687 (slightly revised), by permission of the author and the publisher. This chapter was originally prepared as a review article. The studies analyzed herein are Jan F. Triska and David D. Finley, *Soviet Foreign Policy* (New York: Macmillan Company, 1968) and Adam B. Ulam, *Expansion and Coexistence: The History of Soviet Foreign Policy, 1917 – 67* (New York: Praeger, 1968), two widely adopted texts on Soviet foreign behavior.

In sharp contrast to Ulam's traditional-historical approach, Triska and Finley concern themselves with the systematic study of recurring patterns in Soviet policies and especially with the dissection of the decision-making process in the Soviet system. Disaffected by contradictory interpretations, they strive to overcome the primary limitation of historical and intuitive knowledge, that of "perceptive relativity" — the fact that different observers perceive the same phenomenon differently. Therefore, they look for causal relationships by means of statistical inference and experimentation, assuming that the facts, relationships, and conclusions thus established will compel agreement by all observers. To accomplish their objective, they employ a wide variety of empirical methods and approaches such as content analysis, decision theory, role theory, bargaining and game theories, a "multiple-symmetry" model, as well as elaborate statistical and mathematical techniques. To the social scientist they demonstrate the attraction and usefulness of systematic empirical research in the study of Soviet politics. To the historian and the humanist who is unaccustomed to the language, symbols, typologies, and techniques of modern social science, *Soviet Foreign Policy* may well seem overwhelming at first, surprising later, but probably provocative and stimulating in the end; at the very least, the authors will have imparted a concern for precision and refinement in Soviet studies.

2.

Broadly speaking, there are two types of data used in all political and historical research: "words" and "deeds." Of the two, scholars generally rely on words since they seldom have the opportunity to observe deeds. In the study of Soviet foreign policy, our sources therefore inevitably include the Soviet political elite's communications about the goals, instruments, and implementation of foreign policy. The crucial methodological question — one that is explicitly raised by Triska and Finley — is *how* to use the voluminous Soviet literature on foreign policy.

The importance of this question lies in our preoccupation with, and perhaps somewhat uncritical acceptance of, what the Soviet leadership professes to be doing or would do in the future. What Samuel L. Sharp once called the "doubtful art of quotation" has long characterized not only the Kremlinological literature but a good many other scholarly works on Soviet foreign policy as well. In varying degrees, the impression is created that Soviet communications more or less accurately reflect Soviet behavior. This assumption, taken literally, is questionable. Suppose that a Soviet leader says to an American audience, "We will bury you!" Do we interpret his statement to mean that *(a)* he will definitely do it; *(b)* he would like to do it and do it now; *(c)* he would like to do it in the future; *(d)* he would do it now or in the future but only if and when the opportunity arose and he had the resources to do it? And can we even assume that he is using the word "bury" in the same way as his audience and his country's decision-makers? Surely there can be no correct or valid answer to these questions, insofar as the Soviet leader could also have intended to make the statement for many purposes — for example, to communicate with his own bureaucrats, to pacify the Chinese, or to warn the American military establishment.

The public statements of foreign policy-makers, then, represent a hazardous source of information about foreign policy *behavior*. But they represent a particularly hazardous source for understanding foreign policy *intentions*. For there is a seemingly perpetual discrepancy between what any man or group would like to do and what he or the group may actually decide to do or be capable of doing. To the extent that Soviet leaders appear particularly committed to the perfection of man and his environment and hence promote high hopes about the future, such discrepancy may be especially acute. Accordingly, textual analysis of the Soviet elite's descriptive or prescriptive communications presents a major methodological challenge to students of the Soviet political system.

How, then, can the printed word emanating from the Soviet Union be used? What do these statements mean generally and in different contexts? How does one know that what he is observing is what he thinks he is observing, and that what he is measuring is what he thinks he is measuring? In the language of the social scientist, these are questions of validity.

Significantly, these are questions on which the historian and the social scientist begin to part. The former seeks to be primarily "discriminating and judicious," the latter "methodical and systematic." There is a difference. For example, in his chapter on Khrushchev's foreign policy from 1956 to 1965, Ulam discusses the 22nd Congress of the CPSU. He observes, *inter alia*, that "Khrushchev's language was still opprobrious (the West, previously referred to as 'the capitalist nations,' was now almost invariably described as the 'imperialist' ones), his tone threatening (as in his relating of the latest and biggest Soviet atomic tests). But there was a hint of moderation in the language about Germany. . ." (p. 656). Ulam then conveys the conclusion that the Soviet leadership experienced a period of hesitation and perhaps confusion in regard to foreign policy at this time. While his argument seems sound and the reconstruction of the background of the Congress is well rounded, another analyst may well take issue with Ulam's selection of what constituted the important parts of the various speeches dealing with foreign policy and ask for "hard" or more conclusive evidence to support his conclusions.

In contrast, Triska and Finley examined the printed record of the 22nd Party Congress with a view of seeking *verifiable generalizations* about a specific question: that of the role of doctrine in the formulation of Soviet foreign policy. They were interested in the frequency of doctrinal stereotypes in the various speeches on foreign policy. For this reason, they prepared fourteen specific "propositions" (pp. 119 – 122) to find out, for example, if the impact of doctrine was generally greater in the Soviet public analysis of long-range policies than in the analysis of short-term policies (Proposition #8; p. 120). Or, they asked if the older members of the foreign policy elite speaking at the Congress used doctrinal stereotypes more frequently than did the younger members of the elite (Proposition #14; p. 122). Their data, derived from elaborate content analysis of the documents, "clearly confirmed" both propositions. How?

> Quantitative content analysis of public statements is one imperfect but promising method by which modern social scientists seek to overcome the obstacles to investigating motivation in human behavior. Basically, quantitative content analysis discovers the frequency of use of selected verbal symbols and semantic formulations and uses this information as one ground for concluding some of the attitudes or beliefs of the speaker [p. 116]. . . . [I]nstances of words or phrases prejudged to have a high doctrinal loading [were counted]. . . . A word/phrase list for this purpose was developed and amended during the analysis. Terminology was included or rejected according to our prior judgment as to whether or not it constituted a short-hand symbol for a concept or relationship or characteristic property clearly derived from Marxist-Leninist theoretical formulation. The results of this analysis were then expressed by a fraction representing the number of doctrinally stereotyped words or phrases in proportion to the total number of words in the statement analyzed. We called this fraction a *Doctrinal Stereotype Quotient* (DSQ) [pp. 118 – 119].

What did the DSQ reveal about the role of Marxist-Leninist ideology as an "active ingredient" in foreign policy decisions? The substantive conclusions which emerged indicated that the older members of the elite and those whose lives had been devoted mainly to Party work tended to use doctrinal formulations more frequently than others. Those with a primary preoccupation with domestic politics also adopted Marxist-Leninist terminology more often than those primarily concerned with foreign affairs. Moreover, the authors report that broad generalizations about the international situation and about Soviet foreign policy intentions seem to have led to the inclusion of more ideological referents than specific conclusions about a particular policy situation. (In fact, analysis of additional data about Khrushchev's communications during the 1962 Cuban missile crisis offers the optimistic conclusion that the possibility of recourse to ideology in time of international crisis is not very great at all.)

Such generalizations are based on three assumptions: first, that there exists a properly identified foreign policy elite in the Soviet Union, an assumption whose validity Triska and Finley convincingly demonstrate in a chapter on "The Men Who Make Soviet Foreign Policy" (pp. 75 – 106).

The second, infinitely more complex, assumption is that political communications in the Soviet Union (or, for that matter, elsewhere) actually reflect the leaders' *thought*. Linguists and psychologists have confirmed the existence of a positive relationship between communications and thought patterns; indeed, if such relationships could not be postulated, there would be little or no substance to scholarly research in the social sciences and humanities, which are based, as such research must be, on the printed word.

But the relationship confirmed is that between language and thought and *not* necessarily between language and *action.* In other words, we know that what one communicates has an impact on others and is an expression of his thought patterns; we do not know whether one's political communication discloses that which he is *doing* or intends to do. Given this uncertainty, the strictly policy-oriented student of Soviet foreign behavior may well be somewhat disappointed by, and skeptical about, the ultimate practical or applied value of textual analysis of any sort. For at best it can reveal what the Soviet leaders think and not necessarily what they do. Thus, even systematic textual analysis raises a number of perplexing questions about language, thought, policy, and their relationships — questions which become particularly troublesome in the study of any country's foreign policy.

Third, the generalizations offered by Triska and Finley not only raise the question of validity, but also of reliability. The reliability of all generalizations must be ascertained by further testing with different observers utilizing the same instruments. If such tests produce similar results, we shall have gained partial confirmation of important propositions about the functions and place of doctrine in the thought processes of the Soviet foreign policy elite.

Soviet communications about foreign policy, then, lend themselves to different modes of analysis. The historical-traditional approach provides the reader with commentary about the *inputs* and the *outputs* of Soviet foreign policy, stressing the probable causes and consequences of the most dramatic developments of each period. Given the emphasis on that which is unique, there is no attempt to reach such generalized conclusions which would hold true in the future as well. As utilized by Triska and Finley, social science approaches offer, or seek to offer, verifiable propositions, primarily about the decision-making process (even if some of these propositions are gained from nonrecurring data), that provide insights mostly about the *inputs* of Soviet foreign policy: how incoming information is selected and interpreted, goals formulated, and decisions reached. Substantively, both books point to the presence of divergent opinions and contending forces within the Soviet foreign policy-making apparatus.

3.

The mode of analyzing Soviet foreign policy actions or deeds also separates the historian and the social scientist. Understandably enough, Ulam is interested in, and is fascinated by, the great events and conflicts of the past fifty years: the conclusion of World War I, relations with Germany and with the Allies before World War II, the origins and development of the Cold War, the significance of Stalin's death, the emerging Sino-Soviet conflict, the confrontation over Cuba — events whose uniqueness he explicitly recognizes. While he does offer occasional generalizations about Soviet policy, Ulam prefers to concentrate on the concrete event and the leading personality. His method is in good part intuitive. While he seeks objectivity and fairness in the treatment of Soviet actions or deeds, Ulam's handling of the data suggests he finds impartiality beyond reach if not actually repugnant.

On the whole, Ulam's judgments are based on an appreciation of the relationships between Soviet domestic and foreign policies; on the impact of the Russian tradition; on the role of leading personalities (rather than the larger foreign policy elite); and on the conviction that Soviet behavior abroad can best be understood in terms of power politics. His treatment of the Cold War, for example, is thus "conventional" in the sense that he accepts Soviet policies as essentially inevitable — as if, given Soviet goals and perceptions and Western policies, the Soviet leaders had no real options other than those they actually chose. *To suggest inevitability in retrospect but at the same time deny the possibility of generalizations of the "if . . . then" variety concerning future Soviet actions is the historian's self-imposed, and perhaps unnecessary, limitation.*

In contrast, Triska and Finley seek to ascertain the relative importance of factors or the impact of major events in the international system on the formulation of Soviet foreign policy. In order to arrive at generalizations, they examine fifteen recent international events, ranging from the civil war in Laos to the COMECON integration problems of 1961 – 1963 (pp. 127 – 148). They classify the Soviet leadership's perception of these events as indications of success, failure, threat, or opportunity, and conclude — on the basis of subsequent Soviet reactions — that perceptions of failure and threat are "more likely to induce abrupt changes" in Soviet policy than perceptions of success and opportunity. In other words, "failures" and "threats" abroad constitute an important factor to which Soviet leaders respond and adapt policies accordingly. Significantly, relatively few such events perceived as failures or threats are thought to have led to lasting change in Soviet policy (p. 145). Thus Triska and Finley emphasize continuity and stability, stipulating that radical change can be expected only with a change of elite personalities. "If an 'ideological purist' were to attain 'dictator' status in the USSR," they observe, "we might expect an abrupt rise in the application of doctrinal propositions, especially in the crisis context." However, since only the older members of the elite are said to be doctrine-oriented, Triska and Finley consider the prospect of such change unlikely (p. 147).

Thus, Triska and Finley focus on the permanent and repetitive elements in Soviet behavior. They are far more concerned with verifying empirical generalizations than with analyzing the causes and consequences of unique historical events. Although the evidence they have so diligently collected is restricted in both time and place, their qualifications are not always sufficient to dispel an unfortunate impression of finality. Paradoxically, the qualifications they do introduce significantly weaken the scope and degree of confirmation of their generalizations, in part because of the great number of complex variables on which they depend.

What we have, then, are two impressive and stimulating studies of Soviet foreign policy. Their substantive conclusions are certainly compatible, although their views on what constitutes understanding, what questions should be studied, and what kinds of information should be gathered are profoundly different. One is conventional and highly readable, the other experimental. Primarily, Ulam seeks understanding of *what, when,* and *who*; Triska and Finley of *what, who,* and *how.* Both books address themselves to questions of *why* — Ulam by informed and sophisticated speculation, Triska and Finley by systematic and controlled investigation of propositions about presumed relationships. Together, the two books underline the increasing gap in Soviet studies between the methodologies of history and social science.

Elite Perspectives and the
Explanation of Soviet Foreign Policy*

1.

Analysts have vacillated between two major orientations in explaining foreign policy behavior. Theorists of international politics have generally adopted a macro-analytic approach in which the internal dynamics of a state's behavior — including such factors as the particular political structure of the polity, the perspectives and personalities of the decision-makers, and the articulated attitudes and demands of the citizenry — are "black-boxed" in the name of analytic parsimony. They anthropomorphize the state, treating it as a unitary rational decision-maker whose behavior is explained largely as a response *(a)* to the anarchic quality of politics in an international arena devoid of international government, *(b)* to changes in the structure of the international system (e.g., changes in the number of major actors — the great powers, in the distribution of power among the major actors, or in the relative power differential separating the major actors from the "bit" players on the international scene), or *(c)* to calculated moves by rival states.

In contrast, those whose interest in international politics has developed out of an initial comparative politics or area studies concern have shown themselves more prone to adopt micro-analytic approaches to foreign policy analyses. These men view the attributes of foreign policy as resultants of internal political processes or as resultants of the interplay of phenomena particular to

*Copyright by the Board of Editors of the *Journal of International Affairs,* reprinted from volume XXIV, Number 1, pages 84 – 98, 1970. Permission to reprint is gratefully acknowledged to the Editors of the *Journal* and the author.

the state in question. According to these analysts, policy attributes may grow out of entirely *nonhuman factors* such as a state's geopolitical position or its natural resource endowment. Or they may stem from *domestic societal forces* such as a state's national character, "modal personality," political culture, belief system or ideology, or social structure. Or they may have their origins in factors which shape the *effective structure of a state,* factors ranging from the state's formal constitutional framework on the one hand to structural impacts on information flows within the state on the other, or finally according to our *micro-analysts,* foreign policy attributes may be thought to originate in the *idiosyncrasies of particular decision-makers* — their anxieties, their aspirations, and their perceptions. In short, the *micro-analysts* have tended to regard the nature of the individual *components* of a polity, such as those we have just enumerated, and not situationally induced general propensities of a state as providing the most important clues to a proper understanding of any state's foreign policy. This has been particularly true in western analysis of Soviet foreign policy.

There has, of course, always been a willingness on the part of western observers to recognize Moscow's sensitivity to the global distribution of power (macro-analysis). Arnold Horelick and Myron Rush in *Strategic Power and Soviet Foreign Policy* (1966), for instance, argued that the strategic superiority of the United States provided an external environment in which the Soviet Union was not prone to resort to "the dangerous employment of . . . strategic power for political ends."[1] Indeed, as early as 1951, Raymond Garthoff had affirmed this centrality of the balance of power concept in Soviet foreign policy calculus. At times Soviet decision-makers have been thought by western observers to retreat or otherwise adapt their tactics when confronted by an asymmetrical and unfavorable power configuration, and then to return to the fray under more propitious circumstances. Only recently, though, has the consistently *reactive nature* of Soviet foreign policy been stressed, first by Marshall Shulman in *Stalin's Foreign Policy Reappraised* (1963), and then more elaborately by Jan Triska and David Finley in their stimulus-response model of Soviet-American interaction.[2]

The prevailing orientation to the explanation of Soviet foreign policy in the West, however, has been micro-analytic. There have been several reasons for the western emphasis on the internal origins of Soviet international behavior. The cold war created an atmosphere conducive to stressing the extent to which the foreign policy of the Soviet Union differed from that of other states, while

---

1. Arnold Horelick and Myron Rush, *Strategic Power and Soviet Foreign Policy* (Chicago: University of Chicago Press, 1966), p. 218.
2. Marshall D. Shulman, *Stalin's Foreign Policy Reappraised* (Cambridge, Mass.: Harvard University Press, 1963); and Jan Triska and David Finley, "Soviet-American Relations: A Multiple Symmetry Model," *The Journal of Conflict Resolution,* IX, No. 1 (March, 1965), pp. 37 – 53.

Soviet studies remained somewhat divorced, conceptually and methodologically, from the mainstream of comparative politics and international relations
inquiry. But more importantly, there was compelling evidence to suggest that
Soviet foreign policy did differ from that of other states and that the explanation for the unique in Soviet policies, goals, and instrumentalities was to be
found in the radical transformation of the Russian polity and Russian society
brought about by or after the Bolshevik seizure of power in 1917.

That this was the conclusion of Soviet specialists may be seen by identifying
the themes and preoccupations which have been at the core of the scholarly
dialogue on Soviet foreign policy. One central theme has been that of historical
comparison or "continuity and change." There has been a major preoccupation with the Soviet Union's international performance capability, with the
general tendency being to stress the Soviet Union's ability to act efficaciously
in international politics. A third central theme has pertained to the role of
ideology in shaping Soviet foreign policy.[3] Implicit in these themes were several assumptions about the nature of the Soviet political system. The focus on
continuity and change obviously reflected an assumption that Soviet foreign
policy differed substantially from the foreign policy of the antecedent Tsarist
regime. Beyond that, it revealed an assumption that the major variable war-
ranting attention in foreign policy analysis was the Soviet political system —
perhaps as shaped by a particular leader. (There was of course a wide range
of opinion within the broad consensus. Interpretations varied from the emphasis of Robert Tucker on the idiosyncratic psychodynamics of the leader to the
structural focus of Marshall Shulman.)[4] Similarly, the significance attached to
the Soviet political system in explaining Soviet foreign policy underlay the
attention paid to the international performance capability of the Soviet Union,
for central to western calculations of this capability was the notion that the
Soviet Union was an archetypical totalitarian mobilization system. It was
assumed that the Soviet Union was impermeable to extra-national influences
and insulated from the constraints of an open, pluralist society whose decision-
makers are obliged to take the opinions of domestic critics into account.
Furthermore, many experts argued that the Soviet Union, as a totalitarian
system, was favored in its competition with an "instrumental" system like that
of the United States because the Soviet elite could secure greater social mobilization of society.

It was the attention of ideology, however, which most revealed the assumptions about the Soviet Union which disposed scholars to a micro-analytic

    3. Definitions of ideology abound. Usage here follows that of Zbigniew Brzezinski and
Samuel Huntington in *Political Power USA/USSR* (New York: Viking Press, 1964), in which they
distinguish between Soviet *ideology* and more traditional *belief systems*. Ideology is a revolutionary belief system which is explicit and simplified and which conveys fairly general but direct
perspectives about the future good society, the antecedent reality, and the means whereby the
present reality might be transformed into a better future society.
    4. See Robert C. Tucker, *The Soviet Political Mind* (New York: Praeger, 1963); and Mar-
shall D. Shulman, *op. cit.*, Chapter 2.

interpretation of Soviet foreign policy. This attention partly stemmed from a sense that the peculiar quality of Soviet beliefs gave the USSR an advantage in its global competition with the United States. Scholars noted the preoccupation of Soviet ideology with violence, conflict, and qualitative change, and also the lesser role attributed to nation-state interaction in the overall world historical process. They contrasted this to the allegedly legalistic and ahistorical belief system of American decision-makers disposed to assume a natural international harmony of interests, to view stability rather than conflict as a norm (both in the sense of the expected and the desired), and to believe in the efficacy of incremental and intra-systemic change. More specifically, western analysts focused on Soviet ideology because it was thought that the all-encompassing character of Soviet beliefs — embracing a critique of the existing order, notions about a better future society, and policy prescriptions for transforming the real into the desired — provided the key to the seemingly uniquely purposive character of Soviet behavior.

Indeed, the belief was widespread that ideology would retain its significance in explaining Soviet foreign policy long after it had ceased to play a significant role domestically in a Soviet Union developed beyond the era of collectivization and mass purges. One reason for this belief was, as Adam Ulam argued, that "while the Soviet citizen, including the indoctrinated party member, has numerous occasions to discover the contradictions or irrelevances of Marxism in his daily life, he enjoys no such tangible experience insofar as the world outside the USSR is concerned."[5] For an ordinary citizen as well as for a party ideologue, international relations lacked the salience of domestic affairs; therefore beliefs about the structure of the international system, the nature and identity of the Soviet Union's major antagonists, and the future transformations of international politics were less likely to be called into question. A second argument also buttressed the assumption of the continued significance of ideology and its implication for the continued preeminent role of the Soviet political system in explaining foreign policy behavior. It was acknowledged that, at least in the long run, ideological erosion domestically was to be anticipated in the complex large-scale Soviet industrial society. In order to maintain the institutionalized revolutionary zeal integral to the nature of the Soviet regime, foreign policy would become a surrogate for rapid industrialization. In the post-industrialization phase of Soviet society the barricades to be stormed would be found in the international arena.

2.

Compelling as all the arguments for continued attention to the unique impact of ideology on Soviet foreign policy are, the dominant cast to Soviet perspectives on international relations during the 1960's provides little support for

5. Adam Ulam, *The New Face of Soviet Totalitarianism* (New York: Praeger, 1965), p. 74.

such a conclusion and much evidence which points in the opposite direction. Not only do the main trends in Soviet perspectives on the international system bear a marked similarity to western conventional wisdom, but the evidence indicates that Moscow's reading of the contemporary international scene has led the Soviet leadership to propositions and steps inconsonant with any determination to maintain the institutionalized revolutionary zeal which many have thought the most characteristic feature of the Soviet system.

Conventional Bolshevik assumptions about international relations constituted a logical adaptation of Marxism to early twentieth-century reality and to the fact that, contrary to expectation, the communist revolution occurred in Russia alone. As a result, the imagery of fundamental conflict was altered from that of a struggle waged within a state between the dominant but moribund capitalists and the emerging proletariat to one taking place in the horizontally structured environment of international politics. Vertical, class, and economic concepts were transposed and adjusted to account for the basically horizontal, international, and political arena in which the Soviet leaders were to engage their class enemies. Once the Bolsheviks were in power, capitalism became equated with a system of states as well as with a global socio-economic system. Marxism as modified by Leninist and Stalinist experience was projected onto the international arena. Soviet notions about the actors in international politics became inextricably linked with Soviet assumptions concerning the major agents in the historical process. Given the assumption that classes are the movers of history, it was only natural that, as Zbigniew Brzezinski has noted, "the interplay of nation-states" was considered "merely one, and often only a formal aspect of international affairs."[6]

Traditional Soviet ideas about the hierarchical structure of the international order were strongly conditioned by Bolshevik conceptions of power. Since the key question of politics is *kto-kogo* (who [eliminates] whom), the very notion of non-hierarchical power relations was anathema. States, classes, and individuals, except for historically brief moments in which one actor supplanted another, were either on top or not, and values were allocated accordingly. Similarly, traditional Soviet appraisals of the motives and behavior of the major imperialist powers illustrated the extent to which, to paraphrase Alfred G. Meyer, Soviet commentators on the international scene let Lenin do their thinking for them. The bourgeoisie, it was assumed, made the key political decisions; the state was little more than a front organization for Wall Street. As the major imperialist power, the United States' motives were easily understood: the capitalist ruling circles, animated by considerations of power and profit, were seeking to dominate the world and destroy socialism. And finally, Soviet assumptions about the transformation of the international system were

6. Zbigniew Brzezinski, *Ideology and Power in Soviet Politics* (New York: Praeger, 1962), p. 105.

also reflective of doctrinal projections. Whereas western analysis has tended to assume that the natural condition of a multi-sovereign system is equilibrium, both doctrinal predispositions and experiences encouraged Soviet observers to expect violence, revolution, qualitative change, and disequilibrium. Because the revolution was inevitable, there was but a single outcome to the international "equation." Ultimately, the contemporary international system would be displaced by "international relations of a new type."

In the late 1950's and the 1960's, however, a significant transformation in Soviet perspectives on international relations took place.[7] By the end of Khrushchev's tenure, *states* had taken precedence over the *world systems* of capitalism and socialism as the main actors in the international arena. In part, the change reflected Soviet adjustment to the passing of rigid bipolarity and to fissiparous tendencies evident within the two camps. In addition, Soviet observers in the 1960's seemed to attach somewhat greater significance than previously to the role of institutions in the determination of actor capability.

Perhaps the most striking aspect of the transformation in Soviet perspectives pertained to the new depiction of the hierarchical structure of the modern international system, one which diverged fundamentally from conventional Bolshevik expectations about power relations. According to Soviet commentary, in the "new, third stage of capitalism's general crisis," it was no longer the case that the international system was a rigidly hierarchical order headed by a single dominant power. Now there were two leading states, the two superpowers, the United States and the Soviet Union. Their competition provided the framework within which, in the views of some Soviet observers, even small, formally independent states, although economically tied to imperialism and politically linked to the United States, need not always be considered dependent countries. In the last years of Khrushchev's rule, moreover, Soviet observers, responding to their accurate perception of the increased assertiveness of the second-level great powers in the two camps, began to evidence increasing concern over the danger of catalytic war, and thus to recognize that the question of war and peace was no longer solely a matter of relations between the leaders of the imperialist and socialist camps.

The main contradiction in the world, nevertheless, continued to consist of the relationship between the imperialist and socialist camps, and it was to this relationship that Soviet observers looked in analyzing the global distribution of power. Here an interesting progression occurred. Prior to 1959, the term of reference utilized in describing the balance of power was "distribution of power" (usually *sootnoshenie sil,* occasionally *rasstanovka sil*). In 1959, although formulations involving the generic phrase "distribution of power"

---

7. The summary of the evolution of Soviet perspectives in the Khrushchev and post-Khrushchev periods was drawn heavily from my *Soviet Perspectives on International Relations, 1956–1967* (Princeton: Princeton University Press, 1969), especially pp. 276–280.

prevailed quantitatively, formulations containing *pereves sil* (favorable balance or preponderance of power) also made their appearance. After late 1961, the focal term of reference became *ravnovesie sil* (equilibrium). This progression corresponded to changing Soviet appraisals of existing as well as ontological reality; that is, to changes in the Soviet perception of the distribution of power and in Soviet expectations of the imminence of revolutionary advance. These shifts in formulation had distinct limits. At the height of revolutionary optimism in 1958 – 60, Soviet observers continued to accord the United States world power status. In 1962 – 64, while acknowledging implicitly that a reversal in socialist fortunes had occurred, these same observers continued to insist on the Soviet Union's position as a world power, at the same time integrating this temporary reversal into their perception of the world historical process by elongating their time perspective.

The evolution of Soviet views about American foreign policy behavior was equally profound during the last years of Khrushchev's rule. The analysis of American capabilities was increasingly explicit and detailed. The depiction of the American decision-making process reflected a shift in focus from Wall Street to Washington and implied a belated recognition that the Keynesian revolution had indeed transformed the relationship between the political and economic systems in the capitalist world. It also revealed an awareness that the enhanced role of international relations in world events had greatly augmented the position of the state and especially the institution of the Presidency. The most dramatic change in Soviet perceptions was with respect to the characterization of the motives of the majority of the American ruling elite ("the realists"). Khrushchev himself professed to detect a "reappraisal of values" within the American ruling group and thus, in effect, asserted that the motives of American imperialism had changed. In the atomic age under conditions of mutual deterrence, security was considered the primary value of the dominant element within the American leadership. The United States, while doubtless the major adversary, was no longer to be regarded as the main enemy, largely because the realistic elements of her leadership could be expected to prevent the outbreak of general war.

Khrushchev's "prettification" of American imperialism — as the Chinese Communists described his reappraisal — was tied directly to his efforts to sustain a belief in the inevitability of revolution under atomic age conditions; to sustain, in other words, the expectation that the contemporary international system would in fact be transformed into a socialist "international relations of a new type." The dilemma posed by the constraints Soviet decision-makers considered operative in the atomic age — tersely summarized in July, 1963, by the observation that "the atomic bomb does not observe the class principle" — was as simple as it was intractable. In doctrinal terms, the dilemma constituted a challenge to the unity of theory and practice. How could the triumph of socialism be secured without general war? How could the creation of an "international relations of a new type" be accomplished while avoiding the violent destruction of the existing international system? Khrushchev's answer contemplated that Soviet missiles would deter the outbreak of general war and deprive imperialism of its capacity to impede artificially (through the "export of counter-revolution") processes taking place within states as a result of the disequilibrating tendencies inherent in a revolutionary epoch. The plausibility of such a vision, however, relied on the behavior of the decision-makers in the leading capitalist power, the United States, that is, on a contingency neither "objectively" determined by the "world historical process" nor sufficiently subject to the influence of *right-thinking* communists. Under nuclear age conditions, the unity of theory and practice was ruptured. Even accepting Soviet postulates, international relations could no longer be considered a closed system, a general theory with a predictable solution at a single point.

To proceed one step further, it was not only the inevitability of the desirable which was called into question by international developments in the 1960's. The Sino-Soviet conflict even produced open misgivings about the very desirability of a communist international system. In the words of one Soviet spokesman:

> The new world system of Socialist states is now in the making. Entirely new, previously unknown relations are being established between them, and these relations are a prototype of the relations soon to be established all over the world.... Will this be a truly fraternal alliance of the nations, completely free of hostility and mistrust, or a system of states still tainted with mistrust between peoples, without real fraternal mutual assistance and help for each other, a system with trends to isolation and autarchy?[8]

And with these misgivings, Soviet leaders began to regard the contemporary international system more favorably, as was most vividly evident in the aftermath of the Cuban missile crisis when Moscow declared:

> gone are the days when the working men rising in struggle against capitalism had indeed nothing to lose but their chains. Through selfless, heroic struggle, the masses have won immense material, political and cultural gains, gains that are embodied in the socialist world system. Tomorrow the whole world and the civilization created by their labor will belong to the working people.[9]

Developments in the years following Khrushchev's ouster were generally not as dramatic as those of the early 1960's. After 1965, Khrushchev's successors showed little enthusiasm for affirming the clearly revisionist statements to which Khrushchev and the specialists in the Academy of Sciences' Institute of World Economy and International Relations had given voice. Khrushchev's successors, for multiple reasons, did not repudiate the slogan, "workers of the world unite, you have nothing to lose but your chains." While in 1963 – 64 the

8. V. G. Korionov, "Proletarian Internationalism — Our Victorious Weapon," *International Affairs* (Moscow), No. 8 (August, 1963), p. 13
9. See "The Policy of Peaceful Coexistence Proves Its Worth," *World Marxist Review*, No. 12 (December, 1962), p. 6.

Clausewitzian dictum that war is the continuation of politics by other means was increasingly subject to criticism in the Soviet Union, it was generally rendered token obeisance in the years immediately following Khrushchev's ouster. Indeed, Khrushchevian doctrine that peaceful coexistence was the general line of Soviet foreign policy was abandoned.

Nevertheless, despite the fact that Khrushchev's successors were markedly less prone than he to engage in explicit doctrinal innovation, the trend of Soviet analysis of the structure of the international system, their projections for the future development of the international system, and even of American foreign policy, followed the pattern of the last years of the Khrushchev era. That direction had been toward a closer approximation of reality — or to western perceptions of reality — and to an evident cynicism with respect to a future communist international order. The emphasis in post-Khrushchevian commentary has been on the state and the state system. Increasingly, there has been a tendency to dissociate the world historical process from analyses of world politics. It has recently been asserted that "Ultimate victory on a world scale belongs to Socialism as the most progressive social system. . . . The operative word is *ultimate.* Meanwhile it is the ups and downs of the struggle that in the main constitute the content of international affairs."[10]

In analogous fashion, the changes in the Soviet depiction of the global hierarchy are largely explained by the capacity of Soviet observers to react to changes in the international order. In Soviet commentary the gap between the superpowers and other great powers narrowed, and the border separating the lesser-ranked great powers and the "major independents" became more ill-defined. Khrushchevian claims about the global distribution of power were consciously reduced while his calculation of the situational aspects of power was retained. Even post-Khrushchevian commentary on American foreign policy, which after the American bombing of North Vietnam moved away from Khrushchev's benign assumption that the "realists" constituted a majority within the American ruling group, could be said to constitute a step toward a more realistic appraisal of American actions. Certainly, post-Khrushchevian utterances about the rate of historical development were more realistic. Khrushchev had spoken of the full-scale building of communism and in 1960 – 61 had held high expectations for major revolutionary advances in the 1960's and 1970's. His successors, in contrast, consoled themselves that "Marxist-Leninists" had no "grounds for regretting the tempo of the development of the revolutionary processes in the world" by pointing to the time required to displace feudalism with capitalism:

The replacement of feudalism by capitalism occupied an epoch which embraced several centuries. . . . *In comparison with this replacement* [italics added], the replace-

10. S. L. Sanakogev, "The World Socialist System and the Future of Mankind," *International Affairs* (Moscow), No. 10 (October, 1960), p. 62.

ment of capitalism is taking place at a significantly more rapid tempo, spreading simultaneously over an immeasurably larger zone.[11]

In a sense, post-Khrushchevian commentary has retained the belief that ours is a revolutionary epoch while simultaneously postponing the time when the "international relations of a new type" would be created so far into the future as to be of little operative significance for Soviet foreign policy at the onset of the 1970's.

All things considered, there has been a marked tendency for Soviet perspectives to converge with western analysis. Western analysis traditionally has tended to underplay the internal elements affecting the foreign policy of the main actors in the international system; the early Soviet view gave inadequate weight to national interests *per se* and obfuscated the existential realm of international relations and the allegedly ontological realm of the world historical process. Both traditional appraisals postulated a single solution to the international relations equation: generalizing from one historically limited vantage point, the western solution postulated equilibrium; operating from an entirely different vantage point, the Bolsheviks expected disequilibrium. At the onset of the 1970's, neither western nor Soviet observers consider international relations a closed system. Instead, both maintain open-ended perspectives on the process of world politics — even though one might be more disposed to view equilibrium, and the other disequilibrium, as the norm. Western and Soviet perspectives on the basic structure of the modern international system are essentially similar. Soviet analysis of the internal politics of American foreign policy seems to accept basic western assumptions pertaining to the locus of decision-making within a capitalist state. Soviet commentary reveals, moreover, the same preoccupation with the political significance of technology — especially weapons technology — generally found among western analysts and an analogous attention to the constraints imposed on the behavior of states in the atomic age.

3.

It seems evident that much of the importance attached to ideology in explaining Soviet foreign policy has been misplaced. Ideology continues to serve as the language of politics — "proletarian internationalism" masks and legitimates Soviet imperial politics as surely as "law and order" masks and legitimates the repression of American blacks. To a considerable extent it remains the language of analysis, although there was a growing tendency in the 1960's for specialists to adopt the vocabulary and tools of their western counter-

11. M. Marinin, "Sotsialisticheskii internationalizm; politika voinstvuiushchego imperializma," *Mirovaia ekonomika i mezhdunarodnye otnosheniia,* No. 6 (June, 1966), p. 16.

parts.[12] Significantly, however, ideology has neither hindered nor enhanced the general Soviet appraisal of international relations. Aside from the Soviet assessment of relations among communist states, the maintenance of *elan* domestically through the retention of doctrinal purity internationally has been consistently sacrificed to the aspiration to pursue foreign policy goals rationally and efficiently. In the atomic age international relations have had a salience for Soviet "high priests" which has confounded the predictions of those who assumed that international relations would be the last doctrinal redoubt.

Consequently, it seems equally clear that the traditional rationale for the attention accorded to the internal origins of Soviet foreign policy can no longer be considered tenable. Indeed, one can go further and assert that in principle one ought to accord as much weight to international system-level explanations of Soviet foreign policy as one would in the case of any other state. A model of Soviet foreign policy which takes into account the impact of the international system only in the sense that it pays attention to Moscow's likely tactical policy changes in response to alterations in the global power configuration is analytically incomplete. It ignores the extent to which changes in the international environment alter elite attitudes and affect the goals and purposes for which decision-makers exercise power. The Soviet Union has proved more penetrable than conventional wisdom supposed. Changes in the international environment and in the USSR's role and status in the international system, by producing changes in Soviet perspectives, have altered Soviet foreign policy behavior. A reactive approach will presumably provide a better framework for understanding Soviet behavior in the 1970's precisely because of international system-generated changes in Soviet perspectives, with their attendant changes in Soviet goals. Attention to the international system has the distinct advantage that it calls attention to an important if obvious point, namely, that what other actors do (especially the United States) affects Soviet foreign policy, both directly and indirectly. Moscow *qua* unitary rational decision-maker does react; more than this, the context of policy debates in the conflict-ridden, oligarchic Kremlin is altered by American actions.

The difficulty with all this is that an international system-level explanation, while essential for an understanding of the major reorientation in Soviet thinking in the post-Stalin period, provides little in the way of guidance for the prediction of day-to-day state behavior. While calling attention to the interactive nature of nation-state behavior, it provides no criteria for anticipating *what kind* of reaction will be forthcoming from *which persons* in Moscow under *what circumstances*, and no standards for estimating which responses within

---

12. The emergence of international relations as a discipline in the Soviet Union is treated in Zimmerman, *op. cit.*, pp. 27 – 74. For an extensive discussion of problems of theory in international relations, see "Problemy teorii mezhdunarodnykh otnoshenii," in *Mirovaia ekonomika i mezhdunarodnye otnosheniia,* No. 9 (September, 1969), pp. 88 – 106.

a broad range of options are most and least probable under specified conditions. Nor does it take into account the fact that organizational behavior everywhere is frequently such that policies are continued in blithe disregard of a changing milieu.

Hence we have come full circle, back *inter alia* to the cognitive and affective maps of particular decision-makers — but at a greater level of specificity than in the summary of Soviet assessments presented in this essay, and within a general framework which stresses the impact of external factors on Soviet behavior. Rather than describe what in the 1960's has been the dominant strand in Soviet commentary, one is directed *(a)* to an analysis of differences in Soviet perspectives, and *(b)* to a search for propositions which relate external and internal variables to the perspectives and perceptions of the decision-makers. Here one is no longer concerned with how communists or even Soviet communists think, but with how which Soviet policy-maker with what career background occupying which political role assesses the international system and the actors in that system.

The evidence of the past decade amply demonstrates that, the general re-orientation in Soviet perspectives notwithstanding, there are divergent assessments of considerable policy relevance. Such divergences often seem only to concern nuances in interpretation. Yet even a dispute over what seems a nuance, for example, the difference between those who affirm that the global distribution of power *has shifted* and those who assert that it is shifting in favor of socialism, may portend crucially divergent policy choices. At other times there is no question that divergent assessments have immense policy consequences. Witness the consequences of asserting that: *(a)* there can be "no more dangerous illusion" than to believe that nuclear war can be an instrument of foreign policy (General Nikolai Talenskii, May, 1965), as opposed to *(b)* it is "mistaken and even harmful" to assert there can be no victors in a "world nuclear-rocket conflict" (Colonel I. Grudinin, July, 1966).

Unfortunately, while students of Soviet foreign policy have become reasonably aware of ongoing divergences in perspective within the Politburo and among various sub-elites, we are only in the initial stages of developing propositions which account for the differences detected. A few points have become clear. In international affairs as elsewhere, the reacquisition of old attitudes requires appreciably less information inflow than does the reinforcement of new insights. Thus there is a strong propensity among Soviet policy-makers to grasp at the belief that it is somehow possible (perhaps by general and complete disarmament, perhaps by an effective anti-ballistic missile) to eliminate the mutual vulnerability characteristic of the atomic age. Those persons directly involved professionally with international affairs seem to be among those who sense most keenly the imperatives of the atomic age, while among the least inclined to accept these imperatives are those whose status and influence are threatened by new and less doctrinaire modes of thought.

These few points of enlightenment show that much remains to be done. Only the slightest beginnings have been made with respect to several basic issues. With regard to Soviet perceptions of western signals, it is now presumably accepted that some western actions will be "read" in Moscow as evidence of an accommodating temper rather than as a sign of political weakness or as a Machiavellian maneuver. When this "proper reading" is most likely to occur is far less well established. No considerable literature exists which attempts to clarify the impact of recruitment patterns on Soviet foreign policy. How do past career experiences color the perspectives of Politburo members? In particular, does the Komsomol-secret police route to the Politburo encourage a more hostile assessment of the outside world than that adopted by persons with other career progressions?[13] Does it matter, for instance, whether the Central Committee and Politburo are made up predominantly of persons whose first major political appointment came during the years 1936 – 1940 as a direct result of the Great Purge rather than in the period 1941 – 45, when to identify with the Party was to identify with the nation?

It is to questions such as these that Soviet specialists will have to address themselves if we are to anticipate Soviet behavior with reasonable accuracy. The Soviet Union is no longer a purposeful political system ruled by leaders sharing an outlook on international events which the label "Bolshevik" aptly describes. It is precisely because it is now so difficult to anticipate Soviet leaders' thinking without an examination of the specific international context, the roles of particular individuals and institutions in the Soviet system, and the recruitment patterns which particular occupants of leadership positions may have experienced, that the empirical investigation of contemporary Soviet assessments of the international scene matters so much in our efforts to explain Soviet foreign policy.

13. For a provocative essay suggesting that this may not be the case, see Jerry F. Hough, "Ideology and Ideological Secretaries as a Source of Change in the Soviet Union," a paper delivered at the Mid-West Association for the Advancement of Slavic Studies, April 11, 1969, at Lincoln, Nebraska.

PART II

Domestic Politics and the
Formation of Soviet Foreign Policy

This is the first of two sections on domestic or internal influences on Soviet foreign policy. The present section is devoted to internal influences from "the operational environment"; the next section analyzes domestic inputs from "the psychological environment" (see the conceptual framework page 8 above). At the outset, it must be emphasized that one cannot discuss the impact of "domestic politics" on "Soviet foreign policy" without first stipulating which internal factors and which aspects of Soviet international behavior one is talking about. Some domestic influences have greatly affected major Soviet foreign policy decisions, while other domestic factors have had little or no discernible effect on the same decisions. *Which* factors have *what kind of* influence under *what* conditions during *which* time periods are empirical questions, albeit difficult ones. Informed observers, in efforts to identify and confirm these relationships, can and do differ. But one cannot meaningfully analyze "the" influence of domestic politics on international behavior.

In an important anthology, *Domestic Sources of Foreign Policy,* a central premise and basic dilemma are clearly stated. "The premise is that domestic sources of foreign policy are no less crucial to its content and conduct than are the international situations toward which it is directed. The dilemma is that the links between the domestic sources and the resulting behavior — foreign policy — are not easily observed and are thus especially resistant to coherent analysis."[1] In the Soviet context, this dilemma is particularly acute. One has no a priori reason to reject the central premise, but verification of the presumed relationships has relied heavily on informed speculation and generalization from one or two cases. The conceptualization and measurement of "influence" are particularly intractable problems. For example, it is exceedingly difficult to ascertain the calculations of Soviet leaders and the information they have at their disposal when they make their decisions. And it is equally difficult to determine which factors are decisive in their final selections (or compromises) among perceived alternatives. The analyst's sources of information are almost always limited to a handful of written documents, from which inferences must be made with utmost care and sophistication.

Professor Dallin, in his essay below, suggests five sets of domestic factors that may influence Soviet foreign policy behavior. Particularly important is his emphasis on the changing nature of the Soviet political system. In the course of the past fifty years, the structure and functions of the Communist Party have undergone significant transitions. This suggests that domestic sources of foreign policy — and their relative importance in different situations — have also undergone major changes.[2] For example, since 1956 there has been a dramatic increase in the quantity and quality of Soviet research on international affairs. This is perhaps especially true of research on the United States and on the developing countries, which "are being increasingly studied within the context of their own specific requirements and possibilities rather than according to preconceived dogmatic theories."[3] Whether this fresh information is being used in the formulation and implementation of policy is a very difficult empirical question. But the fact remains that large quantities of accurate information are now available to Soviet decision-makers — information of the kind that was simply not available prior to 1956. Good scientific and social science research institutes are not automatically major "domestic" influences on Soviet foreign policy, but they are surely very important potential factors in most policy areas.

The identification of potentially significant influences on Soviet foreign policy does not constitute verification of their actual impact under different conditions. Nor does identification of variables that may be related to one another warrant undocumented assertions about the nature of these relation-

1. James Rosenau, "Introduction," in James Rosenau (ed.), *Domestic Sources of Foreign Policy* (New York: Free Press, 1967), p. 2. See also Henry Kissinger, "Domestic Structure and Foreign Policy," in James Rosenau (ed.), *International Politics and Foreign Policy* (New York: Free Press, 1969), pp. 261 – 275.

2. See Edward Morse, "The Transformation of Foreign Policies: Modernization, Interdependence, and Externalization," *World Politics,* XXII, 3 (April, 1970), pp. 371 – 392.

3. Elizabeth Valkenier, "Recent Trends in Soviet Research on the Developing Countries," *World Politics*, XX, 4 (July, 1968), p. 659. See also William Zimmerman, *Soviet Perspectives on International Relations, 1956 – 1967* (Princeton: Princeton University Press, 1969), especially pp.

ships. The formulation and testing of unconfirmed empirical generalizations (hypotheses) are highly desirable, but one must very carefully distinguish among generalizations that are well confirmed, partially confirmed, or not at all confirmed by the data available.

The article by Professor Ploss focuses on the relationships between domestic and foreign policy in the post-Stalin era. His central hypothesis is that Soviet international behavior is significantly influenced by "domestic politics in the form of bureaucratic group struggle over functions and funds." In another context, a respected student of American politics concludes that "interest group influence on foreign policy is slight."[4] Professors Armstrong and Pipes[5] would perhaps agree that this is also true in the Soviet Union. Professors Dallin and Linden,[6] on the other hand, would probably argue that certain institutional and nonassociational groups in Soviet society have vested interests in different foreign policies, and that some of these groups significantly influence the formulation of policy alternatives and actual decisions. Professor Aspaturian emphasizes that Soviet behavior in this respect is very similar to that of all nations. "Foreign policy, including external defense, is more a function of preserving the social order and the interests of its dominant groups than of the state or the national interests in the abstract . . . [and] functions more to serve tangible internal interests than intangible or abstract ideological interests abroad."[7] For example, the Russian military heavy-industrial "complex" in fact and/or in rhetoric favors an aggressive foreign policy. Other coalitions of interests clearly favor a less militant posture and less defense spending.[8]

The analysis of "Interest Group" and "Political Structure" influences (see the conceptual model above) on Soviet foreign policy is hazardous for both empirical and conceptual reasons. Not only is "influence" exceedingly difficult to measure, but Soviet specialists simply do not agree on what constitutes an "interest group."[9] Therefore, one must very carefully examine the way that this concept is used before evaluating the descriptive accuracy or explanatory power of propositions employing the concept.

Professor Armstrong suggests that one aspect of domestic politics — the

4. Lester Milbrath, "Interest Groups and Foreign Policy," in Rosenau (ed.), *Domestic Sources of Foreign Policy,* p. 251.

5. See the chapter by John Armstrong below. Also Richard Pipes, "Domestic Politics and Foreign Affairs," in Ivo Lederer (ed.), *Russian Foreign Policy: Essays in Historical Perspective* (New Haven: Yale University Press, 1962), pp.145 – 169.

6. See the chapter by Alexander Dallin below. Also Carl Linden, *Khrushchev and the Soviet Leadership, 1957– 1964* (Baltimore: The Johns Hopkins Press, 1966).

7. Vernon Aspaturian, "Internal Politics and Foreign Policy in the Soviet System," in R. Barry Farrell (ed.), *Approaches to Comparative and International Politics* (Evanston, Ill.: Northwestern University Press, 1966), p. 230. Also see Linden, *op. cit.*

8. See Linden, *op. cit.* ; and Aspaturian, *op. cit.* , especially pp. 256 – 287.

9. See Philip Stewart, "Soviet Interest Groups and the Policy Process," *World Politics,* XXII, 1 (October, 1969), pp. 29 – 50.

competition for power among political leaders — is generally the most important factor influencing Soviet international behavior, and that foreign policy issues tend to be manipulated not in the interests of the USSR as a whole, or even of congeries of interests, but primarily to the personal benefit of individual Politburo members and cliques. Professor Pendill, in his article below, challenges this view. On at least one major issue (Soviet policy toward the Third World) resolved during an intense power struggle (1953 – 1956), he finds far-reaching decisions that may have been "truly collective" or "bipartisan." Careful investigation reveals little evidence that this issue was used as a "pawn" in personal rivalry for power and position.

There is probably more agreement among scholars that group influence on foreign policy varies with the *issue*.[10] Ploss and Linden emphasize that genuine policy choices are always present, and that since Stalin's death the power and prestige of Soviet leaders are dependent on the success of their policies, domestic and foreign. Perhaps this was more true of Khrushchev than of the present leadership. However, high Party officials, individually and collectively, often appeal to bureaucratic institutions and groups for political support and technical expertise in the constant competition over policy alternatives and resource allocation. Thus, institutional and nonassociational interests can and do exert considerable influence on *some* policy issues — generally and in single instances.

Furthermore, political leaders who hold certain views on foreign policy often hold distinct sets of views on domestic policy. There may not be any apparent logical connection between the two (for example, Barry Goldwater's simultaneous call for a weak Federal Government and an aggressive foreign policy), but political attitudes do cluster. As Linden persuasively argues, competing Soviet views on domestic and foreign policy also tend to cluster:

> The antagonism in the post-Stalin period between those leaning toward orthodoxy and conservatism, on the one hand, and those disposed to reform and innovation, on the other, can be roughly defined in terms of an internal versus an external orientation in policy. The more orthodox emphasize the necessities of the world struggle and the dangers from the outside enemy. Those inclined toward reform stress internal problems, the prospects for a relatively stable international environment, and the possibilities of developing less dangerous forms of struggle with the adversary abroad. In domestic policy the orthodox stress the ideological function of the party, doctrinal continuity, the need for limits on de-Stalinization, maintenance of centralized control of the economy, close supervision of the intelligentsia, and a heavy industry-defense weighted resource allocation policy. The reformers, by comparison, lean toward innovation in theory and practice, pragmatic solutions to economic problems, greater reliance on material rewards than on ideological stimuli, more local initiative and less centralization, and concessions to the consumer.[11]

10. See Milbrath in Rosenau (ed.), *Domestic Sources of Foreign Policy,* p. 248.
11. Linden, *op. cit.,* pp. 18 – 19.

How these attitudes and interests affect Soviet policy in different "issue areas" is the key question. Professor Rosenau hypothesizes that "The more an issue encompasses a society's resources and relationships, the more will it be drawn into the society's domestic political system and the less will it be processed through the society's foreign political system."[12] But this hypothesis and others have not been and perhaps cannot be rigorously tested in the Soviet context. For the time being, at least, conceptual confusion and inadequate evidence place a premium on insightful, informed speculation and on cautious inferences from available data. There is little general theory about the relationships between domestic and foreign policies, and even data on American politics are sometimes difficult to muster.[13] In the study of Soviet foreign policy, these problems are compounded.

12. James Rosenau, "Foreign Policy as an Issue-Area," in Rosenau (ed.), *Domestic Sources of Foreign Policy,* p. 49.
13. For an important study of pressure groups, public opinion, and foreign policy-making in the United States, see Raymond Bauer, Ithiel Pool, and Lewis Dexter, *American Business and Public Policy: The Politics of Foreign Trade* (New York: Atherton, 1963).

Soviet Foreign Policy
and Domestic Politics:
A Framework for Analysis*

Soviet foreign policy has usually been analyzed in terms of the leaders' objectives, their perceptions and initiatives in the outer environment of world politics, and their responses to developments abroad. Far less attention has been paid to another complex of variables which shapes Soviet policy — those internal to the USSR. These include not only resources and strategic capabilities but also intangible elements such as national style and tradition, elite conflicts, and a variety of domestic pressures exerted, directly or indirectly, on Soviet decision-makers. While it would be an oversimplification to think of Soviet foreign policy as purely and simply a dependent variable of domestic inputs, such an approach might well be a lesser error than to assume (as was generally done in the Stalin era and is often still an operative assumption) that Soviet leaders are immune to various constraints, diverse opinions, and political pressures arising out of their own polity and society.[1]

*Copyright by the Board of Editors of the *Journal of International Affairs,* reprinted from Volume XXIII, Number 2, pages 250 – 265, 1969. Permission to reprint is gratefully acknowledged to the Editors of the *Journal* and the author.
    1. Of those who have dealt explicitly with this problem, John Armstrong has tended to write off domestic social and political constraints on Soviet foreign policy (e.g., in his "The Domestic Roots of Soviet Foreign Policy," *International Affairs* (London), January 1965, pp. 37 – 47), as has Richard Pipes (e.g., in his contribution to Ivo Lederer, ed., *Russian Foreign Policy* [Yale University Press, 1962]). Robert M. Slusser (e.g., in his paper in Peter Juviler and Henry Morton, eds., *Soviet Policy-Making* [Praeger, 1966] concentrates heavily on "Kremlinological" aspects, of

This essay explores some aspects of the interaction between Soviet domestic political processes and foreign policy. It is not concerned with the impact of "objective" factors such as geography and natural resources, nor does it seek to probe the reverse phenomenon — the effect of external forces (real, imagined, or contrived) — on Soviet internal development. This process has been more satisfactorily identified and illustrated, as in the Soviet manipulation of the image of the "enemy," and in the assumptions underlying Western thinking about the Soviet Union that fomented the "containment" policy.

1.

American scholarship has in recent years seen various attempts to bring foreign policy studies into the ambit of contemporary political science. Some studies have focused on decision-making; others have probed the "linkages" of domestic and foreign policies by means of original and imaginative constructs. However, little effort has been made thus far to test the applicability of such concepts to Soviet politics.[2] Similarly, attempts have only just begun to look upon general hypotheses about modernization as providing relevant categories and insights for an understanding of communist systems as well as those of the "underdeveloped" states. It is from the literature of development that we adapt the following hypothetical trends for our point of departure.

(1) All developing systems tend to bring an increasing part of the population into (passive or active) political participation.

(2) Such systems eventually tend to produce integration at the level of the nation-state, at the expense of both parochial and internationalist preoccupations.

(3) Over time, developing systems tend to focus priority of attention, resources, and operationally relevant objectives on the domestic, rather than foreign, arena.[3]

While we would assert that all three of these dynamic tendencies can be identified in the Soviet case, too, there are also countervailing forces at work due to the inherent structure or systemic characteristics of totalitarianism. Among these, two are particularly noteworthy:

---

varying or uncertain degrees of verifiability. Two approaches closer to the assumptions implicit in the present essay are Sidney Ploss, "Studying the Domestic Determinants of Soviet Foreign Policy," *Canadian Slavic Studies,* I, no. 1 (spring, 1967); and, at greater length, Vernon V. Aspaturian, "Internal Politics and Foreign Policy in the Soviet System," in R. Barry Farrell, ed., *Approaches to Comparative and International Politics* [Northwestern University Press, 1966], pp. 212–87.

2. Two exceptions are Jon D. Glassman, "Soviet Foreign Policy Decision-Making," *Columbia Essays in International Affairs,* III (Columbia University Press, 1968); and David Finley, unpublished doctoral dissertation, Stanford University (1966).

3. See, for instance, Karl W. Deutsch, "Social Mobilization and Political Development," *American Political Science Review,* September 1961, pp. 497–500.

(4) Of all sectors of public policy, foreign affairs are least susceptible to direct involvement by broader strata of the population and to verification of official pronouncements. They inevitably require, in Communist as in other polities, greater reliance on authoritative institutions.[4]

(5) Of all political systems, the totalitarian is best able to override, delay, or distort the typical tendencies of modernizing systems to bring about certain changes in political development. It does so, for instance, by reducing participation to ritualistic ratification and explication, and by seeking to limit pluralism and the delegation of decision-making to functional-instrumental, rather than to political problem-areas.

We face in the Soviet experience, therefore, contradictory trends. It is our contention here that the specific weight of these and other relevant elements has tended to change over time, and that the dynamics of change tend to follow a plausible and intelligible pattern. This does not imply a deterministic perspective: we merely contend that Soviet development can be usefully examined in relation to an ideal type and that deviations from it are susceptible to rational explanation by identifying intervening variables responsible for such departures from it.

At the risk of oversimplification, these relevant political variables may be categorized according to the following schema.

(1) "Unwitting" elements, such as continuities in political cultures and projections of domestic experience and categories of perception onto the international arena.

An example of the former (as E. H. Carr has pointed out) is the Russian tradition of strong central authority in the state. The latter is illustrated by the prevalence of hierarchical relations between superiors and subordinates within the Party and state bureaucracy, making Soviet officials relatively unprepared to deal as coequals with representatives of other sovereign units in international intercourse. On the other hand, such features are of varying persistence: the assumption of the unilinear parallelism of revolutions, axiomatic in the early years of the Soviet regime (and still pronounced in Chinese analyses) appears to have lost much of its erstwhile policy relevance.[5]

(2) Perceptions and assumptions of the policy-makers regarding popular attitudes and, in particular, the existence or absence of either diffuse or specific support at home.

This aspect of the leadership's decision-making calculus has generally been ignored, perhaps because we have no certain knowledge of the assessments made by Soviet authorities. Still, there are some indirect indicators that may be resorted to: other estimates may be inferred or, frankly, guessed. Relevant dimensions include (a) the expected stress to which loyalty and compliance would be subjected under crisis conditions — what might be called the assumed support/alienation quotient of various social groups — such as behavior in case of war; and (b) reaction to particular foreign policy moves — what V. O. Key referred to as the decision-makers' anticipation of "contingent opinion"[6] — such as the probable response to an armed conflict with China.

(3) Elite cleavages and policy conflicts relevant to foreign affairs. This element includes *(a)* policy disputes and differences directly related to foreign policy and typically expressed either in bureaucractic politics or in esoteric debate; *(b)* policy conflicts focusing primarily on other areas but with inevitable implications for foreign relations; and *(c)* cleavages in the elite due primarily to power struggles, factionalism, and personality conflicts.

The Soviet record suggests that   at least until quite recently — policy and power conflicts have tended to overlap quite extensively. Thus the Stalin-Trotsky duel in the 1920's, the Malenkov-Zhdanov struggle in 1946 – 48, and the Khrushchev-Molotov fight in 1955, each involved all these facets: conflicts over domestic and foreign policies, differences in ideological formulations, and the struggle for power. Indeed, communist labels, such as "revisionism," "dogmatism," and the "general line," typically refer to syndromes comprising all these dimensions, though their relative prominence may vary from case to case. An unpublicized foreign policy debate, for example, preceded the shift from the "anti-Versailles" orientation which prevailed in the 1920's to the anti-Nazi alignment sought in 1934; another example is the split over the inevitability of a new "two-camp" polarization between the communist and capitalist systems in 1945 – 46 (as reported by Maxim Litvinov); a third, the debate over the desirability (and possibility) of a relaxation of tensions with the West, in the post-Stalin years. Among the many political conflicts with significant implications for foreign policy but dealing first of all with other matters, the most continuous and contested is the fight over resource allocation, the national budget, and investment policy. Under conditions of resource scarcity in a centralized command economy, decisions regarding procurement of weapons systems, foreign economic assistance, space programs, massive investment in chemical fertilizer production, or significant expansion of housing construction or consumer goods are all bound to have reciprocal consequences for foreign affairs.

Another useful way of distinguishing among policy conflicts is suggested by the labels employed by Robert Levine[7] and others, separating "systemic"

---

6. V. O. Key, *Public Opinion and American Democracy* (Knopf, 1961), p. 13.
7. Robert Levine, *The Arms Race* (Harvard University Press, 1963), pp. 28 – 29, 46ff.

from "marginalist" differences. While the former relate to fundamental differences over policy objectives, the latter describe conflicts over alternative ways of achieving shared goals. Methodologically, this distinction raises special difficulties in the Soviet case. Not only is overt dissent over foreign policy even less permissible than public differences on internal affairs, but even when couched in indirect, esoteric argument, systemic differences — to be voiced at all — must be cloaked in "marginalist" terms. It follows that technical differences in judgment regarding the relative cost, desirability, or effectiveness of particular tactics may (or may not) conceal more profound differences over policy objectives. This is also true of Soviet debates over strategic posture, in which (much as in the United States) differences over technical matters often conceal fundamentally divergent assumptions regarding the prospects of international war and peace.

(4)   Attempts by individuals and groups outside the circle of policy-makers to make themselves heard or to be consulted before basic decisions are made. There was virtually none of this in the Stalin era, but the proliferation of such efforts in recent years constitutes one of the most intriguing developments in Soviet foreign as well as domestic affairs. Here one should differentiate between those officially consulted as experts — such as military men, academic specialists on foreign areas, and scientists — and those who volunteer their advice and opinion.

This element includes, in particular, the Soviet equivalent of interest groups as well as the initiative of personalities of high public visibility (such as prominent scientists, novelists, and poets) to make known their views. The most significant among the groups involved, for our purposes, are the military and the creative intelligentsia; but it should be borne in mind that such groups are themselves by no means homogeneous in political orientation. Possibly others have similarly begun to exert influence on foreign policy decisions, largely through personal and informal access to policy-makers and their staff. Finally, in the most recent period there have been instances of incipient opinion groups, cutting across occupational and generational lines, taking the initiative to submit petitions or protests on a wide range of issues, from miscarriages of justice to the Soviet intervention in Czechoslovakia.

(5)   The broadening base of participation may, in theory, extend to public opinion — at least to the general mass of the "politically relevant" (or, to use Gabriel Almond's phrase, the "attentive public"), who constitute a growing share of the population. If the crystallization of interest groups is still at an early and informal stage, the vocal articulation of independent public opinion has never been and still is not sufficient to inhibit Soviet decision-makers.

The impact of these five categories has been quite uneven and unequal. Among the significant trends has been not only a slow widening of the circle of those consulted, but also increasing intercommunication and interaction among diverse elements, both within the same category and among different categories. This tendency was perhaps most visible in the Khrushchev days, illustrated by the informal alliances of certain civilian and military leaders against other civilian and military leaders over divergent approaches to both domestic and foreign affairs;[8] and in the occasional efforts of authority figures to secure the tacit support of particular interest groups.

To point to these tendencies — some of them, still quite fragile — is not to deny that the power to make final decisions remains normally in the hands of a very few nor that, for instance, during crises abroad (such as the Cuban Missile Crisis of October 1962) the leadership can in effect ignore "outside" opinion and function with only a minimum of concern for its subsequent accountability to formally responsible institutions such as the Party Central Committee and the less influential Supreme Soviet of the USSR.

2.

One perspective on the interactions of these influences on the elite's decision-making evolves from considering the changing focus of Soviet foreign policy during the "modernizing" phase of Soviet domestic development. Throughout this period and until the fifties, Soviet foreign policy required far-reaching adaptation, repeated postponement of goals, and painful compromises with reality. During the early years the Soviet leaders — after wars and revolutions, famines and revolts — were compelled to operate from a perception of their domestic "front" as imposing severe constraints in their pursuit of desired objectives. If some leaders were inclined to dismiss these constraints, the virtually simultaneous shift in early 1921 from the militancy of War Communism to the New Economic Policy at home and to its equivalent of "coexistence" abroad signaled the recognition of such weakness. Along with economic and military factors the sociopolitical fabric of Soviet society was a major source of this perceived inferiority to the outside world.

Indeed, throughout the interwar period Soviet policy generally avoided foreign adventures and involvement in violent conflict abroad. More than once the response of the Soviet regime to potential foreign threats was one of reluctant accommodation, retrenchment, and even appeasement — from the Treaties of Brest-Litovsk (1918) and Riga (1920) to the Litvinov Protocol and the effort to propitiate Japan in 1931 – 32. This policy was especially evident during the phases of intense socio-economic transformations "from above," such as the First Five-Year Plan, collectivization of agriculture, and the Great Purge. The reluctant alliance with France and Czechoslovakia in 1934 – 35 responded to a similar defensiveness born of a quest for time in which to improve the relative power position of the Soviet state.[9] In every instance the

8. See Thomas W. Wolfe, *Soviet Strategy at the Crossroads* (Harvard University Press, 1964); Roman Kolkowicz, *The Soviet Military and the Communist Party* (Princeton University Press, 1967); Carl Linden, *Khrushchev and the Soviet Leadership* (Johns Hopkins Press, 1966).

9. It is well to note, however, that perceived weakness need not always produce a conciliatory

desire to gain time was both pragmatically rational and ideologically rooted in the belief that the "correlation of forces" would necessarily change in the Soviet Union's favor as its enemies were bound to encounter greater "contradictions" while its own power and cohesion were bound to grow.

This policy of relative caution and diplomatic and military restraint reflected among other things a fear of dubious or divided loyalties at home, especially on the part of certain social and ethnic strata. Among these were the "bourgeois" specialists — such as engineers, officers, and intellectuals needed by the regime; the millions of kulaks; later, during World War II, entire nationalities, such as the Volga Germans, Crimean Tatars, Kalmyks, Balkars, and Ingush; and, after 1948, Soviet Jews. These — and others — were deemed politically suspect, whether these assumptions on the part of the leadership were in fact justified or not.[10]

Actually Soviet policy toward such groups tended to undermine the accommodation of their members to the status quo. In effect, "integration from above" (or the forcible removal of such groups) at least temporarily weakened the system still more by generating social and individual destabilization — most dramatically illustrated by the effects of the Great Purge.

Gradually, however, these sources of inherited and man-made weakness of the system vanished. Some of the old "hostile" classes died out; others were effectively absorbed and assimilated; and a general changeover of generations tended to lessen the strains of diffuse hostility. Some of the groups involved (for example, the kulaks) and some of the disruption occasioned by their removal or liquidation (for example, the purge of the Old Bolsheviks) were by definition nonrepetitive. True, alienating effects reverberated for some time after the victimization of the different groups themselves (as became apparent in 1939 – 41), but it remains an open question to what extent Stalin was cognizant of these sources of socio-political stress among his subjects or perceived them as constraints on the making of policy.

Moreover, with the passage of time the Soviet system began to acquire greater popular legitimacy and support as a result of many different processes. One was its very survival and the concomitant accommodation of a citizenry impressed by the absence of viable alternatives to it and the gradual effects of sustained political socialization. Another was the support given the regime by those who found personal success, recognition, or fulfillment within the system. The partial solidarity between state and society born of the shared challenge of foreign invasion and brutality bred legitimacy and a sense of national identification nurtured by the common experience of a victorious war which also saw a revival of national patriotic symbols. The seeming validation of

---

mood in Moscow; nor does a willingness to seek a detente or compromise need to stem from weakness alone.

10. These perceptions are the obverse of Soviet efforts to exploit irredentist sentiments in neighboring areas, e.g., in Moldavia, Karelia, Azerbaidzhan, or Sinkiang ("Eastern Turkestan").

ideological tenets by the course of history, highlighted by communist victories in and after World War II, and including the establishment of a communist "world system" in Eastern Europe and the Far East were significant elements.

Thus, by the 1950's, the earlier sources of widespread popular disloyalty — objectively as well as those perceived by the Soviet leadership — had vanished, particularly after Stalin's death. Yet, ironically, the Soviet system itself, by the logic of its development, had simultaneously begun to manufacture new constraints and sources of dissent as essentially unintended consequences of successful modernization. Creeping pluralism invades totalitarian life as it must invade all developing politics. The growing complexity of society and economy are bound to produce greater functional specialization, greater multiplicity of role conflicts, a greater awareness of divergent group interests, and at least their incipient aggregation. At the same time, political articulation and participation tend to increase while the pressures of forcible social, political, and economic mobilization are somewhat relaxed; while the system has more material resources to spare from its all-out mobilization and survival needs; and as important choices among alternative strategies need to be made. Different elite elements tend to opt for different priorities in resource allocation, reflecting different values with different political implications (even if the options are not, on the face of it, "political"). As terror tends to recede at this stage, dissenting voices may be heard with greater impunity, precisely at a time when the regime must make greater efforts to manufacture a genuine consensus. The more modernized society must rely more heavily on "experts," who in turn tend to press for better information and greater rationality and often seek access to policy-makers, thus introducing notes which clash with the repetitive refrains of the ideologues and the timid, conservative bureaucrats.

In addition, the fear of a return to one-man rule (among those who remember the Stalin era and also among some who deplore the improvisations of the Khrushchev days) supports "collective" decision-making at the highest level, which requires the adjustment of conflicting opinions and preferences — or else stalemate and inaction. Collective leadership invariably creates a situation in which outside influences can more effectively be brought to bear on the narrow circle of decision-makers. And if, by comparison with the Khrushchev era, there has in recent years been a distinct de-emphasis on simple ideological formulae, there is by the same token greater confusion about the shape of things to come and uncertainty about the "proper" priorities and policies to be pursued. There is simply a greater range of choice among possible courses of action. Such open-endedness is heightened still further by the failure of events to conform to prior expectations — neither in what used to be the communist "Bloc," nor in the Third World, nor in the capitalist West. Thus, one unintended consequence of the Sino-Soviet dispute is a further disorientation regarding the international environment: to many Soviet observers it is no longer so axiomatic what the rank order of friends and enemies is, or which strategies and tactics are legitimate and which are taboo.

Thus, as the stage of all-out mobilization and terror is completed, a number of mutually reinforcing processes tend to destroy the earlier "simplicity" of relatively uncontested totalitarian policy-making. But if at the same time Soviet foreign policy is no longer significantly constrained by the leadership's earlier uncertainty regarding the loyalty of its own population, it has tended to become increasingly contested by various elements — more powerful, more autonomous, and more articulate — *within* the system. As the Soviet Union moves into the 1970's, it is hardly an exaggeration to say that there are within the Soviet elite conflicting perceptions and images of the outside world; conflicting priorities and values regarding foreign objectives; and advocates of conflicting foreign policy strategies and tactics — either explicitly voiced or else implied in their stated goals.[11]

3.

It is significant, while we chart the increasing range of choice and the commensurate freedom of alternative of the Soviet elite, to pause momentarily over the salient continuities as well as the marked changes in Soviet foreign policy formation. One tendency which, though persistent, has often been underestimated abroad, is to give priority to domestic over foreign objectives unless a manifest threat or crisis looms abroad — a low-risk strategy that has satisfied both the present-minded pragmatists and the ideologically committed who expect greater things in the future. A related practice — rarely spelled out — has been to give clear priority to the interests of the Soviet state over those of revolutionary movements abroad. Despite charges of "selling out" its comrades and of "betraying" its verbal commitment to "internationalism," Soviet policy has been typically guided by a *sacro egoismo* not unfamiliar to other states.

There has also been a significant continuity in the terms and categories in which foreign policy alternatives have been perceived and discussed. While the traditional dichotomy into "Left" and "Right" is an inadequate diagnostic tool, it is descriptive of profoundly divergent attitudes which, in their extreme manifestations, reflect conflicting values and orientations. Communists themselves have, of course, continued to use these terms and, while they frequently serve as pejorative labels, it is important to realize how often there has been a congruence of cleavages over foreign policy approaches with those over other issues. More recently (and most obviously, in the Sino-Soviet dispute) such differences have been replicated among communist states as well.

11. See, e.g., William Zimmerman, *Soviet Perspectives on International Relations* (Princeton University Press, 1969).

These divergencies should not suggest that the spectrum of expressed opinions always extends from one polarity to the other, nor that there are not various intermediate positions. Nor *must* there be such congruence at all times: in American politics not all "doves" are liberals; not all politicians assume ideologically coherent or consistent postures on all issues that arise. Under Soviet conditions, when the range of alternatives is never publicly ventilated and when information and sophistication are far more unevenly distributed within the elite, it would be naive to expect such consistency, even if there are in the ideological set strong compulsions in the direction of such totalism. All the more striking, then, is the extent to which (just as in China and Yugoslavia) shifts in Soviet domestic, foreign, and ideological positions have tended to go hand in hand: this was as true of the turn to the "Right" in 1921, as it was of the turn to the "Left" in 1946–48, and of the turn to the "Right" in 1955–56.[12]

Some significant elements of this cleavage may be presented schematically in dichotomic form.[13]

PRIORITIES AND COMMITMENTS

Left	Right
Goal-orientedness (utopianism)	Pragmatism
Optimism	Pessimism
"Red" (partisanship)	"Expert" (rationality)
Transformation	Stability
Monolithism	Pluralism
Politics	Economics
Mobilization	Normalcy
Heavy industry	Consumer goods
Uneven ("breakthrough") development	Even development
Central command economy	Market economy
Cultural revolution	Tradition persistence
Tension-management	Consensus-building
Dialectic ("The worse, the better")	Linear ("The better, the better")
Centralization	Decentralization
Violence	Gradualism
Three-class alliance strategy	Four-class alliance
Inevitability of international conflict	Avoidability of conflict
Voluntarism	Determinism

12. Such parallel "fever curves" also extend, in the interwar period, to the "general line" dictated to the Communist International. The one significant exception — which confirms the rule — relates to the 1928–33 period when Soviet foreign policy remained "rightist" while at a time of drastic domestic transformation foreign communist parties pursued an "ultra-leftist" course intended to paralyze the potential enemy's rear in case of a showdown.

13. It is, of course, not being suggested that this is an exhaustive enumeration of divisive

Against this background one can see both the predisposition to make different assessments of the "correlation of forces" in world politics (or in individual foreign countries) and the tendency to link certain "readings" of reality to other, seemingly unrelated policy positions. Thus, the "Left" has invariably perceived opportunities to be exploited where the "Right" has seen none (and has charged the former with adventurism): this was the case with Zinoviev's associates in the Communist International until at least 1923; with the militant line symbolized by Andrei Zhdanov and Josip Tito in 1947 – 48; and with the Maoists seeking to convince the Khrushchevites after 1957.

A subsidiary aspect of this divergence has been the debate over Soviet strategy toward the non-communist world, with positions at different times ranging from advocacy of communist equivalents of "rollback," liberation, and deterrence, to détente, bluff, and compromise. These differences have given rise to specific disagreements over the intentions of other powers, such as the war scare of 1927, Stalin's views of Hitler's intentions in 1939 – 41, and the vigorous disagreement in the 1960's over U.S. intentions (with the polar positions represented, on the one hand, by the advocates of *ad hoc* agreements with the U. S. — since "men of reason" were in charge both "here" and "there" — and by those, on the other hand, who, like Marshal Malinovsky, insisted on the intrinsic, unchanging aggressiveness of American imperialism).

The question of whether one can do business with capitalism (literally or figuratively) is also of old vintage. It arose in Lenin's lifetime in connection with disagreements in the Soviet leadership over the foreign trade monopoly and foreign economic concessions. It was intensely disputed at the time the Kellogg-Briand Pact was concluded. It reemerged in the Khrushchev era in the arguments over the desirability of maximizing scientific and cultural relations abroad, the reliability of other powers as treaty partners (for instance, in regard to disarmament), and the risks of inviting foreign enterprises (like French, Italian, or Japanese) to help develop the Soviet economy.

Similarly related to basic ideological orientations has been the disagreement over the very nature of international tensions, involving a difficult search for satisfactory answers to whether tension is functional or dysfunctional:[14] a dilemma reminiscent of the ultra-left phase starting in 1928 as well as of the Maoist commitment to the dialectical belief in "the worse, the better."

Still another complex of policy disagreements has concerned the search for the wisest alliance strategy — both for the Soviet state and for communist parties abroad with the pivotal element (wooed as an ally in "Rightist" phases, and spurned as alien in "Leftist" ones) as the uncommitted, unpolarized

---

variables. Moreover, in addition to pseudo-rational elements, a variety of other factors — from personality elements to great-power compulsions — need to be considered in a fuller catalog.

14. See, for instance, Roman Kolkowicz, "The Dilemma of Superpower: Soviet Policy and Strategy in Transition" (IDA Research Paper P-383, October 1967).

middle: the nationalist movements, the peasantry, Social-Democracy, and the neutralist powers.

The tendency to link policy positions in regard to seemingly unrelated fields was most pronounced in the final years of the Khrushchev era. A more detailed study could show the interlocking nature of alignments over such varied issues as de-Stalinization, the new CPSU Program of 1961, the doctrine of peaceful transition to power, the debate between consumer-goods advocates and those whom Khrushchev derisively called "metal-eaters," the Albanian heresy, the role of non-party experts in advising the Chairman, reconciliation with Tito, the "spirit of Camp David," the shift from reliance on Soviet ground forces to stress on the rocket command, the proper response to Maoist charges against the Soviet leadership, the release of manpower from the armed forces to the civilian economy, freedom of artistic expression in the Soviet Union, and the nuclear test-ban treaty. To be sure, not all advocates of policies on any one of these took explicit positions on all other issues; and on many of the issues the alternatives were not even discussed esoterically in any detail. For this reason the military have been in a somewhat privileged position. Since strategic debates have been quasi-legitimate since 1954, the range of opinions voiced in them has tended to skew arguments somewhat toward the "hawkish" end of the political spectrum.

If policy disagreements within the Soviet elite since 1965 have been harder to identify, we should not conclude that their scope or intensity has lessened. Time and again we have learned in retrospect that what seemed to be policy consensus actually concealed bitter debates and that what appeared to be "marginalist" differences easily escalated into more fundamental cleavages.[15] While a fuller analysis would identify the limits of dissent as well, it is surely a safer course to assume the existence at all times of significant disagreements in the Soviet elite over objectives and policies than to accept at face value the professed commitment to common orthodoxy and the ritual appeal to concord and continuity.

Of course, not all differences over foreign policy can be explained in terms of a Left/Right spectrum. Many are typical of great-power dilemmas and frustrations.[16] Others are characteristic of divergencies between practitioners in the field and policy-makers at home.[17] Some stem from different functional orientations and jurisdictional biases of the actors.[18] And, of course, some are

15. It would be rewarding to re-examine the foreign-policy positions of men like Leonid Krasin, Nikolai Bukharin, and Maxim Litvinov.

16. It is suggestive of the shared problems of superpowers that some Soviet debates, especially over strategic problems, have virtually paralleled American discussions, on such questions as, "Is nuclear war unthinkable?" or "The political uses of military power," or the possibility of effective arms control and arms limitation, or the parity vs. superiority debate.

17. As the differences between Soviet negotiators in the ENDC negotiations in Geneva and decisions made, in apparent contradiction, by the authorities in Moscow.

18. Soviet experience provides a long list of such cases, ranging from "marginalist" differences

apparently rooted in honest differences in individual perceptions, judgments, and priorities.

4.

Soviet society becomes increasingly permeated by an awareness of multiple truths, multiple interests, and multiple forces at work both at home and abroad. In foreign affairs there is as yet lacking any institutionalized mechanism by which "outsiders" can affect policy formation legitimately and overtly: major influence thus continues to be exerted informally and indirectly. Resource allocation serves, however, as a quasi-institutionalized arena in which interest groups feel relatively free to do battle from time to time — with obvious implications for foreign affairs, but also with inherent limits on the specificity of policy articulation and with unequal opportunities for various groups. Military-industrial elements, for instance, have easier access to the budgetary trough than members of the creative intelligentsia, not to say spokesman for the kolkhoz peasantry.

The Party bureaucracy, which, until recently, appeared fairly indifferent to foreign-policy problems, now seems to be taking a more active part in silencing rivals and in promoting an essentially conservative line toward the Soviet-oriented parts of the communist camp — a line perhaps congruent with the orientation of traditionalist-military elements as well. Still, the efforts of the bureaucracy cannot be expected to stem the general tendency toward broader participation in the discussion of alternatives in foreign affairs. Indeed, in future domestic crises in the Soviet Union success may well go to him who is able to articulate the policy preferences of a greater range of elite groupings.

Such an increase in participation — even if it does not extend to policy-making proper — must be considered generally a healthy development, for reasons that scarcely require elaboration. But it is well to bear in mind some possibly counterproductive consequences. Since broader participation carries no assurance of moderation, the regime may find it harder to execute retreats in foreign relations — and an intense nationalist streak might prove more congenial to a large sector of the influential elite than would a liberal, cosmopolitan position. While the resultant multiplicity of perspectives may assure the avoidance of dangerously biased inputs, it also tends to circumscribe rationality in policy-making. Herbert Dinerstein has suggested that *both* ideology and factional politics have tended to limit or undermine rationality

---

between different desks of the Soviet Foreign Ministry (e.g., over Korea and Cyprus) to fundamental rivalry dating back to the 1920's. More than once the diplomats were disturbed and felt undercut by the efforts of the Comintern; while the foreign trade officials generally tended to have an even more pronounced conservative bias than political negotiators. A unique role, worthy of closer study, was of course occupied by the Beria machine and its representatives in the diplomatic and intelligence services — often at variance with that of the Foreign Ministry.

in Soviet foreign policy.[19] If the impact of "ideology" continues to weaken as elements of pluralism multiply, the simultaneous growth in the pressures exerted by elite factions and interest groups sets the stage for bargains and compromises which are apt to produce policy decisions well shy of clear and rational behavior. (To give but one recent example: it seems probable that the partial ABM system erected around Moscow was precisely the result of a compromise between the advocates of a larger system and its opponents.)

It would be foolish, however, to assume that present trends are bound to continue unchanged. As the economy develops, for instance, the reciprocal linkage between military and investment decisions and foreign policy may no longer be so simple or direct. Already the earlier assumption of the Soviet option as "guns versus butter" has proved to be vastly oversimplified — as indicated by Western surpise at Soviet ability, in the 1960's, to increase strategic capabilities while also raising the standard of living.

As the Soviet system matures, it may also happen that the compulsion toward totalism in policy orientation will yield to a more relaxed and sophisticated tolerance of ambiguity. But it would be premature to see the kernel of such a development in the recent attempt to pursue a repressive policy at home and in the "Bloc" while striving for limited accommodation and agreements with the United States. Nor should one as yet detect such a trend in the changed response to Peking: the proclivity of the Khrushchev era to move toward greater domestic "liberalization" as Sino-Soviet positions polarized seems to have been supplanted by an attitude which permits a confrontation with the Maoists without requiring any adjustment in Soviet domestic policy.

In the short run there may, of course, be all manner of reversals and zigzags. In the long run, however, "monolithic" policy-making is bound to remain — indeed, to become even more of — a myth. The increased influence of wider elements of Soviet society is likely to be exerted in support of a national policy of reasonable security, but it is also likely to express priority for welfare and prosperity objectives at home over expensive, risky, and decreasingly compelling goals of a "forward" foreign policy, whatever the ideological rationale.

No less importantly, while the circle of effective actors may remain restricted for some time to come, in the long run the professional and personal contacts of scientists and scholars, of novelists and poets, of tourists and technicians who become conversant with the outside world, and the growing familiarity of Soviet youth with foreign heroes and achievements, as well as cultural and academic exchanges, may well have as great a cumulative impact in fundamentally restructuring the image of the outside world in the minds of Soviet citizens. This is especially true for the younger generation who some day will be making the crucial decisions over life and death.

19. Herbert S. Dinerstein, *Fifty Years of Soviet Foreign Policy* (Johns Hopkins Press, 1968).

The Domestic Roots
of Soviet Foreign Policy*

In any country the nature of the relationship between internal and external affairs, if it can be determined, provides a significant clue to the future development of foreign policy. Aside from this general consideration, several special circumstances have recently heightened interest in the relation between Soviet domestic politics and foreign policy. The upheavals in Soviet ruling circles in the mid-1950's raised the question of whether equally drastic changes in foreign policy might follow. The open friction between the USSR and other Communist countries — particularly China — induces one to speculate about the nature of internecine rivalry in the Communist world. The sudden removal of Nikita Khrushchev from his positions as head of the Soviet Communist Party and Government has made the relationship between internal and external affairs in the USSR one of the most urgent questions confronting political observers everywhere.

Is it feasible, though, to analyze, to generalize, about the relationship between Soviet domestic and external policies? Certainly it is hard to study this relationship even in democratic, "open" societies. The problem is greatly complicated by the obscurity in which policy formation in the USSR is deliberately hidden. Not only is current policy consideration concealed, but there is

*Reprinted from *International Affairs,* XLI, 1 (January, 1965), pp. 37 – 47, by permission of the author and the publisher.

no systematic disclosure, through legislative investigation, publication of official records, or writing of personal accounts, of the factors behind policy decisions even in the distant past. Nevertheless, the exigencies of the Soviet struggle for power lead contestants to reveal more than their normally secretive tendencies would lead one to expect, especially in periods of upheaval like the last 12 years.

Another obstacle is almost as hard to overcome as the veil of official secrecy. Soviet society is rapidly changing. Many generalizations which held good even in the early 1950s are now subject to question, and one can anticipate even more rapid change in the future. Most observers would probably agree, however, that the essential nature of the Communist power structure has not basically changed. This power system now has a history of almost half a century — a far longer experience than that of any other modern totalitarianism. Much of this history remains obscure, but important aspects are now reasonably determinable. While one cannot hope to base fully confident predictions upon analysis of the Soviet experience in the relation of internal to foreign affairs, attentive examination of this experience is an indispensable step in the process of reasonably probable inferences about the future.

The question at issue is the relation between domestic politics, in the sense of internal competition for power, and foreign policy, not the relation between the interests of the USSR (or the Russian nation) and world Communism. An example may help make the distinction clearer. Lenin's decision to make peace with Germany at Brest-Litovsk basically represented a choice between the immediate security of the Soviet state and the immediate, all-out promotion of world revolution. Lenin evidently decided in favor of the former on the basis of a rational calculation that the best chance for eventual triumph of Communism throughout the world was its secure establishment in Russia — a calculation which eventually led to Stalin's doctrine of "socialism in one country." It is true that Lenin had to engage in a short, sharp struggle with his colleagues to secure acceptance of the Brest-Litovsk concessions. Lenin's personal position of leadership was never, however, in danger because of this policy difference.[1] Consequently, the dispute must be regarded entirely as one concerning choice of alternative policies, not as an issue of domestic politics in the sense of conflict between competitors for power.

Probably such competition for personal power did not seriously affect the conduct of foreign policy as long as Lenin dominated the Soviet regime. The situation changed rapidly when Stalin began his protracted conflict with "opposition" groups in the twenties. Stalin could not rest his claim to power upon the charisma, the intense personal devotion which had been Lenin's

---

1. See especially Louis Fischer, *The Soviets in World Affairs* (New York: Jonathan Cape, 1930), I, Chapter 1.

major instrument in dominating the party leadership. Instead, Stalin was obliged to resort to manipulation and trickery; and it seems clear that he personally enjoyed these tactics. At the same time, because his hegemony was not based on the respect of his followers, Stalin never felt secure. Hence, his insistence, approaching paranoia, on eliminating all opposition or potential opposition to his authority, regardless of the cost.

Three instances of Stalin's subordination of Soviet foreign policy objectives to his personal interests stand out. One of the best known is the sharp reversal of policy in China in 1927. Stalin had insisted that the Chinese Communist Party collaborate with non-Communist nationalists, first with Chiang Kai-shek and then (after Chiang attacked the Communists) with the "left" group of the Kuomintang in Wuhan. Eventually even the latter group turned upon its Communist allies. The whole prospect of Communist association in a victorious anti-Western nationalist front vanished. Stalin's critics at home — particularly Trotsky — seized on the manifest failure in China to demonstrate Stalin's incompetence. Although his personal power was not really endangered, Stalin wanted to recoup his prestige prior to the opening of the 15th Congress of the Soviet Communist Party. Blaming the Chinese failure upon the local Communist leadership was not enough; he needed the appearance of spectacular success. Consequently, he sharply reversed the earlier cautious line by ordering violent uprisings against the Chinese nationalist leadership, especially in Canton.[2] These rebellions were bloodily suppressed, and Chinese Communism remained in eclipse for almost a decade.

Stalin's sacrifice of Soviet objectives during the Spanish Civil War in order to destroy those he distrusted was a considerably more complicated affair. Many of Stalin's critics have contended that the destruction of the Anarchist and semi-Trotskyite forces in Catalonia in the spring of 1937 was designed merely to serve Stalin's personal interests. There is some merit in this argument, but it is quite possible that the defeat of the extreme left-wing forces was desirable from the standpoint of Soviet efforts to secure Western support for a policy of collective security to restrain Germany and Italy. Stalin's subsequent liquidation of the Communist control apparatus in Spain had no such rational justification. Old Bolshevik political leaders like Antonov-Ovseenko were purged because Stalin feared they might retain their earlier association with Trotsky. Skilled NKVD control agents were purged (unless, like Alexander Orlov, they successfully fled) as collaborators of Stalin's disgraced police chiefs.[3] Outstanding military officers, who (as Khrushchev later noted) had

2. Robert C. North, *Moscow and Chinese Communists* (Stanford: Stanford University Press, 1953), Chapter 7; Conrad Brandt, *Stalin's Failure in China* (Cambridge, Mass.: Harvard University Press, 1958), Chapters 4, 5.

3. David C. Cattell, *Communism and the Spanish Civil War* (Berkeley: University of California Press, 1955), pp. 102 *et seq.*, 208 *et seq.*; John A. Armstrong, *The Politics of Totalitarianism* (New York: Random House, 1961), pp. 42–43; and Il'ia Ehrenburg, "Liudi, gody, zhizn'," in

acquired invaluable experience in combat in Spain, were executed.[4] As a result, the remnants of the Communist control apparatus were unable to dominate the Spanish Republic during its last months. Even more important, from the standpoint of Soviet interests, was the loss of painfully acquired military experience.

The most spectacular and, in the long run, the most important example of Stalin's sacrifice of foreign policy interests to his mania for undisputed control was the break with Josip Tito in 1948. It is true that one cannot be sure that Stalin's motive in this instance was "domestic" politics, though there are good reasons for thinking that he believed Tito's defiance was related to the covert deviation of certain high Soviet officials. Given the complete dependence of the European satellites upon the USSR at that time, however, the quarrel with Tito was scarcely distinguishable from a domestic controversy. The damaging repercussions for Soviet foreign policy scarcely need recounting here. Aside from the considerable injury to the Soviet strategic position in southeast Europe, the complete split with Yugoslavia was a very severe blow to the prestige of the USSR and Communism in general. It is, of course, possible that Stalin calculated that these liabilities were offset by monolithic control of the remaining European satellites. That this was not a wise calculation is fairly well demonstrated by the frantic efforts which his successors made to repair the breach.

As was just suggested, it is possible that Stalin consciously thought that he was promoting the interests of the Soviet Union and of world Communism by his ruthless pursuit of personal power. It is conceivable that he may have reasoned that only absolute, rigid control by the "indispensable" leader would preserve the unity and strength of the Communist world.[5] After the revelations which Khrushchev and other Soviet spokesmen have made about Stalin, it is hardly possible to argue that his more extreme actions, such as those outlined above, can be rationally regarded as in accord with Soviet interests.[6] Of course, it is possible that Stalin's mind was so warped that he could not distinguish his personal position from the interests of the regime as a whole. Whether or not this was the case, his objective sacrifice of Soviet foreign policy interests seems indisputable. One should not, however, carry this interpretation too far; certainly many of Stalin's errors — including, probably, the Nazi-Soviet pact

Novyi Mir, June 1962, p. 124. Ehrenburg's "Kotov" was really Orlov's successor, the NKVD officer Eitingon.

4. The "secret speech" at the 20th Party Congress, in *Current Soviet Policies II* (New York: Praeger, 1957), p. 181.

5. "He may be given the dubious credit of the sincere conviction that what he did served the interest of the revolution and that he alone interpreted those interests aright." Isaac Deutscher, *Stalin: A Political Biography* (New York: Oxford University Press, 1949), p. 378.

6. In other words (to use the convenient terminology advanced by Herbert Simon in *Administrative Behavior* [New York: Macmillan, 1957], p. 76), Stalin's behavior may have been "personally rational," but it was not "organizationally rational."

of 1939 — were the result of genuine miscalculation of Soviet and Communist interests, rather than the result of personal obsession.

But Stalin's ruthlessness in subordinating all policy considerations to his personal aims was sufficiently frequent and evident (at least to his major lieutenants) to leave a deep impress on the mentality of the Soviet elite. Today it is easy to forget that two-thirds of the life span of the Soviet system was passed under the shadow of Stalin. Every major figure (and nearly all of the minor ones) in the present elite spent most of his active career in Stalin's service. The effect of Stalin's teaching and, more significantly, his example will not be erased as long as this group remains in power.

The harshest lesson which the elite has learned is that the consequence of defeat in the struggle for power is personal destruction. This grim lesson was reinforced soon after Stalin's death by the execution of Beria and his followers. It is instructive to note that Beria apparently anticipated what his fate would be if he became powerless, and drew the "Stalinist" conclusion that his own survival was the paramount consideration. The steps he took in internal Soviet affairs are too complicated to relate in detail here, but some, at least, might have been very injurious to the system. Apparently Beria, working through the police apparatus, tried to gain effective control of a broad belt of territory on the periphery of the USSR, including, in addition to his Transcaucasian stronghold, Latvia, Lithuania, the Ukraine, and the Central Asian republics. If he had been successful in doing this he could have assured his own safety, but only at the cost of disrupting the monolithic pattern of the Soviet system. In foreign affairs, Beria's policies are not so clear, but there is reason to believe that he contemplated major concessions to the Western powers and the European satellite populations in order to secure personal support.[7]

It is harder to be certain that any of the contestants for power in the USSR since 1953 has jeopardized Soviet foreign policy interests in order to attain personal objectives. The coincidence of the sudden war scare, which Khrushchev initiated by threatening Turkey in the autumn of 1957, and his disgracing the popular Marshal Georgi K. Zhukov, is suspicious, but there is no direct evidence to indicate that Khrushchev was trying to divert the Soviet public from his domestic political move. It appears certain that Khrushchev remained relatively free from Stalin's obsessive fear of potential opposition. Aside from the Beria group, Khrushchev's opponents were allowed their lives. If rumors are accurate, however, at least some of Khrushchev's defeated rivals suffered great personal hardship as well as humiliation.[8] In any case, their careers were ruined, at least as long as Khrushchev remained master of the country, for in a totalitarian state there is no alternative position for a man whom the

7. Armstrong, *op. cit.,* pp. 244 – 247.
8. "Les Droits de l'Homme selon les Communistes (Le Sort de D. T. Chêpilov)," in *Est et Ouest,* May 16 – 31, 1962, pp. 17 – 18.

regime rejects. Under these circumstances, it seems reasonable to predict that ambitious and determined future contestants for power will not hesitate to juggle foreign interests to secure domestic political victory.

In a very important sense the subordination of Soviet interests abroad to the demands of the domestic power struggle is only a special case of the more general practice of Soviet leaders of making policy a pawn in personal contests. In order to illustrate this general tendency, it is scarcely necessary to go further back than the period following Stalin's death. It will be recalled that a major criticism directed against Georgi M. Malenkov before his forced resignation as premier in early 1955 was his emphasis on the development of consumer-goods industries at the same rate as heavy industry. Scarcely was Malenkov's defeat sealed, however, before Khrushchev and his associates muted this criticism; at the 20th Party Congress only a year later practically nothing was heard of it. On the contrary, within a very short time Khrushchev was stressing the production of consumer goods in terms which were virtually identical to those Malenkov had used.[9] One is bound to conclude that Khrushchev and his faction recognized the pressing need for diversion of industrial facilities to relieve the more urgent needs of the Soviet consumer, though they had earlier found the shibboleth of priority for heavy industry a convenient lever to dislodge Malenkov.

The issue of industrial reorganization in 1956–57 developed in a very similar fashion, though here Khrushchev and his group were the innovators. The functional need for reorganization of the cumbersome ministerial system was fairly obvious, but the *manner* of reorganization carried major political implications. The central ministerial bureaucracies were the stronghold of supporters of Malenkov and Lazar M. Kaganovich. If the ministries were only partially broken up, or replaced by broad regional economic directorates, the economic bureaucracies might retain much of their power. If, on the other hand, the reorganization involved transfer of industrial direction to the provincial level, Khrushchev's supporters in the territorial party machine would assume dominant positions. Consequently, Khrushchev's decision (after some hesitation) to demand the latter type of reorganization was a sharp thrust at Malenkov, Kaganovich, and their associates. As speakers at the 22nd Party Congress later complained, this incident was a major factor impelling the "anti-Party" group to make its disastrous attempt in June 1957 to depose Khrushchev.[10] Only a few months had elapsed after Khrushchev's spectacular

9. In 1953, Malenkov advocated developing heavy and light industry "at the same rate," while Khrushchev emphasized heavy industry as the basis of further development; in 1962 Khrushchev declared that "in the future light and heavy industry will develop at the same pace."

10. See the speeches by E. A. Furtseva and A. I. Mikoyan in *XX S'ezd Kommunisticheskoi Partii Sovetskogo Soiuza, Stenograficheskii Otchet* (Moscow: Gosudarstvennoi Izdatel'stvo Politicheskoi Literatury, 1962), pp. 396, 449.

victory, however, before it became apparent that transfer of industrial direction to the provincial level — where more than 100 control units were established — had led to fragmentation of economic activity and the danger of provincial autarky. After 1958 Khrushchev, having attained his political objectives, moved steadily in the direction of constituting larger economic control units. In a word, the functionally efficient solution lay about midway between those which the contending factions sought, for political reasons, to impose in 1957.

In the field of foreign policy, the reversals of policy were not so sharp, but the tendency of a competitor to adopt his defeated rivals' policies has nevertheless been apparent. One of the secret charges (corroborated by considerable circumstantial evidence) brought against Beria was that he tried to send a clandestine personal emissary to effect a reconciliation with Tito.[11] But Beria's elimination did not mean that these conciliatory efforts were abandoned; on the contrary, throughout Malenkov's direction of state affairs there was a notable *rapprochement* between Yugoslavia and the Soviet Union. It must have been apparent to the great majority of the Soviet leaders (Molotov, hopelessly compromised by his involvement in Stalin's vicious attacks on Tito, was the exception) that closer ties between the two countries would be useful to Soviet foreign policy. Moreover, Tito's prestigious position in the world Communist movement meant that the Soviet leader who restored *Party* relations between Yugoslavia and the USSR would gain a notable advantage in the contest for power in the Soviet Communist Party.

As soon as Malenkov was deposed as head of government, Khrushchev devoted extraordinary effort to attaining this objective; his partial success in the summer of 1955 received almost unprecedented stress in local Party meetings throughout the Soviet Union. During the next two years (despite some friction over the Hungarian revolution) Tito and Khrushchev exchanged visits and Tito gave Khrushchev moral support in his struggle with his rivals. After the defeat of the "anti-Party" group, the *Party* aspect of Yugoslav-Soviet relations rapidly cooled. At the state level (with some exceptions) cordiality has continued. It would appear that Khrushchev as a contestant for Soviet power no longer needed to draw on Tito's prestige as a Communist leader; but Khrushchev as leader of Soviet Communism continued to foster Yugoslav-Soviet cooperation in the interests of Soviet foreign policy, particularly in relation to China.

Finally, one may note the attitudes of Soviet leaders toward the effects of nuclear weapons. Early in 1954 Malenkov said that nuclear war would mean the "destruction of civilization." This was a novel thesis for a Leninist, for it clearly implied that the march of history toward Communism could be terminated by an "accidental" factor. Khrushchev, by implication, sharply

11. Armstrong, *op. cit.,* p. 248.

refuted Malenkov's assertion, maintaining that nuclear war would destroy capitalism, but not "socialism." Leading military figures like Marshal Zhukov took the same position. After the rout of the "anti-Party" group (followed a few months later by the dismissal of Marshal Zhukov) Khrushchev moved to adopt a position closer to Malenkov's, though not precisely identical with it: that, though "socialism" would prevail, nuclear war would mean destruction of "major centers of civilization."

It seems clear that any Soviet leadership is now compelled by the logic of facts to accept the catastrophic implications of general nuclear war. Indeed, Khrushchev stressed repeatedly the need for avoiding such a war, even going so far as to revise explicitly Leninist teachings on the inevitability of war while capitalist states exist. Certainly it would have been just as logical for Khrushchev to have taken this position in 1954 when the USSR's weakness in nuclear weapons made it even more important for the country to avoid nuclear war. But then Khrushchev stood to gain by picturing Malenkov as "weak" in his foreign policy stand. Khrushchev, having eliminated all rival power alignments at home, had sufficient leeway to take a position which is more rational from the standpoint of Soviet interests.

On the basis of these examples, one can generalize — with at least a fair measure of probability — that *in the short run* contestants for leadership in the Soviet Union will manipulate policy issues to strengthen their domestic power positions. This manipulation (which sometimes involves at least marginal sacrifice of Soviet interests) will, however, last only as long as the power struggle is in doubt. Thus the "short run" is a matter, at most, of a very few years. In the *longer run*, any victorious contestant tends to take the position which is consonant with a rational calculation of Soviet interests. This is not the place to discuss at length what those interests may be, but one may summarize them very generally as the maximization of the power of the Communist system in the USSR and abroad. From the tactical standpoint, the pursuit of these interests is characterized by a delicate mixture of dynamic expansionism and caution. Taken as a whole this policy is functionally rational from the standpoint of the Communist ideology (though in any given instance it may be based on an error in judgment), however little one may think it serves the true interests of the Soviet peoples and others whom it affects.

One can, of course, speculate that a leader with quite different objectives and personality might arise in the USSR. Such a man might, conceivably, be genuinely devoted to liberalism and peace as they are understood in Western democratic countries. Conversely, he might be a fanatic like Hitler, eager to gamble on quick victory. Such types do not, however, appear to be produced by the selection process which has brought forth the contestants for supreme power in the Soviet Union. There are those who argue that broad, secular changes in Soviet society will alter the personality types who attain leadership positions. Possibly this is true — but in this instance it would seem most prudent to interpret "secular" in its most literal sense. For the foreseeable future, neither the liberal statesman nor the *fanatic* adventurer appears likely to assume direction of Soviet affairs.

One possibility does, however, deserve serious consideration. An individual contestant in the power struggle may see his only hope for victory in taking a desperate step which would jeopardize the existence of the Soviet system, or even the peace of the world. As was briefly discussed above, Lavrenti Beria seems to have been in this position in 1953; but his moves jeopardized Soviet stability rather than world peace. It is possible that a future contestant for power might calculate that his only hope for personal safety lay in a dramatic diversion in the foreign field. Between 1953 and 1957 there was a tendency for widening circles of officials to play a role on the periphery of the power struggle. These broader groups have had no direct voice in the selection of leaders, except in crises like the June 1957 plenary session of the Party Central Committee, and (though the evidence is not yet clear) in the Central Committee session which ousted Khrushchev on October 14, 1964. Nevertheless, the contestants for power have evidently paid close attention to attitudes among such circles of higher- and medium-level officials. Consequently, these attitudes may be regarded as a sort of oligarchic public opinion which may influence the development of policy and especially the manner in which it is expressed. Given the permanent elimination of the terror which cowed officials under Stalin, the increase in their sense of self-importance and assertiveness seems to be an irreversible trend. Now that Khrushchev has passed from the Soviet scene, this "public opinion" is even more significant; a future contestant for power may find it crucially important to impress these officials with his ability to achieve rapid and striking successes. For a contestant who is in an insecure position at home, the temptation to seek such a dramatic success in foreign policy may be very great — given the high personal cost of failure in the power struggle. Obviously, the cost of such an adventure to the Soviet Union and to the world could be appalling.

It would be interesting to extend the discussion of the relation between internal strife and foreign policy to the controversies which are prevalent today in the Communist bloc as a whole. As the example of Tito's relations to Stalin and Khrushchev suggests, there is no clear line of demarcation between the domestic politics of a single Communist country and intra-bloc politics. One is tempted to generalize that, insofar as the personal positions of rival leaders may be threatened by intra-bloc disputes, the same rules would apply to such controversies as to internal Soviet power struggles. Differences in national charactertistics — which affect even Communist regimes — and the widely varying stages of development of the Communist systems, should make one very cautious in reaching conclusions based on evidence drawn from the Soviet system alone. For example, the more recent the seizure of power by a Communist regime, the stronger seems its tendency to seek radical solutions in foreign affairs. Consequently, policy disputes between Communist bloc regimes on the timing of expansionist moves and the degree of risk to be taken quite possibly reflect differing perceptions of what are the appropriate tactics for the Communist movement as a whole, rather than manipulation of policy for the sake of enhancing either personal or national power.

A special case, however, is worth noting. Most observers of the current controversy between the Soviet and the Chinese Communist regimes have concluded that both have too many interests in common (particularly in opposition to the Western democratic powers) to permit their cleavage to go to the extreme of armed conflict. From the standpoint of world Communist interests, and very probably even the interests of the individual Communist regimes, this is true. If one can apply the generalizations elaborated earlier in this article, however, what is rational for the Communist system is not necessarily determinative for individual Communist leaders. Recent Chinese attacks on Khrushchev's leadership and retaliatory Soviet denunciations of the ruling group in Peking indicate that both sides have been playing the dangerous game of intervention in the internal affairs of the rival regime. If a Soviet or Chinese Communist leader in a key position were seriously threatened by the influence which the other country's regime could exercise among his own elite, he might feel obliged to take drastic action against the other Communist regime, including even the use of force. While such action would almost certainly be highly dysfunctional from the standpoint of his own regime as a whole, it would be a wholly rational personal response to extreme danger. Khrushchev's removal may temporarily diminish the force of the Chinese denunciation of Soviet leadership. It is conceivable that the new Soviet leadership may make far-reaching concessions to the Chinese position, but resumed hostility between the two Communist powers appears more probable. In the near future, however, any Soviet leader is likely to be less secure than Khrushchev was when his quarrel with Peking began. Consequently, the scope for Chinese Communist intrigue among the Soviet elite will broaden. Apparently the reverse is not true, for the Chinese ruling group has been able to maintain a much more "monolithic" front than the Soviet equivalent. Under these circumstances, it is possible, though hardly probable, that a Soviet leader might decide on forcible action against the Chinese Communist regime.

If the above analysis of the effects of the current instability in Soviet politics is correct, what are the implications for Western policy? There is probably little that the Western statesmen can do to avert the extreme contingency — the precipitation of a catastrophic world war by a desperate contender in the Soviet power struggle. This possibility (fortunately, it does not seem more than a possibility) is a chastening reminder that even the best Western policy cannot avoid catastrophe in extreme contingencies. The best that can be done — and it is extremely important that it be done — is to study the development of the Soviet power struggle closely and continuously.

The more likely contingency is a repetition of the short-run manipulation of Soviet foreign policy in the course of an internal power struggle. Here, too, direct intervention by Western policy-makers is scarcely feasible. It is possible that such a situation would permit the West to make small gains; it is also possible that the Western powers might rationally calculate that small concessions were desirable. If it is true that in the long run (and not such a *very long run* at that) any Soviet leader victorious in the power struggle will return to the basic interests of Soviet policy, the West cannot gain by making important concessions to "help" a contestant in this struggle. Careful observation of Soviet internal political developments, but steadfast adherence to major Western interests, is far safer than an attempt to adjust our policies to the changing of the guard in the Kremlin.

"Bipartisanship" in Soviet
Foreign Policy-Making

What influence, if any, do factional differences within the Kremlin leadership have on Soviet foreign policy? Are foreign policy issues used as political footballs in the succession game of *kto-kovo* (who gets whom) in the USSR? How "collective" is Soviet collective leadership when decisions are being made which result in an about-face in Soviet economic, political, military, propaganda, and ideological policies toward the outside world? Can we find evidence that Soviet decision-makers are motivated more by considerations of their own careers and power position? Or do they look primarily at matters of the overall "national" interest? These are the types of questions which have aroused the curiosities of Sovietologists particularly since the death of Stalin ended the "cult of the personality" and Khrushchev's "subjectivism" culminated in his ouster over five years ago.

In an attempt to gain an empirical handle on this important yet elusive aspect of Kremlinology, one period has been isolated for study.[1] Between the 19th and 20th Congresses of the CPSU, factionalism within the Soviet leadership was pronounced — Stalin died, Beriya was eliminated, Malenkov and Molotov were effectively reduced in power, and Khrushchev emerged trium-

1. This paper is based upon the author's doctoral dissertation, *Foreign Policy and Political Factions in the USSR, 1952–1956: The Post-Stalin Power Struggle and the Developing Nations* (Ann Arbor, Michigan: University Microfilms, 69–21, 415), supervised by Alvin Z. Rubinstein.

phant. Simultaneously there was a pronounced long-term shift of emphasis in Soviet policy toward expanding the influence of the USSR in the under-developed areas of the world.[2] This aspect of changing foreign policy was chosen because Soviet moves were true initiatives in the sense that the rulers were not obliged to act in order to preserve the national security of the USSR. There was wide latitude. Decisions involved taking advantage of opportunities which presented themselves rather than reacting to threats on Soviet territory, established interests, or even prestige. Therefore, one could suppose that con-tenders for power within the CPSU leadership might be more willing to use policy-making in this area of foreign policy as a means for weakening the authority of their opponents and strengthening their own positions than in more crucial Cold War areas.

For research purposes, we postulated that early post-Stalin foreign policy decisions about the underdeveloped world were strongly influenced by differ-ences among those Soviet leaders aspiring to ruling primacy. There are a number of ways in which foreign policy decisions could be used by leadership factions for internal purposes as suggested by this hypothesis. In order to prove (or disprove) the hypothesis, however, two steps need to be taken. First, links must be found which join factions with specific foreign policies. Once such links are established then covariance can be looked for. Yet some types of covariance would substantiate the hypothesis while others would refute it or leave it in limbo, dealt with only inconclusively. What criteria can we use to evaluate the validity of the hypothesis?

In order to assert that foreign policy decisions concerning the under-developed world were "strongly" influenced by factional rivalries, we ought to find a faction of the Soviet leadership closely associating itself with a particular approach toward the underdeveloped world while opposed in this approach by a contending faction. Then, if the policy approach were pursued in such a way as to give one or the other of the factions an advantage in the power struggle, we could conclude that this facet of foreign policy was being "strongly" influenced by factional differences.

There are variations on this theme. A faction could initiate a certain policy in an attempt to weaken an opponent or it might oppose an innovation by the opponent for the same purpose. Credit for the success of a policy might be taken by a faction or, conversely, blame for a failure could be shifted onto a factional contender. In a more indirect manner, a foreign policy approach, for example, a vociferous propaganda campaign, may be used as a diversion to draw attention away from the final *coup de grace* in a battle for primacy.[3]

---

2. This term has been used as a catch-all for all the economically developing countries of Asia, Africa, and Latin America — former colonies and independent aligned and nonaligned nations.

3. Vernon V. Aspaturian, "Internal Politics and Foreign Policy in the Soviet System," in R. Barry Farrell (ed.), *Approaches to Comparative and International Politics* (Evanston, Ill.:

There are a number of circumstances under which we would have to conclude that this working hypothesis had not been supported, that Soviet policies toward the underdeveloped world were not subject to factional influences. One would be if there appeared to be no differences among the Soviet leaders over foreign policy matters, that is, that they agreed on approaches to be taken toward the developing nations. Similarly, it might be possible to detect differences over policies yet determine that these disagreements were not used by any faction to enhance its own position or detract from that of a rival faction. This would be the epitome of Leninist "democratic centralism," which postulates that only rational, selfless considerations motivate Communist policy-makers. Such conditions would be observable if differences of opinion were expressed and changes in policy came about but the balance of power did not change. Again, we could find that, while some foreign policy issues are used as weapons between warring factions, policies bearing on the underdeveloped world are not involved. In such a case the assumption that Soviet policies toward the Third World might be more susceptible to factional usage than intra- or inter-bloc policies would have to be questioned. Finally, lack of information or absence of links between power and policy could leave us unable to draw any meaningful conclusions.

Having spelled out the circumstances under which one could judge whether or not the working hypothesis had been substantiated, let us consider the approach taken in this study. One of the major methodological problems has been to establish links between the two variables — factions and foreign policies. A number of the links are quite straightforward. Soviet leaders who are members of a faction, or closely identified with one, may, through their words or actions, take a position in favor of or opposed to a particular policy alternative. This could take the form of announcing a new policy, attacking an old policy, accepting credit for success, or admitting guilt for past faults. Similar action may be taken, in a more indirect manner, not by the factional leader himself but by a cohort or in a publication which is identified with a faction.

However, because power struggles within the Soviet leadership generally became known *post factum,* and then in all-too-sketchy partisan terms, and because Soviet foreign policy decisions are arrived at under conditions of secrecy, circumstantial evidence has to be used extensively. Ties may be inferred from a congruency of Soviet policies and events within the power struggle. Changes in a policy may come about as a result of changes in the personnel responsible for its implementation. The coincidence of the time factor may be the only lead we can find to relate the two variables. Though fragile links, if many such ties of coincidence are found to support each other, they can open doors to understanding.

In order to obtain as full a picture as possible of both policies and factions

Northwestern University Press, 1966), pp. 247–248.

and then relate them, we adopted an interdisciplinary approach utilizing a variety of methods in the full study. These included a computer program designed to facilitate the analysis of over 9,000 press items devoted to the underdeveloped areas in *Pravda* and *Izvestiya,* a graphic presentation of changes in diplomatic representations and ambassadorial assignments, a statistical summary of foreign trade, and historical descriptions of changing attitudes in international groupings and of doctrinal revisions.

Since some investigation of these separate topics, by themselves, has been published by reputable experts, and since the purpose of this study has been to discover relationships rather than to unearth new primary data, we relied heavily on secondary sources.[4] The tasks have been to choose from the secondary (and primary) materials those data and findings which are relevant for our present purposes and then to summarize and combine them into integrated data banks which we could then draw on for purposes of synthesis. The remainder of this paper will be drawn from the synthesis of the detailed study.

Stalinist Background

During Stalin's last years factionalism was at a minimum. Rather, the autocrat was manipulating his lieutenants. Soviet relations with the underdeveloped areas were at a low ebb yet not stagnant. Trade was down and declining from a postwar high in 1948.[5] The USSR was feeling the effect of the Western embargo imposed during the Korean War. In order to obtain required raw materials, the sale of Soviet goods was promoted beginning in late 1951. However, Stalin took a strictly businesslike view of this trade — a tactical necessity — for, as he made clear in his "two parallel world markets" thesis of October 1952, these underdeveloped areas were still part of the capitalist world market and any aid to them was a form of aid to the enemy.

Through the Cominform Stalin shifted the tactics of international Communism during 1951 – 52 away from violent revolution and toward the establishing of a broad anti-imperialist front in India, Burma, Pakistan, Ceylon, and Indonesia.[6] In spite of certain successes, such as Communist gains in Indian elections in late 1951 and 1952, Stalin was not ready to follow through and permit a full parliamentary strategy. During the 19th CPSU Congress he gave Soviet support to the "fraternal" parties of the dependent countries and called for a strengthening of a "democratic antiwar front of supporters of peace," yet

4. We have selected the footnotes in this paper from the original manuscript with the hope of giving the reader a sampling of the major works utilized as well as offering support for the argumentation.

5. Joseph S. Berliner, *Soviet Economic Aid* (New York: Praeger, 1958), p. 84.

6. John H. Kautsky, *Moscow and the Communist Party of India* (New York: Wiley, 1956), pp. 140, 147.

the national parties were not to go so far as actively to seek alliances with the leaders of the "bourgeois" parties.[7]

Stalin's lack of interest in the underdeveloped areas was reflected in the relatively limited amount of press coverage devoted to these areas by *Pravda* and *Izvestiya* during 1952 and its predominantly "anti-" character, according to our computer categories.[8] The 19th Congress had introduced some "pro-" bias into the press, but in November this reverted to a very strong "anti-" content which continued through that winter until after Stalin's death.

Beriya's Bid for Power

Stalin's heirs wanted to extricate themselves from the the rigid, dangerous situation which the dictator left when he died in March 1953. A number of conciliatory moves were made toward the West in the spring of 1953, culminating in the settlement of the Korean War. There were differing emphases within the party Presidium, however, with Molotov in a strong position and not inclined to move away from Stalin's policies and Beriya apparently ready to make concessions in relations with the satellites, the West, and to some extent the underdeveloped world.[9]

The basis for this latter contention may be found in Soviet policies toward Iran during the spring of 1953 after Premier Mossadegh had broken diplomatic relations with Great Britain and legalized the Communist Tudeh party Stalin had supported Mossadegh's defiance of the West and was extremely critical of the Shah. Then in March and April 1953, right after Stalin's death, the Soviet press shifted its coverage dramatically, dropping criticism of the Shah while praising both Mossadegh and the Tudeh. This constituted a significant new approach stressing local nationalists.

This policy change may be linked to Beriya in two ways. First, the only person to be brought into the reduced Soviet governing bodies after Stalin's death was a Presidium candidate, Jafar Bagirov, who was a close associate of Beriya, had been first secretary of the Azerbaydzhan party since 1933,[10] and

---

7. Marshall D. Shulman, *Stalin's Foreign Policy Reappraised* (Cambridge, Mass.: Harvard University Press, 1963), pp. 247, 253.

8. The computer analysis was a quantitative measure, consisting of a month-by-month count of press items and words in *Pravda* and *Izvestiya*, with a printout presentation both in figures and in histograms with the 50 months along the horizontal axis. A qualitative element was introduced by dividing the press coverage into three broad types of contents, reflecting different Soviet attitudes toward events or personalities: (1) "anti-," including "anti-U.S.," "anti-West," "anti-local authorities," and "anti-local conditions"; (2) "pro-," including "pro-Soviet," "pro-Communism," "pro-local Communist party," and "pro-local progressive events"; and (3) "neutral," which applies to objective reporting without value judgments.

9. Zbigniew K. Brzezinski, *The Permanent Purge* (Cambridge, Mass.: Harvard University Press, 1956), p. 161; Robert Conquest, *Power and Policy in the U.S.S.R.* (New York: St. Martin's Press, 1962), p. 215.

10. John A. Armstrong, *The Politics of Totalitarianism* (New York: Random House, 1961),

was reported to have had great influence on the Tudeh party over a considerable time, including the early postwar period when the USSR attempted to
annex Azerbaydzhani Iran. It is not unreasonable to expect that Bagirov, with
Beriya's support, was playing an important if not decisive role in Soviet policy
toward Iran. A second link, again of an indirect nature, was the recall of
Ambassador Sadchikov in late June 1953 — at the same time Beriya was
arrested and just before both Beriya and Bagirov were denounced at the July
party plenum. Sadchikov was replaced by a career diplomat who had served
under the new Soviet Foreign Minister, Molotov.[11]

In spite of this evidence, Beriya's downfall was due to much more important
factors related to internal affairs and policies toward the Communist bloc.[12]
Therefore, we are not able to assert that there was a strong relationship
between Beriya's power struggle and policies toward the underdeveloped nations.

Initial Malenkov-Molotov Policy Formulation

The expansion of Soviet economic ties with the underdeveloped world, initiated by Stalin, continued through 1953 on a broader, more organized basis,
unaffected by Beriya's downfall. The USSR ceased its criticism of the UN's
Expanded Program of Technical Assistance in July 1953[13] and during the
latter half of the year concluded trade negotiations with many countries,
including Egypt, Argentina (first credit extended to an underdeveloped nation), India, and Israel.[14] Malenkov's report of August 8, 1953 placed these
economic moves into the context of his "new course," the first stage of which
concentrated on importation of necessary foodstuffs and raw materials. Malenkov also made favorable remarks toward many of the non-Communist governments of developing countries, omitting the usual criticism of the national
bourgeoisie.[15]

The volatile course of events in Iran during the summer of 1953 forced the
Soviet leadership to face a crucial decision. While the Soviet government was
making a series of cooperative gestures toward Premier Mossadegh, the Shah
and General Zahedi lost out in an attempt to replace the Premier and were

p. 247.
   11.   William B. Ballis, "Soviet-Iranian Relations during the Decade 1953 – 64," *Bulletin of
the Institute for the Study of the USSR,* XII (November, 1965), pp. 9 – 10.
   12.   Edward Crankshaw, *Russia without Stalin* (New York: Viking Press, 1956), p. 90; Boris
Nicolaevsky, *Power and the Soviet Elite* (New York: Praeger, 1965), pp. 118, 134; Myron Rush,
Political Succession in the USSR (New York: Columbia University Press, 1965), pp. 58 – 59.
   13.   Alvin Z. Rubinstein, *The Soviets in International Organizations* (Princeton, N. J.: Princeton University Press, 1964), p. 32.
   14.   Robert L. Allen, *Soviet Economic Warfare* (Washington, D. C.: Public Affairs Press,
1961), p. 129.
   15.   J. M. Mackintosh, *Strategy and Tactics of Soviet Foreign Policy* (London: Oxford University Press, 1962), pp. 77, 119 – 120, 130.

forced to flee. The Tudeh obtained freedom of action and Communist demonstrations broke out across the country. The "bourgeois nationalist" Mossadegh and the Communist Tudeh were ready to take over. Soviet support of both might have led to victory. However, the Tudeh was not satisfied with the prospects of sharing power and the Soviets may have gained confidence from the world reaction of awe at the first Soviet hydrogen bomb test, announced August 12. The Soviets chose a "dogmatic" course, putting their support behind the Tudeh and urging the bypassing of Mossadegh. With the division of these two anti-Western forces, the takeover failed.[16]

It would be reasonable to assume that those Soviet leaders most closely concerned with relations with foreign Communist parties, Secretaries Khrushchev and Suslov, and also Foreign Minister Molotov, favored support for this revolution, yet there is no evidence that this was an issue of factional difference. Soviet interest in these events was high (greater press coverage on Iran than in any other period from 1952 to 1956). Yet there was probably considerable wavering on the entire Iranian situation, as the high proportion of "neutral" press content would indicate. The failure of this coup must certainly have cooled down those "dogmatic" Soviet leaders who favored quick results in the form of Soviet takeovers and victories for Communist parties in the underdeveloped countries, and tended to give more credence to the practical advisability of cooperating with the liberation movements even though they were bourgeois.

During 1953 there was a significant discrepancy between the types of content emphasized by the two Soviet newspapers. The computer program indicated only one other such period, the winter of 1954–55. From May through November 1953 *Pravda* averaged 16.6 percentage points more "anti-" content than *Izvestiya*, although *Pravda* had been more "pro-" the preceding year. *Izvestiya*, on the other hand, averaged 14.0 percentage points more "neutral" than *Pravda* between June and November. If we assume that *Pravda* represented the party apparat and *Izvestiya* was the organ of the government at this time, then these differences mean that there were rather different approaches being advocated toward the underdeveloped world by the Khrushchev (party) and Malenkov (government) factions. *Pravda* was sticking to the "dogmatic" hard line of criticizing Western imperialism while *Izvestiya* was initiating a "revisionist" approach by introducing more objective reporting and editorializing less. Malenkov and his supporters were apparently more willing to revise the Stalinist approach to the "dependent" areas than were Khrushchev and those party *apparatchiki* aligned with him. This hypothesis is further supported by the finding that, in October 1953, the month after

16. David J. Dallin, *Soviet Foreign Policy after Stalin* (Philadelphia: Lippincott, 1961), pp. 213, 220, 294.

Khrushchev was recognized as the first secretary by the party Central Committee plenum, *Izvestiya* fell back into an "anti-" line.

These different emphases were apparently worked out within the collective leadership and resolved by "democratic centralism."

A Coordinated Policy Drive — 1954

Once differences between the newspapers had been resolved, analysis of the press indicates that after several months of caution and uncertainty a carefully organized, controlled, broad propaganda campaign was undertaken to lay a basis for an expansion of Soviet relations with the underdeveloped world through diplomacy and trade and in international organizations. Afghanistan was the object of an extensive drive through relief, assistance, conferences, and exchanges. Turkey was subjected to both weaning and cajoling in an attempt to turn her away from Western ties. Conciliation with Iran had little favorable results, as did vacillation toward Nasser, who was hard on Egyptian Communists. Arms were furnished to Colonel Arbenz in Guatemala but that revolution failed.

There were difficulties in implementing this new policy of expanding governmental relations when applied to countries which had influential national Communist parties. In India the Soviets had trouble in influencing the Communist party of India to cooperate somewhat with the Nehru government and to focus on American imperialism rather than on British colonialism. However, developments in Syria supported those Soviet leaders who favored a positive attitude toward the "national bourgeoisie." The secretary of the Syrian Communist party was elected to the parliament in September 1954 with the backing of petty bourgeois, nationalist elements whose cooperation he had encouraged.[17]

The most significant gain for the Communist movement during 1954 was the conclusion of the Geneva Indochina accord, which brought the first territorial gain to the Communist bloc since Czechoslovakia and mainland China. It came about as a result of an amalgamation of both the "dogmatic" approach through armed struggle and a "revisionist" willingness to come to terms with the capitalist enemy. The hard-line approach of Molotov appeared dominant at first, as the French were losing militarily.[18] Khrushchev took a very aggressive position, probably to align himself with Molotov, and Malenkov was forced in early 1954 to shift to a less conciliatory attitude toward the West. As the possibility of U.S. "massive retaliation" became more real and the

17. Walter Z. Laqueur, *The Soviet Union and the Middle East* (London: Routledge & Kegan Paul, 1959), pp. 198 – 199, 250 – 251.
18. Herbert S. Dinerstein, *War and the Soviet Union* (New York: Praeger, 1959), pp. 100, 115.

French deadline approached, Soviet concern rose and they began to encourage their Communist allies to find a diplomatic solution.[19] The computer analysis indicates that in May 1954 Soviet press coverage shifted from an "anti-U.S." emphasis to an "anti-West" one, suggesting that criticism was to be concentrated on the immediate French colonizers rather than on the overall threat of U.S. "imperialism." This success may have encouraged Soviet leaders to combine different approaches into a flexible policy toward the underdeveloped world that could lead to more than just obtaining raw materials or reducing Western influence.

The 1954 policy of expansion was a quantitative, not qualitative, change and does not appear to have been subject to factional differences. Malenkov was leading the way and Molotov was cooperating, with Khrushchev's support. The motivations may have differed — Molotov more concerned with blocking the West out of these areas or supporting Communist takeovers, Malenkov more interested in first obtaining raw materials needed by the USSR and then pursuing long-term gains for Communism — but they could agree on the overall desirability of extending Soviet influence into the underdeveloped world.

Factional Strife and Policy Reevaluation, 1954 – 1955

The period of October 1954 to March 1955 was one in which differences between Malenkov and Khrushchev came out into the open and during which there were foreign policy controversies also. An intense anti-American campaign was undertaken by the Communists in late 1954 over issues such as West German rearmament within NATO, the formation of SEATO, the Chinese "offshore islands," and the Turkish-Iraqi defense treaty which was followed by the Baghdad Pact. The Khrushchev-oriented Soviet delegation which went to Peking in September 1954 probably gained Chinese Communist support for a coordinated hard line against the United States and opposition to Malenkov's concepts of mutual deterrence, conciliation with the capitalist world, and consumer production.[20] By insisting that international tensions were mounting and undertaking these moves, Khrushchev was implementing a plan to win support against Malenkov from Molotov, Mikoyan and Shepilov (who were included on the China trip), and from the military-heavy industrial complex.

Patterns of press coverage of the developing nations offer some interesting sidelights on these overall developments. In October 1954 a cautious shift away from the previous "pro-" content appeared and then developed during the next two months into a definite shift away from this "pro-" to an "anti-U.S."

19. Boris Nicolaevsky, "Battle in the Kremlin," *The New Leader* (August 12, 1957), p. 7.
20. Donald S. Zagoria, *The Sino-Soviet Conflict, 1956 – 61* (Princeton, N. J.: Princeton University Press, 1962), pp. 405 – 406.

content, a reversion to the Stalinist hard line. At the same time, during November and December there was the second significant divergency between *Pravda* and *Izvestiya*, *Pravda* being considerably more "anti-" than *Izvestiya*. This occurred congruently with the heavy-industry – consumer-goods debate, supporting our thesis that once again the Malenkov *(Izvestiya)* faction favored a positive approach toward the underdeveloped world, stressing Soviet achievements and potentials, while Khrushchev *(Pravda)* and his allies were at this time putting greater emphasis on the negative goal of opposing the West.

Throughout the heightened international tensions propaganda campaign of late 1954 to early 1955, Soviet policy toward the underdeveloped nations appeared to become polarized. The Soviet leaders began to recognize that they could profitably cooperate with some of these nations and not with others if they ceased to lump them together. Those countries firmly tied to the West were included as targets for vilification.

On the other hand, the scope and depth of Soviet conciliatory moves were impressive and indicate a coordinated program. A decree was issued against crude anti-Islamic propaganda, signaling a change in attitude toward the Arab world. Criticism of Nasser was dropped and Soviet-Egyptian trade and aid relationships were established. Soviet concessions toward Iran and Turkey were made in an attempt to dissuade them from joining the Baghdad Pact. For the first time Nehru was given clearly favorable written praise, and India was granted the most significant foreign aid yet offered to a non-Communist country by the USSR for the Bhilai steel plant. In January 1955 an article appeared in the Cominform publication which laid the basis for doctrinal innovation in regard to the "national bourgeoisie." Foreign Minister Molotov summarized the combined "hard-soft" policy in his February report to the Supreme Soviet and it was applied the next month to the Pushtunistan issue when, for the first time, Moscow overtly supported Afghan claims against Pakistan.

These events can be related to factionalism within the Soviet leadership. After the divergency between *Pravda* and *Izvestiya* was reconciled in January 1955, *Pravda* assumed a leading role. Apparently Shepilov, editor-in-chief of *Pravda*, received policy-making authority in foreign propaganda matters and Pospelov, the party Secretariat head of *Agitprop*, switched from his somewhat neutral, pro-Malenkov inclination to Khrushchev's side. This shift in the press also supports the contention that the decision to reduce Malenkov from the premiership was not made at the Central Committee plenum in late January but rather early in the month. Molotov undoubtedly favored the "hard," anti-West aspect of the new "hard-soft" line while Mikoyan would have preferred the "soft" position toward local nationalists.

The overall contradiction between word and deed in this period leads one to suspect that the belligerent propaganda campaign was manipulated to hold the West at bay and divert attention from internal difficulties as Khrushchev weakened Malenkov's prestige.

Khrushchev's New Offensive Unfolds
during the Pre-summit Thaw

Not long after Khrushchev and Bulganin had taken over from Malenkov in February 1955, an all-out peace campaign was launched toward the West. The rapidity of this switch supports the hypothesis that the war scare had been trumped up to facilitate factional interests. In April the press coverage of the underdeveloped world shifted most significantly from its previously strongly "anti-" content to a predominantly "pro-" orientation, most of which was "pro-Soviet." The preparation for a new campaign was seen in the Soviet Foreign Ministry "Statement on Security in the Near and Middle East" of April that encouraged Arab opposition to Western alliances and, more significantly, expressed a willingness to cooperate with Arab nationalists. Coming right after the Baghdad Pact and just before the Afro-Asian Bandung Conference, it indicated to the underdeveloped countries that those which cooperated could count on the USSR for assistance. An important conference of Soviet Orientologists was held and their journal came out again for the first time in eighteen years. Finally, the Bandung Conference, which the USSR supported even though not invited, had a special influence upon Soviet policy.[21] Its impact upon world opinion must have given support to those Soviet policy-makers who were opting for greater latitude in dealing with national governments of underdeveloped countries.

Beginning after the Bandung Conference, a new energy, flexibility, and sometimes reckless willingness to experiment were introduced into Soviet policies toward the developing areas. A highly authoritative editorial appeared in *Kommunist* on May 25th criticizing previous evaluations of the role of the "national bourgeoisie" in colonial and semi-colonial areas. Shortly thereafter Khrushchev and Bulganin agreed with Tito's implicit rejection of the "two-camp" thesis when they recognized his neutral, unaligned position which was similar to that of many of the underdeveloped nations.[22] A number of traditional diplomatic and economic exchanges were undertaken, including Nehru's unprecedented visit to the USSR.

Of a much more radical nature was the encouragement the USSR gave to Egypt's interest in purchasing arms from the Communist bloc. Nasser had long wanted to achieve a truly independent position, which implied adequate military armament. Inquiries had received no encouragement from either East or West. After the agreement with the British in the fall of 1954 Nasser expected — in vain — Western help. The formation of the Baghdad Pact and Israel's attack on the Gaza Strip added an urgency to Nasser's perceived military needs. Soviet Ambassador Solod responded to Nasser's approaches in late

21. George M. Kahin, *The Asian-African Conference* (Ithaca, N. Y.: Cornell University Press, 1956), pp. 129 – 130.
22. Richard Lowenthal, *World Communism* (New York: Oxford University Press, 1964), p. 16.

May. It appears, however, that no final decision was made until after the July 1955 Central Committee plenum, indicating that the Soviet leaders realized the gravity of this extension of previous gradualistic expansion and wanted to have a firm position at home before taking this risky step.

The temporary coalition between Khrushchev and Molotov, formed during late 1954 as Malenkov was demoted, broke down very shortly after the immediate factional aim was achieved and fell completely apart at the July 1955 plenum. There had been differeuces within this coalition over several issues, including personal precedence, the appointment of party officials as diplomats, and particularly Yugoslav Communism. A gradual rapprochement had been undertaken with Tito after Stalin's death. Then in February 1955 Molotov critcized Tito and the latter's rebuttal was unexpectedly published in Shepilov's *Pravda* along with a mild editorial implying that Molotov's "dogmatic" position was no longer acceptable. In May, Shepilov — not Molotov — was included in the high-level Soviet delegation which visited Yugoslavia, indicating that Molotov's opposition to establishing party ties with Tito had been overruled. At the July plenum Molotov was isolated and forced to acknowledge his shortcomings.[23] It appears that he was relieved of many important functions and Shepilov, newly elected party secretary, took on greater responsibility in foreign affairs, particularly as concerned the underdeveloped world.

Khrushchev-Shepilov Underdeveloped Nations Policy in Full Bloom

Khrushchev used the July 1955 plenum to obtain support for his new campaign aimed at taking full advantage of opportunities in the underdeveloped world. Khrushchev is said to have described the very favorable situation on the "periphery of capitalism" as containing the possibility of sealing the fate of capitalism if India followed China in joining the socialist camp. Khrushchev's aim was to draw these underdeveloped areas away from the capitalist camp into that of socialism. The first explicit indication of a break with the Stalinist "two-camp" thesis was carried by *Kommunist* in an article which listed four categories of countries in Asia.[24]

Shortly thereafter Molotov made a second confession, this time of errors in theory. This allowed Khrushchev to reconcile the concept of "different roads to socialism," important for the underdeveloped world, with that of the leading role of the USSR. Molotov, an old Bolshevik, was reduced as an expert in ideological matters and the way was opened for further doctrinal changes. Molotov's humiliation gave Khrushchev and Shepilov more authority over foreign affairs. Khrushchev, together with Bulganin, took over high-level

23. George D. Embree, *The Soviet Union between the 19th and 20th Party Congresses, 1952 – 1956* (The Hague, The Netherlands: Martinus Nijhoff, 1959), p. 263.
24. V. Mikheev, "Novaya Aziya" [New Asia], *Kommunist,* August 25, 1955, pp. 85 – 88.

negotiations almost completely after the July plenum, and Molotov was apparently not among those Soviet leaders who met in October to plan the Geneva Foreign Ministers' Conference and its implications for the Twentieth Party Congress. Changes in diplomatic assignments to underdeveloped countries during the winter of 1955 – 56[25] indicate that Khrushchev and Shepilov were strengthening their authority to implement policy through the Ministry of Foreign Affairs at the expense of Molotov. Finally, it was Shepilov, not Molotov, who delivered the report on foreign affairs to the Twentieth Congress.

The spirit of Geneva characterized Soviet relations with the West in late 1955 and early 1956. The rather mild Western position may have encouraged Khrushchev to pursue a forceful, active campaign in the underdeveloped world. In addition to a series of moves which fit into the Malenkov pattern of cautious expansion of contacts through international groupings and meetings as well as diplomatic and economic relations, Shepilov brought the Egyptian arms deal to completion. Through this military aid coup the new Soviet leadership succeeded in hurdling the Baghdad Pact, creating a military counterforce within the Arab world, and encouraging "positive neutralism," a policy for the underdeveloped world which was not only anti-imperialist, but also leaning toward or indebted to the Communist bloc.[26]

The Khrushchev-Bulganin trip through India, Burma, and Afghanistan in November-December 1955 was the most publicized activity undertaken by the USSR throughout the entire four years under consideration and the prototype of Khrushchev's new style. In preparation for the Indian tour the "Shepilov letter" was allegedly sent to the Indian Communist party, with instructions not to interfere in Soviet diplomatic efforts aimed at courting the Indian government while advising the Indian comrades not to take all the public professions at face value. In spite of these machinations of international Communism, Khrushchev and Bulganin made a joint political statement with Premier Nehru and concluded a trade agreement which resulted in India's ranking first among the underdeveloped nations as a trading partner with the USSR, both in imports and exports. There appears to have been some criticism of this trip within the Soviet leadership, but the glowing reports of success overcame all objections and made the trip an impressive victory for Khrushchev's offensive.

Just as the Egyptian arms deal and the trip to the Far East may be regarded as the culmination of the implementation of Khrushchev's policy, so may the Twentieth Party Congress be looked upon as the high point of doctrinal readjustment. Many of the Stalinist concepts had been changed in practice over the three years since the dictator's death, yet not until the Twentieth

25. Andrey I. Lebed (ed.), *Key Officials of the Government of the USSR and Union Republics,* Series II, No. 81 (Munich: Institute for the Study of the USSR, Research Section, 1962), *passim;* Boris Meissner, "Der Auswärtige Dienst der UdSSR" [The Foreign Service of the USSR], *Osteuropa,* III (February, 1953), 49 – 54; IV (April, 1954), 112 – 118; V (February, 1955), 42 – 44.
26. Keith Wheelock, *Nasser's New Egypt* (New York: Praeger, 1960), p. 231.

Congress were the necessary changes in theory made and integrated into the doctrinal generalization of "peaceful coexistence." War was not a "fatalistic inevitability" because of the deterrent effect of socialist forces. Encirclement of the USSR had ended and a "peace zone" had emerged from the "two-camp" thesis. "Different roads to socialism" were recognized, as was the important role of the "national bourgeoisie" in achieving independence.

Although Khrushchev and his colleagues had only begun to apply their innovative policies toward the underdeveloped world by the time of the Twentieth Congress, they did have some results to show for their efforts. In this way, policies toward the underdeveloped world did assist them in establishing themselves as successful victors in the factional struggle within the Soviet leadership.

Conclusions

Our purpose has been to summarize the relationship between political factions and foreign policy in the USSR from 1952 to early 1956. We postulated that early post-Stalin policies toward the underdeveloped world were strongly influenced by factional differences between the Soviet leaders.

I must conclude that the hypothesis was substantiated only in part and that much of the evidence until 1955 negated it. Although there were very significant changes in Soviet policies toward the developing nations between the Nineteenth and Twentieth Party Congresses and intense struggles for power during the same period, policies toward the underdeveloped world were not "strongly" influenced by factional differences. Rather, they were generally developed collectively.

On occasion, however, some of the issues involved in the changing policies vis-à-vis the developing areas were used for factional advantages. Once Khrushchev had achieved his initial victories over Malenkov and Molotov in his struggles during early 1955, then the evidence clearly supports our hypothesis as policies toward the underdeveloped world were specifically used to broaden his power. Khrushchev took over Malenkov's careful extension of Stalin's trade expansion and added his own energetic, sometimes reckless style. He tried to make such a success of this "new" campaign — one of economic and military aid, political and propaganda captation, and doctrinal revisions — that his leadership position would be unassailable.

Khrushchev was strongly aided in this program by Shepilov, who had seen the potentialities for Soviet incursions into the underdeveloped world and used these issues as a means for reducing the prestige of Molotov and raising his own. Starting in late 1954, Shepilov had hitched his horse to the Khrushchev wagon and pulled especially hard in the direction of revising the Molotov approach toward the former colonies. The Twentieth Party Congress gave evidence of the success of the Khrushchev-Shepilov campaign as Khrushchev's broad doctrinal revisions were accepted and Shepilov's authority in foreign affairs rose over Molotov's.

Thus during the final year of our study, policies toward the underdeveloped world were used by one faction not so much to gain power over another faction as to retain an advantage previously won.

If policies toward the underdeveloped areas were not "strongly" influenced by factional differences, then one must deduce that these issues were decided by the Presidium in a "collective" or "bipartisan" manner, based on the merits as seen by the oligarchy. Policy alternatives would have been formulated through the various levels of the party and state hierarchies. Soviet leaders were able to disagree with one another on approaches in this area of foreign policy primarily on the basis of advantages which could accrue to the USSR and only secondarily in terms of their own power positions.

The conclusion that factional differences did not have a very pronounced effect upon foreign policies toward the underdeveloped world can have some important implications for Western evaluation of Soviet foreign policy-making in general. Those "bipartisan" policies arrived at and pursued under a truly "collective" leadership could be expected to be more deliberate, cautious, and open to rational influences, from within the decision-making body as well as from without. During such periods the organizational framework of foreign policy-making takes on added importance, indicating the advisability of keeping abreast of changes in such formal structures and their staffing.

In times when foreign policies are being used as weapons in a struggle for power, however, different guidelines prevail. A propaganda campaign may not be a substantial policy expression, but rather a front to keep the West at bay while the Soviet leadership is weakened by internal rivalry and strife. At other times a faction may choose to take a risky course which could have dangerous consequences yet promises brilliant successes in order to project itself ahead of opposing factions. If Western policy-makers are alert to the varying relationships which exist between Soviet foreign policies and leadership factions they will be in a better position to deal effectively with critical situations of various kinds.

Studying the Domestic Determinants
of Soviet Foreign Policy*

Some 15 to 20 years have passed since George F. Kennan and Barrington
Moore, Jr., expressed the basic viewpoints of American students of Soviet
affairs on the subject of the forces which shape Soviet foreign policy. In the
meantime, important political and social changes have occurred on the Soviet
scene. The autocratic form of government which Stalin personified has been
replaced by an oligarchic regime headed by less omnipotent figures. A population which is more loosely controlled resorts to work slow-ups and petitions
to demand a better and freer life. More information has become available about
the sections of opinion and configuration of interests in bureaucratic quarters.
The aim of these preliminary notes is accordingly to reexamine the viewpoints
of Kennan and Moore in the light of contemporary history, and to suggest a
possibly useful mode of inquiry into a slightly explored but perhaps important
area of scholarship.

In his "Sources of Soviet Conduct," which first appeared in 1947, Kennan
argued that the process of political consolidation of the Soviet regime was
never completed and that the men in the Kremlin were always preoccupied
with the struggle to secure and make absolute their power over Russian

*Reprinted with permission from *Canadian Slavic Studies,* I, 1 (Spring, 1967), pp. 44 –
59. This article was originally prepared for discussion at the Inter-university Research Col-
loquium on the Soviet Union and Eastern Europe, held at the Institute for Sino-Soviet Studies
of George Washington University.

society. The Soviet leaders endeavored to secure their power primarily against forces at home, but also against the outside world, since ideology taught them that the outside world was hostile and that it was their duty eventually to overthrow the political forces beyond their borders. Kennan felt that as the remnants of capitalism were liquidated in Russia, one of the most basic of the compulsions which came to act upon the Soviet leaders was the necessity to justify the retention of dictatorial authority at home by stressing the menace of capitalism abroad. Moreover, Kennan held that many of the phenomena which Americans found disturbing in the conduct of Soviet foreign policy — secretiveness, lack of frankness, and duplicity — were essential to "the internal nature of Soviet power," by which he apparently meant the moral climate of the regime, and would endure until "the internal nature of Soviet power" had changed.[1]

Moore in 1950 found acceptable the argument that the authoritarian nature of the Soviet regime is a source of an aggressive and expansionist foreign policy insofar as the real or imagined threat of potential attack made it easier to drive the Russian masses through one set of Five-Year Plans after another. In this sense, the Soviet rulers were more desirous of creating an illusion of the threat of general war rather than fomenting general war itself as a means of maximizing their power. But these were afterthoughts, overshadowed by Moore's central thesis that the main outlines of Soviet foreign policy were reactions to alterations in the distribution of political power in the world at large. As far as internal factors like specific historical background, cultural tradition, and ideology(gies) were concerned, Moore emphasized the conditioning influence which they might have in molding the Soviet's response to an international situation. It should be added that in his outstanding book, Moore did suggest that Soviet foreign policy was made not only by the impersonal interplay of social forces but also by the personal ambitions of individual leaders. For example, he attributed a lag in Soviet recognition of the danger of Nazism to factional struggles within the Russian Communist party, centering around differing evaluations of the political situation abroad as well as personal rivalries, and suspected that at all times during the 1930's there was a group of Soviet leaders who believed in the possibility of good relations with the Hitler regime.[2]

Since Kennan and Moore wrote their essays a division of opinion has persisted over the relative weight to be given to internal and external happenings and stimulants of the Kremlin's international policy. Robert C. Tucker has adhered to the general concept of Kennan, focusing upon domestic political development and the impact of the personality of Soviet leaders, mainly

1. George F. Kennan, *American Diplomacy*, 1900 – 1950 (Chicago, 1952), pp. 107 – 128. See also Kennan's remarks in Carl J. Friedrich, ed., *Totalitarianism* (New York, 1964), p. 35.
2. Barrington Moore, Jr., *Soviet Politics — The Dilemma of Power: The Role of Ideas in Social Change* (New York, 1963), pp. 350 – 383.

Stalin.[3] Marshall D. Shulman, like Moore a decade earlier, has interpreted Soviet foreign policy largely in terms of responsiveness to changes in world power relationships. Doubtlessly alluding to Tucker, Shulman claims that his own analysis has merit because "it departs from familiar interpretations of Soviet policy which emphasize enigmatic and occult characteristics or the psychology of particular Soviet leaders" and "reveals patterns of behavior which bear some relationship to what we know of human behavior elsewhere in the world." Unlike Moore, however, Shulman deplores and avoids any attempt to investigate the mainsprings of Soviet policy from the angle of internal power politics, which he terms "the shenanigans in the Kremlin."[4]

While acknowledging the contribution which each of the aforementioned scholars has made to our understanding, it seems to me that the speculative model of Kennan and Tucker has more heuristic and predictive value than that of Moore and Shulman. Its underlying assumptions encourage us to search for information which helps to clarify matters of importance like influential trends of thought and the process of decision-making in the USSR, as well as the interaction of domestic and foreign policy considerations. Specifically, the analyst is challenged to find answers to questions of evidence along the following lines: What do Soviet sources have to say about the relationship of the internal and foreign policies of a Communist government? Are there different appraisals among Soviet policy-makers and subtleties regarding the consolidation of interior rule and, if so, of corresponding shades of opinion on foreign affairs? And is there a repeated coincidence of movement towards both the reform of domestic institutions and a variety of limited accommodation with the U.S.? Having derived partial answers to such questions, we may be in a better position to evaluate Soviet conduct and frame policy proposals which are sensible and statesmanlike.

A general discussion of the problem in recent Soviet literature[5] states that the internal and foreign policies of all governments are interconnected and puts emphasis on internal factors as the determinants of a government's transactions in the international field. The following elements are seen at work in the Soviet case, as in any other: (1) economics; (2) politics; (3) ideology; (4) personality of leaders; and (5) chance. Lenin is cited to the effect that "the very deepest roots of both the internal and foreign policy of our state are shaped

---

3. Robert C. Tucker, *The Soviet Political Mind: Studies in Stalinism and Post-Stalin Change* (New York, 1963), *passim*.

4. Marshall D. Shulman, "Some Implications of Changes in Soviet Policy toward the West: 1949 – 1952," *Slavic Review,* XX, No. 4 (December, 1961), 630 – 640 and *Stalin's Foreign Policy Reappraised* (Cambridge, Mass., 1963). See also the disdainful reference to "the mental exercise of analyzing obscure signposts indicating behavior and thinking within the Kremlin," in Bernhard J. Bechhoefer, "The Soviet Attitude toward Disarmament," *Current History,* No. 266 (October, 1963), 193 – 199.

5. "Nauchnye osnovy vneshnei politiki," in A. A. Arzumanyan *et al., Stroitel'stvo Kommunizma i mirovoi revoliutsionnyi protsess* (Moscow, 1966), pp. 409 – 415.

by economic interests," and the original adds: "by the economic situation of the dominant classes of our state." This apparently signifies that the holders of power who rule in the name of the so-called dominant classes of workers and peasants give priority to tasks of internal construction, the fulfillment of which will sooner or later improve the material lot of Soviet citizens, over schemes to aggrandize the Soviet Union abroad. That much can be inferred from the 1961 party program, which declares that "The CPSU considers that the chief aim of its foreign policy activity is to provide peaceful conditions for *the building of a Communist society in the USSR* and developing the world socialist system, and together with the other peace-loving peoples to deliver mankind from a world war of extermination" (italics added).[6] More recently, the idea of the preeminence of domestic policy in the USSR was conveyed as follows: "The central problem of the internal policy of the Communist party is systematic improvement of the material and cultural conditions of the life of all the toilers of our country and creation of the essential economic preconditions for this. . . . Of course, for the successful fulfillment of the tasks which are set by internal policy it is essential to assure a favorable international atmosphere for the peaceful labor of the people building communism."[7]

The element of domestic politics, which admittedly enters into the calculations of Soviet policy-makers, is not spelled out in the discussion of Arzumanyan *et al.,* and the reader is led to believe that such phenomena as palace intrigue and parliamentary deals are completely alien to the Soviet milieu. Other Soviet propagandists have alleged that only capitalist states are concerned mostly about the political function of maintaining internal control of their population and subordinate the expansion of borders or defense of territory to this main, domestic function of the state.[8] Still others have claimed apropos of politics that the absence in the USSR of a privately owned munitions industry which is operated for private profit and the existence of party controls over the armed forces, prohibits the advent of a military-industrial lobby and its unwarranted influence in governmental chambers.[9] What Arzumanyan *et al.* may have in mind in their reference to the politics of Soviet foreign policy is how Soviet leaders handle the political question of "non-antagonistic contradictions of socialism" like the discrepancy between limited production of consumer goods and rising popular demand, something related to the perennial issue of guns or butter (about which, more below). By "ideology," the authors plainly allude to the theories of social development which fall under the rubric of "Marxism-Leninism," and they imply that old habits of thought may sometimes be operative. The haphazard impact of

6. *Pravda,* November 1, 1961.
7. V. Stepanov, *ibid.,* August 10, 1966.
8. Iu. M. Borodai, ed., *Marksizm-leninizm — teoreticheskaia osnova stroitel'stva Kommunizma* (Moscow, 1965), p. 101.
9. Iu. Zhukov, *Pravda,* March 29, 1964.

personalities and chance is pointed up through the use of a Marxian letter of 1871 to the effect that "accidents" and "the character of people who at first stand at the head of the movement" might seriously accelerate or retard the inevitable course of history.

At the same time, the authors take into account the possibility of exterior initiatives, calling the tune and therefore reject the view of some that foreign policy is nothing more than a function of internal events. An unprovoked act of aggression committed against a state may impose upon its ruling circles a number of tasks which are not inherent in their philosophy or method of government. There is reciprocity between internal and foreign policy, since class relations are not limited to the national level, but have expanded into a worldwide system of economic and political entanglements. The capitalist system of states indeed exerts an "enormous" — but not "decisive" — influence on the internal and foreign policy of every state on the globe. Summarizing, the authors instruct that, "It follows from the Marxist-Leninist proposition about the system of states that internal policy is determined not only by the class relations inside a given country, but also by international class relations on the scale of the entire system of states; that the foreign policy of a given country is an integral part of the entire existing system of international relations; and that internal and foreign policy are inseparable from one another, both on the national scale and on the scale of the entire system of states."

There is merit to the Soviet disquisition, as far as it goes. The Soviet leaders' preoccupation with internal affairs is suggested by a number of materials which are designed for the orientation of CPSU officials. It is approvingly recalled that in the Leninist golden age of 1923 – 24 the Politburo examined almost 4,000 questions and only about one-fifth were related to the activities of the commissariat of foreign affairs, Comintern, and trade union International.[10] The curriculum of the Higher Party School in 1963 featured 1,500 hours of study, only 80 of which were devoted to the international Communist, labor, and national-liberation movements.[11] A survey of the lead articles in *Pravda* has disclosed that on an average there are seven a month on general domestic policy, five on industry, five on agriculture, five on political indoctrination and party organization, one on cultural policy, and seven on foreign policy.[12]

The effect of Stalin's warfare mentality on the conduct of Soviet foreign relations has been reasonably if not elaborately pointed out in party literature. Diplomatic contacts, especially at the highest level, were sharply reduced in view of Stalin's prophecy that the U.S. and USSR would ultimately engage in armed conflict.[13] Stalin aroused the displeasure of Communist China, Ru-

10. *Trinadtsatyi s'ezd RKP (b), Mai 1924 goda, stenograficheskii otchet* (Moscow, 1963), p. 73.

11. *Spravochnik partiinogo rabotnika, Vypusk piatyi* (Moscow, 1964), p. 258.

12. Wolfgang Leonhard, *The Kremlin Since Stalin* (New York, 1962), p. 22.

13. N. M. Druzhinin *et al., Sovetskaia istoricheskaia nauka of xx k xxii s'ezdu KPSS*

mania, Bulgaria, and Hungary by creating joint-stock companies, and instead of patiently discussing points of difference with Yugoslavia, he caused a rift.[14] In conformity with his mistrust of national reformers and line of self-isolation, Stalin kept the Soviet Union aloof from the newly emancipated nations in the underdeveloped regions.[15] Khrushchev's "subjectivist" errors in foreign policy have been hinted, but never pinpointed, in Soviet media. Western correspondents reported at the time of the premier's fall that his successors reproached him for personal initiatives which resulted in the serious loss of national prestige *vis-à-vis* Washington (the Cuban missile crisis) and good will inside the Eastern bloc (the Rumanian oil issue), as well as aggravation of the dispute with Peking.[16]

The record as viewed from Moscow and corroborated by independent sources also lends some support to the contention that the Kremlin must adjust its internal policy to modifications in the structure of world politics. The 17th CPSU(B) Congress in 1934 endorsed a five-year plan which called for higher rates of growth of light rather than heavy industry, but for a number of reasons, including German rearmament and hostility, these directives to ensure economic balance were altered.[17] (True, Hitler's rise to power was facilitated by the tactics of Stalin's Comintern with respect to the German social-democrats, but those tactics presumably were not decisive.) Soviet investment policy in 1949 underwent another drastic shift away from the renewed direction of balancing heavy and light industry.[18] The postwar forcing of military production which may be traced to 1949 can be related to the formation of NATO, which to be sure was a U.S. response, or maybe over-response, to the Communist political militancy in Central Europe. The argument of Soviet defensiveness appears to become more strained, however, once Moscow in the 1960's justified increases of its military budget in terms of American policy in Berlin and Southeast Asia. In those instances, the U.S. moderately answered Communist challenges to its overseas commitments and made no gesture which could be classified as detrimental to Soviet security concerns, no matter how liberally those concerns might be interpreted.

The fact that Soviet publicists deem it necessary to dispute "the simplified formula that 'foreign policy is a function of internal' events" suggests that certain members of the home audience raise the question of why a "peace-loving" state like the Soviet Union must habitually deny to its rank and file citizens a wide assortment of consumer durables and nourishing foodstuffs for

---

(Moscow, 1962), p. 494.

14. V. A. Zorin, ed., *Vneshniaia politika SSSR na novom etape* (Moscow, 1964), pp. 42–43.
15. *Ibid.,* p. 8.
16. Cf. *Le Monde,* October 30, 1964, *Neue Zuercher Zeitung,* October 30, 1964, and the *New York Times*, October 31, 1964.
17. Druzhinin, *op. cit.,* p. 412.
18. *Narodnoe Khoziaistvo SSSR v 1958 godu* (Moscow, 1959), p. 139.

the sake of building industrial-military power. *It cannot be stressed too heavily that the traditional patterns of investment and resource allocation which greatly favor the interest of industrial-military power over the interest of popular consumption are essentially legitimized in terms of international imperatives*. The 1961 party program held out the prospect of eliminating the national shortage of housing in ten years and providing an abundance of material benefits for the whole population in twenty years. But the qualification was made that, "The set program can be fulfilled with success under conditions of peace. Complications in the international situation and the resultant necessity to increase defense expenditures may hold up the fulfillment of the plans for raising the living standard of the people. An enduring normalization of international relations, reduction of military expenditures, and, in particular, the realization of general and complete disarmament under an appropriate agreement between countries, would make it possible greatly to surpass the plans for raising the people's living standard."

Once the preeminence of internal affairs and the dependence of investment policy upon an estimate of the international situation are accepted, the commanding influence of domestic politics in the form of bureaucratic group struggle over functions and funds may be hypothesized. Such a hypothesis rests on our knowledge of simultaneous and obviously interrelated conflict over economic and foreign policy within the Soviet hierarchy. This knowledge is derived to some extent by cross-checking the statements of topmost leaders on relevant issues and official decisions with accusations made against these leaders after they have fallen from power and the policies in force at the time of the denunciations. This inductive procedure will enable the analyst to discern only the contours of the dual struggle over power and policy, but that seems better than relying on deductive or intuitive processes.

The Malenkov-Khrushchev dispute of 1953 – 54 is one example of how bureaucratic infighting over issues of personal power and resource allocation can be a strong undercurrent of the formulation of foreign policy. Malenkov uniquely disputed the validity of the practice of giving preferential treatment to heavy industry, telling the USSR Supreme Soviet in August 1953 that "Heretofore we have not had the opportunity to develop light industry and the food industry *at the same rate* as heavy industry. Now we can and, consequently, must speed up the development of light industry in every way in order to secure a faster rise in the living standards and cultural level of the people" (italics added).[19] Malenkov gained the upper hand for a time, and in 1953 the rate of growth of the output of light industry not only matched but exceeded that for heavy industry.[20] Malenkov's determination to enforce his

19. *Pravda,* August 9, 1953.
20. See the official data cited in Leonard Schapiro, *The Communist Party of the Soviet Union* (New York, 1960), p. 553, note 1.

will on the issue of economic priorities apparently moved him to indicate that external risks had to be avoided lest East-West tension increase and require the Soviet to raise its military expenditure, which would be detrimental to the cause of bolstering light industry. The indicator was provided in Malenkov's unilateral and controversial statement of March 12, 1954 that nuclear war would result in "the destruction of world civilization."[21] On the practical level, the party Presidium headed by Malenkov stabilized defense spending and conducted vigorous diplomatic activity to settle the war in Indochina and redefine security arrangements in Europe so as to prevent the adherence of West Germany to NATO.

Khrushchev, a personal rival of Malenkov's since at least 1951, had a different set of objectives which interlaced ambitions of power and policy. First, the majority of the members of the party Presidium had to be persuaded to transfer from Malenkov to the party first secretary the right to steer the work of the Presidium. Second, the presidial majority had to be convinced that the interests of agriculture and defense required the expansion of heavy industry. Third, the U.S. had to be represented as an implacable antagonist which had to be restrained by a consistent military buildup in the Soviet Union and strengthening of the industrial base in Communist China. Khrushchev's opposition was expressed at the time by distinctive nuance in public speeches which acquired political meaning after his ascendancy in the Presidium was attended by appropriate changes of state policy.

Only a few weeks after Malenkov approved of developing light and heavy industry at equal rates, Khrushchev in his report on agriculture to the Central Committee plenum refused to endorse this viewpoint. Khrushchev instead accented the role of heavy industry in equipping agriculture, the sharp upswing of which was the most vital and important task in economic life.[22] Khrushchev, and especially his allies Bulganin and Voroshilov, spared no black paint in imaginatively depicting the U.S. as a plotter of surprise attack on the USSR, and they insisted upon a further strengthening of Soviet defenses.[23] Moreover, Khrushchev, Bulganin, and Mikoyan visited China in September 1954 and made agreements for technical assistance which put a further drain on the resources of Soviet heavy engineering.

The position of Khrushchev's group could only be reinforced by the U.S. determination to rearm West Germany and bring it into NATO. Shortly afterward, in January or February 1955, decisions were reached to oust Malenkov from the premiership and under the stewardship of Khrushchev to resume the policy of forcing the heavy and defense industries. The "theoreticians" who were denounced for having favored light industry were identified a few years later, when one of Khrushchev's lieutenants directly attacked Malenkov on

21. *Pravda*, March 13, 1954.
22. *Ibid.*, September 15, 1953.
23. See the citations in the Soviet press as noted in Arnold L. Horelick and Myron Rush, *Strategic Power and Soviet Foreign Policy* (Santa Monica, 1965), pp. 31ff.

this score.[24] In foreign policy, Malenkov in 1955 was obliquely discredited as "weak-nerved" and Khrushchev combined flexibility on the Austrian peace treaty with the launching of a risk-fraught course of politico-military adventure in the Middle East.[25]

Shortly after Malenkov was deposed, a philosophical argument over the stages of Communist development which had implications for Soviet domestic and foreign policy raged between Khrushchev and Molotov. Molotov, true to his reputation as a devoted follower of Stalin and insular Great Russian, urged a circumspect policy at home and abroad. He did so publicly in esoteric fashion by denying in a speech to the Supreme Soviet on February 8, 1955 that socialism had been built in the USSR and that the Communist regimes of Europe and Asia had taken more than the first steps toward socialism. It followed from these premises that bolder measures could not be adopted to increase free ("Communist") services to the Soviet people, deny the inevitability of world war, and self-assuredly bargain with the West, or hope for expanding the zone of Sovietization without the assistance of the Red Army. Khrushchev's counter-thesis that socialism had irrevocably triumphed in the Soviet Union was a doctrinal sign that conditions were ripe for a more equal distribution of wealth in the country, that Soviet power could prevent world war, and that under the Soviet nuclear shield, Communist regimes might emerge anywhere without fear of Western intervention to throttle them.[26]

Molotov's apprehension about the Kremlin's base of strength would probably have never created a political uproar unless it had been shared by various representatives of the elite and in the context of oligarchic politics had to be discredited so as to neutralize the influence of these representatives. One such leader of conservative opinion was the writer Kochetov, whose novel *Brothers Yershov* (1957) deplored the lack of ideological clarity after the attack on Stalin at the 20th Congress and insinuated that a popular revolution in the Soviet Union could not be excluded. In Kochetov's novel, a Soviet party member tells another in October 1956: "Is Hungary really cut off from us by an impenetrable wall? Do not the enemies of Communism harass us all they can? Of course they do, it's an all-out offensive, and a fierce one. And what are we going to do? Are we going to sit and wait till they start hanging us by the feet on the very same trees that we have planted?" Kochetov's adherence to circles which are especially hostile towards the U.S. was later suggested by the fact that shortly after the aborted summit conference in May, 1960, he condemned those interested in East-West dialogue as "some simpletons" who had become "too ecstatic over the murky and devious utterances of the

    24. L. F. Ilyichev, *Pravda*, October 26, 1961.
    25. See the instructive articles of Boris I. Nicolaevsky, "Malenkov's Heyday and Deposition," *The New Leader*, August 12, 1957, pp. 6 – 8, and "The Meaning of Khrushchev's Victory," *ibid.*, September 2, 1957, pp. 5 – 8.
    26. See the speech of A. I. Mikoyan to the 22nd CPSU Congress in *Pravda*, October 22, 1961.

[American] President."[27] It may be hazarded that the Molotovs and Kochetovs would not be adverse to using cold war stereotypes for the purpose of maintaining time-honored institutions and ideological clarity in the USSR.

The interconnection of domestic and foreign policy may also be surmised from Khrushchev's repeated advocacy of internal reform and *détente* with the U.S. at one and the same time. In January 1958, Khrushchev publicly advised the sale of state-owned agricultural machinery to the collective farms, thus embarking on a course of raising collective farm income. Khrushchev in the same speech proposed a heads-of-government meeting, evidently to induce the kind of external atmosphere needed to liberate investment funds earmarked for conventional military projects.[28] After high-level talks in July 1963 to conclude an agreement to limit nuclear testing, Khrushchev implied the linkage of effort to pull up weak sectors of the economy and curtail military procurement by telling a delegation of American farm experts: "Now we shall reduce expenditure on defense, and this money as well we shall direct to the production of chemical fertilizers."[29] Once more, in August 1964, the premier fought for new approaches to the chronic peasant question, including a scheme for the decentralization of marketing practices in the socialized sector, and he told the British publisher Lord Roy Thomson that he was ready for a summit meeting to ease the burden of military spending.[30]

Significantly, Khrushchev's willingness to parley with the American president in 1964 was expressed after U.S. planes had bombed shore installations in North Vietnam (the Tonkin Gulf incident) which suggested that the premier was bent on furthering domestic experimentation even at the cost of impairing the Soviet's renown as a bulwark of "anti-imperialism." Khrushchev furthermore was drumming up support for a new international conference of the pro-Moscow parties in order to read out of the movement the Chinese Communists, who noisily held that the CPSU was betraying the cause of world revolution for the sake of domestic reconstruction. True, the Sino-Soviet dispute went on after the fall of Khrushchev, albeit in subdued tones until Peking's massive anti-Soviet campaign in the summer of 1966. Moscow, however, adopted a more forward tactic in its foreign policy and, as if in criticism of Khrushchev's final demarches, it was argumentatively stated that, "It would be an error to assume that at some stage the foreign policy of the USSR is guided exclusively or predominantly by the principle of proletarian internationalism and at some other stage by the principle of peaceful coexistence. . . . The paramount role in the foreign-policy activity of socialist states belongs, in our view, to proletarian internationalism."[31] The observer might be war-

27. *Pravda*, May 23, 1960.
28. *Pravda*, January 25, 1958.
29. N. S. Khrushchev, *Stroitel'stvo Kommunizma v SSSR i razvitie sel'skogo khoziaistva* (Moscow, 1964), VIII, 51.
30. *Pravda*, August 11 and 17, 1964.
31. V. Trukhanovskii, *Mezhdunarodnaia zhizn'*, no. 8, 1966, pp. 76 and 82.

ranted in suspecting that the events surrounding the ouster of Khrushchev confirmed the opinion and prediction which David J. Dallin ventured in 1955: "In a way the nearly four decades of Soviet history may be viewed as a very slow process of divorce of the Russia which is a part of World Communism and the Russia which is a new post-revolutionary national formation. The painful evolution still in its beginnings will not be completed without a resounding fight at the top of the Soviet regime."[32]

The sway of group and personal ambitions and manipulation of images of the outer world in the making of a Communist government's foreign policy is further suggested by the nature of Moscow's criticism of Peking in the 1960's. Whether the specific charges are truthful cannot be ascertained and is not actually relevant; what counts is the plausibility of the indictment in the circle of Soviet officials. According to the report of CPSU Central Committee Secretary Suslov to the Committee in February 1964, "the adventurous course of the Chinese leaders in the international arena is connected with their errors in domestic policy." The Great Leap campaign was allegedly motivated by nationalistic ambition to catch up rapidly with other socialist countries and occupy a dominant position in the world socialist system. The same nationalistic tendency was seen in Peking's agitation of passions over border questions, use of inflammatory propaganda during the Cuban missile crisis, and desire to build a nuclear arsenal. More personally, Suslov averred that Chinese Communist domestic and foreign policy could not be understood without realization that Mao Tse-tung craved recognition as the chief of the world Communist movement and a classicist of Marxism-Leninism.[33] A speaker in the discussion of Suslov's report added that Peking blamed outsiders for its internal difficulties: "instead of seriously analyzing the reasons for their own failures and finding correct means to overcome the effects of miscalculations, the Chinese splitters, concealing from their people the real state of affairs, try to shift the responsibility for their errors on to the Communist parties and leadership of other socialist countries."[34] Similarly, Academician B. G. Gafurov told a conference of ideological functionaries in June 1964: "I should like only to emphasize that the chauvinistic and adventurous course of Chinese foreign policy was especially activated after a series of reversals in the economy. This foreign-policy course was to distract the popular masses from internal reversals, hunger, and poverty. The CPC leadership sees a panacea for all its ills in the kindling of nationalism and chauvinism."[35]

To sum up, the Soviet viewpoint is that a Communist government ordinarily seeks to apply most of its energies to the solution of its domestic

---

32. David J. Dallin, *The Changing World of Soviet Russia* (New Haven, 1956), pp. 349 – 350.

33. *Plenum TsK KPSS, 14 – 15 fevralia 1964 goda, stenograficheskii otchet* (Moscow, 1964), pp. 543 – 544.

34. A. D. Skaba, *ibid.,* p. 593.

35. *Za chistotu marksizma – leninizma* (Moscow, 1964), p. 232.

problems and for that reason will not assume a belligerent posture toward other states unless it feels threatened by them. However, Soviet sources attest that the spirit of domestic leadership and politics in a Communist state may introduce serious complications into the international environment. The Communist leader of policy may be fatalistic and underrate diplomacy, thereby contributing to the rise of world tensions. He may intimidate and take unfair advantage of alliance partners, which can generate resentment and suspicion between nations. The leader is also capable of inspiring militaristic enterprises with a view towards channeling popular discontent into a direction which he thinks beneficial for the structure of internal power. While CPSU literature explicitly denies that there are professional groups in the Eastern bloc which have a vested interest in the manufacture of armaments and the endurance of international frictions, it provides circumstantial evidence of factional conflict inside the Soviet party over germane matters like estimates of the world situation, levels of military expenditures, and the stability of interior rule.

All this suggests that the dynamics of Soviet foreign policy that Kennan attributed to the inner workings of the Stalin regime almost twenty years ago have since provided the stuff of controversy in the closed system of committee politics which replaced the narrowly court politics of the Stalin era. Under Malenkov and Khrushchev, a unified viewpoint was lacking on the extent to which the Kremlin commands the allegiance of its subjects and needs to harp on the theme of vigilance in the face of outside perils as an instrument to promote mass dicipline. Cohesion was less than total on the doctrinally stipulated hostility of the West and the urgency of subverting its worldwide positions. Some notable collisions also occurred over the extent to which Stalin should be criticized, and this issue has involved questions of social morality and publicity of governmental business — questions bearing on what Kennan termed "the internal nature of Soviet power."

The Kremlin's deliberations and controversies over foreign policy in the 1950's and 60's hardly transpired in isolation from the outer world, and in updating our constructs we might do well to combine the one-dimensional insights of Kennan and Moore, simultaneously keeping in mind the primacy of domestic power considerations. Some practitioners have outdistanced many theorists in reaching this assumption. During the Cuban missile crisis in 1962, for example, an awareness of multi-sided interaction guided the counsel which U.S. roving ambassador Averell Harriman proffered to the White House. Arthur M. Schlesinger, Jr., who was then a presidential assistant, recalls that at the peak of the crisis he received a telephone call from Harriman at the U.S. mission in New York to the effect that Khrushchev "was desperately signaling a desire to cooperate in moving toward a peaceful solution." Harriman further said of Khrushchev: "We must give him an out. If we do this shrewdly, we can downgrade the tough group in the Soviet Union which persuaded him to do this. But if we deny him an out, then we will escalate this business into a nuclear war." Schlesinger adds that, "These words from the most experienced of all American diplomats seemed utterly convincing to me."[36]

One wonders what might have happened if President Eisenhower's speech-writers had not filtered out of the draft text of a public message of April 16, 1953 "a presidential offer to travel abroad to meet Malenkov" and exchange of American and Soviet airtime to allow the leaders of each nation to address the people of the other."[37] Or if West Germany was not rearmed and brought into NATO? Or if concern for his image as an alert chief executive had not prompted Mr. Eisenhower to declare that he was responsible for the decision to make the U-2 overflight of Soviet territory on the eve of the Paris Confer-ence in May 1960? Or if in June 1961, President Kennedy had not refused to accept the Soviet proposal that the communique of the Vienna summit meeting indicate that he and Khrushchev had made some progress towards peace settlements? Or if the circumstance of the U.S. presidential campaign of 1964 had not made it impolitic for the American leader to respond to Khrushchev's latest bid for a summit conference? This is not to say that the U.S. Government acted wrongly in all of these complex situations, but that in some of them a display of flexibility may have had as important an effect on the collective mind of the Kremlin as did the adaptability shown with respect toward the Cuban missile affair and limited nuclear test-ban treaty.

If these impressions have any virtue, it follows that the student of Soviet foreign relations who wishes to go beyond mere description might find it profitable to look for causation in the intermeshing of various systems of national politics and policies. He may investigate foremost the conflicts of bureaucratic and philosophic interest within the Soviet political community and the effect of diplomatic and military decisions taken in world capitals like Washington, Peking, and Bonn on the resolution of those conflicts of rival interests. Of course, this is a matter of the skillful utilization of those methodo-logical techniques which were originally devised by Boris I. Nicolaevsky and Franz Borkenau to shed a measure of light on the secret intrigues of the Kremlin and subsequently enabled analysts such as Donald S. Zagoria and Victor Zorza to track the vicissitudes of the Sino-Soviet conflict before it rose to the surface. The failure of most commentators to utilize those techniques in studying the struggle for power in the Soviet Union may be regarded as one of the foremost reasons why the demise of Khrushchev came as so rude a shock to many "experts," not to speak of interested laymen. It is to be hoped that in the future we shall not see a repetition of the error of 1957 – 64, when it was usually said that "Khrushchev is no Stalin," but the party leader was nonethe-less viewed by many as unchallengeable.

36. Arthur M. Schlesinger, Jr., *A Thousand Days: John F. Kennedy in the White House* (Cambridge, Mass., 1965), pp. 821 – 822.
37. Emmet John Hughes, *The Ordeal of Power: A Political Memoir of the Eisenhower Years* (New York, 1963), pp. 108 – 109.

The following pointers on methodology are by no means exhaustive, but will give the student who has a command of the Russian language and the factional history of Communism a few working tools, and he can later make all kinds of refinements. To begin, an official reappraisal of investment, defense, and foreign policies may be reasoned from a combination of factors. One is the publication in the Soviet press of a direct statement that the heavy financial burden of producing nuclear weapons has had an adverse effect on proper development of the Soviet economy. Such a statement takes on added meaning if accompanied by agitation of the question of economic imbalance in the professional journals such as *Voprosy Ekonomiki* and the appearance of various doctrinal formulas on the subject of purchasing power and production in party political magazines such as *Kommunist.* The acrimonious nature of policy reappraisal may be inferred if such a statement about nuclear weapons and economic health is reported in a press organ which slants the foreign news in a way that conveys an impression of U.S. reasonableness and if the statement is ignored by another which selectively emphasizes U.S. firmness. This slanting of the news, a common feature of the press in authoritarian states such as Spain under Franco, also extends to coverage of how economic priorities are handled in other lands of the Eastern bloc. Policy debate may furthermore be signalled by the presentation of conflicting lists of diplomatic priorities in the articles and speeches of Central Committee members and diverse patterns of verbal approval or reservation by Committee members, with special reference to such items as disarmament and arms control.

At this point, Borkenau would probably add his maxim that "Spricht man von Kämpfen, muss man auch die Kämpfenden identifizieren" (If we talk about struggles, we must also identify the antagonists). A pitfall to be avoided is the foregone conclusion that a topmost leader's adherence to any one of the major apparatuses of Soviet rule presupposes his orientation as a "world revolutionist" or "coexistence man." There are certainly grounds for believing that the party apparatus harbors many officials who are of the opinion that world war is inevitable or that it can be prevented only by developing the industrial and military power of the USSR and expanding the zone of Sovietization. It would follow that any leader whose "constituency," or base of power, was in the party apparatus would unhesitatingly urge a line of doctrinaire intransigence toward the U.S. This apparently was true of party secretary Zhdanov in the postwar period and perhaps is true of Brezhnev today, but hardly seems applicable to Khrushchev, at least by the time his official career was ended. Which, of course, is to suggest that the party apparatus is subject to divisions of opinion and may be led in directions which may not conform to its "objective" interest. Similarly, diverse pressures of a functional and ideological nature are intrinsic to the state apparatus by virtue of its organization into civilian and industrial-military departments. One has only to inspect the record of the ups and downs in the political fortunes of business executives such as Voznesenskii and Saburov in the 1940's and later Mikoyan and Kosygin to suppose that Russia's technocratic class — distinguished as it is by general class interests — is no more cohesive than any other. In view of these circumstances, which give rise to temporary alignments of party and state leaders on various issues, the analyst may best ground his pertinent speculations on a detailed comparison of the differential verbal behavior and prominence of Soviet political personalities.

PART III

Communist Ideology,
Belief Systems,
and Soviet Foreign Policy

Observers of Soviet behavior have long been vexed by the question of the motivational role of Communist ideology. Many writers on this subject can be located on a spectrum running between two extreme positions based on certain assumptions about the motives of Soviet leaders: (1) that Communist ideology is a post facto rationalization of actions motivated by other considerations (personal power, national interest, imperialism, etc.); or (2) that ideology motivates Soviet leaders to take particular kinds of actions, or at least serves as "a guide to action."[1] Several of the chapters in this section represent positions which approach one or the other extreme, while others implicitly or explicitly reject this dichotomy and approach the question of the motivational role of Communist ideology from quite different perspectives.

Professor Sharp (see Chapter 7 below) comes down clearly on the side of national interest as the key to Soviet politics, including foreign policy. Sharp rejects the view that "the *ultimate* aims of the Communist creed are operative

1. Several articles have appeared in the last decade or so that classify the literature on Soviet ideology and foreign policy, and the student should consult them for a more detailed categorization. For example: William Glaser, "Theories of Soviet Foreign Policy: A Classification of the Literature," *World Affairs Quarterly*, XXVII, 2 (July, 1956), pp. 128 – 152; Daniel Bell, "Ten Theories in Search of Reality," *World Politics*, X, 3 (April, 1958), pp. 327 – 365; Adam Bromke, "Ideology and National Interest in Soviet Foreign Policy," *International Journal*, XXII, 4 (Autumn, 1967), pp. 547 – 562.

in policy determinations" and function as "a guide to action." He would probably concur with the findings of two major recent studies which conclude that "At no point does it appear that Leninist theory excludes a significant range of policy choices from being considered by the Soviet leadership,"[2] and that Soviet political leaders and analysts "rather than let Lenin do their thinking for them, found they could utilize Lenin to legitimate their thinking no matter how un-Leninist those thoughts might be. . . . [For] the ideological high priests under Khrushchev created the doctrinal legitimation for regarding *Leninism* as irrelevant to atomic age international politics by declaring that the period when the nature of imperialism determined the style of international politics had been historically transcended."[3]

While admitting that Communist ideology may be significant for the internal working of the regime, Professor Daniels (see Chapter 9) concludes that "foreign policy is one of the least ideological aspects of Soviet politics, in reality if not in words. Rather than foreign policy being governed in any substantial way by ideological requirements, the chief connection of the two lies in the decisions and situations which foreign policy considerations bring about and require the ideology to justify or explain away." For both Sharp and Daniels, ideology serves mainly as a post facto rationalization for policy.

However, R. N. Carew Hunt (in Chapter 7) contends that both ideology and "power politics" have a significant impact on Soviet foreign policy. He emphasizes that Soviet ideology affects the thinking and perceptions of Soviet leaders, whose actions are often influenced by the concepts and principles "to which all Communists subscribe." Indeed, Hunt maintains that certain Marxist beliefs have "led the Soviet rulers to take so distorted a view of the world as to make it harder to deal with them than with any government in the annals of diplomacy; and this . . . is just what may be expected from an 'ideology' in the sense in which Marx originally used the term." Hunt concludes that "There is no yardstick that permits a measure of the exact relation between power politics and ideology in the policies that result; but surely neither factor can be ignored."

David Forte also believes that "Soviet ideology bears an intimate relationship to Soviet foreign policy . . . and is not a mere philosophical rationalization for basically nationalist designs."[4] In support of these views, Forte presents a

2. Michael Gehlen, *The Politics of Coexistence* (Bloomington, Ind.: Indiana University Press, 1967), p. 294.

3. William Zimmerman, *Soviet Perspectives on International Relations, 1956–1967* (Princeton: Princeton University Press, 1969), pp. 287, 290.

4. David Forte, "The Response of Soviet Foreign Policy to the Common Market, 1957–63," *Soviet Studies,* XIX, 3 (January, 1968), p. 373. Cf. Barrington Moore, Jr., "The Relations of Ideology and Foreign Policy," in Barrington Moore, Jr., *Soviet Politics — The Dilemma of Power* (Cambridge, Mass.: Harvard University Press, 1951), pp. 384–401 (reprinted in Alexander Dallin [ed.], *Soviet Conduct in World Affairs* [New York: Columbia University Press, 1960], pp. 75–91); and Bertram D. Wolfe, "Communist Ideology and Soviet Foreign Policy," *Foreign*

detailed study of the Soviet response to the early development of the European Economic Community (the Common Market). Significantly, he found that shifts in ideological premises nearly always *preceded* changes in policy; ideological change thus "set the stage for new practical policies."[5] Far from rationalizing or legitimizing policies already initiated, Soviet leaders and ideologists — at least on this crucial issue and during this period — played important parts in assessing the situation, planning new courses of action, and reformulating ideological principles in anticipation of policy changes.

In his contribution to the debate with Sharp and Hunt, Richard Lowenthal emphasizes three exceedingly important ideas: first, that some parts of an ideology have a much greater influence on elite perceptions, beliefs, and behavior than others; second, that a crucial question to ask about any ideological statement or belief is, "What *functions* does it perform?"; and, third, that the "operative" parts of Soviet ideology are those that maintain and justify the predominant role of the Communist Party in the Soviet political system.

Lowenthal is by no means the only scholar to distinguish among the component elements of Soviet ideology and to suggest that certain parts perform different functions under various circumstances.[6] Zbigniew Brzezinski, in his monumental study *The Soviet Bloc: Unity and Conflict,* carefully distinguishes among the "philosophical component," the "doctrinal component," and the "action program" of Soviet ideology. Brzezinski notes that these three elements "cannot always be neatly compartmentalized and will often overlap," but he stresses that their susceptibility to change and their impact on policy vary considerably.[7] J.M. Bochenski also identifies three basic aspects of Marxism-Leninism: "the basic dogma," "the systematic superstructure," and "the declassified doctrines."[8] Other scholars distinguish among "ideology," "dogma," and "doctrine"; "operational ideology" (the way Soviet leaders think), "official ideology" (what the people are told), and "national ideology"

Affairs, XLI, 1 (October, 1962), pp. 152 – 170.

5. Forte, *op. cit,* pp. 373, 386ff.

6. For example, Alfred G. Meyer, "The Functions of Ideology in the Soviet Political System," *Soviet Studies,* XVII, 3 (January, 1966), pp. 273 – 285. For general discussions of the functions performed by attitudes, opinions, values, and beliefs, see M. Brewster Smith, Jerome Bruner, and Robert White, *Opinions and Personality* (New York: John Wiley, 1964); and Daniel Katz, "The Functional Approach to the Study of Attitudes," *Public Opinion Quarterly,* XXIV, 2 (Summer, 1960), pp. 163 – 204.

7. Zbigniew K. Brzezinski, *The Soviet Bloc: Unity and Conflict* (Cambridge, Mass.: Harvard University Press, 1967), p. 489: from the important chapter "Ideology and Power in Relations among Communist States," pp. 485 – 512. See also Brzezinski's *Ideology and Power in Soviet Politics* (New York: Praeger, 1967), especially Chapter 5. On the important subject of *change* in the content and functions of Marxist theory and ideology, see Robert C. Tucker, *The Marxian Revolutionary Idea* (New York: Norton, 1969), especially "The Deradicalization of Marxist Movements," pp. 172 – 214.

8. J. M. Bochenski, "The Three Components of Communist Ideology," *Studies in Soviet Thought,* II, 1 (March, 1962), pp. 7 – 11.

(what the people believe); and even "popular ideology," "cadre ideology," and "ideologists' ideology."[9]

Assessing the impact of Soviet ideology on foreign policy, Professor Ulam (see Chapter 8 below) identifies three potential *uses* of Marxism: (1) "implied prescriptions (implied, because Marx and Engels never devoted much attention to the problem of the foreign policy of a socialist state)"; (2) "an analytical discipline for viewing international as well as domestic politics"; and (3) "a symbol and quasi-religion giving its practitioners the sense that they are moving forward with the forces of history and that the success of their state is predicated upon the truth of the doctrine." The first of these, he argues, no longer plays a significant part in the conduct of Soviet foreign policy, "while the analytical and symbolical uses of Marxism remain important and necessary to the understanding of Soviet policy." Ulam would perhaps agree that even the *"Realpolitik"* pursuit of "national interest" is "totally conditioned by the way in which the policy-makers apprehend reality."[10]

Ulam also anticipates Alfred G. Meyer's important arguments on the "legitimizing" and "self-legitimizing" functions of Soviet ideology — that is, the use of ideological statements "to convince the citizenry that the party and its leaders have a legitimate claim to rule them," and as "a continual attempt on the part of the rulers to convince *themselves* of their legitimacy."[11] Ulam's essay, published over a decade ago, retains a special significance in that it is written by the author of *Expansion and Coexistence*, by far the most comprehensive and influential interpretive history of Soviet foreign policy by any Western scholar.

Careful readers have undoubtedly noted that we have yet to present a precise, lucid, and succinct definition of the concept "ideology." David Joravsky, in a stimulating and insightful paper, offers just such a definition: "When we call a belief ideological, we are saying at least three things about it: although it is unverified or unverifiable, it is accepted as verified by a particular group, because it performs social functions for that group." Joravsky explains that "'Group' is used loosely to indicate such aggregations as parties, professions, classes, or nations," and "'Because' is also used loosely, to indicate a functional correlation rather than a strictly causal connection between acceptance of a belief and other social processes."[12]

Joravsky's distinction between unverifiable beliefs ("grand ideology") and verifiable but unverified beliefs ("petty ideology") is important. Beliefs of the former kind include powerful emotional appeals such as "All men are created equal," whereas more specific and perhaps verifiable derivatives of this precept

9. For example, Kurt Marko, "Soviet Ideology and Sovietology," *Soviet Studies*, XIX, 4 (April, 1968), pp. 465 – 481.

10. Forte, *op. cit.*, p. 373.

11. Meyer, *op. cit.*, especially pp. 279 – 281.

12. David Joravsky, "Soviet Ideology," *Soviet Studies*, XVIII, 1 (July, 1966), p. 3.

include propositions such as, "Universal suffrage would allow the poor to control or even take the property of the rich."[13] Fundamental Soviet beliefs at the level of grand ideology include: "matter is all that exists, reality is essentially dialectical, the triumph of communism is inevitable, the aims of communism coincide with the aims of working mankind, the Party is the vanguard of mankind and will lead it to communism."[14] Beliefs at the level of petty ideology include many of Khrushchev's major doctrinal innovations: "Wars are not inevitable," "violent revolutions are not inevitable," "peaceful coexistence with the West is possible and desirable," "different roads to socialism are possible and desirable," "countries of the Third World 'peace zone' are unaligned and uncommitted to either the socialist or capitalist 'camps.'" In short, petty ideology consists of the more "specific, verifiable beliefs that cluster about the grand ideologies," and both the content and the social functions of petty ideology are more susceptible to change than those of grand ideology.

Theoretical ideology, in both its grand and petty forms, must be sharply distinguished from "political realism," which Joravsky defines as "a constantly shifting jumble of commitments to particular judgements and persons."

Perhaps the most basic, the golden rule of the "realistic" politician, is his practical way of recognizing that politics is the business of arranging people in hierarchies of power. . . . His basic principle, though rarely stated, is evident in his behaviour: If a belief reduces one's influence in one's group, it is wrong; if it increases one's influence, it is right. This is an ideological principle.[15]

Joravsky goes on to observe that "it is clear to most Western students of Soviet affairs that grand and petty ideology have been giving way to political 'realism' in the thinking of the Soviet elite. This is the process that Meyer calls 'the routinization of indoctrination'; others have called it the erosion, exhaustion, or even the end of ideology."[16] The latter phrases are very misleading, Joravsky argues, because they suggest that "political realism" is devoid of ideology merely because it does not contain serious philosophical or theoretical statements.

This gradual transformation has created difficult problems for analysts of Soviet ideology and political behavior. In essence, "political realism" consists of the "basic rules of thought" that shape the motives, beliefs, judgments, and actions of Soviet leaders. But the lack of data on the belief systems of Soviet officials, the nature of the Soviet policy-making process, and the organizational, social, and psychological constraints on Party leaders, make it exceedingly difficult to study the "operative" political beliefs of Soviet elites, individually or collectively.

13. *Ibid.*, pp. 3–8.
14. Richard DeGeorge, *Patterns of Soviet Thought* (Ann Arbor, Mich.: University of Michigan Press, 1966), pp. 234ff.
15. Joravsky, *op. cit.,* p. 9.
16. *Ibid.*, p. 10.

In view of these problems, the contribution by Alexander George (see Chapter 10 below) is particularly important. For George attempts to reconstruct both the philosophical and the instrumental beliefs that comprise "the operational code" of Soviet leaders, especially in the Lenin and Stalin eras. In far greater detail than Lowenthal and others, George describes the maxims or "approaches to political calculation" that seem to have shaped Soviet decisions and behavior. "Knowledge of the actor's beliefs helps the investigator to clarify the general criteria, requirements, and norms the subject attempts to meet in assessing opportunities that arise to make desirable gains, in estimating the costs and risks associated with them, and in making utility calculations." These considerations greatly influence foreign policy decisions, and are almost certainly what Joravsky had in mind when he referred to "political realism," as distinct from theoretical ideology.

George's reformulation of Soviet "optimizing strategy" is particularly interesting in light of past and present Soviet performance, for example, the "dual policy" of the 1920's and "peaceful coexistence" of the 1950's and 1960's. George argues that knowledge of belief systems and the ways in which they change provides "one of the important inputs needed for behavioural analyses of political decision-making and leadership styles. The 'operational code' construct does this insofar as it encompasses that aspect of the political actor's perception and structuring of the political world to which he relates, and within which he attempts to operate to advance the interests with which he is identified. This approach should be useful for studying an actor's decision-making 'style,' and its application in specific situations."

The chapter by Kelly and Fleron examines some of the important research questions explicitly and implicitly raised by George; it is a sort of lament for what is not known about the motivational linkage between Communist ideology and behavior. The authors point to the tradition among "experts" on Communist affairs to treat their subject as a more or less unique phenomenon. This has had the adverse effect, they argue, of isolating the study of Communist ideology from the conceptual, empirical, and theoretical advances in psychology and social psychology in recent decades.

Analysis of the psychological dimension of individual political leaders was *au courant* in the study of Soviet foreign policy two decades ago, but fell into disrepute after the appearance of Nathan Leites' *The Operational Code* and *A Study of Bolshevism,* which some felt were at least premature and not firmly data-based, and others viewed as utterly bizarre. Recently, however, George and others have shown renewed interest in this aspect of inquiry, not only in the study of Soviet foreign policy, but also in the study of foreign policy more generally.[17] Both the general theorist and the area specialist will benefit if this renewed interest is pursued jointly, rather than separately as in the past.

Kelly and Fleron present some hypotheses drawn from psychological theories which may describe the relationship of Communist ideology to the political behavior of Soviet leaders. So little has been done in the area of applying that literature to the study of Communist ideological beliefs that it is easy to dip into various theories and extract small parts for purposes of illustration. Extreme eclecticism characterizes the Kelly-Fleron chapter, some parts of which may be contradictory, empirically if not logically (for example, the conclusions of Davies and those of the positivist learning theorists). Each theory would have to be analyzed separately and in greater depth to have significant utility for the study of the relationship between Communist beliefs and behavior. In essence, Kelly and Fleron identify some possibilities for the application of psychological theory to the study of Communist ideology and behavior.

When the question of the motivational role of Communist ideology for Communist behavior is placed in the broader context of the relationship between belief systems and behavior, one finds a huge set of potentially relevant variables and important questions which have not been applied in the Soviet context. And although psychological theories are not the only source of such variables and questions (the same could be said of Marxist theory, Christian theology, and many others), it does seem that there is more systematic evidence for psychological theory than there is for any of the others. It may be that our insistence on such "evidence" is epistemologically unsound, but that evidence is nevertheless the main standard of usefulness and proof currently employed in science and philosophy.

In the study of international relations, then, the key issue "is not *whether* psychological processes are relevant, but *how* they are relevant."[18] Fundamen-

17. Cf. William Zimmerman, "Elite Perspectives and the Explanation of Soviet Foreign Policy," Chapter 2 above; Jan F. Triska and David D. Finley, *Soviet Foreign Policy* (New York: Macmillan, 1968), especially Chapters 4 and 9; Robert C. Angell and J. David Singer, "Social Values and Foreign Policy Attitudes of Soviet and American Elites," *Journal of Conflict Resolution*, VII, 4 (December, 1964), pp. 329–491; Ralph K. White, "Images in the Context of International Conflict: Soviet Perceptions of the U.S. and the U.S.S.R.," in Herbert C. Kelman (ed.), *International Behavior: A Social-Psychological Analysis* (New York: Holt, Rinehart & Winston, 1965), pp. 236–276; J. David Singer (ed.), *Human Behavior and International Politics* (Chicago: Rand McNally, 1965); David Finlay, Ole Holsti, Richard Fagan, *Enemies in Politics* (Chicago: Rand McNally, 1967); Joseph De Rivera, *The Psychological Dimension of Foreign Policy* (Columbus, Ohio: Merrill, 1968); "Leadership: The Psychology of Political Men," *Journal of International Affairs*, XXIV, 1 (1970), "Image and Reality in World Politics," *Journal of International Affairs*, XXI, 1 (1967); Michael Brecher, Blema Steinberg, and Janice Stein, "A Framework for Research on Foreign Policy Behavior," *Journal of Conflict Resolution*, XIII, 1 (March, 1969), pp. 75–101.

18. Herbert C. Kelman, "The Role of the Individual in International Relations: Some Conceptual and Methodological Considerations," *Journal of International Affairs*, XXIV, 1 (1970), p. 4. See also John G. Gunnell, "The Idea of the Conceptual Framework: A Philosophical

tal questions concerning the psychological environment of Soviet foreign policy-makers (see the conceptual framework, page 8 above) include: How do
Soviet leaders perceive their "national interests"? How do they perceive the
interests, capabilities, and intentions of other nations? To what extent does
Soviet ideology shape these perceptions? Which parts of the ideology shape
attitudes, images, and beliefs more than others? What effects do these attitudes,
images, and beliefs have on Soviet behavior? Why do they have these effects?
When do they do so? In short, "whose images count, under what conditions,
and at what points in the international policy-making process"?[19]

Thus, if ideology is "a broad system of concepts with educational and
integrative functions,"[20] and if "the chief function of ideology — whether
theoretical, 'realistic', or a mixture of the two — is to rationalize a group's
readiness to act, or to refuse to act,"[21] some parts of Soviet ideology may
significantly influence the social-psychological processes of Soviet leaders (e.g.,
"those relating to motivation, perception, trust and suspicion, definition of the
situation, stress, communication, leadership, influence, norm formation, role
prescription, group cohesiveness, loyalty").[22] For foreign policy-makers, particularly important general processes include defining the nature of a situation,
formulating possible initiatives and responses, assessing threats, risks, and
likely consequences of different policies, and developing criteria for choosing
among alternative courses of action. Hence Zimmerman concludes (see his
essay above) that the serious researcher finds himself returning to the study
of "the cognitive and affective maps of particular decision-makers — but at a
greater level of specificity . . . and within a general framework which stresses
the impact of external factors on Soviet behavior."

Herbert C. Kelman, a distinguished social psychologist, adds an important
caveat. He warns that the study of foreign policy-making should not be based
entirely on psychological variables. Such an analysis would be inadequate
because "it ignores the role of situational constraints (i.e., constraints deriving
from the specific context in which national decision-makers arrive at their
decision and in which they interact with their counterparts in other nations)
and/or structural constraints (i.e., constraints deriving from the structure of
national and international political systems)."[23] But Kelman also argues that
certain social-psychological processes can and should "enter importantly into

Critique," *Journal of Comparative Administration,* I, 2 (August, 1969), pp. 140–176.

19. Herbert C. Kelman, "Social-Psychological Approaches: The Question of Relevance," in
Kelman (ed.), *International Behavior,* p. 456.

20. Rudolf Schlesinger, "More Observations on Ideology," *Soviet Studies*, XIX, 1 (July,
1968), p. 87.

21. Joravsky, *op. cit.*, p. 15.

22. Herbert C. Kelman, "Social-Psychological Approaches to the Study of International
Relations: Definition of Scope," in Kelman (ed.), *International Behavior*, p. 17.

23. Kelman, "The Role of the Individual in International Relations: Some Conceptual and
Methodological Considerations," *op. cit.,* p. 9.

various general conceptualizations of the interaction between nations and foreign policy-making" — particularly those internal constraints and personality dispositions of important decision-makers. Situational and psychological constraints both

> may operate to varying degrees, depending on the occasion for the decision and on numerous other factors, and they may interact with one another in various ways. Structural factors may create dispositional constraints, and dispositional factors, in turn, may create structural constraints. We are dealing here with societal and inter-societal processes and with the complex functioning of national and international systems. These processes, however, can be in part illuminated by a microanalysis of the cognitive and social processes that occur at the locus of decision-making, as long as we recognize that these merely represent the culmination of a large array of prior events and interactions. Most important, by studying the perceptions and action tendencies of the decision-maker and the interactions within the decision-making unit, we can learn a great deal about the nature of the constraints that operate in different situations and the way in which they affect each other and the final decision outcome.[24]

For the researcher, then, it is very difficult to ascertain what Soviet leaders believe and which perceived factors and beliefs actually shape policies and behavior under different circumstances. Joravsky notes that after the first five or ten years of Soviet rule, Party leaders ceased to make serious efforts to state their operative political beliefs in explicit theoretical form, and, as a result, a significant portion of the political process ceased to be publicly documented. "After that brief period, the increasing replacement of theoretical ideology by closemouthed 'realism', and the growing passion for closed politics, limited the Western student to very gross inferences about the interaction of political beliefs and political processes."[25]

As a result of this situation, Joravsky argues, "The Western student of Soviet ideology faces a choice. He can limit himself to areas of thought where Soviet ideology can be identified from the vantage point of genuine knowledge and its social functions discovered by rigorous empirical scholarship. Or he can turn boldly to the political process, where ideology is most important — and nearly impossible to study in a rigorously empirical scholarly fashion. He can aspire to a scientific analysis of Soviet ideology or to an ideological critique of it. The choice can hardly be thoroughly rational; it is unavoidably influenced by one's ideological hopes and fears concerning the relationship between politics and scholarship."[26]

For the most part, students of Soviet ideology have chosen the latter approach — they have engaged in ideological critiques of Communist ideology rather than in scientific analysis. In some cases these ideological critiques (or "counter-ideologies") have masqueraded as "scientific" analysis, especially by

24. *Ibid.,* pp. 9 – 10.
25. Joravsky, *op. cit.,* pp. 12 – 13.
26. *Ibid.,* p. 15.

some American academics who wish to market their "services" to American policy-makers. As Kelly and Fleron point out, every "expert" on Communist affairs is expected to have some answer to the question of the motivational link between Communist ideology and Communist behavior. However, the locked door of the archive and the paucity of candid interviews have made impossible rigorous scientific analysis of the social functions performed by Soviet ideology. Hence it is impossible for the more objective scholar to refute the theories (and rantings and ravings) of anti-Communist counter-ideologists.[27] Yet concerted efforts in these directions must be made. For, as a respected social psychologist reminds us, "situations defined as real are real in their consequences."[28]

27. Not surprisingly, this latter form of ideology may also perform important social functions. See the chapter by Spiro and Barber below.

28. W. I. Thomas, quoted in Urie Bronfenbrenner, "Allowing for Soviet Perceptions," in Roger Fisher (ed.), *International Conflict and Behavioral Science* (New York: Basic Books, 1964), p. 166. For evidence that Soviet international perceptions are becoming increasingly similar to Western perceptions, see Zimmerman, *Soviet Perspectives on International Relations, 1956 – 1967.* For another example, consider the following comments of the distinguished Soviet Academician, N. N. Inozemtsev, from an article justifying the importance of American area studies programs in the USSR: "One of the important tasks of our American area studies is the concrete analysis of the complex and in many ways contradictory process of the elaboration and formulation of the course of U. S. foreign policy. This process is influenced by external and internal factors; it reflects changes in the international situation and in the domestic situation within the United States. It is affected by the internal struggle among various groupings in the ruling elite of the U. S. A. and by the nature of foreign-policy doctrines and concepts." From "The U. S. A. Today and Soviet American Area Studies," *Ekonomika, politika, ideologia,* I, 1 (January, 1970), pp. 6 – 14, translated in *The Current Digest of the Soviet Press,* XXII, 11 (April 14, 1970), p. 5.

SEVEN

Ideology and Power Politics:
A Symposium *

The Importance of Doctrine
R. N. CAREW HUNT

The term "ideology" is one which is more often used than defined. As the present study will be concerned with what the Russian Communists, and Communists in general, mean by it, a definition taken from a Soviet source is in order. The *Filosoficheskii Slovar* (Philosophical Dictionary, 1954 ed.), calls ideology "a system of definite views, ideas, conceptions, and notions adhered to by some class or political party," and goes on to say that it is always "a reflection of the economic system predominant at any given time." In a class-divided society the ideology will be that of one or another of the struggling classes, but under socialism, when there is no longer any class division, it will be that of society as a whole. A quotation from Lenin is added to the effect that there can be no "middle way" between the ideology of the bourgeoisie and that of the proletariat. The one is false and the other true.

Such a summation, albeit neat, is not altogether satisfactory. Broadly speaking, Marx was right in contending that the ideology of a society — the complex of ideas which determine its "way of life" — will be that of its dominant class, that is, of those whose abilities (whether used rightly or wrongly is irrelevant in this context) have raised them above the common herd. But this sociological fact applies equally to the Soviet Union, where the party certainly

*Reprinted from *Problems of Communism,* VII, 2 (March-April, 1958), pp. 10–30, and VII, 3 (May-June, 1958), pp. 50–52, by permission of the authors and the publisher.

constitutes such a class and indeed is assigned the duty of fertilizing the masses with its ideas. Undoubtedly the current Soviet ideology is intended to strengthen the party and reinforce its claim to rule. But one must probe further to explain why the party should have adopted the particular body of doctrine that it has. The fact is that the ideology has been largely determined by the type of collective society which has been established in the Soviet Union.

The authors of the October Revolution were Marxists, and were thus committed to abolishing the capitalist system and replacing it by a nationwide planned economy. For a brief period the experiment of allowing the workers to take charge was tried out, but, when this led to chaos, the party assumed control and has ever since retained it.

If a Communist regime is to be set up in a backward country, the first prerequisite, as Lenin saw, is industrialization; this is likely to be carried out as rapidly as possible, since the quicker the country is developed, and particularly its war potential, the stronger will be the position of its rulers. The execution of such a program of necessity demands the centralization of power in the hands of a small group of leaders, along with the adoption of such unpopular measures as the fixing of wages, the direction of labor, and the prohibition of strikes. And as large-scale planning geared to an expanding economy is impracticable if the plan is liable to be upset at any moment by a vote in a popular assembly, it is not to be expected that the planners will long tolerate any opposition. Furthermore, they will be tempted to interfere in one branch of human activity after another, seeing that all can be so manipulated as to assist the execution of their grand design.

All this has happened in the Soviet Union, and the outcome has been an ideology which derives from the logic of collectivism. Its basic principles are to be found in Marx's revolutionary doctrine, the implications of which were spelled out by Lenin and Stalin when confronted with the practical problem of setting up the type of social order Marx had advocated. Communist literature and propaganda have made us familiar with the doctrine, and there is no need to analyze it here even if space permitted. The issue to be decided is what role ideology plays today, and how far it influences Soviet policy.

Myths and the Masses

Virtually all analysts would agree that in the years of struggle before the October Revolution the Bolsheviks took the theory which lay behind their movement in deadly earnest; there is also general agreement that in the 1920's the doctrine acted as a stimulus to the workers, who took pride in building up their country. In the 1930's, however, the situation changed. Stalin assumed absolute power. The machinery of the state and of the secret police was greatly strengthened, and all prospect of establishing a genuine classless society disappeared. With the Stalin-Hitler Pact, if not before, the Soviet Union entered an era which can plausibly be represented as one of naked power politics, perpetuated after World War II in the aggressive and obstructive policies pursued by the regime. Hence it is sometimes argued that Communist ideology has now ceased to possess any importance; that it is simply a top-dressing of sophistries designed to rationalize measures inspired solely by Soviet interests; and that apart from a few fanatics, such as may be found in any society, no one believes in the doctrine any longer, least of all the leaders themselves.

Yet such unqualified assertions are erroneous. Consider, first, the outlook of the ordinary Soviet citizen *vis-à-vis* the ideology. Day in, day out, he is subjected to intensive and skillfully devised propaganda through every known medium, designed to demonstrate that the ideology on which the Soviet Union is based makes it the best of all possible worlds, and that on this account it is encircled with jealous enemies bent on its destruction. The Soviet leadership has always considered it essential that every citizen possess as deep an understanding of Communist principles as his mind is capable of assimilating, and those holding positions of consequence are obliged recurrently to pass through carefully graded schools of political instruction.

It is significant that whenever the leaders feel themselves in a tight corner — as in the recent aftermath of de-Stalinization and the intervention in Hungary — their invariable reaction is to intensify indoctrination in an attempt to refocus public attention on "first principles." As hard-headed men they would certainly not attach such importance to indoctrination if they did not know that it paid dividends — and experience has proved that the persistent repetition of a body of ideas which are never challenged is bound to influence the minds of their recipients. Of course, the present generation does not react to the formal ideology with the same fervor as did its forebears who made the revolution, and there are doubtless those who view official apologetics with a large degree of cynicism. But between total commitment and total disillusionment there are many intermediate positions; it is quite possible for a man to regard much of what he is told as nonsense while still believing that there is something of value behind it, especially if he identifies that "something" with the greatness of his country as "the first socialist state" and believes in its historic mission.

Leadership Credence — A Hope or a Habit?

More significant, in the present context, than the attitude of the ordinary citizen is that of the ruling elite which is responsible for policy. What its top-ranking members believe is a question which no one, of course, can answer positively. But before surmising, as do some analysts, that the Soviet leadership cannot possibly believe in the myths it propounds, we should remind ourselves that no class or party ever finds it difficult to persuade itself of the soundness of the principles on which it bases its claim to rule.

The Soviet leaders are fortified in this conviction by the very nature of their creed. They have been nurtured in it from birth, and it would be strange indeed if they had remained unaffected. It has become second nature to these men to regard history as a dialectical process — one of incessant conflict between progressive and reactionary forces which can only be resolved by the victory of the former. The division of the world into antagonistic camps, which is an article of faith, is simply the projection onto the international stage of the struggle within capitalistic society between the bourgeoisie, which history has condemned, and the proletariat, whose ultimate triumph it has decreed. The leaders seem to be confident that history is on their side, that all roads lead to communism, and that the contradictions of capitalism must create the type of situation which they can turn to their advantage.

Democratic governments desirous of recommending a certain policy normally dwell upon its practical advantages. But in the Soviet Union this is not so. Any important change of line will be heralded by an article in *Pravda* often of many columns, purporting to show that the new policy is ideologically correct because it accords with some recent decision of a party congress, or with Lenin's teaching, or with whatever other criterion may be adopted. How far the policy in question will have been inspired by considerations of ideology as opposed to others of a more mundane nature can never be precisely determined. This, however, is not an exclusive feature of the Communist system; in politics, as for that matter in personal relations, it is seldom possible to disentangle all the motives which determine conduct. The policies of any party or government are likely to reflect its political principles even if they are so framed as to strengthen its position, and there is no reason why the policies adopted by the Soviet leaders should constitute an exception.

Analysts of the "power politics" school of thought hold that the Kremlin leaders are concerned solely with Soviet national interest, and merely use the Communist movement to promote it. Yet here again the difficulty is to disengage factors which are closely associated. The future of the Communist movement cannot be disassociated from the fortunes of the Soviet Union. If the Soviet regime were to collapse, that movement would count for little, and whether it would long survive even in China is doubtful. Recognizing this, non-Russian Communist parties generally have remained subservient to Moscow even when threatened with large-scale defections of rank-and-file members in the face of particularly odious shifts in the Moscow line.

The "Separate Paths" Issue

The quarrel between the Soviet and the Yugoslav Communist parties — which an intergovernmental agreement of June 1956 has failed to resolve — is a good example of the interpenetration of ideological and non-ideological factors in policy determinations. The immediate occasion of the quarrel was Tito's unwillingness to allow the spread of Soviet influence through the presence of

Soviet military officers and technological experts on Yugoslav soil. As a result Stalin determined to crush Tito, and resorted to various political and economic measures in an unsuccessful attempt to do so. It was at least a year before the struggle was extended to the ideological plane. But that it should have been was inevitable. One may well sympathize with Tito's desire for independence and hope that other national leaders will follow his example. Yet from the Communist point of view, if the movement is to be an international one, it must have an international center, and upon historical grounds alone Moscow has a strong claim to the mantle. Ever since Communist parties were formed, it was in fact to Moscow that their internal disputes were referred for settlement, just as it was Moscow which directed their general policy. Whether this role was performed well or ill is beside the point.

Hence the principle of "separate paths to socialism," approved by the Twentieth CPSU Congress for tactical reasons, is one which Moscow can accept only with reservations. If it merely means that in establishing communism in a given country consideration must be given to local conditions, and that every country's experience adds to the common store, then it is not only unobjectionable but is a salutary corrective to the earlier dogmatism which insisted on the universal applicability of the Russian experience. Such is the attitude nowadays expressed by Soviet theoreticians, though they insistently stress the dangers of exaggerating the importance of national characteristics, denying "the common laws of socialist development," or playing down the October Revolution. The official Soviet position is best expressed in an article in *New Times,* March 1956, which states that "while *serving as an example* to other working-class parties, the CPSU *draws upon their experience and formulates it in general theoretical principles* for the benefit of all working-class parties."

Clearly the Soviet leaders are on the defensive in this matter. They recognize that concessions must be made, but will make no more than they can help. The desire to perpetuate their own power doubtless influences their stand, but considering the fact that communism professes to be a world movement, it would be unreasonable to conclude that either national or personal interests are the sole factors motivating them.

Inefficiency — An Index of Ideology

Indeed, if the analysis given earlier in this article of the genesis of the Communist ideology is correct, the attitude of the Soviet leaders *must* be attributed at least in part, to the theoretical principles which distinguish Communist regimes from other forms of dictatorship. Certainly the leaders shape and phrase their domestic and foreign policies to fit the general framework established by these principles, and the latter often do not allow much room for maneuver. In fact, their application may sometimes weaken rather than strengthen the country.

To take a simple example, much waste would be avoided if small traders were permitted to operate on a profit basis; the fishmonger, for instance, would have an incentive to put his fish on ice, which he frequently fails to do to the discomfort of the public. Allowance of profits, however, would constitute a return to private enterprise, which cannot be tolerated.

Similarly, in the Communist view it has long been regarded as indefensible to subordinate a higher to a lower form of socialized enterprise. Thus, while it has been apparent for years that Soviet agriculture would be more efficient if the Machine Tractor Stations were handed over to the collective farms, the issue has been consistently dodged, because the MTS are fully state-owned organs and therefore "higher" than the farms, which still belong in part to the peasants. When the economist Venzher advocated this measure some years ago, he was slapped down at once by Stalin, the fact that it had already been adopted in Yugoslavia only making his suggestion the more objectionable. Just two years ago Khrushchev launched an extensive program to strengthen the organization and power of the MTS. Very recently, however, he indicated that the regime was — at long last — prepared to yield to practical necessity on this point; in a speech on farm policy, he advocated the transfer of farm machinery to the collectives, and although his proposals are not yet legalized, it would appear that a number of MTS have already been dissolved.

The principle of hierarchy has not been repudiated, however, and still governs other aspects of agricultural organization — for example, the relative status of the two forms of agricultural enterprise. From the standpoint of productive efficiency the collective farms are bad, but the state farms are worse. Nonetheless, the latter represent a "higher type" of organization, and thus the present virgin lands campaign has been based upon them.

Dogmatism in Foreign Policy

The same point can be scored by examining the Soviet Union's treatment of its satellites. Poland affords a good example. With the country at its mercy after World War II, the Soviet regime decided, among other measures, to integrate the Polish economy with its own. Now had Poland been regarded merely as a colony to be exploited, the operation would have been viewed primarily as a business proposition, and due attention would have been paid to such questions as the nature of the country's resources and the aptitudes of its people. The need to proceed with caution was very evident. The traditional hostility of the Poles to everything Russian should have been taken into account, as well as the fact that the Polish Communist Party had no public support (due in part to the liquidation of its established leaders during the Great Purges). Yet it was decided that the country must pass through, in shorter time intervals, precisely those stages of development which the Soviet Union had traversed. The result was a serious disruption of the economy through the erection of a top-heavy industrial structure on the basis of a depressed agriculture. This policy cannot be attributed to Stalin alone as it was continued after his death. It proved disastrous, and is only intelligible on the assumption that it was primarily motivated by ideological considerations.

The argument can be carried further. By its behavior throughout its history, the Soviet Union has incurred the hostility, or at least the suspicion, of the entire free world. Yet there was no practical reason why it should have done so. After the October Revolution the Bolshevik regime was faced with appalling domestic problems, and it had nothing to gain by courting the animosity of the West. The Soviet leaders might well have built up their country in accordance with the principles to which they were committed without exciting such widespread hostility. What governments do at home is commonly regarded as their own affair. Fundamentally, the regime in Yugoslavia is as Communist as that of the Soviet Union, and was established with an equal ruthlessness. But Tito, having asserted his independence from Moscow, has muffled his attacks on the West, and in turn the Western governments have demonstrated their desire — albeit tempered with caution — to believe in his good faith.

What no country will tolerate is the attempt, deliberately engineered by a foreign power, to overthrow its form of government; this has been the persistent aim and effort of the Soviet regime in defiance of its express diplomatic guarantees of noninterference. It is hard to see how this strategy has assisted the development of Soviet Russia, and that it has never been abandoned cannot be dissociated from those messianic and catastrophic elements in the Communist creed which influence, perhaps impel, the Soviet drive for world power.

In conclusion, it is frequently stated that communism has created an ideological cleavage between the West and the Soviet bloc. Yet this statement would be meaningless if the issue today were, as some believe, simply one of power politics. An ideology is significant only if it makes those who profess it act in a way they would not otherwise do. The fact that large numbers of persons accept communism would not constitute a danger if it did not lead them to support policies which threaten the existence of those who do not accept it. It is true that many people, especially in backward countries, call themselves Communists without having any clear idea of what it means. Yet the movement would not be the force it has become were there not in every country men and women who sincerely believe in the ideas behind it which form collectively what we call its ideology.

To represent this ideology as a species of opium with which the Soviet leaders contrive to lull the people while taking care never to indulge in it themselves is to attribute to them an ability to dissociate themselves from the logic of their system — an ability which it is unlikely they possess. For the concepts which make up that system, fantastic as many of them appear to be, will be found on examination to be interrelated, and to be logical extensions of the basic principles to which all Communists subscribe.

To turn it the other way around, Communists claim a theoretical justification for the basic principles in which they believe. But these principles must
be translated into appropriate action; and action, if directed by the rulers of
a powerful country like the Soviet Union, will take the form of *Realpolitik.*
There is no yardstick which permits a measure of the exact relationship
between power politics and ideology in the policies which result; but surely
neither factor can be ignored.

National Interest: Key to Soviet Politics
SAMUEL L. SHARP

An enormous body of Western research and analysis focuses on Marxist-
Leninist ideology as a clue to understanding Kremlin policy. This extensive and
intensive preoccupation with matters doctrinal is, at least in part, the result
of a rather widely circulated belief that the democratic world was guilty of
neglect when it refused to take seriously the "theoretical" writings and pronouncements of Adolf Hitler. It has been alleged that these writings later
guided Hitler's actions and that a ready key to his conduct was thus overlooked.

When, at the end of World War II, the Soviet Union appeared on the
international scene as a power — and a menace — of the first order, led by a
group consistently claiming its adherence to a body of doctrine as a guide to
action, legions of experts began to dissect that body in a search for a key to
Soviet behavior, current and future. The material at hand was certainly more
promising than the intellectually scrawny homunculus of Nazi or Fascist
"ideology." After all, Marxism has its not entirely disreputable roots in legitimate Western thought. Even in terms of sheer bulk there was more to operate
on, what with Lenin's and Stalin's additions and modifications of the original
scriptures and the voluminous exegetic output of a generation of Soviet propagandists.

The massive study of Communist ideology has had one happy result in that
some serious scholarly output has been provided to counterbalance party-line
apologias, thereby destroying a number of primitive notions concerning the
Soviet system and what makes it tick. At the same time, in this writer's view,
preoccupation with the search for a formula of interpretative and predictive
value has produced its own distortions. These distortions seem to be the
composite result of cold-war anxieties, faulty logic, and disregard of some of
the elementary principles and practices of international relations. To these
causes must be added the human tendency to look beyond the simple and

obvious for the complicated and mysterious in attempting to explain any condition which is exasperating and which is therefore perceived as strange and unique. Baffled by the Soviet phenomenon, millions in the Western world have found a negative consolation of sorts in the famous statement by Winston Churchill that Russian policy is "a riddle wrapped in a mystery inside an enigma." But how many have bothered to read the qualifying words which followed? Having disclaimed ability to forecast Soviet actions, Churchill added: *But perhaps there is a key. That key is Russian national interest.* [1]

Clearly implied in this observation was the logical supposition that the policy-makers of the Soviet Union act in what they believe to be the best interest of the state over whose destinies they are presiding. In this sense the Soviet Union is to be looked upon as an actor, a protagonist, on the stage of international politics; and in this writer's view, its actions can be interpreted most fruitfully in terms of behavior *germane* to the practice of international politics. Without denying the possible pitfalls of this approach, the writer proposes to argue its usefulness as a key to understanding a phenomenon which the non-Communist world can ill afford to envelop in a fog of self-generated misinterpretation.

The Doubtful Art of Quotation

Whenever the suggestion is made that the concept of national interest be applied as an explanation of Soviet behavior on the international scene, objections are raised in many quarters. The most vigorous protests come, of course, from Soviet sources. It is a standard claim of Soviet spokesmen that their state is by definition something "different" (or "higher") and that the foreign policy of this entity is different in principle *(printsipialno otlichna)* from that of other states because the latter are capitalist and the former is socialist. [2] It would seem that only uncritical adherents of communism could take such statements seriously. Yet non-Communists very often cite them as a convenient *ipse dixit* in support of their own claim that the Soviet Union is indeed "different," though not in the way Soviet propaganda wants one to believe. The claim is that the Soviet Union is, at best, "a conspiracy disguised as a state" and cannot be viewed as a "normal" member of the world community of nations. There is no attempt to explain on what basis some Soviet statements are to be taken as reliable indices of regime motivations, while other statements, no less abundantly scattered throughout the Marxist-Leninist scriptures, are rejected as lie and deception.

1. Radio broadcast of October 1, 1939, reprinted in W. Churchill, *The Gathering Storm* (Boston: Houghton-Mifflin, 1948), p. 449. Author's italics.
2. To quote just one recent source, cf. V. I. Lissovskii, *Mezhdunarodnoe Pravo* [International Law], (Kiev, 1955), p. 397.

It is surely dubious scholarship to collect quotations (sometimes reduced to half a sentence) from Lenin and Stalin without regard to the time, place, circumstances, composition of the audience, and, whenever ascertainable, immediate purposes of such utterances. What results from such compilations, no matter how laboriously and ingeniously put together, is, as a thoughtful critic has pointed out, "a collection of such loose generalizations and so many exceptions and contradictions that few readers can find much guidance in it."[3] Stalin, for example, can be quoted as once having said that "with a diplomat words must diverge from facts" and that "a sincere diplomat would equal dry water, wooden iron"; yet this not too astute observation was made in 1913 in an article dealing with bourgeois diplomacy written by an obscure Georgian revolutionary who probably had never met a diplomat. His view in this instance is identifiable as a variant of the classic image of the diplomat as "an honorable gentleman sent abroad to lie for his country." This image may very well have stayed with the congenitally suspicious and pessimistic Stalin in later life, and thus might indeed afford us a clue to his "real" nature. However, sound scholarship would seek to reconstruct the attitudes of the Kremlin ruler out of words and deeds of a more relevant period of his life rather than from this loose piece of Djugashvili prose torn out of context.

The Vital Factor of Feasibility

Some objections to the interpretation of Soviet policies in terms of national interest are rooted in the aforementioned line of analysis which conjures up the ghost of Adolf Hitler. The democracies erred, did they not, in initially looking upon Hitler's aims as an expression of "legitimate" (we will return to this phrase in a moment) — however distasteful — national aspirations, only to discover later that they were dealing with a maniac whose appetites were unlimited. Since it is generally agreed that Soviet policy, like Hitler's, belongs to the totalitarian species, would it not be impardonable to repeat the same mistake by looking upon the aims of the Soviet leaders as the expression of the aspirations of a "normal" nation-state?

Two points should be made here. First, Hitler bears comparison with no

3. Marshall Knappen, *An Introduction to American Foreign Policy* (New York: Harper & Bros., 1956). The quote is from the chapter entitled "Capabilities, appeal and intentions of the Soviet Union" and refers specifically to the well-known effort by Nathan Leites in *A Study of Bolshevism* (Glencoe, Ill.: Free Press, 1953) to construct out of thousands of quotes from Lenin and Stalin bolstered with excerpts from nineteenth-century Russian literature, an "image of Bolshevism" and an "operational code" of the Politburo. See also the remarks on "Difficulties of content analysis" and "The problem of context" in John S. Reshetar, Jr., *Problems of Analyzing and Predicting Soviet Behavior* (New York: Doubleday & Co., 1955). In all fairness to Leites and his prodigious undertaking it must be pointed out that he was aware of a "spurious air of certainty" in his formulations, which were intended to be only "guesses about the mind of the Soviet Politburo" (*op. cit.,* p. 27).

one; there is no other leader in history who has combined his precise mental makeup with his enormous concentration of power. He was, as his biographer Allan Bullock pointed out, a man "without aims," that is, without *limited* and therefore tractable aims.[4] At one point in his career Hitler began to disregard the cardinal rule of politics — the necessity of aligning ambitions with capacity to translate them into reality. He broke the barrier of the *feasible,* motivated by what could most likely be diagnosed as the death-wish. Whatever else may be said about the Soviet leaders, no one, including people who suspect them of ideological self-deception, has denied them the quality of caution. Far from seeking self-destruction, they are lustily bent on survival. This in itself, even in the complete absence of scruples, makes their aims *limited.*

Mr. Carew Hunt argues elsewhere in these pages that there are "messianic and catastrophic elements in the Communist creed which influence . . . the Soviet drive for world power." While there may indeed be a degree of messianism in the Soviet leadership's view of its mission, the "catastrophic" tendency seems to be held carefully in check. Hitler was propelled by the absurd notion that he had to accomplish certain aims before he reached the age of sixty — an arrogant and, from the point of view of German national interest, totally irrelevant assumption. Granted that the Soviet leaders aim at "world power" (a concept which in itself should be defined more explicitly than it usually is), they have long since decided not to fix any specific time limit for the achievement of this ultimate aim. Certainly the present generation of leaders has acted to modify (perhaps "refine" is a better word) the aggressive drive for power abroad at least to an extent which will allow some enjoyment at home of the tangible fruits of the revolution this side of the Communist heaven. Even back in the early days of Bolshevik rule, Lenin, though at times carried away by expectations of spreading revolution, never sacrificed practical caution to missionary zeal; repeatedly he warned his followers to look after the "bouncing baby" (the Soviet state), since Europe was only "pregnant with revolution" (which it wasn't).

An Applicable Concept of Interest

The second point to be made is a crucial one. Reluctance to analyze Soviet aims in terms of national interest is due, in part, to the aura of legitimacy which surrounds the "normal" run of claims of nation-states, giving rise to the notion that the term itself infers something legitimate. However, suggesting that Kremlin moves can best be understood in terms of what the leaders consider advantageous to the Soviet state by no means implies subscribing to their aims or sympathizing with them. In international relations the maxim *tout comprendre c'est tout pardonner* does not apply. The concept of national interest, by

4. Allan Bullock, *Hitler – A Study in Tyranny* (New York: Harper & Bros., 1953).

focusing attention on the *objective sources of conflict* — that is, those which *can* be explained rationally as issues between nations — permits us to view the international scene in terms of a global problem of power relations rather than a cops-and-robbers melodrama. We can then perceive which are the *tractable* elements in the total equation of conflict, and devote our energies to reducing or altering these factors.

This approach seems to the writer to be indispensable both to the scholar and to the statesman. The scholar who accepts the "natural" (in terms of the nature of international politics) explanation for Kremlin behavior is not likely to violate the "law of parsimony" by unnecessarily piling up hypotheses which are unprovable and which in any case simply confuse the issue, insofar as dealing practically with the Soviet Union is concerned. The statesman finds that he is coping with a phenomenon which he knows how to approach both in accommodation and in opposition, rather than with some occult and other-worldly force.

Those who object to the framework of analysis here proposed would say, as does Mr. Hunt, that there are many cases on record when the Soviet leaders have acted in a way clearly inconsistent with the Russian national interest and intelligible only in terms of ideological dogmatism. The answer to this argument is simple: it does not matter what Mr. Hunt — or anybody else — considers to be the Russian national interest; as the term is defined here, the only view which matters is that held by the Soviet leaders. By the same token it is a rather fruitless thing to speak of "legitimate" vs. "illegitimate" Soviet interests. One of the essential attributes of sovereignty (and the Soviet leaders are certainly jealous where their own is involved!) is that it is up to the sovereign to determine what serves him best.

Yet doesn't this reasoning render pointless the entire conceptual approach proposed? If Soviet national interest is what the Soviet leaders take it to be, and if one agrees — as one must — that their view of the world is derived largely from their adherence to Marxism-Leninism, isn't this another way of saying that Soviet behavior is the result of ideological conditioning? Not quite. The point at issue is whether the "pure" Soviet view of the world is important *as a guide to action,* whether the *ultimate* aims of the Communist creed are operative in policy determinations. In the present writer's view they are not; the fault of the opposing line of analysis is that in dwelling on the supposed impact of ideology on the leadership, it tends to ignore the degree to which the pursuit of ultimate goals has been circumscribed in time and scope by considerations of *the feasible*. In simple arithmetic, doctrine minus those aspects which are not empirically operative equals empirically determined policy. If a policy action is called "revolutionary expediency," it is still expediency. Why then introduce into the equation an element which does not affect the result?

A supporting view in this respect is W. W. Rostow's characterization of Soviet foreign policy as a series of responses to the outside world which, especially before 1939, "took the form of such actions as were judged most likely, *on a short-range basis,* to maintain or expand the national power of the Soviet regime." Despite the Soviet Union's vastly greater ability to influence the world environment in the postwar era, says Rostow, "there is no evidence that the foreign policy criteria of the regime have changed."[5] If some instances of Soviet behavior appear to have produced results actually detrimental to the Soviet interest, we must not only refrain from applying our view of Soviet interest but also — as Rostow's viewpoint suggests — judge the policy decisions involved in terms of their validity at the time they were made and not in the light of what happened later (remembering, too, that mistakes and miscalculations are common to all policy-makers, not just those who wear "ideological blinders").

The words "on a short-range basis" have been underscored above to stress that the term "policy," if properly applied, excludes aims, ambitions, or dreams not accompanied by action visibly and within a reasonable time capable of producing the results aimed at or dreamed of. In the case of the Soviet leaders, concentration on short-range objectives and adjustment to political realities has, in the brilliant phrase suggested by Barrington Moore, Jr., *caused the means to eat up the ends.*[6]

The objection will still be raised that the Soviet leaders mouth every policy decision in terms of ideological aims. Enough should have been said on this score to obviate a discussion here; as able students of the problem have pointed out, the Soviet leaders' claim to rule rests on their perpetuation of the ideology and their insistence on orthodoxy; they have no choice but to continue paying lip-service to the doctrine, even if it is no longer operative. The liberal mind somehow balks at this image of total manipulation, of an exoteric doctrine for public consumption which has no connection with its esoteric counterpart — that is, the principles or considerations which really govern Kremlin behavior. Yet allowance must be made for this possibility.

Moscow and International Communism

One serious argument of those who reject the image of the Soviet Union as a "legitimate" participant in the balance-of-power game played in the arena of international politics is that the Soviet leaders consistently violate the rules of the game by enlisting out-of-bounds help from foreign Communist parties.

5. W. W. Rostow *et al., The Dynamics of Soviet Society* (New York: W. W. Norton & Co., 1952), p. 136. Author's italics.
6. Barrington Moore, Jr., *Soviet Politics — The Dilemma of Power* (Cambridge: Harvard University Press, 1950).

This point invites the following brief observations:

1) Early in its history the Communist International was transformed into a tool of Soviet foreign policy, at a time when few other tools were available to Moscow.

2) As soon as the Soviet state felt at all sure of its survival (after the period of civil war, foreign intervention, and economic chaos), it reactivated the apparatus of foreign policy along more traditional lines.

3) Under Stalin, the Third International was reduced to a minor auxiliary operation. An index of his attitude toward it is the fact that he never once addressed a Comintern congress. Probably the International was kept up in the interwar period because it seemed to produce marginal dividends in terms of nuisance value. Moreover, Stalin could hardly have divorced himself from it officially at a time when he was jockeying for total power inside Russia, since this would have helped to confirm his opponents' accusations that he was "betraying the revolution." But he certainly did everything to show his belief in the ineffectiveness of the organization and its foreign components as against the growing power of the Soviet state.

4) When the entire record of Soviet success and failure is summed up, the achievements are clearly attributable to Soviet power and diplomacy with no credit due to the international Communist movement. Furthermore, the ties between the Soviet Union and foreign parties have never deterred Moscow from useful alliances or cooperation with other governments — including, from one time to another, the astutely anti-Communist Turkish government of Ataturk; the more brutally anti-Communist regime of Adolf Hitler; and, during World War II, the Western powers. That the Soviet leaders, by virtue of their doctrine, entertained mental reservations about the durability of friendly relations with these governments can hardly be doubted. But it is equally clear that the cessation of cooperation was due in each case to the workings of power politics rather than Soviet ideological dictate — that is, to the historical tendency of alliances to disintegrate when what binds them (usually a common enemy) disappears.

5) Finally, it might be argued that the Soviet appeal to foreign Communist parties is not dissimilar to the practice of various governments of different periods and persuasions to appeal for support abroad on the basis of some sort of affinity — be it Hispanidad, Slav solidarity, Deutschtum, or Pan-Arabism. The Soviet appeal is admittedly broader and the "organizational weapon" seems formidable, but their importance should not be exaggerated. Actually, there is no way at all to measure the effectiveness of the appeal *per se* since Communist "success" or "failure" in any situation always involves a host of other variables — including military, geographical, social, political, or economic factors. In the last analysis, virtually every instance where Moscow has claimed a victory for communism has depended on Soviet manipulation of traditional levers of national influence.

An Exception to Prove the Rule

There remains one area of Soviet "foreign policy" where the Soviet leaders have supplemented power politics — or more accurately in this instance naked force — with an attempt to derive special advantage, a sort of "surplus value," from claiming ideological obeisance to the Soviet Union as the seat of the secular church of communism. This area is the so-called Soviet orbit in Eastern Europe.

The term "foreign policy" is enclosed in quotation marks here because Stalin obviously did not consider areas under the physical control of Soviet power as nations or governments to be dealt with in their own right. He was clearly impatient with the claim of at least some Communist parties that their advent to power had changed the nature of their relationship to Moscow, and that the party-to-party level of relations must be separated from the government-to-government level (as Gomulka argued in 1948). In Stalin's thinking, especially after 1947, the East European regimes were not eligible for more real sovereignty than the "sovereign" republics of the Soviet Union. He attempted to extend the principle of *democratic centralism* (a euphemism for Kremlin control) to these countries, allowing them only as much of a façade of sovereignty as was useful for show toward the outside world.

One need not necessarily dig into doctrine to explain this attitude; in fact, doctrine until recently said nothing at all about relations between sovereign Communist states. The explanation lies to a large extent in Stalin's personal predilection for total control, plus the need to tighten Moscow's bonds to the limit, by whatever means or arguments possible, in the face of the bipolarization of global power after World War II.

Stalin's successors began by pressing the same claims of ideological obeisance from the satellites. But rather striking — in the same period that their foreign policy has scored substantial successes in other areas in traditional terms of diplomatic advances and manipulation of the economic weapon[7] — they have failed in the one area where they attempted to substitute the ties of ideology for the give-and-take of politics. Communist parties in power, it turned out (first in the case of Yugoslavia, while Stalin still reigned, and later in Poland, not to mention the very special case of China), claimed the right to be sovereign — or at least semi-sovereign — actors on the international scene. Whether or not this makes sense ideologically to the Soviet leaders is unimportant; they have recognized the claim.

It is not necessary to review here the post-Stalin history of fluctuating Soviet relations with Eastern Europe which began with the B. & K. pilgrimage to Belgrade. Let us take only the most recent attempt to reformulate the nature of relations between the USSR and other Communist countries — the inter-party declaration issued on the occasion of the fortieth anniversary of the

7. Samuel L. Sharp, "The Soviet Position in the Middle East," *Social Science,* National Academy of Economics and Political Sciences, Vol. 32, No. 4, October, 1957.

Bolshevik revolution. On the surface, the declaration, published in the name of twelve ruling Communist parties, seems to reimpose a pattern of ideological uniformity as well as to recognize the special leadership position of the Soviet Union.[8] However, the circumstances of the gathering and the internal evidence of the declaration, together with the reports of some of the participants, show a far more complex situation.

The following aspects of the conference deserve attention: First, the very fact that the parties representing governments of sovereign countries were singled out for a special meeting and declaration instead of being lumped together with the mass of parties (many of them illegal, some leading no more than a paper existence) is a significant departure from past practice. Second, the Yugoslav party, though represented at the festivities, refused to sign the declaration, apparently after long negotiations. Third, attempts to revive in any form an international, Moscow-based organization resembling the Comintern were unsuccessful. Gomulka's report on the meeting made it clear that the Polish party opposed both a new Comintern (for which it nevertheless had a few good words) and a new Cominform (for which it had nothing but scorn.)[9]

A point of particular significance was the revelation that future international gatherings of Communist parties, especially those in power, are to be based on previous agreements concerning the agenda. According to Gomulka, problems which each party thinks it can best solve *for itself and its country* will not be decided by interparty conferences.[10]

Perhaps most significant for the purposes of the present discussion was a statement by Mao Tse-tung, who next to Khrushchev and Suslov was the main speaker at the meeting of the "ruling" parties and was billed as co-sponsor of the declaration. Mao bolstered his argument for the recognition of the leading position of the Soviet Union in the "socialist camp" with the remark that "China has not even one-fourth of a sputnik while the Soviet Union has two."[11] Now, the possession of a sputnik is a symbol of achievement and a source of prestige for the Soviet Union, but certainly not in terms of ideology. It was Soviet national power to which Mao paid deference.

In sum, the entire circumstances of the gathering indicate a disposition on the part of the Soviet Union to substitute — wherever it has to — the give-and-take of politics for its former relationship with the orbit countries, which relied on naked power to enforce demands of ideological subservience.

8. The text of the declaration, adopted at a meeting held on November 14–16, 1957, was published in *Pravda* on November 22. A separate "peace manifesto" issued in the name of all of the Communist parties present at the congregation appeared in *Pravda* a day later.

9. Gomulka's report was published in *Trybuna Ludu,* Warsaw, November 29, 1957.

10. Gomulka, *ibid.* See also an analysis of the conference entitled, "Gescheiterte Komintern-Renaissance" [Failure of Comintern Revival], *Ost-Probleme,* Bad Godesberg, X, No. 1 (January 3, 1958).

11. Cited in Friedrich Ebert's report to the East German party (SED), published in *Neues Deutschland,* East Berlin, November 30, 1957, p. 4.

From all the foregoing, it should be clear that the task of the non-Communist world is not to worry itself sick over the ultimate goals of the Soviet leadership or the degree of its sincerity, but to concentrate on multiplying situations in which the Soviet Union either will be forced or will choose to play the game of international politics in an essentially traditional setting. How the Kremlin leaders will square this with their Marxist conscience is not really our problem.

The Logic Of One-Party Rule

RICHARD LOWENTHAL

To what extent are the political decisions of the Soviet leadership influenced by its belief in an official ideology — and to what extent are they empirical responses to specific conflicts of interest, expressed in ideological terms merely for purposes of justification? The phrasing of the question at issue suggests the two extreme answers which are *prima facie* conceivable — on the one hand, that ideology provides the Kremlin with a ready-made book of rules to be looked up in any situation; on the other, that its response to reality takes place without any reference to ideology. Yet any clear formulation of this vital issue will show that both extremes are meaningless nonsense.

A ready-made book of rules for any and every situation — an unvarying roadmap to the goal of communism which the Soviet leaders must predictably follow — cannot possibly exist, both because the situations to be met by them are not sufficiently predictable, and because no government which behaved in so calculable a manner could conceivably retain power. On the other hand, empirical *Realpolitik* without ideological preconceptions can exist as little as can "empirical science" without categories and hypotheses based on theoretical speculation. Confronted with the same constellation of interests and pressures, the liberal statesman will in many cases choose a different course of action from the conservative — and the totalitarian Communist's choice will often be different from that of either.

It seems surprising, therefore, that at this late stage of discussion Professor Sharp is apparently in earnest in defending the extreme of the *Realpolitik* interpretation and in denying completely the relevance of Communist ideology for the formation, and hence the understanding, of Soviet foreign policy. The latter, he assures us, can be adequately understood in terms of national interest, just as with any other state. When reminded by Mr. Carew Hunt of certain irrational features of Soviet foreign policy, he replies that what matters is not any outsider's concept of Soviet interests, but the Soviet leaders' own. Yet this reduces his thesis to a tautology: he "proves" that national interest motivates Soviet foreign policy by the simple device of labeling whatever motivates it "national interest."

Surely Professor Sharp cannot have it both ways. Either there are objective criteria of national interest, recognizable by the scholar — and then the view that these interests explain Soviet actions is capable of proof or refutation; or else it is admitted that different statesmen may interpret national interest in different but equally "legitimate" ways — and then the concept of a self-contained study of international relations collapses, because a consideration of the internal structures of different national communities and of the "ideologies" reflecting them becomes indispensable for an understanding of their foreign policies.

The latter observation does not, of course, apply to Communist states alone, although it is only reasonable to expect the influence of the monopolistic ideology of a single-party state to be specially pervasive. Mr. George Kennan, in his 1950 lectures on American diplomacy, has convincingly shown the relevance of ideological factors to an understanding of modern United States foreign policy as well. To deny this influence *a priori* and to admit, as Professor Sharp apparently would, only the *Ding an sich* of national interest on one side, and the accidental element of human error or pathology (such as Hitler's "death-wish") on the other, seems to this writer to be an unjustifiable renunciation of one of the limited roads to understanding which are available to present-day political science.

The Function of Doctrine

Assuming, then, that the Soviet leaders' ideology is relevant to their conduct, the real problem remains to discover which are the actual operative elements in it, and in what way they affect policy decisions. Clearly it would be folly to expect that Soviet policy could be predicted solely from an exegetic study of the Marxist-Leninist canon. Not only is it impossible for any group of practical politicians to base their decisions on an unvarying book of rules; there is any amount of historical evidence to show that the rules have been altered again and again to fit the practical decisions *ex post facto*. Moreover, there are vast parts of the Communist ideological structure, such as the scholastic refinements of "dialectical materialism" or the labor theory of value, which in their nature are so remote from the practical matters to be decided that their interpretation cannot possibly affect policy decisions. They may be used in inner-party arguments to *justify* what has been decided on other grounds, but that is all.

How, then, are we to distinguish those elements of Soviet ideology which are truly operative politically from those which are merely traditional scholastic ballast, linked to the operative elements by the historical accident of the founding fathers' authorship? The answer is to be found by going back to the original Marxian meaning of the term "ideology" — conceived as a distorted reflection of social reality in the consciousness of men, used as an instrument of struggle. The fundamental, distinctive social reality in the Soviet Union is the rule of the bureaucracy of a single, centralized, and disciplined party, which wields a monopoly of political, economic, and spiritual power and permits no independent groupings of any kind. The writer proposes as a hypothesis that the operative parts of the ideology are those which are indispensable for maintaining and justifying this state of affairs: "Marxism-Leninism" matters inasmuch as it expresses, in an ideologically distorted form, the logic of one-party rule.[1]

Totalitarian Parallels

There are a few interconnected ideological features which are common to all the totalitarian regimes of our century — whether of the nationalist-fascist or of the Communist variety. We may designate them as the elements of chiliasm, of collective paranoia, and of the representative fiction. Each totalitarian regime justifies its power and its crimes by the avowed conviction, first, that its final victory will bring about the Millennium — whether defined as the final triumph of communism or of the master race — and second, that this state of grace can only be achieved by an irreconcilable struggle against a single, omnipresent, and multiform enemy — whether Monopoly Capitalism or World Jewry — whose forms include every particular opponent of the totalitarian power. Each also claims to represent the true will of the people — the *volonté générale* — independent of whether the people actually support it, and argues that any sacrifice may be demanded from the individual and the group for the good of the people and the defeat of its devilish enemies.

The Communist version of these basic beliefs is superior to the Nazi version in one vital respect. Because the appeal of racialism is in its nature restricted to a small minority of mankind, the Nazis' goal of world domination could not possibly have been attained without a series of wars, preferably surprise attacks

---

1. While this comes close to the position outlined in Mr. Carew Hunt's paper, I cannot follow him in his assumption that the totalitarian party monopoly is a by-product of the attempt to establish collectivist economic planning or to achieve the speedy industrialization of a backward country. This neo-Marxist view, held by such otherwise divergent authors as Professor Hayek and Milovan Djilas, is contradicted by the fact that the Bolshevik party monopoly, including the ban on inner-party factions, was fully established by Lenin at the time of the transition to the "New Economic Policy" (1921), when economic planning was reduced to a minimum and forced industrialization not yet envisaged. Independent of the concrete economic program, totalitarianism was implicit in the centralized, undemocratic structure of a party consciously created as an instrument for the conquest of power, and in the ideological characteristics resulting (to be discussed further in this article). Of course, totalitarian power, once established, favors total economic planning and the undertaking of revolutionary economic tasks by the state; but this is a consequence, not a cause. Marx never developed a concept of total planning, and even Lenin never imagined anything of the kind before 1918. But Marx in his youth at least equated the "dictatorship of the proletariat" with the Jacobin model, and Lenin followed this model throughout.

launched against isolated opponents. Because the appeal of communism is directed to all mankind, it can be linked with the further doctrine of the inevitable victory of the rising forces of socialism over the imperialist enemy, which is disintegrating under the impact of its own internal contradictions. This central ideological difference, and not merely the psychological difference between Hitler and the Soviet leaders, explains why the latter are convinced that history is on their side and that they need not risk the survival of their own regime in any attempt to hasten its final triumph: they believe in violence, revolutionary and military, as one of the weapons of policy, but they do not believe in the inevitability of world war.

Awkward Aims and Claims

Yet the Communist version of totalitarian ideology also suffers from some weaknesses and contradictions from which the Nazi and Fascist versions are free. In the first place, its vision of the Millennium has more markedly utopian features — the classless society, the end of exploitation of man by man, the withering away of the state — which make awkward yardsticks for the real achievements of Communist states. Second, in a world where nationalism remains a force of tremendous strength, an internationalist doctrine is bound to come into conflict with the interests of any major Communist power, or with the desire of smaller Communist states for autonomy.

Third, by rejecting the "Fuehrer principle" and claiming to be "democratic," Communist ideology makes the realities of party dictatorship and centralistic discipline more difficult to justify; yet because appeal to blind faith is not officially permitted, justification is needed in "rational" terms. It is precisely this continuous need for the pretense of rational argument — the awkward heritage of communism's origin from revolutionary Western democracy — which has led to the far greater elaboration of its ideology compared to that of "irrationalist" right-wing totalitarianism, and which gives its constant interpretation so much greater importance in preserving the cohesion of the party regime. Due to the fictions of democracy and rationality, the morale of party cadres has been made dependent on the appearance of ideological consistency.

The result of these inherent weaknesses of Communist ideology is that the component doctrines — dealing with the "dictatorship of the proletariat," the party's role as a "vanguard" embodying the "true" class consciousness, "democratic centralism," "proletarian internationalism," and the "leading role of the Soviet Union" — become focal points of ideological crises and targets of "revisionist" attacks whenever events reveal the underlying contradictions in a particularly striking way. Yet these are the very doctrines which the regime cannot renounce because they are the basic rationalizations of its own desire for self-preservation.

We can expect, then, that Communist ideology will have an effective influence on the policy decisions of Soviet leaders when, and only when, it expresses the needs of self-preservation of the party regime. We can further expect that ideological changes and disputes within the Communist "camp" will offer clues to the conflicts and crises — the "contradictions" — which are inseparable from the evolution of this, as of any other, type of society. The fruitful approach, in this writer's view, consists neither in ignoring Communist ideology as an irrelevant disguise, nor in accepting it at its face value and treating it as a subject for exegesis, but in using it as an indicator of those specific drives and problems which spring from the specific structure of Soviet society — in regarding it as an enciphered, continuous self-disclosure, whose cipher can be broken by sociological analysis.

Two Camps — One Enemy

Let us now apply this approach to the doctrine of the "two camps" in world affairs. The "two-camp" concept was not, of course, a Stalinist invention, although this is sometimes supposed. The postwar situation with its alignment of the Communist and Western powers in two openly hostile politico-military blocs merely gave plausibility to a world image which was inherent in Leninism from the beginning, but which attracted little attention in the period when the Communist "camp" was just an isolated fortress with several outposts. Nor has the doctrine disappeared with the post-Stalin recognition of the importance of the uncommitted, ex-colonial nations and of the tactical value of incorporating them in a "peace zone;" it remains one of the basic ideas of the Moscow twelve-party declaration of last November and one of the fundamental subjects of ideological disagreement between the Soviets and the Yugoslav Communists.

The Yugoslavs can reject the "two-camp" doctrine because they admit the possibility of "roads to socialism" other than Communist party dictatorship — "reformist" roads for advanced industrial countries with parliamentary traditions, "national revolutionary" roads for ex-colonial countries. It follows from this view that Communist states have no monopoly on progress, and that alliances have no ultimate ideological meaning.

The Soviets still assert that while there can be different roads to Communist power, and minor differences in the use of power once gained, there is no way of achieving socialism except by the "dictatorship of the proletariat exercised by its vanguard." It follows that tactical agreements with semi-socialist neutrals are not different in kind from the wartime alliance with the Western "imperialists," or the prewar pact with Hitler — maneuvers which are useful in dividing the forces of the "class enemy" but which remain subordinate to the fundamental division of the world into the Communists versus the Rest.

In other words, the "two-camp" doctrine is the Communist version of what we have called the element of "collective paranoia" in totalitarian ideology — its need for a single, all-embracing enemy which is assumed to pull the wires of every resistance to the party's power. The term "paranoia" is used here not to infer that the phenomenon in question is due to psychotic processes in either the leaders or the mass following of totalitarian parties, but merely to describe, through a convenient psychological analogy, the ideological mechanism of projection which ascribes the regime's drive for unlimited power to an imagined all-enemy. The essential point is that in the nature of totalitarianism, any independent force — either inside or outside the state — is regarded as ultimately hostile; the concept of "two camps" and that of "unlimited aims" are two sides of the same phenomenon.

Moscow's Double-Indemnity Tactics

Now Professor Sharp is, of course, entirely right in asking where this doctrine impinges on actual Soviet foreign policy — given the undoubted facts that actual Soviet aims, and the risks incurred in their pursuit, are limited at any given moment; that the Soviets are perfectly capable of concluding "temporary" alliances with "bourgeois," "imperialist," or even "fascist" states; and that most other alliances in this impermanent world are proving to be "temporary" as well, for quite nonideological reasons. The present writer would suggest to him that the difference has manifested itself in the peculiar suspicion with which the Soviets treated their "imperialist" allies even at the height of the war, seeking in particular to isolate their own population from contact; in the manner in which they sought to create additional "guarantees" for the reliability of those allies by the use of local Communist parties wherever this was possible; and above all, in the difference between the traditional and the Communist concepts of "spheres of influence" as illuminated by the different interpretations of the Yalta agreements.

The peculiar forms taken by Moscow's suspicion of its wartime allies are too well known to need elaboration here; but it is less generally realized that such behavior was merely the reverse side of Soviet efforts to "strengthen" such temporary alliances where possible, by the use of party ties. Existence of the party channel has not, of course, been a *sine qua non* for Moscow's intragovernmental deals, as is shown by the examples of Russo-Turkish cooperation after World War I, the Stalin-Hitler pact, and perhaps also present Soviet cooperation with Egypt. But wherever Communist parties were tolerated by the partner, Soviet foreign policy has assigned to them a vital role. Indeed, the implication that Stalin never used the foreign Communists for any important purposes is perhaps the most astonishing aspect of Professor Sharp's article.

In the 1920's, Stalin's Chinese policy was openly run in double harness; diplomatic support for the Nationalist advance to the North was supplemented by an agreement of affiliation between the Chinese Communist Party and the Kuomintang, enabling the Communist to occupy influential political and military positions — an attempt no less serious for its ultimate total failure in 1927.

In the 1930's, a variant of the same "dual policy" was evident when Moscow supported the League and "collective security," while Communist parties in France and Spain pursued "popular front" policies which soft-pedalled economic and social demands for the sake of influencing governmental foreign policy. In the Spanish case the Communists, aided by the Republicans' dependence on Soviet supplies, ended up in virtual control of the republic on the eve of its final collapse.

Again during World War II, Communists in the resistance movements and in the free Western countries were ordered to pursue the same tactics of social moderation and occupation of key positions as were practiced in China in the 1920's and Spain in the 1930's. Wartime military and political cooperation between "Soviet China" and Chiang Kai-shek was urged in the same spirit, with considerable success. All these are the foreign policy methods of a state *sui generis* — a one-party state enabled by its ideology to make use of a disciplined international movement organized for the struggle for power. To compare them — and the secondary opportunities for infiltration and espionage which they offer in addition to their main political objectives — to the use of vague cultural influences like "Hispanidad" is to show a notable degree of innocence.

Yalta — A Historic "Misunderstanding"

The crucial example to illustrate the role of ideology in Soviet foreign policy, however, remains the history of the postwar division of Europe. The writer is not concerned here with the political controversy over whether this division, as first laid down in the wartime agreements at Teheran and Yalta, was inevitable in the light of the military situation as seen at the time, or whether the Western statesmen committed an avoidable mistake of disastrous dimensions. What matters in the present context is the different meaning attached by the Western and Communist leaders, in concluding these agreements, to the concept of "spheres of influence," and the consequences of this "misunderstanding."

That Great Powers are in a position to exert a measure of influence over their smaller neighbors, and that they use this influence in one way or another to increase as far as possible their security against attack by other Great Powers, is an experience general in the politics of sovereign states and unlikely to be superseded by any amount of declamation about "equality of rights"; hence, the fact that the wartime allies, in drawing a military line of demarcation from north to south across the center of Europe, should have tried to agree about their postwar spheres of influence is, by itself, proof of realistic foresight rather than of morally reprehensible cynicism.

To Mr. Roosevelt and Mr. Churchill, however, these spheres of influence meant what they had traditionally meant in the relations of sovereign states — a gradual shading over from the influence of one power or group of powers to that of the other, a shifting relationship which might be loosely described in terms of "percentages of influence," ranging from 50/50 to 90/10. To the Soviets, "spheres of influence" meant something completely different in the framework of their ideology — the ideology of the single-party state. To them there could be no securely "friendly" government except a government run by a Communist party under their discipline; no sphere of influence but a sphere of Communist rule; no satisfactory percentage short of 100. Hence the consistent Soviet efforts, which began even before the end of the European war, to impose total control by Communist parties in every country on their side of the demarcation line — an effort that was finally successful everywhere but in Finland and Eastern Austria; hence also the indignant protests of the Western powers that the Soviets had broken the agreements on free elections and democratic development, and the equally indignant Soviet retort that they were only installing "friendly governments" as agreed, that theirs was the truly "democratic" system, and that they had kept scrupulously to the essential agreement on the military demarcation line.

A large section of Western opinion has concluded from this experience that agreements with the Soviets are useless in principle, because "you cannot trust them"; and Professor Sharp's insistence on national interest as the sole key to Soviet policy is probably at least in part a reaction against this emotional and moralizing approach. In fact, any interpretation of the postwar experience overlooking the fact that the Soviets have for reasons of national self-interest, kept to the "self-enforcing" agreement on the demarcation line, would be as seriously one-sided as one overlooking the fact that they have, for reasons of ideology or party interest, broken every agreement on "percentages" and free elections.

There is no need, however, to base future policy on either of two one-sided views equally refuted by experience. Nobody in the Western world has argued more powerfully against the "moralizing" approach to foreign policy, and for a return to the give-and-take of diplomacy based on real interests, than George Kennan; yet in his recent Reith lectures as before, he insists that the specific ideological distortion in the Soviet leaders' image of the world, far from being magically cured by a return to diplomacy, has to be taken into account continuously in judging which kind of agreements are possible and which are not. After all, the peoples of Eastern Europe are still paying for the illusion of the West that the Soviet Union was a state like any other, pursuing its power interests without regard to ideology.

The Soviet Dilemma in Eastern Europe

If we now turn to interstate and interparty relations within the Communist camp, we seem at first sight to have entered an area where ideology is adapted quite unceremoniously to the changing requirements of practical politics. Lenin, having barely seized power in Russia and looking forward to an early spreading of Communist revolution, could talk airily enough about the sovereign equality and fraternal solidarity of sovereign "socialist" states. Stalin, having determined after the failure of short-term revolutionary hope to concentrate on "socialism in a single country," came to regard international communism as a mere tool of Soviet power, and to believe that revolutionary victories without the backing of Soviet arms were neither possible nor desirable; he wanted no sovereign Communist allies, only satellites, and he got them in postwar Eastern Europe.

The independent victories of the Yugoslav Communists at the end of the war and of the Chinese Communists in 1949 nevertheless posed the problem he had sought to avoid, and thus required a revision of policy and ideology. But, so one argument goes, the stubborn old man had lost the flexibility to accept the situation; he precipitated a needless quarrel with the Yugoslavs and generally prevented the necessary adjustment while he lived. His heirs, however, hastened to correct his mistakes and to put inter-Communist relations back on a basis of sovereign equality and diplomatic give-and-take, not only with China and Yugoslavia but, after some trial and error, with all Communist states. Or did they?

In the above "common-sense" account, not only the facts of the final phase are wrong; by deliberately neglecting the ideological aspect, it loses sight of all the real difficulties and contradictions which remain inherent in the situation. Because the Soviet Union is both a great power and a single-party state tied to an international ideology, it cannot be content either to oppress and exploit other Communist states or to come to terms with them on a basis of expediency; it must act in a way that will ensure the ideological unity of the Communist "camp" and its own authority at the center.

Stalin's insistence on making the "leading role of the Soviet Union" an article of the international creed expressed not just the idiosyncrasies of a power-mad tyrant, but his perception of one side of the dilemma — the risk that a recognition of the sovereign equality of other Communist states might loosen the solidarity of the "camp" in its dealings with the non-Communist world, and weaken the ideological authority of the Soviet party leaders, with ultimate repercussions on their position in the Soviet Union itself. His successors disavowed him because his Yugoslav policy had failed, and because they perceived the other side of the dilemma — that rigid insistence on Soviet hegemony might break up the unity of the "camp" even more quickly, and might in particular lead to open conflict with China. But by going to Peiping and Belgrade and admitting the "mistakes" of Stalin's "Great Russian chauvinism" (as well as the "mistakes" of his internal terrorist regime), they precipitated the very crisis of authority which he had feared.

The Reassertion of Soviet Primacy

Even Khrushchev and his associates, however, never intended to grant effective sovereign equality to the other Communist satellite regimes of Eastern Europe, which in contrast to Yugoslavia and China had come into being exclusively through the pressure of Soviet power; they merely had planned to make the satellite regimes more viable by reducing Soviet economic exploitation and administrative interference, while maintaining full policy control. In the one case in which not full sovereignty, but at least effective internal autonomy, was in fact granted — the case of Poland — the Soviet leaders were forced to act against their will as a result of open local defiance in a critical international situation. To say that the other East European participants in the Moscow twelve-party meeting of last November, or for that matter the participants from Outer Mongolia and North Korea, represented "governments of sovereign countries" is to mistake the fancies of Communist propaganda for political facts. Nor do the facts bear out Professor Sharp's interpretation that the outcome of the conference showed the Soviet leaders' willingness to rely in their future relations with these "sovereign governments" on the give-and-take of diplomacy. Rather, they confirm Mr. Carew Hunt's view that the need for a single center of international authority is inherent in the Soviet Communist Party's conception of its own role and in its ideology.

The real purpose of that conference was to exploit the recent successes of the Soviet Union as a military and economic power in order to restore the indispensable but lately damaged ideological authority of its leaders in the international Communist movement. The principle of "proletarian internationalism" — that is, unity in foreign policy — had been recognized by all participants, including for the first time in many years the Yugoslavs, before the conference started. Now Moscow was aiming at the further recognition both of its own leadership role and of the need for doctrinal unity, a joint struggle against "revisionism" on the basis of common principles, abolishing once and for all the heresy of "polycentrism" (that is, the concept of a plurality of truly autonomous Communist movements).

As it turned out, the Yugoslavs refused both propositions, while the Polish Communists and the non-ruling but important Italian Communist Party accepted them only with mental reservations, insisting in practice on their right to decide for themselves how the "common principles" would be applied in their own countries. As opposed to this partial failure, however, Moscow was successful in winning full acceptance of the new dispensations by the Chinese Communists and the satellites, as well as in getting agreement on a new, elaborate international liaison machinery within the secretariat of the Soviet Communist Central Committee, in implementation of its renewed claim to international authority.

Moscow's partial failure, therefore, does not indicate that the Soviets will be content with less than they demanded, but that conflict continues. The Soviet press has already reactivated its campaign against Polish "revisionist" ideologies, insisting to Mr. Gomulka that revisionism is the chief internal danger in *all* Communist movements, including that of Poland. Moreover, the proposition defending a Communist party's autonomy in deciding its policy — conceded in principle at the time of Khrushchev's Belgrade visit and at the Twentieth CPSU Congress — is now singled out as a "revisionist" heresy; increasingly the example of Imre Nagy is invoked to show how a demand for autonomy led him down a "road" of "betrayal" and finally "counterrevolution." While the methods of Khrushchev remain conspicuously different from those of Stalin, the logic of the one-party regime, which requires insistence on Soviet authority as a precondition for unity both in foreign policy and in ideological principles, has forced the present first secretary to reassert some of the very doctrines he rashly threw overboard in 1955 – 56.

Ideology on the Home Front

Ultimately, the need to fight "revisionism" in Eastern Europe, even at the price of renewed difficulties with both Yugoslavia and Poland, arises from the need to strengthen the ideological defenses of the party regime in Russia itself. To admit that in Hungary the workers rose against a Communist government would call into question the basic identification of the ruling party with the working class — the fiction of the "dictatorship of the proletariat." To let Yugoslav propaganda for "workers' management" pass unchallenged would confirm the implication that Soviet factories, having no workers' councils with similar rights, are managed in the interest not of the workers but of the privileged bureaucracy. To keep silent when the Poles proudly report the improvement of their agricultural yields since the dissolution of most of their collective farms would encourage Soviet peasants to dream of similar reforms. To condone the increased, if still limited, freedom of artistic, literary, and philosophical discussion now permitted in Poland and Yugoslavia would strengthen the demands of Soviet writers and scholars for similar freedom.

The obvious and intended implication here is that Soviet reconciliation with Yugoslavia and the near-revolutionary changes in Poland merely aggravated pressures for change which *already* existed in Russia itself. Thus the present account would be incomplete without some attempt to indicate, however sketchily, how ideological changes can be used as aids in interpreting the Soviet domestic scene as well as Kremlin foreign policy and bloc relations.

Earlier in the paper, reference was made to some of the basic tenets which seem inseparably bound up with the preservation and justification of a Communist one-party regime. But within this unchanging framework, considerable variations in detail have taken place in the history of the Soviet Union. The appearance or disappearance of one of these "ideological variables" may be a valuable indicator of the kind of pressures which are exerted on the regime by the growing society and of the manner in which the leaders try to maintain control, sometimes by partly ceding to such pressures and seeking to canalize them, other times by a sharp frontal counterattack.

The "Permanent" Revolution

Among the most revealing of these variables are Soviet doctrines dealing with the economic role of the state and with the "class struggle" within Soviet society. The underlying reality is that a revolutionary party dictatorship, once it has carried out its original program and by this contributed to the emergence of a new privileged class, is bound to disappear sooner or later — to fall victim to a "Thermidor" — unless it prevents the new upper class from consolidating its position by periodically shaking up the social structure in a "permanent revolution from above." The ideological expression of this problem is the classical doctrine that the dictatorship of the proletariat should gradually "wither away" after it has succeeded in destroying the old ruling classes; thus, if continued dictatorship is to be justified, new goals of social transformation must be set and new "enemies" discovered.

In the early period of Stalin's rule, the new "goal" was the forced collectivization of the Russian countryside; the prosperous peasants — the *kulaks* — took the place of the former landowners and capitalists as the "enemy class" which had to be liquidated. Summing up the achievement in 1937, Stalin wrote in his "Short Course" on party history that collectivization had been a second revolution, but a revolution carried out from above, by state power "with the help of the masses," not just by the masses from below. The ideological groundwork was thus laid for assigning the state a function of continuous economic transformation from above, in addition to its terminable revolutionary task.

The second step, also taken by Stalin in 1937, at the height of the Great Blood Purge, consisted in proclaiming the doctrine that the "class struggle" in the Soviet Union was getting more acute as the "construction of socialism" advanced, because the "enemies" were getting more desperate. This was the ideological justification of the purge itself; at the same time, it was a veiled indication that another revolution from above was in effect taking place, though Stalin refrained this time from trying to define the "enemies" in social terms. In fact, what Stalin accomplished was a mass liquidation of both the bearers of the party's older revolutionary tradition — considered unsuited to the tasks of a bureaucratic state party — and of the most confident and independent-minded elements of the new privileged bureaucracy; the end result was a transformation of the party's social and ideological composition through the mass incorporation of the surviving frightened bureaucrats.

Stalin's final ideological pronouncement was contained in his political testament, "Economic Problems of Socialism," published in 1952. In this work he mapped out a program for the further revolutionary transformation of Soviet society, with the taking over of *kolkhoz* property by the state as its central element.

Khrushchev's Formula for Perpetual Rule

The first major renunciation of these Stalinist ideological innovations was made by Khrushchev in his "secret speech" at the Twentieth Congress. Apart from his factual disclosures concerning Stalin's crimes, he denounced Stalin's doctrine of the sharpening class struggle with societal progress as dangerous nonsense, calculated to lead to the mutual slaughter of loyal Communists after the real class enemy had long been liquidated. This statement affords the master clue to the puzzle of why Khrushchev made the speech: it was a "peace offering" to the leading strata of the regime in the party machine, army, and managerial bureaucracy alike — a response to their pressure for greater personal security. But by his concession, Khrushchev reopened the problem which Stalin's doctrine and practice had been intended to solve — that of preserving and justifying the party dictatorship by periodic major shakeups of society.

By the spring and summer of 1957, Khrushchev showed his awareness of the practical side of the problem: his dismantling of the economic ministries, breaking up the central economic bureaucracy, and strengthening the power of the regional party secretaries, was another such revolutionary shakeup. By November, he responded to the ideological side of the problem. First he repeated, in his solemn speech on the fortieth anniversary of the Bolshevik seizure of power, his rejection of Stalin's doctrine of ever-sharpening class struggle and ever-present enemies, thus indicating his wish to avoid a return to Stalin's terroristic methods even while following his social recipe of permanent revolution. Then he proceeded to develop his own alternative justification for maintaining the party dictatorship — a unique argument which identified the strengthening of party control with the "withering away of the state" predicted by Lenin.

Reviving this formula for the first time since it was buried by Stalin, Khrushchev explained that the military and police apparatus of the state would have to be maintained as long as a hostile capitalist world existed outside; but he added that the economic and administrative functions of the state bureaucracy would henceforth be steadily reduced by decentralization and devolution, thus strengthening the organs of regional self-government and of national autonomy within the various republics. At the same time, he quietly took steps to strengthen the control of the central party secretariat — his own seat of power — over the republican and regional party organs, thus following the old Leninist principle that the fiction of national autonomy must be balanced by the fact of centralized discipline within the ruling party.

In short, the same aim of maintaining the social dynamism of the party dictatorship and justifying its necessity, which Stalin achieved by exalting the economic role of the state, is pursued by Khrushchev by means of the reverse device of claiming that the state's economic functions have begun to "wither away." On the face of it, this doctrinal manipulation seems to reduce the role of ideology to that of ingenious trickery, obscuring rather than reflecting the underlying social realities. Yet in fact, the very need for a change in the ideological argument reflects the change that is taking place in the underlying social situation — the resistance against a return to naked terrorism, the growing desire for a lessening of state pressure and a greater scope for local activity. Whether in industry or agriculture, in the control of literature, or in relations with the satellite states, the basic conditions which the regime needs for its self-perpetuation have remained the same — but they can no longer be assured in the same way. That, too, is reflected in the variables of the official ideology.

Form and Function
R. N. CAREW HUNT

It seems to me important to distinguish between the *function* of the Soviet ideology and the peculiar *form* it has assumed. In the last analysis, its *function* is to provide a rationalization of the one-party system of government and of the policies to which the Soviet rulers are committed. The doctrine of the party is thus its central theme, and to this are related all its other elements, "proletarian democracy," "proletarian internationalism," "capitalist encirclement," "socialist realism," *etc.* On the other hand, the *form* it has taken derives primarily from Marxism with its insistence upon conflict as the mainspring of history and the force behind all progress within society — a conflict which is teleological and can only end in one way. The division of the world into two antagonistic camps, the one "progressive" and the other "reactionary," and the belief that the victory of the former, as represented by the Soviet Union, is predestined by the logic of history, is simply the Marxist class struggle between the bourgeoisie and the proletariat projected onto the international plane, and it constitutes the basis of all Soviet political thinking. It has led the Soviet rulers to take so distorted a view of the world as to make it harder to deal with them than with any government in the annals of diplomacy; and this, as Mr. Lowenthal says, is just what may be expected from an "ideology" in the sense in which Marx originally used the term.

Professor Sharp argues that Soviet national interests alone count, though his definition of these interests is tautological, as Mr. Lowenthal rightly points out. Yet to take a single example: if the Soviet rulers had consulted their national interests only, how are we to explain their strenuous efforts to promote revolution in China during the 1920's, that is, at a time when their country was weak, and was seeking to strengthen its position by entering into trade agreements and diplomatic relations with the Western powers? Such zeal for the welfare of the Chinese masses is intelligible only on the assumption that the rulers believed that they had a mission to spread the revolution wherever there was a chance of doing so effectively. Lenin had repeatedly declared this to be a primary obligation before he seized power — that is, before there was any question of promoting national interests — while after the revolution he never said a word to suggest that there was any connection between the two.

Naturally, the concepts of an ideology have to be translated into action, and when this action is undertaken by a powerful country such as Russia has now become, it can be plausibly represented as *Realpolitik*. Yet it does not follow that it belongs solely, or even primarily, to this category, or that we can afford to ignore the principles of which it claims to be the expression. The objection to such agreements as that of Yalta is precisely that they failed to take this into account, and assumed that any conflicts which might later arise with the Russians would be of a political nature only.

Further, it is not easy to see what process of logic entitles us to assume that, while the leaders of the West believe in their standard of values and seek to formulate their policies in accordance with them, the Soviet rulers neither believe in theirs nor seek to apply them. Doubtless Professor Sharp is right in saying that they proceed with caution. But this has no bearing upon the matter, as there is nothing in their ideology which requires them to act otherwise.

Finally, I would join issue with Mr. Lowenthal on one point where we disagree. Certainly Marx, who had no interest in social technology, did not develop a concept of total planning. Yet he and Engels consistently advocated the replacement of "the anarchy of social production" under capitalism by production to be carried out upon a "common plan," though who was to do the planning was not explained. Yet this was sufficient to excite the suspicion of his Anarchist opponents. Both the Anarchists and the Marxists agreed that the state must be abolished; but whereas the Anarchists held that the whole object of the revolution was to destroy it, Marx held that its object was to set up a new form of society in which the means of production would be developed in the interests of all, though once it was established, the state would "wither away." The Anarchists reasoned, however, that in any such society it would be necessary to retain some form of coercive authority, and whether it was called the state or something else was immaterial. Subsequent events were to prove how right they were.

From the early days of the revolution Lenin made clear that his objective was a nationwide planned economy, though it was left to his successor to introduce it. My contention is that if such an economy is to be introduced and made effective, the state (or the party) will have to do many unpopular things. The reason why the Soviet Union has become so powerful in so short a time is precisely because its rulers were able to enforce measures which would never have been tolerated under a democracy, and one of the functions of the ideology is to justify their right to act in this manner. Naturally, such a policy has led to the emergence of a bureaucracy which is the virtual owner of the means of production. My criticism of Djilas is that he approves the economic objectives of communism, but objects to the state of affairs to which the attempt to realize them inevitably gives rise. He wants a "democratic communism." It is a contradiction in terms.

The Policy Pie
SAMUEL L. SHARP

The differences of opinion expressed by the participants in the symposium on the roles of ideology and of power politics in Soviet policy decisions bring to mind the story about a product labeled "rabbit pie" which, on closer scrutiny, turns out to be not quite pure rabbit but a mixture of rabbit and horse meat, in the proportion of one horse to one rabbit. Although Mr. Lowenthal insists that I deny "completely" the relevance of Communist ideology to the formation of Soviet policies, or that I overlook "completely" the use made of foreign Communist parties by the Soviet Union, this is not so. The controversy is actually one about the proportions in which the ingredients of ideology and power politics appear in the final product, Soviet policy (especially within the area to which my original arguments were directed, namely foreign policy).

I find it difficult to pick a quarrel with Mr. Hunt since, while seeming to argue that the product is pure rabbit (ideology), he is careful at all times to leave open a gate wide enough for the horse (power politics) to be brought in. At his most specific, Mr. Hunt argues that the significance of ideology lies in that "it makes those who profess it act in a way that they would not otherwise do," presumably with a frequent sacrifice of efficiency for the sake of principle. The burden of proof, of course, rests on him, and in his comments appearing in the current issue he refers to Soviet support of the nationalist revolution in China in the 1920's as obviously the result of "zeal for the welfare of the Chinese masses" (Mr. Hunt is ironical, I hope) or of a sense of "mission" to spread revolution *whenever there was a chance of doing so effectively.* This, he maintains, was a mistake from the standpoint of Soviet state interests because Russia was then seeking trade agreements and diplomatic recognition from the West. His argument, however, is debatable. The establishment of Communist regimes outside Russia, if it could be "effectively" achieved, would have been definitely to the advantage of the weak Soviet state under the circumstances of the time. The case of Soviet "support" for the Chinese revolution ("encouragement" would be more accurate) is, of course, notorious because there was nothing "effective" about it: it was a case of miscalculation to be sure, but not necessarily a miscalculation caused by ideological zeal or a sense of mission. As to the effect of the policy on relations with the West, Stalin apparently was following in the footsteps of nineteenth-century Tsarist foreign ministers who attempted to "bring in the East in order to redress an unfavorable balance in the West" (as suggested, with respect to Lenin's policies, by E. H. Carr).

Since Mr. Lowenthal agrees that ideology will effectively influence policy decisions of the Soviet leaders "when, and only when, it expresses the needs of self-preservation of the party regime" (and I need not remind him that those in charge of a going concern tend to identify the interests of the concern with their own continued tenure), there would be little for me to object to were it not for his previously mentioned distortions of my views, his introduction of the gratuitous compliment of "innocence" (hereby acknowledged as an undeserved but charming relief from the much stronger epithets collected by this writer on other occasions), and for his own excursion into the theory of international relations and recent diplomatic history which — to return the compliment — is not only innocent but presumptuous.

Mr. Lowenthal states that the doctrine of "two camps" was not invented by Stalin, but was "inherent in Leninism." This is unhistorical. The temptation to present the world as divided into "good" and "bad" camps is as old as international conflict itself. And certainly in recent times the "two camps" image has been used on both sides of the dividing line; it fits admirably into a bipolarized world situation. "At the present moment in world history nearly every nation must choose between alternative ways of life," declared President Truman in his message to Congress in March 1947, several months before the late Andrei Zhdanov came out with the first vigorous postwar reformulation of the old cliche on the Soviet side. Politics operates this side of the ultimate. The persistence of the enemy image and the drive for "unlimited power" may well be present in the minds of the Soviet leaders, but the history of future years will be shaped, not by this admittedly unfriendly view of the outside world, but by what the Soviet leaders are *persuaded or compelled* to do; not by their "collective paranoia" (a term given a completely arbitrary definition by Mr. Lowenthal), but rather by their desire for survival and appraisal of the limits of the feasible. I do not doubt that they will grasp every opportunity to press any advantages to the utmost. This makes them unpleasant and tough opponents, but not totally intractable ones. To posit a world that would be animated by general harmony were it not for a single disturber of the peace is to sacrifice all history on the altar of deceptive imagery.

Mr. Lowenthal points out the difference between the "traditional" and Soviet concepts of spheres of influence, ascribing the controversy over the Yalta agreements to this difference. However, there is a built-in and often deliberate vagueness in the concept of spheres of influence, and differences of interpretation are not necessarily rooted in differences of *Weltanschauung*. Examining the historical record, one will find that conflicts of interpretation have usually occurred between those who acquired a sphere of influence and those who conceded one. This is not the time and, Mr. Lowenthal will admit, not exactly the place to enter into a debate over what Yalta meant and whether the representatives of the West were on that occasion laboring under an illusion about the real nature of the Soviet Union, or rather were trying to

military theaters. Nor is it correct to say that complete Communist control was immediately imposed throughout the Soviet sphere of influence. In at least some countries (especially Czechoslovakia, but also, to some extent, Poland and Hungary until 1947) there was the kind of fuzzy situation characteristic of an in-between area. The Soviet Union, for a variety of practical considerations, on some occasions actually seems to have curbed the enthusiasm of local Communists for a speedy transition to full control. The present writer certainly did not err on the side of optimism about the lasting nature of this halfway arrangement. It was obvious that the fuzziness could not survive the onset of the cold war; yet it is wrong to mistake one of the symptoms of the cold war for its cause.

There is no serious controversy between Mr. Lowenthal and myself with regard to recent developments in Eastern Europe, except that I offer a guess while he professes to know for certain what the meaning of these developments is. Of course, the Soviet Union would like to derive advantages in its dealings with "ruling" Communist parties from the magic of ideological control. However, in this case as in others, the intentions of the Soviet leaders, or their views about what would be the optimum situation, do not exclusively determine the outcome. When they saw the need to shift relations with at least some of the countries in the Soviet sphere to a more "traditional" basis, this was done whether graciously or not. If the Soviet Union appears currently to be reassuring its ideological domination over Eastern Europe, this reflects an acknowledgment by the leaders of these countries of Russia's strengthened international power position. Obviously, the Soviet Union, like any big power in a position of leadership, will try to hold together by various means the grouping over which it presides. To the extent that its leaders disregard the general rules of international relations from which no one is exempt, they will be inviting trouble and failure. There are no cut-rate worlds to be had.

A Difference in Kind
RICHARD LOWENTHAL

I am sorry that Professor Sharp should feel that I have distorted his position. He, in turn, has certainly mistaken my meaning if he attributes to me the view that our world would be animated by general harmony were it not for a single disturber of the peace. That view is nothing but a reflection of the Leninist dogma of the two camps, which consists precisely in the delusion of seeing all conflicts, and ultimately all independent forces, as manifestations of a single enemy. It is not unhistorical to regard this outlook as characteristic of the totalitarian movements of our time; on the contrary, it is unhistorical to confuse it with the age-old tendency to regard one's own side in a given conflict as good and the enemy as bad.

I agree with Professor Sharp on one point of great practical importance — that the Soviets are not intractable in his sense, that is, that they are tough politicians liable to be influenced by the hard facts of power and the processes for negotiation, rather than madmen pursuing a preordained plan of world conquest regardless of risk. But while Soviet policy differs from Hitler's in this vital respect, I hold that it is also different in kind from that of nontotalitarian great powers. Professor Sharp persists in seeking to blur this difference, while I wish to show that it is not confined to motives and ultimate aims, but constantly affects the Soviets' *modus operandi.*

For instance, Professor Sharp accepts my formula that Soviet ideology influences policy decisions only when it expresses the needs of self-preservation of the party regime, but adds that it is normal for any government to identify the interests of its country with its own. But my point is that the interests of a one-party government which uses an international movement as a weapon are highly peculiar, and I gave examples to show just how they affect its foreign relations. Since we wrote, the new Soviet quarrel with Yugoslavia — a quarrel which both Khrushchev and Tito would have liked to avoid for realistic reasons, but which was forced on them by Tito's need to justify ideologically his position outside the Warsaw pact, and Khrushchev's need to restore ideological unity and discipline within the bloc — has further illustrated my thesis.

Again, Professor Sharp claimed in his article that taking the entire Soviet record to date, the achievements are clearly attributable to Soviet power and diplomacy with no credit due to the international Communist movement. I find it impossible to fit into this formula the victory of communism in China, which has been to an overwhelming extent the outcome of the struggle of indigenous forces under indigenous leadership, but has resulted in a major shift in the balance of world power in favor of the Soviets. Some rabbit!

But we remain farthest apart on the Soviet conquest of Eastern Europe. In referring to Yalta, I explicitly disclaimed any intention to pass judgment on whether the Western statesmen committed an avoidable mistake of disastrous dimensions. I was concerned to show that, whether the concessions were avoidable or not, the later fate of the Soviet sphere of influence was implicit in the nature of Soviet power. Professor Sharp denies this on the ground that the "peoples' democracies" were somewhat fuzzy coalition regimes until 1947, and concludes that their later total sovietization was a symptom and not a cause of the cold war. Yet readers of this journal are familiar with the overwhelming evidence that preparations for total sovietization, such as the occupation of all key positions of power (armed forces, police, press, *etc.*), by Communists and the systematic undermining of the independence of the other parties were begun throughout the area almost from the moment of the first entry of Soviet forces. I can find no evidence to back the hypothesis that these preparations would not have been pursued to their logical conclusions if the West had acquiesced in the first steps instead of reacting to the challenge of the forcible expansion of the Soviet system, nor can I accept the implication that the cold war began only when the West took up the challenge.

Soviet Ideology and
Soviet Foreign Policy*

1.

None of the perplexing problems of contemporary international affairs has given rise to more confusing discussion than the relationship of Soviet ideology to the foreign policy of the USSR. The very vagueness of the term "Soviet ideology" or "Communist ideology" (and are they synonymous?), the uncertainty to what extent this uncertain force motivates the makers of Soviet policies, have compounded our difficulties in understanding the behavior of one of the world's two superpowers. Are Russia's rulers motivated by cynical power politics? Are they ideological fanatics? Is the content of their ideology the gospel of Marx, Engels, and Lenin, or something else? Questions can be compounded ad infinitum.

And this is no academic problem, for the West has sought some way of understanding the basis of Soviet policies, some means of both peaceful accommodation with the USSR and preservation of the confines of the free world. The means hinge on the character of Soviet policy. Mr. John Foster Dulles has formulated one approach to the problem, viewing Soviet ideology as exerting an influence on the foreign policy of the USSR. Proclaiming the peaceful

*Reprinted by permission of Princeton University Press and the author from *World Politics,* XI, 2 (January, 1959), pp. 153 – 172. Copyright 1959 by Princeton University Press. The author wishes to acknowledge his debt to the Russian Research Center, Harvard University.

136

content of democratic ideology, Mr. Dulles wrote: "unhappily, it is otherwise with the creed of Communism, or at least that variety of Communism which is espoused by the Soviet Communist Party." Marx, Lenin, and Stalin have all consistently taught the use of force and violence and Mr. Dulles sees the relationship between ideology and action as a fairly direct one, for he goes on to say, "these teachings of Marx, Lenin and Stalin have never been disavowed by the Soviet Communist Party of which Mr. Khrushchev is now the First Secretary. . . . Therefore, I believe that it is necessary that at least that part of the Soviet Communist creed should be abandoned."[1] And the dependence of the international behavior of the USSR on its alleged philosophy is also maintained by those who, unlike Mr. Dulles, believe that the ideology does not necessarily encourage the use of force or violence. A British political scientist sees the content of the Bolsheviks' ideology as a reassuring rather than a depressing portent for world peace. "They will, while they retain their present philosophy, understand neither our society nor their own. . . . We cannot rely on their good will, but we can, if we act wisely, rely on their patience. Their false philosophy teaches them that time is their ally; and the more they can be persuaded to let time pass quietly the better for us and for them. Let us at least thank God that Hitler is dead and that the dictators we have to deal with are sane."[2]

The crucial problem is the meaning of the term "ideology." Most of us, if asked about the meaning and content of our own ideology, would begin by recognizing that while in many cases it is the product of certain ethical, religious, and political teachings, the relationship is never simple, but modified by a large number of factors, like the conditions of our material and social life, our experience, etc. We do not usually assume that the motives and aims of the policies of the United States or Great Britain can be fully explained by the ideas of John Locke, Thomas Jefferson, or John Stuart Mill. "Freedom," said a famous English jurist, "has been secreted in the interstices of procedure." And, to paraphrase, the Western notions of freedom, of the proper aims of politics, foreign policy included, have been formulated through the experience of life, the experience of trying to realize the precepts of democracy and liberalism. The more sophisticated writers on the Soviet Union and communism have realized that one cannot explain the behavior of the rulers of Russia, or certain aspects of the mentality of Soviet society, by pointing to a passage in the Communist Manifesto or a phrase from Stalin or Lenin. But in our search for the meaning of Soviet ideology, we have not fully recognized that that ideology has been secreted in the interstices of the totalitarian system, which has now existed for over forty years, and that the early millenarian

1. John Foster Dulles in a letter to *The New Statesman*, February 8, 1958.
2. John Plamenatz, *German Marxism and Russian Communism* (London, 1954), pp. 350.

Communist faith has been modified by the experience of almost two generations' application of the original theories to the stubborn facts of life.

We should not, however, go to the other extreme and assume that the rulers
of Russia have remained totally unaffected by the doctrines in which they have
been brought up and which they have been proclaiming. The relationship
between ideology and action eludes a straightforward definition, but it is naive
to assume that a group of men, even when endowed with totalitarian powers
and with what to an outsider appears an infinite possibility of political manipulation, can remain unaffected by their habits of thought and speech, and can
indulge in unrestrained Machiavellian politics. At times, tired of explaining
Soviet politics by quoting from the scriptures of Marxism-Leninism, we assign
the role of ideology to the realm of "propaganda" with which the leaders of
the Communist Party of the USSR beguile their subjects while they themselves
enjoy cynical freedom from ideological scruples. But again, the picture is not
so simple. Stalin, or Khrushchev and his colleagues, may think primarily of
expanding their power and increasing that of the USSR, but their choice of
means to that end is inextricably intertwined with their philosophy of power,
in which again ideology plays a crucial part.

The content of what must be called the working creed of the Soviet leaders
is not easy to define. It is not wise to seek a definition which ignores the
changing character of Soviet society and the changing generations and personalities of the leaders. But it is possible to make certain generalizations and
then to see how they apply in the Soviet evaluation of the outside world.

The original doctrine of Marx-Engels still remains the official creed of the
Soviet Union, but somewhat in the manner in which a modern secularized
society acknowledges being based on religion. Gone in Soviet Russia today is
the sense of the practical immediacy of the socialist doctrine which characterized the ten or fifteen years after the November Revolution. The reasons are
manifold. One of them may be that Marxian socialism, as interpreted first by
Lenin and then by Stalin (and we shall not enter here into the question of
whether this is the "correct" interpretation of Marxism), has as its two main
historical functions, first, the channeling of the revolutionary impulses of a
society undergoing industrialization, and then the guidance of this society
toward the achievement of a modern industrial state.[3] If this be essentially
correct, then Marxian phrases and prescriptions simply have very little immediate relevance to the problems of the Soviet state and society of today.
Paradoxically, the success of Marxism in Russia has meant its decline in
importance, insofar as the original doctrine of Marx-Engels is concerned. If
this statement appears extravagant, let us look at some concrete examples. Is
the average citizen of Russia, or a Soviet leader when not giving an official

---

3. This interpretation is presented in my article, "The Historical Role of Marxism and the
Soviet System," *World Politics,* VIII, No. 1 (October 1955), pp. 20–45.

speech, really concerned with the problem of creating an egalitarian society? Is the world revolution viewed with the same intensity of feeling or related to the internal problems of the Soviet Union as it was in the first few years after the Revolution? It is unlikely that a member of the Presidium loses any sleep over the meaning of Marxian "negation of negation" or over any other subtleties of the dialectic which once constituted the intellectual fare of the Communists and, what is more important, which were bound up with the actual problems of the internal and external politics of the USSR. Phrases from Marx and Engels will still take their place in official speeches, and in the philosophical journals obscure Party hacks will adorn with scriptural invocations the latest economic or political decisions of the government. And the doctrine will be stretched to justify any practical needs of policy. Collaboration with the West was not only the logical outcome of the dire need in which the Soviet Union found itself after the German attack, but also a theoretically correct application of the Marxian injunction to collaborate with the progressive part of the capitalist camp against its reactionary component. The possibility of peaceful coexistence and the unavoidability of a clash "sometime" between the camps of socialism and capitalism are interchangeable ideological interpretations given out with equal facility according to the turn of international events.

What then remains of original Marxism which is pertinent to the actual conduct of Soviet policy as distinguished from the language in which this policy is proclaimed or rationalized? First of all, there is no doubt that the tone of Soviet policies, domestic as well as foreign, is still greatly affected by the original *Weltanschauung* of Marx. The father of modern socialism proclaimed his theory at a time when the tendency of liberalism was to proclaim the eventual solution of international difficulties and the harmonious coexistence of nations. *Without necessarily assimilating all governments to the same pattern,* free trade, the liberals believed (and the term at its broadest meant a free interchange of people and ideas as well as goods), would bring about a degree of international harmony, with such irrational phenomena as war and imperialism gradually withering away. The general tenor of Marx's philosophy was to discount the notion of an automatic harmony of interests within an industrial society and, by the same token, in international relations. He held that in the world at large, just as within an individual society, growth, development, and clashes of interests and struggles were unavoidable and would continue until socialism became the predominant, if not the only, form of social and political organization.

This legacy of Marxism has become an important part of the Soviet habitual view of international relations. It has expressed itself in two general characteristics of Soviet foreign policy. The first has been an unusual sensitivity to economic and social developments in states playing a major role in international relations. The United States or France, for instance, does not appear in Soviet eyes primarily as a state having certain historical and power interests *qua* state, but as a conglomeration of class interests and certain social and economic pressures which determine the policy of the capitalist state, regardless of the dressing-up of these postulates in terms of national interests or honor. This instinct of Soviet international policy has contributed both to its strength and to its weakness. It has endowed the Russian policy-makers with a degree of sophistication about international relations surpassing the old platitudes of the diplomatic art; it has also, at times, made them the dupes of the rigid dogmatisms which they have erected to account for the international situation. Thus the belated recognition of the threat of Hitlerism which, according to a dogmatic oversimplification, should have proved but a prelude to a Communist revolution in Germany. Thus the initial underestimate of the strength of national and democratic impulses which made the West stand up to Hitler, an underestimate which almost proved fatal to the Soviet Union. In a subsequent passage, we shall discuss what has happened in recent years to this Marxian technique of viewing the world outside the Soviet Union.

The second aspect of the legacy of Marxism to the policy-makers of the Soviet Union is subtler and more paradoxical in its effect. While the technique of viewing the world through the prism of Marxian categories of economic development and class conflict may be narrow and lead to serious miscalculations, it is still a rationalist technique. The other Marxian element is quasi-religious in its manifestations. It consists in an attachment to the symbols and phrases of the doctrine rather than to its analytical content. Just as in internal Soviet politics the official doctrine has been considered infallible and any errors or shortcomings in Soviet politics, economy, or culture have been attributed to mistakes or malevolence on the part of an individual, so in external relations the Soviet state has pursued the injunctions of Marxism-Leninism and any departure from them (read a reversal in the foreign policy of the USSR) has been attributed to an individual's inability to apply Marxism-Leninism correctly to the given situation, or to his malice and treason. The terror of the Stalin era has been ascribed by his successors not to certain organic features of a totalitarian system but solely to the pathological tendencies of the aging despot. When trying to reestablish a *modus vivendi* with Yugoslavia in the spring of 1955, Khrushchev felt constrained after arriving in Belgrade to blame the whole tangled story of the difficulties between the two states on the sinister malevolence of one man, Lavrenti Beria. To a Western commentator, grounded in the iconoclastic liberal tradition, the tendency of the Soviet leaders to invoke the magic formula of their doctrine as an explanation and guide to everything, *at the same time that they increasingly ignore and reject certain specific prescriptions of Marxism-Leninism,* smacks either of calculated hypocrisy or of a facile propaganda device. Yet such judgments are often oversimplified. The practitioners of the world's most totalitarian system must feel the need to believe in the infallibility of their doctrine; that the doctrine itself has become blurred or irrelevant to current situations does not change their tendency to use the magic incantation of Marxism. In both 1948 and 1958, in trying to account for their difficulties with Yugoslavia, the Soviets fell back upon the same ideological device: in 1948 the Yugoslav Communist Party was accused of the betrayal of Marxism-Leninism; in 1958, of revisionism. The whole complex of grievances against Tito and his regime has been reduced to an infraction of orthodoxy, of which the Communist Party of the Soviet Union is the only and infallible exponent. Three years of efforts by the Khrushchev regime to alter through diplomacy and compromise what they themselves had branded as Stalin's erroneous and paranoiac condemnation of the Yugoslavs have ended for the time being in a milder version of the Stalinist fiat: since Yugoslavia is a source of trouble for the Soviet Union, since her anomalous position is in itself an open encouragement of independent-minded Communist satellites, the Yugoslavs obviously cannot be bona fide Communists. Once again the Soviets have demonstrated that they cannot regard an international situation as essentially a series of concrete issues between states, but rather as an ideological conflict or betrayal.

If we think of the potential uses of Marxism for actual politics, we might separate three main strains: first, as a body of implied prescriptions (implied, because Marx and Engels never devoted much attention to the problem of the foreign policy of a socialist state); second, as an analytical discipline for viewing international as well as domestic politics; and, finally, as a symbol and quasi-religion giving its practitioners the sense that they are moving forward with the forces of history and that the success of their state is predicated upon the truth of the doctrine. It is asserted here that the first strain no longer plays any significant part in Soviet foreign policies, while the analytical and symbolical uses of Marxism remain important and necessary to the understanding of Soviet policy. In pondering the interconnection of the three elements of the ideological inheritance of the Soviet system, we are immediately struck by certain parallels to a society undergoing the process of secularization: when specific points of a religious creed lose their veracity or relevance for people, can they for long retain a general religious outlook and belief in the doctrine as a whole? Similarly, if the Marxian doctrine loses its specific relevance, can the frame of mind engendered by it and the belief itself endure? It is tempting for a Western observer to answer this question in the negative and to envisage a time when the realities of the world will bring about a reorientation of Soviet values. Mr. Kennan in his famous essay postulated the possibility of a change in the Soviet outlook consequent upon the failure of their assumptions about capitalism: "the palsied decrepitude of the capitalist world is the keystone of Communist philosophy. Even the failure of the United States to experience the early economic depression which the ravens of the Red Square have been predicting with such complacent confidence since hostilities ceased would have deep and important repercussions throughout the Communist world."[4] And further: "For no mystical Messianic movement — and particularly not that of the Kremlin — can face frustration indefinitely without eventually adjusting itself in one way or another to the logic of that state of affairs."[5]

Mr. Kennan overlooked, perhaps, the natural intransigence of religious millenarian movements to purely rational objective facts. *Credo quia absurdum* is not entirely atypical of the attitude of religious or political fanaticism. But the most fundamental objection to the postulating of an erosion of the ideology by contact with reality is that this ideology is propagated within a totalitarian system. If the rulers of this system see in the ideology, as we have seen, not only the rationale of their absolute power but a source of their inner security and effectiveness, then the doctrine will not be soon or easily repudiated just because the West increases its material welfare. Furthermore, while the Soviet citizen, including the indoctrinated Party member, has numerous occasions to discover the contradictions or irrelevancies of Marxism in his daily life, he enjoys no such tangible experiences insofar as the world outside the USSR is concerned. And to the Soviet leaders, the field of foreign relations offers the best opportunity to attempt to demonstrate the viability of Marxism, conscious as they are of the necessity of preserving and developing the ideological *élan* of the Communist Party and of the regime. Marxism may be irrelevant to the problems of the Soviet Union now that its industrialization is accomplished and the state has shown no signs of withering away or becoming, in essence, less authoritarian. If some meaning is to be attached to the ideology, if it is not to fade out completely in the minds of the Soviet people, then it must show its effectiveness in propelling Soviet society into economic and scientific development at a *faster pace* than that achieved by societies inspired by the rival creed. And most important of all, the Soviet brand of Marxism must be shown to be advancing in the world at large, proving alluring to societies emerging from backwardness and colonial rule. The battle to preserve Soviet ideology in the USSR and with it the rationale of the totalitarian system is thus being fought in a world context, and the spread of Soviet ideology, influence, and prestige throughout the world becomes increasingly crucial to the preservation of the Soviet system as we know it.

The latter statement sounds like a truism. But we may best put it in perspective by contrasting the present situation with that which prevailed in the first decade after the Revolution. The Russian Communists, a group devoted much more literally to their ideology than the current rulers of Russia, were confronted with the seeming failure of the ideological premises on which the Revolution had been undertaken. It was only their own weak and backward country which remained under the rule of their version of socialism. Elsewhere in the world the wave of revolutionary feeling had subsided and

---

4. "The Sources of Soviet Conduct," reprinted in *American Diplomacy, 1900–1950* (Chicago, 1951), p. 123.

5. *Ibid.,* p. 124.

capitalism appeared to be stabilized. The logical response to the situation was to build the prerequisites of socialism in Russia; and the ideology was vindicated by the industrialization of the Soviet state. The terrible cost of the transformation and the increasingly ruthless totalitarian methods employed cannot obscure the fact that Marxism, and the ideological fervor generated by it, were crucial factors in the achievement. And conversely, the achievement appeared to vindicate the ideology, and the totalitarian system of the USSR. Today, it may be flatly asserted that the growth of the USSR can proceed on its own momentum. If the ideology is to become increasingly decorative and meaningless, in terms of concrete problems of Soviet life, where, in the last resort, will be the rationale for the totalitarian system, for the assumed omnipotence and omniscience of the highest councils of the Communist Party of the USSR? The focus of "proving" Marxism-Leninism, and by the same token of preserving something of the old ideological *élan* and sense of mission without which the most efficient totalitarian regime runs the danger of internal disintegration, has shifted once again beyond the geographical confines of the USSR.

2.

To the outsider, the shifting trends of Soviet policy appear almost incomprehensible. The Khrushchev who in 1955 and 1956 proclaimed the legitimacy of seeking various roads to socialism is the same person who in the spring of 1958 led the attack upon the "revisionism" of the Yugoslav Communists.[6] In 1956, in his "secret" report on Stalin and Stalinism, Khrushchev bluntly blamed the Yugoslav situation on the pathological characteristics of the late despot.[7] And yet in 1958 the charge advanced against the Yugoslav Communist Party repeated many points of the Stalinist indictment of 1948 – 1949. The Yugoslavs indulged in revisionism by stressing the possibility of separate roads to socialism; they implied that the Soviet Union could also be guilty of increasing international tension, etc. As a matter of record, the Yugoslav Party program for its 7th Congress in 1958 did not say anything that Tito and his

6. From Khrushchev's report to the 20th Party Congress: "As far back as on the eve of the great October revolution, V. I. Lenin wrote 'All nations will arrive at socialism — this is inevitable — but not all will do so in exactly the same way.' . . . Historical experience has fully confirmed this brilliant precept of Lenin's. . . . In the Federal People's Republic of Yugoslavia, where power belongs to the working people and society is founded on public ownership of the means of production, unique specific forms of economic management and organization of the state apparatus are arising in the process of socialist construction." *Current Soviet Policies, II,* ed. by Leo Gruliow (New York, 1957), pp. 37 – 38.

7. "The July plenary session of the Central Committee studied in detail the reasons for the development of conflict with Yugoslavia. It was a shameful role that Stalin played there. The 'Yugoslav affair' contained no problems that could not have been solved through Party discussions among comrades. . . . No matter how much or how little Stalin shook not only his little finger but everything else that he could shake, Tito did not fall. Why? The reason was that in this case of disagreement with the Yugoslav comrades, Tito had behind him a state and a people who had gone through a severe school of fighting for liberty and independence, a people who gave support to their leaders." Quoted in *ibid.,* p. 183.

group had not been saying before, and most of which had been acquiesced in by Khrushchev and his colleagues in 1955 and 1956. Even the charge that the Soviet Union was contributing to world tension had been acknowledged by Khrushchev, though blamed on Stalin, and the indictment against Molotov, Kaganovich, and Malenkov upon their expulsion from the Central Committee of the CPSU in July 1957 accused them of attempting, as high officials of the Soviet Union, to perpetuate international tensions. There is no phrase in the Yugoslav program the truth of which had not been conceded by the present leadership of the Soviet Union during the past three years.

Explanations of this *volte-face* by the Soviet leadership have ranged from the alleged pressure exerted by the Chinese Communists on behalf of Communist orthodoxy, to the existence of a Stalinist group in the Central Committee which out of nostalgia for the late dictator and his policies continues to embarrass Khrushchev and compels him to resort to former policies and tactics. Yet there is no tangible evidence in support of either thesis. True, attacks upon the Yugoslavs began to appear in the Chinese Communist press before the Soviets made a full-fledged attack. But it is perfectly natural that this should have occurred, if a joint attack upon Tito had been determined sometime before. Ever since the rise of Communist China, the satellites have looked upon it hopefully as the best means of eventually obtaining a modicum of independence from the Russians. Long after Yugoslavia's breach with the Russians in 1948, the Yugoslav press continued to extol Communist China. If once again the Yugoslav experiment had to be branded as unsocialist, and the satellites again be called to task, it was sound strategy and psychology that the initiative should appear to come from China rather than from the USSR.

The notion of a Stalinist faction in the Presidium and the Central Committee also requires a qualification. As in any political and particularly any totalitarian situation, there is no doubt that the inside group at the summit of power in Russia is split up into, if not open, then latent factions. Every faction will exploit its opponents' failures, whether these failures are grounded in alleged "liberalism" or in alleged "Stalinism." But there is no iota of evidence to indicate the existence of a specific "Stalinist" faction. The complex of methods of governing associated with Stalin is so abhorrent, even in the eyes of high Party officials in the USSR, that it has been part of a sound psychological campaign by Khrushchev to brand his opponents as would-be renovators of Stalinism. It is clear, for example, that Malenkov, Molotov, and Kaganovich plotted against Khrushchev, and that during the winter of 1956–1957 they probably came close to replacing him by Shepilov or Pervukhin. But that they did so in the name of abstract Stalinism is as little probable and worthy of belief as the charge in their indictment that they opposed the USSR's attempting to catch up with and overtake the United States in the production of butter, milk, and meat.

The reasons for Russia's reversal of attitude toward Yugoslavia are to be sought in the reappraisal of policies toward the satellites which the Soviet leadership as a whole seems to have undertaken during recent years. The history of this reappraisal provides the best illustration of the interweaving of ideology, power motives, and internal politics in the making of Soviet foreign policy.

At the time of Stalin's death, Russian domination of the satellites was absolute and extended to the smallest details of their internal policies. Whatever changes the rulers were forced to make in the Stalinist pattern insofar as internal Soviet politics was concerned, there appeared no logical reason, granting their totalitarian premises, to change substantially the system of terror and close control which held Eastern Europe in subjugation to the USSR. Yet parallel with so-called liberalization in Soviet Russia, a new course was set in the satellites. Terror was relaxed and some semblance of internal autonomy was granted to the local Communists, who, at first incredulously, listened to their Russian masters urging them to do certain things on their own. Many satellite Communist leaders most closely associated with the Stalinist era of repression were either pushed to the second rank (e.g., Chervenkov in Bulgaria, Cepicka in Czechoslovakia, Berman in Poland, and others) or obligingly died (this being the case with Gottwald and Bierut). The highest Party and state offices in the satellites were separated and the local Stalins were either fired or told to share their power with a wider circle of Party colleagues.[8] Soviet pressure for show trials of "deviationists" and other morbid paraphernalia of Communist statecraft of the Stalin era disappeared. For the first time since 1948 the satellite regimes enjoyed some power of decision on such issues as the pace of collectivization, cultural policies, etc.

Now, it is easy to see in the new course of 1953 – 1956, which was not consistent and uniform insofar as all the European satellites of the USSR were concerned, the reflection of internal dissension and uncertainty within the Kremlin circle itself. But it is reasonably clear that the new policies represented a measure of consensus among the successors of Stalin. Just as in internal politics they decided to eliminate the most oppressive measures and techniques of Stalin, so in their relations with the satellites they tended to substitute the ties of mutual interest and ideology for the most stringent aspects of foreign control. In both cases, one of the main reasons was ideological. Stalin's tech-

---

8. The satellite Parties were told in 1953 – 1954 that the office of Secretary-General could no longer be combined with that of President or Prime Minister. In Imre Nagy's statement, which appears well authenticated, he mentions the discussion of Malenkov, Molotov, and Khrushchev with the Hungarian leaders in May 1953, which was designed among other things to end Rakosi's absolute domination of Hungarian communism: "Comrade Khrushchev noted 'the matter involved was that the leadership of the Party and the state should not be concentrated in the hands of one man or a few men, this is not desirable.'" Imre Nagy, *On Communism, in Defense of the New Course* (New York, 1957), p. 250.

niques, his successors held, were partly pathological, partly obsolete in their severity. The maximum of control which they obtained did not compensate for the sapping of the vital forces of the Communist parties at home and abroad, for the impairing and tarnishing of the attraction of revolutionary socialism in the uncommitted parts of the world.

This ideological element was twofold in character. One side of the decision was the feeling that the Communist parties in the Soviet Union and the Soviet bloc could not be allowed to ossify and to become nothing but bodies of bureaucrats and spies driven by compulsion and ritualistic obeisances without, in the long run, creating a basic danger to the regime. The phrase "contact with the masses" is not used by the Communists entirely hypocritically. To give up some degree of control in exchange for popularity was deemed to be a reasonable gamble. The other side of the ideological element in the new course was the apparent conviction of the masters of the Kremlin that, when stripped of its worst excesses, communism possessed enough historical truth and popular attraction to secure the devotion of even those who had suffered for years under its "errors." In the immemorial manner of politicians, the Soviet leaders assumed that they could have their cake and eat it, too; that the fundamental features of internal totalitarianism and essential control over the satellites could be preserved, and yet the removal of the worst abuses would procure them genuine loyalty, would release new creative impulses and ideological fervor among the Communists at home and abroad.[9] In an ideological revival, Stalin's successors wanted to anticipate and forestall two great dangers. The first was that the gradual erosion of ideology through the continuance of methods of the Stalin era would strip the Party entirely of its meaning and its *esprit de corps.* If that happened, the Party, while nominally in existence and in power, could in fact be supplanted by another organization, the security apparatus or the army. In foreign affairs the prevalence of the 1948 – 1952 pattern of relations could lead to the second danger — the complete attenuation of ideological ties between the Communist Party of the USSR and the foreign Communists, whether in the satellites or in other countries. If that were to happen, what of the future relations of the USSR with the Communists in China, what of the loyalty of other Communists in the eventuality of a clash with the West? Thus what are, from the perspective of the West, rather intangible theoretical categories had for the Soviet leaders concrete ideological meaning readily translatable into considerations of power.

9. While there was general agreement on the overall character of domestic reforms and the shift in foreign tactics, the pace and methods of the modification of Stalinism were the subject of considerable maneuvering within the Soviet elite. Thus the fall of Beria in the summer of 1953 was not unconnected, it is safe to say, with his attempt to claim the main credit for the alleged return to "socialist legality" and more liberal nationality policies. Malenkov's fall from the premiership was expedited by the other leaders' alarm over his identification with the policy of increased consumers' goods. In addition to administrative and inner-Party intrigues, the struggle for power in the USSR has consisted during the last five years in each faction's trying to claim credit for the more liberal policies — policies on which all of them in principle were agreed.

The new course in inter-Communist relations was thus to parallel the de-Stalinization at home. But on this count Stalin's successors, as they must have ruefully realized by the fall of 1956, fell into the very error of their dreaded predecessor. It was Stalin who applied without any inhibitions the methods he found workable in the USSR in dealing with non-Soviet Communists. And the post-Stalin regime, which by relaxation of terror reaped the dividends of a certain popularity and increased *esprit de corps* among the Communists and the population at large in the USSR, blithely expected the same results from similar policies in other Communist states. Stalin could be denounced and his regime, in which the present rulers had been important figures, could be revealed as having indulged in wholesale murder and atrocities, and yet the totalitarian structure could be preserved and Soviet communism appear stronger for having acknowledged its errors. It appeared equally simple to proclaim Tito as having been unjustly denounced, Gomulka mistakenly imprisoned, and Rajk judicially murdered, and to expect a growth in the popularity of communism and affection toward the USSR in Yugoslavia, Poland, and Hungary. Being intelligent men, the Soviet leaders must have expected some form of shock to result from the revelations and the institution of the new course, but having been imprisoned within the Soviet system and within their own ideological premises for forty years, they evidently did not expect that the shock would take the form of revulsion toward communism, demoralization of local Communist parties, and even open hostility toward the Soviet Union.

Having decided upon the modification of Stalinist practices, the Soviet leaders proceeded boldly. The visit of Khrushchev and Bulganin to Belgrade in the spring of 1955 was a stroke of diplomacy as startling in terms of what had gone before as would be a visit of Eisenhower and Dulles to Peking or of Macmillan and Selwyn Lloyd to Cairo! But quite apart from the assumed humility of the Soviets toward the man and regime they had tried for years to overthrow, and against which they had hurled the most fantastic accusations and insults, the visit dramatized the importance attached by the Soviet Union to the principle of the ideological unity of the Communist world. Again, being realists, the Soviet leaders must have realized that the Communists in the satellites would draw their own conclusions from the Soviets bowing in effect to the defier of Stalin. A premium would be put upon a certain amount of nationalist intransigence, and the Communists of Poland or Rumania would no longer be terrified of standing up to their Soviet colleagues. But if the Yugoslav gamble worked, what was lost in absoluteness of control would be counterbalanced by the growth of genuine ideological unity. Soviet Russia could resume the ideological and diplomatic offensive in Asia and Africa without a Communist state standing as visible proof that the USSR was dominated by imperialist rather than ideological motives. To liquidate the Yugoslav defection, this time through diplomacy, became one of the main Soviet objectives, and the reasons for it are to be found not only in the "propaganda" aspects of Soviet foreign policy but in the need for ideological self-assurance. An outside observer may have from the beginning foreseen the gross psychological error inherent in the method of rapprochement with Tito. He may have argued, as undoubtedly some have argued in the Politburo, that a more gradual and cautious reestablishment of friendly relations with Yugoslavia would have produced less of a shock on the satellites (and the same observation applies to the unmasking of Stalin by Khrushchev). Yet one is left with some appreciation of the boldness of the move and of the new demonstration of the flexibility of Soviet policy. The policy initiated by the post-Stalin Presidium had, however, this distinguishing characteristic: it freely envisaged the abandonment of a certain amount of control — something the old despot had been unwilling to do — in the expectation of considerable ideological gains.

Khrushchev and Co., then, took a fairly long-run point of view: the Communist bloc would be reconstructed, this time with Yugoslavia as a valued member. Day-to-day control of the satellites' affairs would be abandoned by the Russians, but their foreign and defense policies would be more effectively synchronized with those of the USSR. Their internal sovietization would proceed ever so much more intensely and healthily, now that it was not being accomplished under extreme duress. The new policies would obviate, or at least postpone, a clash with the Chinese Communists which would have been unavoidable had the old Stalinist policies been rigidly adhered to. The united Communist bloc would be much more attractive to the new uncommitted nations, and Asian and African leftists would not have the dismaying example of the Soviet-Yugoslav dispute to dampen their pro-Communist inclinations. Finally, within the Soviet Union the fact that the Communist states were united and more freely associated on the international scene would help in the ideological reactivation of communism in Russia.

Within two years the main premise of the new Soviet policies was exposed as hollow. The tie of ideology did not prove strong enough to hold the Communist bloc together and subservient to Russia in the absence of more tangible means of control. The return of Yugoslavia to the Soviet bloc could not simply obliterate the seven years during which the Yugoslav leaders had learned to be independent. For ideological and power reasons of his own, Tito was only too glad to arrive at a *modus vivendi* with the Russians. The continued isolation from the Communist bloc was slowly undermining the morale of the CPY, the main support of his totalitarian regime, as witnessed by the Djilas affair. But the Yugoslav Communists could not now settle for what they would gladly have taken from Stalin in 1948: internal autonomy, but in other respects unquestioning adherence to the USSR. This time the Yugoslavs were ready to reenter the Soviet bloc only as representatives and propagators of the idea of equality of socialist states. The Soviet Union as the leading socialist state would still enjoy primacy, but each member of the bloc should be granted external and internal independence. What was implicit in the Soviet *theory* of the new course the Yugoslavs were eager to make explicit in *practice.*

The imperfect reconciliation became an additional disruptive influence within the Soviet sphere. The events of October 1956 represented a serious blow to Soviet policies. Again the policy habit acquired within the Soviet context proved almost disarmingly naive when applied to another country. It was easy for the Russians to imagine that with the worst repression abolished in Poland and the deviant Communists rehabilitated, Soviet influence would be made more secure and Polish communism would become even more loyal to the USSR. But Gomulka was not only readmitted to the Communist Party but was carried to power, and the Polish army passed from the control of Soviet officers. And finally the events of Hungary demonstrated vividly that not only Soviet influence but communism in Eastern Europe rest mainly upon force, and that any weakening in the network of Soviet controls and terror would not readily be compensated by an enhanced ideological solidarity with the Soviet Union. It is not too much to assume that the events in Eastern Europe had a certain unsettling effect upon the Russian Communists, and that their intellectual and artistic side effects, which spilled over the borders of the Soviet Union, went in the opinion of the leaders beyond the legitimate and safe limits of liberalization.

The balance sheet of the new policy was therefore largely negative. But it is instructive to see that the Soviets did not panic at the failure of their design. We have no means of knowing what discussions went on in Moscow after the Polish and Hungarian events. But it is unlikely that the Soviets would have or could have implemented the policy of complete return to Stalinism either in their internal affairs or in dealing with Eastern Europe. The pendulum had swung too far, and the decision was taken in the winter of 1956–1957 to restore a form of balance between the old and the new policies. It was hoped that the fortieth anniversary of the October Revolution in 1957 would see the beginning of a new Communist International to replace the Cominform, dissolved in 1956 as a relic of the Stalinist era and discredited in its only major undertaking: the attempt to undermine and overthrow Tito. The Cominform had been organized in the summer of 1947 mainly to give an international appearance to the Soviet control of the Communist parties in power, and thus to obviate the trouble which the Soviets already discerned in the Yugoslav situation.[10] Now, in a different atmosphere, the new Communist organization, in which various ruling and perhaps other Communist parties would associate in apparent equality, would again give an international appearance to Soviet guidance. But, as we know, the Yugoslav Communists for obvious reasons refused to participate in a new Cominform. Their refusal, it seems, was supported by the Poles, and thus for the time being no international Communist

10. Adam B. Ulam, *Titoism and the Cominform* (Cambridge, Mass.), 1952, p. 68.

agency would be created to "internationalize" Soviet control of the satellites' policies. The new method of "domesticating" Tito proved no more successful than the previous ones. Furthermore, the carrier of the Titoist virus had again been taken into the Communist camp as a bona fide member, visiting the satellite capitals and entertaining in Yugoslavia delegations of the Polish, Hungarian, and Rumanian Communists.

It is in the light of these developments that the Soviet decision to denounce the Yugoslav Communists, in terms considerably milder than those of 1948, becomes understandable. If in 1948 Tito and his group were denounced as followers of Bukharin and Vollmar, and then as agents of Western imperialism, they are in 1958 "revisionists" and fence-sitters. Again obscure doctrinal excommunications are pronounced by the Soviet Communists to account for the failure to solve their own ideological dilemma: how can an international political movement be genuinely international and yet be run and controlled by a single state? And that problem is but the other side of the internal dilemma: how can you have ideological fervor and socialist *élan* in a totalitarian and bureaucratic state? These seemingly intangible theoretical questions appear to the Soviet leaders with the increasing urgency of problems of power. It is almost pathetic to observe the Soviets' attempting to develop within the last few years some of the paraphernalia of popular government. Stalin never went abroad, with the exception of the wartime trip to Teheran. The current leaders travel assiduously, especially in the satellite areas. They do not confine themselves, as was the pre-1953 pattern, to conferences with high state and Party officials. They address themselves to crowds. The visit of Voroshilov to Poland in the spring of 1958 was an exhibition of the new technique. The aged titular head of the USSR visited factories, farms, and Party gatherings. He was accompanied by a retinue of dignitaries, including — most significantly — high officials of the Byelorussian, Ukrainian, and Lithuanian parties, who shared in the frantic visiting and speech-making. It is unlikely that this search for popularity will lead the Soviets to put it to test by removing the more tangible forms of insurance of their satellites' loyalty. Veiled threats accompany professions of ideological brotherhood, as during Khrushchev's tour of Hungary. But in the speeches and activities connected with the satellites there has definitely been a new tone since 1955: an attempt by the Soviet leaders to convince not only others but, one might almost say, themselves that the Communist commonwealth of states is based upon ideological ties rather than upon force or threats of force. Even the reversal of the new course, the stiffened Soviet attitude toward manifestations of satellite "nationalism," does not change that tendency basically.

The problem of working out a feasible pattern of relations between the states in the "camp of socialism" is increasingly becoming one of the main problems of Soviet policy, and not only of *foreign* policy. The earlier attempted solution — strict subordination by force — has proved impractical, and no matter how much is said about the return to Stalinism, the situation prior to 1953 simply cannot be reproduced. Enough of Marxist historical sophistication remains to the rulers of the Kremlin to prevent them from attempting to turn back history. Not because of any increased humanitarianism, but because of changed conditions, they will try to supplement force with diplomacy and with an increased community of interests between themselves and their satellites. Much has been said about the "erosion" of Soviet ideology, but ideologies and social movements are not eroded by the mere passage of time or the impact of statistics. Nineteenth-century liberalism was eroded, and with it much of the influence of the West in other parts of the world, largely by the abrasive force of nationalism. Communism has up to now managed to turn this abrasive force to its own uses, but it has begun to experience its unsettling effect within its own system.

3.

The example of Soviet policy within the Communist bloc is perhaps sufficient to point out the involved nature of the ideological element in the policy as a whole. The contribution of the ideology is not simply to endow the Soviet rulers with a propensity for violence and conquest. Nor is Marxism-Leninism an unsubstantial line of fortifications separating the Soviet Union from the rest of the world, quite ready to collapse at repeated trumpetings of the facts of the West's material and political stability and peaceful intentions toward the USSR. Soviet ideology in the sense discussed here is neither a detailed guide to action nor a superficial creed vulnerable to exposure. Quite apart from its textual content, belief in this ideology represents the most cohesive force in the Soviet system, one which has enabled Communist Party rule and the dynamics of industrialization to persist through decades of oppression, misrule, and economic suffering. It has been observed that Communist ideology now has but little relevance insofar as domestic problems of the Soviet Union are concerned. Were the USSR to cease being a one-party state equipped with totalitarian paraphernalia, the process of industrialization and modernization would go on under the aegis of another ideology and another political system. There has been no change or reform in the social or economic field in the last six years which might not have been effected in the USSR for purely pragmatic reasons. If the ideology is to remain demonstrably important to the Soviet citizen, and demonstrably correct to the Party members, and the perpetuation of the Communist Party rule rests in the long run upon these assumptions, then there must be another dimension than the domestic one in which Communist ideology does make a difference. Successful proselytizing becomes an important factor in the preservation of the faith. Foreign successes, the preservation and expansion of collaboration within the Communist bloc, become important insofar as the preservation of the present pattern of communism in the USSR is concerned.

If this hypothesis is correct, then there is little foundation in the hope often expressed in the West that the growth and maturity of the USSR as a modern and industrial state will necessarily be reflected in more peaceful and less expansive policies. As we have seen, the growing power and prosperity of the USSR *as a state,* even the increased material well-being of its citizens, accentuate rather than diminish the ideological crisis. This ideological crisis is not, as is often imagined, simply the matter of everyday reality of Soviet life not conforming to the precepts of Marx and Lenin, but of the existence and growth of social and economic forces which impinge upon the foundations of the totalitarian system in Russia. At the height of the collectivization struggle, Stalin propounded his famous formula, then the rationalization for the ruthless suppression of the peasants, that the closer the goal of socialism the sharper becomes the character of the class struggle. This terrible formula, pronouncing in effect that increased success will necessitate more terror, was declared un-Marxist by Stalin's successors.[11] But it unwittingly contained an important insight; in the measure that the Communist movement achieves its objectives, it becomes increasingly difficult to preserve the totalitarian system, to continue to exact sacrifices and deny basic freedoms and amenities of life. The program of ideological revival devised by the despot's successors has aimed at preventing communism from "withering away," and thus at preserving the rationale of Soviet totalitarianism. An increasingly great part in this revival has been played by the renewed missionary character of communism. Thus the success of communism as a self-proclaimed worldwide liberation and peace movement, and as a tenable basis for the association of Communist states, becomes increasingly important to the continuance of the present form of the Communist regime in the USSR.

Most studies of Soviet foreign policy imply or state the question: What can the West do about it? And in the process of asking this question, we very often and unavoidably distort the problem according to our hopes or fears, or indulge in a natural irritation because the drift of world affairs has not gone according to our plans and expectations. We have attempted here to sketch the connection between Soviet ideology, so different now and yet descended in many ways from the prototypes of Marxism and Leninism, and actual Soviet policies. All that a study of this kind can do is to suggest a certain range of problems and characteristics of Russian policies. It cannot, nor can the most detailed scheme of the politics of the USSR, predict or outline the eventuality of either a peaceful resolution of the East-West conflict or of its catastrophic settlement. Nor is it possible to sketch an "unavoidable" pattern of development of Soviet policies either toward a repetition of the Stalinist pattern, or

11. See Khrushchev's speech quoted in *Current Soviet Policies, II,* p. 177.

toward an erosion of totalitarianism. Very often in our analyses we tend to be more deterministic than our antagonists.

Yet, within a shorter range of time and without attempting to answer the really unanswerable and, alas, most important questions, it is possible to outline some basic difficulties of the Soviet international position. It has been suggested here that the ideological crisis created, paradoxically, by the successes of the Communist system impels it to seek a justification of the ideology in the international sphere. Thus, and not only because of the natural tendency of a totalitarian system, the USSR is bent upon ideological and power expansion. Here we encounter one of those "inherent contradictions" with which the Marxists upbraid the capitalist system, but of which their own offers glittering examples. Just as within the Soviet Union the reality of a modernized and industrialized society clashes with the ideological premises, and the contradiction is encompassed only by the chains of totalitarianism, so within the Communist bloc the reality of Soviet domination clashes with the ideological premise of the equality of socialist states, and the contradiction is concealed (imperfectly, as Yugoslavia, Hungary, and Poland have demonstrated) only by an enormous preponderance of power, which is for the time being on the side of the USSR. Here, then, are the Algerias and Cypruses of the Soviet camp, and the proverbial forces of history which appear to be working for the Soviets in disrupting the liberal world are impinging upon the combination of socialism and totalitarianism which is Soviet ideology.

Doctrine and Foreign Policy*

Soviet Russia under Khrushchev and since his fall has not ceased to bear out the paradoxical reality of a dogmatic movement that is hardly ever doctrinaire. Particularly in the realm of official utterances about foreign policy, the Soviet authorities continue to exemplify both terms of this seeming contradiction: they cling to the rigid self-righteousness of Marxist-Leninist orthodoxy, and they bend or twist the orthodoxy in innumerable practical applications to make it yield the interpretation that squares with prudence, challenge, or opportunity. In specific statements about the West as well as in general pronouncements about the communist movement, but above all in the context of the Sino-Soviet schism, the leadership has hewed to the old Stalinist use of doctrine as an instrument of policy rationalization and justification, however much it tries to sustain the illusion of unyielding doctrinal rigor in the eyes of the world communist movement, the Soviet masses, and itself as well.

Communist ideology, particularly in its foreign policy aspect, is often discussed but seldom defined. "Ideology," "doctrine," and "theory" are commonly used as synonyms, with little effort to distinguish them. Theory, in the ordinary usage, denotes a hypothesis or guess that might be true or might not.

*Reprinted from *Survey: A Journal of Soviet and East European Studies,* 57 (October, 1965), pp. 3 – 13, by permission of the author and the publisher. Copyright 1965, *Survey*, London, England.

Doctrine suggests a hard-and-fast teaching or policy on any particular subject. Ideology designates a general system of doctrine and belief that is professed by a particular political movement or regime. All three terms are used by the Russians — *teoriya, uchenie,* and *ideologiya* — but in their usage the meanings of the first two are virtually identical with the definition of ideology. There is certainly nothing tentative or partial in the official communist commitment to Marxism-Leninism.

According to official communist spokesmen ever since Lenin's time, Marxism-Leninism offers both a scientific prediction of the course of history and a guide to successful revolutionary action. In particular, it is supposed to give the analytic key to understanding the weaknesses of capitalist society and the forces that can overthrow it. It is also supposed to be the vital factor in clarifying the class consciousness of the proletariat and galvanizing its will to seize power.

Contained in this official view of the ideology are several different conceptions of its actual political role. These different conceptions are inherent, in turn, in the unacknowledged contradiction within the original corpus of Marxism, between the scientific-analytic-predictive-deterministic side of the ideology, and its revolutionary-moralistic-hortatory-activist side.[1] From the analytic standpoint, Marxism may have the force of prophecy, or, more modestly, it may serve to interpret political and social situations around the world and suggest to the policy-maker whether a given move will work or not. From the moralistic standpoint, Marxism may be the categorical imperative to fight and risk death for revolution and the worldwide victory of the proletariat, or it may be simply an instrument of propaganda to get the workers or anybody else to do what the communists want.

All four of these functions of ideology have figured in Soviet foreign policy at one time or another, though with different weights. The trend has been clearly and heavily toward the propaganda function, with some residual role for the interpretive function. The most important function of all, however, is not inherent in the origins of the ideology but developed historically during the early years of the Soviet regime. This is the function of legitimizing the regime and its authority in the eyes of the communist rulers themselves, however much the specific acts of the regime may appear to deviate from the original spirit of Marxism-Leninism. Ideology thus becomes a self-justifying dogma of a quasi-religious nature, totally dependent for its day-to-day meaning on the interpretations which the political authorities decide to lay down.

Lenin himself began the practice of dogmatic ideological restatement, beginning with his propositions about the role of the conspiratorial party in

---

1. Cf. Alfred G. Meyer, *Marxism: The Unity of Theory and Practice* (Cambridge, Mass., 1954), and R. V. Daniels, "Fate and Will in the Marxian Philosophy of History," *Journal of the History of Ideas,* October 1960.

bringing about revolution, and culminating in his retraction of the revolutionary war commitment in 1918 in favor of the Russia-first "citadel of revolution" doctrine. Stalin merely spelled out the implications of Lenin's policy with his own doctrine of "socialism in one country," according to which Russia could overcome its own relative backwardness and progress through "socialism" to "communism" independently of any proletarian success elsewhere.

The legacy of ideological manipulation during the period of Lenin's leadership and Stalin's rise was to tie both the meaning and the function of Marxist-Leninist theory to the authority of the communist party-state. The leader has had the power since Stalin's time to establish the meaning of ideology in an absolutely binding way. Criticism of his interpretation is heresy or treason, literally a crime against the state. There is no force to keep his interpretations honestly in conformity with the original meaning of the ideology; on the other hand there is every temptation to modify the meaning of the ideology, through reinterpretation, to make each new practical policy or expedient appear consistent with the original ideology. Thus, as the analysis of some recent Soviet policy shifts will show, ideology cannot determine or limit action except for some short-run rigidities; it is action, rather, that eventually supplies the up-to-date meaning of ideology.

While ideology is consequently very flexible over the years, it is rigid and dogmatic at any given moment. The authorities cannot admit that their reinterpretations are novelties, since this would defeat the whole purpose of doctrinal rationalization of new policies as the supposedly imperative application of Marxism-Leninism. To sustain their self-justification, they are compelled to enforce their interpretation of ideology with all the power at the disposal of the state. In no realm of thought can they tolerate the autonomy that might allow the party's ideological authority to be questioned — hence the principle of party decision in art and science that has stood for thirty-five years.

Despite the administrative burden and intellectual stifling that this entails, it nevertheless constitutes an element of major strength for the regime. The imposed ideology serves as a vehicle of mental discipline, to enforce the tests and demands of political conformity on every citizen in the land. It matters not so much what particular idea or ideology or verbal formula is proclaimed, but that some official thought is available to answer every public question and that the regime constantly exacts conformity. The exercise of doctrinal authority therefore becomes a necessary element in sustaining the general authority of the regime, a permanent fixture in the communist system of totalitarian rule.[2]

It follows from the foregoing that communist ideology is primarily signifi-

2. For a fuller development of this point, see my studies, *The Conscience of the Revolution: Communist Opposition in Soviet Russia* (Cambridge, Mass., 1960), pp. 248–52, and "What the Russians Mean," *Commentary,* October 1962.

cant for the internal working of the regime. Foreign policy is one of the least ideological aspects of Soviet politics, in reality if not in words. Rather than foreign policy's being governed in any substantial way by ideological requirements, the chief connection of the two lies in the decisions and situations which foreign policy considerations bring about and require the ideology to justify or explain away.

There is one respect in which foreign developments have struck more deeply at the system of ideological authority in the USSR. This is the factual emergence of new power centers in the communist world, in the now well-recognized phenomenon of polycentrism, above all as represented by China. The establishment of a communist regime in China strong enough to rival the Soviet Union for influence in the world communist movement has had a serious effect not only on the unity of the movement from country to country, but also on the intrinsic character of the movement. China, by challenging the single ideological authority of the leaders of Soviet Russia, threatened the entire system of mental discipline formerly imposed by the single authoritative interpretation of doctrine. Such a challenge may not have been intended by the Chinese or foreseen by the Russians, but it was inherent in the emergence of a second power center within the single ideological movement.

Far from ideology's serving as a bond between Russia and China, inhibiting their conflict, it was bound by its nature to force the conflict to the open cleavage the world has witnessed since 1961. The communist system, with its peculiar imposition of a constantly revised ideology, depends on a single authority that will hand down authoritative interpretations of doctrine to fit the practical needs of each new development on the world scene. Given two centers of power, each strong enough to issue its own interpretations of doctrine, and each seeing the practical requirements of policy in a different light, each is led to make theoretical pronouncements inconsistent with the view of the other. By its nature the movement cannot tolerate such differences, though neither center is willing to make the symbolic surrender of authority implicit in a recognition of the rival's theoretical correctness. Therefore every hair-splitting theoretical issue becomes the potential source of a major political clash, no less than the theological subtleties that led up to the Great Schism between the churches of Rome and of Constantinople in the eleventh century. The problem cannot logically be resolved until each center has anathematized the other and read it out of the movement — so splitting the movement into two, each with its own authoritative center issuing its own binding interpretations of a once common ideology. The dogmatic ideology of revolution may be compatible in practice with peaceful coexistence with the anti-revolutionaries, but it is a direct cause of rupture with all co-revolutionaries who are able and willing to proclaim their independence.

Khrushchev's career bears eloquent witness to the function of Soviet ideology as the instrument of political authority and justification after the fact.

For all his railing at the perversions of Stalinism, Khrushchev did little to alter the basic workings of the Stalinist state, and in the manipulation of doctrine as the Marxist high priest he all but outdid his former boss. In one central area of theory after another, Khrushchev laid down new pronouncements to accommodate his foreign policy or to embarrass his communist challengers, and when his startling overthrow ended his tenure of power in 1964, the principles of the Marxist philosophy of politics were in a shambles. No one in Russia could criticize the mess while he was in power, nor have they so far done so since his fall, but in the name of battling "revisionism," the Peking wing of the movement has done us the service of calling attention to most of Khrushchev's arbitrary modifications of theory.

Khrushchev was involved in ideological manipulations in the very first phase of his maneuvering for the succession, between 1953 and 1956. The area of theory he moved into was, significantly, international; the particular issue he raised was the Marxist assessment of the capitalist powers and the prospects for war and victory. Khrushchev chose his stand as a maneuvering point against his rival Malenkov, and proceeded to stress the possibility of war, the assurance that communism could emerge even from a nuclear conflict, and the necessity of continuing Russia's heavy industry stress and military buildup.

How contrived Khrushchev's interpretations were became obvious when, as soon as he had humbled Malenkov in 1955, he reversed his field and adopted most of his rival's views in order to force the hand of his next victim, the hard-liner Molotov. The whole maneuver was strongly reminiscent of Stalin's manipulation of the issue of economic development in the 1920's, first to defeat Trotsky with a moderate line and then to break Bukharin by pressing an exaggerated version of Trotsky's program.

The maneuvers of 1955 were only the prelude to Khrushchev's grand slam of theoretical innovation, the twentieth congress of the CPSU in February 1956. The congress is justly famous for his not-so-secret "secret speech" denouncing the excesses of Stalinism. For the theoretical guidelines of the Soviet Union and the world communist movement, however, the most significant new interpretations were contained in Khrushchev's open report to the congress. Regarding the international relations of the communist movement, Khrushchev proclaimed three sweeping innovations, couched of course in the language of undeviating Leninist orthodoxy: the doctrine of peaceful coexistence and non-inevitability of war; the doctrine of separate national roads to socialism; and the doctrine of non-violent communist revolution. All these propositions were radical breaks with Leninism; all were prompted by pragmatic temptations of foreign policy or domestic politics; and all were instrumental in precipitating the schism and polycentrism that subsequently sapped the strength and resolve of the communist movement.

"Peaceful coexistence" was Khrushchev's doctrinal sanction for policies to reduce tension with the West and lessen the threat of nuclear war. He tried to make it look like an old idea:

The Leninist principle of peaceful coexistence of states with different social systems has always been and remains the general line of our country's foreign policy. It has been alleged that the Soviet Union puts forward the principle of peaceful coexistence merely out of tactical considerations, considerations of expediency. Yet it is common knowledge that we have always, from the very first years of Soviet power, stood with equal firmness for peaceful coexistence. Hence it is not a tactical move, but a fundamental principle of Soviet foreign policy. . . . Indeed, there are only two ways: either peaceful coexistence or the most destructive war in history. There is no third way.

Interestingly, Khrushchev gave the Chinese a credit line for peaceful coexistence as it had been enunciated in their 1955 "five principles" agreement with India. He was sufficiently aware of the novelty of his line to try to dispose of doctrinaire doubts: "There is, of course, a Marxist-Leninist proposition that wars are inevitable as long as imperialism exists." But now, Khrushchev contended, the "degree of organization and the awareness and determination of the people" could offset the "economic basis of wars under imperialism." This was hardly consistent with Marxist teaching about the influence of economic base on political superstructure, but for Khrushchev it was enough to observe,

Now there is a world camp of socialism, which has become a mighty force. In this camp the peace forces find not only the moral, but also the material means to prevent aggression.

The notion of separate roads to socialism, meaning the possibility of independent decisions and policies on the part of various communist governments, was anathema in Stalin's time. Tito's line in Yugoslavia after 1948 was the first attempt at such a separate road, and even this came only after Stalin had read Tito out of the communist movement. A greater problem for the integrity of Stalin's unilinear conception of communism came with the accession of the Chinese communists in 1949, though they were content for the time being to confine their separate roads to the realm of practice and not to challenge Soviet doctrinal supremacy. Khrushchev's embrace of the separate-roads doctrine followed as the obvious corollary of his rapprochement with Tito in 1955 (and as an effective move in his maneuvering against Molotov). "Alongside the Soviet form of reconstructing society on socialist lines," Khrushchev told the twentieth congress, "we now have the form of people's democracy." ("People's democracy" had hitherto been regarded by the Russians as a preliminary to socialist construction, not an alternative route.) Khrushchev's gestures to both Peking and Belgrade were explicit:

Much that is unique in socialist construction is being contributed by the People's Republic of China. . . . Having taken over the decisive commanding positions, the people's democratic state is using them in the social revolution to implement a policy of peaceful reorganization of private industry and trade, and their gradual transformation into a component of socialist economy.

The leadership of the great cause of socialist reconstruction by the Communist Party of China and the communist and workers' parties of the other people's democracies, exercised in keeping with the peculiarities and specific features of each country, is creative Marxism in action.

In the Federal People's Republic of Yugoslavia . . . specific concrete forms of economic management and organization of the state apparatus are arising in the process of socialist construction.

Khrushchev's third line of departure from Lenin followed closely on the separate-roads idea:

It is probable that more forms of transition to socialism will appear. Moreover, the implementation of these forms need not be associated with civil war under all circumstances. Our enemies like to depict us Leninists as advocates of violence always and everywhere. True, we recognize the need for the revolutionary transformation of capitalist society into socialist society. It is this that distinguishes the revolutionary Marxists from the reformists, the opportunists. There is no doubt that in a number of capitalist countries the violent overthrow of the dictatorship of the bourgeoisie and the sharp aggravation of class struggle connected with this are inevitable. But the forms of social revolution vary. It is not true that we regard violence and civil war as the only way to remake society.

Though the practical import of all this was restricted — Khrushchev had in mind as the "non-violent" model the communist takeover in Czechoslovakia in 1948 — it was nonetheless a far cry from Lenin's insistence that the "bourgeois" state must everywhere be "smashed" with revolutionary force.

Altogether, Khrushchev's modifications of the international theory of communism constituted a long step towards the revisionism that the Chinese were soon to charge him with. His purpose was pragmatic — a restatement of theory so that it would not impede his realistic or opportunistic foreign policy in the two directions he proposed to push: accommodation with different communist states which he could not control; and the reduction of the danger of nuclear war with the United States.

The international doctrines of 1956 served Khrushchev sufficiently well for the rest of his career, though they did not prevent his great diplomatic setback, the loss of China. The Chinese communists, for their part, seized upon Khrushchev's interpretations as an object of power contest, so that they might assert their independence of Soviet doctrinal authority by taking issue with the new Moscow line.

The Chinese revolt built up gradually between 1956 and 1960. Its particular foci were the appraisal of Stalin and (of more relevance to foreign policy) the question of unity or autonomy within the communist movement — i.e., the issue of separate roads to socialism. Preferring not to attack Khrushchev head-on the Chinese made Yugoslavia the butt of their critique of tendencies that weakened "international proletarian solidarity." In the spring of 1958, in the face of a projected state visit to Yugoslavia by Soviet Chief of State Voroshilov, the Chinese opened their blistering attack on the new program of the League of Communists of Yugoslavia — a document of surrender to capitalism, in Peking's view.

By this point the Chinese clearly had the ideological initiative. Khrushchev endorsed Mao's attack on revisionism, and could only add (in his Sofia speech of June 1958) that "attempts to find different shades in the criticism of present-day revisionism on the part of the fraternal parties are in vain." Mao, his appetite for authority in the movement whetted by Khrushchev's gestures of appeasement, immediately struck out in another direction — the transition to communism. The actual move, in the fall of 1958, was the program to reorganize the loosely-collectivized Chinese peasants into tightly knit communes, and with this the strong theoretical suggestion that China was leaping ahead of Russia on the path of transition from the socialist to the communist form of society.

This time the Russians rebelled, and dismissed the Chinese commune experiment as an aberration entirely irrelevant to the transition to communism. Khrushchev then threw himself into a glowing exposition of the Soviet transition to communism, in his report to the twenty-first congress of the CPSU in January 1959. This was the first Soviet treatment of the subject since Stalin's speeches of the 1930's, and Khrushchev's motive of countering the Chinese commune claims came clearly through the lines:

> The Marxist-Leninist party considers the setting up of a communist society its final aim. But society cannot switch over to communism from capitalism without passing through the socialist phase of development. From capitalism, Lenin said, mankind can switch over directly only to socialism, that is, to communal ownership of production means and distribution of products to individuals in accordance with their work. Our party looks farther ahead. Socialism must inevitably develop gradually into communism, on the banner of which is written: From each according to his abilities, to each according to his needs.

As to the concrete details of the stateless society of communism, Khrushchev took pains to rule out any expectations that might interfere with the practical operations of the Soviet state. For him, as for Stalin, there would be no equalizing of rewards for the foreseeable future of the transition period: "One cannot fail to see that equalization would lead to unjust distribution. Both the good and bad workers would receive the same. . . . Equalization would mean not a transition to communism but the discrediting of communism."

From the old promise of the "withering away of the state," Khrushchev escaped by defining the future regime "dialectically" as "communist public self-government," with "certain public functions . . . analogous to present state functions." He thus anticipated the doctrine, spelled out in the party program of 1961, of the permanence of the communist state in everything but name, and of the Communist Party in name as well as in fact.

During the following year Khrushchev vigorously pursued the line of

peaceful coexistence, capped in September 1959 by his visit to the United
States and his guarded censure of the Chinese in their first clash with India.
In Peking following his American tour, he spoke forcefully against the use of
war to expand communism:

> We must think realistically and understand the contemporary situation correctly.
> This, of course, does not by any means signify that if we are so strong, then we must
> test by force the stability of the capitalist system. This would be wrong: the peoples
> would not understand and would never support those who would think of acting in
> this way. We have always been against wars of conquest. Marxists have recognized,
> and recognize, only liberating, just wars; they have always condemned, and con-
> demn, wars of conquest, imperialist wars.

After some mutterings of disquiet about revisionism and the exclusion of
China from international agreements, Peking finally drew up its lines of ideological battle against Moscow in April 1960. On the occasion of the ninetieth
anniversary of the birth of Lenin, the Chinese theoretical journal *Red Flag*
published, under the title "Long Live Leninism," an extended attack on the
errors of "modern revisionism":

> Are the teachings of Marxism-Leninism now "outmoded"? Does the whole, inte-
> grated teaching of Lenin on imperialism, on proletarian revolution and proletarian
> dictatorship, on war and peace, and on the building of socialism and communism
> still retain its vigorous vitality? . . . Is it that there can be no question of war even
> if imperialism and the system of exploitation are allowed to survive for ever?
>
>   As long as the peoples of all countries enhance their awareness and are fully
> prepared, with the socialist camp also mastering modern weapons, it is certain that
> if the US or other imperialists refuse to reach an agreement on the banning of atomic
> and nuclear weapons and should dare to fly in the face of the will of all humanity
> by launching a war using atomic and nuclear weapons, the result will be the very
> speedy destruction of these monsters encircled by the peoples of the world, and the
> result will certainly not be the annihilation of mankind. We consistently oppose the
> launching of criminal wars by imperialism. . . . But should the imperialists impose
> such sacrifices on the peoples of various countries, we believe that, as the experience
> of the Russian revolution and the Chinese revolution shows, those sacrifices would
> be repaid. On the debris of a dead imperialism, the victorious people would create
> very swiftly a civilization thousands of times higher than the capitalist system and
> a truly beautiful future for themselves. . . .
>
>   We believe in the absolute correctness of Lenin's thinking: War is an inevitable
> outcome of systems of exploitation and the source of modern wars is the imperialist
> system. Until the imperialist system and the exploiting classes come to an end, wars
> of one kind or another will always occur.

In their efforts to discredit Khrushchev, the Chinese had (perhaps deliberately)
confused the Lenin and Stalin doctrine of inevitable war among capitalist
countries, with the question of likely war between capitalist and communist
states. (On this the Soviet leaders had never been dogmatic. Stalin himself had
maintained in his valedictory article of 1952 that the rivalries among the
capitalists were stronger than the contradictions between the capitalist camp
and the socialist camp.) The purpose of the Chinese communists, again, was

to raise a theoretical point which the Russians could not accept without acknowledging Chinese initiative, but could not reject without risking the appearance of softness and revisionism.

The now familiar political clash between the Russians and the Chinese began soon after this ideological challenge, with the confrontation at the Rumanian Communist Party congress in June 1960, and the acrimony surrounding the Albanian problem. There followed the decisive conference of 81 communist parties in November 1960, with its bitter behind-the-scenes exchanges and its expression of superficial unity in the statement published in December.

In 1961, to offset the Chinese pretensions to Marxist superiority and keep his foreign policy free of strictures about inevitable war, Khrushchev gave renewed attention to the updating of ideology. This time he put emphasis on the theory of the internal development of the communist society, with the occasion for discussion provided by the proposal and adoption of the new program of the Soviet Communist Party.

In his presentation of the program (notably in his address to the twenty-second congress in October 1961), Khrushchev made it official that Soviet Russia had entered on the stage of the all-out building of communist society. Like Stalin before him, he was at pains to square the revised vision of the communist utopia with his practical intentions regarding Soviet internal development and leadership in the communist camp. As he spelled out the expected provisions of communism, it was evident that he envisaged only more of the same Soviet reality, ameliorated by an American living standard.

Khrushchev complicated the problem of accommodating the utopian theory of communism by enunciating a new political doctrine, devoid in fact of any textual roots in Marxism. As this was stated in the program, "The dictatorship of the proletariat has fulfilled its historic mission and has ceased to be indispensable in the USSR. . . . The state . . . has . . . become a state of the entire people. . . . The state as an organization of the entire people will survive until the complete victory of communism." Such a non-class notion of the state had been explicitly rejected by Marx in his criticism of the German social-democrats. At an opportune moment Peking picked up the cry of orthodoxy:

> In the view of Marxist-Leninists, there is no such thing as a non-class or supra-class state. So long as the state remains a state, it must bear a class character; so long as the state exists, it cannot be a state of the "whole people." As soon as society becomes classless, there will no longer be a state. . . . In calling a socialist state the "state of the whole people" is one trying to replace the Marxist-Leninist theory of the state by the bourgeois theory of the state? Is one trying to replace the state of dictatorship of the proletariat by a state of a different character? If that is the case, it is nothing but a great historical retrogression.[3]

Finally, Khrushchev's international application of the transition-to-commu-

3. Letter of the CC of the CCP to the CC of the CPSU, 14 June 1963.

nism vision showed an interesting twist. As earlier understood, all socialist states were to accomplish the transition to communism at the same time, which implied that Russia, with its head start, would have to lend a substantial hand to countries such as China. The final draft of the 1961 program got around this: The transition by the various bloc countries could occur merely "in the same historical epoch," no definition being given of the length of an epoch. Separate roads to socialism were thus to carry separate arrival dates, and presumably separate national responsibilities for completing the journey at all. Thus did polycentrism show its mark on what had originated as a movement of international revolution.

The history of official Soviet thinking during the Khrushchev era repeatedly confirms the instrumental character of contemporary communist ideology. Ideology serves foreign policy as justification after the fact, while the principal concern of Soviet policy-makers in the realm of doctrine — since the fall of Khrushchev no less than before — is to retain a free hand for any opportune move, unrestricted by possible theoretical inhibitions.

As an instrument of policy, communist ideology has figured more prominently in the internal politics of the movement than in the more pragmatic area of relations with the non-communist world. Ideology has notably been employed as a device both to provoke and to discredit opposition factions and dissident communist governments. Within the Soviet Union, the ideological statement of foreign policy was adroitly employed by Khrushchev in his political contest with Malenkov and Molotov in the mid-1950's. Within the communist bloc, ideology has provided the most visible arena of political contest between the Soviet Union and the Chinese People's Republic, with a series of ideological initiatives taken by both sides to force the rival either to follow abjectly or to stand and fight.

As in the earlier history of the Soviet Union, the use of ideology as a political instrument in the Khrushchev era had a substantial impact on the meaning of the doctrine itself. Nevertheless, as was the characteristic under Stalin, there was no official acknowledgment that the doctrine was being modified. Every reinterpretation was represented as a mere restating and application of the original orthodoxy.

With the schism between Moscow and Peking, however, this reinterpretation was carried on in different directions, independently. The consequence was, as it could only have been, the crystallization of two distinct and mutually exclusive versions of the Marxist-Leninist orthodoxy. Neither Communist power, after the parting of their ideological ways in 1960, could acknowledge the virtue of the other without undermining its own authority at home as well as abroad. The ideological habits of communism thus had, in a peculiar way, a profound impact on the course of foreign policy, not in uniting the bloc, not in guiding the campaign against the West, but in driving home an unbridgeable wedge into what had once passed as a monolithic revolutionary whole.

The "Operational Code": A Neglected Approach to the Study of Political Leaders and Decision-Making*

In the past two decades the field of international relations studies has become increasingly diversified and is now marked by sharp differences over questions of scope, method, and theory. This heterogeneity, however, should not be allowed to obscure broad agreement on some fundamental propositions of overriding importance. One of these is the feeling shared by traditionalists and scientifically-oriented investigators alike, and by many academic scholars as well as sophisticated policy-makers, that the way in which the leaders of nation-states view each other and the nature of world political conflict is of fundamental importance in determining what happens in relations among states.

Reflecting the perspective of the policy maker, for example, Louis Halle, a former State Department planner, writes that the foreign policy of a nation addresses itself not to the external world, as is commonly stated, but rather to "the image of the external world" that is in the minds of those who make foreign policy. Halle concludes his book on American foreign policy with a sober warning: "In the degree that the image is false, actually and philosophically false, no technicians, however proficient, can make the policy that is

*Reprinted from *International Studies Quarterly,* XIII, 2 (June, 1969), pp. 190–222, by permission of the author and the Wayne State University Press. Copyright 1969 by Wayne State University Press. This article is a slightly modified version of a publication with the same title issued by The RAND Corporation as RM-5427 in August, 1967. The author wishes to express appreciation for permission to reprint.

based on it sound."[1] Essentially the same point has emerged from the work of many scientifically-oriented scholars who, influenced by psychological theories of cognition, have been struck by the role that the subjective perceptions and beliefs of leaders play in their decision-making in conflict situations.

Convergence on this fundamental point provides an opportunity, therefore, for establishing a more fruitful dialogue among academic scholars of various persuasions and policy-oriented researchers. To call attention to this opportunity and to help structure some of the central research questions, I decided a few years ago to reexamine an older study that had pioneered in the analysis of elite belief systems. I refer to Nathan Leites' concept of "operational code." It must be said immediately that this term is a misnomer insofar as it implies, incorrectly, a set of recipes or repertoires for political action that an elite applies mechanically in its decision-making.

A closer examination of what Leites had in mind indicates that he was referring to a set of general beliefs about fundamental issues of history and central questions of politics as these bear, in turn, on the problem of action. The actor's beliefs and premises that Leites singled out have a relationship to decision-making that is looser and more subtle than the term "operational code" implies. They serve, as it were, as a prism that influences the actor's perceptions and diagnoses of the flow of political events, his definitions and estimates of particular situations. These beliefs also provide norms, standards, and guidelines that influence the actor's choice of strategy and tactics, his structuring and weighing of alternative courses of action. Such a belief system influences, but does not unilaterally determine, decision-making; it is an important, but not the only, variable that shapes decision-making behavior. With this caveat in mind, let me recall briefly the origins, nature, and impact of Leites' study before proceeding to indicate how his approach can be codified into a more explicit and usable research model.

I. Background

It is now over fifteen years since Nathan Leites published *A Study of Bolshevism,* [2] which broke important ground in the newly emerging behavioral approach to the study of political elites. During and after World War II, many students of world politics turned their attention to the ways in which different elites approached problems of international conflict and cooperation. They posed questions for research that could not be satisfactorily answered by traditional approaches, such as systematic biographical analysis of a ruling group according to the social origins, education, training, and other background characteristics of its members. Biographical profiles of this kind often

---

1. *American Foreign Policy* (London: G. Allen, 1960), pp. 316, 318.
2. (Glencoe, Ill.: Free Press, 1953), hereafter cited as *Study.*

suggested factors that helped account for the emergence and formation of leadership groups, but they did not illuminate adequately the political orientations, styles of calculation, and behavior of the ruling groups in question.[3]

Leites' book was by no means universally acclaimed. But there were those who welcomed it not merely for its insights into Bolshevik mentality; some thought it introduced a new genre of elite study that might fill some of the needs for a behavioral approach to studies of political leadership.

Thus the eminent anthropologist, Clyde Kluckhohn, praised *A Study of Bolshevism* as being "a work of gigantic stature that is likely to *faire école* in politics and the other behavioral sciences for many years to come."[4] This expectation has not materialized. *A Study of Bolshevism* inspired few efforts at similar research on other leadership groups.[5]

Among the reasons for this, I believe, is the unusually complex nature of Leites' work, which is not one but several interrelated studies that are subtly interwoven. While the complexity of the work adds to its richness and intellectual appeal, it has also made it unusually difficult for readers to grasp its structure or to describe its research mode.[6]

I wish to call particular attention in this paper to that portion of *A Study of Bolshevism* known as the "operational code." Leites employed this phrase to refer to the precepts or maxims of political tactics and strategy that characterized the classical Bolshevik approach to politics. Leites initially published this portion of his larger treatise separately, and in abbreviated form as *The Operational Code of the Politburo.*[7] Two years later his more detailed statement of the "operational code" appeared in the full-scale *A Study of Bolshevism* (1953), but now several new dimensions were added and interwoven with it. Hence, the "operational code" became embedded in a much more ambitious

3. For a useful critique of the systematic multi-biographical study of elite groups, see Morris Janowitz, "The Systematic Aspects of Political Biography," *World Politics,* VI (April, 1954). A comprehensive critical appraisal of elite theories and related empirical researches is provided in Dankwart A. Rustow, "The Study of Elites," *World Politics,* XVIII (July, 1966).

4. In his review article, "Politics, History, and Psychology," *World Politics,* VIII (October, 1955), p. 117

5. An early attempt was made by Theodore Chen to apply the "operational code" approach to Communist Chinese leaders. More recently, in December 1966, Robert North organized a conference of Chinese area specialists at Stanford University to consider again the utility and feasibility of doing a study of the Chinese Communist operational code. Other studies pursue similar research objectives, though not modeled on the operational code: see, for example, Davis B. Bobrow, "The Chinese Communist Conflict System," *Orbis,* IX (Winter, 1966); Howard L. Boorman and Scott A. Boorman, "Strategy and National Psychology in China," *The Annals,* 370 (March, 1967); Tang Tsou and Morton H. Halperin, "Mao Tse-tung's Revolutionary Strategy and Peking's International Behavior," *American Political Science Review,* LIX (March, 1965).

6. A helpful effort to identify the several components of *A Study of Bolshevism* is provided by Daniel Bell, "Bolshevik Man, His Motivations: A Psychoanalytic Key to Communist Behavior," *Commentary,* XIX (1955), pp. 179–87; much of this essay was reproduced in the same author's "Ten Theories in Search of Reality: The Prediction of Soviet Behavior in the Social Sciences," *World Politics,* X (April, 1958).

7. New York: McGraw-Hill, 1951.

socio-psychological account of the historical origins and meanings of Bolshevism. The reader was provided not only with the "operational code" but, as Daniel Bell noted, also with a special kind of history of the changing moral temper of an important element of the radical reform-minded Russian intelligentsia. A third component of the study, in some ways the most ambitious, was Leites' delineation of the "Bolshevik character" which, he suggested, constituted in some respects a distinct type in social history in the sense that any individual is unique though resembling others in important respects.[8]

Hence *A Study of Bolshevism* emerges as far more than a list of maxims of political strategy. Rather, the "operational code" blends and merges at many points with the discussion of "Bolshevik character." The maxims of political strategy that comprise the "operational code" take on the character of *rules of conduct* held out for good Bolsheviks and *norms of behavior* that, ideally, are internalized by the individual who thereby acquires a new and different character structure — that of the reliable, "hard-core" Bolshevik. In the terminology of modern ego psychology, the individual who succeeds in internalizing this preferred character structure thereby accomplishes an "identity transformation."

Leites dealt briefly, and necessarily speculatively, with the origins of the "Bolshevik character." He saw it as being, in part, a *reaction* to those qualities of the reform-minded Russian intelligentsia of the nineteenth century that had, in Lenin's judgment, proven to be quite unsuitable for the task of making a successful revolution.

In dealing with the origins of the Bolshevik character and, in particular, with its "reactive" aspects, Leites employed a method that drew in part, but only in part, on psychoanalytic theory. This has further complicated the task of understanding the research model on which his complex study is based. Since the question is germane to the task of "disentangling" the operational code portion of the work, some clarification of the role psychoanalytic theory played in Leites' study is necessary before proceeding.

It is true that Leites felt that the full significance of important elements of the emergent Bolshevik character could be better understood by regarding them as "reaction formations" (and other ego defense mechanisms) to powerful unconscious wishes that had helped to shape the older character structure of Russian reform-minded intellectuals.[9] But, according to Leites, the Bolshevik character also represented a *conscious* effort by Lenin and his associates

---

8. In this connection see, for example, Michael Walzer's study of the origins of modern radical politics in the sixteenth century and his effort to construct a general model of radical politics that encompasses Bolshevism as well as Puritanism. *The Revolution of Saints* (Cambridge, Mass.: Harvard University Press, 1965).

9. The psychoanalytic hypotheses employed by Leites were touched upon at various points in *A Study of Bolshevism* and discussed more fully in his article, "Panic and Defenses Against Panic in the Bolshevik View of Politics," in *Psychoanalysis and the Social Sciences,* IV (New York: International Universities Press, 1955), pp. 135–44.

to reverse certain traditional aspects of Russian character. Leites therefore employed psychoanalytic theory to illuminate the unconscious significance of Bolshevik beliefs; but he noted explicitly that his "delineation of the preconscious and conscious content" of Bolshevik doctrine and the operational code did not require the reader either to accept the theory of psychoanalysis or to agree with the particular use Leites made of it in his admittedly speculative attempt to illuminate the possible unconscious significance of some of these Bolshevik beliefs.[10]

What emerges from this is that the set of beliefs about politics associated with the concept, "operational code," can be investigated without reference to psychoanalytic hypotheses. These beliefs, implicitly or explicitly held by the political actor, can be inferred or postulated by the investigator on the basis of the kinds of data, observational opportunities, and methods generally available to political scientists. In this respect, the "operational code" approach does not differ from research efforts to identify many other beliefs, opinions, and attitudes of political actors. Leites' use of psychoanalytic theory, therefore, offers no impediment to "factoring out" the operational code part of his study.

At the same time, it is one of the attractive features of the operational code construct for behaviorally-inclined political scientists that it can serve as a useful "bridge" or "link" to psychodynamic interpretations of unconscious dimensions of belief systems and their role in behavior under different conditions.[11] Thus, once an actor's approach to political calculation has been formulated by the researcher, he can proceed — if he so wishes and is able to do so — to relate some of the beliefs in question to other motivational variables of a psychodynamic character. With the belief system of the political actor in hand, the investigator can move more easily than would otherwise be possible into the sphere of unconscious motives and defenses against them that affect the strength and operation of these beliefs in the actor's political behavior in different circumstances, and to an assessment of the extent to which these beliefs are subject to reality-tests of various kinds. An elite's fundamental beliefs about politics are probably resistant to change for various reasons, of which unconscious motivations are but one factor.[12]

10. *Study*, p. 22. Daniel Bell, *op. cit.*, also called attention to the fact that Leites regards Bolshevik character as both a conscious and unconscious reaction to features of the earlier pre-Bolshevik character.

11. I have suggested elsewhere ("Power as a Compensatory Value for Political Leaders," *Journal of Social Issues*, XXIV [July, 1968]) that political scientists interested in applying personality theories to the study of political leaders need to build a number of conceptual "bridges" that reflect the problems, theoretical interests, and available data of their discipline in order to make more effective use of personality theories rooted in psychoanalysis. The "operational code" construct is one such "bridge." The belief system about politics is part of the cognitive and affective portion of the ego structure of personality; as such it serves an adaptive function for coping with reality. But at the same time the emergence of a belief system may be affected by developmental problems encountered in personality formation; if so, beliefs may then also serve ego defensive functions *vis-à-vis* unconscious wishes and anxieties.

12. In this connection, Leites argued that the fact that beliefs comprising the operational code

Another shortcoming of the *Study* should be mentioned. Leites did not structure and synthesize the various beliefs, rules, and maxims about politics associated with his concept of "operational code." The relationship of the different elements of the Bolshevik view of politics to each other and to the problem of making specific choices of action remained somewhat obscure.[13] That is, he did not clarify sufficiently the order, hierarchy, and interrelationships among the various elements of the "code." I will attempt to redress this by reinterpreting various components of the so-called code and restructuring it into a more tightly knit set of beliefs about fundamental issues and questions associated with the classical problem of political action. To repeat, it is in this sense — as a set of premises and beliefs about politics and not as a set of rules and recipes to be applied mechanically to the choice of action — that the "operational code" construct is properly understood.

II. The "Operational Code" and Cognitive Limits on Rational Decision-Making

A political leader's beliefs about the nature of politics and political conflict, his views regarding the extent to which historical developments can be shaped, and his notions of correct strategy and tactics — whether these beliefs be referred to as "operational code," "Weltanschauung," "cognitive map," or an "elite's political culture" — are among the factors influencing that actor's decisions. The "operational code" is a particularly significant portion of the actor's entire set of beliefs about political life.[14] Not all the beliefs and attitudes that influence a political actor's behavior, then, will be considered here. A comprehensive model of decision-making behavior, for example, would also consider the actor's ethical and normative beliefs.[15]

It is widely recognized that there are important cognitive limits on the

---

appeared to be held with unusual stubbornness, exaggeration, and intensity raised the presumption that adherence to them was reinforced by defenses against strong unconscious wishes or fears and, hence, that they were relatively impervious to many kinds of rational tests. (We shall return to this point below.)

13. This point was well made recently by John Weakland in a perceptive and balanced appraisal of *A Study of Bolshevism*. Weakland notes that Leites' work is "remarkably simple in overall organization, and for a work aiming to present a code, it gives little attention to synthesis and systematization. . . . We are presented with a list of themes, but these parts of the code are not interrelated. . . . And there is even less attention given to questions of more complex structure, such as possible relationships between themes or principles of different levels . . ." John H. Weakland, "Investigating the Operational Code of the Chinese Communist Leadership," an unpublished paper written for the Politburo Feasibility Study Conference, Stanford University, 16 – 18 December, 1966.

14. For a more general discussion of political belief systems, see Lucian W. Pye and Sidney Verba (eds.), *Political Culture and Political Development* (Princeton, N.J.: Princeton University Press, 1965), particularly the "Introduction" by L. Pye and "Conclusion: Comparative Political Culture" by S. Verba.

15. These were considered by Leites in *Study,* especially pp. 99 – 144.

possibility of rational decision-making in politics as in other sectors of life.[16] In contrast to models of "pure" rationality in statistical decision theory and formal economics, efforts at rational decision-making in political life are subject to constraints of the following kind: (1) The political actor's information about situations with which he must deal is usually incomplete; (2) his knowledge of ends-means relationships is generally inadequate to predict reliably the consequences of choosing one or another course of action; and (3) it is often difficult for him to formulate a single criterion by means of which to choose which alternative course of action is "best."[17]

Political actors have to adapt to and try to cope with these cognitive limits or "boundaries" to rational decision-making. There are, no doubt, a variety of ways in which different political leaders deal with this problem in similar or different political settings. This is, indeed, an aspect of comparative political research that has received little systematic attention.[18] How do political leaders in varying political cultures and institutional structures approach the task of making calculations, of deciding what objectives to select, and how to deal with uncertainty and risk — that is, more generally, how to relate means and ends, etc.? What styles of political calculation and strategies are developed for this purpose by different leaders? This has to do, of course, with the familiar problem of the relation of knowledge to action on which many observers and practitioners of politics have reflected. What is proposed here is that this classical problem be conceptualized more rigorously and studied more systematically than in the past.[19]

16. In recent years a number of social scientists have attempted to draw upon the field of cognitive psychology in order to elaborate better decision-making models for studies of world politics. While cognitive theory is relevant and suggestive, it does not lend itself readily to the task. Considerable adaption and development are needed. In particular, investigators will have to articulate the substantive beliefs and cognitive problems that are relevant in decision-making in political settings, and they will also have to define more specifically the special contexts in which these political beliefs originate, operate in decision-making, and change. For a useful discussion and statement of a still quite general model, see Richard A. Brody, "Cognition and Behavior: A Model of International Relations," in O. G. Harvey (ed.), *Experience, Structure, and Adaptability* (New York: Springer, 1966).

17. For useful discussions of these cognitive limits and some of their implications in the area of political decision-making, see James G. March and Herbert A. Simon, *Organizations* (New York: John Wiley, 1958); and Charles E. Lindblom, "The Science of Muddling Through," *Public Administration Quarterly,* XXIX (Spring, 1959), pp. 79 – 88. Lindblom's views have been elaborated in subsequent publications.

18. For interesting developments in this direction, however, see Albert Hirschman's effort to identify some characteristic features of the problem-solving and decision-making styles of Latin American reform leaders, in his *Journeys Toward Progress* (New York: Twentieth Century Fund, 1963); and the research by Wendell Bell and James Mau on "images of the future," as a key variable in social change in developing countries.

19. For insightful essays on some of these questions, see, for example, David S. McLelland, "The Role of Political Style: A Study of Dean Acheson," in Roger Hilsman and Robert C. Good (eds.), *Foreign Policy in the Sixties* (Baltimore: Johns Hopkins University Press, 1965); Peter Gourevitch, "Political Skill: A Case Study," in John D. Montgomery and Arthur Smithies (eds.), *Public Policy* (Cambridge, Mass.: Harvard University Press, 1965), especially pp. 266 – 68; Erwin C. Hargrove, *Presidential Leadership: Personality and Political Style* (New York: Macmillan,

The issues and questions referred to in the preceding paragraph comprise one part of the "operational code" construct. We shall refer to the "answers" given by a political actor to these questions as his "instrumental beliefs," that is, his beliefs about ends-means relationships in the context of political action.

There is another set of more general issues and questions that are part of an operational code. These are what may be called the political actor's "philosophical" beliefs, since they refer to assumptions and premises he makes regarding the fundamental nature of politics, the nature of political conflict, the role of the individual in history, etc.[20]

It is in terms of these two sets of beliefs — the specific contents of which will be discussed shortly — that I have redefined and restructured the concept of "operational code." What emerges is a research construct for empirical work on decision-making that focuses more clearly than did *A Study of Bolshevism* on the interrelated set of beliefs about the nature of political conflict and an effective approach to calculation of political strategy and tactics.

A Study of Bolshevism emphasized the "answers" that, in Leites' judgment, the old Bolsheviks gave to these central questions about politics and the relation of knowledge to action. However, he did not explicitly state all the issues and questions themselves. This I shall attempt to do here in order to facilitate similar studies of other leaders and other leadership groups, and thereby lead to systematic comparative studies.

There are, of course, difficult problems in employing knowledge of a leader's "operational code," or belief system about politics, for purposes of explaining or predicting his behavior in specific instances.[21] The investigator's knowledge of the actor's general belief system can assist, but not substitute for, analysis of specific situations and assessment of institutional and other pressures on the political actor's decisions. Knowledge of the actor's approach to calculating choice of action does *not* provide a simple key to explanation and prediction; but it can help the researcher and the policy planner to "bound" the alternative ways in which the subject may perceive different types of situations and approach the task of making a rational assessment of alternative courses of

1966); Michael Brecher, "Elite Images and Foreign Policy Choices: Krishna Menon's View of the World," *Pacific Affairs,* XL (Spring and Summer, 1967). Systematic research on presidential leadership styles is currently being undertaken by Professor James David Barber, Department of Political Science, Yale University.

20. I have borrowed here and adapted the general distinction between "epistemological" and "instrumental" beliefs made by O. G. Brim, D. C. Glass, D. E. Lavin, and N. Goodman, *Personality and Decision Processes: Studies in the Social Psychology of Thinking* (Stanford: Stanford University Press, 1962). In attempting to apply their useful distinction to the subject matter of the "operational code" I have found it necessary to formulate differently the specific issues and questions related to the problem of political action.

21. Leites himself did not overlook these problems or oversimplify the task of utilizing the operational code, with its ambiguous and inconsistent prescriptions, for explaining or predicting Soviet behavior. See *Study,* pp. 16–18.

action. Knowledge of the actor's beliefs helps the investigator to clarify the general criteria, requirements, and norms the subject attempts to meet in assessing opportunities that arise to make desirable gains, in estimating the costs and risks associated with them, and in making utility calculations.

Whether it be from the standpoint of philosophy, history, psychology, sociology, economics, or political science, students of human behavior have long agreed that any individual must necessarily simplify and structure the complexity of his world in order to cope with it. In everyday life as in the laboratory, problem-solving often requires deliberate or unwitting simplification of a more complex reality. This applies also to the political actor, for he too must somehow comprehend complex situations in order to decide how best to deal with them.[22] In doing so, the actor typically engages in a "definition of the situation," that is, a cognitive structuring of the situation that will clarify for him the nature of the problem, relate it to his previous experience, and make it amenable to appropriate problem-solving activities. The political actor perceives and simplifies reality partly through the prism of his "cognitive map" of politics. This includes the belief system that has been referred to in the past as the "operational code" of a political actor.

We turn now to the content of an operational code. I have identified a number of questions about politics that, together, hopefully cover most of the central issues connected with the problem of knowledge and action. The "answers" a political actor gives to these questions serve to define his fundamental orientation towards the problem of leadership and action. Before proceeding, we take note of the possibility that in some non-Western cultures the problem of knowledge and its relation to the calculation of political action may be approached differently and, hence, the list of fundamental questions identified here may not be entirely applicable.

Most of the observations Leites made about the classical Bolshevik approach to political calculation can be subsumed under one or another of these questions. We will not take up here whether Leites' construction of the classical Bolshevik belief system was valid in all respects. But we shall consider later the question of the extent to which some of the old Bolshevik beliefs have since changed. And we shall suggest some of the ways in which knowledge of this belief system relates to the task of explaining or predicting Soviet behavior.

The immediate objective of this paper — to explicate in detail the nature of the belief system associated with the concept of operational code — does not require us to delve deeply into these additional questions. Of more immediate concern is the adequacy of our explication and restructuring of the code. One useful way of assessing this is to see whether the Bolshevik beliefs described in the *Study* can be subsumed under the various philosophical and instrumen-

22. This point has been emphasized particularly in the writings of Charles E. Lindblom. See also March and Simon, *op. cit.*, pp. 139, 151.

tal questions we have formulated. We need deal only summarily with Leites' study for this purpose; we shall ignore those dimensions of his multifaceted study that do not constitute the operational code *per se* but comprise related questions concerning the "Bolshevik character," the social-psychological origins of the Bolshevik belief system, and the underlying psychodynamic processes about which Leites speculated.

III. The Philosophical Content of an Operational Code

1. *What is the "essential" nature of political life? Is the political universe essentially one of harmony or conflict? What is the fundamental character of one's political opponents?*[23]

A political actor's belief system about the nature of politics is shaped particularly by his orientation to other political actors. Most important of these are one's opponents. The way in which they are perceived — the characteristics the political actor attributes to his opponents — exercises a subtle influence on many other philosophical and instrumental beliefs in his operational code.[24] In the classical Bolshevik belief system the "image of the opponent" was perhaps the cornerstone on which much of the rest of their approach to politics was based. The old Bolsheviks perceived the capitalist opponent as thoroughly hostile at bottom, whatever facade he might display, and possessed of great shrewdness and determination to annihilate his class opponent.

Accordingly, for the old Bolsheviks the political universe was one of acute conflict. The fundamental question of politics and history, as formulated by the Bolsheviks, was "who [will destroy] whom?" This conflict between Communists and their class enemies was viewed as fundamental and irreconcilable. It was not attributable to particular historical personages but sprang from the "objective" historical conditions described by Marxist dialectics.

Consistent with these views was another Bolshevik belief regarding the instability of any "intermediate" historical position between being annihilated or achieving world hegemony. So long as the Bolsheviks had not yet achieved world hegemony, the danger of being annihilated by the enemy would remain an ever-present one.

Other answers to the first question posed here are possible and have been given by different elites. For example, the traditional "idealist" conception of international affairs postulates a fundamental harmony of interests among peoples and nations that is only temporarily disrupted because of the wickedness or weakness of certain individuals and the lack of adequate institutions, a view with which "realists" have increasingly taken issue.[25]

---

23. The summary presented here is drawn from *Study,* pp. 27 – 30 ("Politics Is a War") and pp. 429 – 41 ("Who-Whom?").

24. For this reason, it is of particular interest that in his more recent work Leites has found indications of an amelioration in the Soviet leaders' image of their opponent. (See below.)

25. On this point see, for example, Robert E. Osgood, *Ideals and Self-Interest in America's*

It is important to recognize that on this issue as on other elements of the belief system, not all members of a ruling group will necessarily agree; moreover, beliefs can change significantly over a period of time. Thus, in research since the publication of *A Study of Bolshevism* Nathan Leites noted various indications of an important modification in this basic Bolshevik belief which, in turn, has potentially far-reaching implications for the Soviet style of political behavior.

2. *What are the prospects for the eventual realization of one's fundamental political values and aspirations? Can one be optimistic, or must one be pessimistic on this score; and in what respects the one and/or the other?*[26]

The conventional Bolshevik position was optimistic, drawing as it did upon ideological-doctrinal premises regarding the eventual triumph of Communism on a worldwide scale. Yet, it was an optimism tinged with conditional pessimism, that is, an underlying belief that catastrophe could not be excluded and was an ever-present danger. One had to be constantly aware of the possibility of catastrophe and avoid contributing to its actualization by defective calculations and inept political behavior.

3. *Is the political future predictable? In what sense and to what extent?*[27]

The classical Bolshevik position on this issue reflected the strong "determinist" streak in the Marxist view of history; but this view was balanced by strong "indeterminist" conceptions. Thus, the Bolsheviks believed that while the direction and final outcome of the major historical development from capitalism to Communism are predictable, nonetheless the rate of this development and its particular paths are not. At many junctures or branch points of historical development, therefore, more than one outcome is "objectively possible."

This general belief has had important implications for the way in which Bolsheviks approached the problem of "action." The passive orientation to action that was logically and psychologically implicit in the "determinist" view of history was counterbalanced by the "indeterminist" conception of the many zig-zags that historical developments could take prior to reaching their predictable final outcome. From an operational standpoint the latter, "indeterminist," component of the belief dominated in that it emphasized the importance of intelligent, well-calculated action as a means of expediting the historical

---

Foreign Relations (Chicago: University of Chicago Press, 1953); and Kenneth Waltz, *Man, the State and War* (New York: Columbia University Press, 1959).

26. The summary which follows draws from *Study,* pp. 404–16 ("The Incessant Danger of Attack," and "The Uncertainty of Survival Before Victory").

27. The summary presented here draws from *Study,* pp. 32, 77–85 ("Unpredictable Aspects of the Future").

process. As a result, the Bolshevik answer to this question encouraged and, when reinforced by the other beliefs already referred to, even drove its adherents towards "voluntarism" and initiative rather than fatalism and passivity.

Elaborating on this philosophical theme, the Bolsheviks believed that "objective conditions" from time to time create certain "opportunities" for the Party to advance its interests at the expense of its opponents. However, it was regarded as not predictable and by no means certain that the Party would succeed in "utilizing" these opportunities for advance and in transforming them into realities.

> 4. *How much "control" or "mastery" can one have over historical develop-
>   ment? What is one's role in "moving" and "shaping" history in the
>   desired direction?*[28]

The classical Bolshevik answer to this question follows from beliefs held with respect to the preceding issues. Thus, in the Bolshevik view, the Party is obliged to seize and utilize any "opportunity" for advance, for men can determine within fairly wide limits the cost and duration of an "inevitable" social change. The answer to this question, therefore, emphasizes the role that dedicated, disciplined, and intelligent political actors can play in "moving" history in the desired direction.

> 5. *What is the role of "chance" in human affairs and in historical develop-
>   ment?*[29]

The classical Bolshevik answer was that all politically important events are explainable by the laws of Marxism-Leninism; therefore, that history can be importantly shaped by "accidental" events is rejected.

Consistent with this general belief was the Politburo's tendency, often noted by Western observers, to perceive connections between events where we see none; to regard unrelated details as symptomatic of major political trends; and to believe there is complicated planning behind events which we know to be fortuitous. Bolshevik thought minimized the role of chance — with all its unsettling implications for their belief system — by distorting the image of the opponent and perceiving him as preternaturally calculating and powerful, which, in turn, had other unsettling implications.

Related to this was the emphatic negative the Bolsheviks gave to the question: Can one "muddle through"?[30] It is not only not possible to "muddle through," they believed, but extremely dangerous to try to do so. Accompanying this was the related belief that there is in every situation just one "correct" line or policy. All other policies or choices of action may result in, or tend to

28. See *Study*, pp. 85 – 92 ("Transforming Opportunities into Realities").
29. See *Study*, pp. 67 – 73 ("The Denial of Accidents").
30. See *Study*, pp. 49, 264 – 68.

lead to, ruin — that is, the "catastrophe" held to be an ever-present possibility, as noted above. In the Bolshevik belief system, moreover, political mistakes were rarely harmless or anything less than acutely dangerous. ("Every small step has to be carefully weighed.")

As the preceding discussion has suggested, these beliefs about the major philosophical issues concerning politics are related to each other. This set of beliefs, in turn, is logically and psychologically related to a set of "instrumental" beliefs that refer more specifically to key aspects of the problem of knowledge and action. What should be stressed before proceeding is that the answers different political leaders or elite groups give to the basic questions implicit in the traditional problem of knowledge and action are affected by their philosophical beliefs about the nature of politics.

IV. The Instrumental Beliefs in an Operational Code

1. *What is the best approach for selecting goals or objectives for political action?*[31]

The classical Bolshevik answer to the question of how best to set one's goals in embarking upon action was influenced by two of the general philosophical beliefs already alluded to: the mixture of determinist and indeterminist conceptions regarding future historical developments and the view of one's role in "moving" history in the right direction. Recall in this connection, too, the general injunction implicit in the Bolshevik answer to the third and fourth of the philosophical beliefs noted earlier, namely that the Party is obliged to seize all "opportunities" that arise for making advances. How, then, did the Bolsheviks orient themselves more specifically to the critical question of determining what one should strive for, and what the goals and objectives of action should be when an "opportunity" to make gains arises?

The classical Bolshevik "answer" (perhaps partly at the preconscious level) was along the following lines:

(a) One should *not* approach the task of setting the objective or goal of political action by trying first to calculate precisely the probability of achieving each of the alternative objectives that might be pursued in a given situation.

(b) Further, one should not limit the objective one strives for in a particular situation to that which, on the basis of such calculations, appears to be quite likely or rather certain of being achieved by the means at one's disposal. (Note here the Bolshevik admonition against the tend-

31. The discussion of this question draws from and freely interprets materials in *Study,* pp. 32, 77 – 92, 47 – 49, 514 – 24.

ency to allow assessments of available means and their presumed limited efficacy unduly to circumscribe and limit the magnitude of the objective or goal to be pursued.)

(c) In setting one's goals, therefore, one must counter tendencies towards an overly conservative approach to political action: a reluctance to push for useful gains against seemingly difficult odds, and the related tendency to "pare down" the goals of action to those that seem highly feasible and likely to be achieved.

(d) Against this conservative approach to calculation of ends-means relationships to politics, the Bolsheviks argued on behalf of a strategy of attempting to optimize or maximize the gains that might be derived in a given situation. (Note here the Bolshevik tendency to reject what has been called the "satisficing" strategy that many other decision-makers often prefer to an "optimizing" one.)[32]

Let us consider now how some of the familiar cognitive limits on rational decision-making are dealt with in support of the preference for an optimizing strategy rather than a more conservative approach. In Bolshevik thinking on this central issue, the problem of uncertain or incomplete knowledge relevant to choice of action is "bounded" in a special way. In behalf of the preferred optimizing approach, the Bolshevik code argues — not unrealistically, it may be said — in the following vein:

(a) Political action often has to begin with incomplete knowledge about possible outcomes; it is action itself and only action that will increase knowledge.

(b) What can be achieved in a particular situation cannot be predicted in advance — it can only become known in the process of "struggle" in which one attempts to get the most out of a situation.

(c) In choosing the goals or objectives of a particular course of action, therefore, one should limit them only by assessing what is "objectively possible" in that situation — that is, not impossible to achieve by intelligent use of resources at one's disposal.

The operative belief, restated, is that in initiating an action the Party must be concerned only with ascertaining that the goals it sets are "objectively possible" (in the general and somewhat vague sense already indicated) — not that they can be achieved with high probability. For what can be achieved cannot be predicted in advance; it depends on the "relationship of forces" which can be known only in the process of "struggle" carried out "to the end."

---

32. On this point see, for example, March and Simon, *op. cit.,* pp. 140 – 41, 169.

What is important, therefore, is that the limited knowledge available to assess the likely consequences of alternative courses of action should not lead the political actor who engages in ends-means calculations to make an overly conservative choice of what to strive for.

Applying these beliefs to the problem of action, the Bolsheviks developed *a special kind of optimizing strategy.* In undertaking an initiative to advance their interests, they often set for themselves not a single objective but a set of graduated objectives. The standard task faced by all decision-makers — namely, that of attempting to reconcile what is desirable with what is thought to be feasible — is not over-determined in this optimizing strategy. Rather, action is oriented in a specific situation to a series of objectives embracing payoffs that are graduated (but perhaps inversely related) in degree of utility and feasibility. The optimizing strategy calls for striving simultaneously for a maximum payoff — even though the probability of achieving it appears to be low — and the more modest payoffs which appear to be less difficult and more probable. There seems to be an implicit assumption that such a strategy not only provides an opportunity to achieve the maximum payoff in a given situation but, should that prove infeasible or emerge as too costly or risky, it will enable one to settle, if necessary, for one of the lesser of the graduated objectives that will constitute the largest payoff that could have been squeezed out of the "opportunity" the situation afforded. The contrast here is with "adventures" where there are no lesser objectives, but only a maximum payoff or a severe loss. (See below.)

Such an optimizing strategy, therefore, is consonant with the general philosophical belief alluded to earlier: namely, that what can be achieved in a particular situation cannot be predicted in advance, that action must begin with incomplete knowledge and a measure of uncertainty regarding possible outcomes, and that it is only through "struggle" that one can find out how much a given "opportunity" to advance will yield.[33]

It should not be assumed that resort to an optimizing strategy of this kind necessarily implies neglect of risk and cost calculations. On the other hand, adherents of this strategy may not give due recognition to the possibility that striving for the maximum possible payoff in a given situation may well entail special costs and risks. Thus, if the optimizing strategy is not correctly perceived as such by the opponent, it may well unduly arouse his sense of danger and mobilize his potential for resistance and counteraction in a way that pursuit of more modest objectives might avoid doing.[34]

---

33. During the course of efforts to assess Soviet intentions in placing missiles in Cuba, Charles Bohlen, a leading U. S. specialist on the Soviet Union, cited one of Lenin's adages which compared national expansion to a bayonet drive: "If you strike steel, pull back; if you strike mush, keep going." Theodore C. Sorensen, *Kennedy* (New York: Harper & Row, 1965), p. 677.

34. For a discussion of the possibility that the Bolshevik tendency to push to the limit led

We shall shortly discuss Bolshevik beliefs about calculation, control, and acceptance of risks. Here we note that the general Bolshevik answer to the question under discussion proclaimed the need for important limits to this preferred optimizing strategy. Thus, the injunction to optimize was "bounded" by the somewhat contradictory maxim: "Avoid adventures." This maxim, or rule of action, conveys several different imperatives:

(a) A generalized injunction not to embark on forward operations against an opponent that are not carefully calculated in advance to exclude complacent overestimates of one's own strength and underestimates of his strength. Complacent miscalculations of this kind reflect a failure to assess properly whether the "objective conditions" permit a responsible effort to make gains of any kind, and, if so, what the range of objectives should be that one can safely pursue in the given situation.

(b) A generalized injunction against undertaking action that has an uncertain chance of yielding any payoff but is coupled, at the same time, with a large risk of severe loss if it fails. Actions to advance one's interests should be avoided when they cannot utilize the optimizing strategy noted above in which graduated objectives and payoffs are pursued. An action is "adventuristic" if it has no lesser objectives and no possibility of lesser payoffs — that is, one for which the expected outcomes are limited to a maximum payoff or a severe loss.

(c) A generalized injunction against permitting one's calculations and choice of action to be dominated by prospects of immediate or short-term gains while ignoring the possibility of the longer-range costs and risks attached to the same action.

We may summarize our discussion of the first instrumental belief in the Bolshevik code as follows: Choose an optimizing strategy that pursues graduated objectives, but "avoid adventures."

The fact that not one but several graduated objectives may serve to orient Soviet action in conflict situations is particularly important in the sphere of world politics. The optimizing strategy that lies behind Soviet initiatives in foreign policy from time to time has evidently complicated the task of Western governments in trying to assess Soviet intentions and to devise appropriate countermeasures. On various occasions in the past, unfamiliarity with this aspect of the Soviet operational code seems to have resulted in unnecessary perplexity, confusion, and alarm in attempts to assess Soviet intentions. Western observers have responded to Soviet initiatives (such as the Berlin blockade

---

to an underestimation of the undesired consequences of such conduct, see Leites, *Study,* pp. 33 – 34, 36 – 37, 39.

of 1948) on the assumption that Soviet leaders were pursuing a single objective.

Equivocal indications of what the Soviets were after were variously interpreted in terms of what "the" Soviet intention really was, as if the Soviets were pursuing only a single objective rather than a set of graduated objectives. Some Western interpretations focused on indications that the Soviets were pursuing an extremely ambitious objective, thus heightening apprehensions regarding the aggressive bent of Soviet policy, the "risks" Soviet leaders were willing to take, and the "danger" of war. Other interpretations focused on indications that the Soviets were pursuing only a quite modest, even "defensive" objective, thus encouraging the belief that the crisis could be quickly and easily terminated if only the Western policies that had "provoked" the Soviets were altered and concessions made to satisfy them.[35]

It is not possible to discuss in detail here the consequences of Western responses based upon misperception of the nature of Soviet optimizing strategy. One might assume that Western responses in such situations would be more effective if based on awareness that the opponent is pursuing a set of graduated objectives ranging from relatively modest to quite ambitious goals, and that he relies heavily on feedback in deciding how far to go. But we must also consider the possibility that Western responses to Soviet initiatives have occasionally been more effective precisely because they focused on the most ambitious gains the Soviets may have had in mind in pursuing this kind of optimizing strategy.

2. *How are the goals of action pursued most effectively?*

The classical Bolshevik answer to this question can be summarized in three maxims: "push to the limit," "engage in pursuit" of an opponent who begins to retreat or make concessions, *but* "know when to stop."[36]

The first part of the answer, "push to the limit," enjoins that maximum energy be exerted to attain the objectives of action. The "struggle" to attain them should not be curtailed prematurely; pressure should be maintained against the opponent even though he doesn't give signs of buckling and even though it seems to stiffen his resistance at first.

The second part of the answer invokes the principle of "pursuit." Once some progress, some weakening of the opponent's position has been achieved, it is imperative not to yield to the temptation of relaxing pressure. When an opponent begins to talk of making some concessions or offers them, it should be recognized that this is a sign of weakness on his part. Additional and

35. In the Cuban missile crisis, U.S. policy-makers at first entertained various theories, partly overlapping and partly divergent, as to Soviet intentions. They seem to have settled on an interpretation that avoided attributing to the Soviet leaders a single motive in favor of a theory that the Soviets expected that the deployment of missiles would give them prospects for a variety of specific gains in foreign policy. See particularly Roger Hilsman, *To Move a Nation* (New York: Doubleday, 1967), pp. 161–65, 201–02; and Sorensen, *op. cit.,* pp. 676–78.

36. See *Study,* pp. 30–34, 505–12, 442–49, 52–53, 514–24.

perhaps major gains can be made by continuing to press the opponent under these circumstances.

Once again, however, the Bolshevik operational code set important limits, though of a generalized character, to the preceding two maxims. These limits are, characteristically, embodied in a general injunction, "know when to stop," which is directed against the psychological danger of being carried away by one's success to the point of failing to calculate soberly and rationally the costs and risks of continuing efforts to press forward. Once again, a general injunction of this type lacks operational content; it does not suggest how the maxim is to be applied meaningfully in specific situations; but it is presumably a valuable part of the cognitive and affective makeup of a good Bolshevik.

It has been of considerable value on occasion to Western leaders to understand that their Soviet counterparts structure the problem of action with a set of beliefs and maxims that seem to contradict or, rather, oppose one another. There is, as a result, what might be called a "tension of opposites" in their cognitive structuring of the problem of action. We saw this already in the beliefs held with respect to the first of the instrumental issues: attempt to optimize gains, but don't engage in "adventures." And we see it again here with reference to the second instrumental issue: "push to the limit" and "pursue" a retreating opponent, but "know when to stop."[37]

Another "tension of opposites" may be discussed at this point that applies to situations in which a Bolshevik leader feels himself put on the defensive by some action of the opponent. The maxims which "bound" this problem of action and create a tension are "resist from the start" any encroachment by the opponent, no matter how slight it appears to be; *but* "don't yield to enemy provocations" and "retreat before superior force."[38]

"Yielding" to an opponent is so worrisome a danger in the classical Bolshevik code (and, presumably, so anxiety-arousing a fantasy in the old Bolshevik psyche) that it gave rise to a strong injunction to be ultra-sensitive to encroachments of any kind. No matter how trivial they seem, the opponent's encroachments are to be opposed because failure to "resist from the start" may encourage him to step up his attack. (This is related to fears associated with the second of the philosophical beliefs in which ideological/doctrinal optimism regarding the final triumph of Communism is mixed with a certain pessimism, that is, an underlying belief that nonetheless catastrophe and major setbacks cannot be excluded.)

3. *How are the risks of political action calculated, controlled, and accepted?*

The Bolsheviks' answer to this question was importantly influenced by their experience in struggling against vastly stronger, dangerous opponents — first

---

37. A similar "tension of opposites" has been noted in the Chinese Communist approach to the problem of strategy and action. See Tang Tsou and Morton H. Halperin, *op. cit.*, p. 89.

38. For a discussion of these maxims, see *Study*, pp. 55 – 57, 449 – 61, 46 – 47, 57 – 60, 475 – 503. See also N. Leites, *Kremlin Thoughts: Yielding, Rebuffing, Provoking, Retreating*, The RAND Corporation, RM-3618-ISA (May, 1963).

the Tsarist government and then, after the revolution, the leading capitalist powers. If we recall the Bolshevik answer to the earlier question on choosing one's objectives in embarking in political action, the present question can be reformulated as follows: *How does one pursue an optimizing strategy while at the same time knowing how to calculate and control its risks?*

(a) The Bolsheviks recognized that it was of course possible, in principle, to "provoke" a strong opponent into a major attack designed to crush the Bolshevik party (or, later, the Soviet Union). Behavior that might have this effect upon the opponent, therefore, was to be avoided. Nonetheless, it was believed that considerable scope was left short of this for lesser, well-calculated efforts to advance at the stronger opponent's expense. The opponent, it was believed, would be deterred by various constraints from lashing back in an effort to crush the Bolsheviks. The opponent's evaluation of his overall self-interest would keep him from translating his basic hostility — always present — into an operational plan for liquidating the Bolshevik party (and, later, the Soviet Union).

(b) It is often safe to pursue even quite major objectives at the expense of a stronger opponent (as in the Berlin blockade of 1948 – 1949 and in the Cuban missile crisis). In the Soviet view, the risks of offensive actions of this kind can often be controlled by *limiting the means* they employ on behalf of their ambitious objectives. In the Soviet view, it is possible to pursue quite large gains at an enemy's expense in this fashion without triggering a strong, undesired reaction.

We digress briefly at this point to take note of an important difference that often characterized Soviet and U.S. approaches to the calculation and acceptance of risks during the period of the Cold War. The question of how to keep conflicts between them safely limited was answered somewhat differently in the "limitations" theories of the two sides. The U.S. theory, strongly reinforced by our reading of the lessons of the Korean War, has been that a limitation on one's objectives is essential to keep limited conflicts from expanding dangerously.[39] This seemed to be borne out by the consequences — that is, Chinese Communist intervention — of our failure to keep the U.S. objective limited in the Korean War. After defeating the North Koreans we enlarged our war aims to include unification of North Korea and South Korea by force of arms, which triggered the Chinese Communist intervention.

The Soviet theory of limitations, on the other hand, holds that it is often

39. See, for example, R. E. Osgood, *Limited War* (Chicago: University of Chicago Press, 1957); W. W. Kaufmann, "Limited Warfare," in Kaufmann (ed.), *Military Policy and National Security* (Princeton: Princeton University Press, 1956); Morton H. Halperin, *Limited War in the Nuclear Age* (New York: John Wiley, 1963).

safe to pursue even large, far-reaching objectives in limited conflicts without immediate danger or undue risk of their expanding. What is critical in the Soviet view is not so much the limitation of one's objectives but rather limitation of the means one employs on their behalf. (Examples of this theory of limitations are Soviet behavior in the Berlin blockade and Chinese behavior in the Quemoy crisis of 1958. In both cases far-reaching objectives were evidently among those being pursued, but the risks of doing so were controlled by limiting the means employed against the two Western outposts.)

(c) It is a Soviet belief that the fact that risks of high magnitude are in some sense present in a conflict situation — e.g., the danger of war between the Soviet Union and the United States — is less important than (1) whether that undesired consequence is immediately at hand or at some remove in time, and (2) whether the Soviet leaders believe themselves able to control the intermediate events of the sequence that could result in war. Soviet leaders have displayed considerable confidence in their ability to control and avoid quite unacceptable, more distant risks in this way. Their approach to risk calculation is often more sophisticated than that of Western leaders in that Soviet leaders distinguish not only the magnitude of risks but also between risks that are immediate and those which are more remote.

Hence Soviet leaders believe, and often act on the premise, that in a struggle to make important gains one can accept seemingly high risks so long as the undesired event is several steps removed in a possible temporal sequence and so long as, in addition, they believe they can control the sequence of events leading to it. In a number of cases (the North Korean attack on South Korea, some of the Berlin crises, the Cuban missile crisis) the Soviets acted in ways that seemed to indicate to Western leaders and publics that Soviet leaders were prepared to risk and indeed were risking general war. The risk of general war, however, was in fact several steps removed; and Soviet leaders could well believe that they retained the possibility of calling off the crisis or redirecting it into safer channels, if necessary.

In other words, Soviet leaders do not settle for a single probability estimate of unwanted risks that may develop in the future; rather, they attempt to subject such estimates of probability to sequential analysis. We may contrast this style of risk calculation with the tendency of Western leaders and publics to blur the time component of the different risks created by a Soviet initiative, or by their own actions, a tendency which disposes Westerners in some situations to magnify their estimates of the prevailing risks and to greater conservatism in risk acceptance.

In this respect, therefore, as in others previously noted, Soviet and U.S. approaches to risk calculation and risk acceptance have often differed. Soviet understanding of the ways in which undesired risks could be calculated and controlled often constituted an advantage. As for Western leaders and publics, their tendency to perceive and interpret Soviet risk acceptance behavior erroneously from the standpoint of their own approach to risk calculation inclined them to make distorted judgments regarding Soviet intentions and the riskiness and significance of Soviet Cold War initiatives. (One may note briefly that, over time, Western leaders have perhaps come to understand better the Soviet approach to risk calculation and risk acceptance.)

4. *What is the best "timing" of action to advance one's interest?*[40]

Once again the Bolshevik answer displays a tendency to state the matter in terms of opposites (excluding middle positions). Thus, the Bolshevik code says, somewhat enigmatically or tritely: "There must be neither procrastination nor precipitate action." The Party must be able to bide its time indefinitely, if need be. But it is forbidden to defer an advance that is feasible now (even though difficult) in the necessarily uncertain expectation that advance would be easier at some later date. Action, therefore, tends to be either required or impermissible; there is nothing in between.

5. *What is the utility and role of different means for advancing one's interests?*

Of a number of Bolshevik views about the utility of different means, mention will be made here of one that has been rather unfamiliar to Westerners and is perhaps more idiosyncratic than other Bolshevik beliefs about means. This is the belief that in order to deter a powerful enemy "it often pays to be rude."[41] Rude and even violent language, which may or may not be accompanied by small damaging actions, is expected to serve this purpose by heightening the opponent's estimates of one's strength and determination and/or by weakening the mass support for his policies. The tactic of rudeness was believed to be not overly risky because, in Bolshevik thought, a "serious" powerful opponent is expected not to allow himself to become emotionally aroused by such tactics.

V. Changes in the Belief System

Even a belief system that reflects well-considered evaluations of past political experience is subject to change under certain conditions. Resistance to chang-

40. See *Study,* p. 34.
41. See *Study,* pp. 34–42.

ing beliefs may be accentuated by personality rigidities, which may be greater in some members of a ruling group than in others; but a variety of other factors may be operative.

Some political elites have a pronounced tendency to perceive and to deal with present problems in the light of authoritative diagnoses they have made of past experiences. They attach considerable importance to making correct diagnoses of past events which, they feel, provide usable "lessons" of history in the form of models and precedents. The tendency to approach calculation of present policy in this manner is particularly pronounced in radically oriented elites, such as the Marxists, who claim to have a special understanding of history and historical development. As a result, a body of general beliefs develops about the nature of political conflict and basically correct or incorrect approaches to dealing with opponents that takes on a doctrinal character. Special precautions may be taken to safeguard the content of such beliefs from arbitrary, unauthorized changes. Beliefs about politics, then, become part of the sacred political culture of the elite that is systematically transmitted to new leaders. Change in such an elite's belief system, then, does not follow simply from the fact that the composition of the top leadership changes.

As noted earlier, indications are available that some changes in important elements of the classical Bolshevik operational code took place or became noticeable in the Khrushchev era. I believe that the restructuring and synthesis in this paper of the major elements of this kind of belief system facilitates inquiry into the possibility of changes in its content and of their implications. Thus, as was suggested earlier, the first philosophical belief in our list appears to be of critical importance in shaping the character of the belief system as a whole and in regulating its impact on the actor's political behavior. Particularly close attention should be given, therefore, to possible shifts in the political actor's image of his opponent and, related to this, his view of the fundamental nature of political conflict.[42]

Let us look briefly now at Leites' more recent research on the Soviet elite from this standpoint. Leites studied statements by Khrushchev and other contemporary Soviet leaders in order to establish whether they held the same set of beliefs regarding the nature of political conflict and the same image of the opponent as Lenin and Stalin had earlier held. He noted various indications that a somewhat more moderate view had emerged of the basic "who-whom" problem that Lenin had so starkly formulated (see p. 174 above), and that the

---

42. This would appear to apply also to the Chinese Communist leadership. (See the forthcoming report by Robert C. North on the Stanford University conference which considered the feasibility of research on the Chinese politburo.) Among those scholars who have examined the problem of evaluating and changing beliefs about the opponent are Morton Deutsch, William Gamson, Andréa Modigliani, John Kautsky, Charles E. Osgood, Amitai Etzioni, Ralph K. White, Milton Rokeach, and Joseph deRivera.

related fear of annihilation had softened. The hypothesis of a change in these beliefs was stated cautiously by Leites.

> When one strikes a balance . . . it would seem that Bolshevik fears of annihilation have declined, which presumably decreases the urgency of total victory as an antidote against extinction.[43]

Such change would be of considerable significance since, as Leites noted, the aggressiveness and expansionist drive in the older variant of Bolshevism had probably been motivated to a significant extent by this basic view of the nature of political conflict and the related fear of annihilation.[44]

If this fundamental belief was attenuated over time, one would expect that such a change would influence other components of the belief system as well. Leites found indications that this was the case. Examining evidence bearing on the question: "Are They Relaxing?" Leites concluded, again cautiously: "Despite the Cuban affair, it cannot be excluded that they are relaxing, to some limited extent."[45] Posing another question: "Are They Mellowing?" and reviewing relevant statements by Khrushchev and other leaders, Leites concluded:

> Thus it would seem that the Bolshevik fear of yielding has, after all, declined, and the insistence on "utilizing possibilities" weakened. . . . contemporary Soviet leaders probably feel less constrained to push forward into any possible accessible space without regard for delayed and indirect consequences. They may even have gained for themselves some slight liberty to concede without an immediate concession in return.[46]

We turn briefly now to the task of accounting for an amelioration in elements of the older Bolshevik belief system. This task is admittedly formidable; the following remarks are by no means intended as an authoritative explanation. Any effort to explain such a change should probably consider several factors and the interactions among them. Changes in top Soviet leadership following Stalin's death in 1953 were undoubtedly of great importance. As Leites noted, Stalin had bent some of the Bolshevik beliefs of Lenin's time in a harsher direction. Even before the accentuation of Stalin's paranoid tendencies in his later years, idiosyncratic elements of his personality had probably rendered his adherence to the Bolshevik belief system relatively impervious to reality-testing.[47] Khrushchev's mind was apparently less "closed" in this respect than Stalin's; he was more receptive to recognizing relevant experi-

43. *Kremlin Moods,* The RAND Corporation, RM-3535-ISA (January, 1964), p. 126.
44. *Ibid.,* p. 91.
45. *Ibid.,* pp. 164 – 66.
46. *Ibid.,* p. 211.
47. The importance of Stalin's personality for his political behavior has been emphasized particularly by Robert Tucker. See his "The Dictator and Totalitarianism," *World Politics* (July, 1965), and his earlier analysis, "Stalinism and the World Conflict," *Journal of International Affairs,* VIII, No. 1 (1954).

ences and historical changes as being in some sense "critical tests" of basic components of the belief system, and also more capable of cautiously modifying some of these beliefs.

While the difference between Stalin's and Khrushchev's personalities was perhaps critical in this respect, other factors also must be taken into account. The growth of Soviet power may have contributed to Khrushchev's reassessment of the "danger of annihilation." Perhaps of greater importance was the fact that historical experience demonstrated, more during Khrushchev's rule than in Stalin's, that perhaps after all the United States would not engage in an unprovoked war with the Soviet Union. U.S. leaders had not only failed to wage preventive war while the Soviet Union was weak in the immediate post-World War II period, they also seemed prepared to allow it to approach parity with the United States. Well might these historic developments encourage post-Stalin leaders to alter somewhat the earlier image of the U.S. elite as an overwhelmingly hostile, shrewd, determined opponent and to permit themselves to feel a somewhat greater sense of security.[48]

In accounting for changes in the Soviet belief system, therefore, it appears necessary to give weight not only to changes in personality variables but also to the impact of significant historical developments. In addition to those already mentioned, reference should be made to events such as the emergence of greater independence and conflict within the international Communist movement after Stalin's death. It is probably the case that changes in top leadership made it easier to reconsider older beliefs in the light of new developments.

Changes in the belief system that manifested themselves during Khrushchev's period are indeed of considerable significance for world politics. But it is necessary to note that they evidently constituted modifications of the classical Bolshevik belief system, not its abandonment or radical transformation. There remained substantial elements of continuity with the past in the belief system and political culture of post-Stalin Soviet leadership.[49]

VI. Conclusion

This paper has formulated and illustrated the set of beliefs about basic issues concerning the nature of politics and political action that have been heretofore

48. Interestingly, Khrushchev's period also saw the emergence of a less favorable image of the United States as an opponent. There was both less idealization of, and less respect for, the U.S. elite than in the old Bolshevik view. This historic class enemy was not perceived as an "aging," "declining" elite, one which was weaker, less intelligent, less determined than in the past. The changed characteristics imputed to the United States leadership, however, were seen as making it in some respects possibly more dangerous. (See *Kremlin Moods*, pp. 91 – 126, 1 – 13.)

49. This point was emphasized in Leites' *Kremlin Moods*. There is, in the writer's knowledge, no similar study of further changes in the belief system that may have emerged in the post-Khrushchev era. However, Vernon V. Aspaturian is studying Soviet images of the Kennedy Administration.

implied by the term "operational code." This term is a misnomer in important respects; it should probably be replaced by some other way of referring to these beliefs, such as "approaches to political calculation." I have tried in this paper to codify the general issues and questions around which such a belief system is structured in the hope that it will encourage and facilitate systematic efforts to apply this research approach to a variety of other ruling groups and individual political leaders as well. The possibility emerges of a useful new dimension for comparative studies of different leaders and elite groups.

I have argued in this paper that knowledge of this belief system provides one of the important inputs needed for behavioral analyses of political decision-making and leadership styles. The "operational code" construct does this insofar as it encompasses that aspect of the political actor's perception and structuring of the political world to which he relates, and within which he attempts to operate to advance the interests with which he is identified. This approach should be useful for studying an actor's decision-making "style," and its application in specific situations.

As noted earlier, this paper focuses on the political actor's orientation towards opponents (domestic and international) rather than towards other types of political actors. I believe this focus is justified; a belief system about politics is influenced particularly by the actor's assumptions about the nature of political conflict and by his image of opponents.

Of course, the image of the opponent may play a less central and a somewhat different role in the belief systems of elites who do not attribute (as did the Bolsheviks) an irreconcilable hostility to their political enemies. When political opponents are perceived as limited (and perhaps temporary) adversaries, important consequences may be expected to follow for other elements in the belief system. Particularly in such cases is it desirable to supplement attention to the actor's image of the opponent with observations about his orientation towards political friends and followers.

There remain, of course, important questions concerning data and methods to be employed for research directed towards constructing a political actor's belief system about politics. These problems are not considered here; I would suggest here merely that questions of data and methods be approached in an eclectic and pragmatic spirit. Even provisional answers to the research questions encompassed by the operational code are likely to be useful. Opportunities for research of this kind vary considerably, depending on the particular leaders or elite groups that happen to be of interest. Different research methods may be employed for using materials that are already available and, when opportunities permit, for acquiring new data more systematically. Data relevant to the operational code may be obtained from various kinds of content analysis — both via qualitative analysis of texts (as in Leites' study) or more rigorous quantitative analysis (as by Professor Ole Holsti in his study of John

Foster Dulles' image of the Soviet opponent).[50] Similarly, when interviewing is possible, several variants of open-ended, in-depth, or structured interview techniques might be employed. Useful data and inferences on these matters are likely to be obtained also by those who have opportunities to engage in "participant observation," whether as researchers, political journalists, or political participants. Finally, inferences about various aspects of an actor's operational code are possible from case studies of his behavior in particular situations.[51]

50. Ole Holsti, "Cognitive Dynamics and Images of the Enemy," in D. J. Finlay, O. R. Holsti, and R. R. Fagen, *Enemies in Politics* (Chicago: Rand McNally, 1967).

51. For example, Arnold Horelick, "The Cuban Missile Crisis: Analysis of Soviet Calculations and Behavior" (see Chapter 21 below).

ELEVEN

RITA M. KELLY AND
FREDERIC J. FLERON, JR.

Personality, Behavior, and Communist Ideology*

Ever since Western scholars have been trying to analyze the political behavior of Communist leaders, they have felt compelled to present some answer to the question: in what ways does the official ideological system affect the actions and decisions of these leaders? After fifty years of Communist rule in the Soviet Union, however, there is no one consistent answer. Confusion and contradiction still reign.[1] In the literature on the subject one finds that the position a scholar takes is very often related to his particular field of specialization. For example, if one has an anthropological or psychoanalytic bent, then one tends to follow the point of view advocated by Dicks and Leites. The ideology fulfills important functions for the maintenance of the leader's ego and, hence, the official ideology is a strong, dominant motivating force, not easily subject to

*This chapter is an expanded version of an article which appeared under the same title in *Soviet Studies,* XXI, 3 (January, 1970), pp. 297 – 313. Reprinted by permission of the authors and the publisher. Copyright © 1970 by Rita M. Kelly and Frederic J. Fleron, Jr.

1. The best summary of the many different theories which attempt to interpret and explain what determines Soviet political behavior is still Daniel Bell's "Ten Theories in Search of Reality: The Prediction of Soviet Behavior," *World Politics,* X, 3 (April, 1958), pp. 327 – 365. Cf. William Glaser, "Theories of Soviet Foreign Policy: A Classification of the Literature," *World Affairs Quarterly,* XXVII, 2 (July, 1956). A collection of articles which quickly illustrates that the debate has ranged from a complete denial of any motivational impact of ideology to views verging toward ideological determinism is the Hunt-Sharp-Lowenthal symposium reprinted above from *Problems of Communism.*

change.[2] Political scientists, although they vary considerably, tend to take a more pragmatic and cynical point of view. Avid Kremlinologists generally discount the official ideology as a major motivating force and concentrate on "who is doing-in whom." To many of them ideology is almost entirely a polemical and political weapon or a useful opium for the masses.[3] A geopolitical theorist tends to claim that traditional national and strategic interests constitute the main motivating force for behavior. Ideology is only added verbiage justifying what the leaders would do in any case.[4] Historians emphasize the similarity between contemporary behavior and the traditional Slavic character and institutions, saying the latter determine most of Soviet behavioral patterns.[5] The social psychologists and sociologists seem to take a more intermediate position, i.e., ideology is sometimes only a polemical tool and at other times a major determinant of how the Soviets think and act.[6]

Rigid compartmentalization of inquiry, whether by academic discipline or geographic area, greatly hampers the construction of empirical theory. Without such theory, we are unable either to explain or to predict phenomena.

2. See Henry V. Dicks, "Observations on Contemporary Russian Behavior," *Human Relations,* V, 2 (1952), pp. 111 – 175, and Nathan Leites, *A Study of Bolshevism* (Glencoe, Ill.: Free Press, 1953). Jan Triska, Zbigniew Brzezinski, and others have held similar positions, even though they are not anthropologists or psychoanalysts by training. See Triska's article, "A Model for Study of Soviet Foreign Policy," in *The American Political Science Review,* LII, 2 (March, 1958), pp. 64 – 83, and just about any of Brzezinski's articles and books.

3. Examples of Kremlinologists who seem to incline toward this view are Myron Rush, *The Rise of Khrushchev* (Washington, D. C.: Public Affairs Press, 1958), and R. Conquest, *Power and Policy in the USSR: The Study of Soviet Dynastics* (New York: St. Martin's Press, 1961). Cf. also Conquest, *The Politics of Ideas in the USSR* (New York: Praeger, 1967).

4. The clearest spokesman for the position has been Samuel Sharp. See "National Interest: Key to Soviet Politics," Chapter 7 above. Barrington Moore, Jr., in "The Relations of Ideology and Foreign Policy," *Soviet Politics: The Dilemma of Power* (Cambridge: Harvard University Press, 1950), takes a similar but more qualified position. While the ideology did not force the Soviet Union to join or abandon any alliance that it would not have joined or abandoned simply on the basis of national interest, in some cases it slowed or speeded up the process.

5. Scholars who have represented this group include Nicholas Berdyaev, Sir Bernard Pares, Sir John Maynard, Edward Crankshaw, Ernest Simmons, and Cyril E. Black. A good but brief illustration of how present-day historians tend to view the problem is found in Black, "The Modernization of Russian Society," *The Transformation of Russian Society* (Cambridge: Harvard University Press, 1960), pp. 661 – 680.

6. See Raymond A. Bauer, Alex Inkeles, and Clyde Kluckhohn, *How the Soviet System Works* (Cambridge: Harvard University Press, 1956), pp. 29 – 35. Though sociologists tend to be more moderate in the positions they hold with regard to how ideology influences political behavior, a great deal of diversity exists about the question of how ideology influences scientists. For a view which asserts that science and ideology are bound to oppose each other, see Bell's "The End of Ideology in the Soviet Union?" in Milorad M. Drachkovitch (ed.), *Marxist Ideology in the Contemporary World* (New York: Praeger, 1966), pp. 76 – 112. For the opposite position see George Fischer's article "Sociology," in George Fischer (ed.), *Science and Ideology in Soviet Society* (New York: Atherton Press, 1967). Those interested in this issue of how science and ideology are related should also consult David Joravsky, "Soviet Ideology," *Soviet Studies,* XVIII, 1 (July, 1966), pp. 2 – 19; "Ideology, Science and the Party," *Problems of Communism,* XVI, 1 (January-February, 1967), pp. 67 – 75; *The Lysenko Affair* (Cambridge: Harvard University Press, 1970).

Previous discussions of the motivational role of ideology in Communist systems illustrate some of the factors contributing to such an outcome. The question of the relationship between Communist ideology and Communist behavior has been discussed in isolation from more general empirical theory. Most students of Communist ideology and behavior have tended to view the relationship between *Communist* thought and action as a unique problem.[7] However, any discussion of the motivational role of *Communist* ideology is merely part of the more general question of the motivational role of ideology in determining or at least influencing behavior in any political system. Therefore, research done on the more general question must be relevant to the specific question.

But there has been felt, in the United States in particular, a special urgency about answering the question of what behavioral consequences the Communist ideology has. This demand for immediate answers has contributed to a tendency to proceed to generalizations about Communist ideology after examining only the available empirical data on Communist systems, and without undertaking the more arduous (but certainly more fruitful) task of studying the motivational role of Communist ideology in the context of general empirical theory. The pronounced policy science orientation of Communist studies in the United States has had serious effects on both the questions asked about ideology in Communist systems and the answers given to those questions. The position taken seems to be: "If we are to be relevant as Soviet or Communist 'experts,' we have to be able to give some immediate answer concerning the motivational role of ideology in Communist systems because, whatever the answer, it has critical implications for U.S. policy decisions." For one reason or another, Communist ideology is viewed as a relevant variable in this context and must be taken into account by American policy-makers. So every Communist "specialist" has an answer to this vital question of the motivational role of Communist ideology and seeks to justify it usually by pointing to certain actions in the past which conformed to his interpretation of the motivational role of Communist ideology. Most frequently these interpretations have been based on very scanty, impressionistic data. Relatively few attempts have been made to apply our rich variety of reliable contemporary research techniques to systematically collected data. The frequently heard argument is that the research methods and techniques of modern social and behavioral science cannot be systematically applied to the study of Communist systems because we do not have open access to those systems. Although this is often true, there are many areas which have been left unexplored despite the availability of techniques which would permit us to analyze available data relevant to the

---

7. . For example, see P. B. Reddaway, "Aspects of Ideological Belief in the Soviet Union," *Soviet Studies*, XVII, 4 (April, 1966), p. 472.

testing of basic propositions from empirical theory. The recent study by Triska and Finley is an excellent example of innovation in this regard.[8]

What follows is based on our conviction that scarcity of data concerning relevant variables does not justify sloppy methodology or exclusion of relevant variables. Inaccessibility of data is a frustrating problem, but it is a pragmatic, technical one. It is not a legitimate excuse for lowering standards for the evaluation of empirical research. Further, the absence of available data on relevant variables does not make those variables any less relevant; it merely means that we ought to be more cautious in our conclusions and more re-strained in our prognostications to policy-makers. The purpose of this chapter is to discuss some variables which psychological theory suggests are relevant to the relationship between ideology and behavior, but which have been gener-ally absent in previous discussions of the motivational impact of Communist ideology on Communist behavior.

Problems of Conceptualization

Unfortunately, as Nathan Glazer has observed, one of the pressing conceptual problems of social psychology is that "no study of the relation between atti-tudes and personality has yet . . . solved the problem of distinguishing ideology — the views one picks up — from character — the orientations that are basic to a person.[9] This statement refers to the fact that very few individuals in a society will have a belief and value system that coincides exactly with that of the official ideological system, and that many of the variables relating to why such a divergence exists involve the specific personality traits and personality processes of each individual. Although the conceptual problem is still not satisfactorily resolved in the eyes of most psychologists, progress has been made in establishing a framework for what variables and distinctions must be considered in attempts to relate a formal ideology to an individual's or a group's ideology.

In an attempt to clarify the relationship of an ideological system to an individual, Milton Rokeach introduced the concept of "belief-disbelief sys-tem." In his discussion of this concept he points out that as the term "belief-disbelief system" is applied to individuals and to groups, it necessarily must include "*all* of a person's beliefs and therefore is meant to be more inclusive than what is normally meant by ideology. Ideology refers to a more or less institutionalized set of beliefs — 'The beliefs someone picks up.' Belief-disbelief systems contain these too but, in addition, they contain highly personalized pre-ideological beliefs."[10]

8. Jan F. Triska and David D. Finley, *Soviet Foreign Policy* (New York: Macmillan, 1968).
9. Nathan Glazer, "New Light on the Authoritarian Personality," *Commentary,* XVII (March, 1954), p. 293.
10. Milton Rokeach, *The Open and Closed Mind* (New York: Basic Books, 1960), p. 35. For

Since ideological beliefs constitute much less than the total belief-disbelief system of an individual or a group, it obviously is grossly insufficient to study only the content and structure of the ideological system when one is looking for determinants of human behavior. One must first and foremost look at the content and structure of the individual's entire belief system.

When looking at the belief system of an individual or group, one must be as concerned about the various content levels within that belief system. One way the former distinctions can be made is by presenting a broad definition of beliefs that allows the notion of hierarchy to be built into it. One group of scholars has proposed that beliefs be generally defined as follows: beliefs "are existential propositions held by individual human beings regarding the structure and operation of the social and physical universe and one's place in it. . ." They are "vectors which bear upon an individual as he confronts a choice of conduct." Within the context of this broad definition, they suggest that four distinctions be made:

1. *Cognitive Standards:* the existential propositions which serve as criteria to establish the validity and/or the applicability of information and are not themselves subject to ultimate verification.

2. *Appreciative Standards:* existential propositions which serve as criteria to evaluate the potential results of an act particularly in reference to its gratificatory significance.

3. *Knowledge:* an existential proposition than an individual accepts as established fact which is subject to further empirical verification.

4. *Power:* an existential proposition regarding man's perception of his relative capacity to influence and/or control the structure and operation of the social and physical world.[11]

These four subdefinitions of beliefs are given because they provide not only useful distinctions for the study of belief-disbelief systems in general (and of Communist ideologies in particular) but also because they introduce the notion of content hierarchy within belief systems. An examination of the four subdefinitions should suggest, for example, that those elements of a belief system or ideology that fall in the categories of (4) *Power* and (3) *Knowledge* would be much more susceptible to change through scientific discovery and changing circumstances over time than (1) *Cognitive Standards* and (2) *Appreciative Standards*. It is also a feasible and testable hypothesis that Appreciative

---

a more recent discussion of the relationship between ideology and belief systems, see Samuel H. Barnes, "Ideology and the Organization of Conflict: On the Relationship between Political Thought and Behavior," *Journal of Politics*, XXVIII, 3 (August, 1966), pp. 513–530.

11. Philip E. Jacob and James J. Flink, "Values and Their Function in Decision-Making," *The American Behavioral Scientist*, V, Supplement No. 9 (May, 1962), p. 23.

Standards will change before Cognitive Standards will change. Hence, if one could identify in either an individual's or a group's belief system (or in the Marxian ideological system) those aspects which would fall in which of the above categories, then one could proceed to the formulation and testing of hypotheses regarding them. In addition, one could hypothesize which elements of the belief system in Marxian ideology are set for individuals and groups by *(a)* the socialization process during childhood, *(b)* educational and higher vocational training, *(c)* indoctrination of Party doctrine, *(d)* the role individuals perform in society, or *(e)* any other variable considered relevant. As will be shown below, all these variables plus many others help to determine what an individual's, or a group's, or a nation's operative ideology will be.

Once the distinctions in terms of content are understood, one can further try to determine the consistency with which an individual holds specific beliefs at each structural level of the belief-disbelief system. This endeavor can be accomplished by evaluating whether that belief fits into the structure of the individual's belief system at (1) the specific opinionation level, (2) the habitual opinionation level, (3) the attitudinal level, or (4) the ideological level. If beliefs are held at the specific opinionation level, it means that they "are not related in any way to other opinions, . . . are not in any way characteristic of a person who makes them, . . . and are not reproducible in the sense that if the same or a similar question were asked again under different circumstances, the answer might be different."[12] In other words, such opinions would not be very likely to influence behavior. If they did, they would do so in a random, inconsistent fashion.

The chief characteristic of habitual opinions is that they are reproducible and "form a relatively constant part of an individual's make-up. In other words these are opinions which are voiced in the same or a similar manner on different occasions, and which are not subject to sudden arbitrary changes, such as are opinions at the lowest level."[13] At the more general attitudinal level, "we find not only that an individual holds a particular opinion with regard to a particular issue with a certain degree of stability; we also find that he holds concurrently a large number of other opinions on the same issue which in combination define his attitude towards that issue."[14]

Finally, at the most general level are found "ideologies" which Eysenck defines as clusterings of attitudes. Beliefs held at these latter three levels are quite likely to influence behavior, with those at the "ideological" level being the most likely to do so. The higher the level the greater value the individual places on the belief and the larger is his vested interest in the belief.

    12. H. J. Eysenck, *The Psychology of Politics* (London: Routledge & Kegan Paul, 1954), p. 111.
    13. *Ibid.*, pp. 111–112.
    14. *Ibid.*, p. 112.

Although Eysenck's use of the ubiquitous and ambiguous word "ideologies" is unfortunate in the above context, it should not blur the rather obvious point that is being made, which is: no individual can or does hold all beliefs with equal strengths and no person can simultaneously and consistently act on all his beliefs. Specific circumstances, his own physical and mental limitations and those of the system in which he operates, simply make this impossible. Moreover, some beliefs become more internalized and habitual than others, and some are held more dogmatically than others. In terms of trying to answer questions regarding which beliefs are operative and which are most susceptible to change, attention must be directed to this problem of how beliefs are held and structured.

Sources of Personal Ideology

The map on the following pages, created by M. Brewster Smith,[15] provides a paradigm for viewing the many different general classes of variables which can influence personal behavior in general and political behavior in particular. As this map shows, three out of the five broad classes of variables involve variables from the social environment, most of which cannot be controlled by the individual. The least controllable class of variables by far is that involving the distal social antecedents such as the prior history of one's country before one was born and while one was growing up, its existing economic and political system, and other broad social determinants such as the existence of a formal, established ideological system like Marxism-Leninism-Stalinism. All of these "givens" can affect the motivating forces of an individual, but the extent to which they either can or will do so is largely determined by the variables listed under II, i.e., the more immediate social environment as it affects an individual as he is reared, educated, and socialized into the society and its culture.

It is obvious from the vast literature on socialization that the socio-economic status of an individual's family will, in part, determine how a child or even an adult will perceive objective reality.[16] It more often than not will partly determine his opportunities for educational and occupational training which,

---

15. A discussion of the main sections of this map and their connections can be found in M. Brewster Smith, "A Map for the Analysis of Personality and Politics," *Journal of Social Issues,* XXIV, 3 (July, 1968), pp. 15–28. An expanded version of this article appears as "Personality in Politics: A Conceptual Map with Application to the Problem of Political Rationality," in Oliver Garceau (ed.), *Political Research and Political Theory: Essays in Honor of V. O. Key, Jr.* (Cambridge: Harvard University Press, 1968), pp. 77–101, reprinted in M. Brewster Smith, *Social Psychology and Human Values* (Chicago: Aldine Publishing Co., 1969). The other essays in the above issue of *The Journal of Social Issues* are relevant to the present discussion, especially the introductory essay by Fred I. Greenstein, "The Need for Systematic Inquiry into Personality and Politics: Introduction and Overview," pp. 1–14. Cf. also Fred I. Greenstein, *Personality and Politics: Problems of Evidence, Inference, and Conceptualization* (Chicago: Markham Publishing Co., 1969), esp. chapter 2.

16. Two good studies of political socialization are: Herbert H. Hyman, *Political Socialization:*

in turn, will also help to determine how much, and what forms of, the official, formal ideology he (or she) will be exposed to. Obviously, exposure to the formal ideology is a prerequisite to its becoming any sort of a motivational force in behavior. It is true, of course, that most Soviet children are exposed to at least the essential elements of the formal ideology through the school system, the Octobrists, the Pioneers, and the Komsomol organization, but even this exposure does not guarantee that the belief and value systems of the formal ideology will be internalized by the individuals receiving that exposure. It is always possible, and quite likely, that the other socialization experiences and interactions with one's fellow human beings will lead one to internalize and, as an adult, act upon a belief quite different from the one formally taught. For example, while the national or Party ideology may assume that human beings are basically good and perfectable, an individual's early childhood and adult experiences may lead him to believe otherwise. As an adult, he may find it politically necessary and expedient to affirm the official ideological position, but in his decision-making and behavior he will be motivated by his belief based on experience rather than by the stated ideological position.[17]

Figure 1. General Schematic Map*

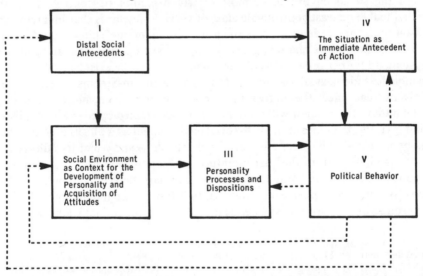

*Adapted from M. Brewster Smith, "A Map for the Analysis of Personality and Politics," *The Journal of Social Issues,* XXIV, 3 (July, 1968), 17. Reprinted by permission of the author and publisher.

A Study in the Psychology of Political Behavior (New York: The Free Press, 1959), and Fred I. Greenstein, *Children and Politics* (New Haven: Yale University Press, 1965).

17. Philip Worchel in "Social Ideology and Reactions to International Events," *Journal of Conflict Resolution,* XI, 4 (December, 1967), pp. 414–431, found, for example, that the ideological orientation toward others that a person develops through the socialization process is definitely related to the way one reacts toward alternative resolutions of international conflict situations.

Figure 2. Detailed Schematic Map*

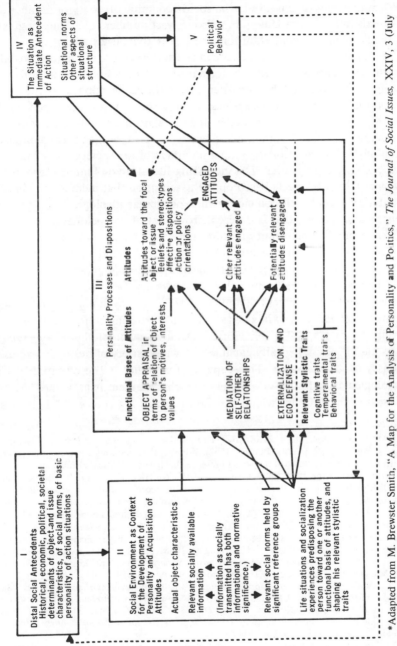

*Adapted from M. Brewster Smith, "A Map for the Analysis of Personality and Politics," *The Journal of Social Issues,* XXIV, 3 (July 1968), p. 25. Reprinted by permission of the author and publisher.

When one considers not only the socio-economic diversity of families and individuals in the Soviet Union, but also its vast numbers of ethnic, linguistic, and religious groups and traditions, one sees that, even among those who become leaders and a part of the elite in the society, there is a high probability that whatever part of the written, formal ideology does become a motivating force for them will not be consistent, and the same applies to the whole decision-making group. Since an individual's personal attitudes, beliefs, and values are often largely determined by the social norms, beliefs, etc., of his peer and reference groups, the amount of diversity in terms of the degree of internalization of the formal ideology among members of the society and of the elite group becomes even greater. The increasing literature on "interest groups" in the Soviet Union is largely based on the assumption that membership in such an "interest group" will coincide with a particular ideological and political emphasis and outlook that is different from that of one belonging to another "interest group."[18] Important questions here, however, are to what extent can the members of an "interest group" be expected to hold similar beliefs, and what scholars should look for in trying to answer this question.[19]

Psychologists generally hold that the diversity and conformity of an individual's beliefs and values are limited by the basic psychological and biological limits of *Homo sapiens* in general. The limits to conformity are determined basically by man's biological nature. "As a member of the *Homo sapiens* species man is physiologically capable of a wide variety of mutually exclusive responses to given stimuli. This capacity for choice is the essential physio-psychological basis for the development of what we identify as 'values,' namely standards of the desirable which men apply in making choices."[20] This means

18. See, for example, the work of Roger Pethybridge, *A Key to Soviet Politics: The Crisis of the Anti-Party Group* (New York: Praeger, 1962). Sidney I. Ploss has found evidence that this split in beliefs and values is reflected in the Soviet press. See his paper, "Political Conflict and the Soviet Press," presented at the 1964 Annual Meeting of the American Political Science Association, Chicago, Illinois, September 1964. For some additional recent research on groups and group values in Soviet politics, see the following: H. Gordon Skilling, "Interest Groups and Communist Politics," *World Politics,* XVIII, 3 (April, 1966), 435–451; Milton Lodge, "Soviet Elite Participatory Attitudes in the Post-Stalin Period," *American Political Science Review,* LXII, 3 (September, 1968), pp. 827–839; Milton Lodge, "'Groupism' in the Post-Stalin Period," in *Midwest Journal of Political Science,* XII, 3 (August, 1968), pp. 330–351; Sidney I. Ploss,"Interest Groups," in Allen Kassof (ed.) *Prospects for Soviet Society* (New York: Praeger, 1968), pp. 76–103; Michael P. Gehlen, "Group Theory and the Study of Soviet Politics," in Sidney I. Ploss (ed.), *The Soviet Political Process: Aims, Techniques, and Examples of Analysis* (Waltham, Mass.: Blaisdell Publishing Co., 1970); Philip D. Stewart, "Soviet Interest Groups and the Policy Process: The Repeal of Production Education," *World Politics,* XXII, 1 (October, 1969), pp. 29–50; H. Gordon Skilling and Franklyn Griffiths (eds.), *Interest Groups in Soviet Politics* (Princeton: Princeton University Press, 1971).

19. For a further discussion of this point along somewhat different lines, see Frederic J. Fleron, Jr., "Representation of Career Types in the Soviet Political Leadership," in R. Barry Farrell (ed.), *Political Leadership in Eastern Europe and the Soviet Union* (Chicago: Aldine Publishing Co., 1970), pp. 108–139.

20. Jacob and Flink, *op. cit.,* p. 13.

that the norms governing the responses of individuals or groups to given stimuli vary widely. Values and beliefs are not, in fact, universally shared phenomena. Individuals deviate from the norm. Moreover, since beliefs and values are learned and, hence, transmitted by one generation to another by socially agreed upon symbols, they are more likely to change than biological phenomena. Communicating an official, ideological system such as Marxism-Leninism-Stalinism can seldom be uniform and precise whether it be from one age group to another, from one occupational or elite group to another, or, as polycentrism has revealed, from one nation to another. In addition, whatever is internalized by the individual or the group is interpreted in terms of his or their own past experiences and is continually reevaluated and changed as a result of new experiences. Consequently, even within "interest groups," a good deal of diversity can and should be expected.

It is, nonetheless, generally true that a great many of the beliefs and values that influence decision-making are determined for an individual by the groups to which he belongs, for the limits of diversity in beliefs and values are of a psychological and sociological nature. Yet, simple membership in a group (including "an interest group") does not seem to be so significant a determination of an individual's beliefs and values as the specific roles he plays in the society. There are a great number of specialized roles in human societies which make individuals dependent and less than self-sufficient and autonomous.

> Each of these specialized roles involves specific rights and obligations on the part of the person to whom they are assigned. These rights and obligations are expectancies held by the person playing the role which, if they are to be adequately filled, must be inculcated in the individual role player as moral imperatives in his socialization into the role. . . . Ultimately, most human norms, especially those which apply to public policy decisions, can be conceived as role expectancies and variations in "value" profiles can be understood as differences in role expectancies.[21]

What this means for students of Communist political systems is that less emphasis should probably be put on studies of "interest groups," defined as broad occupational groupings, and more emphasis should be placed on the types of roles individuals play within such groupings.[22] It also seems to indicate that if one really wants to know what importance ideology has in decision-making in the Soviet Union, one must identify and specify the role expectancies of individuals in various decision-making positions in the Soviet Union.[23] If existential propositions from the ideological belief system and normative

---

21. *Ibid,* p. 14. Cf. Seymour Lieberman, "The Effects of Changes in Roles on the Attitudes of Role Occupants," and Robert K. Merton, "Occupational Roles: Bureaucratic Structure and Personality," in Neil J. and William T. Smelser (eds.), *Personality and Social Systems* (New York: John Wiley & Sons, 1963), pp. 264–279 and 255–263, respectively.

22. For an excellent discussion related to this point, see John Wilson Lewis, "Chinese Communist Party Leadership and the Succession to Mao Tse-tung: An Appraisal of Tensions" (Washington, D.C.: U.S. Department of State, Bureau of Intelligence and Research, Policy Research Study, January 1964), esp. p. 2.

23. Cf. Erik P. Hoffmann, "Role Conflict and Ambiguity in the Communist Party of the

propositions from the ideology constitute an important and integral part of these role expectancies, then the chances are high that these role expectancies are those parts of the ideology that will influence political decision-making.

Ideology and Behavior

In political science, as well as in the field of Communist studies in particular, there is a great tendency to equate values and ideology with supposed purposes of actions or with different outcomes. Following in the tradition of Lasswell and Kaplan in *Power and Society,* [24] many scholars of Communist systems use what can be called a "motive-belief" type of explanation to link ideology, values, or belief systems to political behavior and decision-making. The logic of this type of explanation is something as follows: A desired event — or a goal event — often thought to be set by an ideology is said to be the motive or the cause for a certain action or series of actions. This is very often done when it can be found in a written statement that this or that is part of an action program or this or that is a stated goal and over a period of time this or that actually is fulfilled. In other words it is assumed that "if X values Y, it means that X acts so as to bring about the consumption of Y."[25] At worst, such types of explanation mean: "Y happened, therefore, X must have valued Y."

Unfortunately, the demonstration of such a causal relationship is not so easily accomplished. Psychologists have known for a long time that neither words nor actions are invariably accurate reflections of underlying beliefs, attitudes, or goals. A person's beliefs and attitudes prejudice an issue by determining his *set,* that is, his way of reacting to new facts and experiences. They become *mental habits* which, *if aroused,* determine actions. But since attitudes are intervening variables and must be measured indirectly, to assert that a particular attitude regarding a goal, object, or belief motivated a person, one must be able to link that attitude with his antecedent conditions and

---

Soviet Union," in Roger E. Kanet (ed.), *The Behavioral Revolution and Communist Studies: Applications of Behaviorally-Oriented Political Research on the Soviet Union and Eastern Europe* (New York: Free Press, 1971).

24. Harold Lasswell and Abraham Kaplan, *Power and Society* (New Haven: Yale University Press, 1950).

25. An example of the use of the motive-belief type of explanation in Soviet studies can be found in Myron Rush, *Political Succession in the USSR* (New York: Columbia University Press, 1965), p. 67, where he tries to explain why Khrushchev became the leader of the anti-Malenkov group in 1954-55. For an analysis and criticism of Rush's use of motive-belief explanation, see Frederic J. Fleron, Jr., "Soviet Area Studies and the Social Sciences: Some Methodological Problems in Communist Studies," *Soviet Studies,* XIX, 3 (January, 1968), pp. 336 – 337. (This article is reprinted in Frederic J. Fleron, Jr. [ed.], *Communist Studies and the Social Sciences: Essays on Methodology and Empirical Theory* [Chicago: Rand McNally,, 1969], pp. 1 – 33.) For a more detailed general discussion of motive-belief explanation, see Quentin Gibson, *The Logic of Social Enquiry* (London: Routledge & Kegan Paul, 1960), chapter 4.

consequent behavior. It is not sufficient to study just the verbal statements of attitudes or just the consequent behavior. One must analyze all of the above plus the need level and drives of the individual or of the individuals that compose a group.[26] It is known, for example, that two people can hold the same belief with the same degree of strength and intensity and still behave differently. Obviously, something besides "ideology" is involved even when an individual ostensibly acts as though "ideology is motivating" his behavior.

The use of this motive-belief type of explanation causes other problems as well. At the group level of analysis there is the very real problem of determining empirically whether or not a group actually believes that a stated or written goal, such as the withering away of the state, is an operative one, that is, that it is a goal actually desired and thought possible. If there is such a thing as a group goal, it can only be a composite of the goals of the individuals that constitute the group. It is true that one can speak of a goal as a property of the group without worrying in detail about its origins. However, before one can go further and assert that a particular stated goal is operative, one must determine the extent to which the group members do in fact accept the group goals.

This question of whether or not groups can have properties separate and distinct from the individuals who compose them is one to which scholars of Communist systems should pay more attention. When the issue involves evaluation of an official statement to the effect that the Communist Party represents the "will of the people," even though only one person is generally allowed to run for an office, Western scholars generally follow the principle of Methodological Individualism, that is, they assert the statement is false because there can be no such group characteristic as "will of the people" unless it can be demonstrated that each and every member of the electorate (the people) has had the opportunity to express this individual will in a truly democratic, secret election. In this context, the group property, "will of the people," is said to be dependent upon counting the different "wills" of each person and coming up with a majority. When the issue involves ideology, on the other hand, scholars often disregard the scientific principle of Methodological Individualism. In this context statements such as "the Party believes," or "the army took the position," or the "economic managers acted on the basis of," etc., are often made. Yet here the basic methodological issue is the same. The "will of the people" refers to the beliefs and values of individuals within a group. The operative beliefs and values of the Party, of the army, etc., also refer to the beliefs and values of individuals within these groups. Since all groups are composed of aggregates of individuals, the characteristics or properties of all groups must be dependent upon the characteristics and properties of the individuals who compose them. Hence, group concepts of the behavior

26. Eysenck, *op. cit.*, pp. 238–39.

of groups must refer to the complex patterns of descriptive, empirical relations among individuals.[27]

Whether or not the group as such actually has a particular goal or part of the belief system as an operative basis of reference or action will be a function of a number of things. To go back to Smith's map, it depends, first of all, upon how the individual mediates the "self-other" relationships within his own particular group and his perception of society, as well as his objective position, role, and function in society.

A second circumstance affecting whether or not a goal or belief will become operative for a group is the position of the group itself, its habitual pattern of behavior, and its roles and functions in society.[28] A good illustration of how these variables can mediate the possible impact upon a stated belief or goal is the decision-making situation of an economic manager in the Soviet Union. It has been often asserted that the main reason that the profit motive was not introduced into the Soviet economic system was the ideological belief in the superior value of the Marxian theory of surplus value. While historically this may well be true, it is largely irrelevant to a contemporary discussion of decision-making for most Soviet political and economic leaders. The decisions and responses of an economic manager, for example, would more likely be determined by the habit of conforming to "success indicators" and group norms for managers than they would be by any ideological belief or goal considerations. Even for the planning officials in Gosplan this ideological problem is not an immediate criterion for their decisions. Their goals have already been set for them. Until recently, the vast majority accepted these goals and the supposed rationale behind them without question.[29] The same was probably true even for the Politburo members. The ideological belief only became important for decision-making when economists such as Liberman demonstrated that it had to be questioned in order to enable the economy to perform efficiently, and provided an alternative to it. Once they had demonstrated that the Marxian theory of surplus value was not supported by facts at the knowledge level in the belief system, then the political question arose: do we or do we not accept these findings even though they disprove and reject some of our most basic ideological tenets? An important point must be noted here. Even at this point no part of the written content of the ideology per se becomes the criterion for decision-making! What happens is that some other criteria are used to accept or reject this element of Marxian ideology.

Other circumstances which help to determine whether or not a stated goal or belief will become operative for a group are: (1) the motives of each in-

27. May Brodbeck, "Methodological Individualism: Definition and Reduction," *Philosophy of Science,* XXV, 1 (January, 1958), pp. 1–22.

28. C. N. Cofer and M. H. Appley, *Motivation: Theory and Research* (New York: Wiley, 1963), pp. 779–780.

29. For important discussions of the variables related to density of doctrinal stereotypes, see Triska and Finley, *op. cit.,* pp. 119–127.

dividual for behavior in general; (2) each individual's judgment of the relative positive and negative weights for him of engaging in the activities necessary to achieve the group goal; (3) each individual's subjective estimate of the probability that a group goal can and will be achieved; (4) the clarity of the group goal; and (5) the amount of interdependency and cohesiveness of the group members.[30] Unmentioned still is perhaps the most important consideration — what motivated the individual to accept the goal (or belief) to begin with. An individual's motive for accepting the goal or belief will generally be as influential in determining whether or not it affects his political behavior as the actual goal or belief itself.[31]

Motivation

Psychologists generally assert that motivation for human behavior can be broken down into the following categories: (1) within the human organism itself there exist a variety of internal urges, whims, wishes, feelings, emotions, drives, instincts, wants, desires, demands, purposes, interests, aspirations, needs, and/or "motives"; (2) on the basis of interaction between the organism and its environment there develop incentives, goals, or object values which attract or repel the organism; and (3) there are strictly environmental determinants, e.g., the application of some irresistible force which of necessity leads to a particular response. Categorizing these types of motivation somewhat differently, one finds that some (emotion, force, drive, instinct, need) are at a biological level; others (urge, wish, feeling, impulse, want, striving, desire, demand) have significant "mental" import; and still others (purpose, interest, intention, attitude, aspiration, plan, motive, incentive, goal, value) require interaction with objects or states in the environment.[32] To satisfy any one of these items is, in a sense, to behave in a manner to fulfill a goal or, better, a "need." All are an inherent part of an individual's total personality; and all will at some time or another become the motivation or a part of the motivation for behavior, including political behavior. The question is: when?

One theory of motivation that has recently gained prominence in the discipline of political science is Abraham Maslow's theory of five main categories of human needs.[33] This theory of motivation, more than any other, makes a clear distinction among the different goals (or needs) of human beings and tackles directly the problem of when various needs are capable of motivating behavior. Hence, although the theory is not empirically proven, it does provide

30. Cofer and Appley, *op. cit.*, pp. 779–780.

31. Cf. Fred I. Greenstein, *Personality and Politics.*

32. For a good discussion of the different theories of motivation and the extent to which evidence exists to support them, see Cofer and Appley, *op. cit.*,

33. Abraham Maslow, "A Theory of Motivation," *Psychological Review,* L (1943), pp. 370 –396. The theory was applied to political behavior by James C. Davies in *Human Nature in Politics: The Dynamics of Political Behavior* (New York: Wiley, 1963).

a very useful model and aid for illustrating some of the basic issues involved in the study of motivation.

According to Maslow, all human beings have the following levels of needs: (1) individuals have basic *physical needs,* such as the need for food, water, and sex; (2) they also have *safety needs,* that is, a need for order, predictability, and dependability of their environment; (3) they have a *need for belonging,* which includes the need to be loved, to have affection, and friends; (4) they have a *need for self-esteem,* such as feeling equal to others; and (5) they have a *need for self-actualization,* i.e., a need to fulfill themselves. In Maslow's opinion, individuals pursue these five needs for their own sake throughout their lives. The needs are universal to the human organism regardless of the culture in which it lives or the ideology it is said to have embraced. In addition, these needs, which establish "goals" for an individual (consciously or unconsciously), are in a hierarchical arrangement. This notion of hierarchy means the following: until there is a substantial and relatively durable satisfaction of the physical needs, it will not be possible for the second level of needs, the safety needs, to emerge fully. Before the third level of needs, the need for belonging, can manifest itself as a strong force of motivation, the safety needs must be reasonably well met; and before the need for self-esteem can blossom forth, the need for belonging must be fairly well satisfied; and finally, before an individual can attain the highest level of motivation, which falls under the broad category of the need for self-actualization, all of the other four types of needs must be adequately fulfilled.

Maslow's hierarchical theory has many implications for the study of politics and the study of ideology. It helps one realize, for example, that neither politics nor any written, official ideological system necessarily performs any directly significant function in the fulfillment of the more basic needs. To satisfy their physical needs, the needs of belonging, and even basic safety needs, individuals usually turn to the local grocery store and to their family and friends. It is true that the political and economic system and the stage of development of a country will determine how well these needs can be met, but, nonetheless, whether one is a peasant in the Soviet Union or a member of the Politburo, the sources for fulfillment of these needs tend to be one's immediate family, circle of friends, and professional colleagues. In the words of Davies, "It is only when the achievement of these needs is threatened by individuals or groups too powerful to be dealt with privately that people turn to politics to secure their ends. Politics is generally only an indirect and instrumental means to the attainment of these ends. In other words, from a psychological point of view, politics is a form of exceptional, non-routine human behavior.[34] It might be added that in most political systems it would be even more exceptional and non-routine to find that a person's manner and motivation for fulfilling these lower needs were directly influenced by the official ideological system, for

34. Davies, *op. cit.,* p. 10.

when individuals do not have these basic needs met, they tend to withdraw not only from any concern from politics, but also from a formal system of ideology.

Maslow's theory implies (and research on various revolutions tends to support this implication) that extreme deprivation of either the physical or safety needs can and often will lead to depoliticization.[35] There are numerous examples in the history of the Soviet Union to support this contention. Bauer, for example, found that in the 1930's and 1940's the physical and safety needs of the Soviet populace were so severely unfulfilled that most of the people simply withdrew from politics, creating the illusion and, in fact, the reality that the Soviet political system was very stable. It was stable, to a very large extent, simply because the people withdrew from either supporting or opposing it. Marxian ideology and/or any correspondence or discrepancy between that ideology and the practices of the Party were, for all practical purposes, irrelevant to their actual political behavior.[36]

The same can be said for what happened in the Ukraine during Hitler's invasion. Initially the population's hostility to the Soviet system (at perhaps an ideological level) led them to greet the Nazi army joyously. When, however, they found that the Nazis were quite willing to starve and kill them, the Ukrainians chose to support the Soviet military and to fight Hitler. It does not appear that this was an ideological decision. It was a very basic human necessity of survival.

At the decision-making level these same hierarchical needs may apply. It is thought that most individuals who engage in politics have successfully attained the self-actualization level.[37] This means that the most common level of motivation for intense political participation is one in which the other needs have already been well met. In other words, as Davies argues, most political actors may enjoy intense political participation for its own sake and "not primarily because [they] thereby feed or protect [themselves] or because [they] can give socially acceptable vent to [their] aggressions, gain great deference, or bend people to [their] will."[38] While there are certainly exceptions to this generalization (and these will be discussed below), it seems reasonable to assume that many aspects of an ideological belief system can become operative only when the key decision-makers have attained this level. It is highly unlikely, for example, that any political leader will worry about implementing

---

35. The more empirical studies on revolution consistently show that revolutions based on the masses occurred only after a significant increase in economic development had prevailed for a number of years. The sudden drop in prosperity immediately prior to the revolutions, while perhaps a necessary condition for the occurrence of a revolution, did not constitute severe deprivation. Cf. Crane Brinton, *The Anatomy of Revolution* (New York: Vintage Books, 1952), and Raymond Tanter and Manus Midlarsky, "A Theory of Revolution," *Journal of Conflict Resolution*, XI, 3 (September, 1967), pp. 264–280.

36. Bauer, Inkeles, and Kluckhohn, *op. cit.*

37. Davies, *op. cit.*, p. 59.

38. *Ibid.*

immediately a stated ideological goal or tenet if he thinks his life, livelihood, or professional position is in danger (as seems often to have been the case in the Soviet Union, particularly during the various succession crises). It is also highly unlikely that a preference for one version of an ideological position will receive high consideration if a political actor feels his sense of belonging to the in-group and personal self-esteem are being threatened. Under these circumstances ideology is likely to become not a goal or criterion for behavior, but rather a tool, polemical or otherwise, to achieve a more basic human need.

What all this means is that before one can successfully analyze the function of ideology in decision-making, one probably must know not only the content of the ideology and the existing rules and norms of the political process in a system but also at what level of the human need hierarchy the political actors can act and are acting, because the criteria for making decisions and acting will vary according to these need levels. And to repeat, ideological goal considerations are highly unlikely to become criteria for decision-making until and unless political actors have most of their lower-level needs fairly well met and do not fear that they will suddenly no longer be so.

One very good illustration of how severe deprivation or the fear of such deprivation can lead even the most political members of a society to abandon considerations of principle and ideology in order to satisfy lower-level needs is found in the behavior of some of the victims of the Great Purge Trials in the 1930's in the Soviet Union. The individuals who were forced to confess to sins against Marxism, the Party, the government, and the state were severely deprived of the food, sleep, and any order or predictability regarding when they would be fed or allowed to rest, or how they would be treated. They were additionally deprived of any clear sense of belonging, even to a group of persecuted prisoners. Having been cut off from their families and persuasively told they were traitors to the system and to the society, they were further isolated from their fellow victims and allowed to learn of their welfare only from periodical screams and reports that the others had confessed to the alleged crimes. This severe deprivation along with a simultaneous severe lowering of their own feelings of self-esteem and dignity as human beings certainly reduced their physical and mental capability of being strongly motivated by any "orthodox" ideological considerations and, indeed, perhaps even higher-level ethical values. As Davies, in somewhat stronger terms, put it:

> At no time did they in any usual sense actually become social or political. They confessed their sins against society not so much because of a sense of social responsibility as to get sleep and bread. . . . In short, they had a stark, naked, physical need to survive, however hopeless, and to gain some sense of identity and worth, however contemptible.[39]

When these basic needs are not met, a human being ceases to be "political." If they are not ever adequately met, human beings will never become "poli-

39. *Ibid.*, p. 19.

tical." Although it is true that some of the lower-level human needs, such as the need for self-preservation, can become the main motivating force for political behavior and can obstruct the potential motivating force of an individual's basic beliefs and values, these needs usually are satisfied and play little or no motivating role in often mundane day-to-day political situations.

PERSONALITY PROCESSES AND MOTIVATION

At the lower left corner of III in Smith's map (Figure 2), under the heading "Externalization and Ego Defense," one finds, in a somewhat different form, an illustration of how the basic human needs elaborated by Maslow fit into a total motivational framework. Individuals have these needs. However, the manner in which specific individuals will try to cope with threats to the meeting of these needs will depend upon their previous life and personality development. Individuals who are more prone to be anxiety-ridden and to have more internal conflicts than others will probably have their belief and value systems as well as their political decisions determined, to a higher degree than other individuals, by their need to defend their ego rather than by the objective facts.[40] Beliefs and values for them would be more likely to fulfill the function of ego defense than the function of object appraisal. Such individuals may latch onto and subscribe to an ideological system because of these needs. They may also reject the formal ideology for the same reason. (It would be interesting to compare and analyze in these terms the members of *Agitprop* and the dissident writers and intellectuals in the Soviet Union. Basic personality needs and processes certainly must account for much of the divergence in beliefs, values, and behaviors. While it may be that members of these two groups differ substantially in their basic personality traits and the functions which their beliefs and values fulfill for their personality maintenance, it is equally possible that a similar proportion within each group are using, in different ways, the official ideological system as a means of justifying a particular manner of satisfying and defending needs and egos.)

The heading "Mediation of Self-Other Relationships" refers not only to the nature and type of interaction one has with others, but also to the need an individual has for identifying with and being similar to or different from one's peers and reference groups. The role this personality process can have in motivating political behavior should be fairly obvious. Individuals who have a need to conform or who have habituated themselves to conforming will be more likely to adopt as their own large segments of a formal and official ideological system than those who do not. Also, an intense dislike for a person or the converse, a strong liking for a person, could lead to either the rejection or the acceptance of a particular ideological point of view in a given situation.

Certainly one of the needs human beings have is the need to know and to

---

40. Nathan Leites' work, *A Study of Bolshevism,* is a detailed and elaborate application of this generalization to the Soviet leadership group.

feel that the beliefs they hold are based on the "truth." The personality process related to "Object Appraisal" refers to this need. Most individuals, including "Communist" ones, like to assert that they hold this or that belief or opinion because they have objectively analyzed a problem and on the basis of existing knowledge and experience have reached an objective conclusion regarding what means will lead to what ends. If an individual does hold a belief because of this motivation, however, it means only that that particular belief is not a function of his other needs, but rather the end product of what the individual perceives to be the objective situation based upon his previous experience and present knowledge. It does not necessarily mean that the belief held will be any more "operative," i.e., acted upon more consistently, than other beliefs which are held because they fulfill some other function for the maintenance and operation of the personality of the individual concerned.[41]

This point is important to note because when most scholars of Communist systems talk about ideology as a motivating force in decision-making, they do so largely in terms of what seems to them to be a means-end relationship among beliefs, values, and goals. To most scholars an aspect of the ideological system is considered to be "operative" when, ostensibly at least, the actors involved have made something of an objective appraisal of the situation and then take concrete political actions in terms of goal attainment or instrumental action which can be related to some element in the written ideological system. If such a relationship is observed often, it is argued that the political actors actually "believe" in the ideology. It is also sometimes argued that if the leaders act irrationally or inefficiently and a correspondence between this behavior and some element in the ideological system can be seen, then they also must "believe" in that ideological tenet. Hence, the question of objective appraisal is very important.

Apparently, it is thought that if and only if significant elements of the official ideology are held as either objective truths or attainable goals and values, the ideology or elements of it will be "operative" for an individual, group, or society. One of the crucial questions here is what is meant and perhaps what should be meant by the term "operative." If that term refers to the functions an official ideological system fulfills, then it should be obvious by now that an official ideology can and probably does fulfill quite different functions for individuals, groups, and indeed nations. While a specific decision-making body may act as though all or most of its members believe in a particular tenet or goal in one circumstance, it may well be that all or sections of the group are acting that way for quite different reasons. In another, ostensibly similar, situation, the majority of these individuals may take quite a different stand, giving the impression that this aspect of the ideology is not "operative." The reason for taking the different stand could have nothing to do with belief or

---

41. *Ibid.* Cf. Milton Rokeach, *Beliefs, Attitudes, and Values: A Theory of Organization and Change* (San Francisco: Jossey-Bass Inc., 1968); and Rokeach, *The Open and Closed Mind.*

lack of it in a particular ideological tenet or goal. It could simply mean, and probably often does mean, that in the new situation different motivating forces were at work and the strength of one force simply overrode another.

From this brief discussion of motivation it seems clear that one of the most important reasons for the existing controversy over the motivational role of the Communist official ideological system in political behavior is, indeed, the fact that the positions advocated by different scholars are based on limited methodologies and on limited views of what variables need to be considered. The anthropological and psychoanalytic schools tend to concentrate on character and ego development, which in turn leads them to emphasize temperamental and stylistic traits and ego defenses in the personality. In terms of Smith's map these variables concern primarily only small sections of I, II, and III. Kremlinologists tend to concentrate most on the variables relating to IV, the immediate situational context, and on intense conflict situations. In the past at least, intense conflict in the Soviet Union has often posed severe dangers to individuals and forced them to be concerned about protecting what Maslow would call their lower-level needs. Given this framework, it is not surprising that Kremlinologists are inclined to believe that ideology is primarily a polemical tool. Much the same can be said for the geopolitical theorists, only they tend to pay more attention to the distal social determinants (I) than the Kremlinologists do. The historians obviously study the distal social determinants most intensely. Since the ideological system is only one of numerous variables in this class of variables and historians do not, unless they are doing a study involving biographical data, usually concern themselves with personality dispositions and processes, it would be expected that they would stress the importance of non-ideological determinants of behavior. The social psychologists and sociologists, whose theoretical and methodological orientations encourage them to look to empirical theories of motivation, naturally take a more intermediate position, for as it has been demonstrated, motivation is extremely complex. What will be a strong motivating force in one context will not be in another. Until and unless scholars of Communist ideologies recognize this fact and also develop a methodological and theoretical orientation which will take into consideration all of the different aspects of the problem, progress will not be made. It is hoped that this paper will stimulate thought in the direction of developing such an orientation.

PART IV

Western Diplomacy, International Communism, and Soviet Foreign Policy: The Origins of the Cold War

This is the first of three sections on the influence of international politics on Soviet foreign policy. There is much disagreement about *whether* external factors significantly shape Soviet behavior, *which* factors exert influence under various circumstances, and *in what manner* they do so. "Traditional" historians contend that external factors had little effect on Soviet policies and actions during and immediately after World War II. "Revisionist" historians assert that external influences — especially American diplomacy — had a significant impact on Soviet behavior. The former emphasize the aggressive, inflexible, inexorable, inevitable nature of Soviet policies, especially in Eastern Europe; the latter stress the adaptive, responsive, reactive, flexible nature of Soviet policy, particularly Stalin's willingness to consider alternative courses of action and to negotiate certain crucial issues with his American and British allies. The chief implication of the former interpretation is that Soviet "expansionism" was the primary cause of the breakdown of Allied cooperation and the onset of the Cold War; the latter view concludes that unrealistic and sometimes truculent Western diplomacy (especially between 1945 and 1947) was a major cause of the Cold War in that it reduced policy alternatives open to Stalin and thus induced him to choose "hard-line" policies (for example, the satellization of *all* of Eastern Europe) he might not have chosen otherwise.

Thanks to Professor Graebner's review of the literature on the origins of the Cold War, these introductory notes can be brief. One of his major points is that there are various "orthodox" and "revisionist" interpretations; few analysts of either persuasion fully agree on the relative importance of key factors. A second significant observation is that a definitive analysis of Cold War origins is impossible without more information from *Russian* sources.

Evidence concerning Western intentions and behavior is more accessible, although subject to varying interpretations. In his famous "X" article, George F. Kennan unwittingly provided the rationale for more than two decades of American foreign policy. His language suggested that military "containment" of Russian "expansive tendencies" should be the cornerstone of American policy.[1] But Kennan and fellow members of the State Department's Policy Planning Staff did not in 1947 see any danger of Soviet military expansion into Western Europe. What they did consider a serious threat was that large Western European countries and major industrial centers might come under Soviet control by internal political changes — that is, by local Communist parties seizing power.

The military implications of the "containment" doctrine had a vastly greater impact on American foreign policy than did its political or ideological implications. As Kennan ruefully observed in his memoirs, a "serious deficiency of the X-Article — perhaps the most serious of all — was the failure to make clear that what I was talking about when I mentioned the containment of Soviet power was not the containment by military means of a military threat, but the political containment of a political threat."[2]

Professor Schlesinger, in his article below, presents a classic "traditional" or "orthodox" interpretation of the origins of the Cold War. He stresses three factors often de-emphasized or omitted in other assessments — "the intransigence of Leninist ideology, the sinister dynamics of a totalitarian society, and the madness of Stalin" — and concludes that "The Cold War could have been avoided only if the Soviet Union had not been possessed by convictions both of the infallibility of the communist word and of the inevitability of a communist world."

Professors Williams and Lasch, in contrast, present "revisionist" viewpoints. Directly addressing himself to Schlesinger, Williams sharply criticizes the view that Stalin's paranoia was "a primary operational factor" in the genesis of the Cold War. Even if Stalin had been paranoid, Williams contends, other factors would be equally crucial to an accurate historical explanation of the Cold War's origins. For example, he observes that no major American policy-maker in the mid-1940's seems to have perceived Stalin's paranoia and acted on this belief — in other words, United States' policies and counterresponses were not adapted accordingly. Had flexible American initiatives failed

1. X (George F. Kennan), "The Sources of Soviet Conduct," *Foreign Affairs,* XXV, 4 (July, 1947), pp. 566 – 582.
2. George F. Kennan, *Memoirs: 1925 – 1950* (Boston: Atlantic-Little, Brown, 1967), p. 358.

because of Stalin's intransigence, this might well constitute indirect evidence of Stalin's "madness." But Williams concludes that Stalin was not intransigent and, considering American policies, Soviet actions cannot be accurately described as paranoid.

Lasch is particularly critical of the view that misunderstandings, misperceptions, and "communication problems" were major factors contributing to the inception and escalation of the Cold War. Russian leaders probably understood Western policies very well and had good reason to consider them hostile, Lasch implies. Indeed, revisionists argue that the primary goal of American policy in 1945 was "to force the Soviet Union out of Eastern Europe," and Lasch would very likely contend that this view gains considerable credence in light of Allied decisions at Teheran (November – December, 1943), the Moscow "percentages" agreement (October, 1944), the Allied armistice agreements with Rumania, Bulgaria, and Hungary (September, 1944 – January, 1945), and the decisions, "nondecisions," and unresolved issues at Yalta (February, 1945) and Potsdam (July-August, 1945).

To the "orthodox" observer, the famous Yalta "Declaration on Liberated Europe" was a major Allied policy agreement that the Soviet Union repeatedly violated in subsequent months and years; to the "revisionist," this document was merely rhetoric intended for domestic consumption in the democracies, a statement whose real purpose was to mask previous explicit and implicit agreements regarding separate Allied "spheres of influence" in Western and Eastern Europe. Revisionist historians dare suggest that the American decisions to drop atomic bombs on Japan may have been a show of force primarily intended to dislodge the Red Army from Eastern Europe and to renege on previous Allied agreements. Orthodox historians retort that this argument stands or falls on the crucial assumption that there *was* in fact "atomic diplomacy," and that no convincing evidence has been produced to confirm this because no such bargaining or threats took place.[3]

Professor Starobin's article is an important contribution because it emphasizes one factor — international Communism — virtually ignored in previous explanations of Cold War origins. Starobin describes the real and "incipient" diversity in the nonruling Communist parties, "among whom the changes produced by the war had outmoded earlier ideological and political premises," and he notes the apparent indecisiveness of Soviet policy toward this "nascent polycentrism" as late as 1947. Starobin argues that probably the most important single factor shaping Soviet foreign policy was Stalin's wish to unify and

3. Adam Ulam, "Re-reading the Cold War," *Interplay,* II, 8 (March, 1969), pp. 51 – 53. Cf. Gabriel Kolko, *The Politics of War: The World and United States Foreign Policy, 1943 – 1945* (New York: Random House, 1968); Barton Bernstein and Allen Matusow (eds.), *The Truman Administration: A Documentary History* (New York: Harper & Row, 1966); and the references listed by Graebner at the end of his article (especially Gar Alperovitz, *Atomic Diplomacy,* and Herbert Feis, *The Atomic Bomb and the End of World War II*).

control the international Communist movement. To do this, the Soviet leader could hardly create close economic and political ties with the major "imperialist" and "colonial" states, or accept greater ideological and institutional diversity within the USSR. All of these considerations were interrelated, and in many ways the policies chosen were logically consistent with one another. Each of these factors may well have contributed to Stalin's eventual decision to reconstruct the shattered Soviet economy in the time-tested autarkic manner, with assistance from the new satellite regimes in Eastern Europe, rather than await possible (but improbable) large-scale American assistance or German reparations.

In short, the implications of the Starobin argument are that American "hard-line" policies under President Truman may have made Stalin's basic decisions somewhat easier, but that Western diplomacy and actions were probably not the decisive factor in shaping Soviet policy. Cooperation with the United States, "different roads to socialism" in the world Communist movement and in Eastern Europe, greater internal diversity at home — all were new and untried paths. In time of war, these paths were worth exploring, and some had to be explored. In time of peace, old policies were less risky and probably more in line with Stalin's personal goals and those of other Soviet leaders. Above all, the Red Army remained in Eastern Europe, which it had occupied before the end of the war by virtue of its military victories over Nazi Germany and by explicit agreements with the other Allied powers. James F. Byrnes touched on a crucial issue when he said of Yalta, "It was not a question of what we would *let* the Russians do, but what we could *get* the Russians to do."[4]

What is the Cold War? How did it originate? What were its consequences? Was it avoidable? Why condemn it? Has it ended? These are among the important questions analyzed from various points of view in the next two sections.

4. Quoted in John Bagguly, "The World War and the Cold War," in David Horowitz (ed.) *Containment and Revolution* (Boston: Beacon Press, 1967), p. 110. For an important new study of Yalta, see Diane S. Clemens, *Yalta* (New York: Oxford University Press, 1970).

TWELVE

Cold War Origins and the Continuing Debate: A Review of the Literature*

More than twenty years have passed since scholars and journalists began their examination of the Cold War to explain its existence. Despite the ensuing flood of literature, much of it excellent by any standards, the Cold War remains the most enigmatic and elusive international conflict of modern times. Writers differ in their judgments of causation and responsibility in 1968 as greatly as they did when the examination began; twenty years of scholarship have produced no consensus. Nor are those who have committed themselves along the way inclined to alter their assumptions and conclusions. The record of national behavior has been clear enough. But beyond the recognition of day-to-day events the quest for meaning leads to a realm of secrecy and confusion where national purposes and individual motivations are reduced to conjecture. This absence of certainty encourages many who are attracted to the Cold War, as actors and students, to hold fast to established intellectual preferences. It is not strange that scholars, editors, politicians, and statesmen choose to disagree. And the resolution of the quarrel is nowhere in sight.

Since 1945 the great confrontation between the United States and the USSR has been the central fact of international life, perhaps no less so than the Brit-

*Reprinted from *The Journal of Conflict Resolution,* XIII, 1 (March, 1969), pp. 123–132, by permission of the author and the publisher. Copyright © 1969 by The University of Michigan.

ish – French struggle for world leadership in the Second Hundred Years' War. But any historic conflict between two giants, always diplomatically unsettling and potentially disastrous, would of necessity separate those who view such struggles as fundamental, even inevitable, from those who prefer to dwell on the immediate issues and the possibilities of their avoidance or solution. Those who accept the Cold War as an historic confrontation which always pits any two nations, recently elevated to prominence, in a struggle for power can find respectability for their view in the prophecies of Alexis de Tocqueville. This French traveler wrote over a century ago that one day the United States and Russia would each sway the destinies of half the globe; and it is doubtful that the two nations could have reached such positions of primacy except as rivals. If the struggle for power and prestige between the United States and the USSR is the logical product of modern history, its significance far transcends what is known as the Cold War. Those who interpret the Cold War as an imperial struggle might, as does Desmond Donnelly (1965), find its inception in the British – Russian conflict across Central Asia in the nineteenth century. Or, according to Walter LaFeber (1967), the historian might find the origins in the Russo – American rivalry over Manchuria at the turn of the century.

Those who attribute the Cold War to ideology — be it the Soviet-based doctrines of Communist expansion and revolution or the anti-Soviet attitudes which such doctrines produced — discover the origins of the Cold War in the Second Russian Revolution of 1917. John F. O'Conor (1961), who attributes the Cold War to Soviet expansionism, began his study of origins with the murder of the Romanov family in July, 1918. Similarly André Fontaine, in his more recent *History of the Cold War, 1917–1950* (1967), attributes Soviet aggressiveness to Communist ideology which, he believes might have been uprooted by a more concerted military effort against the Red Army in 1918 and 1919. For Frederick L. Schuman (1962) and D. F. Fleming (1961), two critics of American policies, the Cold War indeed began in 1918, not in any Bolshevik declaration of ideological warfare against the West, but in the Western invasion of Russia and the international ostracism of the Bolshevik regime which followed.

Still, most students of the Cold War find its origins in the events of the Second World War. If to some degree the Great War of 1914 was the cause of the Second, many historians would consider it even truer that the Second World War produced the Cold War. On April 25, 1945, Russian and American forces met along the Elbe in the middle of Europe. "This symbolic event," John Lukacs has written (1962, p. 3), "marks the supreme condition of contemporary history. . . . That supreme condition is not the Atomic Bomb and not Communism; it is the division of Germany and of most of Europe into American and Russian spheres of influence. The so-called cold war grew out of this division." Even those writers who find the Soviet – American confrontation more thoroughly grounded in history agree that the struggle entered a new stage of intensity with the rise of Russia to predominance on the European continent after the battle of Stalingrad.

Russia's penetration of Europe to the Elbe in April 1945 upset Western calculations on two fronts. Germany's total destruction, the high purpose of Allied wartime policy, had permitted the Red Army to challenge the traditional European balance of power. Second, Russia's military dominance of Slavic Europe, the result not of aggression but of victory, gave the Soviets the power, if not the intention, to impose their will on the states of eastern Europe. What is more, Stalin had made clear throughout the war years that Russia would interfere in the postwar politics of Slavic Europe to the extent of insuring pro-Soviet governments along Russia's western periphery. Thus the Kremlin gave the United States and Britain the ultimate choice of recognizing Soviet political and strategic interests in eastern Europe or accepting the postwar disintegration of the Grand Alliance as the price of clinging to their principles of self-determination. It is in these Soviet demands and their fundamental rejection by the Western world that such writers as Herbert Feis (1957), William H. McNeill (1953), Martin F. Herz (1966), Norman A. Graebner (1962), and even Frederick L. Schuman (1962) find the origins of the Cold War.

Was this giant political and military confrontation across Europe in 1945 avoidable? Did it result from unacceptable Soviet behavior or from the West's refusal to recognize the results of its neglect of eastern and central Europe during the months following Munich? Were military strategies available to the Western allies which might have disposed of Nazi power without placing Slavic Europe under direct Soviet control? Or was the division of Europe the necessary price of victory? Judgments on such questions are crucial to any interpretation of the Cold War. Despite their complexities, those judgments are basically three. Those who are concerned less with Soviet power than with Soviet behavior quite logically place the burden of wartime and postwar disagreement on the Soviet Union. Schuman, on the other hand, recalls that Munich gave Hitler a free hand in eastern Europe and permitted him to invade Russia in June 1941 with ample preparation and on his own terms. The West, in abdicating its responsibilities in 1938, concludes Schuman, had no right, after 20,000,000 Russian deaths, to demand equal rights in liberated Europe seven years later. Placing his emphasis on the realities of a divided Europe, Louis B. Halle, in *The Cold War as History* (1967), eschews moral judgment and views the Soviet – American confrontation in 1945 as a tragic and unavoidable condition created by the war itself, not unlike that which faces a scorpion and a tarantula in a bottle, each compelled to protect itself by seeking to kill the other. "This," writes Halle (1967, p. xiii), "is not fundamentally a case of the wicked against the virtuous . . . and we may properly feel sorry for both parties, caught, as they are, in a situation of irreducible dilemma."

Those charged with the formulation of American policy toward Europe from 1945 until 1947 created the intellectual foundations of orthodoxy. They rejected as immoral, and thus diplomatically unjustifiable, Soviet actions in eastern Europe, the Soviet refusal to permit free elections or accept the principle of four-power agreement on German reconstruction, the Soviet failure to disarm or withdraw forces to the old Russian border, the Soviet rejection of any agreement on the control of atomic energy, and eventually the Soviet resort to the veto to prevent action in the United Nations. What was the significance of this Russian behavior beyond a rejection of the Western blueprint for the postwar world? In defending their policies the Soviets claimed no more than the right to manage the political evolution of liberated Europe in terms of their own security interests. From the beginning, however, American officials interpreted Soviet defiance as evidence of a more sinister design, aimed not alone at the protection of Soviet commitments in eastern Europe, but also at the extension of Soviet power and influence beyond the regions of direct Soviet control. George F. Kennan warned from Moscow in May 1945 that Russia was an imperialistic nation, now in possession of great power and time, already determined "to segregate from the world economy almost all the areas in which it has been established" (quoted in Kennan, 1967, p. 537). The Soviets, wrote Kennan, were determined to gain Western recognition of their security interests in eastern Europe. By standing firm in rejecting the Soviet position the West would exert pressure on Soviet control and prevent any further Russian advances toward the west.

During April 1945, Ambassador Averell Harriman returned from Moscow and reported to President Harry Truman that the Soviets, having broken the Yalta agreements, would proceed to create additional pressures on world diplomacy. Harriman feared, moreover, that Stalin was prepared to exploit the devastation and economic dislocation of western Europe to extend Soviet influence into that region. Several weeks later Harriman complained that Hitler had opened "the gates of Eastern Europe to Asia." Similarly State Department offical Joseph M. Jones declared that the USSR "had demonstrated beyond any doubt that it was aggressive and expanding, and that its immediate design for dominion included as much of Europe and Asia and North Africa as it could get away with short of war with its Western allies" (Jones, 1955, p. 41). By 1947 many United States spokesmen no longer limited the Soviet challenge to an imperialistic design but rather to a Moscow-centered ideological crusade aimed at the total destruction of the Western traditions of government and society. They viewed Stalin's ruthless transformation of the eastern European nations into Russian satellites, following the Truman Doctrine and the Marshall Plan, as proof less of Soviet insecurity than of the unlimited ambitions of Soviet Communism, demanding after 1948 a Western policy of military containment in Europe.

What policy choices were available to Western leaders in the formulation of an allegedly *defensive* policy designed to blunt Soviet expansionism? The simplest decision, one overwhelmingly acceptable to concerned Americans and confirmed at Potsdam in July – August, 1945, was the refusal to recognize the Soviet sphere of influence. Western leaders, secondly, made it clear that Soviet expansion would not extend beyond the region of Soviet control in Europe; nor would it remain in Iran or reach Japan. Beyond setting the limits of Soviet expansion in a divided world, American spokesmen recognized the need to create some new international equilibrium that would offset Russia's military preponderance on the European continent. This would demand a new balancing role, one formerly conducted by Britain, for the United States. Such cabinet spokesmen as Secretary of the Navy James V. Forrestal and Secretary of War Henry L. Stimson had no interest in ideological policies. For Stimson the issue in Soviet-American relations was not self-determination as much as the established limits of power and change. Finally, Western leaders recognized in past Soviet actions no threats to Western security which required any specific settlements of major issues or any resort to force. These decisions established the character of the Cold War. On the one hand the positions taken and the interests at stake eliminated any concessions to Soviet demands through diplomatic negotiation. To gain objectives not achievable through the normal devices of diplomacy, the contestants would exert pressure on the will of their opponents by every means available short of war. In practice such behavior would comprise a tacit admission by Western leaders that both the political price of recognizing the status quo and the military price of undoing it exceeded by far the cost of sustaining the diplomatic, economic, and military policies of the Cold War.

Historians of the fifties tended to accept the Cold War orthodoxy laid down by United States and British officials in speeches, writings, memoirs, communications, and recorded conversations between 1945 and 1950. Such writers accepted the notion of Soviet aggressiveness as valid and of Western firmness as necessary. They accepted the logic of U. S. containment policy and regarded it generally as the most successful of the nation's postwar decisions, both in concept and in execution. Feis, in his judicious volume *Between War and Peace,* recognized the failures of Western purpose at Potsdam, but he accepted the orthodox position that the Soviets must bear the responsibility for the breakdown of Allied unity. "The western allies," ran his conclusion, "were standing out against both Soviet expansionism and Communist social ideals" (Feis, 1960, p. 322). From the challenge of Soviet aggressiveness there could be no retreat. "The survival of freedom was dependent solely upon the United States," wrote John W. Spanier in 1960 (p. 33). More recently such students of postwar United States foreign policy as Charles Burton Marshall (1965), Dexter Perkins (1967), and David Rees (1967) have continued in the sixties to view the Soviet Union as an expansive force and have regarded Stalin as the exponent, not of Russian security, but of the Communist program. This is not to say that any of these writers laud every American decision or accept the rationale of every official utterance. They do, however, agree that the nation's general reaction to a divided Europe in 1945 and thereafter — both in rejecting any agreement on spheres of influence and in creating a countering strategy — was the proper one.

Those who have rejected one or more aspects of the official, or orthodox, interpretation of the Cold War are not of one mind. Their disagreement with official doctrine is not over the nature, or even the morality, of Soviet behavior, but over its meaning. Soviet policies in eastern Europe following Yalta had been anticipated by both British and American leaders as early as 1943 with the knowledge that they would not be prevented. Then why were they not accepted? E. H. Carr, the British historian, raised the question of Soviet behavior in *The Times* of London on November 6, 1944. Denying that Russia had any greater expansionist designs toward Europe than England, he warned not only that the Soviets would seek security guarantees in eastern Europe but also that "it would be foolish, as well as somewhat hypocritical, to construe insistence on this right as the symptom of an aggressive policy." This theme — that a postwar Russian sphere of influence was a logical expression of the times and no danger to Western security — Walter Lippmann developed fully in *The Cold War* (1947). Lippmann recognized the existence of a Russian problem but rejected the official concept. Permitting the record to speak for itself, assigning no blame or assigning it equally, a number of writers have accepted both a more limited view of the Soviet challenge and the need for policies which reflect the limited choices which have confronted the West since 1944. For it was quite clear from the outset that the mere rejection of Soviet behavior in eastern Europe would in no way influence the course of events in the regions under Russian control.

In varying degrees such writers as Hans J. Morgenthau (1951), John Lukacs (1962), Isaac Deutscher (1966), Louis B. Halle (1967), Paul Seabury (1967), Charles O. Lerche (1965), Marshall Shulman (1966), and Wilfrid Knapp (1967) have questioned the fears and the ideological assumptions which guided the evolution of United States policy in the postwar years.[1] Seabury, for example, in *The Rise and Decline of the Cold War,* traces the development of many American Cold War attitudes and questions their usefulness as the bases of policy. From writings such as these Stalin emerges less an expansionist than a realist, determined to pursue a spheres of influence policy as the surest guarantee of Russian security. Most would agree with Deutscher that the Western dread of Soviet expansionism was mistaken. Employing a different analysis, Morgenthau, in *The Defense of the National Interest,* separated the issue of imperialism from that of world revolution and insisted that the USSR represented the former and not the latter threat. George F. Kennan's official

1. In this connection see Luard (1964), another valuable study of the Cold War. The essays in this volume were prepared by British scholars.

communications of 1945 – 1947 warned official Washington of Soviet belligerence toward the outside world and suggested the countering policy of containment. His *Memoirs, 1925 – 1950,* published in 1967, restated his underlying assumptions of the postwar years. But he made it clear that he did not, either in 1947 or afterward, approve of the intensity, the militarization, or the crusading zeal which came to characterize the American response to the Soviet challenge. This criticism of containment — that it embodied no clear, precise objectives and thus eliminated any genuine effort at negotiation — characterized the views of many writers who nevertheless have insisted that the power and the ambitions of the USSR, even if limited, necessitated some Western response.

Kennan's dissatisfaction with United States policy increased with the passage of time. Indeed, many whose writings have praised the Truman Doctrine and the Marshall Plan, as prudent and necessary reactions to the Soviet presence in central and eastern Europe, believe that the United States soon lost its balance and restraint. After 1950, and especially after the Korean war, a new globalism encouraged the national executive to extend United States commitments into Asia and the Pacific under the doubtful assumption that the West faced, not a limited if powerful antagonist in Europe, but rather an international conspiracy emanating from the Kremlin and designed to establish Soviet influence over the entire world.

During the sixties another group of scholars has rejected the precepts of orthodoxy completely. Beginning with the assumption that a war-battered Soviet Union had the right to demand friendly buffer states as a defense against Western encirclement, these revisionists have charged U.S. policy with provoking and sustaining the Cold War. They argue that the USSR emerged from the war weak and insecure, that it desired an accommodation with the West based on the minimum acceptance of a Soviet sphere of influence. It was the repeated British and American protests against the imposition of a Soviet hegemony in eastern Europe that inaugurated the successive responses which led to the Cold War. The United States, charge the revisionists, was not powerless to prevent the Cold War. Lippmann had argued the revisionist case in *The Cold War* (1947). The British physicist, P. M. S. Blackett, stated it differently a year later in his *Military and Political Consequences of Atomic Energy.* The USSR, declared Blackett, had a right not only to defend her western frontiers but also to extend her frontiers as far as possible in response to the Baruch Plan for the control of atomic energy. That plan, the Russians believed, would have rendered them vulnerable to Western military power. K. Zilliacus, a British official and writer, carried the revisionist cause forward another step with the publication of his book, *I Choose Peace* (1949). Zilliacus argued that British wartime and postwar policy, from Munich to Churchill's Fulton speech of March 1946, had been as much anti-Soviet as anti-German.

It was the anti-Communist bias of Churchill and Bevin in 1945 that made agreement with the Kremlin impossible.

In large measure the American revisionism of the sixties found its inception in D. F. Fleming's *The Cold War and Its Origins, 1917–1950* (1961). Critics have termed Fleming's book as little more than a collection of contemporary comments. In large measure the charge is true. But Fleming's massive Cold War studies illustrate, as have no other published volumes, the extent to which every fundamental American decision after 1944 created doubts in the nation's intellectual community, especially among leading members of the press. Much of that early criticism followed a pattern, suggesting conceptual weaknesses in policy that would become more obvious, embarrassing, and costly with the passage of time. Employing a succession of unilateral (purely American) explanations for the origins of the Cold War, Fleming consistently attributes Soviet suspicion and misbehavior to Western aggressiveness. "From the first," he writes (1961, p. 31), "it was the West which was on the offensive, not the Soviets." If Fleming's detailed and often disturbing catalogue of American editorial, official, and semi-official opinion offers some explanation of United States policy, it avoids any analysis of Soviet purpose and ignores the anti-American polemics of Soviet officials. Fleming traces forty years of American opposition to Soviet ideas and actions, but he makes no effort to account for it except in the general terms of anti-Communism.

But David Horowitz, in his *Free World Colossus* (1965), explains the unity of American policy in the Cold War by characterizing it as "counterrevolutionary" rather than "counterexpansionary." The purpose of American policy since 1945, writes Horowitz (p. 423), is to crush any movement anywhere in the world that threatens radical change against the will of the United States government. To prevent change, the nation has employed the concept of containment and has built up vast excesses of power in order to force a showdown with the USSR and thereby terminate the processes of revolution elsewhere in the world. It was this purpose that led to the extension of American power and American commitments into Asia and Latin America after 1950. Thus Horowitz, no less than Fleming, sees the United States in the role of the aggressor and demonstrates, as do others, that Stalin's disturbing policies of 1947 and 1948 — the rejection of the Marshall Plan, the establishment of the Cominform, the Czech coup, and the Berlin blockade — were the result rather than the cause of U.S. containment policy.

William A. Williams, in *The Tragedy of American Diplomacy* (1959, revised edition 1962), likewise finds a single and persistent motive in American Cold War policy — the determination to compel the Kremlin to accept this nation's concept of itself and the world. This purpose, writes Williams, comprises especially the expansion of the open door principle of trade and investment into areas under Soviet control. The Marshall Plan as originally conceived, he believes, would have given the United States considerable influence over the internal and external affairs of the USSR. Soviet rejection, therefore, should have been anticipated. When the Marshall Plan failed to open eastern Europe, the Truman administration adopted both the concept of negotiating from strength and the buildup of American power to achieve the dismantling of the Iron Curtain. In their ultimate failure, Washington officials underestimated the strength and determination of the Soviet opposition (Williams, 1962, pp. 205 – 209).

More recently Walter LaFeber has adopted the concept of the open door to explain United States aggressiveness *vis-à-vis* the Soviet Union in 1945 and the years that followed. Opposed to the formation of political blocs, writes LaFeber, the United States government, led by Secretary of State James F. Byrnes, attempted to use its predominant economic power to penetrate Europe. Whereas that policy, culminating in the Marshall Plan, triumphed in western Europe, it failed to penetrate the Iron Curtain. Meanwhile the United States, with its vast economic power, might have extended credit to the Soviet Union in 1945 to relieve its economic plight. Instead the Truman administration cancelled Lend-Lease abruptly and without explanation; in March 1946 Stalin announced another five-year plan to rebuild Russian industry and assure the technological and financial independence of the Soviet Union. Again the quest for the open door failed to achieve anything except the breakdown of diplomacy (LaFeber, 1967, pp. 6 – 20).

If American economic power could not penetrate the Soviet sphere, perhaps another force was available in 1945 to turn the Russians out of eastern Europe. Gar Alperovitz, in his *Atomic Diplomacy: Hiroshima and Potsdam* (1965), has discovered the origins of the Cold War in the atomic diplomacy which led to Potsdam and the decision to use the bomb against Japanese targets. Alperovitz develops three specific themes. First, he argues along with Fleming, Horowitz, and Williams that U.S. policy toward Russia changed precipitously under Truman in April, 1945, when the new administration sought to impose an immediate settlement on Russia over eastern Europe. Second, he believes that this change to a tough policy occurred because of Truman's assumption that the atomic bomb, then being developed, would strengthen his diplomacy with the Kremlin, making the desired settlement possible without war. Third, Alperovitz attempts to explain why Truman delayed the Potsdam Conference, attending ultimately only with reluctance, and then used the atomic bomb against Japan long after he knew of the Japanese premier's willingness to surrender provided its emperor were retained. While admitting that such questions cannot be answered with complete confidence for lack of evidence, he suggests that Truman delayed his trip to Potsdam until the bomb had been fully developed and then used it, not to end the war in the Pacific, but to demonstrate this new power to the Soviet Union. As one American official explained in May 1945, "Mr. Byrnes did not argue that it was necessary to use the bomb against the cities of Japan in order to win the war. . . . [His] view

[was] that our possessing and demonstrating the bomb would make Russia more manageable in Europe."[2] Still, if the President hoped to exert diplomatic pressure on Stalin he failed to exploit the bomb either at Potsdam or thereafter. Indeed, the bomb had no appreciable effect on Soviet policy whatever. The showdown over eastern Europe never came.

Late in 1966 Arthur M. Schlesinger, Jr., wrote a letter to the *New York Review of Books:* "Surely the time has come to blow the whistle before the current outburst of revisionism regarding the origins of the Cold War goes much further." Then in the autumn of 1967 Schlesinger published a full article in *Foreign Affairs* in which he argued for greater orthodoxy and insisted that Stalin's paranoia and rigidity were sufficient to explain the failure of postwar accommodation. Still the revisionist attack on U.S. Cold War policy has tended to become increasingly pronounced with the passage of time.[3] As long as much of the American and most of the Russian evidence remains hidden from view the final judgment on Cold War origins will remain elusive. But the publication of British and American memoirs and documents over the past decade reveals both an inflexible opposition to Soviet behavior and an illusion that somehow the postwar Soviet dominance in Europe could be undermined without the price of war. Revisionist studies, moreover, have traced the descent into the Cold War through a series of cause-and-effect relationships in which key Soviet decisions throughout the postwar era appear to be reactions to, not the causes of, Western demonstrations of power and determination. After more than twenty years of Cold War, the quest for understanding raises one fundamental and still unanswered question: Why did the United States after 1939 permit the conquest of eastern Europe by Nazi forces, presumably forever, with scarcely a stir, but refused after 1944 to acknowledge any primary Russian interest or right of hegemony in the same region on the heels of a closely won Russian victory against the German invader? When scholars have answered that question fully the historical debate over Cold War origins will be largely resolved.

References

Alperovitz, Gar. *Atomic Diplomacy: Hiroshima and Potsdam.* New York: Simon & Schuster, 1965.
Deutscher, Isaac. "Twenty Years of Cold War." In *Ironies of History,* London, 1966.
Donnelly, Desmond. *Struggle for the World: The Cold War and Its Causes.* London: St. Martin's Press, 1965.

2. Alperovitz, 1967, p. 242. Feis (1961) has challenged this interpretation of the use of the atomic bomb against Japan. He believes that Truman ordered its employment against Hiroshima as another weapon, however destructive, to terminate the war promptly and thus save American and Japanese lives.
3. For a popular defense of revisionism, see Lasch (1968).

Cold War Origins: A Review of the Literature   227

Feis, Herbert. *Churchill, Roosevelt, Stalin: The War They Waged and the Peace They Sought.* Princeton, N.J.: Princeton University Press, 1957.
——. *Between War and Peace: The Potsdam Conference.* Princeton, N.J.: Princeton University Press, 1960.
——. *Japan Subdued.* Princeton, N.J.: Princeton University Press, 1961. [Revised edition appeared as *The Atomic Bomb and the End of World War II.* Princeton, N.J.: Princeton University Press, 1966. Eds.]
Fleming, D.F. *The Cold War and Its Origins, 1917–1950.* Garden City, N.Y.: Doubleday, 1961.
Graebner, Norman A. *Cold War Diplomacy, 1945–1960.* Princeton, N.J.: Princeton University Press, 1962.
Halle, Louis B. *The Cold War as History.* New York: Harper & Row, 1967.
Herz, Martin F. *Beginnings of the Cold War.* Bloomington: Indiana University Press, 1966.
Horowitz, David. *The Free World Colossus: A Critique of American Foreign Policy in the Cold War.* New York: Hill & Wang, 1965.
Jones, Joseph Marion. *The Fifteen Weeks.* New York: Viking Press, 1955.
Kennan, George F. *Memoirs, 1925–1950.* Boston: Little, Brown, 1967.
Knapp, Wilfrid. *A History of War and Peace, 1939–1965.* London: Oxford University Press, 1967.
LaFeber, Walter. *America, Russia, and the Cold War, 1945–1966.* New York: Wiley, 1967.
Lasch, Christopher. "The Cold War, Revisited and Re-Visioned," *New York Times Magazine,* January 14, 1968.
Lerche, Charles O., Jr. *The Cold War and After.* Englewood Cliffs, N.J.: Prentice-Hall, 1965.
Luard, Evan (ed.). *The Cold War. A Reappraisal.* New York: Praeger, 1964.
Lukacs, John. *A History of the Cold War.* Rev. edn. Garden City, N.Y.: Doubleday, 1962.
Marshall, Charles Burton. *The Cold War: A Concise History.* New York: Franklin Watts, 1965.
McNeill, William H. *America, Britain, and Russia: Their Cooperation and Conflict, 1941–1946.* London: Oxford University Press, 1953.
Morgenthau, Hans J. *In Defense of the National Interest.* New York: Knopf, 1951.
O'Conor, John F. *The Cold War and Liberation.* New York: Vantage Press, 1961.
Perkins, Dexter. *The Diplomacy of a New Age.* Bloomington: Indiana University Press, 1967.
Rees, David. *The Age of Containment: The Cold War, 1945–1965.* London: St. Martin's Press, 1967.
Schuman, Frederick L. *The Cold War: Retrospect and Prospect.* Baton Rouge: Louisiana State University Press, 1962.
Seabury, Paul. *The Rise and Decline of the Cold War.* New York: Basic Books, 1967.
Shulman, Marshall D. *Beyond the Cold War.* New Haven: Yale University Press, 1966.
Spanier, John W. *American Foreign Policy Since World War II.* New York: Praeger, 1960.
Williams, William A. *The Tragedy of American Diplomacy.* Rev. edn. New York: World Publishing, 1962.

Origins of the Cold War*

I

The Cold War in its original form was a presumably mortal antagonism, arising in the wake of the Second World War, between two rigidly hostile blocs, one led by the Soviet Union, the other by the United States. For nearly two somber and dangerous decades this antagonism dominated the fears of mankind; it may even, on occasion, have come close to blowing up the planet. In recent years, however, the once implacable struggle has lost its familiar clarity of outline. With the passing of old issues and the emergence of new conflicts and contestants, there is a natural tendency, especially on the part of the generation which grew up during the Cold War, to take a fresh look at the causes of the great contention between Russia and America.

Some exercises in reappraisal have merely elaborated the orthodoxies promulgated in Washington or Moscow during the boom years of the Cold War. But others, especially in the United States (there are no signs, alas, of this in the Soviet Union), represent what American historians call "revisionism" — that is, a readiness to challenge official explanations. No one should be surprised by this phenomenon. Every war in American history has been fol-

*Reprinted from *Foreign Affairs*, XLVI, 1 (October, 1967), pp. 22–52, by permission of the author and the publisher. Copyright 1967 by the Council on Foreign Relations, Inc., New York.

lowed in due course by skeptical reassessments of supposedly sacred assumptions. So the War of 1812, fought at the time for the freedom of the seas, was in later years ascribed to the expansionist ambitions of Congressional war hawks; so the Mexican War became a slaveholders' conspiracy. So the Civil War has been pronounced a "needless war," and Lincoln has even been accused of maneuvering the rebel attack on Fort Sumter. So too the Spanish-American War and First and Second World Wars have, each in its turn, undergone revisionist critiques. It is not to be supposed that the Cold War would remain exempt.

In the case of the Cold War, special factors reinforce the predictable historiographical rhythm. The outburst of polycentrism in the communist empire has made people wonder whether communism was ever so monolithic as official theories of the Cold War supposed. A generation with no vivid memories of Stalinism may see the Russia of the forties in the image of the relatively mild, seedy, and irresolute Russia of the sixties. And for this same generation the American course of widening the war in Vietnam — which even non-revisionists can easily regard as folly — has unquestionably stirred doubts about the wisdom of American foreign policy in the sixties which younger historians may have begun to read back into the forties.

It is useful to remember that, on the whole, past exercises in revisionism have failed to stick. Few historians today believe that the war hawks caused the War of 1812 or the slaveholders the Mexican War, or that the Civil War was needless, or that the House of Morgan brought America into the First World War or that Franklin Roosevelt schemed to produce the attack on Pearl Harbor. But this does not mean that one should deplore the rise of Cold War revisionism.[1] For revisionism is an essential part of the process by which history, through the posing of new problems and the investigation of new possibilities, enlarges its perspectives and enriches its insights.

More than this, in the present context, revisionism expresses a deep, legitimate, and tragic apprehension. As the Cold War has begun to lose its purity of definition, as the moral absolutes of the fifties become the moralistic clichés of the sixties, some have begun to ask whether the appalling risks which humanity ran during the Cold War were, after all, necessary and inevitable; whether more restrained and rational policies might not have guided the energies of man from the perils of conflict into the potentialities of collaboration. The fact that such questions are in their nature unanswerable does not mean that it is not right and useful to raise them. Nor does it mean that our sons and daughters are not entitled to an accounting from the generation of Russians and Americans who produced the Cold War.

1. As this writer somewhat intemperately did in a letter to *The New York Review of Books,* October 20, 1966.

II

The orthodox American view, as originally set forth by the American government and as reaffirmed until recently by most American scholars, has been that the Cold War was the brave and essential response of free men to Communist aggression. Some have gone back well before the Second World War to lay open the sources of Russian expansionism. Geopoliticians traced the Cold War to imperial Russian strategic ambitions which in the nineteenth century led to the Crimean War, to Russian penetration of the Balkans and the Middle East, and to Russian pressure on Britain's "lifeline" to India. Ideologists traced it to the Communist Manifesto of 1848 ("the violent overthrow of the bourgeoisie lays the foundation for the sway of the proletariat"). Thoughtful observers (a phrase meant to exclude those who speak in Dullese about the unlimited evil of godless, atheistic, militant communism) concluded that classical Russian imperialism and Pan-Slavism, compounded after 1917 by Leninist messianism, confronted the West at the end of the Second World War with an inexorable drive for domination.[2]

The revisionist thesis is very different.[3] In its extreme form, it is that, after

2. Every student of the Cold War must acknowledge his debt to W. H. McNeill's remarkable account, *America, Britain and Russia: Their Cooperation and Conflict, 1941–1946* (New York, 1953) and to the brilliant and indispensable series by Herbert Feis: *Churchill, Roosevelt, Stalin: The War They Waged and the Peace They Sought* (Princeton, 1957); *Between War and Peace: The Potsdam Conference* (Princeton, 1960); and *The Atomic Bomb and the End of World War II* (Princeton, 1966). Useful recent analyses include André Fontaine, *Histoire de la Guerre Froide* (2 v., Paris, 1965, 1967); N. A. Graebner, *Cold War Diplomacy, 1945–1960* (Princeton, 1962); L. J. Halle, *The Cold War as History* (London, 1967); M. F. Herz, *Beginnings of the Cold War* (Bloomington, 1966); and W. L. Neumann, *After Victory: Churchill, Roosevelt, Stalin and the Making of the Peace* (New York, 1967).

3. The fullest statement of this case is to be found in D. F. Fleming's voluminous *The Cold War and Its Origins* (New York, 1961). For a shorter version of this argument, see David Horowitz, *The Free World Colossus* (New York, 1965); the most subtle and ingenious statements come in W. A. Williams' *The Tragedy of American Diplomacy* (rev. ed., New York, 1962), and in Gar Alperovitz's *Atomic Diplomacy: Hiroshima and Potsdam* (New York, 1965), and in subsequent articles and reviews by Mr. Alperovitz in *The New York Review of Books*. The fact that in some aspects the revisionist thesis parallels the official Soviet argument must not, of course, prevent consideration of the case on its merits, nor raise questions about the motives of the writers, all of whom, so far as I know, are independent-minded scholars.

I might further add that all these books, in spite of their ostentatious display of scholarly apparatus, must be used with caution. Professor Fleming, for example, relies heavily on newspaper articles and even columnists. While Mr. Alperovitz bases his case on official documents or authoritative reminiscences, he sometimes twists his material in a most unscholarly way. For example, in describing Ambassador Harriman's talk with President Truman on April 20, 1945, Mr. Alperovitz writes, "He argued that a reconsideration of Roosevelt's policy was necessary" (p. 22, repeated on p. 24). The citation is to pp. 70–72 in President Truman's *Years of Decision*. What President Truman reported Harriman as saying was the exact opposite: "Before leaving, Harriman took me aside and said, 'Frankly, one of the reasons that made me rush back to Washington was the fear that you did not understand, as I had seen Roosevelt understand, that Stalin is breaking his agreements.'" Similarly, in an appendix (p. 271) Mr. Alperovitz writes that the Hopkins and Davies missions of May 1945 "were opposed by the 'firm' advisers." Actually the Hopkins mission was proposed by Harriman and Charles E. Bohlen, who Mr. Alperovitz

the death of Franklin Roosevelt and the end of the Second World War, the United States deliberately abandoned the wartime policy of collaboration and, exhilarated by the possession of the atomic bomb, undertook a course of aggression of its own designed to expel all Russian influence from Eastern Europe and to establish democratic-capitalist states on the very border of the Soviet Union. As the revisionists see it, this radically new American policy — or rather this resumption by Truman of the pre-Roosevelt policy of insensate anti-communism — left Moscow no alternative but to take measures in defense of its own borders. The result was the Cold War.

These two views, of course, could not be more starkly contrasting. It is therefore not unreasonable to look again at the half-dozen critical years between June 22, 1941, when Hitler attacked Russia, and July 2, 1947, when the Russians walked out of the Marshall Plan meeting in Paris. Several things should be borne in mind as this reexamination is made. For one thing, we have thought a great deal more in recent years, in part because of writers like Roberta Wohlstetter and T. C. Schelling, about the problems of communication in diplomacy — the signals which one nation, by word or by deed, gives, inadvertently or intentionally, to another. Any honest reappraisal of the origins of the Cold War requires the imaginative leap — which should in any case be as instinctive for the historian as it is prudent for the statesman — into the adversary's viewpoint. We must strive to see how, given Soviet perspectives, the Russians might conceivably have misread our signals, as we must reconsider how intelligently we read theirs.

For another, the historian must not overindulge the man of power in the illusion cherished by those in office that high position carries with it the easy ability to shape history. Violating the statesman's creed, Lincoln once blurted out the truth in his letter of 1864 to A. G. Hodges: "I claim not to have controlled events, but confess plainly that events have controlled me." He was not asserting Tolstoyan fatalism but rather suggesting how greatly events limit the capacity of the statesman to bend history to his will. The physical course of the Second World War — the military operations undertaken, the position of the respective armies at the war's end, the momentum generated by victory, and the vacuums created by defeat — all these determined the future as much as the character of individual leaders and the substance of national ideology and purpose.

Nor can the historian forget the conditions under which decisions are made,

elsewhere suggests were the firmest of the firm — and was proposed by them precisely to impress on Stalin the continuity of American policy from Roosevelt to Truman. While the idea that Truman reversed Roosevelt's policy is tempting dramatically, it is a myth. See, for example, the testimony of Anna Rosenberg Hoffman, who lunched with Roosevelt on March 24, 1945, the last day he spent in Washington. After luncheon, Roosevelt was handed a cable. "He read it and became quite angry. He banged his fists on the arms of his wheelchair and said, 'Averell is right; we can't do business with Stalin. He has broken every one of the promises he made at Yalta.' He was very upset and continued in the same vein on the subject."

especially in a time like the Second World War. These were tired, overworked, aging men: in 1945, Churchill was 71 years old, Stalin had governed his country for 17 exacting years, Roosevelt his for 12 years nearly as exacting. During the war, moreover, the importunities of military operations had shoved postwar questions to the margins of their minds. All — even Stalin, behind his screen of ideology — had became addicts of improvisation, relying on authority and virtuosity to conceal the fact that they were constantly surprised by developments. Like Eliza, they leaped from one cake of ice to the next in the effort to reach the other side of the river. None showed great tactical consistency, or cared much about it; all employed a certain ambiguity to preserve their power to decide big issues; and it is hard to know how to interpret anything any one of them said on any specific occasion. This was partly because, like all princes, they designed their expressions to have particular effects on particular audiences; partly because the entirely genuine intellectual difficulty of the questions they faced made a degree of vacillation and mind-changing eminently reasonable. If historians cannot solve their problems in retrospect, who are they to blame Roosevelt, Stalin, and Churchill for not having solved them at the time?

III

Peacemaking after the Second World War was not so much a tapestry as it was a hopelessly raveled and knotted mess of yarn. Yet, for purposes of clarity, it is essential to follow certain threads. One theme indispensable to an understanding of the Cold War is the contrast between two clashing views of world order: the "universalist" view, by which all nations shared a common interest in all the affairs of the world; and the "sphere-of-influence" view, by which each great power would be assured by the other great powers of an acknowledged predominance in its own area of special interest. The universalist view assumed that national security would be guaranteed by an international organization. The sphere-of-interest view assumed that national security would be guaranteed by the balance of power. While in practice these views have by no means been incompatible (indeed, our shaky peace has been based on a combination of the two), in the abstract they involved sharp contradictions.

The tradition of American thought in these matters was universalist — that is, Wilsonian. Roosevelt had been a member of Wilson's subcabinet; in 1920, as candidate for Vice President, he had campaigned for the League of Nations. It is true that, within Roosevelt's infinitely complex mind, Wilsonianism warred with the perception of vital strategic interests he had imbibed from Mahan. Morever, his temperamental inclination to settle things with fellow princes around the conference table led him to regard the Big Three — or Four — as trustees for the rest of the world. On occasion, as this narrative will show, he was beguiled into flirtation with the sphere-of-influence heresy. But in principle he believed in joint action and remained a Wilsonian. His hope for Yalta, as he told the Congress on his return, was that it would "spell the end of the system of unilateral action, the exclusive alliances, the spheres of influence, the balances of power, and all the other expedients that have been tried for centuries — and have always failed."

Whenever Roosevelt backslid, he had at his side that Wilsonian fundamentalist, Secretary of State Cordell Hull, to recall him to the pure faith. After his visit to Moscow in 1943, Hull characteristically said that, with the Declaration of Four Nations on General Security (in which America, Russia, Britain and China pledged "united action . . . for the organization and maintenance of peace and security"), "there will no longer be need for spheres of influence, for alliances, for balance of power, or any other of the special arrangements through which, in the unhappy past, the nations strove to safeguard their security or to promote their interests."

Remembering the corruption of the Wilsonian vision by the secret treaties of the First World War, Hull was determined to prevent any sphere-of-influence nonsense after the Second World War. He therefore fought all proposals to settle border questions while the war was still on and, excluded as he largely was from wartime diplomacy, poured his not inconsiderable moral energy and frustration into the promulgation of virtuous and spacious general principles.

In adopting the universalist view, Roosevelt and Hull were not indulging personal hobbies. Sumner Welles, Adolf Berle, Averell Harriman, Charles Bohlen — all, if with a variety of nuances, opposed the sphere-of-influence approach. And here the State Department was expressing what seems clearly to have been the predominant mood of the American people, so long mistrustful of European power politics. The Republicans shared the true faith. John Foster Dulles argued that the great threat to peace after the war would lie in the revival of sphere-of-influence thinking. The United States, he said, must not permit Britain and Russia to revert to these bad old ways; it must therefore insist on American participation in all policy decisions for all territories in the world. Dulles wrote pessimistically in January 1945, "The three great powers which at Moscow agreed upon the 'closest cooperation' about European questions have shifted to a practice of separate, regional responsibility."

It is true that critics, and even friends, of the United States sometimes noted a discrepancy between the American passion for universalism when it applied to territory far from American shores and the preeminence the United States accorded its own interests nearer home. Churchill, seeking Washington's blessing for a sphere-of-influence initiative in eastern Europe, could not forbear reminding the Americans, "We follow the lead of the United States in South America"; nor did any universalist of record propose the abolition of the Monroe Doctrine. But a convenient myopia prevented such inconsistencies from qualifying the ardency of the universalist faith.

There seem only to have been three officials in the United States Government who dissented. One was the Secretary of War, Henry L. Stimson, a classical balance-of-power man, who in 1944 opposed the creation of a vacuum in Central Europe by the pastoralization of Germany and in 1945 urged "the settlement of all territorial acquisitions in the shape of defense posts which each of these four powers may deem to be necessary for their own safety" in advance of any effort to establish a peacetime United Nations. Stimson considered the claim of Russia to a preferred position in Eastern Europe as not unreasonable: as he told President Truman, "he thought the Russians perhaps were being more realistic than we were in regard to their own security." Such a position for Russia seemed to him comparable to the preferred American position in Latin America; he even spoke of "our respective orbits." Stimson was therefore skeptical of what he regarded as the prevailing tendency "to hang on to exaggerated views of the Monroe Doctrine and at the same time butt into every question that comes up in Central Europe." Acceptance of spheres of influence seemed to him the way to avoid "a head-on collision."

A second official opponent of universalism was George Kennan, an eloquent advocate from the American Embassy in Moscow of "a prompt and clear recognition of the division of Europe into spheres of influence and of a policy based on the fact of such division." Kennan argued that nothing we could do would possibly alter the course of events in Eastern Europe; that we were deceiving ourselves by supposing that these countries had any future but Russian domination; that we should therefore relinquish Eastern Europe to the Soviet Union and avoid anything which would make things easier for the Russians by giving them economic assistance or by sharing moral responsibility for their actions.

A third voice within the government against universalism was (at least after the war) Henry A. Wallace. As Secretary of Commerce, he stated the sphere-of-influence case with trenchancy in the famous Madison Square Garden speech of September 1946 which led to his dismissal by President Truman:

> On our part, we should recognize that we have no more business in the *political* affairs of Eastern Europe than Russia has in the *political* affairs of Latin America, Western Europe, and the United States. . . . Whether we like it or not, the Russians will try to socialize their sphere of influence just as we try to democratize our sphere of influence. . . . The Russians have no more business stirring up native Communists to political activity in Western Europe, Latin America, and the United States than we have in interfering with the politics of Eastern Europe and Russia.

Stimson, Kennan, and Wallace seem to have been alone in the government, however, in taking these views. They were very much minority voices. Meanwhile universalism, rooted in the American legal and moral tradition, overwhelmingly backed by contemporary opinion, received successive enshrinements in the Atlantic Charter of 1941, in the Declaration of the United Nations in 1942, and in the Moscow Declaration of 1943.

IV

The Kremlin, on the other hand, thought *only* of spheres of interest; above all, the Russians were determined to protect their frontiers, and especially their border to the west, crossed so often and so bloodily in the dark course of their history. These western frontiers lacked natural means of defense — no great oceans, rugged mountains, steaming swamps, or impenetrable jungles. The history of Russia had been the history of invasion, the last of which was by now horribly killing up to twenty million of its people. The protocol of Russia therefore meant the enlargement of the area of Russian influence. Kennan himself wrote (in May, 1944), "Behind Russia's stubborn expansion lies only the age-old sense of insecurity of a sedentary people reared on an exposed plain in the neighborhood of fierce nomadic peoples," and he called this "urge" a "permanent feature of Russian psychology."

In earlier times, the "urge" had produced the tsarist search for buffer states and maritime outlets. In 1939 the Soviet-Nazi pact and its secret protocol had enabled Russia to begin to satisfy in the Baltic states, Karelian Finland and Poland, part of what it conceived as its security requirements in Eastern Europe. But the "urge" persisted, causing the friction between Russia and Germany in 1940 as each jostled for position in the area which separated them. Later it led to Molotov's new demands on Hitler in November 1940 — a free hand in Finland, Soviet predominance in Rumania and Bulgaria, bases in the Dardanelles — the demands which convinced Hitler that he had no choice but to attack Russia. Now Stalin hoped to gain from the West what Hitler, a closer neighbor, had not dared yield him.

It is true that, so long as Russian survival appeared to require a second front to relieve the Nazi pressure, Moscow's demand for Eastern Europe was a little muffled. Thus the Soviet government adhered to the Atlantic Charter (though with a significant if obscure reservation about adapting its principles to "the circumstances, needs, and historic peculiarities of particular countries"). Thus it also adhered to the Moscow Declaration of 1943, and Molotov then, with his easy mendacity, even denied that Russia had any desire to divide Europe into spheres of influence. But this was guff, which the Russians were perfectly willing to ladle out if it would keep the Americans, and especially Secretary Hull (who made a strong personal impression at the Moscow conference), happy. "A declaration," as Stalin once observed to Eden, "I regard as algebra, but an agreement as practical arithmetic. I do not wish to decry algebra, but I prefer practical arithmetic."

The more consistent Russian purpose was revealed when Stalin offered the British a straight sphere-of-influence deal at the end of 1941. Britain, he suggested, should recognize the Russian absorption of the Baltic states, part of Finland, eastern Poland, and Bessarabia; in return, Russia would support any special British need for bases or security arrangements in Western Europe. There was nothing specifically communist about these ambitions. If Stalin achieved them, he would be fulfilling an age-old dream of the tsars. The British reaction was mixed. "Soviet policy is amoral," as Anthony Eden noted at the time; "United States policy is exaggeratedly moral, at least where non-American interests are concerned." If Roosevelt was a universalist with occasional leanings toward spheres of influence and Stalin was a sphere-of-influence man with occasional gestures toward universalism, Churchill seemed evenly poised between the familiar realism of the balance of power, which he had so long recorded as an historian and manipulated as a statesman, and the hope that there must be some better way of doing things. His 1943 proposal of a world organization divided into regional councils represented an effort to blend universalist and sphere-of-interest conceptions. His initial rejection of Stalin's proposal in December 1941 as "directly contrary to the first, second and third articles of the Atlantic Charter" thus did not spring entirely from a desire to propitiate the United States. On the other hand, he had himself already reinterpreted the Atlantic Charter as applying only to Europe (and thus not to the British Empire), and he was, above all, an empiricist who never believed in sacrificing reality on the altar of doctrine.

So in April 1942, he wrote Roosevelt that "the increasing gravity of the war" had led him to feel that the Charter "ought not to be construed so as to deny Russia the frontiers she occupied when Germany attacked her." Hull, however, remained fiercely hostile to the inclusion of territorial provisions in the Anglo-Russian treaty; the American position, Eden noted, "chilled me with Wilsonian memories." Though Stalin complained that it looked "as if the Atlantic Charter was directed against the USSR," it was the Russian season of military adversity in the spring of 1942, and he dropped his demands.

He did not, however, change his intentions. A year later Ambassador Standley could cable Washington from Moscow: "In 1918 Western Europe attempted to set up a *cordon sanitaire* to protect it from the influence of bolshevism. Might not now the Kremlin envisage the formation of a belt of pro-Soviet states to protect it from the influences of the West?" It well might; and that purpose became increasingly clear as the war approached its end. Indeed, it derived sustenance from Western policy in the first area of liberation.

The unconditional surrender of Italy in July 1943 created the first major test of the Western devotion to universalism. America and Britain, having won the Italian war, handled the capitulation, keeping Moscow informed at a distance. Stalin complained:

> The United States and Great Britain made agreements but the Soviet Union received information about the results . . . just as a passive third observer. I have to tell you that it is impossible to tolerate the situation any longer. I propose that the [tripartite military-political commission] be established and that Sicily be assigned . . . as its place of residence.

Roosevelt, who had no intention of sharing the control of Italy with the

Russians, suavely replied with the suggestion that Stalin send an officer "to General Eisenhower's headquarters in connection with the commission." Unimpressed, Stalin continued to press for a tripartite body; but his Western Allies were adamant in keeping the Soviet Union off the Control Commission for Italy, and the Russians in the end had to be satisfied with a seat, along with minor Allied states, on a meaningless Inter-Allied Advisory Council. Their acquiescence in this was doubtless not unconnected with a desire to establish precedents for Eastern Europe.

Teheran in December 1943 marked the high point of three-power collaboration. Still, when Churchill asked about Russian territorial interests, Stalin replied a little ominously, "There is no need to speak at the present time about any Soviet desires, but when the time comes we will speak." In the next weeks, there were increasing indications of a Soviet determination to deal unilaterally with Eastern Europe — so much so that in early February 1944 Hull cabled Harriman in Moscow:

> Matters are rapidly approaching the point where the Soviet Government will have to choose between the development and extension of the foundation of international cooperation as the guiding principle of the postwar world as against the continuance of a unilateral and arbitrary method of dealing with its special problems even though these problems are admittedly of more direct interest to the Soviet Union than to other great powers.

As against this approach, however, Churchill, more tolerant of sphere-of-influence deviations, soon proposed that, with the impending liberation of the Balkans, Russia should run things in Rumania and Britain in Greece. Hull strongly opposed this suggestion but made the mistake of leaving Washington for a few days; and Roosevelt, momentarily free from his Wilsonian conscience, yielded to Churchill's plea for a three-months' trial. Hull resumed the fight on his return, and Churchill postponed the matter.

The Red Army continued its advance into Eastern Europe. In August the Polish Home Army, urged on by Polish-language broadcasts from Moscow, rose up against the Nazis in Warsaw. For 63 terrible days, the Poles fought valiantly on, while the Red Army halted on the banks of the Vistula a few miles away, and in Moscow Stalin for more than half this time declined to cooperate with the Western effort to drop supplies to the Warsaw Resistance. It appeared a calculated Soviet decision to let the Nazis slaughter the anti-Soviet Polish underground; and, indeed, the result was to destroy any substantial alternative to a Soviet solution in Poland. The agony of Warsaw caused the most deep and genuine moral shock in Britain and America and provoked dark forebodings about Soviet postwar purposes.

Again history enjoins the imaginative leap in order to see things for a moment from Moscow's viewpoint. The Polish question, Churchill would say at Yalta, was for Britain a question of honor. "It is not only a question of honor for Russia," Stalin replied, "but one of life and death. . . . Throughout history Poland had been the corridor for attack on Russia." A top postwar priority for any Russian regime must be to close that corridor. The Home Army was led by anti-communists. It clearly hoped by its action to forestall the Soviet occupation of Warsaw and, in Russian eyes, to prepare the way for an anti-Russian Poland. In addition, the uprising from a strictly operational viewpoint was premature. The Russians, it is evident in retrospect, had real military problems at the Vistula. The Soviet attempt in September to send Polish units from the Red Army across the river to join forces with the Home Army was a disaster. Heavy German shelling thereafter prevented the ferrying of tanks necessary for an assault on the German position. The Red Army itself did not take Warsaw for another three months. Nonetheless, Stalin's indifference to the human tragedy, his effort to blackmail the London Poles during the ordeal, his sanctimonious opposition during five precious weeks to aerial resupply, the invariable coldness of his explanations ("the Soviet command has come to the conclusion that it must dissociate itself from the Warsaw adventure"), and the obvious political benefit to the Soviet Union from the destruction of the Home Army — all these had the effect of suddenly dropping the mask of wartime comradeship and displaying to the West the hard face of Soviet policy. In now pursuing what he grimly regarded as the minimal requirements for the postwar security of his country, Stalin was inadvertently showing the irreconcilability of both his means and his ends with the Anglo-American conception of the peace.

Meanwhile Eastern Europe presented the Alliance with still another crisis that same September. Bulgaria, which was not at war with Russia, decided to surrender to the Western Allies while it still could; and the English and Americans at Cairo began to discuss armistice terms with Bulgarian envoys. Moscow, challenged by what it plainly saw as a Western intrusion into its own zone of vital interest, promptly declared war on Bulgaria, took over the surrender negotiations and, invoking the Italian precedent, denied its Western Allies any role in the Bulgarian Control Commission. In a long and thoughtful cable, Ambassador Harriman meditated on the problems of communication with the Soviet Union. "Words," he reflected, "have a different connotation to the Soviets than they have to us. When they speak of insisting on 'friendly governments' in their neighboring countries, they have in mind something quite different from what we would mean." The Russians, he surmised, really believed that Washington accepted "their position that although they would keep us informed they had the right to settle their problems with their western neighbors unilaterally." But the Soviet position was still in flux: "the Soviet Government is not one mind." The problem, as Harriman had earlier told Harry Hopkins, was "to strengthen the hands of those around Stalin who want to play the game along our lines." The way to do this, he now told Hull, was to be understanding of their sensitivity, meet them much more than half way, encourage them and support them wherever we can, and yet oppose them promptly with the greatest of firmness where we see them going wrong. . . . The only way we can eventually come to an understanding with the Soviet Union on the question of non-interference in the internal affairs of other countries is for us to take a definite interest in the solution of the problems of each individual country as they arise.

As against Harriman's sophisticated universalist strategy, however, Churchill, increasingly fearful of the consequences of unrestrained competition in Eastern Europe, decided in early October to carry his sphere-of-influence proposal directly to Moscow. Roosevelt was at first content to have Churchill speak for him too and even prepared a cable to that effect. But Hopkins, a more rigorous universalist, took it upon himself to stop the cable and warn Roosevelt of its possible implications. Eventually Roosevelt sent a message to Harriman in Moscow emphasizing that he expected to "retain complete freedom of action after this conference is over." It was now that Churchill quickly proposed — and Stalin as quickly accepted — the celebrated division of southeastern Europe: ending (after further haggling between Eden and Molotov) with 90 percent Soviet predominance in Rumania, 80 percent in Bulgaria and Hungary, fifty-fifty in Yugoslavia, and 90 percent British predominance in Greece.

Churchill in discussing this with Harriman used the phrase "spheres of influence." But he insisted that these were only "immediate wartime arrangements" and received a highly general blessing from Roosevelt. Yet, whatever Churchill intended, there is reason to believe that Stalin construed the percentages as an agreement, not a declaration; as practical arithmetic, not algebra. For Stalin, it should be understood, the sphere-of-influence idea did not mean that he would abandon all efforts to spread communism in some other nation's sphere; it did mean that, if he tried this and the other side cracked down, he could not feel he had serious cause for complaint. As Kennan wrote to Harriman at the end of 1944:

> As far as border states are concerned the Soviet government has never ceased to think in terms of spheres of interest. They expect us to support them in whatever action they wish to take in those regions, regardless of whether that action seems to us or to the rest of the world to be right or wrong. . . . I have no doubt that this position is honestly maintained on their part, and that they would be equally prepared to reserve moral judgment on any actions which we might wish to carry out, i.e., in the Caribbean area.

In any case, the matter was already under test a good deal closer to Moscow than the Caribbean. The communist-dominated resistance movement in Greece was in open revolt against the effort of the Papandreou government to disarm and disband the guerrillas (the same Papandreou whom the Greek colonels have recently arrested on the claim that he is a tool of the communists). Churchill now called in British Army units to crush the insurrection.

This action produced a storm of criticism in his own country and in the United States; the American government even publicly dissociated itself from the intervention, thereby emphasizing its detachment from the sphere-of-influence deal. But Stalin, Churchill later claimed, "adhered strictly and faithfully to our agreement of October, and during all the long weeks of fighting the Communists in the streets of Athens not one word of reproach came from *Pravda* or *Izvestia,*" though there is no evidence that he tried to call off the Greek communists. Still, when the communist rebellion later broke out again in Greece, Stalin told Kardelj and Djilas of Yugoslavia in 1948, "The uprising in Greece must be stopped, and as quickly as possible."

No one, of course, can know what really was in the minds of the Russian leaders. The Kremlin archives are locked; of the primary actors, only Molotov survives, and he has not yet indicated any desire to collaborate with the Columbia Oral History Project. We do know that Stalin did not wholly surrender to sentimental illusion about his new friends. In June 1944, on the night before the landings in Normandy, he told Djilas that the English "find nothing sweeter than to trick their allies. . . . And Churchill? Churchill is the kind who, if you don't watch him, will slip a kopeck out of your pocket. Yes, a kopeck out of your pocket!. . . Roosevelt is not like that. He dips in his hand only for bigger coins." But whatever his views of his colleagues it is not unreasonable to suppose that Stalin would have been satisfied at the end of the war to secure what Kennan has called "a protective glacis along Russia's western border," and that, in exchange for a free hand in Eastern Europe, he was prepared to give the British and the Americans equally free hands in their zones of vital interest, including in nations as close to Russia as Greece (for the British) and, very probably — or at least so the Yugoslavs believe — China (for the United States). In other words, his initial objectives were very probably not world conquest but Russian security.

V

It is now pertinent to inquire why the United States rejected the idea of stabilizing the world by division into spheres of influence and insisted on an East European strategy. One should warn against rushing to the conclusion that it was all a row between hard-nosed, balance-of-power realists and starry-eyed Wilsonians. Roosevelt, Hopkins, Welles, Harriman, Bohlen, Berle, Dulles, and other universalists were tough and serious men. Why then did they rebuff the sphere-of-influence solution?

The first reason is that they regarded this solution as containing within itself the seeds of a third world war. The balance-of-power idea seemed inherently unstable. It had always broken down in the past. It held out to each power the permanent temptation to try to alter the balance in its own favor, and it built this temptation into the international order. It would turn the great powers of 1945 away from the objective of concerting common policies toward competition for postwar advantage. As Hopkins told Molotov at Teheran, "The President feels it essential to world peace that Russia, Great Britain, and the United States work out this control question in a manner which will not start each of the three powers arming against the others." "The greatest likelihood of eventual conflict," said the Joint Chiefs of Staff in 1944 (the only conflict which the J.C.S., in its wisdom, could then glimpse "in the foreseeable future" was between Britain and Russia), " . . . would seem to grow out of either nation initiating attempts to build up its strength, by seeking to attach to herself parts of Europe to the disadvantage and possible danger of her potential adversary." The Americans were perfectly ready to acknowledge that Russia was entitled to convincing assurance of her national security — but not this way. "I could sympathize fully with Stalin's desire to protect his western borders from future attack," as Hull put it. "But I felt that this security could best be obtained through a strong postwar peace organization."

Hull's remark suggests the second objection: that the sphere-of-influence approach would, in the words of the State Department in 1945, "militate against the establishment and effective functioning of a broader system of general security in which all countries will have their part." The United Nations, in short, was seen as the alternative to the balance of power. Nor did the universalists see any necessary incompatibility between the Russian desire for "friendly governments" on its frontier and the American desire for self-determination in Eastern Europe. Before Yalta the State Department judged the general mood of Europe as "to the left and strongly in favor of far-reaching economic and social reforms, but not, however, in favor of a left-wing totalitarian regime to achieve these reforms." Governments in Eastern Europe could be sufficiently to the left "to allay Soviet suspicions" but sufficiently representative "of the center and *petit bourgeois* elements" not to seem a prelude to communist dictatorship. The American criteria were therefore that the government "should be dedicated to the preservation of civil liberties" and "should favor social and economic reforms." A string of New Deal states — of Finlands and Czechoslovakias — seemed a reasonable compromise solution.

Third, the universalists feared that the sphere-of-interest approach would be what Hull termed "a haven for the isolationists," who would advocate America's participation in Western Hemisphere affairs on condition that it did not participate in European or Asian affairs. Hull also feared that spheres of interest would lead to "closed trade areas or discriminatory systems" and thus defeat his cherished dream of a low-tariff, freely trading world.

Fourth, the sphere-of-interest solution meant the betrayal of the principles for which the Second World War was being fought — the Atlantic Charter, the Four Freedoms, the Declaration of the United Nations. Poland summed up the problem. Britain, having gone to war to defend the independence of Poland from the Germans, could not easily conclude the war by surrendering the independence of Poland to the Russians. Thus, as Hopkins told Stalin after Roosevelt's death in 1945, Poland had "become the symbol of our ability to work out problems with the Soviet Union." Nor could American liberals in general watch with equanimity while the police state spread into countries which, if they had mostly not been real democracies, had mostly not been tyrannies either. The execution in 1943 of Ehrlich and Alter, the Polish social-ist trade union leaders, excited deep concern. "I have particularly in mind," Harriman cabled in 1944, "objection to the institution of secret police who may become involved in the persecution of persons of truly democratic convictions who may not be willing to conform to Soviet methods."

Fifth, the sphere-of-influence solution would create difficult domestic prob-lems in American politics. Roosevelt was aware of the six million or more Polish votes in the 1944 election; even more acutely, he was aware of the broader and deeper attack which would follow if, after going to war to stop the Nazi conquest of Europe, he permitted the war to end with the communist conquest of Eastern Europe. As Archibald MacLeish, then Assistant Secretary of State for Public Affairs, warned in January 1945, "The wave of disillusion-ment which has distressed us in the last several weeks will be increased if the impression is permitted to get abroad that potentially totalitarian provisional governments are to be set up without adequate safeguards as to the holding of free elections and the realization of the principles of the Atlantic Charter." Roosevelt believed that no administration could survive which did not try everything short of war to save Eastern Europe, and he was the supreme American politician of the century.

Sixth, if the Russians were allowed to overrun Eastern Europe without argument, would that satisfy them? Even Kennan, in a dispatch of May 1944, admitted that the "urge" had dreadful potentialities: "If initially successful, will it know where to stop? Will it not be inexorably carried forward, by its very nature, in a struggle to reach the whole — to attain complete mastery of the shores of the Atlantic and the Pacific?" His own answer was that there were inherent limits to the Russian capacity to expand — "that Russia will not have an easy time in maintaining the power which it has seized over other people in Eastern and Central Europe unless it receives both moral and material assistance from the West." Subsequent developments have vindicated Ken-nan's argument. By the late forties, Yugoslavia and Albania, the two East European states farthest from the Soviet Union and the two in which commu-nism was imposed from within rather than from without, had declared their independence of Moscow. But, given Russia's success in maintaining centralized control over the international communist movement for a quarter of a century, who in 1944 could have had much confidence in the idea of communist revolts against Moscow?

Most of those involved therefore rejected Kennan's answer and stayed with his question. If the West turned its back on Eastern Europe, the higher probability, in their view, was that the Russians would use their security zone, not just for defensive purposes but as a springboard from which to mount an attack on Western Europe, now shattered by war, a vacuum of power awaiting its master. "If the policy is accepted that the Soviet Union has a right to penetrate her immediate neighbors for security," Harriman said in 1944, "penetration of the next immediate neighbors becomes at a certain time equally logical." If a row with Russia were inevitable, every consideration of prudence dictated that it should take place in Eastern rather than Western Europe.

Thus idealism and realism joined in opposition to the sphere-of-influence solution. The consequence was a determination to assert an American interest in the postwar destiny of all nations, including those of Eastern Europe. In the message which Roosevelt and Hopkins drafted after Hopkins had stopped Roosevelt's initial cable authorizing Churchill to speak for the United States at the Moscow meeting of October 1944, Roosevelt now said, "There is in this global war literally no question, either military or political, in which the United States is not interested." After Roosevelt's death Hopkins repeated the point to Stalin: "The cardinal basis of President Roosevelt's policy which the American people had fully supported had been the concept that the interests of the U.S. were worldwide and not confined to North and South America and the Pacific Ocean."

VI

For better or worse, this was the American position. It is now necessary to attempt the imaginative leap and consider the impact of this position on the leaders of the Soviet Union who, also for better or for worse, had reached the bitter conclusion that the survival of their country depended on their unchallenged control of the corridors through which enemies had so often invaded their homeland. They could claim to have been keeping their own side of the sphere-of-influence bargain. Of course, they were working to capture the resistance movements of Western Europe; indeed, with the appointment of Oumansky as Ambassador to Mexico they were even beginning to enlarge underground operations in the Western Hemisphere. But, from their viewpoint, if the West permitted this, the more fools they; and, if the West stopped it, it was within their right to do so. In overt political matters the Russians were scrupulously playing the game. They had watched in silence while the British shot down Communists in Greece. In Yugoslavia Stalin was urging Tito (as Djilas later revealed) to keep King Peter. They had not only acknowledged Western preeminence in Italy but had recognized the Badoglio regime; the Italian communists had even voted (against the Socialists and the Liberals) for the renewal of the Lateran Pacts.

They would not regard anti-communist action in a Western zone as a *casus belli,* and they expected reciprocal license to assert their own authority in the East. But the principle of self-determination was carrying the United States into a deeper entanglement in Eastern Europe than the Soviet Union claimed as a right (whatever it was doing underground) in the affairs of Italy, Greece, or China. When the Russians now exercised in Eastern Europe the same brutal control they were prepared to have Washington exercise in the American sphere of influence, the American protests, given the paranoia produced alike by Russian history and Leninist ideology, no doubt seemed not only an act of hypocrisy but a threat to security. To the Russians, a stroll into the neighborhood easily became a plot to burn down the house: when, for example, damaged American planes made emergency landings in Poland and Hungary, Moscow took this as attempts to organize the local resistance. It is not unusual to suspect one's adversary of doing what one is already doing oneself. At the same time, the cruelty with which the Russians executed their idea of spheres of influence — in a sense, perhaps, an unwitting cruelty, since Stalin treated the East Europeans no worse than he had treated the Russians in the thirties — discouraged the West from accepting the equation (for example, Italy= Rumania) which seemed so self-evident to the Kremlin.

So Moscow very probably, and not unnaturally, perceived the emphasis on self-determination as a systematic and deliberate pressure on Russia's western frontiers. Moreover, the restoration of capitalism to countries freed at frightful cost by the Red Army no doubt struck the Russians as the betrayal of the principles for which *they* were fighting. "That they, the victors," Isaac Deutscher has suggested, "should now preserve an order from which they had experienced nothing but hostility, and could expect nothing but hostility . . . would have been the most miserable anti-climax to their great 'war of liberation.' " By 1944 Poland was the critical issue; Harriman later said that "under instructions from President Roosevelt, I talked about Poland with Stalin more frequently than any other subject." While the West saw the point of Stalin's demand for a "friendly government" in Warsaw, the American insistence on the sovereign virtues of free elections (ironically in the spirit of the 1917 Bolshevik decree of peace, which affirmed "the right" of a nation "to decide the forms of its state existence by a free vote, taken after the complete evacuation of the incorporating or, generally, of the stronger nation") created an insoluble problem in those countries, like Poland (and Rumania) where free elections would almost certainly produce anti-Soviet governments.

The Russians thus may well have estimated the Western pressures as calculated to encourage their enemies in Eastern Europe and to defeat their own minimum objective of a protective glacis. Everything still hung, however, on the course of military operations. The wartime collaboration had been created by one thing, and one thing alone: the threat of Nazi victory. So long as this threat was real, so was the collaboration. In late December 1944, von Rundstedt launched his counteroffensive in the Ardennes. A few weeks later, when Roosevelt, Churchill, and Stalin gathered in the Crimea, it was in the shadow of this last considerable explosion of German power. The meeting at Yalta was still dominated by the mood of war.

Yalta remains something of an historical perplexity — less, from the perspective of 1967, because of a mythical American deference to the sphere-of-influence thesis than because of the documentable Russian deference to the universalist thesis. Why should Stalin in 1945 have accepted the Declaration on Liberated Europe and an agreement on Poland pledging that "the three governments will jointly" act to assure "free elections of governments responsive to the will of the people"? There are several probable answers: that the war was not over and the Russians still wanted the Americans to intensify their military effort in the West; that one clause in the Declaration promised action on "the opinion of the three governments" and thus implied a Soviet veto, though the Polish agreement was more definite; most of all that the universalist algebra of the Declaration was plainly in Stalin's mind to be construed in terms of the practical arithmetic of his sphere-of-influence agreement with Churchill the previous October. Stalin's assurance to Churchill at Yalta that a proposed Russian amendment to the Declaration would not apply to Greece makes it clear that Roosevelt's pieties did not, in Stalin's mind, nullify Churchill's percentages. He could well have been strengthened in this supposition by the fact that *after* Yalta, Churchill himself repeatedly reasserted the terms of the October agreement as if he regarded it, despite Yalta, as controlling.

Harriman still had the feeling before Yalta that the Kremlin had "two approaches to their postwar policies" and that Stalin himself was "of two minds." One approach emphasized the internal reconstruction and development of Russia; the other its external expansion. But in the meantime the fact which dominated all political decisions — that is, the war against Germany — was moving into its final phase. In the weeks after Yalta, the military situation changed with great rapidity. As the Nazi threat declined, so too did the need for cooperation. The Soviet Union, feeling itself menaced by the American idea of self-determination and the borderlands diplomacy to which it was leading, skeptical whether the United Nations would protect its frontiers as reliably as its own domination in Eastern Europe, began to fulfill its security requirements unilaterally.

In March Stalin expressed his evaluation of the United Nations by rejecting Roosevelt's plea that Molotov come to the San Francisco conference, if only for the opening sessions. In the next weeks the Russians emphatically and crudely worked their will in Eastern Europe, above all in the test country of Poland. They were ignoring the Declaration on Liberated Europe, ignoring the

Atlantic Charter, self-determination, human freedom, and everything else the Americans considered essential for a stable peace. "We must clearly recognize," Harriman wired Washington a few days before Roosevelt's death, "that the Soviet program is the establishment of totalitarianism, ending personal liberty and democracy as we know and respect it."

At the same time, the Russians also began to mobilize communist resources in the United States itself to block American universalism. In April 1945 Jacques Duclos, who had been the Comintern official responsible for the Western communist parties, launched in *Cahiers du Communisme* an uncompromising attack on the policy of the American Communist Party. Duclos sharply condemned the revisionism of Earl Browder, the American Communist leader, as "expressed in the concept of a long-term class peace in the United States, of the possibility of the suppression of the class struggle in the postwar period and of establishment of harmony between labor and capital." Browder was specifically rebuked for favoring the "self-determination" of Europe "west of the Soviet Union" on a bourgeois-democratic basis. The excommunication of Browderism was plainly the Politburo's considered reaction to the impending defeat of Germany; it was a signal to the communist parties of the West that they should recover their identity; it was Moscow's alert to communists everywhere that they should prepare for new policies in the postwar world.

The Duclos piece obviously could not have been planned and written much later than the Yalta conference — that is, well before a number of events which revisionists now cite in order to demonstrate American responsibility for the Cold War: before Allen Dulles, for example, began to negotiate the surrender of the German armies in Italy (the episode which provoked Stalin to charge Roosevelt with seeking a separate peace and provoked Roosevelt to denounce the "vile misrepresentations" of Stalin's informants); well before Roosevelt died; many months before the testing of the atomic bomb; even more months before Truman ordered that the bomb be dropped on Japan. William Z. Foster, who soon replaced Browder as the leader of the American Communist Party and embodied the new Moscow line, later boasted of having said in January 1944, "A postwar Roosevelt administration would continue to be, as it is now, an imperialist government." With ancient suspicions revived by the American insistence on universalism, this was no doubt the conclusion which the Russians were reaching at the same time. The Soviet canonization of Roosevelt (like their present-day canonization of Kennedy) took place after the American President's death.

The atmosphere of mutual suspicion was beginning to rise. In January 1945 Molotov formally proposed that the United States grant Russia a $6 billion credit for postwar reconstruction. With characteristic tact he explained that he was doing this as a favor to save America from a postwar depression. The proposal seems to have been diffidently made and diffidently received. Roosevelt requested that the matter "not be pressed further" on the American side until he had a chance to talk with Stalin; but the Russians did not follow it up either at Yalta in February (save for a single glancing reference) or during the Stalin-Hopkins talks in May or at Potsdam. Finally the proposal was renewed in the very different political atmosphere of August. This time Washington inexplicably mislaid the request during the transfer of the records of the Foreign Economic Administration to the State Department. It did not turn up again until March 1946. Of course this was impossible for the Russians to believe; it is hard enough even for those acquainted with the capacity of the American government for incompetence to believe; and it only strengthened Soviet suspicions of American purposes.

The American credit was one conceivable form of Western contribution to Russian reconstruction. Another was lend-lease, and the possibility of reconstruction aid under the lend-lease protocol had already been discussed in 1944. But in May 1945 Russia, like Britain, suffered from Truman's abrupt termination of lend-lease shipments — "unfortunate and even brutal," Stalin told Hopkins, adding that, if it was "designed as pressure on the Russians in order to soften them up, then it was a fundamental mistake." A third form was German reparations. Here Stalin, in demanding $10 billion in reparations for the Soviet Union, made his strongest fight at Yalta. Roosevelt, while agreeing essentially with Churchill's opposition, tried to postpone the matter by accepting the Soviet figure as a "basis for discussion — a formula which led to future misunderstanding. In short, the Russian hope for major Western assistance in postwar reconstruction foundered on three events which the Kremlin could well have interpreted respectively as deliberate sabotage (the loan request), blackmail (lend-lease cancellation), and pro-Germanism (reparations).

Actually the American attempt to settle the fourth lend-lease protocol was generous and the Russians for their own reasons declined to come to an agreement. It is not clear, though, that satisfying Moscow on any of these financial scores would have made much essential difference. It might have persuaded some doves in the Kremlin that the U.S. government was genuinely friendly; it might have persuaded some hawks that the American anxiety for Soviet friendship was such that Moscow could do as it wished without inviting challenge from the United States. It would, in short, merely have reinforced both sides of the Kremlin debate; it would hardly have reversed deeper tendencies toward the deterioration of political relationships. Economic deals were surely subordinate to the quality of mutual political confidence; and here, in the months after Yalta, the decay was steady.

The Cold War had now begun. It was the product not of a decision but of a dilemma. Each side felt compelled to adopt policies which the other could not but regard as a threat to the principles of the peace. Each then felt compelled to undertake defensive measures. Thus the Russians saw no choice but to consolidate their security in Eastern Europe. The Americans, regarding

Eastern Europe as the first step toward Western Europe, responded by asserting their interest in the zone the Russians deemed vital to their security. The
Russians concluded that the West was resuming its old course of capitalist
encirclement; that it was purposefully laying the foundation for anti-Soviet
regimes in the area defined by the blood of centuries as crucial to Russian
survival. Each side believed with passion that future international stability
depended on the success of its own conception of world order. Each side, in
pursuing its own clearly indicated and deeply cherished principles, was only
confirming the fear of the other that it was bent on aggression.

Very soon the process began to acquire a cumulative momentum. The
impending collapse of Germany thus provoked new troubles: the Russians, for
example, sincerely feared that the West was planning a separate surrender of
the German armies in Italy in a way which would release troops for Hitler's
eastern front, as they subsequently feared that the Nazis might succeed in
surrendering Berlin to the West. This was the context in which the atomic
bomb now appeared. Though the revisionist argument that Truman dropped
the bomb less to defeat Japan than to intimidate Russia is not convincing, this
thought unquestionably appealed to some in Washington as at least an advantageous side-effect of Hiroshima.

So the machinery of suspicion and counter-suspicion, action and coun-
ter-action, was set in motion. But, given relations among traditional national
states, there was still no reason, even with all the postwar jostling, why this
should not have remained a manageable situation. What made it unmanage-
able, what caused the rapid escalation of the Cold War and in another two
years completed the division of Europe, was a set of considerations which this
account has thus far excluded.

VII

Up to this point, the discussion has considered the schism within the wartime
coalition as if it were entirely the result of disagreements among national states.
Assuming this framework, there was unquestionably a failure of communication between America and Russia, a misperception of signals and, as time went
on, a mounting tendency to ascribe ominous motives to the other side. It seems
hard, for example, to deny that American postwar policy created genuine
difficulties for the Russians and even assumed a threatening aspect for them.
All this the revisionists have rightly and usefully emphasized.

But the great omission of the revisionists — and also the fundamental
explanation of the speed with which the Cold War escalated — lies precisely
in the fact that the Soviet Union was *not* a traditional national state.[4] This is

4. This is the classical revisionist fallacy — the assumption of the rationality, or at least
of the traditionalism, of states where ideology and social organization have created a different

where the "mirror image," invoked by some psychologists, falls down. For the Soviet Union was a phenomenon very different from America or Britain: it was a totalitarian state, endowed with an all-explanatory, all-consuming ideology, committed to the infallibility of government and party, still in a somewhat messianic mood, equating dissent with treason, and ruled by a dictator who, for all his quite extraordinary abilities, had his paranoid moments.

Marxism-Leninism gave the Russian leaders a view of the world according to which all societies were inexorably destined to proceed along appointed roads by appointed stages until they achieved the classless nirvana. Moreover, given the resistance of the capitalists to this development, the existence of any non-communist state was *by definition* a threat to the Soviet Union. "As long as capitalism and socialism exist," Lenin wrote, "we cannot live in peace: in the end, one or the other will triumph — a funeral dirge will be sung either over the Soviet Republic or over world capitalism."

Stalin and his associates, whatever Roosevelt or Truman did or failed to do, were bound to regard the United States as the enemy, not because of this deed or that, but because of the primordial fact that America was the leading capitalist power and thus, by Leninist syllogism, unappeasably hostile, driven by the logic of its system to oppose, encircle, and destroy Soviet Russia. Nothing the United States could have done in 1944 – 45 would have abolished this mistrust, required and sanctified as it was by Marxist gospel — nothing short of the conversion of the United States into a Stalinist despotism; and even this would not have sufficed, as the experience of Yugoslavia and China soon showed, unless it were accompanied by total subservience to Moscow. So long as the United States remained a capitalist democracy, no American policy, given Moscow's theology, could hope to win basic Soviet confidence, and every American action was poisoned from the source. So long as the Soviet Union remained a messianic state, ideology compelled a steady expansion of communist power.

It is easy, of course, to exaggerate the capacity of ideology to control events. The tension of acting according to revolutionary abstractions is too much for most nations to sustain over a long period: that is why Mao Tse-tung has launched his Cultural Revolution, hoping thereby to create a permanent revolutionary mood and save Chinese communism from the degeneration which, in his view, has overtaken Russian communism. Still, as any revolution grows older, normal human and social motives will increasingly reassert themselves. In due course, we can be sure, Leninism will be about as effective in governing

range of motives. So the Second World War revisionists omit the totalitarian dynamism of Nazism and the fanaticism of Hitler, as the Civil War revisionists omit the fact that the slavery system was producing a doctrinaire closed society in the American South. For a consideration of some of these issues, see "The Causes of the Civil War: A Note on Historical Sentimentalism" in my *The Politics of Hope* (Boston, 1963).

the daily lives of Russians as Christianity is in governing the daily lives of Americans. Like the Ten Commandments and the Sermon on the Mount, the Leninist verities will increasingly become platitudes for ritual observance, not guides to secular decision. There can be no worse fallacy (even if respectable people practiced it diligently for a season in the United States) than that of drawing from a nation's ideology permanent conclusions about its behavior.

A temporary recession of ideology was already taking place during the Second World War when Stalin, to rally his people against the invader, had to replace the appeal of Marxism by that of nationalism. ("We are under no illusions that they are fighting for us," Stalin once said to Harriman. "They are fighting for Mother Russia.") But this was still taking place within the strictest limitations. The Soviet Union remained as much a police state as ever; the regime was as infallible as ever; foreigners and their ideas were as suspect as ever. "Never, except possibly during my later experience as ambassador in Moscow," Kennan has written, "did the insistence of the Soviet authorities on isolation of the diplomatic corps weigh more heavily on me . . . than in these first weeks following my return to Russia in the final months of the war. . . . [We were] treated as though we were the bearers of some species of the plague" — which, of course, from the Soviet viewpoint, they were: the plague of skepticism.

Paradoxically, of the forces capable of bringing about a modification of ideology, the most practical and effective was the Soviet dictatorship itself. If Stalin was an ideologist, he was also a pragmatist. If he saw everything through the lenses of Marxism-Leninism, he also, as the infallible expositor of the faith, could reinterpret Marxism-Leninism to justify anything he wanted to do at any given moment. No doubt Roosevelt's ignorance of Marxism-Leninism was inexcusable and led to grievous miscalculations. But Roosevelt's efforts to work on and through Stalin were not so hopelessly naïve as it used to be fashionable to think. With the extraordinary instinct of a great political leader, Roosevelt intuitively understood that Stalin was the *only* lever available to the West against the Leninist ideology and the Soviet system. If Stalin could be reached, then alone was there a chance of getting the Russians to act contrary to the prescriptions of their faith. The best evidence is that Roosevelt retained a certain capacity to influence Stalin to the end; the nominal Soviet acquiescence in American universalism as late as Yalta was perhaps an indication of that. It is in this way that the death of Roosevelt was crucial — not in the vulgar sense that his policy was then reversed by his successor, which did not happen, but in the sense that no other American could hope to have the restraining impact on Stalin which Roosevelt might for a while have had.

Stalin alone could have made any difference. Yet Stalin, in spite of the impression of sobriety and realism he made on Westerners who saw him during the Second World War, was plainly a man of deep and morbid obsessions and compulsions. When he was still a young man, Lenin had criticized his rude and arbitrary ways. A reasonably authoritative observer (N. S. Khrushchev) later commented, "These negative characteristics of his developed steadily and during the last years acquired an absolutely insufferable character." His paranoia, probably set off by the suicide of his wife in 1932, led to the terrible purges of the mid-thirties and the wanton murder of thousands of his Bolshevik comrades. "Everywhere and in everything," Khrushchev says of this period, "he saw 'enemies,' 'double-dealers' and 'spies.' " The crisis of war evidently steadied him in some way, though Khrushchev speaks of his "nervousness and hysteria . . . even after the war began." The madness, so rigidly controlled for a time, burst out with new and shocking intensity in the postwar years. "After the war," Khrushchev testifies,

> the situation became even more complicated. Stalin became even more capricious, irritable and brutal; in particular, his suspicion grew. His persecution mania reached unbelievable dimensions. . . . He decided everything, without any consideration for anyone or anything.
>
> Stalin's willfulness showed itself . . . also in the international relations of the Soviet Union. . . . He had completely lost a sense of reality; he demonstrated his suspicion and haughtiness not only in relation to individuals in the USSR, but in relation to whole parties and nations.

A revisionist fallacy has been to treat Stalin as just another *Realpolitik* statesman, as Second World War revisionists see Hitler as just another Stresemann or Bismarck. But the record makes it clear that in the end nothing could satisfy Stalin's paranoia. His own associates failed. Why does anyone suppose that any conceivable American policy would have succeeded?

An analysis of the origins of the Cold War which leaves out these factors — the intransigence of Leninist ideology, the sinister dynamics of a totalitarian society, and the madness of Stalin — is obviously incomplete. It was these factors which made it hard for the West to accept the thesis that Russia was moved only by a desire to protect its security and would be satisfied by the control of Eastern Europe; it was these factors which charged the debate between universalism and spheres of influence with apocalyptic potentiality.

Leninism and totalitarianism created a structure of thought and behavior which made postwar collaboration between Russia and America — in any normal sense of civilized intercourse between national states — inherently impossible. The Soviet dictatorship of 1945 simply could not have survived such a collaboration. Indeed, nearly a quarter-century later, the Soviet regime, though it has meanwhile moved a good distance, could still hardly survive it without risking the release inside Russia of energies profoundly opposed to communist despotism. As for Stalin, he may have represented the only force in 1945 capable of overcoming Stalinism, but the very traits which enabled him to win absolute power expressed terrifying instabilities of mind and temperament and hardly offered a solid foundation for a peaceful world.

VIII

The difference between America and Russia in 1945 was that some Americans fundamentally believed that, over a long run, a *modus vivendi* with Russia was possible; while the Russians, so far as one can tell, believed in no more than a short-run *modus vivendi* with the United States.

Harriman and Kennan, this narrative has made clear, took the lead in warning Washington about the difficulties of short-run dealings with the Soviet Union. But both argued that, if the United States developed a rational policy and stuck to it, there would be, after long and rough passages, the prospect of eventual clearing. "I am, as you know," Harriman cabled Washington in early April, "a most earnest advocate of the closest possible understanding with the Soviet Union so that what I am saying relates only to how best to attain such understanding." Kennan has similarly made it clear that the function of his containment policy was "to tide us over a difficult time and bring us to the point where we could discuss effectively with the Russians the dangers and drawbacks this status quo involved, and to arrange with them for its peaceful replacement by a better and sounder one." The subsequent careers of both men attest to the honesty of these statements.

There is no corresponding evidence on the Russian side that anyone seriously sought a *modus vivendi* in these terms. Stalin's choice was whether his long-term ideological and national interests would be better served by a short-run truce with the West or by an immediate resumption of pressure. In October 1945 Stalin indicated to Harriman at Sochi that he planned to adopt the second course — that the Soviet Union was going isolationist. No doubt the succession of problems with the United States contributed to this decision, but the basic causes most probably lay elsewhere: in the developing situations in Eastern Europe, in Western Europe, and in the United States.

In Eastern Europe, Stalin was still for a moment experimenting with techniques of control. But he must by now have begun to conclude that he had underestimated the hostility of the people to Russian dominion. The Hungarian elections in November would finally convince him that the Yalta formula was a road to anti-Soviet governments. At the same time, he was feeling more strongly than ever a sense of his opportunities in Western Europe. The other half of the Continent lay unexpectedly before him, politically demoralized, economically prostrate, militarily defenseless. The hunting would be better and safer than he had anticipated. As for the United States, the alacrity of postwar demobilization must have recalled Roosevelt's offhand remark at Yalta that "two years would be the limit" for keeping American troops in Europe. And, despite Dr. Eugene Varga's doubts about the imminence of American economic breakdown, Marxist theology assured Stalin that the United States was heading into a bitter postwar depression and would be consumed with its own problems. If the condition of Eastern Europe made unilateral action seem essential in the interests of Russian security, the condition of Western Europe and the United States offered new temptations for communist expansion. The Cold War was now in full swing.

It still had its year of modulations and accommodations. Secretary Byrnes conducted his long and fruitless campaign to persuade the Russians that America only sought governments in Eastern Europe "both friendly to the Soviet Union and representative of all the democratic elements of the country." Crises were surmounted in Trieste and Iran. Secretary Marshall evidently did not give up hope of a *modus vivendi* until the Moscow conference of foreign secretaries of March 1947. Even then, the Soviet Union was invited to participate in the Marshall Plan.

The point of no return came on July 2, 1947, when Molotov, after bringing 89 technical specialists with him to Paris and evincing initial interest in the project for European reconstruction, received the hot flash from the Kremlin, denounced the whole idea, and walked out of the conference. For the next fifteen years the Cold War raged unabated, passing out of historical ambiguity into the realm of good versus evil and breeding on both sides simplifications, stereotypes, and self-serving absolutes, often couched in interchangeable phrases. Under the pressure even America, for a deplorable decade, forsook its pragmatic and pluralist traditions, posed as God's appointed messenger to ignorant and sinful man, and followed the Soviet example in looking to a world remade in its own image.

In retrospect, if it is impossible to see the Cold War as a case of American aggression and Russian response, it is also hard to see it as a pure case of Russian aggression and American response. "In what is truly tragic," wrote Hegel, "there must be valid moral powers on both the sides which come into collision. . . . Both suffer loss and yet both are mutually justified." In this sense, the Cold War had its tragic elements. The question remains whether it was an instance of Greek tragedy — as Auden has called it, "the tragedy of necessity," where the feeling aroused in the spectator is "What a pity it had to be this way" — or of Christian tragedy, "the tragedy of possibility," where the feeling aroused is "What a pity it was this way when it might have been otherwise."

Once something has happened, the historian is tempted to assume that it had to happen; but this may often be a highly unphilosophical assumption. The Cold War could have been avoided only if the Soviet Union had not been possessed by convictions both of the infallibility of the communist word and of the inevitability of a communist world. These convictions transformed an impasse between national states into a religious war, a tragedy of possibility into one of necessity. One might wish that America had preserved the poise and proportion of the first years of the Cold War and had not in time succumbed to its own forms of self-righteousness. But the most rational of American policies could hardly have averted the Cold War. Only today, as Russia begins to recede from its messianic mission and to accept, in practice if not yet in principle, the permanence of the world of diversity, only now can the hope flicker that this long, dreary, costly contest may at last be taking on forms less dramatic, less obsessive, and less dangerous to the future of mankind.

The Cold War Revisionists*

It becomes increasingly clear that many of the policies and actions of the New and Fair Deals, and of the upper-class Daniel Boones of the New Frontier, are producing something less than happiness and security. One of the reactions of liberals within the Establishment is to blame that Nasty Old Populist Lyndon, and to regroup with their own kind. That course has its intellectual and moral difficulties, however, as well as its pragmatic risks, and no one has pointed them out more directly than Daniel P. Moynihan.

One has to respect the integrity and the historical accuracy of his remarks to the A.D.A. on September 24. "The war in Vietnam," he candidly announced, "was thought up and is being managed by the men John F Kennedy brought to Washington." Then, addressing his audience directly, he remarked that there were few present "who did not contribute something considerable to persuade the American people that we were entirely right to be setting out on the course that has led us to the present point of being waist-deep in the big muddy. It is this knowledge, this complicity if you will, that requires of many of us a restraint. . . . Who are we to say we would have done better?"

Brave words — and largely true.

But also terribly and dangerously misleading. For there is neither logical nor moral discrepancy between acknowledging responsibility and admitting

*Reprinted from *The Nation,* CCV, 16 (November 13, 1967), pp. 492 – 495, by permission of the author and the publisher.

error. It is neither the act of a trimmer or coward, nor an abstract proposition advanced by an academic. Senator Fulbright and others have done it.

There is no transcendent reason to persist in rationalizing a mistake, or in hanging on to see it through. Explanations can no doubt be found for such action, but they do not speak to the central point. Those who realize that have clearly become increasingly nervous in the service of the Establishment. They know that the primary objective is to discover the where and the why of the mistake, and then rectify it as rapidly and effectively as possible.

A good deal of evidence suggests that Arthur M. Schlesinger, Jr., would like to rectify while at the same time prove that no mistakes were made of major dimensions. His little essays on the war in Vietnam, for example, are interesting exercises in trying to achieve that magical success. He does not succeed because no one can succeed in that enterprise: there are momentum, drift and chance in human affairs, but the initial course determines the effect of the momentum, drift and chance.

The difficulties of Schlesinger's approach are even more evident in his essay on "The Origins of the Cold War," printed in the October issue of *Foreign Affairs* (that *House Beautiful* of the Department of State). The article subtly admits some minor degree of American responsibility for the onset of the cold war as part of a central and overt attempt to modify the attitudes and policies of that era in the knowledge of their clearly dangerous consequences. But he maintains that there were no major American mistakes, and no major American responsibility, because nothing else could have been done. The trouble, he insists, was that "Stalin alone could have made any difference," and Stalin was paranoid.

There is a great book to be written some day explaining how Schlesinger and a good many other historians of his generation came by the power to render such flat-out psychiatric judgments without professional training and without direct access to their subjects. My own candidates for that undertaking are Robert Coles, Abraham H. Maslow, or Rollo May, men who somehow acquired a sense of the limits of their approach even as they mastered its discipline.

Meanwhile, the first point to be made about Schlesinger's attempt to fix the origins of the cold war in Stalin's paranoia is that *no major American policy-maker between 1943 and 1948 defined and dealt with the Soviet Union in those terms.* Schlesinger offers not the slightest shred of evidence that such was the case. The reason is simple: there is no such evidence.

Even if Schlesinger's characterization of Stalin as a paranoid were granted, the argument would still be unable to account either for the nature or the adoption of American policy. There is only one circumstance in which his proposition would become directly relevant: If a different American policy had been carefully formulated and then seriously tried over a significant period of time, only to fail because of Russian intransigence, then Schlesinger's argument that Stalin's paranoia caused the cold war would bear on the case.

It is particularly important to grasp that point because Schlesinger does not introduce paranoia until after he has demonstrated that Stalin was acting on a rational and conservative basis. Long before he mentions paranoia, Schlesinger notes the ambivalence of Soviet leaders toward an accommodation with the United States, and makes it clear that American leaders were operating on that estimate of the situation — not on the proposition that the Russians were paranoid. While entering the caveat that "no one, of course, can know what was really in the minds of the Russian leaders," he nevertheless concludes that "it is not unreasonable to suppose that Stalin would have been satisfied at the end of the war to secure . . . 'a protective glacis along Russia's western border' . . . . His initial objective was very probably not world conquest but Russian security." And he makes it clear that Stalin kept his word about giving the British the initiative in Greece.

Schlesinger does not resort to explaining Soviet action in terms of paranoia until he has to deal with American efforts to exert direct influence on affairs in Eastern Europe. Then he casually asserts that it was a factor: "given the paranoia produced alike by Russian history and Leninist ideology, [American action] no doubt seemed not only an act of hypocrisy but a threat to security."

That offhand introduction of paranoia as a primary operational factor in historical explanation staggers the mind. It is simply not convincing to hold that a man (in this instance, Stalin) who believes he has negotiated a clear security perimeter is paranoid because he reacts negatively when one of the parties to the understanding (in this case the United States) unilaterally asserts and acts on a self-proclaimed right to intervene within that perimeter. When examined closely in connection with foreign affairs, the most that can be made of Schlesinger's argument is that Stalin may have had strong paranoid tendencies, and that the American thrust into Eastern Europe (and elsewhere throughout the world) could very well have pushed him gradually into, and perhaps through, the psychic zone separating neurosis from psychosis.

The most significant aspect of Schlesinger's argument that emerges at this point is his admission that America's assertion of its right to intervene anywhere in the world, and its action in doing so in Eastern Europe, had a primary effect on Soviet behavior. For in saying that, however he qualifies it later, Schlesinger has granted the validity of one of the major points made by the critics of the official line on the cold war. Many criticisms could be made of his description of the nature and dynamism of American global interventionism, which he labels "universalism," but the most important weakness in his analysis is the failure to discuss the explicit and implicit anti-communism that was a strong element in the American outlook from the moment the Bolsheviks seized power in 1917. That omission gravely undercuts the attempt he makes later to substantiate a vital part of his argument.

For, having admitted the reality and the consequences of American interventionism, Schlesinger faces the difficult problem of demonstrating the truth
of three propositions if he is to establish Soviet responsibility for the cold war.
First, he must show that a different American policy could not have produced
other results. Second, he must sustain the thesis that the Soviet response to
American universalism was indeed paranoid. Third, he must prove that the
American counterresponse was relevant and appropriate.

Schlesinger's argument that an alternate American policy would not have
made any difference has two themes. He says that a serious effort to negotiate
around the Soviet bid for a $6 billion loan would "merely have reinforced both
sides of the Kremlin debate" because "economic deals were merely subordinate to the quality of mutual political confidence." That judgment completely
overlooks the impact which a serious American economic proposal would have
made on the "quality of political confidence."

In the end, however, Schlesinger falls back on Soviet paranoia as the reason
that a different approach would have made no difference. Here, however, he
introduces a new factor in his explanation. In the early part of the argument,
he holds that the Soviets "thought *only* of spheres of influence; above all, the
Russians were determined to protect their frontiers, and especially their border
to the west, crossed so often and so bloodily in the dark course of their
history." But later Schlesinger suggests that the paranoia was partially caused,
and significantly reinforced, by the Marxist ideology of capitalist antagonism
and opposition.

However, Soviet leaders did not detect capitalist hostility merely because
they were viewing the world through a Marxist prism. Such enmity had
existed, and had been acted upon, since November, 1917, and anti-communism
was an integral part of the universalism that guided American leaders at the
end of World War II. As Schlesinger demonstrates, willy-nilly if not intentionally, American leaders were prepared to work with Russian leaders if they
would accept key features of the American creed. It is possible, given that
truth, to construct a syllogism proving that Stalin was paranoid because he did
not accept the terms. But that kind of proof has nothing to do with serious
historical inquiry, analysis and interpretation.

The real issue at this juncture, however, is not how Schlesinger attempts
to establish Stalin's paranoia. The central question is whether or not Soviet
actions are accurately described as paranoid. The evidence does not support
that interpretation. Consider the nature of Soviet behavior in three crucial
areas.

First, the Russians reacted to American intervention in Eastern Europe by
consolidating their existing position in that region. Many Soviet actions implementing that decision were overpowering, cruel and ruthless, but the methods
do not bear on the nature of the policy itself. The Soviet choice served to verify

an important point that Schlesinger acknowledges: Stalin told Harriman in October, 1945, that the Soviets were "going isolationist" in pursuit of their national interests. Russian policy at that time in Eastern Europe was neither paranoid nor messianic Marxism.

Second, the Soviets pulled back in other areas to avoid escalating a direct national or governmental confrontation with the United States. They did so in the clash over rival claims for oil rights in Iran; and that policy was even more strikingly apparent in Stalin's attempt to postpone Mao's triumph in China. In the first instance, prudence belies paranoia. In the second, any messianic urges were suppressed in the national interest.

Third, the Soviets acquiesced in the activities of non-Russian Communist movements. While the term *acquiesced* is not perfect for describing the complex process that was involved, it is nevertheless used advisedly as the best single term to describe the *effect* of Soviet action. Stalin and his colleagues no doubt sought results other than those that occurred in many places — China and Yugoslavia come particularly to mind — and clearly tried to realize their preferences. Nevertheless, they did acquiesce in results that fell far short of their desires.

Schlesinger makes a great deal, as do all official interpreters of the cold war, of the April, 1945, article by Jacques Duclos of the French Communist Party. Let us assume that Duclos wrote the article on orders from Moscow, even though the process that produced the action was probably far more complex than indicated by that simple statement. The crucial point about Duclos' article is that it can be read in two ways. It can be interpreted as a messianic cry for non-Soviet Communist parties to strike for power as part of a general push to expand Russian boundaries or the Soviet sphere of influence. But it can as persuasively be read as primarily a call for non-Soviet Communists to reassert their own identity and become militant and disruptive as part of the Russian strategy of consolidation in the face of American universalism.

Official explanations of the cold war generally imply that American leaders heard the Duclos piece as a bugle call for Communist aid in behalf of Soviet expansion. In truth, no significant number of American leaders feared a Russian military offensive at any time during the evolution of the cold war. When the Duclos article appeared, and for a long period thereafter, they were far more concerned with devising ways to use the great preponderance of American power to further the universalism and interventionism of the United States in Eastern Europe and elsewhere.

But the most astonishing use of the Duclos article by any defender of the official line on the cold war is made by Schlesinger when he employs it to avoid any serious discussion of the impact of the dropping of two atomic bombs in August, 1945. In truth, astonishing is a very mild word for Schlesinger's performance on this point. He says merely that the Duclos article came many months before the bombs were dropped, and then proceeds to ignore the *effect* of the bomb on Soviet leaders. All he adds is a flat assertion that the critics are "not convincing" in their argument that "the bomb was dropped less to defeat Japan than to intimidate Russia" (which is a strained interpretation of what they have said). That is not even to the point, for one could agree that the bomb was dropped only to finish the Japanese and still insist that it had a powerful effect on Soviet thought and action in connection with its future relations with the United States.

The argument could be made, of course, that only a Russia gone paranoid would have been upset by the American act. The issue of psychotic behavior might better be raised about the Americans. It could also be maintained that the United States had no responsibility for the effects of the bomb on Soviet leaders because the motive in using it was not anti-Soviet. That is about like saying that a man who constantly interferes in the affairs of his neighbors, and who suddenly starts using a 40-millimeter cannon to kill cats in his back yard, bears no responsibility for the neighbor's skepticism about his good intentions. Schlesinger is fully warranted in making a careful examination of the period before the bomb, but he has no justification for so nearly ignoring the role of the bomb in the origins of the cold war.

Finally, there is the question of the relevance and appropriateness of the American response to the Soviet policy of consolidation in Eastern Europe, and the related call for non-Russian Communists to reassert their identity and policies. The answer, put simply and directly, is that the increasingly militarized holy war mounted by American leaders was grossly irrelevant to the situation and highly conducive to producing problems that were more dangerous than those the policy was supposed to resolve.

The fashion of the moment among those who are nervous in the service of the Establishment is to wring one's hands and explain that George F. Kennan did not mean what he wrote in his famous "Long Letter," first filed as a dispatch to the State Department and then printed as the X-article in *Foreign Affairs*. Poor Kennan, the argument seems to be, the one time he left his style in the inkwell was unfortunately the time he needed it most.

It is a ludicrous argument. In the first place, Kennan had ample opportunity to revise the document before it was declassified and published. Furthermore, style is an expression of thought and the intransigent and quasi-military metaphors of the article do accurately express Kennan's deep, abiding and militant anti-communism. In addition, nothing prevented him from immediately revising and clarifying the article if people were getting an erroneous impression of his ideas from an accurate reading of his language; and nothing prevented him from resigning in urgent protest against the rapid emotional militarization of his strategy. Finally, those liberals who enlisted in the cold war had as much to do with that implementation of his policy as did the conservatives. The truth is that Senator Robert A. Taft made a far more courageous and public fight to prevent that from happening than did either Kennan or those liberals who now wring their hands about the state of the nation and the dangers of the Vietnamese War. And so did the radicals who are now far stronger than they were in 1945, 1946 and 1947 — or even 1948.

It is nevertheless true that the contemporary trauma of Establishment liberals is very real. They have come to recognize, or at least sense, the dangerous consequences of American universalism and the global interventionism that it produces. But they cannot wrench themselves free of the false syllogism by which they equate universal interventionism with internationalism, and they cannot tune out the siren call to save the world. They are still practicing the nonintellectualism (and worse) of pinning the label "isolationist" on anyone who has the temerity to point out that universalism is an extremely dangerous *reductio ad absurdum* of internationalism.

Richard H. Rovere spoke to these points in *The New Yorker* of October 28, where he supplied further documentation of the nervousness within the Establishment. In some respects, at any rate, he speaks more directly and candidly about the issues than does Schlesinger. Thus he says that the war in Vietnam is "an application of established policy that has miscarried so dreadfully that we must begin examining not just the case at hand but the whole works."

He also acknowledges the relationship between foreign aid given within that framework and the rise of anti-Americanism and wars. And he bluntly admits that American democracy "is in many ways a fraud." Most important, Rovere speaks directly to the necessity of acting now to change American attitudes and policies before the mistakes of the past lead to very serious disruption and disaffection.

Unless the liberals abandon universalism, they face the serious possibility of being overpowered by the conservatives inside the Establishment at the same time that they are being shunted aside by the radicals in the society at large. One is reluctant to conclude, once and for all, that Schlesinger has allowed his archaic interpretation of American history to blind him to the essential truth that his beloved Vital Center retains its vitality only as it moves left.

That estimate is difficult to accept because of his great intelligence, but it is even more painful to accept because it means that the liberals are becoming mere role players in a Greek tragedy rather than sustaining their activities as protagonists in the Christian tragedy. If that is the case, it could very well mean that America can renounce universalist interventionism only as it is forced to do so.

The Cold War, Revisited and Re-Visioned*

More than a year has passed since Arthur Schlesinger, Jr., announced that the time had come "to blow the whistle before the current outburst of revisionism regarding the origins of the cold war goes much further." Yet the outburst of revisionism shows no signs of subsiding. On the contrary, a growing number of historians and political critics, judging from such recent books as Ronald Steel's *Pax Americana* and Carl Oglesby's and Richard Shaull's *Containment and Change,* are challenging the view, once so widely accepted, that the cold war was an American response to Soviet expansionism, a distasteful burden reluctantly shouldered in the face of a ruthless enemy bent on our destruction, and that Russia, not the United States, must therefore bear the blame for shattering the world's hope that two world wars in the 20th century would finally give way to an era of peace.

"Revisionist" historians are arguing instead that the United States did as much as the Soviet Union to bring about the collapse of the wartime coalition. Without attempting to shift the blame exclusively to the United States, they are trying to show, as Gar Alperovitz puts it, that "the cold war cannot be understood simply as an American response to a Soviet challenge, but rather as the insidious interaction of mutual suspicions, blame for which must be shared by all."

*©1968 by The New York Times Company. Reprinted by permission of the author and publisher from *The New York Times Magazine,* January 14, 1968.

Not only have historians continued to reexamine the immediate origins of the cold war — in spite of attempts to "blow the whistle" on their efforts — but the scope of revisionism has been steadily widening. Some scholars are beginning to argue that the whole course of American diplomacy since 1898 shows that the United States has become a counterrevolutionary power committed to the defense of a global status quo. Arno Mayer's monumental study of the Conference of Versailles, *Politics and Diplomacy of Peacemaking,* which has recently been published by Knopf and which promises to become the definitive work on the subject, announces in its subtitle what a growing number of historians have come to see as the main theme of American diplomacy: "Containment and Counterrevolution."

Even Schlesinger has now admitted, in a recent article in *Foreign Affairs,* that he was "somewhat intemperate," a year ago, in deploring the rise of cold war revisionism. Even though revisionist interpretations of earlier wars "have failed to stick," he says, "revisionism is an essential part of the process by which history . . . enlarges its perspectives and enriches its insights." Since he goes on to argue that "postwar collaboration between Russia and America [was] . . . inherently impossible" and that "the most rational of American policies could hardly have averted the cold war," it is not clear what Schlesinger thinks revisionism has done to enlarge our perspective and enrich our insights; but it is good to know, nevertheless, that revisionists may now presumably continue their work (inconsequential as it may eventually prove to be) without fear of being whistled to a stop by the referee.

The orthodox interpretation of the cold war, as it has come to be regarded, grew up in the late forties and early fifties — years of acute international tension, during which the rivalry between the United States and the Soviet Union repeatedly threatened to erupt in a renewal of global war. Soviet-American relations had deteriorated with alarming speed following the defeat of Hitler. At Yalta, in February, 1945, Winston Churchill had expressed the hope that world peace was nearer the grasp of the assembled statesmen of the great powers "than at any time in history." It would be "a great tragedy," he said, "if they, through inertia or carelessness, let it slip from their grasp. History would never forgive them if they did."

Yet the Yalta agreements themselves, which seemed at the time to lay the basis of postwar cooperation, shortly provided the focus of bitter dissension, in which each side accused the other of having broken its solemn promises. In Western eyes, Yalta meant free elections and parliamentary democracies in Eastern Europe, while the Russians construed the agreements as recognition of their demand for governments friendly to the Soviet Union.

The resulting dispute led to mutual mistrust and to a hardening of positions on both sides. By the spring of 1946 Churchill himself, declaring that "an iron curtain has descended" across Europe, admitted, in effect, that the "tragedy" he had feared had come to pass: Europe split into hostile fragments, the eastern half dominated by the Soviet Union, the western part sheltering nervously under the protection of American arms. NATO, founded in 1949 and countered by the Russian sponsored Warsaw Pact, merely ratified the existing division of Europe.

From 1946 on, every threat to the stability of this uneasy balance produced an immediate political crisis — Greece in 1947, Czechoslovakia and the Berlin blockade in 1948 — each of which, added to existing tensions, deepened hostility on both sides and increased the chance of war. When Bernard Baruch announced in April, 1947, that "we are in the midst of a cold war," no one felt inclined to contradict him. The phrase stuck, as an accurate description of postwar political realities.

Many Americans concluded, moreover, that the United States was losing the cold war. Two events in particular contributed to this sense of alarm — the collapse of Nationalist China in 1949, followed by Chiang Kai-shek's flight to Taiwan, and the explosion of an atomic bomb by the Russians in the same year. These events led to the charge that American leaders had deliberately or unwittingly betrayed the country's interests. The Alger Hiss case was taken by some people as proof that the Roosevelt Administration had been riddled by subversion.

Looking back to the wartime alliance with the Soviet Union, the American Right began to argue that Roosevelt, by trusting the Russians, had sold out the cause of freedom. Thus Nixon and McCarthy, aided by historians like Stefan J. Possony, C. C. Tansill, and others, accused Roosevelt of handing Eastern Europe to the Russians and of giving them a preponderant interest in China which later enabled the Communists to absorb the entire country.

The liberal interpretation of the cold war — what I have called the orthodox interpretation — developed partly as a response to these charges. In liberal eyes, the right-wingers made the crucial mistake of assuming that American actions had been decisive in shaping the postwar world. Attempting to rebut this devil theory of postwar politics, liberals relied heavily on the argument that the shape of postwar politics had already been dictated by the war itself, in which the Western democracies had been obliged to call on Soviet help in defeating Hitler. These events, they maintained, had left the Soviet Union militarily dominant in Eastern Europe and generally occupying a position of much greater power, relative to the West, than the position she had enjoyed before the war.

In the face of these facts, the United States had very little leeway to influence events in what were destined to become Soviet spheres of influence, particularly since Stalin was apparently determined to expand even if it meant ruthlessly breaking his agreements — and after all it was Stalin, the liberals emphasized, and not Roosevelt or Truman, who broke the Yalta agreement on Poland, thereby precipitating the cold war.

These were the arguments presented with enormous charm, wit, logic, and power in George F. Kennan's *American Diplomacy* (1951), which more than any other book set the tone of cold war historiography. For innumerable historians, but especially for those who were beginning their studies in the fifties, Kennan served as the model of what a scholar should be — committed yet detached — and it was through the perspective of his works that a whole generation of scholars came to see not only the origins of the cold war, but the entire history of 20th century diplomacy.

It is important to recognize that Kennan's was by no means an uncritical perspective — indeed, for those unacquainted with Marxism it seemed the only critical perspective that was available in the fifties. While Kennan insisted that the Russians were primarily to blame for the cold war, he seldom missed an opportunity to criticize the excessive moralism, the messianic vision of a world made safe for democracy, which he argued ran "like a red skein" through American diplomacy.

As late as 1960, a radical like Staughton Lynd could still accept the general framework of Kennan's critique of American idealism while noting merely that Kennan had failed to apply it to the specific events of the cold war and to the policy of containment which he had helped to articulate. "Whereas in general he counseled America to 'admit the validity and legitimacy of power realities and aspirations . . . and to seek their point of maximum equilibrium rather than their reform or their repression' — 'reform or repression' of the Soviet system were the very goals which Kennan's influential writings of those years urged."

Even in 1960, however, a few writers had begun to attack not the specific applications of the principles of *Realpolitik* but the principles themselves, on the grounds that on many occasions they served simply as rationalizations for American (not Soviet) expansionism. And whereas Lynd in 1960 could still write that the American demand for freedom in Eastern Europe, however misguided, "expressed a sincere and idealistic concern," some historians had already begun to take a decidedly more sinister view of the matter — asking, for instance, whether a country which demanded concessions in Eastern Europe that it was not prepared to grant to the Russians in Western Europe could really be accused as the "realist" writers had maintained, of an excess of good-natured but occasionally incompetent altruism.

Meanwhile the "realist" interpretation of the cold war inspired a whole series of books — most notably, Herbert Feis's series (*Churchill-Roosevelt-Stalin; Between War and Peace; The Atomic Bomb and the End of World War II);* William McNeill's *America, Britain and Russia: Their Cooperation and Conflict;* Norman Graebner's *Cold War Diplomacy;* Louis J. Halle's *Dream and Reality* and *The Cold War as History;* and M. F. Herz's *Beginnings of the Cold War.*

Like Kennan, all of these writers saw containment as a necessary response to Soviet expansionism and to the deterioration of Western power in Eastern

Europe. At the same time, they were critical, in varying degrees, of the legalistic-moralistic tradition which kept American statesmen from looking at foreign relations in the light of balance-of-power considerations.

Some of them tended to play off Churchillian realism against the idealism of Roosevelt and Cordell Hull, arguing for instance, that the Americans should have accepted the bargain made between Churchill and Stalin in 1944, whereby Greece was assigned to the Western sphere of influence and Rumania, Bulgaria, and Hungary to the Soviet sphere, with both liberal and Communist parties sharing in the control of Yugoslavia.

These criticisms of American policy, however, did not challenge the basic premise of American policy, that the Soviet Union was a ruthlessly aggressive power bent on world domination. They assumed, moreover, that the Russians were in a position to realize large parts of this program, and that only counterpressure exerted by the West, in the form of containment and the Marshall Plan, prevented the Communists from absorbing all of Europe and much of the rest of the world as well.

It is their criticism of these assumptions that defines the revisionist historians and distinguishes them from the "realist." What impresses revisionists is not Russia's strength but her military weakness following the devastating war with Hitler, in which the Russians suffered much heavier losses than any other member of the alliance.

Beginning with Carl Marzani's *We Can Be Friends: Origins of the Cold War* (1952), revisionists have argued that Russia's weakness dictated, for the moment at least, a policy of postwar cooperation with the West. Western leaders' implacable hostility to Communism, they contend, prevented them from seeing this fact, a proper understanding of which might have prevented the cold war.

This argument is spelled out in D. F. Fleming's two-volume study, *The Cold War and Its Origins* (1961); in David Horowitz's *The Free World Colossus* (1965), which summarizes and synthesizes a great deal of revisionist writing; in Gar Alperovitz's *Atomic Diplomacy: Hiroshima and Potsdam* (1965); and in the previously mentioned *Containment and Change*.

But the historian who has done most to promote a revisionist interpretation of the cold war, and of American diplomacy in general, is William Appleman Williams of the University of Wisconsin, to whom most of the writers just mentioned owe a considerable debt. Williams's works, particularly *The Tragedy of American Diplomacy* (1959), not only challenge the orthodox interpretation of the cold war, they set against it an elaborate counterinterpretation which, if valid, forces one to see American policy in the early years of the cold war as part of a larger pattern of American globalism reaching as far back as 1898.

According to Williams, American diplomacy has consistently adhered to the policy of the "open door" — that is, to a policy of commercial, political, and cultural expansion which seeks to extend American influence into every corner of the earth. This policy was consciously and deliberately embarked upon, Williams argues, because American statesmen believed that American capitalism needed ever-expanding foreign markets in order to survive, the closing of the frontier having put an end to its expansion on the continent of North America. Throughout the 20th century, the makers of American foreign policy, he says, have interpreted the national interest in this light.

The cold war, in Williams's view, therefore has to be seen as the latest phase of a continuing effort to make the world safe for democracy — read liberal capitalism, American-style — in which the United States finds itself increasingly cast as the leader of a worldwide counterrevolution.

After World War II, Williams maintains, the United States had "a vast proportion of actual as well as potential power vis-à-vis the Soviet Union." The United States "cannot with any real warrant or meaning claim that it has been *forced* to follow a certain approach or policy." (Compare this with a statement by Arthur Schlesinger: "The cold war could have been avoided only if the Soviet Union had not been possessed by convictions both of the infallibility of the communist word and of the inevitability of a communist world.")

The Russians, by contrast, Williams writes, "viewed their position in the nineteen-forties as one of weakness, not offensive strength." One measure of Stalin's sense of weakness, as he faced the enormous task of rebuilding the shattered Soviet economy, was his eagerness to get a large loan from the United States. Failing to get such a loan — instead, the United States drastically cut back lend-lease payments to Russia in May, 1945 — Stalin was faced with three choices, according to Williams:

He could give way and accept the American peace program at every point — which meant, among other things, accepting governments in Eastern Europe hostile to the Soviet Union.

He could follow the advice of the doctrinaire revolutionaries in his own country who argued that Russia's best hope lay in fomenting worldwide revolution.

Or he could exact large-scale economic reparations from Germany while attempting to reach an understanding with Churchill and Roosevelt on the need for governments in Eastern Europe not necessarily Communist but friendly to the Soviet Union.

His negotiations with Churchill in 1944, according to Williams, showed that Stalin had already committed himself, by the end of the war, to the third of these policies — a policy, incidentally, which required him to withdraw support from Communist revolutions in Greece and in other countries which under the terms of the Churchill-Stalin agreement had been conceded to the Western sphere of influence.

But American statesmen, the argument continues, unlike the British, were in no mood to compromise. They were confident of America's strength and Russia's weakness (although later they and their apologists found it convenient to argue that the contrary had been the case). Furthermore, they believed that "we cannot have full employment and prosperity in the United States without the foreign markets," as Dean Acheson told a special Congressional committee on postwar economic policy and planning in November, 1944. These considerations led to the conclusion, as President Truman put it in April, 1945, that the United States should "take the lead in running the world in the way that the world ought to be run"; or more specifically, in the words of Foreign Economic Administrator Leo Crowley, that "if you create good governments in foreign countries, automatically you will have better markets for yourselves." Accordingly, the United States pressed for the "open door" in Eastern Europe and elsewhere.

In addition to these considerations, there was the further matter of the atomic bomb, which first became a calculation in American diplomacy in July, 1945. The successful explosion of an atomic bomb in the New Mexican desert, Williams argues, added to the American sense of omnipotence and led the United States "to overplay its hand" — for in spite of American efforts to keep the Russians out of Eastern Europe, the Russians refused to back down.

Nor did American pressure have the effect, as George Kennan hoped, of promoting tendencies in the Soviet Union "which must eventually find their outlet in either the break-up or the gradual mellowing of Soviet power." Far from causing Soviet policy to mellow, American actions, according to Williams, stiffened the Russians in their resistance to Western pressure and strengthened the hand of those groups in the Soviet Union which had been arguing all along that capitalist powers could not be trusted.

Not only did the Russians successfully resist American demands in Eastern Europe, they launched a vigorous counterattack in the form of the Czechoslovakian coup of 1948 and the Berlin blockade. Both East and West thus found themselves committed to the policy of cold war, and for the next 15 years, until the Cuban missile crisis led to a partial détente, Soviet-American hostility was the determining fact of international politics.

Quite apart from his obvious influence on other revisionist historians of the cold war and on his own students in other areas of diplomatic history, Williams has had a measurable influence on the political radicals of the sixties, most of whom now consider it axiomatic that American diplomacy has been counter-revolutionary and that this fact reflects, not a series of blunders and mistakes as some critics have argued, but the basically reactionary character of American capitalism.

Some radicals now construe these facts to mean that American foreign policy therefore cannot be changed unless American society itself undergoes a revolutionary change. Carl Oglesby, for instance, argues along these lines in *Containment and Change.* From Oglesby's point of view, appeals to conscience or even to enlightened self-interest are useless; the cold war cannot end until the "system" is destroyed.

Williams thought otherwise. At the end of the 1962 edition of *The Tragedy of American Diplomacy,* he noted that "there is at the present time no radicalism in the United States strong enough to win power, or even a very significant influence, through the processes of representative government" — and he took it for granted that genuinely democratic change could come about only through representative processes. This meant, he thought, that "the well-being of the United States depends — *in the short-run but only in the short-run* — upon the extent to which calm and confident and enlightened conservatives can see and bring themselves to act upon the validity of a radical analysis."

In an essay in *Ramparts* last March, he makes substantially the same point in commenting on the new radicals' impatience with conservative critics of American diplomacy like Senator Fulbright. Fulbright, Williams says, attracted more support for the position of more radical critics than these critics had attracted through their own efforts. "He hangs tough over the long haul, and that is precisely what American radicalism has never done in the 20th century."

As the New Left becomes more and more beguiled by the illusion of its own revolutionary potential, and more and more intolerant of radicals who refuse to postulate a revolution as the only feasible means of social change, men like Williams will probably become increasingly uncomfortable in the presence of a movement they helped to create. At the same time, Williams's radicalism, articulated in the fifties before radicalism came back into fashion, has alienated the academic establishment and prevented his works from winning the widespread recognition and respect they deserve. In scholarly journals, many reviews of Williams's work — notably a review by Oscar Handlin of *The Contours of American History* in the *Mississippi Valley Historical Review* a few years ago — have been contemptuous and abusive in the extreme. The result is that Williams's books on diplomatic history are only beginning to pass into the mainstream of scholarly discourse, years after their initial publications.

Next to Williams's *Tragedy of American Diplomacy,* the most important attack on the orthodox interpretation of the cold war is Alperovitz's *Atomic Diplomacy*. A young historian trained at Wisconsin, Berkeley, and King's College, Cambridge, and currently a research fellow at Harvard, Alperovitz adds very little to the interpretation formulated by Williams, but he provides William's insights with a mass of additional documentation. By doing so, he has made it difficult for conscientious scholars any longer to avoid the challenge of revisionist interpretations. Unconventional in its conclusions, *Atomic Diplomacy* is thoroughly conventional in its methods. That adds to the book's persuasiveness. Using the traditional sources of diplomatic history — official records, memoirs of participants, and all the unpublished material to which scholars have access — Alperovitz painstakingly reconstructs the evolution of

American policy during the six-month period from March to August, 1945. He proceeds with a thoroughness and caution which, in the case of a less controversial work, would command the unanimous respect of the scholarly profession. His book is no polemic. It is a work in the best — and most conservative — traditions of historical scholarship. Yet the evidence which Alperovitz has gathered together challenges the official explanation of the beginnings of the cold war at every point.

What the evidence seems to show is that as early as April, 1945, American officials from President Truman on down had decided to force a "symbolic showdown" with the Soviet Union over the future of Eastern Europe. Truman believed that a unified Europe was the key to European recovery and economic stability, since the agricultural southeast and the industrial northwest depended on each other. Soviet designs on Eastern Europe, Truman reasoned, threatened to disrupt the economic unity of Europe and therefore had to be resisted. The only question was whether the showdown should take place immediately or whether it should be delayed until the bargaining position of the United States had improved.

At first it appeared to practically everybody that delay would only weaken the position of the United States. Both of its major bargaining counters, its armies in Europe and its lend-lease credits to Russia, could be more effectively employed at once, it seemed, than at any future time. Accordingly, Truman tried to "lay it on the line" with the Russians. He demanded that they "carry out their [Yalta] agreements" by giving the pro-Western elements in Poland an equal voice in the Polish Government (although Roosevelt, who made the Yalta agreements, believed that "we placed, as clearly shown in the agreement, somewhat more emphasis" on the Warsaw [pro-Communist] Government than on the pro-Western leaders). When Stalin objected that Poland was "a country in which the USSR is interested first of all and most of all," the United States tried to force him to give in by cutting back lend-lease payments to Russia.

At this point, however — in April, 1945 — Secretary of War Henry L. Stimson convinced Truman that "we shall probably hold more cards in our hands later than now." He referred to the atomic bomb, and if Truman decided to postpone the showdown with Russia, it was because Stimson and other advisers persuaded him that the new weapon would "put us in a position," as Secretary of State James F. Byrnes argued, "to dictate our own terms at the end of the war."

To the amazement of those not privy to the secret, Truman proceeded to take a more conciliatory attitude toward Russia, an attitude symbolized by Harry Hopkins's mission to Moscow in June, 1945. Meanwhile, Truman twice postponed the meeting with Churchill and Stalin at Potsdam. Churchill complained, "Anyone can see that in a very short space of time our armed power on the Continent will have vanished."

But when Truman told Churchill that an atomic bomb had been successfully exploded at Alamogordo, exceeding all expectations, Churchill immediately understood and endorsed the strategy of delay. "We were in the presence of a new factor in human affairs," he said, "and possessed of powers which were irresistible." Not only Germany but even the Balkans, which Churchill and Roosevelt had formerly conceded to the Russian sphere, now seemed amenable to Western influence. That assumption, of course, had guided American policy (though not British policy) since April, but it could not be acted upon until the bombing of Japan provided the world with an unmistakable demonstration of American military supremacy.

Early in September, the foreign ministers of the Big Three met in London. Byrnes — armed, as Stimson noted, with "the presence of the bomb in his pocket, so to speak, as a great weapon to get through" the conference — tried to press the American advantage. He demanded that the governments of Bulgaria and Rumania reorganize themselves along lines favorable to the West. In Bulgaria, firmness won a few concessions; in Rumania, the Russians stood firm. The American strategy had achieved no noteworthy success. In stead — as Stimson, one of the architects of that strategy, rather belatedly observed — it had "irretrievably embittered" Soviet-American relations.

The revisionist view of the origins of the cold war, as it emerges from the works of Williams, Alperovitz, Marzani, Fleming, Horowitz, and others, can be summarized as follows. The object of American policy at the end of World War II was not to defend Western or even Central Europe but to force the Soviet Union out of Eastern Europe. The Soviet menace to the "free world," so often cited as the justification of the containment policy, simply did not exist in the minds of American planners. They believed themselves to be negotiating not from weakness but from almost unassailable superiority.

Nor can it be said that the cold war began because the Russians "broke their agreements." The general sense of the Yalta agreements — which were in any case very vague — was to assign to the Soviet Union a controlling influence in Eastern Europe. Armed with the atomic bomb, American diplomats tried to take back what they had implicitly conceded at Yalta.

The assumption of American moral superiority, in short, does not stand up under analysis.

The opponents of this view have yet to make a very convincing reply. Schlesinger's recent article in *Foreign Affairs,* referred to at the outset of this article, can serve as an example of the kind of arguments which historians are likely to develop in opposition to the revisionist interpretation. Schlesinger argues that the cold war came about through a combination of Soviet intransigence and misunderstanding. There were certain "problems of communication" with the Soviet Union, as a result of which "the Russians might conceivably have misread our signals." Thus the American demand for self-determination in Poland and other East European countries "very probably" appeared to the Russians "as a systematic and deliberate pressure on Russia's western frontiers."

Similarly, the Russians "could well have interpreted" the American refusal of a loan to the Soviet Union, combined with cancellation of lend-lease, "as deliberate sabotage" of Russia's postwar reconstruction or as "blackmail." In both cases, of course, there would have been no basis for these suspicions; but "we have thought a great deal more in recent years," Schlesinger says, ". . . about the problems of communication in diplomacy," and we know how easy it is for one side to misinterpret what the other is saying.

This argument about difficulties of "communications" at no point engages the evidence uncovered by Alperovitz and others — evidence which seems to show that Soviet officials had good reason to interpret American actions exactly as they did: as attempts to dictate American terms.

In reply to the assertion that the refusal of a reconstruction loan was part of such an attempt, Schlesinger can only argue weakly that the Soviet request for a loan was "inexplicably mislaid" by Washington during the transfer of records from the Foreign Economic Administration to the State Department! "Of course," he adds, "this was impossible for the Russians to believe." It is impossible for some Americans to believe. As William Appleman Williams notes, Schlesinger's explanation of the "inexplicable" loss of the Soviet request "does not speak to the point of how the leaders could forget the request even if they lost the document."

When pressed on the matter of "communications," Schlesinger retreats to a second line of argument, namely that none of these misunderstandings "made much essential difference," because Stalin suffered from "paranoia" and was "possessed by convictions both of the infallibility of the communist word and of the inevitability of a communist world."

The trouble is that there is very little evidence which connects either Stalin's paranoia or Marxist-Leninist ideology or what Schlesinger calls "the sinister dynamics of a totalitarian society" with the actual course of Soviet diplomacy during the formative months of the cold war. The only piece of evidence that Schlesinger has been able to find is an article by the Communist theoretician Jacques Duclos in the April, 1945, issue of *Cahiers du communisme,* the journal of the French Communist Party, which proves, he argues, that Stalin had already abandoned the wartime policy of collaboration with the West and had returned to the traditional Communist policy of world revolution.

Even this evidence, however, can be turned to the advantage of the revisionists. Alperovitz points out that Duclos did not attack electoral politics or even collaboration with bourgeois governments. What he denounced was precisely the American Communists' decision, in 1944, to withdraw from electoral politics. Thus the article, far from being a call to world revolution, "was one of many confirmations that European Communists had decided to abandon violent revolutionary struggle in favor of the more modest aim of electoral success." And while this decision did not guarantee world peace, neither did it guarantee 20 years of cold war.

Schlesinger first used the Duclos article as a trump card in a letter to *The New York Review of Books,* Oct. 20, 1966, which called forth Alperovitz's rejoinder. It is symptomatic of the general failure of orthodox historiography to engage the revisionist argument that Duclos's article crops up again in Schlesinger's more recent essay in *Foreign Affairs,* where it is once again cited as evidence of a "new Moscow line," without any reference to the intervening objections raised by Alperovitz.

Sooner or later, however, historians will have to come to grips with the revisionist interpretation of the cold war. They cannot ignore it indefinitely. When serious debate begins, many historians, hitherto disposed to accept without much question the conventional account of the cold war, will find themselves compelled to admit its many inadequacies. On the other hand, some of the ambiguities of the revisionist view, presently submerged in the revisionists' common quarrel with official explanations, will begin to force themselves to the surface. Is the revisionist history of the cold war essentially an attack on "the doctrine of historical inevitability," as Alperovitz contends? Or does it contain an implicit determinism of its own?

Two quite different conclusions can be drawn from the body of revisionist scholarship. One is that American policy-makers had it in their power to choose different policies from the ones they chose. That is, they could have adopted a more conciliatory attitude toward the Soviet Union, just as they now have the choice of adopting a more conciliatory attitude toward Communist China and toward nationalist revolutions elsewhere in the Third World.

The other is that they have no such choice, because the inner requirements of American capitalism *force* them to pursue a consistent policy of economic and political expansion. "For matters to stand otherwise," writes Carl Oglesby, "the Yankee free-enterpriser would . . . have to . . . take sides against himself. . . . He would have to change entirely his style of thought and action. In a word, he would have to become a revolutionary Socialist whose aim was the destruction of the present American hegemony."

Pushed to what some writers clearly regard as its logical conclusion, the revisionist critique of American foreign policy thus becomes the obverse of the cold war liberals' defense of that policy, which assumes that nothing could have modified the character of Soviet policy short of the transformation of the Soviet Union into a liberal democracy — which is exactly the goal the containment policy sought to promote. According to a certain type of revisionism, American policy has all the rigidity the orthodox historians attribute to the USSR, and this inflexibility made the cold war inevitable.

Moreover, Communism really did threaten American interests, in this view. Oglesby argues that, in spite of its obvious excesses, the "theory of the International Communist Conspiracy is not the hysterical old maid that many leftists seem to think it is." If there is no conspiracy, there is a world revolution and it *"does* aim itself at America" — the America of expansive corporate capitalism.

Revisionism, carried to these conclusions, curiously restores cold war anti-Communism to a kind of intellectual respectability, even while insisting on its immorality. After all, it concludes, the cold warriors were following the American national interest. The national interest may have been itself corrupt, but the policy-makers were more rational than their critics may have supposed.

In my view, this concedes far too much good sense to Truman, Dulles, and the rest. Even Oglesby concedes that the war in Vietnam has now become irrational in its own terms. I submit that much of the cold war has been irrational in its own terms — as witness the failure, the enormously costly failure, of American efforts to dominate Eastern Europe at the end of World War II. This is not to deny the fact of American imperialism, only to suggest that imperialism itself, as J. A. Hobson and Joseph Schumpeter argued in another context long ago, is irrational — that even in its liberal form it may represent an archaic social phenomenon having little relation to the realities of the modern world.

At the present stage of historical scholarship, it is, of course, impossible to speak with certainty about such matters. That very lack of certainty serves to indicate the direction which future study of American foreign policy might profitably take.

The question to which historians must now address themselves is whether American capitalism really depends, for its continuing growth and survival, on the foreign policy its leaders have been following throughout most of the 20th century. To what extent are its interests really threatened by Communist revolutions in the Third World? To what extent can it accommodate itself to those revolutions, reconciling itself to a greatly diminished role in the rest of the world, without undergoing a fundamental reformation — that is, without giving away (after a tremendous upheaval) to some form of Socialism?

Needless to say, these are not questions for scholars alone. The political positions one takes depend on the way one answers them. It is terribly important, therefore, that we begin to answer them with greater care and precision than we can answer them today.

Origins of the Cold War*

I

It is surely a suggestive irony that just at the point when younger American historians had made serious intellectual headway with their reinterpretation of the cold war, fixing historical responsibility in terms of the mistakes, delusions, and imperatives of United States policy, the Soviet Union astonished friends and foes by overwhelming Czechoslovakia and turning its clock of history backwards. If the cold war has not revived, small thanks are due the Soviet leaders. Their extraordinary nervousness, their maneuvers to propitiate both the outgoing and incoming American Administrations, indicate very plainly how much they have feared political retaliation; this in itself is a comment on where responsibility for the cold war today should rest. That Prague should have been the vortex in 1968 as it was in 1948 of critical problems within communism is uncanny, but on deeper examination it may not be fortuitous.

After all, the least credible explanation of Moscow's desperate attempt to resolve the crisis within its own system of states and parties is the one which pictures Czechoslovakia as the helpless Pauline at the crossroads of Europe,

*Reprinted from *Foreign Affairs*, XLVII, 4 (July, 1969), pp. 681–696, by permission of the author and the publisher. Copyright 1969 by the Council on Foreign Relations, Inc., New York.

about to be dishonored by West German *revanchards,* with agents of the CIA grinning in the background, suddenly saved by the stalwart defenders of socialist honor and morality. Today this type of argument is reserved within the communist world for its most backward members — that is, for the Soviet public and the fringes of the most insignificant and expendable communist parties. Yet arguments of this kind had wide currency a generation ago. New Left historians would have us believe that Stalin was simply reacting to external challenge. In their view, the cold war might not have set in if small-minded American politicians had not been determined to reverse bad bargains, if congenital imperialists had not been mesmerized by the monopoly of atomic weapons that statesmen and scientists knew to be temporary. Since all this is so plainly a half-truth when juxtaposed to events of today, then clearly the half-truth of yesteryear will hardly explain the whole of the cold war.

Sophisticated communists, both East and West, are asking why Czechoslovakia, which escaped the upheavals in Poland and Hungary of 1956 after a decade of Stalinist pressure, then experienced such a mounting crisis in the subsequent decade of relative détente and peaceful competition. How is it that twenty years after communist rule had been secured in February 1948 basic verities are now placed in question — whether centralized planning may not be counterproductive, whether a one-party regime can really articulate the needs of a politically evolved people, whether the inner relations of such an unequal alliance as that administered by the Soviet Union are not so inherently antagonistic as to become explosive? Indeed, why did the rebirth of Czechoslovak political life in the first half of 1968 — viewed with hope and excitement by Western communists — raise such menacing ghosts from the past and such fearful question marks for the future that supposedly sober-minded men in Moscow took fright?

Twice within a dozen years the unmanageability of the communist world has been revealed. The crisis which shattered the Sino-Soviet alliance after manifesting itself first in Eastern Europe now rebounds at the supposed strongpoint of Czechoslovakia. And it has done so both in conditions of intense external pressure and times of relatively peaceful engagement. Perhaps it is here, in the dimension of communism as a contradictory and intractable system, that one may find the missing element in the discussions thus far on the origins of the cold war.

II

That world history would someday polarize around two great nations, America and Russia, was a de Tocquevillean insight with which communists were familiar a long time ago. Stalin gave it what seemed like a very clear definition back in 1927 during a talk with an American labor delegation. He envisaged that a socialist center would arise "binding to itself the countries gravitating toward socialism" and would engage the surviving capitalist center in "a struggle between them for the possession of the world economy." The fate of both would be decided by the outcome of this struggle. What appeared at first glance as a sweeping projection was, however, profoundly ambiguous on close examination. Stalin did not spell out how the countries "gravitating to socialism" would get there. Good communists believed this could come about only by the formulas of the October Revolution; yet even Lenin, in 1922, had lamented that perhaps a "big mistake" was being made in imposing Russian precepts on foreign communists. Nor did Stalin elucidate how new nations recruited to socialism would order their relations with Russia as the hub of the socialist center. Presumably "proletarian internationalism" would replace the domination of the weak by the strong which was, in their view, the hallmark of capitalism. Yet even by 1927 the Russification of the international movement had brought catastrophic results — in Germany and China.

Stalin did not, moreover, meet the fundamental intellectual challenge of whether "the struggle for the possession of the world economy" necessarily had to be military in character. On this crucial point, everything could be found in the Leninist grabbag. "Peaceful coexistence" is there, but so is the expectation of "frightful collisions" between the first workers' state and its opponents; the caution that socialism had to be secured in one country first is to be found along with pledges that once socialism was strong enough in Russia, it would raise up revolts in the strongholds of capitalism.

The one possibility which Leninism did not anticipate was a stalemate between rival systems, precluding a "final conflict." The notion was not even entertained that an equilibrium between contending forces might set in, that the subsequent evolution of both contenders under the impact of this equilibrium could alter their distinguishing characteristics and therefore outmode the original Leninist theorems.

Out of such doctrinal ambiguities the Second World War created policy choices affecting most of humanity. The Soviet Union and the international communist movement found themselves allied with democratic-capitalist states among whom public power had grown drastically in an effort to overcome the great depression; the welfare state was expanded by the very demands of warfare while democracy was in fact enhanced. Keynes had made a serious rebuttal to Marx. Would capitalism in the West collapse in a repetition of the crisis of the 1930's after withstanding the test of war? Or had the war itself changed something vital within the workings of capitalism? Moreover, the first global war in history led to the end of colonialism and hence a new relation of metropolitan states to subject peoples. Would the former necessarily collapse because, in Lenin's analysis, they had depended so heavily on colonies? Or might they undergo transformations — short of socialism — to make them viable? Would the countries of the underdeveloped world make socialism the indispensable form of their modernization or might they, dialectically enough, find a new relation with capitalism?

Thus, the war brought on to the world stage a powerful Russia on whose survival a rival system's survival also depended. Simultaneously America came to center stage with a greatly expanded economy no longer limited by laissez-faire economics and inwardly altered by technological change created by the war. America was indispensable to Russia as an ally but formidable as a rival in a sense far deeper than its outward power. This wartime relationship was unexpected, and it challenged ideology and practice on all sides.

Something very particular happened within communism, considered as a most uneven system of a single state and a variety of parties. The fortunes of war, thanks perhaps to Churchill's postponement of the second front, brought the Soviet armies beyond their own borders where they had to be welcomed by the West if only because their help was also being solicited on the plains of Manchuria once Hitler was defeated. Yet at the moment of Russia's greatest need and harshest difficulties, the communist movements *least* helpful to her were those of Eastern Europe; in the one country outside of Russia where a decade before the communists had been a real power — namely, in Germany — the party lay shattered. No anti-Hitler force of any practical significance emerged. On the East European landscape there were only two exceptions. In Yugoslavia a handful of veterans of Comintern intrigue and the hard school of the International Brigades in Spain had succeeded in establishing their power — prior to the arrival of Soviet forces in the Danubian basin. In Czechoslovakia, a communist movement of a very different sort — that is, with a legal and parliamentary tradition — was joined by Slovak guerrillas. Both came to terms with the leadership of the government-in-exile, which both Moscow and the West recognized. A long-term cooperation of diverse social forces was implied.

On the other hand, the communist movements underwent a spectacular resurrection in a wide arc from Greece through Italy, France, the Low Countries, and Scandinavia, while in widely separated corners of Asia they also flourished — in Northwest China, in the peninsula of Indochina, in the Philippines and Malaya. All of them were successful to the degree that they identified with the defense of their nationhood and either subordinated social issues or subsumed them in national ones; where this proved too complicated, as in India, long-term disabilities resulted. But all of these movements grew at a distance from the Soviet armies; their postwar fate could not depend on physical contact. Even parties at the periphery of world politics showed striking changes. They entered cabinets in Cuba and Chile, emerged from prewar disasters with great dynamism in Brazil, became legal in Canada, and stood chance of legitimizing their considerable influence in Britain and the United States. In these latter countries, they could hope to achieve "citizenship" only by ceasing to be propagandist groups reflecting Soviet prestige, and only as they grappled with the specific peculiarities of their societies in rapid change.

Yet for all this success, and perhaps because of it, communism faced the gravest problems. The peculiarity of the moment lay in the fact that some definition of Russia's relation with the West was essential to assure the most rapid conclusion of the war in Europe, and this had to precede a common strategy in Asia. Hence Moscow was obliged to define relations with the communist parties. Simultaneously these movements — of such unequal potential and geographical relation to Russia — had to make a fresh judgment of their strategies in view of those changes within capitalism which challenged their own doctrine. Perhaps the most ambitious attempt to do this came in May 1943 with the dissolution of the Communist International.

Stalin, who had sworn at Lenin's bier to guard this "general staff of the world revolution" like the apple of his eye, was now abandoning it; and in so doing he signaled to Churchill and Roosevelt that he would project the postwar Soviet interest in essentially Russian terms. This decision was consistent with the fact that the Russian Communists had not been able to rely on ideology or internationalism in mobilizing their own peoples for the enormous sacrifices of the war. They had been forced to appeal to the Russian love of soil and the solace of the Orthodox faith. "They are not fighting for us," Stalin had once mused to Ambassador Harriman. "They are fighting for Mother Russia."

All of this would not, of course, make Russia easier to deal with. And in studying the details in the monumental accounts of Herbert Feis or W. H. McNeill, one is struck by Stalin's political opportunism and the enormous part which is played in his calculations by the need to exact material resources from friend and foe. Throughout 1944, Stalin dealt with anyone who would cease fighting, or mobilize men and matériel for the Soviet armies, safeguard their lines, and pledge reparations; and everyone was suitable to Moscow in terms of these objectives — agrarians and monarchists in the Axis satellites, veteran communist-haters in Finland, a Social Democratic old-timer in Austria, Dr. Beneš in Prague, or Comrade Tito in the Yugoslav mountains. Had the putsch against Hitler succeeded in July 1944, Stalin was prepared, by his committee of Nazi generals rounded up at Stalingrad, to bargain.

His only real complication arose over Poland. Here the Soviets had the tactical advantage that a generation earlier the victors at Versailles had been willing to establish the Curzon Line as Russia's western frontier. Churchill and Roosevelt were now obliged not only to ratify this line but to impose it on the intractable London Poles. Moscow's own dilemma lay in the fact that the pro-Soviet Poles, exiled in the USSR, had little political substance; they had one thing in common with their counterparts in London — lack of standing inside Poland. The Polish Communists had been decimated in the great purges and the Polish officer corps had been wiped out in the Katyn murders. Perhaps it was the need to shift the balance in his favor that led Stalin to such extraordinary measures as letting the "Home Army" be wiped out at the banks of the Vistula or continuing to murder Polish Socialists as they came to Moscow as guests. The earlier hope of some prestigious figure who would bridge the gap between Poles and yet be satisfactory to all the great powers had faded with the death in an airplane accident of General Wladislaw Sikorski.

But it is questionable whether this Soviet use of vestigial figures of Comintern experience should be viewed, as of 1944, in terms of "communization." Everything we know of the Kremlin at that time denies this. In the remarkable account by Milovan Djilas in his "Conversations with Stalin," the Kremlin was far from being a citadel of revolution, as this young Montenegrin idealist expected (like so many in Moscow for the first time, before and after him). The Kremlin was really a sort of Muscovite camping-ground such as the great Russian painter, Repin, might have portrayed. Crafty and boorish men, suspicious of all foreigners and of each other, contemptuous of communists who were non-Russian but expecting their obedience, were crowded around the maps of Europe as around some Cossack campfire, calculating how much they could extract from Churchill and Roosevelt, to whom they felt profoundly inferior.

Thus, when Ulbricht and Rakosi, Anna Pauker, and even Dimitroff were being prepared to return to the homelands where they had previously failed, Stalin advised them not to spoil their second chance by their chronic leftism and adventurism.[1] They did not go back as revolutionaries. For all of Moscow's hopes that they root themselves in native soil, they were intended to be the guarantors of control, to stabilize this backyard of Europe and mobilize its resources on Russia's behalf. The troubles with the Yugoslavs began for the very reason that as revolutionaries they would not let themselves be used.

Was Stalin already building a bloc? To be sure he was. But he also knew that the onetime *cordon sanitaire* was a veritable swamp of historic and intractable rivalries and economic backwardness, even though wealthier in immediate resources than the USSR itself. Hoping to transform this bloc, Stalin also entertained most seriously the idea of a long-term relationship with America and Britain based on some common policy toward Germany that would make its much greater resources available to Russia. Thus, when Churchill came to Moscow in September 1944 to work out a spheres-of-influence agreement, demanding 50 – 50 and 75 – 25 ratios in the political control of areas already liberated by the Soviet armies, Stalin agreed by the

---

1. Herbert Feis is the source for the famous and revealing anecdote that when Stalin said farewell to Dr. Beneš, after signing a mutual assistance pact, he urged Beneš to help make Klement Gottwald, the Communist leader now become Premier, "more worldly and less provincial" — an amazing piece of arrogance. Having themselves helped emasculate their foreign friends, the Russians now taunted them and hoped that perhaps the bourgeois world might make men of them (*Churchill, Roosevelt and Stalin,* Princeton: Princeton University Press, 1957, p. 569).

stroke of a pen. He did so without comment. He contemptuously left it to Churchill to decide whether the piece of paper should be retained by him or destroyed. The cobbler's son from Gori, the onetime seminary student, was giving a descendant of the Marlboroughs a lesson in *Realpolitik.*

But as he disposed of Greeks and interposed with Yugoslavs (without asking their consent), the Soviet dictator demanded no quid pro quo in Western Europe where the ultimate world balance could be determined, and where communist movements had powerfully revived, guided by intimates of Stalin — Togliatti and Thorez — whose work he respected. Molotov is on record as inquiring about the disposition of Italian colonies, but not about the operations of the American Military Government in Italy in which Russian participation was passive. At the moment when the French Communists were debating whether to turn in their arms, Moscow recognized the Gaullist regime and invited it to sign a treaty with what de Gaulle was to call "chère et puissante Russie." Churchill's assault on Belgian and Greek Communists was reproved, in private. But no Soviet leverage was employed to help them, and the Greek Communists were advised to strike the best bargain they could to avert civil war. Only much later, when assistance was useless to them, did the Soviets reluctantly help the Greeks, though their hapless plight was useful for cold-war propaganda. Even as late as February 1945, at Yalta, Stalin pledged to renew his pact with Chiang Kai-shek in return for special treaty control of Dairen and the Manchurian railways. Half a year later, the Soviet armies ransacked the industrial installations that were by right Chinese. In central Asia they dickered with warlords, advising them against joining the Chinese Communists. Stalin shied away from the governance of Japan, asking and getting its northern islands instead. All this was accompanied by rather snide references by Molotov to Mao Tse-tung's "margarine communists." American liberals and roving ambassadors may have been more naïve but they were also less offensive in believing the Chinese Communists to be "agrarian reformers."

III

How then did the communist parties respond to the Comintern's dissolution? Its final document had some curious and pregnant phrases, alluding to "the fundamental differences in the historical development of the separate countries of the world" — differences, it was now discovered, which had "become apparent even before the war"; communists were now told most authoritatively that they were "never advocates of the outmoded organizational forms." This suggests that a great watershed had been reached. The implicit self-criticism was bound to encourage those Western communists for whom the "popular front" of the 1930's and the experience of the Spanish Republic were not defensive deceptions but major experiments in skirting the limits of Leninism. The Chinese Communists, as the specialized literature shows, saw in the disappearance of the Communist International a ratification of their own "New Democracy," in which the peasantry and the "national bourgeoisie" had been credited with revolutionary potentials for which no precedent existed in the Russian experience.

The most interesting instance of how new systems of ideas and new organizational forms were bursting the Leninist integument came in the minor party of a major country — among the American Communists. Their leader, Earl Browder, concluded that peaceful coexistence had become obligatory; he saw such coexistence as a whole historical stage in which the contradictions between antagonistic social systems would have to work themselves out — short of war; it is curious that he ruled out war as too dangerous to both sides *before* the advent of the atomic bomb. To give this very novel view some inner logic, Browder postulated a new type of state power, intermediate between capitalism and socialism, which, he thought, would prevail between the Atlantic and the Oder-Neisse Line. Thus he anticipated the "people's democracy" concept which was to have wide currency in the next few years only to be brusquely rejected by the end of 1948, when the cold war demanded rationales of another kind.

To what extent Browder had sanction in Moscow, or only *thought* he had, or whether this sanction was ever intended to be more than temporary, are all fascinating matters; but for our discussion what seems more important is the fact that Browder revealed the incoherence of communism and tried to overcome it. Perhaps America was not so backward as European communists traditionally assumed. The more advanced country was simply showing a mirror to the less advanced of the problems of their own future, to borrow an image from Marx.

One may put this dilemma in very specific terms. In 1944 – 45, a quasi-revolutionary situation prevailed in key areas of Western Europe and East Asia. The communist parties had become mass movements. They were no longer Leninist vanguards but had significant military experience. The old order had been discredited and few charismatic rivals existed. One of two options could be taken, each of them having its own logic. If the communists seized power they might be able to hold it, as in Yugoslavia, with great good luck. But as the Greek experience was to show, the success of a prolonged civil war would involve the rupture of the Anglo-Soviet-American coalition; and the war with Hitler was by no means over, while the Pacific war appeared only begun. To pursue this option meant to oblige the Soviet Union to assist revolutions at a distance from its own armies at a moment of its own greatest weakness and when it seriously entertained the possibility of a long-range postwar relationship with the West. Alternatively, the USSR would be obliged to disavow its own ideological and political allies in an even more explicit way than the dissolution of the Comintern suggested. Stalin's entire diplomacy warned against revolution now. So did his opinion, in a speech of November

6, 1944, that whatever disagreements existed among the great powers could be overcome; he had said flatly that "no accidental, transitory motive but vitally important long-term interests lie at the basis of the alliance of our country, Great Britain, and the United States."

On the other hand, to reject the revolutionary path meant for the Western parties (if not for the Chinese and Vietnamese) forgoing an opportunity that might not return; for a generation this choice caused intense misgivings and internal battles within these parties. To take part in the whole-hearted reconstruction of their societies on a less-than-socialist basis would have involved a revision of fundamental Leninist postulates, a fresh look at capitalism, and presumably a redefinition of their relations with the Soviet Union. Having taken such a sharply Russocentric course, could Stalin give his imprimatur to the embryonic polycentrism of that time? The USSR was in the paradoxical position of trying to be a great power with a shattered economic base, and of trying to lead a world movement whose interests were quite distinct from those of Russia, both in practice and in ideas. The ambiguities inherent in communism, in Stalin's projections of 1927, had come home to roost.

IV

If one tries, then, to make intellectual sense and order out of the bewildering events between early 1945 and mid-1947, the least satisfactory themes are the ones which have been so popular and have dominated the discussion of the origins of the cold war. The revisionist historians are so hung up on the notion that a meticulous rediscovery of America will reveal the clues to the cold war that they ignore the dimension of communism altogether. They have little experience with communism (and perhaps they are better off for it) but they have yet to show the scholarship required to explore it. To say this is not to deny the value of reappraising American policy, especially since so many of today's follies have roots in the past. Communists, anti-communists, and ex-communists have all had troubles with the imperatives of coexistence. But this is quite different from explaining the cold war on one-sided grounds and succumbing to the elementary fallacy of *post hoc, propter hoc*.

On the other hand, the most sophisticated and persuasive rebuttal to the younger historians — that by Arthur Schlesinger, Jr., in these pages[2] — suffered from the limitations of his own major premise: the assumption that communism was a monolithic movement which disintegrated only as the cold war was vigorously prosecuted. Certainly the monolith functioned in a pellmell fashion after 1948 but one wonders whether its explosive decomposition in the late fifties, continuing to the events in Czechoslovakia, can be comprehended without realizing that all the elements of crisis within it were already present

2. *Foreign Affairs*, October, 1967. [See Chapter 13. Ed.]

in its immediate postwar years. It was the futile attempts by Stalin and the communists who everywhere followed him (even if hesitantly and in bewilderment) to stifle the nascent polycentrism and to curtail the inchoate attempts to adjust to new realities which constitute communism's own responsibility for the cold war. Herein also is the key to communism's own disasters.

Thus, the events of 1946 and 1947 were in fact incoherent and contradictory, and for that very reason offer an important clue to the origins of cold war. For example, Earl Browder was roundly denounced by the French Communist leader, Jacques Duclos, in an article written early in 1945 (with data that were available only in Moscow), on the grounds that the very concept of peaceful coexistence and Europe's reconstruction on a bourgeois-democratic basis was heresy; yet the curious thing is that most of the communist parties continued to operate on Browder's assumptions — including the party led by Duclos. Such a state of affairs suggests that the Duclos article was not the tocsin of the cold war but one of the elements of communism's incoherence. By the close of 1946, only the Yugoslavs — and William Z. Foster, who had ousted Browder in the United States — were convinced that even the "temporary stabilization" of capitalism was unlikely. This concept was, of course, an echo from the 1920's. "Relative and temporary stabilization" was Stalin's own justification in the late 1920's for "turning inward" and seeking a truce in external affairs. Ruling out this concept in the 1940's, Foster went even further than Tito in raising the alarum over an ever-more-imminent danger of an American attack on the Soviet Union. It is not generally known that when Browder's successor visited Europe in March 1947 he was amazed to find that few Communist leaders agreed with his views, and one of those who disagreed most sharply was Jacques Duclos.

In studying the French Communists of that period one finds unusual emphasis on the need for a policy of "confident collaboration" with "all of the Allied nations, without exception," and a declaration by Duclos that "we are not among those who confuse the necessity and fertility of struggle with the spirit of adventurism. That is why — mark me well — we ask of a specific historic period what it can give and only what it can give . . . but we do not ask more, for we want to push ahead and not end up in abortive and disappointing failures."

In this same year of 1946, it is sometimes forgotten that the Chinese Communists negotiated seriously for a long-term coalition with Chiang Kai-shek. They did so under the aegis of General George Marshall, which suggests that their own antagonism to "American imperialism" had its limits; their view that the United States was necessarily hostile to a unified China with a large communist component was a later development. During the recent Great Proletarian Cultural Revolution, Chinese historians blamed this coalition strategy on the now-disgraced Liu Shao Chi, alleging that he was under the influence of "Browder, Togliatti, Thorez, and other renegades to the proletariat." But the official Chinese Communist documents show that at the time Mao Tse-tung took credit for it and was himself viewed as a "revisionist" — by the Indian Communists, for example. In those same months, Ho Chi Minh led a coalition delegation to Paris, trying to work out the terms for remaining within the French Union; it is a curious but revealing detail that Ho had the previous winter dissolved his own creation, the Communist Party of Indochina, in favor of an Association of Marxist Studies, without, however, receiving a rebuke from Jacques Duclos.

Throughout 1946, almost every communist leader in the West voiced the view that peaceful roads to socialism were not only desirable but were — because of objective changes in the world — now theoretically admissible. If in Eastern Europe this popularity of the "people's democracy" can be explained in terms of Stalin's attempt to stabilize a chaotic region of direct interest to Russia, in Western Europe it was part of a serious effort to implement the non-revolutionary option which the communists had chosen, and for which they needed a consistent justification.

Nor were the Soviet leaders immune to what was happening within communism. Stalin himself can be cited in contradictory assertions which also stimulated the diversity within the communist world as well as baffling some of its members. Early in February 1946 Stalin declared that wars could not be abolished so long as imperialism prevailed; this came in his election campaign speech which is viewed by Sovietologists as another tocsin of the cold war. Yet throughout 1946 Stalin gave interviews to British and American newsmen, and held a long discussion with Harold Stassen that spring, in which the key theme was the viability of peaceful coexistence. In September 1946 Stalin declared that the ruling circles of both Britain and the United States were *not* in fact oriented toward war — a view which communists from China to Italy hailed, although it baffled Tito and William Z. Foster. Stalin also told a British Labor delegation headed by Harold Laski that socialism might well come to Britain by parliamentary means, with the monarchy remaining as a genuine institution. Earlier in the year, in a polemic with a certain Professor Razin on the significance of the doctrines of Clausewitz, Stalin is quoted as believing "it is impossible to move forward and advance science without subjecting outdated propositions and the judgments of well-known authorities to critical analysis. This applies . . . also to the classics of Marxism." Significantly, this exchange was published a full year later — in February 1947 — on the eve of cold-war decisions which made such thinking heretical throughout the communist movement.

Yet in 1946 Soviet diplomacy was in fact moving "with all deliberate speed" toward settlements of a partial kind with the West — as regards the peace treaties, the evacuation of northern Persia, and other matters. Browder was cordially received in Moscow in May after his expulsion from the American party — a rather unprecedented detail in the annals of communism. The deposed communist leader was heard out by Molotov, at the latter's request, and was given a post which enabled him to work energetically for the next two years in behalf of the proposition that Stalin wanted an American-Soviet settlement.

All students of this period have paused on the famous Varga controversy. The title of the book which the foremost Soviet economist, Eugene Varga, published in November 1946 (it was completed the year before) in itself suggests what was bothering Russian leaders, namely: *Changes in the Economy of Capitalism Resulting from the Second World War.* Within six months, Varga was under severe attack, which he resisted for the following two years. Major issues lay at the heart of the controversy. When might a crisis of over-production be expected in the United States? How severe would it be? And to what extent would rearmament or a program for rebuilding Western Europe affect capitalism's inherent propensity for crisis, which was, of course, taken for granted? Another question was whether the new role of governmental power, so greatly enhanced by the war, might not have a bearing on both the onset of the crisis and the terrain of communist activities. Varga did forecast an early crisis, after a brief postwar boom. In so doing, he surely misled Stalin into one of his most fundamental cold-war miscalculations. But Varga also clung to the view that something important had changed within classical capitalism; he insisted that "the question of greater or smaller participation in the management of the state will be the main content" of the political struggle in the West, and he deduced that people's democracy was in fact a transitional form between the two systems, replacing the "either-or" notions of classical Leninism. There was a plaintive protest in Varga's answer to his critics (one of whom was Vosnessensky, who would shortly disappear because of mysterious heresies of his own). "It is not a matter of enumerating all the facts so that they inevitably lead to the former conclusions of Marxism-Leninism," Varga argued, "but to use the Marxist-Leninist method in studying these facts. The world changes and the content of our work must change also."

V

In what sense, then, did all these crosscurrents determine Stalin's decision for cold war? It would seem that the matter turned on the incompatibility between immediate Soviet objectives and the real interests of the communist parties — or more exactly, in the particularly Stalinist answer to these incompatibilities. The Russians, it will be remembered, had set out to achieve rapid and ambitious reconstruction including, of course, the acquisition of nuclear weapons. They were most concerned with reparations. When it became plain that little help would come by loans or trade with the West (they had used up what was still in the pipelines after the abrupt cessation of lend-lease in mid-1945 and were not getting a response to their $6 billion request to Washington), they needed either the resources of Germany beyond what they could extract from their own Eastern Zone, or a desperate milking of their friends and former foes in Eastern Europe. At home, moreover, they could not rely on the ultrachauvinist themes which had served them during the war; rejecting liberalization of Soviet society, they tightened the screws and fell back on the doctrine of the primacy of the Soviet party, the purity of its doctrine, and the universal validity of that doctrine. Consistent with these objectives, the Soviet leaders wanted to erase all sympathy for America which until then was widespread in the Soviet Union.[3]

These objectives, taken together, ran counter to all the tendencies among the foreign communist parties. Both the revolutionary ambitions of the Yugoslavs, their jealous quest for autonomy as well as the emphasis on peaceful non-Soviet roads to socialism — that is, the "revisionist" themes so urgently needed by the parties in the West — could be countenanced by Moscow only if it were prepared to accept diversity within international communism. This very diversity (which they had themselves half entertained) now became an obstacle. The Stalinist premise that what was good for Russia was good for all other communists (a notion which he himself considered abandoning) was now reaffirmed.

The origins of the cold war lie deeper, however, than any analysis of Russia's own interest. Nor can they be understood only in terms of an attempt to prevent economic recovery and political stability in Western Europe. The cold war's origins must be found in a dimension larger than the requirements of Soviet internal mobilization or the thrust of its foreign policy; they lie in the attempt to overcome the incipient diversity within a system of states and parties, among whom the changes produced by the war had outmoded earlier ideological and political premises. The conditions for the transformation of a monolithic movement had matured and ripened. The sources of the cold war lie in communism's unsuccessful attempt to adjust to this reality, followed by its own abortion of this attempt. For Stalin the cold war was a vast tug-of-war with the West, whereby not only internal objectives could be realized but the international movement subordinated; its constituent parts went along — bewildered but believing — on the assumption that, in doing so, they would survive and prosper. The price of the Stalinist course was to be fearsome indeed; and by 1956 the Soviet leaders were to admit that the cold war had damaged the USSR more than the West, that a stalemate of systems had to

---

3. This task was assigned to the late Ilya Ehrenburg following his 1947 visit to the States, when he deliberately oversimplified everything American with the crudest methods. The pattern for this had been set late in 1946 by Andrei Zhdanov.

be acknowledged, and ineluctable conclusions had to be drawn. Thus, the cold war arose from the failure of a movement to master its inner difficulties and choose its alternatives.

The analysis could be continued to the turning-point of mid-1947 — the Marshall Plan decision and Stalin's riposte, for example, in humiliating his Czechoslovak and Polish partners, who thought in terms of what might be good for them, and indirectly for the Soviet Union. Such an analysis would take us through the near-insurrections of late 1947 in France and Italy, adventurist upheavals in Asia, the Berlin blockade, and the coup in Prague in 1948. But this involves another subject — how the cold war was fought. It was indeed fought by both sides. But to say this cannot obscure the crisis within communism, where its origins lie. The record would show how recklessly entire communist movements were expended and to what a dangerous brink the Soviet Union itself was brought. In 1956, Khrushchev was to lament these miscalculations but he did so with such a *désinvolture* as to leave a memory-bank of disasters and skeletons that still rattle in communism's closets. Was the cold war but a test of strength between systems? Or has it not also been the process whereby communism disclosed such an intellectual and political bankruptcy that a dozen years after Khrushchev's revelations, the issues still agonize — as in Czechoslovakia — all the states and parties involved? A world movement claiming to comprehend history and accepting the responsibility for "making history" still grapples with the alternatives opened by the Second World War. It has yet to face what it has tried to avoid at such a heavy cost to coexistence — namely, understanding itself.

PART V

Western Diplomacy and Soviet Foreign Policy:
Competitive Coexistence and the Cold War

The *internal* characteristics of the Soviet and American political systems are probably not becoming increasingly similar or "converging."[1] But there does seem to be an increasing convergence of mutual interest in *international* affairs — that is, there are more and more areas where Soviet-American cooperation is in fact, and is perceived as being, mutually beneficial. To be sure, there are many geographical and issue areas where Soviet and American objectives collide. Competition for influence in different parts of the Third World is one example. But "peaceful coexistence," in Soviet theory and practice, consists of both competition (conflict) *and* cooperation with major Western powers.[2] Under Khrushchev "peaceful coexistence" was the cornerstone or "general line" of Soviet foreign policy; under Brezhnev and Kosygin it has been reduced to equal status with lesser goals and "principles." Yet the basic components of the concept and of the policy — competition and cooperation — remain the same.

1. For example, see Zbigniew Brzezinski and Samuel Huntington, *Political Power: USA/ USSR* (New York: Viking Press, 1964); and Frederic J. Fleron, Jr., "Toward a Reconceptualization of Political Change in the Soviet Union: The Political Leadership System," in Frederic J. Fleron, Jr. (ed.), *Communist Studies and the Social Sciences: Essays on Methodology and Empirical Theory* (Chicago: Rand McNally, 1969), pp. 222 – 243.
2. See Professor Robert C. Tucker's chapter below and his "Dialectics of Coexistence," in *The Soviet Political Mind* (New York: Praeger, 1963), pp. 201 – 222. See also Michael Gehlen, *The Politics of Coexistence* (Bloomington: Indiana University Press, 1967).

There has been considerable debate within and among Communist countries about the meaning and practical implications of "peaceful coexistence." Russian and Chinese leaders have very different ideas about its content, for example. In 1947 Andrei Zhdanov could still write of possible "cooperation" and "reciprocity" among capitalist and socialist systems.[3] But serious Soviet discussion of the cooperative elements of this concept did not begin until the mid- and late 1950's.[4] Not surprisingly, the area of mutual interest first emphasized was the avoidance of nuclear war and self-destruction. In the 1960's the Soviet Union and the United States made greater efforts to infuse this concept with positive content (for example, the Nuclear Test-Ban Treaty). Arms control, curtailment of nuclear proliferation, peace-making efforts in Third World trouble spots, Soviet-American trade, assistance to developing countries, scientific and technological collaboration, environmental, population control, and space exploration programs — these are some of the major areas of possible Soviet-American cooperation.[5]

It has often been argued that most international actions are reactions. Professors Triska and Finley observe: "we know of no significant example in East-West relations where a challenging initiative, if perceived as disturbing the pre-existing harmony within a relevant sector, has not brought about an attempted response in kind to redress the balance. . . . But to proceed further, it appears that the response, to be effective, must match the stimulus in *magnitude* as well as in kind."[6] The emphasis on perception is important. For threats must be perceived as such to provoke responses, and constructive initiatives must be so perceived to induce reciprocity. Triska and Finley conclude that if both "superpowers" persistently strove to acquire the skills and capacity to alleviate international tensions and to expand cooperative efforts in many areas, each would probably be confronted with essentially the same task: "(1) realistically perceiving and then meeting [each other's] challenges without striving to surpass them in such dimensions as that of military-weapons systems and (2) devoting at the same time a sufficient portion of scarce resources to the initiation of its own challenges in more acceptable sectors."[7]

    3. Andrei Zhdanov, *The International Situation,* excerpts in Alvin Rubinstein (ed.), *The Foreign Policy of the Soviet Union* (New York: Random House, 1966), p. 237.
    4. See Tucker, "Dialectics of Coexistence."
    5. See the chapter by Tucker below. Also Andrei Sakharov, *Progress, Coexistence and Intellectual Freedom* (New York: Norton, 1968); Vincent Rock, *A Strategy of Interdependence: A Program for the Control of Conflict between the United States and the Soviet Union* (New York: Charles Scribner's Sons, 1964); and Marshall Shulman, *Beyond the Cold War* (New Haven: Yale University Press, 1966).
    6. Jan Triska and David Finley, *Soviet Foreign Policy* (New York: Macmillan, 1968), p. 301. See also Walter LaFeber, *America, Russia, and the Cold War, 1945-1966* (New York: Wiley, 1967).
    7. Triska and Finley, *op. cit*, p. 308. Robert F. Kennedy argues along much the same lines in his analysis of a major conflict situation, the Cuban missile crisis of 1962. He stresses the importance of "placing ourselves in the other country's shoes" and trying "not to disgrace

Professors Eckhardt and White carefully examine the perceptions of two key decision-makers in the United States and the USSR. It has often been observed that average Soviet and American citizens have strikingly similar distorted impressions of each other's political systems and ways of life. But the views of political leaders, who determine their country's foreign policies, are crucial factors in explaining and understanding international behavior (see the conceptual framework above). For this reason, the findings of Eckhardt, White, and Bronfenbrenner, although not based on sufficient evidence to confirm or refute conclusively the "mirror-image" hypothesis, are nevertheless significant and suggestive.[8]

Also revealing are the findings of Professor Forte.[9] Analyzing Soviet policy toward the European Economic Community or Common Market, he finds it highly flexible, responsive, and reactive. In fact, he identifies seven distinct stages in Soviet policy between 1957 and 1963. The possibility of an economically and politically unified Europe, with increasingly close ties to the United States, clearly was perceived as a threat of major proportions. Soviet ideological and political responses to this threat seem to have been carefully calculated and very receptive to new information and external influences. For policies were constantly reappraised and altered in light of changing economic and political conditions within the Western countries and within the Common Market itself.

Professor Morris focuses on American perceptions and their impact on Soviet-American relations. Our policies have responded more to Soviet ideology than to Soviet actions, he argues, and consequently this has mis-shaped our conception of national security, impaired our will and capacity to cooperate with the USSR, and generally exacerbated Cold War tensions. In the name of "containment," he contends, the United States has committed itself to resist, by force if necessary, allegedly aggressive acts by any Commu-

---

Khrushchev, not to humiliate the Soviet Union, not to have them feel they would have to escalate their response because their national security or national interests so committed them." Kennedy concludes: "Miscalculation and misunderstanding and escalation on one side bring a counterresponse. No action is taken against a powerful adversary in a vacuum. A government or people will fail to understand this only at their great peril. For that is how wars begin — wars that no one wants, no one intends, and no one wins." *Thirteen Days* (New York: Norton, 1969), pp. 124 – 125. On the extent to which the United States followed these principles in this particular case, cf. Ronald Steel, "Endgame," *New York Review of Books,* March 13, 1969, pp. 15 – 22.

8. See the chapter by Eckhardt and White below. Also Urie Bronfenbrenner, "The Mirror Image in Soviet-American Relations: A Social Psychologist's Report," *Journal of Social Issues,* XVII, 3, pp. 45 – 56; Urie Bronfenbrenner, "Allowing for Soviet Perceptions," in Roger Fisher (ed.), *International Conflict and Behavioral Science* (New York: Basic Books, 1964), pp. 161 – 178; and Ralph K. White, "Images in the Context of International Conflict: Soviet Perceptions of the U.S. and U.S.S.R.," in Herbert Kelman (ed.), *International Behavior: A Social-Psychological Analysis* (New York: Holt, Rinehart & Winston, 1966), pp. 236 – 276.

9. David Forte, "The Response of Soviet Foreign Policy to the Common Market, 1957-63," *Soviet Studies,* XIX, 3 (January, 1968), pp. 373 – 386. Cf. Thomas Wolfe, *Soviet Power and Europe, 1945-1970* (Baltimore: The Johns Hopkins Press, 1970).

nist country and any domestic Communist minority in any part of the world, regardless of the strategic significance of the area or the political and economic importance of the issue to the United States.

As is well known, American Presidents have sometimes acted on this belief — in Greece, Turkey, Korea, Vietnam, the Dominican Republic, and elsewhere. Often they have explicitly invoked the doctrine of "containment" to explain and justify these actions. Ironically, during the Eisenhower-Dulles era, when the advocates of "roll-back" called for a more militant policy than "containment," Soviet leaders were beginning to reemphasize and revitalize the concept of "peaceful coexistence" and gingerly exploring the theoretical and practical implications of its cooperative aspects. Elsewhere, Morris has written: "It is to the credit of Khrushchev that, coming to terms with the nuclear reality, he proposed to liquidate the cold war. In his attempt to do so, he precipitated the deepest and probably most lasting schism in the history of the international communist movement, sacrificing the Chinese alliance to efforts at accommodation with the United States."[10] The theory and practice of "containment," Morris concludes, have prevented American leaders from seizing Soviet initiatives and have impeded cooperative efforts in an era when increasingly urgent problems demand imaginative and skillful Soviet-American collaboration. For better or worse, American policy can and does significantly influence Soviet policy, and vice versa.

"Totalitarianism" is another important concept in the lexicon of the Cold War. In a thought-provoking article, Professors Spiro and Barber contend that this concept, by affecting the attitudes, images, and behavior of American foreign policy-makers (see the conceptual framework on p. 8 above), may have played a major role in perpetuating the Cold War. Their emphasis is on the *functions* performed by the concept of "totalitarianism" — primarily its usefulness in "explaining" perplexing and disturbing events since World War II. Spiro and Barber argue that this concept has performed profoundly important social functions by rationalizing the United States' international behavior and by identifying interests, enemies, and issues. If Spiro and Barber are correct, the current debate among political scientists concerning the utility of this concept has far greater implications than commonly recognized.[11] For together with Soviet ideology, dogma, and doctrine, the concepts of "totalitarianism" and "containment" may have played a very significant role in transforming "a storm of miscalculations, misunderstandings, and conflicts of interest into a quagmire of enmity: The Cold War," and may continue to undermine the

10. Bernard S. Morris, *International Communism and American Policy* (New York: Atherton, 1966), p. 151.
11. See, for example, Carl Friedrich, Michael Curtis, Benjamin Barber, *Totalitarianism in Perspective: Three Views* (New York: Praeger, 1969); and Frederic J. Fleron, Jr., "Introduction," in Fleron (ed.), *op. cit.*, pp. 1–33.

"mutual trust" Professor Tucker considers essential to achieving sustained Soviet-American cooperation.

Perhaps no East-West problem is more urgent than the limitation of strategic weapons. Professor Horelick analyzes Soviet behavior in a single instance — the momentous decision to implant strategic missiles in Cuba. What were Khrushchev's calculations? Why did he think the risks were worth taking? Why did he retreat so quickly? These are some of the critical questions discussed. In *Expansion and Coexistence,* Professor Ulam offers alternative answers to these questions. Careful analysis of Soviet-Chinese and Soviet-German relations — especially Khrushchev's efforts to create "atom-free" zones in the Far East and in West Germany — provides the foundation of Ulam's original interpretation.[12]

Professors Rathjens and Kistiakowsky raise crucial issues of an even broader nature. What are the technological problems impeding Soviet-American control of nuclear weapons and ever-expanding defense systems? What are the political problems, domestic and foreign? In what areas are limited agreements most feasible? The authors vividly illustrate certain practical difficulties involved in Soviet-American cooperation and the Strategic Arms Limitation Talks (SALT) in particular. To advocate collaboration in principle is one thing; to implement it is another — especially with rapid changes in weapons technology and kaleidoscopic international political developments. For several compelling reasons, the authors conclude that "Time is of the essence," and that "the superpowers [cannot] afford to delay attacking the strategic-arms race while trying to solve political differences." In light of our growing knowledge of the Cuban missile crisis and the nearness of the disaster avoided, the arguments and evidence of these respected scientists merit the utmost serious consideration by political leaders and concerned citizens of all countries, especially the United States and the Soviet Union.[13]

12. Adam Ulam, *Expansion and Coexistence: The History of Soviet Foreign Policy, 1917–67* (New York: Praeger, 1968). Cf. Michel Tatu, *Power in the Kremlin from Khrushchev to Kosygin* (New York: Viking Press, 1969); and Carl Linden, *Khrushchev and the Soviet Leadership, 1957–1964* (Baltimore: The Johns Hopkins Press, 1966).

13. See Arnold Horelick and Myron Rush, *Strategic Power and Soviet Foreign Policy* (Chicago: University of Chicago Press, 1966); Lincoln Bloomfield, Walter C. Clemens, Jr., Franklyn Griffiths, *Khrushchev and the Arms Race: Soviet Interests in Arms Control and Disarmament, 1954–1964* (Cambridge, Mass.: MIT Press, 1966); Thomas Larson, *Disarmament and Soviet Policy, 1964–1968* (Englewood Cliffs, N. J.: Prentice-Hall, 1969); and Walter C. Clemens, Jr., "Underlying Factors in Soviet Arms Control Policy: Problems of Systematic Analysis," *Peace Research Society: Papers,* VI, Vienna Conference, 1966, pp. 51–70.

SEVENTEEN

United States – Soviet Cooperation:
Incentives and Obstacles*

One of the most significant realignments of the recent past, East and West, is a *rapprochement* between the United States and Soviet Russia, an uncertain move by the two military superpowers and erstwhile cold-war adversaries into limited collaborative relations for purposes of maintaining international peace and security.

This realignment was made possible, on the Soviet side, by the death of Stalin and ensuing reorientation of Soviet policy in both internal and external affairs. It emerged slowly in the course of a post-Stalin dialogue between leaders of the two countries. The Geneva summit meeting of 1955 and the Camp David talks in 1959 between President Eisenhower and Premier Khrushchev were landmarks in the growth of this dialogue. The late 1950's and early 1960's witnessed a series of concrete steps that gave substance to the new trend in the relations between the two countries.

These steps included the limited nuclear test-ban agreement of 1963, the previous year's agreement on neutralization of Laos, the creation of the permanent direct communication channel between Moscow and Washington (called the "hot line"), the agreement on peaceful uses of the Antarctic, the agreement not to place bombs in orbit, the recently concluded multilateral treaty on

*Reprinted from *The Annals of the American Academy of Political and Social Science,* 372 (July, 1967), pp. 2 – 13, by permission of the author and the publisher.

principles for the use by all states of outer space, the growth of cultural and scientific exchange, the regularizing of contacts and discussion between the political leaders and diplomatic officials of the two countries, the continuing negotiations on arms control and disarmament, the talks on measures to prevent proliferation of nuclear weapons, the United States-Soviet agreement on direct air connections, and the conclusion of the consular convention. At the same time, there have also been a number of setbacks to the new trend in United States-Soviet relations. The U-2 episode of 1960 and the Cuban missile crisis of 1962 are both noteworthy examples. In the middle 1960's, moreover, the growth of Soviet-American political cooperation has been seriously retarded and complicated by war in Vietnam, and especially by the United States policy, initiated in early 1965, of bombing raids on North Vietnam, a Soviet ally. At this time of writing (May 1967), the future of Soviet-American cooperation is deeply clouded.

Even without these serious setbacks, the *rapprochement* between the two great powers would by no means have been describable as a "condominium," not to mention the conspiratorial "collusion" for joint Soviet-American world rule which has been conjured up in various statements emanating from Peking. On the other hand, we should not minimize the potential importance of the emergence in the post-Stalin era of a new Soviet-American relationship, the replacement of the old cold-war antagonism with a more complex and constructive interaction in which competition and cooperation are conjoined. What I wish to do in what follows is to explore the possible meaning of this realignment, and to consider some requisites of stable cooperative relations between the two countries.

The Historical Background

Although ideologically at opposite poles, the United States and Soviet Russia were not wholly unprepared in a psychological sense for the new trend in their relations which developed after Stalin. There was no tradition of enmity between their peoples. America has always enjoyed great popularity in the minds of many Russians, and even the Soviet Communist regime, speaking through Stalin, once defined the Bolshevik "style" in work as a combination of "Russian revolutionary sweep" with "American efficiency."[1] Americans, for their part, were perhaps less inclined to positive feelings toward Russia. But during the Second World War, they generally admired the Russian war effort, and ordinary Russians were more aware than their government ever acknowledged of the contribution of American Lend-Lease assistance to that effort. A large fund of mutual good will resulted.

1. J. Stalin, *Works* (Moscow, 1953), p. 194. The statement was made in Stalin's lectures of 1924 on "The Foundations of Leninism."

Not surprisingly, the idea and, to some extent, the fact of Soviet-American political collaboration have a history going back to that period. For in 1941 the two countries suddenly became involved in a "cooperative relationship" of the most elementary kind — a coalition war for survival against a common enemy. It was only natural under those conditions that some should conceive of a continuing cooperative relationship in the postwar period. Such a concept entered into the architecture of the United Nations as an organization, the Security Council in particular. Optimistic expectations were not borne out, however, and the wartime alliance gave way to the cold-war hostilities of 1946 – 1953. Not until after Stalin's death did a change in the Soviet leadership and political outlook begin to make possible the more hopeful and constructive pattern of United States-Soviet relations that some had envisaged during World War II. The prerequisites for this development had been present in the Soviet internal situation ever since the end of the war. But Stalin, the most absolute of twentieth-century dictators, was for psychological reasons unable to recognize and accept them, and continued to the end of his days to press the Cold War against the manifold "enemies" with which his paranoid personality and hostile actions peopled the world.[2]

The men who came to power in the Soviet system after Stalin's death represented a generation of somewhat younger leaders who, unlike Stalin himself, had never been revolutionaries. Rather, they had come up in political life as executives and managers. They were typified by Malenkov and Khrushchev and, more recently, by Brezhnev and Kosygin. Communist in ideology, the post-Stalin leaders give little evidence of being radical in their outlook; they are an essentially *postrevolutionary* leadership presiding over a relatively deradicalized Soviet Marxist movement, one that has gone very far toward accommodating itself to the world that it remains ideologically committed to transform.

The deradicalization of Soviet communism has certain obviously important foreign-policy implications. They could be summed up by saying that fifty years after the Bolshevik Revolution, the Soviet Union can no longer accurately be described as a "revolutionary power." Its leadership remains ideologically committed to the goal of a world-wide Communist revolution, but the pattern of Soviet conduct in world affairs has increasingly become that of a status-quo power rather than a revolutionary one.[3] Of course, "status-quo power" is itself a concept with a range of possible meanings. In the Soviet case, we do not have a power so rigidly wedded to the international status quo that

2. This thesis has been elaborated with supporting evidence in this writer's *The Soviet Political Mind* (New York: Frederick A. Praeger, 1963), Chapters 2 and 8.
3. This refers, of course, to the pattern of action in the non-Communist part of the world. Soviet policy toward the *Communist* part has long been protective of the status quo, as was best shown by the Soviet intervention in Hungary in 1956 to keep communism intact in a country where its fortunes were uncertain owing to popular revolution.

it would actively resist revolutionary change in the non-Communist part of the world. As its response to the Cuban revolution makes clear, for example, Soviet Russia, even in this era of deradicalization, is still willing to welcome and give assistance to a regime moving on its own into the Communist orbit. The thesis here being advanced is simply that the commitment to world Communist revolution, while still intact ideologically, has become very weak as a political motivation and has ceased to be a mainspring of Soviet initiative in world affairs. Soviet ideological behavior has registered the trend in question through emphatic pronouncements against "export of revolution" and through affirmation of the idea that Communist revolution should occur, if at all, as an indigenous development in the country concerned and, if possible, as a nonviolent one.

If the contemporary Soviet Union is no longer to any significant extent a revolution-making power but rather one which finds the international status quo not hard to live with, the explanation is to be sought not solely in the change of leadership and outlook attendant upon the death of Stalin and the passing from the political scene of the remnants of the Bolshevik old guard (such as Molotov) who had survived in power with Stalin. Among other factors reinforcing the status-quo tendency is the growing polycentrism of the Communist world in our time. The fourteen Communist-ruled states and the eighty or so Communist parties elsewhere in the world are no longer under Soviet control as in Stalin's time. Moreover, Soviet political and ideological ascendancy in the polycentric world of Communist states and parties has been powerfully challenged by Communist China under Mao. Further enlargement of the sphere of Communist political power could, in these conditions, complicate the Soviet effort to retain an ascendant position. Indeed, Moscow's position as capital of world communism could be further undermined rather than bolstered by Communist revolutions that brought to power parties looking to China for leadership. The otherwise curious spectacle of Soviet support for a non-Communist India in its latter-day hostilities with Communist China finds part of its explanation here.

Still another force behind the evolution of the Soviet state from the role of a revolutionary power to that of a status-quo power is the need for international stability as a setting for internal Soviet development and reform. The post-Stalin leadership inherited from Stalin a country in internal crisis caused by the long regime of terror, bureaucratic stultification, gross mismanagement, neglect of crying welfare needs of the people, and resulting catastrophically low morale. In Stalin's final years, all these problems had gone largely unrecognized in an atmosphere of relentless pursuit of the Cold War abroad. Indeed, it may have been in part Stalin's unwillingness to face the necessity for change and reform inside the Soviet Union which spurred him to keep the nation's attention constantly fixed upon the machinations of foreign "enemies." With his death, there was an underlying change in the relationship of internal and external politics of the Soviet regime.

Instead of predicating the internal policy upon the needs of the Cold War abroad, the post-Stalin leadership, under Malenkov and Beria at first and subsequently under Khrushchev and others, tended to give the position of priority to internal needs and problems and to seek a cold war *détente*. Not only would such a *détente* relieve external dangers to Soviet security (for example, by ending the Korean War); it might also make it possible to reallocate scarce Soviet funds to internal developmental needs, and especially to the long neglected consumer-goods industries. Thus, the commitment to internal development and reform was a factor favoring international stabilization.

Nor is this, as might be supposed, a strictly short-term proposition. A Soviet regime attempting, as part of its reform policy, to rule Russia without the terror that was the hallmark of Stalinism must necessarily seek substantial and continuing improvement in the living standards of the Soviet population, and the pressure to do this rises as public opinion emerges as a force in the no-longer-totalitarian single-party system. But with a gross national product far lower than America's, Soviet Russia can divert large resources to welfare needs only if it can substantially reduce or control defense expenditures. These considerations point to *détente* and international stabilization as a long-range Soviet interest, to arms control and negotiated disarmament measures as a way of enabling Russia to control arms outlays without falling behind in relative military power vis-à-vis the United States, and to a new political relationship with the United States as a precondition of achieving such ends.

Competitive Coexistence

The new foreign orientation of the post-Stalin Soviet leadership reflected these underlying realities. Ideologically, it expressed itself in the doctrine of "competitive coexistence," which was advanced in the time of Khrushchev and incorporated into the Program of the Soviet Communist party in 1961. That doctrine portrays the United States and the Soviet Union as, respectively, the leaders of two ideologically opposed "systems" competing by peaceful means — economic, political, cultural — for dominant world influence, the chief stake in the contest being the future development of the underdeveloped countries of the Third World toward either Soviet communism or American capitalism. Internal economic development is a principal arena of this external competition, for it is a question of which developmental model, the Soviet or the American, will prove more compellingly attractive in the long run.

But competitive coexistence was presented in the post-Stalin Soviet doctrine as involving a measure of cooperation between the competitors. Rather in the manner in which our economists have described "oligopolistic competition," in which two or more dominant firms cooperate to prevent price wars and maintain general market stability while competing (for example, through advertising) to improve their relative shares of the market, Soviet theorists of competitive coexistence have envisaged the Soviet Union and the United States as engaging in political cooperation to prevent war and maintain overall international stability while they carry on long-range nonmilitary competition (for example, through propaganda and ideology) to enhance their relative influence in the world. Being Marxist, they have presented this notion of a dual competitive-cum-cooperative relationship with America as a "dialectical" approach to coexistence. The basis of the cooperation, according to the Soviet view, as formulated by both political leaders and theoretical specialists, is the shared vital interest of the two great powers in reducing the chances of war. Cooperation for this purpose would involve the development of close and regular contact on all problems of mutual concern, the attempt to negotiate solutions of issues concealing threats to peace, the defusing of trouble spots in various parts of the world (Laos, for example), and the stopping of local conflicts before they grow into great conflagrations threatening to involve the major powers. In effect, the new Soviet doctrine has seen in United States-Soviet political cooperation a way of keeping competitive coexistence peaceful, of maintaining a relatively stable international environment within which the nonmilitary competition for influence can proceed.

The United States government has, since President Eisenhower's time, tended to respond favorably to the concept of a changed relationship involving some cooperation as well as continued political rivalry with Soviet Russia. It, too, has shown awareness that such cooperation could prove a requisite for cosurvival in the nuclear age. It, too, has an interest in curbing the astronomical costs of modern military technology, the spiral of the arms race. Without some success along that line, it can no more get to what is now called the "Great Society" than Soviet Russia can get to what it calls "Full Communism" (two visions of the social goal which have, by the way, more than a little in common). So, the new Soviet foreign orientation of the post-Stalin period found a receptive audience in Washington. President Kennedy's speech at American University, "Toward a Strategy of Peace," was one of the significant markers of this trend in United States official thinking. President Johnson, too, has strongly endorsed the concept of a cooperative relationship with Russia. "We've got to get into the habit of peaceful cooperation," he said, for example, in a public pronouncement of September 1966 to the Soviet people, emphasizing the common interest of the two countries in the avoidance of war, the historical record of friendliness between the two peoples, and the desirability of extending cooperative relations beyond what had so far been accomplished.[4]

4. *The New York Times,* September 28, 1966, p. 14.

Obstacles to Cooperation

Taking stock of the outcome so far, we must admit that the experiment in Soviet-American collaboration has not yet borne great fruit in deeds or brought about a stable *entente* between the two governments. Although by no means insignificant in their cumulative entirety, the cooperative acts and agreements noted earlier are little more than a series of tentative and cautious beginnings. Let us consider, for example, some of what has *not* yet been done. So far, progress on arms control and disarmament has been small. The treaty on nonproliferation of nuclear weapons would, it is true, be a very great step forward in this field. But at present it still remains under negotiation, and the outcome is uncertain. Part of the responsibility for that rests with the failure of the United States and Soviet Union to match the renunciation being asked of others with some renouncing on their own parts — such as the renouncing of the right of *first use* of nuclear weapons — and to give guarantees to the nonnuclear states against nuclear blackmail or nuclear attack by governments which might try to violate the system.

What is more, the United States and Soviet Union may be on the threshold of another fateful round of the arms race, involving the deployment of anti-ballistic missiles systems and resulting further development of offensive weapons by both sides, all of which may represent a serious setback for the cause of arms control (for example, by necessitating a resumption of nuclear tests above ground). They have not so far been willing to transform the costly competitive race to the moon into a cooperative venture. They have done next to nothing to place economic assistance to underdeveloped countries on a cooperative and multilateral basis, although the emerging crisis of economic growth and overpopulation makes the need for a cooperative approach to the problem painfully obvious.

There is no single or simple explanation for the tentativeness of United States-Soviet cooperation and for the modest character of the positive results so far. One of the explanations, however, lies in the strength of the resistances and obstacles on both sides to a working accord between the United States and Soviet governments on important international problems. Realism not only compels us to acknowledge the existence of these obstacles, but also to admit that they make themselves felt on both sides. Thus, both great powers encounter resistances within their respective alliance systems to a Soviet-American *entente*. They emanate in particular from certain governments whose leaders fear that United States-Soviet cooperation could be injurious to their own national interests. The importance that both the United States and Soviet Union attach to the preservation of their alliance structures forces them to take account of these counter-pressures. Soviet policy-makers have had to contend in particular with Communist Chinese objections to the relationship with the United States; and the United States government has had especially to contend with concern in West Germany over the possible impact of Soviet-American cooperation upon German reunification and other interests.

A further obstacle to collaborative relations between the two great powers is the persistence on both sides of old habits of mind born in the era of the Cold War, habits of ingrained hostility and distrust, habits of seeing the struggle against the other side as the supreme proper concern of national policy, and cooperation between Russia and America as unnecessary for security purposes, or undesirable, or both. To make matters still more complicated, these habits of mind are unevenly distributed on both sides. Some American and Soviet political leaders are more flexible and conciliation-minded, more able and willing to conceive of collaborating with adversaries and to experiment along those lines, whereas others are more rigid and doctrinaire, more inclined to rely on military might in relations with the other side, more convinced that the only effective way to talk to them is in the language of cold power. In the jargon of recent times, we have the "soft-liners" and the "hard-liners," the "doves" and the "hawks." These terms are obvious oversimplifications, but the divisions to which they point are real and enormously important facts of political life in *both* of the capitals. The recent United States Senate debate over ratification of the consular convention with the Soviet Union made the division on the American side more dramatically apparent than before. Because of the single-party system and official control of the press on the other side, the division is less apparent in the Soviet leadership. Yet those of us who regularly study the Soviet press have found abundant evidence that it exists.

And so, on both sides, there are influential elements who oppose a Soviet-American working relationship and who resist efforts in that direction to the extent that they can. In a curious way, moreover, they reinforce each other. For insofar as the Soviet hard-liners gain the ascendancy inside the Soviet Union's regime, the policy orientation that they pursue tends to support the arguments of their opposite numbers in Washington about the difficulty of working cooperatively with the Russians. The same process also works in reverse: ascendancy of those who favor a hard-line policy in Washington plays into the hands of the Moscow opponents of Soviet-American cooperation, for it leads to actions by the United States government which make the latter's argument in the internal policy debate on the Soviet side more plausible. Thus, the tough policy that the United States government has pursued in Vietnam during the last two years has resulted, among other things, in a growth of influence of hard-line elements inside the Soviet government and a worsening of the position of the proponents of better relations with Washington.

Still a further serious obstacle to a stable and self-sustained United States-Soviet working relationship is the continuance of political rivalry between them at the level of intensity that has marked it during the past decade. Both great powers have vigorously engaged in a political influence contest, particularly in the Third World, employing diplomacy, economic assistance, arms exports, technical aid, propaganda, and so on. Experience makes it quite clear that this influence contest can create situations that, in turn, impose great strain upon the fabric of Soviet-American relations. Thus, for example, Moscow, pursuing political influence, has in recent months created an arms imbalance in North Africa by shipping much military equipment to Algeria, which has led to a plea from Morocco to the United States for matching arms assistance. The dynamics of situations of this kind contain within themselves the potentiality of armed conflicts which, in turn, create more international tension and threaten to involve the superpowers. The earlier history of present events in Indochina bears witness in its way to the relevance of this proposition.

So, the whole concept of a "nonmilitary" Soviet-American competition for influence in the uncommitted countries has a certain unreality. For competitive coexistence tends to remain peaceful only so long as neither side is conspicuously or irretrievably *losing*. The game shows a dangerous tendency to cease being peaceful when: (1) a change of regime seriously adverse to one or the other side occurs or threatens to occur within a given country that has been an object of competition, and (2) circumstances permit the application of force to prevent or reverse this adverse outcome. An intense competitive struggle to draw uncommitted countries into one orbit of influence or another is, therefore, a serious bar to the development of stable cooperative relations between the United States and Soviet Union.

All of these obstacles to Soviet-American cooperation have made themselves felt in recent years and help to explain why more has not been achieved. In this connection, special mention must be made of the war in Vietnam. On the surface, this war has not completely put a stop to United States-Soviet political collaboration. Yet, in a deeper way, the war, and especially the bombing of North Vietnam which began in early 1965, has had a very depressing effect upon the whole post-Stalin growth of working relations between Moscow and Washington. Changes that slowly were taking place in the official Soviet image of the American political leadership have been set back or reversed, and an image of the American leadership that resembles the old cold-war stereotypes has reemerged in the Soviet official press. A relapse into old suspicions, old animosities, and old anti-American Soviet reflexes may be reflected in this. In part, it may reflect increased influence of the hard-line element in the Soviet leadership under the impact of Vietnam, and in part it may express a general tendency of the Soviet political mind to reconsider its earlier more hopeful view of American leaders. Furthermore, in the general atmosphere of West European apathy or opposition to America's Vietnamese action, the Soviet leadership has been presented with fresh opportunities to cultivate political relationships in Europe that might not otherwise have existed or have been so beckoning, and consequently we have seen in the past two years a tendency for Moscow to exploit centrifugal forces in the Western alliance structure, to give the emphasis not to closer relations with Washington but rather to closer relations with West European capitals, Paris included. Finally, the dialogue between Soviet and American leaders, a dialogue which lies at the core of the cooperative relationship, has suffered and greatly been diminished as a result of Vietnam. On the whole, the injury done to the emergent *entente* with the Soviet Union may be far from the least of the tragedies of the Vietnamese war from the American point of view.

Yet I do not believe that the new Soviet-American relationship is or need be permanently impaired. Given in the near future a negotiated peace in Vietnam, the underlying forces in the world situation which impel the two super-powers to collaborative action should reassert themselves. Fundamental security interests of both powers, and indeed of all peoples, are involved. Hence it seems premature to assume a permanent shift of Soviet diplomatic emphasis to the Western European scene or to treat the whole venture of cooperative relations between the United States and the Soviet Union as a matter of historical interest only. What may be useful, then, is to reflect on the experience of the past decade in this field, and try to draw some lessons from it.

Requisites of Soviet — American Cooperation

(1) It appears that, notwithstanding all the obstacles explored above, the incentives to cooperative action by the two superpowers are quite strong, sufficiently so to provide a basis for greater success in this field than has been achieved so far. The fundamental incentive is the common interest in reducing the danger of a thermonuclear holocaust. This primary common interest, reinforced by a further common interest in curtailing the cost of military preparations and establishments, dictates United States-Soviet cooperation in all feasible measures of arms control and disarmament. Further, the primary common interest in preventing a general war gives rise to a set of secondary common interests in stabilizing or settling crisis situations in which the threat of armed violence is latently present.

Beyond these shared interests in avoiding war, in bringing the arms race under control, and in the defusing of world trouble-spots, the United States and the Soviet Union have an underlying, although as yet imperfectly cognized, common interest in working together to meet certain other problems and dangers. The population explosion, the growing disparity between the wealthy nations and the poor nations and the associated problem of economic development, and the problem of air and water pollution are high on the list of situations that contain a mounting threat of disorder on a world scale, situations of unprecedented urgency and seriousness. Only through international cooperation can these dangers be contained, much less allayed, and without cooperation between the two most powerful and wealthy of industrialized nations, no efforts by the United Nations or regional associations of states can bear great fruit. In effect, international cooperation is becoming a vital necessity in the face of the rise of a plethora of problems that, by their very nature, cannot be satisfactorily resolved within the confines of the nation-state. In the continuing absence of an effective system of world order, the United States and Soviet Russia can alone provide by their cooperative action an interim response to the need for a cooperative international approach to these problems. It is not only, then, the danger of war which provides the underlying motivation for their cooperation, but also the political, demographic, economic, and technological challenges to prolonged meaningful human living on this planet.

(2) A cooperative arrangement between the United States and the Soviet Union cannot easily be enduring and stable unless it becomes more close and extensive than political leaders on either side have apparently envisaged, and unless it takes precedence over such important competing concerns as the integrity of their regional alliance structures. Up to now, the tendency on both sides has been to think in terms of a modicum of cooperation combined with a high level of continued political rivalry throughout the world. The experience of the past decade suggests, however, that unless the cooperative working relationship transcends this, unless it goes beyond a *détente* and becomes an *entente,* it may not be viable at all.

This view is admittedly at variance with the thinking of some respected American specialists in foreign-policy problems. They take a continued intense process of Soviet-American competition for influence as a constant and feel, in part because of pressures from within the Western alliance system, that cooperative relations with Moscow neither need be nor ought to be extended beyond a minimum of mutually advantageous action, chiefly in the sphere of arms control, to reduce the hazards of nuclear war.[5] However, such a scenario for American-Soviet relations may be more of a utopia than the just-mentioned *entente.* For it overlooks the essential indivisibility of these relations, the virtual impossibility of maintaining stable cooperative arrangements in one field — the delicate and difficult area of arms control — while pursuing as vigorously as ever a worldwide political competition for influence which keeps the competitors mutually estranged and periodically generates high tension between them. The cooperative links between Washington and Moscow cannot be expected to prosper if frequently subjected to extreme political turbulence in a world of intense Soviet-American political rivalry.

This is not to argue that some sort of global bargain between the two powers is the precondition of their successful cooperation in world affairs. An antecedent general settlement of outstanding international issues, however desirable in the abstract, does not appear realistically attainable in the near future.

---

5. See, for example, the argument of Marshall D. Shulman in "'Europe' versus *Détente?,*" *Foreign Affairs* (April, 1967).

Undoubtedly, there are various issues — and German reunification is almost certainly one of them — which will have to be lived with until the slow passage of time and efforts of diplomacy can bring possibilities of resolution that do not now exist. The point being made here is simply that the competitive process, although it clearly cannot altogether be stopped, need not on the other hand be taken as a simple given, an unalterable fact of international life, something over which the two governments have no control. Rather, it has an interactive dynamic of its own which can be curbed and brought under control, given the settled will on both sides to do so. It is something to which limits can be set. And difficult as this might be to achieve, it would probably be less difficult than to achieve progress on the terribly complex technical problems of arms control and disarmament *without* curtailment of the power rivalry between the two principals. On the other hand, progress on arms-control measures should become increasingly feasible in a setting of lessened political competition between the chief governments concerned.

The theory of competitive coexistence, as elaborated on the Soviet side and more or less accepted with much ideological rationalization on the American side, envisages an indefinitely prolonged process of political competition tempered by cooperative steps to keep this competition peaceful. But that is a formula for an inherently unstable and deeply troubled United States-Soviet relationship. To stabilize it, the cooperative aspect will have to be given primacy over the competitive aspect. The two governments will have to show a settled disposition to reach settlements where possible. They will have to neutralize or otherwise defuse various danger points in world politics, such as Southeast Asia; to forestall the eruption of crisis situations that place great strain upon their relations; to avoid getting into conflicts which give rise to domestic pressures against cooperative relations; and, in general, to adopt a conflict-resolving posture in their interrelations and their approach to world problems. Clearly, this would imply certain significant modifications in the habitual modes of thought and conduct of both main powers on the international scene. Above all, instead of regarding the promotion of a particular form of society as their highest mission in history, the leaders would have to conceive it as their supreme goal to serve the cause of order in human affairs, pending the slow creation in time of order-maintaining institutions on a world scale.

(3) This raises the whole question of the form that a United States-Soviet *entente* might take. Manifestly, close relationships between great powers can take a multitude of forms, depending upon the purposes that animate them and other factors. A United States-Soviet working relationship could conceivably fall into the pattern of imperialistic great-power alliances of the past, with a division of Soviet and American spheres of influence in the world. In effect, the interests of the two powers, narrowly conceived, would become the touchstone of their cooperative action. Although the United States and Russia have

the combined physical power to enforce such a condominium, an attempt to cooperate along those lines would not, for a great many reasons, be likely to succeed for long. Not only would it be beset by manifold resistances from smaller states whose interests were being overridden by the great powers; it would conflict with the aspirations of the two peoples themselves, and would encounter resistances, both internal and external.

An alternative form of *entente,* although historically unprecedented, would be more in accord with the needs of the situation and the spirit of the two peoples. Instead of cooperating politically in their own national interests, narrowly conceived, the governments of the United States and Soviet Union would seek to exert their influence separately and jointly on behalf of the growth of order, which is in the interest not simply of these two major nations but of all. They would work not only in their bilateral relations but in the United Nations and its working bodies, in their regional alliances, and in every aspect of foreign policy, to promote constructive change and peaceful solutions of world problems. In effect, the United States-Soviet cooperative relationship would become a kind of trusteeship under which the two governments would jointly act as sponsors of international order pending the creation of a workable formal system of world order in the future. They would form, as it were, an informal interim system of order, a holding operation to help man survive long enough to move into the new form of international life that is needed but does not yet exist.

Such an undertaking would tap the deeper sources of idealism present in both the American and Russian peoples. Among contemporary nations, these two are notable for the stubborn streak of idealistic aspiration that marks them both in very different ways. Both have a universalism and a commitment to world order. They conceive it differently, it is true. Americans tend to think in terms of a world order under law, whereas Russians, insofar as they are Communists, tend rather to think in terms of a world order under ideology. No easy reconciliation of these disparate approaches to world order will be possible. But the younger generations, those who come to positions of power and influence in ten or fifteen years time, may find it easier than their elders did to make the necessary mutual adjustment. What their elders can do is to give them a chance to try.

(4) Finally, it is, in my opinion, an essential requisite for stable cooperation between the United States and Soviet Union that an element of mutual trust be built over time into their mutual relations. The foundation of this trust might be the recognition by leading persons on both sides that the two countries have acquired, by virtue of modern military technology, not only certain common security interests but a *mutual* security interest. That is to say, given the unheard-of possibilities of destruction inherent in total thermonuclear war in our time, each of the two superpowers has, whether it recognizes this or not, acquired a certain interest in the *other's* security, or (what amounts to the same

thing) its sense of security. For nervousness, tension, insecurity on either side have become dangerous to both. It is in this context that the growth of mutual trust becomes a factor of great potential importance.

Considering the heritage of mutual mistrust and suspicion born of the Cold War and the whole past history of our relations, the idea of building trust into Soviet-American relations may seem wildly unrealistic. Moreover, there is a certain tendency to suppose that the sole proper basis for Soviet-American relations, including cooperative action in arms control, is the rationally calculated self-interest of both parties, their common desire to survive. This may be so, but it is not self-evidently so. For it may be that in certain situations now emerging on the horizon of Soviet-American relations, the dictates of calculated self-interest will depend on what image of the other side goes into the calculation: the picture of a malevolent force operating only on the basis of calculated self-interest, or, alternatively, that of a force moved by certain human feelings and not foreign to benevolence. If this is so, then the growth of trust — the kind of trust that may have been emerging, for example, in the relations between Kennedy and Khrushchev — could prove of decisive significance.

To build mutual trust into United States-Soviet relations will at best be a long slow process, and probably never complete, at least in the present generation. But without it, there can be no genuine *entente,* and many problems will be far harder to resolve. In particular, the arms race will probably not be brought under control.

EIGHTEEN

WILLIAM ECKHARDT AND
RALPH K. WHITE

A Test of the Mirror-Image Hypothesis:
Kennedy and Khrushchev*

Many Americans seem to assume that the tone of Communist propaganda is similar to Khrushchev's celebrated statement, "We will bury you." This statement has usually been interpreted to reflect the assumed Communist intention to conquer the world by force of arms. In this context it has been interpreted to mean, "We will kill you and then bury you." However, in its own context the statement could be better interpreted as meaning: "We will outlast you and be present at your funeral when you die a natural death." In other words, it would seem that Khrushchev was simply boasting, in accordance with classical Communist theory, that socialism would outlast capitalism in the process of social evolution.

As opposed to the interpretation of Communist propaganda emphasizing offensive uses of military methods to achieve Communist purposes, Bronfenbrenner (1961) has suggested that the Cold War attitudes of Russians are very similar to those of Americans. As a result of many conversations with Russian people in the Soviet Union, Bronfenbrenner came to the conclusion that the Russians' distorted picture of us was similar to our view of them, that there was a "mirror image" in the reciprocal perception of the American and Russian people, and that this image represented serious distortions by each party of realities on the other side.

*Reprinted from *The Journal of Conflict Resolution,* XI, 3 (September, 1967), pp. 325 – 332, by permission of the author and the publisher. Copyright 1967 by The University of Michigan.

Oskamp (1963) investigated the attitudes of American students toward identical actions described as taken by both the U.S. and the USSR. On the basis of the mirror-image hypothesis, he expected to find that most actions would be rated much more favorably when ascribed to America than when they were ascribed to Russia. The results were in accord with these expectations.

Jecker (1964) read a *New York Times* newspaper article concerning a Russian defector to the U.S. to one class of students. Using the same article, but changing identities so that it became an article about an American defector to the USSR, he read this "reversed" article to another class. Significantly more favorable attitudes were expressed in relation to the original article. These students tended to feel that it was right and morally acceptable for a Russian to defect to the U.S. but that it was wrong and morally unacceptable for an American to defect to Russia.

These two studies, showing as they do the use of a double standard by American students in the judgment of American and Russian actions, would provide some confirmation of Bronfenbrenner's hypothesis. The purpose of the present study was to test this hypothesis further through the public speeches of political leaders in both countries.

Methods and Subjects

The subjects chosen for this study were John F. Kennedy and Nikita Khrushchev. It was realized that what these men said in public speeches might not necessarily represent their own private feelings and values. But it seemed reasonable to assume that what they said probably represented the prevalent attitudes in their respective countries.

The six speeches of Kennedy used in this study had been selected by Thonssen (1961, 1962, 1963) for their rhetorical value for inclusion in his annual series of representative American speeches. This criterion for selection, being relatively independent of political content, suggested that this selection of speeches should be a relatively random one from the political point of view. The rhetorical criterion should also free this selection from some of the American bias evident in the "double-standard" studies previously mentioned. All of Kennedy's speeches selected by Thonssen were used as subject matter for this analysis.

The speeches of Khrushchev used in this study had been selected by Mager and Katel (1961), whose explicit intention was to present a critical analysis of Communist intentions. Although this intention might have introduced some bias into their interpretations, the sheer quantity and wide assortment of their source material (all of which was used as subject matter for this analysis) suggested that this would be at once fairly representative of Khrushchev's speeches and fairly free of American bias.

The method of value-analysis (White, 1951) was used to analyze the values explicitly stated or clearly implied in the speeches of Kennedy and Khrushchev. Value-analysis is a form of content-analysis in which a "value," the unit of analysis, was defined as *any goal or standard of judgment which in a given culture is ordinarily referred to as if it were self-evidently desirable* (White, 1951, p. 13). Since White's values were regarded as pervading "not only our own culture but also many other cultures, including that of the Soviet Union" (White, 1951, p. 21), the use of this method to compare the values of Kennedy and Khrushchev would seem to be justified. The values used in this study have been defined by White (1951, pp. 44 – 55).

The limitations of this method should be made quite clear at the outset. The validity of value-analysis is necessarily limited to the manifest content. It is merely a method of categorizing what people say about what they want. Such a categorization has the advantage of reducing various and diverse materials to somewhat comparable terms. Whether these "values" reflect sincere beliefs, or how they will be expressed in action, cannot be determined by value-analysis as such, but is a matter of inference and interpretation. Verbal analyses, such as this one, are necessarily less crucial than an interpretation of goals and values based on a study of actions. However, where a problem has to do with what people are saying about their own values and those of others, then value-analysis is a useful and appropriate method of study.

The reliability of value-analysis, like that of any other statistical technique, is partly a function of the number of units analyzed. In the present case, 1,400 of Kennedy's value-judgments and 2,564 of Khrushchev's value-judgments were categorized into 31 values, which meant that the percent of each of Kennedy's expressed values was based on an average of 45 judgments and the percent of each of Khrushchev's expressed values was based on an average of 83 judgments. These figures would suggest a fair amount of reliability in this respect.

So far as reliability between analysts is concerned, White (1951, p.81) has reported a correlation of .93, significant at the .01 level of confidence, on the ranking of 50 values analyzed in a ten-page autobiography. "The reliability also appears to be relatively high for percentage figures which involve only a twofold classification" (White, 1951, p. 81), such as the percent of denunciation to be discussed later in this paper. The reliability between two analysts is lower on values as such (r=.67 to .72, significant at the .01 level of confidence), and in percent of agreement on individual items (.62 to .67). However, "the final conclusions have to do with item-totals, and minor discrepancies have a tendency to cancel out when totals are computed" (White, 1951, p. 82).

Eckhardt (1965, p. 346) has checked his own analysis-reanalysis reliability on the same material over a six-month interval, and has obtained a correlation of .80, significant at the .01 level of confidence, between two sets of frequencies on 32 values. He has also checked the reliability of subject-matter in the case of Winston Churchill's speeches, whose expressed values in 1933 – 1938, 1938 – 1940, 1940 – 1941, and 1944 were all correlated with each other about .80, significant at the .01 level of confidence (Eckhardt, 1965, p. 346). His average reliability with ten other analysts on a variety of material was .84, significant at the .01 level of confidence.

Table 1. Relative Frequency of Reference to Various Values by Kennedy and Khrushchev.

Values	Kennedy (N=1400)		Khrushchev (N=2564)
Strength			
Freedom	2.5%		0.4%
(W) Achievement	0.9		8.3
(W) Recognition	0.0	=	0.0
Dominance	2.6		0.7
(W) Aggression	2.9		4.0
(W) Military strength	11.3		1.8
(W) Patriotism	1.5		3.2
Determination	8.1		1.0
(W) Sovereignty	6.4	=	5.7
Obedience	0.9		0.0
Democracy (bad)	0.0	=	0.0
	37.1		25.1
Morality			
(P) Morality	1.3		0.0
(W) Truth	4.6		2.8
(W) Justice	1.6		6.5
Religion	0.8		0.0
(P) Democracy	0.8	=	0.8
(W) Aggression (bad)	8.2	=	7.6
(W) Dominance (bad)	4.0	=	5.3
(P) Friendship	5.3		2.7
(W) Tolerance	0.1		2.7
Generosity	0.9	=	0.6
Carefulness	0.8		0.0
	28.4	=	29.0
Economic values			
(P) Economic welfare	5.2		12.6
(W) Ownership	0.0		4.4
(P) Work	0.0		2.7
	5.2		19.7
Miscellaneous			
(P) Peace	19.8		12.4
(P) Knowledge	4.5		6.6

Table 1. Continued.

	Values	Kennedy (N 1400)		Khrushchev (N 2564)
(W)	Practicality	2.3	=	3.5
	Security	2.4		0.0
	Culture	0.1		1.8
(P)	Value-in-general	0.0	=	1.5
		29.1	=	25.8

*Figures in the body of the table are percentages of the total N (number of value-judgments coded) given at the top of each column. Equal signs indicate values between which there is no significant difference at the .05 level, according to a chi-square test. Values preceded by (W) are "war values" in the sense that they were found to be significantly higher in Hitler's speeches than they were in Roosevelt's speeches. Values preceded by (P) are "peace values" in that they were found to be significantly higher in Roosevelt's speeches than they were in Hitler's speeches.

Results

KENNEDY'S VALUES

The values Kennedy expressed most often were peace, military strength, nonaggression (denunciation of aggression in others), and determination (to defend peace and freedom), as shown in Table 1.

Kennedy's emphasis upon peace and freedom was illustrated by statements such as these: "We do not want to fight" (Thonssen, 1962, p. 10). "Freedom can prevail — and peace can endure" (1962, p. 17). "We far prefer world law . . . to world war. . . . [We] challenge the Soviet Union, not to an arms race, but to a peace race" (1962, pp. 44 – 45). "Our goal is not the victory of might, but the vindication of right — not peace at the expense of freedom, but both peace *and* freedom" (1963, p. 15).

Military strength was described as essential to defend the peace: "Only when our arms are sufficient beyond doubt can we be certain beyond doubt that they will never be employed" (1961, p. 38). "If there is one path above all others to war, it is the path of weakness" (1962, p. 17). "We make our [peace] proposals today, while building up our defenses over Berlin. . . . we are compelled against our will to rearm" (1962, p. 46).

Even as the United States was presented on the side of peace and freedom, the Soviet Union was presented as the enemy of peace and freedom: "The source of world trouble and tension is Moscow, not Berlin" (1962, p. 17). "Self-determination has not reached the Communist empire" (1962, p. 50). "They will not settle for . . . a peaceful world but must settle for a Communist world" (1963, p. 162). "These constant desires [of the Communists] to change the balance of power in the world, that is what . . . introduces the dangerous element" (1963, p. 165).

KHRUSHCHEV'S VALUES

The values Khrushchev expressed most often were economic welfare, peace, achievement, and nonaggression (denunciation of aggression in others), as shown in Table 1.

The values of peace and freedom were combined in the concept of "peaceful coexistence," which "implies complete renunciation of war as the means of settling questions at issue, as well as noninterference in the internal affairs of other countries" (Mager and Katel, 1961, p. 60). "Freedom" here clearly meant national freedom, national independence, or national sovereignty. Khrushchev often said that socialism would defeat capitalism not by means of a hydrogen bomb but by means of its ideology (p. 51), for the propagation of which peace was required (p. 68). Peace was also required by socialism for the sake of economic development (p. 63). In fact, "all people on earth are bound to benefit economically from disarmament" (p. 298). Peace and freedom were virtually equated with socialism: "The policy of peace is inseparable from socialism" (p. 279) and "There are no people more resolute and loyal to the struggle against colonialists than the Communists" (p. 139). "Colonialists" here clearly referred to those who were seen as opposing national freedom or independence or sovereignty.

Even as socialism was presented on the side of peace and freedom, capitalism was described as being opposed to these values: "The policy of peace is inseparable from socialism in the same way as aggression and war are inseparable from imperialism" (Mager and Katel, 1961, p. 279). Western nations were said to be "saber-rattling" (p. 444), and were described as having "nightmarish plans for world domination" (p. 92). "Capitalism cannot exist without plundering the masses of the people, without oppression and exploitation" (p. 122).

Capitalism was held responsible for the Cold War: "The monopolists see an advantage in the arms race. . . . In order to insure the continuance of such profits in the future, they use every means to keep the Cold War at a certain height, increase international tension and intimidate people with the 'communist menace'" (p. 285). Communist strength was justified as a defensive necessity: "The Soviet Union is in a capitalist encirclement and must be ready to deal a crushing blow to any attempts by the aggressors to hinder our peaceful construction" (p. 24).

Although international warfare was renounced except in self-defense, class warfare was not renounced, and capitalism was challenged to engage in ideological, economic, and peaceful competition: "Our task is tirelessly to expose bourgeois ideology, reveal how inimical it is to the people, show up its reactionary nature" (p. 309). At the same time, "We are confident that our two states and our two peoples can live in friendship and work in common for an enduring peace" (p. 265).

CORRELATION OF VALUES

Kennedy's and Khrushchev's expressed values, as shown in Table 1, were positively and significantly correlated with each other, $r = .56$, significant at the .01 level of confidence.

There were no significant differences in the values placed upon aggression (fighting for one's own values) and sovereignty by Kennedy and Khrushchev, as determined by a chi-square test as shown in Table 1. There was also no significant difference in their denunciation of each other as being aggressive and dominant, as shown in Table 1 under the moral category. However, in their moral judgments of each other, Kennedy more often described Communists as being untruthful, and Khrushchev more often described capitalists as being unjust as shown in Table 1. In spite of the overall similarity (correlation) in the distribution of their values, two-thirds of their value-frequencies differed significantly according to the chi-square test results shown in Table 1. Although significantly similar in their overall value-distributions, they were also significantly different on two-thirds of their individual values.

INDICES OF CONFLICT-MINDEDNESS

According to White (1951, p. 6), the percent of total judgments involving the denunciation of others for not wanting or respecting certain values was "the best single objective indicator of conflict-mindedness."

Table 2. Indices of Conflict-Mindedness.

Index*	Kennedy (N≂1400)	Khrushchev (N=1400)	Hitler (N=4077)	Roosevelt (N=1249)	Mean of 15 subjects (N=15006)
Denunciation %	17	21	32+	10	15
Justified aggression %	2	3	3	0	2
Strength %	37	25	38	16−	35
Nonwelfare %	77	64	75	50	59
War/peace ratio	1.2	1.4	4.2+	0.3	1.5
Average T score of all indices	51	50	59+	44	49

*These indices were derived from White's (1949) study of Hitler and Roosevelt, which was also the basis of the figures in the third and fourth columns. Plus and minus signs indicate differences of more than one standard deviation from the mean of 15 subjects (Eckhardt, 1965). See the text for the meaning of the indices.

White's original study (1949) showed that Hitler's denunciation of others constituted 32 percent of his total value-judgments, while Roosevelt's denunciation of others (in the speeches analyzed) was 10 percent of his total judgments. Table 2 shows that Kennedy's denunciation was 17 percent and that Khrushchev's denunciation was 21 percent. Kennedy's and Khrushchev's percents of denunciation were not significantly different from each other, but they were both significantly lower than Hitler's percent and relatively higher than Roosevelt's percent, but not significantly so.

Kennedy and Khrushchev were also not far from average on other indices of conflict-mindedness originally developed by White (1949), further validated by Eckhardt (1965), and shown in Table 2. Justified aggression was defined as the percent of total value-judgments in which aggression was described as necessary in order to defend peace, freedom, and other values. Strength was the percent of values shown in the strength category in Table 1. The "war/peace ratio" was defined by Eckhardt (1965) as the sum of "war values" (indicated by a "W" in Table 1) divided by the sum of "peace values" (indicated by a "P" in Table 1). "War values" were defined as those values which Hitler invoked significantly more often than Roosevelt did, and "peace values" were defined as those values which Roosevelt invoked significantly more often than Hitler did. The welfare percent was the percent of "welfare values" (obtained from analysis of interviews with 15 public assistance cases) shared by Kennedy and Khrushchev. "Welfare values" emphasized health, work, and economic welfare (Eckhardt, 1965, p. 353). Justified aggression, strength values, "war/peace ratio," and nonwelfare percent were all accepted as indices of conflict-mindedness because they were all significantly correlated with the percent of denunciation, significant at the .05 level of confidence (Eckhardt, 1965).

Kennedy and Khrushchev were not significantly different from each other on any of these indices, as shown in Table 2. When all of these indices were transformed into T scores and averaged, the average T scores of Kennedy and Khrushchev were not significantly different from each other, as shown at the bottom of Table 2. Kennedy's and Khrushchev's average T scores on all indices were significantly lower than that of Hitler, and relatively higher than that of Roosevelt, but not significantly so.

Discussion

Even as Kennedy identified Communism with imperialism (dominance) and militarism (aggression), Khrushchev identified capitalism with imperialism and militarism. To be sure, Kennedy displayed some detachment in the following statements: "The combination of these two systems in conflict around the world in a nuclear age is what makes the sixties so dangerous. . . . the Communists have a completely twisted view of the United States, and . . . we don't comprehend them, that is what makes life in the sixties hazardous" (Thonssen, 1963, p. 163). Even this limited detachment, however, was far from typical.

The typical statements on both sides would be consistent with the mirror-image theory of the Cold War, according to which the United States' perception of itself in relation to the Soviet Union resembles, in many ways, a mirror image of the Soviet Union's perception of itself in relation to the United States. This theory is in some degree confirmed by the value-judgments made by Kennedy and Khrushchev, both of whom presented their respective nations as champions of peace and freedom, and as wanting disarmament, but as requiring military strength to defend themselves against the aggression of the other. In each case, the speaker's own nation, and his bloc, was described as unified (patriotism) in spite of diversity. Its foreign aid was referred to as an act of friendship, and never as an attempt to interfere with the internal affairs of other nations (dominance). In both countries the government was described as democratic, at least in the sense of being for the people.

On the other hand, both Kennedy and Khrushchev depicted the other side as the enemy of peace and freedom, and as not wanting disarmament in spite of the fact that the enemy's military expenditures were undermining the enemy's economy. The other side was pictured as suffering from inner conflicts. The other nation's foreign aid was seen as an act of imperialism (dominance), their workers were slaves, their press had no real freedom, and their government was undemocratic.

The mirror-image theory is also confirmed to some degree by the fact that Kennedy's and Khrushchev's overtly stated values were positively and significantly correlated with each other. This was especially true of those moral values used as standards of judging and of the mutual denunciation for not wanting certain values, especially peace and freedom, although truth and justice were also mentioned on both sides with some frequency.

Kennedy and Khrushchev were also similar on five indices of conflict-mindedness, which showed them striking an approximate average between Hitler's significantly high scores and Roosevelt's relatively low scores on these same indices, suggesting that their conflict-mindedness was of average or moderate intensity, and about equally so in both cases, as shown by their average T scores in Table 2.

Summary and Conclusions

Bronfenbrenner's mirror-image theory of the Cold War received partial confirmation from the studies of Oskamp (1963) and Jecker (1964) which suggested a double standard in the American judgment of identical actions taken by both the U.S. and the USSR. The present study investigated the mirror-image phenomenon through the value-analysis of public speeches made by Kennedy and Khrushchev, whose verbally expressed values were found to be positively and significantly correlated with each other at the .01 level of confidence. They were about equally aggressive in defending their own nation's sovereignty, and equally denunciatory of each other's aggression, dominance, and immorality in general (total number of moral judgments). Their scores on five indices of conflict-mindedness were in general intermediate between those of Hitler and Roosevelt, and not significantly different from each other.

These studies would suggest that, on both sides of the Cold War, each nation sees itself on the side of values that are not — at this level of analysis — strikingly different. For instance, both sides often invoke such values as peace and national freedom or sovereignty. Each nation appears to see the opposing nation as an enemy of these values, and leaders of both nations sometimes express willingness to use force (in spite of their general devotion to peace) to preserve these and other values. A psychological interpretation of this mirror-image relationship might include at least the mechanisms of denying and ignoring one's own national faults and the mechanism of projecting these faults upon the enemy.

References

Bronfenbrenner, U. "The Mirror-Image in Soviet-American Relations," *Journal of Social Issues,* 17, 3 (1961), p. 45.

Eckhardt, W. "War Propaganda, Welfare Values, and Political Ideologies," *Journal of Conflict Resolution,* 9, 3 (Sept. 1965), pp. 345 – 58.

Jecker, J. D. "Attitudes toward Political Defection." Paper read at Midwestern Psychological Association, St. Louis, May 1964.

Mager, N. H., and J. Katel (eds.). *Conquest without War.* New York: Simon & Schuster, 1961.

Oskamp, S. "Attitudes toward U.S. and Russian Actions: A Double Standard." Paper read at California Psychological Association, San Francisco, Dec. 1963.

Thonssen, L. (ed.). *Representative American Speeches.* New York: Wilson, 1961, 1962, 1963.

White, R. K. "Hitler, Roosevelt, and the Nature of War Propaganda," *Journal of Abnormal and Social Psychology,* 44 (1949), pp. 157 – 74.

——. *Value-Analysis: Nature and Use of the Method.* Ann Arbor, Mich.: Society for the Psychological Study of Social Issues, 1951.

Ideology and American Policy*

Containment has been a hallmark of American policy toward the Soviet Union for the past two decades. Articulated by George F. Kennan, the famous "X," in *Foreign Affairs,* July 1947, as American rationale for countering Soviet post-World War II policy in Europe, the containment doctrine subsequently was generalized as a policy toward international Communism. Containment remained the essential doctrine of the Eisenhower Administration despite cries for "liberation" and "rollback." Containment or containment plus remains the official American dogma toward Communism. Yet the behavior of the Kennedy-Johnson Administration, as distinguished from its formal assurances of undying hostility to Communism, suggests that American policy toward the Soviet Union is in fact undergoing a reappraisal.

The late President Kennedy's commencement address at The American University in June 1963, calling for a reexamination of the American attitude toward the cold war was a significant, if ambiguous, indication of the Administration's thinking. Continuity in this trend of thought after Johnson's succession to the Presidency was maintained in Secretary Rusk's public defense of the Administration's differentiated approach to various Communist countries.

*Reprinted from *The Virginia Quarterly Review,* XL, 4 (Autumn, 1964), pp. 531 – 541, by permission of the author and the publisher. Copyright by *The Virginia Quarterly Review,* The University of Virginia, Autumn 1964.

On February 25, 1964, the Secretary informed a world affairs conference of the International Union of Electrical, Radio, and Machine Workers that the Soviet Union was beginning to behave more nearly like a normal state. The United States representative at the United Nations, Adlai E. Stevenson, used the 1964 Dag Hammarskjold Memorial Lecture to suggest that "we have begun to move beyond the policy of containment" to a "policy of cease-fire, and peaceful change," and within days Senator J. W. Fulbright was heard criticizing the divergence between myth and reality in United States foreign policy. In other words, picking its way cautiously through the highly emotional and politically-charged landscape of anti-Communism in this country, the Administration appears to be rationalizing its position in a more systematic way before the American public. But precisely how does the Administration regard the Soviet Union and the problem of Communism in general? Has Soviet policy changed significantly to warrant a corresponding shift in American policy? Does Soviet motivation appear different from the official or quasi-official reading given it in the immediate postwar period? Or has the change taken place more within the American outlook on the Soviet Union than in any specific changes in the Soviet Union or in world Communism themselves? Since American foreign policy has, to a large degree, been conditioned by its reading of Soviet ideology, this inquiry into the present Administration's thinking will take off from Kennan's classic statement on containment, in which American strategy appears to derive in large measure from Soviet ideology.

The main lines of the containment argument, as developed by Mr. Kennan, proceed as follows: Ideology provides the framework for Soviet internal and foreign policy. Since Communist ideology views world history as a continuous conflict between opposing social forces inexorably moving toward a final synthesis — the perfection of Communist society — the inference is that capitalism, doomed by History, is innately antagonistic to Communism. From this it would seem to follow that the conflict between capitalism and socialism is inherently irreconcilable.

If this were only the speculation of a political philosopher, one could take one's chances with the *Weltgeist*. However, the argument continues, Marx's Bolshevik disciples developed the idea of a disciplined party, claiming a monopoly of truth and power, and dedicated to the purpose of forcing the change ordained by History. But, like the Church, the Kremlin is under no ideological compulsion to accomplish its purposes in a hurry. Existing achievements are not sacrificed "for the sake of vain baubles of the future." Armed with iron discipline and infallibility, the Kremlin is free to adopt any thesis it sees fit. It is completely free tactically, which means that it shares no common assumptions or purposes with the West. Hence facts — what you do or can do — speak louder than words to the Kremlin. Soviet diplomacy is therefore sensitive to contrary force, more ready to yield on individual sectors of the diplomatic fronts when that force is felt to be strong, but on the other hand not easily discouraged by a single victory on the part of its opponents. Therefore "the main element of any United States policy toward the Soviet Union must be that of a long-term, patient but firm and vigilant containment of Russian expansive tendencies." Soviet pressure "can be contained by the adroit and vigilant application of counterforce at a series of constantly shifting geographical and political points, corresponding to the shifts and maneuvers of Soviet policy. . . ." Anticipating the criticism that containment might appear to be too negative a course of action, Kennan contended that the pursuit of such a policy does not merely limit us to "holding the line and hoping for the best"; the United States has the power to force a far greater degree of moderation and circumspection on the Kremlin and "promote tendencies which must eventually find their outlet in either the breakup or the gradual mellowing of Soviet power."

The containment doctrine was a rational reflection of the strategic possibilities open to United States foreign policy in the late forties. As the dominant world power and unscarred by war, the United States was then in a position to deploy its economic resources and atomic superiority to build a Western Alliance and to counteract any pressure exerted by the Soviet Union and Communist movements in Western Europe, Greece, Turkey, and Iran. In fact, though the world which Mr. Kennan analyzed in 1947 has changed drastically and he himself has offered new policy prescriptions, the cogency of his analysis on rereading is remarkable in the light of the post-Stalin changes within the Soviet Union and the moderation of its foreign policy.

Nevertheless, containment, advanced as a doctrine essentially limited to the European theatre, was transformed into a doctrine of pure and simple anti-Communism. Communism everywhere became the concern of the United States government. "Containment" was institutionalized into an "extended siege" of the Soviet Union enforced by a multiplicity of treaty arrangements. By ascribing unlimited ambitions to the USSR, the United States, barely out of its isolationism, undertook a policy without limits. Containment, as extended, has associated the United States with unpopular and weak governments and, above all, has deprived the United States of flexibility and initiative in conducting policy, particularly so since it has inhibited negotiated settlement of major problems. It has involved the United States in the internal affairs of other countries in direct or indirect attempts to "contain" domestic Communism. Moreover, its consequence at home has been the development of a pervasive, unthinking anti-Communism which now ironically serves to immobilize new departures.

One of the most damaging consequences of Kennan's method of analysis, intended or not, has been the tendency to draw a cause-effect relationship between Soviet ideology and foreign policy and to dismiss all seeming departures from this nexus as "tactical." This approach assumes a rigidity in Communist ideology that it does not have and dismisses the "tactical" as intrinsically unimportant and incapable of influencing the actual course of developments. In short, these theorists deal in ultimates and abstractions from which any course of action may be derived and which are therefore useless as guides to what the Soviet leaders can or wish to do in any given situation. If there is any doubt about the scholastic quality of this reasoning, one need only refer to the present conflict between the Soviet Union and Communist China. Both the Soviet and Chinese Communists claim to be privy to the Marxist-Leninist secret of salvation for the human race, but this has not prevented them from subscribing to almost diametrically opposite conceptions of what global Communist policy should be like today.

To be sure, ideological conceptions color all rulers' vision of the national interest. That the Soviet leaders see the future as the triumph of socialism over capitalism and will try to accelerate the process if it does not jeopardize their national security is understandable. But the assumption that the idea of irreconcilable capitalist-socialist antagonisms is a guide to the day-by-day, month-by-month operations of Soviet diplomacy is a misreading of history. Ideology notwithstanding, the Soviet leaders have bargained and maneuvered and made diplomatic commitments with all types of governments (with the Weimar Republic and with Nazi Germany, with Japan and against Japan) to protect the security of their own country. The integrity and defense of the Soviet Union were the paramount considerations, to which the interests of international Communism were sacrificed time and again. Foreign policy decisions were dictated by domestic requirements and the realities of the world situation. That they could be — and were — rationalized ideologically is irrelevant. To claim that these were "necessary" moves to protect and expand world Communism is a tautological argument, even if the power and influence of Communism were expanded. Within the terms of the particular decision, they were beside the point. While appreciation of the ultimate ideological objectives is not irrelevant to an understanding of Communism, to be useful it must be subordinated to the imperatives of national security and the inevitable limitations within which Soviet diplomacy has to work. American obsession with Communist ultimate objectives only beclouds the issues presently at stake and endows the Communists with an omniscience they do not have. The impossibility of a "permanent settlement" need not be an impasse between the United States and the USSR any more than it ever has been between other Great Powers. What is at stake is not a "permanent" settlement, but the elimination, palliation, or neutralization of specific and immediate issues, beginning with the old-fashioned ones of territory and prestige, to minimize the possibility of war now and in the foreseeable future.

Not only have cold-war theorists mistaken the nature of the relationship between ideology and foreign policy; they have also mistaken ideology as a fixed quantity, as if ideological conceptions were not subject to change. No doubt they can cite in support of their position Soviet texts on foreign policy which present classic expositions of class-angled foreign policy. Communist ideology is not, however, immutable and no one is more adamant than the Communist in denying the static nature of his creed. Marxism is, in the last analysis, a *method* of observing the environment — even Soviet Marxism, one might add. The interaction of ideas and the environment has been productive of new notions, and the last few years have witnessed startling innovations affecting the Soviet view of the capitalist world.

Of fundamental importance for Soviet-American relations has been the change in Soviet doctrine on war and peace and the nature of the conflict between "capitalist" and "socialist" states. To summarize the argument briefly: capitalism, according to Leninist theory, breeds war. Caught between the quest for profits and a declining market at home, the capitalist states must resort to war against each other to carve out an imperial domain and thus secure cheap sources of labor and raw materials and a market for their manufactured goods. Capitalism has no choice in the matter; it must take this step to maintain its own position and to stave off revolution. With the establishment of the Soviet state, Lenin's theory was extended to mean that the new socialist state would be the chief target of imperialist attack. The idea of the inevitability of war between socialism and capitalism derives from this circumstance and it has obsessed both Russians and Westerners ever since. Yet, while the weak Soviet state's fear of capitalist attack in the interwar years had some basis in fact, the fear that the USSR would attack Western Europe after 1945 and thus become involved in a war with the United States was born of fright, disillusionment, and inexperience. On the contrary, Stalin assiduously avoided, if not always successfully, involvement in war with the Great Powers.

In any case, the doctrine of the inevitability of war between capitalism and Communism has been discarded by Khrushchev. The Soviet leader has laid it down that, even though the essential nature of capitalism has not changed, the Communist system is now powerful enough to force the capitalist states to remain peaceful.

The operative part of Khrushchev's formula holds that war is avoidable; the characterization of capitalism as unchanged is *pro forma* lip service to an article of faith. For if "predatory" capitalism is unable to act out its essential purpose because of objective factors, in what essential sense can it be urged that capitalism has not changed? More pertinently still, the Soviet estimate of capitalism's capability has changed in that it is now regarded as too weak to wage a successful war against the Soviet Union. Since the Soviet Communists by definition — and by their behavior — do not want war and any warlike ambitions on the part of the capitalists can be contained by Soviet might, war is therefore avoidable.

It may of course be argued that Khrushchev's rejection of the doctrine of the inevitability of war is simply tactical or propagandistic, a deception merely reflecting the newly-acquired strength of the USSR. But for those who hold that ideology determines Soviet policy, to refuse to recognize changes in ideology when they occur is simply an untenable position. In Communist terms, where ideology is supposed to reflect reality, the changed balance of power has been reflected in the reformulation of the doctrine on war and, willy-nilly, on the nature of capitalism. Even if the ultimate irreconcilability of capitalism and socialism, as still postulated in Communist doctrine, were a controlling factor in the conduct of Soviet foreign policy — and this has not been true historically — the resort to war for reasons of doctrine of historical necessity is ruled out. What remains is that the Soviet leaders believe in — or say that they believe in — the replacement of capitalism by Communism as the prevailing world social system. Here the argument is placed in its true ideological context, far transcending the role of foreign policy. On this level what is at stake is the kind of social system that will evolve in the future as a result of the competition between American capitalism and Soviet socialism — and the requirements of other states; but this is another matter which has no necessary relation to the problem of war.

The containment doctrine, analytically suspect because it was derived from the metaphysics of Historical Materialism, was nevertheless strategically sound because it reflected the possibilities of United States foreign policy in the situation prevailing in 1945 – 50. It was also a comfortable policy because it permitted the United States to externalize some favorite characteristics: optimism that solutions can be found for all problems, particularly if American modes and institutions are engaged; and reliance on the economic weapon as a major instrument of its foreign policy. In consequence, it enabled the United States for a time to enjoy the role of a Don Quixote to the "Free World."

Events of recent years, however, have destroyed the myth of American omnicompetence and have shown containment and its version of pure and simple anti-Communism to be a sterile policy. *Sputnik* symbolized the end of American scientific primacy, as Soviet atomic and hydrogen bombs ended American assumptions of military supremacy. Even if the United States remains relatively superior to the USSR in aggregate military power, it nevertheless faces, for the first time in its history, the possibility of immediate devastation of its territory and population in the event of general war. Arranging the world to its liking could easily become too costly.

If the nuclear equilibrium has placed crippling restraints on the pursuit of policy by force or threat of force, the nature of the Communist-capitalist confrontation has changed, as the State Department has long since recognized in its policy toward Yugoslavia and Poland. The ideological war against Communism is too simplistic a rationale for American foreign policy. Within the Communist states, institutions, ideas, and hopes are changing. Yugoslavia is an obvious case in point. The Sino-Soviet conflict reflects more basically serious differences over domestic institutions and values as well as over approaches to foreign policy. Khrushchev's Russia emerges as a conservative state fending off the pressures for a policy of uncompromising hostility to the West, uncompromising support of Communist against capitalist, and uncompromising support of so-called national liberation movements. What primarily motivates the Soviet Union are the material and technical demands of its own society, which in international terms requires peace not revolution, accommodation not adventurism.

If the above analysis is anywhere near accurate, it follows that the policy of containment of Russia should be replaced by a policy of cooperation with Russia in order to limit, as a minimum, the possibility of war. Such a shift in policy would require the correction of pathological thinking on the USSR and an effort to de-indoctrinate the American public or at least to make it more aware of the practical requirements of policy and less subject to the manipulation of ideological anti-Communism.

The destructive potential of nuclear weapons prods the United States and the USSR into closer relations and cautions them in the pursuit of policies that might lead to war. Yet the threat of mass destruction may deter but does not eliminate the suicidal tendencies in national policies, witness the Kennedy-Khrushchev confrontation in Cuba. To avoid war or the threat of war, the underlying irritants to Soviet and American national security must be removed or reduced. This implies both a clear understanding of what constitutes the national security and the willingness to negotiate settlements. It is not unfair to point out that neither official Washington nor, consequently, the American public has a clear idea of what is involved in the defense of our national security. Is South Vietnam vital to the security of the United States? Is.it more vital to the security of the United States than Cuba? If Cuba is vital to the security not only of the United States but of the Western Hemisphere also, a fraction of the effort expended in South Vietnam by the Kennedy Administration could have eliminated Castro. Power begins at home. If, on the other hand, the United States can tolerate a Communist regime off its coast, why can't it tolerate a neutral or Communist regime in Vietnam?

However explosive the situation may be in Vietnam or the Congo or Zanzibar, Europe remains the most crucial area in Soviet-American relations. Is it in the American national interest to refuse to settle formally the problems remaining from World War II? Does the profit in maintaining tension in Europe overbalance the advantage of removing obvious sources of conflict? No doubt it seems odd to suggest that American policy in Europe is based on the deliberate maintenance of tension against the Soviet Union.

If there is any area in which the Soviet Union may feel insecure, it is in Europe. Soviet preoccupation with formalizing the status quo in Europe instead of merely relying on a tacit acceptance of the situation there underscores its concern, whether based in fact or not. What is at stake here is the recognition of the Central and Eastern European states as part of the Soviet sphere of influence, the existence of two Germanies, the Oder-Neisse as a permanent boundary line, and the Baltic states as an integral part of the USSR. Crucially involved also is some new — more or less satisfactory — arrangement for West Berlin which the Russians might be willing to trade against concessions in other spheres. West Berlin is admittedly the toughest problem.

In coldest analytical terms the maintenance of the status quo in West Berlin provides the United States with a lever to exact the required performance from West Germany in the Western Alliance; at the same time the present arrangement places the United States in the intolerable position of a hostage to that enclave. The easement of the situation by some modest agreement with the USSR which guarantees the integrity of West Berlin and its access would at least serve as a fresh attempt to make the best of an "insolvable" problem.

But why should it be necessary at all to make concessions on West Berlin since the Russians know that force will be met by force? The answer is precisely to avoid that contingency by reducing tension and the source of conflict. Moreover, in the event of mounting Soviet-American tension over Berlin and Germany, the Russians — not the United States — hold the trump card, *i.e.*, the possibility of permitting German unification. It is a fantastic possibility, but one that cannot be excluded from diplomatic calculation. The probabilities are easier to deal with: a formal settlement of the issues in Europe would make the Soviet Union more tractable in its relations with the United States on high policy, disarmament, and the peripheral problems in the underdeveloped areas. But first the United States must know what it wants and be willing to compromise on certain issues to achieve its main objectives.

Containment as an adequate expression of United States policy is outdated; it no longer reflects accurately the international political environment of the sixties. A more appropriate slogan would be *"modus non moriendi"* or, to quote a more recent Kennan: ". . . our foremost aim today should be to keep it [the world] physically intact in an age when men have acquired, for the first time, the technical means of destroying it."

TWENTY

HERBERT J. SPIRO AND
BENJAMIN R. BARBER

Counter-Ideological Uses

of "Totalitarianism"*

Totalitarianism is a youthful concept. The first edition of the *Encyclopedia of the Social Sciences,* a comprehensive inventory of the conceptual vocabulary of 1933, does not list the word. The *Oxford English Dictionary* takes its first citation of the term only from an April 1928 number of the *Contemporary Review.* In the *Times* of November 1929, the word referred simply to "the unitary state, whether fascist or communist."

Since that time, *totalitarianism* has become popular in both ordinary and academic parlance. Each of the social sciences has contributed significantly to the vast body of literature which has grown up around the concept, especially since World War II. In keeping with this growth, the second edition of the *ESS* does contain an article on "Totalitarianism."[1] Although that article is critical of the concept, a large number of scholars are enthusiastic about the construct, and would probably concur in Klaus Epstein's judgment that Friedrich and Brzezinski's *Totalitarian Dictatorship and Autocracy* (Cambridge, 1956) represents a "promising beginning" for the building of a "science of the comparative study of totalitarianism."[2]

*Herbert J. Spiro and Benjamin R. Barber, "Counter-Ideological Uses of Totalitarianism'," *Politics and Society,* I, 1 (November 1970). Copyright 1970, Geron-X, Inc., Publishers. Reprinted by permission of the authors and publisher.

    1. By Herbert J. Spiro; see *International Encyclopedia of the Social Sciences,* 1968.
    2. Klaus Epstein, "Shirer's History of Nazi Germany," *The Review of Politics,* XXIII, No.

Others have questioned the utility of the concept as an analytic category, and some have even challenged its intelligibility. "I still do not know," writes R. Robinson in a review of Karl Popper's *The Open Society and Its Enemies,* "what he (Popper) or anyone else means by Totalitarianism."[3] There is, in fact, considerable disagreement even among those who employ the term. John Kautsky, who has tried to put it to good use in his study of nationalism and communism in developing nations, has complained that "the term 'totalitarianism' has been applied so loosely as to become virtually meaningless in communicating any specific meaning."[4] Although Karl Popper and a number of American scholars have contrasted totalitarianism with democracy and lawful rulership, for J. D. Mabbott (an Englishman) "the opposite of Totalitarianism is neither democracy nor beneficent law, but laissez-faire."[5] Barrington Moore has recently taken still another approach to the concept,[6] but in general there is agreement neither about the mode of usage nor the objective utility of "totalitarianism."

For these and other reasons, the authors of this paper have, in separate studies, raised serious questions about the term's value as a tool for systematic comparative analysis and as a starting point for "laws of development."[7] But these charges are not the subject of this essay. Even if acceptable parameters for use of the term could be set, and its analytic utility demonstrated, the meteoric rise in the popularity of "totalitarianism," especially among American scholars and policy-makers, would remain a phenomenon worthy of study. Even the late Martin Luther King was moved to speak of "communism's political totalitarianism."[8] It is then to a different order of questions that this

---

2 (April, 1961) p. 241.

3. R. Robinson, "Dr. Popper's Defense of Plato," *Philosophical Review,* October, 1951.

4. John H. Kautsky, *Political Change in Underdeveloped Countries: Nationalism and Communism* (New York: John Wiley & Sons, 1966), p. 190.

5. J. D. Mabbott, *The State and the Citizen* (London: Arrow Books, 1958), p. 61.

6. Cf. Barrington Moore, Jr., "Totalitarian Elements in Pre-Industrial Societies," *Political Power and Social Theory: Six Studies* (Cambridge, Mass.: Harvard University Press, 1958), and *Social Origins of Dictatorship and Democracy: Lord and Peasant in the Making of the Modern World* (Boston: Beacon Press, 1966).

7. See Spiro, Note 1 above; and Benjamin R. Barber, "Conceptual Foundations of Totalitarianism," in C. J. Friedrich, M. Curtis, and B. R. Barber, *Totalitarianism in Perspective: Three Views* (New York: Praeger, 1969), a work which also includes a provocative critique of the concept as applied to the Soviet Union by Michael Curtis, and an interesting and thoughtful reevaluation by Carl J. Friedrich.

8. Martin Luther King, Jr., *Stride towards Freedom* (New York: Harper Torchbook, 1964), p. 72. The term has been most widely used by social scientists engaged in Soviet area research; it has been a primary analytic construct in studies of communism and the Soviet Union by Adam B. Ulam, Bertram D. Wolfe, Barrington Moore, Jr., Frederick Schuman, Merle Fainsod, Alex Inkeles, Z. K. Brzezinski, W. W. Rostow, Hans Kelsen, and Peter Wiles, *inter alia.* But it has also been employed to describe Germany — for example, Hans Buchheim, *Totalitarian Rule: Its Nature and Characteristics* (Middletown, Conn.: Wesleyan University Press, 1968), or Sigmund Neumann, *Permanent Revolution: Totalitarianism in the Age of International Civil War,* 2nd ed. (New York: Praeger, 1965); to describe Italy — for example, Dante Germino, *The Italian Fascist Party in Power: A Study in Totalitarian Rule* (Minneapolis: University of Minnesota Press, 1959);

essay addresses itself: What have been the justificatory uses of the concept of totalitarianism since World War II? Why has the term become so very popular both among policy-makers and policy-scientists? How has the theory been employed in explaining the contemporary political world? These questions are intended not to raise the very thorny problem of the relationship between politicians and political scientists — a critical related question beyond the scope of the essay. Nor do they encompass the problem of what determines a foreign policy; the theory of totalitarianism *may* have acted as an input, but it may have been no more than a convenient rationalization for policies which would have been pursued in any case. The answers to the questions raised here then can only be used to help in understanding the ways in which the theory of totalitarianism has been used to explain the postwar world. The motives of those proffering the explanations, their relationship to policy-makers, and the real impact on actual policy decisions of their theories, can at best only be inferred from the arguments which follow.

I

Americans have generally regarded themselves as pragmatists in the conduct of their politics, both domestic and foreign; although this self-image is subjective and one-dimensional, it does reflect one aspect of reality in that up until World War II the international political environment had appeared to Americans to be both rational and accessible to pragmatic manipulation. Thus, both isolationists and interventionists assumed the explicability of European international relations in the thirties; they differed only on the question of how best to manipulate a rational situation in the American interest — by intervention or by abstention. Most Americans subsequently assumed, following — indeed, partly because of — World War II, that international relations in the postwar world would continue to be explicable and would become, quite probably, still more susceptible to manipulation than ever before. After all, the war had resulted in the defeat of the most powerful hostile coalition the United States had ever faced; moreover, the second installment of that defeat, victory over Japan, had been achieved in part through the use of a new and infinitely destructive order of weapons, exclusive control over which the United States expected to retain for the foreseeable future.

America had forged together an alliance which, with the help of unprecedented military power, had overcome an *entente* thought to embody evil in

to describe political parties — for example, B. E. Lippincott, *Democracy's Dilemma: The Totalitarian Party in a Free Society* (New York: Ronald Press, 1965); and of course to describe a broad spectrum of ideas — for example, Hannah Arendt, *The Origins of Totalitarianism* (Cleveland: Meridian ed., 1958); J. L. Talmon, *The Origins of Totalitarian Democracy* (New York: Praeger, 1961); Karl Popper, *The Open Society and its Enemies,* 4th ed. (Princeton: Princeton University Press, 1963); R. D. MacMaster, *Danilevsky: A Russian Totalitarian Philosopher* (Cambridge, Mass.: Harvard University Press, 1967); and A. James Gregor, *Contemporary Radical Ideologies: Totalitarian Thought in the Twentieth Century* (New York: Random House, 1968).

its most radical form. It had won the greatest war in its history. It had, moreover, in concert with its wartime allies, established the United Nations — an institution designed both to rest upon and to enhance rationality in international relations, and thus to subject international events still more to calculated (and, it was hoped, nonviolent) manipulation. As part of this process the United States and its allies among the Charter members of the United Nations dedicated themselves to granting early independence to their colonial possessions. There seemed good reason to look forward to a rational and peaceful international future.

But actual events disappointed these sanguine expectations. The international "order" became less rather than more orderly; the behavior of other nations appeared to come ever more under the influence of irrational principles inaccessible to American understanding and impervious to American manipulation. The ground on which America's wartime alliance with the Soviet Union rested — always muddy and uncertain — was transformed by a storm of miscalculations, misunderstandings, and conflicts of interest into a quagmire of enmity: the Cold War. Stalin's behavior, relatively predictable in the uncomplicated setting of a common war against fascism, appeared to be erratic and at times brutal in this unfamiliar and unprecedented new setting. The loss of China by the Kuomintang to the Communists who were thought to be totally dependent on the Soviet Union, and the Korean War which pitted the United States against this dangerous new coalition in a hot war that ended in stalemate rather than victory, added to America's growing sense of apprehension and frustration.

Less inimical but equally inexplicable was the political alchemy by which, with the Cold War as a catalyst, America's enemies in World War II Germany and Japan — were metamorphosized into its most reliable supporters. Even America's nuclear monopoly proved to be a frustrating and self-defeating asset: in the new illogic of the Cold War, atomic and thermonuclear weapons were simply *too* powerful to be used as instruments of pragmatic manipulation. To respond to a limited Russian political probe with threats of Armageddon lacked credibility; and when the Russians developed their own nuclear force, far sooner than had been expected, such threats ceased to be conceivable. Indeed, mutual deterrence not only established a "delicate balance of terror" which tended to paralyze foreign policy in general, but raised the unpleasant specter — given the alleged unpredictability and irrationality of Communist behavior — of a possible "first-strike" strategy for the Soviet Union.

The United Nations, the last best hope of the rationalists, proved to be inadequate and ineffective in dealing with the issues raised by the Cold War; indeed, at times it appeared to be more the theater for, than the arbiter of, big-power conflict. As long as the West controlled a majority of votes in the General Assembly, the Communists either ignored it or fought it as a "tool of imperialism" — in one instance, by resort to war. In time they grew less obstreperous, but in part because the United States had lost its automatic majority in the Assembly; Americans noted with bitter irony that control of the Assembly had passed from their hands precisely because of the admission of scores of new members whose independence the United States had helped to achieve. The Secretariat was still less manageable: the second and third Secretaries-General took positions increasingly at odds with those of the United States. If the new nations put aside the gratitude of their infancy in favor of an opportunism that America regarded as adolescent if not wicked, not even the mature and reliable nations of Europe could be trusted to remember that the United States had provided first military salvation and then economic resuscitation in the great hour of need; instead there was talk of a "Third Force," economic independence, and military self-sufficiency outside of NATO, at least in some quarters.

It was in this environment of increasing frustration, diminishing comprehension, and waning political effectiveness that theories of totalitarianism became increasingly useful — as a major instrument of explanation for political scientists, and as a convincing justification for the changing policies of statesmen whose expectations of rationality and manipulability in international relations had been betrayed by the perverse and unaccommodating realities of the Cold War world.

II

Until World War II America's foreign policy had succeeded without really trying; after the war no amount of trying seemed to bring success. With traditional explanations being contravened by events, many statesmen felt the need for a new set of explanations which would help to reinvest world politics with comprehensibility while at the same time they provided a basis and justification for an effective American role in the world arena. The theory of totalitarianism seemed adaptive to these purposes. It explained and it rationalized American policy in terms which both preserved America's pragmatic self-image *and* carried a moral conviction which pragmatism by itself lacked. For the concept totalitarianism suggested an American policy founded on counter-ideology understood in two vital but distinctive senses: counter-ideology as anti-ideology (or non-ideology), and counter-ideology as anti-totalitarianism, the former implying rejection of all ideology (whatever its content), and the latter suggesting only substantive rejection of totalitarianism — which is itself a species of ideology, that is to say, the ideology of anti-totalitarianism.

Counter-ideology as non-ideology represented the best tradition of American pragmatism: for as exponents of the politics of the "vital center" Americans saw in the anti-ideological stance a reflection of their antipathy to extremes of the right or the left, and their admiration for the politics of compromise and consensus.[9]

On the other hand, anti-totalitarian implications of theories about totalitarianism could be used both as a persuasive moral justification for what otherwise might be considered precipitous or unwarranted intervention in international affairs, and as an explanation for the otherwise inexplicable moral acrobatics of America's one-time friends and some-time enemies. In this manner, theories of totalitarianism helped the United States to re-rationalize a complex and unpredictable world in simplistic terms of Good and Evil, while at the same time they could be used to condone — indeed, encourage — intervention in the name of the preservation of "freedom"; the preservation, that is, of the principle of having no absolute principles.[10] Interest and principle, the two great poles of political theory to which successive generations of American students of foreign policy have alternately tried to tie American foreign relations, were thus seemingly reconciled.

The uses to which new theories of totalitarianism could be put, whether intended by scholars or not, were as numerous as the problems which American foreign policy had to confront; but there were four dominant uses which corresponded to the four predominant problems facing postwar America. First, theories of totalitarianism helped to explain away Japanese and German behavior under the wartime regimes and thereby to justify the radical reversal of alliances which followed the war. Second, they provided (or purported to provide) an explanation of all communist behavior in the unerring terms of what became called the "logic of totalitarianism." This analysis helped in turn — and this was the third major use of theories of totalitarianism — to explain trends in the developing countries and thus to justify the progressive alienation between the United States and the Third World. Fourth, theories of totalitarianism served both to demonstrate the inadequacies of international law and organization, and to justify the consequent necessity of considering the use of force — even thermonuclear force — in the settlement of world issues.

In explaining each of these four sets of phenomena, theories of totalitarianism also were explaining the United States itself. In explaining postwar German behavior, America justified its own somewhat fuzzy theory of alliances, and at the same time — using the ample cosmetics of moralism — glamorized its role in World War II. In discrediting communist motives and behavior in general, and specifically condemning intervention in international affairs, America was crediting itself with higher moral purpose and legitimizing its own intervention. As E. H. Carr has written, "the converse of [the] propaga-

---

9. Until the recent spate of writings by "revisionists," American historiography has been dominated by the notion of consensus; see, for example, the works of Louis Hartz, Arthur Schlesinger, Jr., or Daniel Boorstin.

10. A principle which constitutes one aspect of the "genius of American politics," according to Daniel Boorstin.

tion of theories designed to throw moral discredit on an enemy is the propagation of theories reflecting moral credit on oneself and one's own policies."[11] In
explaining the failure of international institutions it had helped to create,
America legitimized its own apostasy to the nonviolent principles upon which
they depended (although in doing so it contributed to that failure).

In brief, theories of totalitarianism brought order to the confused international affairs of the postwar world by rigidly defining the nature of the issues
at stake and identifying friends, enemies, and even American political character in terms of those issues. In this fashion, theory and practice, principle and
interest, were forged into one. The precise manner in which this transpired
becomes clearer as the four convergent services performed by the concept of
totalitarianism are spelled out.

1. RATIONALIZATION OF EX-ENEMY BEHAVIOR

The needs of the Cold War — especially following the blockade of Berlin and
the Korean War — led to a reversal of the military occupation policy of the
United States in Germany and Japan. In Germany, of the "Four D's" —
demilitarization, decartellization, de-Nazification, and democratization —
only the latter two were retained; and de-Nazification, once it had been turned
over to the West Germans, was pursued with declining vigor. Ten years after
the Allied victory over Germany and Japan, West Germany had been encouraged, against considerable initial domestic resistance, to rearm; and Japan
had been permitted to establish a "Self-Defense Force." America's arch-ene-
mies had become trusted friends and potential allies of considerable significance. Given the bitter enmity of the war, how was this to be explained? Could
history be so easily forgotten?

Theories of totalitarianism made possible not a forgetting but a reinterpretation of history; for the concept of totalitarianism offered a novel and generous
analysis of individual (and even national) responsibility and guilt which tended
to exonerate both individuals and whole nations from culpability for "war
crimes" whose lingering memories might otherwise have tainted postwar relations. The inherent laws of totalitarianism developed by political scientists not
only explained but implicitly justified the lack of resistance within totalitarian
regimes. In the "atmosphere of fear" generated by the Nazi state (or, by
analogy, the Japanese militarist government) "opponents of the regime become
isolated and feel themselves cast out of society. This sense of loneliness, which
is the fate of all, but more especially of an opponent of a totalitarian regime,
tends to paralyze resistance and make it much less appealing."[12] Can one
reasonably expect "captive populations," living in conditions where "terror

11. E. H. Carr, *The Twenty Years' Crisis* (New York: Harper Torchbook, 1964), p. 72.
12. Carl J. Friedrich and Zbigniew K. Brzezinski, *Totalitarian Dictatorship and Autocracy*
(Cambridge, Mass.: Harvard University Press, 1956), p. 137.

embraces the entire society, searching everywhere for actual or potential deviants from the totalitarian unity" and where "total fear reigns," to oppose the totalitarian monolith that has enslaved them?[13]

By this logic, then, a totalitarian regime could be overthrown only from the outside. Resistance being at best useless (and thus tragic in the classical sense) and at worst completely impossible, Americans and other non-Germans had no right to condemn the common man for his failure to oppose Hitler (or Japanese imperialism); indeed, even active support was something less than a crime against humanity, since, as Friedrich and Brzezinski point out, "totalitarian regimes insist that enthusiastic unanimity (and not merely passive acquiescence) characterize the behavior of the captive populations."[14] If it was the regime and not the people, the system and not the nation, that was responsible for the "radical evil" perpetrated by the war governments in Berlin and Tokyo, then with the disappearance of the regime and the defeat of the system there was no reason why the Japanese people and the German nation (or its free Western branch) could not be viewed as innocent and trustworthy friends. Carried to their logical conclusion, theories of totalitarianism could serve to exculpate the Germans entirely from responsibility for the policies and actions of the Nazi government, as this excerpt from the late Klaus Epstein's critique of William Shirer's *The Rise and Fall of the Third Reich* suggests:

> His [Shirer's] exclusive preoccupation with Nazi Germany prevents him from attempting any *comparative* analysis of modern totalitarian regimes. His favorite theory that Naziism is the natural culmination of a peculiar German historical tradition precludes him from drawing insights from other "totalitarian societies" such as Soviet Russia. Shirer never seeks to penetrate the "universal significance" of Naziism — what it can teach us about the terrifying recesses of human nature and the precarious structure of modern civilization — in short, what Max Picard called the "Hitler in ourselves," a phenomenon unhappily not limited to Germany.[15]

With a deft intellectual ambidexterity Epstein suggests on the one hand that Naziism is discontinuous with past and future German history, and in this

---

13. *Ibid.,* pp. 132, 137. A similar passage from another theorist of totalitarianism reads: "Total terror, the essence of totalitarian government, exists neither for nor against men. It is supposed to provide the forces of nature or history with an incomparable instrument to accelerate their movement. This movement, proceeding according to its own law, cannot in the long run be hindered." Hannah Arendt, *op. cit.,* p. 466.

14. Friedrich and Brzezinski, *op. cit.,* p. 132.

15. Epstein, *op. cit.* The late Professor Epstein would perhaps be even more disturbed by Heinz Höhne's study of the S. S., entitled *The Order of the Death's Head* (New York: Coward-Mc Cann, 1970), which treats the supposedly proto-totalitarian heart of Hitler's total state as a diversified, self-interested bureaucracy that was fragmented from within by mundane administrative cleavages wholly unrelated to the "terrifying recesses of human nature." Indeed, just as the past decade has been one in which Soviet area specialists like Frederic Fleron, Robert Tucker, and A. G. Meyer have begun to seek modes of explanation which do not require the uncritical acceptance of totalitarian theory, the coming years may see an increase of German historical scholarship eschewing theories of totalitarianism once thought to be indispensable.

sense episodic and epiphenomenal, while on the other hand it represents psychological forces which — far from being peculiar to Germans — are universal archetypes crouching in the soul of Everyman. No one man or nation is to blame, for Hitler is, in this logic, a psychic facet of the universal man which humanity must confront collectively.

Comparative "totalitarianology" thus begs the crucial comparative question of why, even if we accept man's ubiquitous potential for radical evil, this potential has been realized politically exclusively in certain periods and places in history but not in others (where one assumes the capacity for evil was just as pervasive).

As they refurbish the national image of America's wartime enemies, theories of totalitarianism also enhance America's own image by adding a certain moral luster to American objectives in World War II. The United States, if one pursues the logic of these arguments, by engaging the Germans and the Japanese in combat, did for them what they, by the nature of things, could not do for themselves. If totalitarianism cannot be successfully deposed from within, it must be vanquished from without. The United States can hence be said not only to have overcome enemies of its own national interest, but also to have rescued peoples hopelessly enslaved by totalitarianism. America went to war not only for itself but also to serve the higher purposes of humanity. If reverberations of Wilsonian idealism can be detected here — "we went down to Mexico to serve mankind," Wilson proclaimed following the bombardment of Vera Cruz in 1914 — they are but faint and distant echoes; for though all wars engender a patriotic idealism which generally identifies itself with abstract universal goals, theories of totalitarianism provided a concrete description of real political evils whose defeat would truly serve mankind (and not simply a nation in the guise of mankind).

But however intimate the relations between the United States and the reconstructed postwar democracies of West Germany and Japan, and however much the individual and national guiltlessness posited by theories of totalitarianism exonerated the two nations from responsibility for the built-in and continuing atrocities of their respective regimes, and thus legitimized their new place in the American sun, other factors were ultimately decisive in the reversal of alliances which followed the war. On the whole, it is a nation's enemies which determine its friends, and not the other way around. Theories of totalitarianism functioned only secondarily as justifications for the choice of America's friends; their primary and crucial function was the identification of enemies.

2. EXPLANATION OF COMMUNIST BEHAVIOR

Some Americans were misled by the experience of the wartime alliance with the Soviet Union into expecting permanent postwar international collaboration with it, and these expectations may have actually hastened their own disappointment. The concept of totalitarianism became especially useful in these circumstances because it could be used both to explain in a relatively systematic, comprehensive, and logical way the otherwise erratic and inexplicable behavior of the Soviet Union under Stalin in the eight years preceding his death, and to rationalize America's postwar enmity towards its wartime ally — to rationalize, that is, the Soviet-American aspect of the postwar reversal of alliances.

The explanation was founded upon an initial analogy between Hitler's rule in Germany and Stalin's in the Soviet Union. Though different writers took varying positions on the extent to which the analogy could be carried, most seemed persuaded that similarities outweighed differences — as use of the generic term "totalitarian dictatorship" for both regimes indicates. The structural and behavioral similitude of regimes of the Right and Left postulated by theories of totalitarianism derived from an ineluctable "logic of totalitarianism" whose "laws" governed all totalitarian movements however dissimilar their ideologies. Thus, in a popular text, Adam B. Ulam wrote (as recently as 1962): "The logic of totalitarianism as well as that of socialism make the U.S.S.R. a bureaucratic state."[16] In the same vein Ulam argues that the "hard political facts that are, in reality, the essence of the Soviet political system," are not "transient aberrations arising out of the willful and illegal acts of individuals," but are, rather, "imposed by the logic of totalitarianism."[17] For the logic of totalitarianism implies immutable laws such as the one that "in a totalitarian state terror can never be abolished entirely."[18]

Similar passages recur throughout this work, all of them suggesting that totalitarianism serves as Ulam's chief explanatory category. Events occur or fail to occur according to the discoverable laws of totalitarianism; history, and, more precisely, the role of the Soviet Union and its allies in it, becomes predictable and thus, in the pragmatic American understanding of predictability, manageable.

If theories of totalitarianism help to explain and rationalize communist behavior, they also provide the user with a pair of monoscopic glasses which bring the multi-dimensional political reality of the world to the viewer with monolithic one-dimensional simplicity. *The New Republic,* a journal reputed for its liberalism, stated several years ago in commenting on the Middle Eastern War of June 1967, that all that had happened there "was in the cards, because the laws governing totalitarian movements — whether communist, fascist or Arab socialist — require an offensive along the entire front, once there is a breakthrough in one sector."[19] If communist, fascist, and Arab

16. Adam B. Ulam, "The Russian Political System," in Samuel H. Beer and Adam B. Ulam (eds.), *Patterns of Government: The Major Political Systems of Europe* (New York: Random House, 2d rev. ed., 1962), p. 670.
17. *Ibid.,* p. 656.
18. *Ibid.,* p. 646.
19. *The New Republic,* CLVI, No. 24 (June 17, 1967), p. 1.

socialist [!] totalitarianism are governed by the same laws, then surely countries within the communist bloc can be considered as a single totalitarian monolith — not in the sense that they are cooperative (or even friendly) in their mutual relations, but in that they are but several competing manifestations of the same nefarious threat.

Although it appears that the monolithic view has finally been discarded, to approach communist totalitarianism in this fashion was typical of both official policy and public opinion in the United States up to and into the most recent times. The identification of the National Liberation Front, the government of North Vietnam, and the government of China (and for some earlier observers, even the Soviet Union), as a single monolithic power representing an international communist totalitarian conspiracy, which — despite the more subtle and complicated reality presented by empirical evidence — lies at the roots of America's original involvement in East Asia, is only one expression of the role totalitarianism has played in rationalizing, simplifying, and explaining "communist imperialism" and at the same time making possible an active American military intervention to prevent its spread.[20] Theories of totalitarianism manage then to justify American intervention in the name of counter-ideology (in the guise, here, of "freedom"), while simultaneously condemning all communist undertakings as, by definition, illegitimate.

With the old enemies of the United States exonerated and its new ones indicted, it became a mere exercise in inference to catalog the other nations of the world.

3. JUSTIFICATION OF POLICY TOWARD THE DEVELOPING COUNTRIES

Of the Charter members of the United Nations, America had probably the most flexible and liberal attitude during the war toward the question of the postwar destiny of colonial territories. Even before the war, America had declared its intentions to grant independence to its own colonies, and these commitments were honored in at least one major instance in the Philippines. Japan and Italy, the Netherlands and Great Britain, and eventually France and Belgium were moved — in some cases, compelled by circumstances — to "liberate" their colonies in Asia, the Middle East, Africa, and the Caribbean in the years following the war. However, the new states did not — indeed, could not possi-

---

20. As long ago as 1950, Dean Acheson, in announcing American support of France in Vietnam, invoked the specter of "Soviet Imperialism." The so-called "domino theory" is a more recent manifestation of the same basic reading of the situation. In 1967, President Johnson defended the American presence in Vietnam by affirming that the United States' commitment in Asia was made "because we do believe that no man, whatever the pigmentation of their [sic] skins, should ever be delivered over to totalitarianism" (*New York Times,* October 26, 1967). Some critics have argued that the days of such justification have passed, but President Nixon declared on April 30, 1970, that the American invasion of Cambodia had been undertaken as a demonstration of America's "will and character" to "the forces of totalitarianism and anarchy [which] threaten free nations and free institutions throughout the world" (*New York Times,* May 1, 1970).

bly — live up to expectations in the United States of rapid, American-style internal economic and political development, and friendly external involvement in the "family of nations" within and outside of the United Nations.

Internally, many of the new states turned toward various forms of socialism, public planning, and state control in areas which most Americans believed were best left to private enterprise. A number of new states achieved independence under the leadership of powerful — in some cases even charismatic — men who so dominated the politics of their countries that they became *de facto* dictators (whatever form their rule took in name or in law). Even where internal development was patterned after the "democratic" forms prescribed by America and the West, countries often took positions in world politics hostile to what was conceived to be the American national interest and incompatible with the American version of the ideal international order. Nehru, for example, despite his success in maintaining constitutional government in India, was *persona non grata* in the United States for part of his career as Prime Minister because of his policy of non-alignment in the Cold War and his efforts to build a Third World bloc from the nations which had participated in the Bandung Conference of 1955.

Theories of totalitarianism provided attractive explanations for these untoward and disappointing developments in the new states. In the struggle against monolithic communist totalitarianism by the United States, at the head of the "Free World," there clearly could be no middle ground. Those not with America had, in the inexorable logic of totalitarianism as articulated by John Foster Dulles (as well as by his more retiring but no less adamant successors), to be against it. Neutralism, Third Worldism, and other forms of indifference to the global struggle between Good and Evil were unconvincing disguises for a policy which in fact gave aid and comfort to the enemy. The evolution of one-party states under one-man dictatorships, espousing philosophies of socialism and anti-capitalist anti-colonialism, and professing cynicism toward America's moral struggles, was but a phase of the subversive international campaign of communist totalitarianism to establish a global system. A firm foundation for American alienation from the less cooperative of the developing countries, and for increasing American intervention in what might otherwise be considered the domestic affairs of apparently (but not truly!) independent countries was discovered then in the concept of totalitarianism. In an odd parallel to Marxism, where the great class struggle was thought to supersede national borders, theorists of totalitarianism asserted that totalitarian regimes knew no frontiers and that the struggle against them had to display a similar disregard for the illusory claims of legalists about formal national independence.[21]

21. Friedrich and Brzezinski thus point to "the inability of democratic states to adjust themselves to the fact that the totalitarians completely reject the traditional patterns of diplomatic

With the concept of totalitarianism came a touchstone for making ticklish decisions about foreign aid and alliances. Those nations which leaned toward the Free World and tended to be at least publicly hostile to international communism were worthy of friendship, military aid, and economic assistance — whatever the character of their domestic regimes. (Even a one-party system could be overlooked, if that party was firmly committed to the destruction of world communism; indeed, a single party often achieved a monopoly over government through the liquidation of all opposition in the name of exterminating the local "agents" of communism.) Those countries that opposed the Free World, and even those refusing to take sides, however democratic in form, were not simply refused aid, but often subverted in turn by the mostly covert undertakings of official and less official branches of the United States government.

In justification of support for friendly but autocratic regimes, the theory of totalitarianism postulated a fundamental distinction between traditional dictatorship and totalitarian dictatorship. A traditional, corrupt, "merely" authoritarian dictatorship, based upon an alliance between landowners and religious and military hierarchies, which did not display such features of the "totalitarian syndrome" as commitment to a chiliastic ideology or a "technologically conditioned near-complete monopoly of control . . . of all means of mass communication,"[22] could be welcomed into the camp of the Free World. On the other hand, a "mobilization regime," bent on rapid industrialization and committed to some regional variant of communism (e.g., Arab or African socialism), under the leadership of a hierarchically structured, ideological mass party, represented — whatever its pretensions in the United Nations and other world councils — a tentacle of the totalitarian octopus. As such, it disqualified itself as a legitimate state in the international system and became fair game for America's strategy of "defensive" intervention — whether overt, as in Cuba, the Dominican Republic, and the Far East, or covert, as in Guatemala (1954), Indonesia, and (the precise number can by definition only be surmised) many other uncooperative states. While there may have been some problems in fact, theories of totalitarianism precluded (in theory) the possibility of such contradictions arising as the appearance of a regime that simultaneously exhibited home-grown totalitarian features and professed a firm commitment to anti-communism in the international arena. A regime opposed to international communism could not, by definition, be totalitarian.[23]

---

behavior in the international arena" (*op. cit.,* p. 58).

  22. Carl J. Friedrich, ed., *Totalitarianism* (Cambridge, Mass.: Harvard University Press, 1954), p. 53.

  23. It is difficult to tell whether such usage does more damage to empirical reality or to language; the point here, however, is to explicate the uses of "totalitarianism" and not to criticize its analytic utility.

The concept of totalitarianism — like some latter-day Noah — provided for everything in pairs: there was an acceptable kind of dictatorship and an unacceptable totalitarian mate, a necessary ideology (counter-totalitarianism) and a perverse one (totalitarianism itself), a kindly imperialism which "would not stand for such measures" as "administrative massacres," and which "preferred to liquidate the empire" when the empire threatened to damage the democratic nation,[24] and a totalitarian imperialism which represented the kindly British version run amok. For every evil tool in the kit of totalitarianism there was an anti-totalitarian mate which, while identical in substance, was contrary in purpose. Everything was legitimate as long as it was used in the struggle against totalitarianism — covert as well as overt action, violent as well as nonviolent intercession, subversive counter-aggression as well as open ideological counter-propaganda. This was the logic of counter-totalitarianism as an ideology unto itself with its own laws of development and survival. Ultimately, this logic pointed to a final dualism: an acceptable form of destruction to counter totalitarianism's unacceptable and pernicious proclivity toward globalism through the destruction of others:

> It is . . . quite evident that the possibility for peaceful coexistence of the nations peopling this world presupposes the disappearance of totalitarian dictatorships. Since, according to their own loudly proclaimed professions, their systems must be made worldwide, *those who reject the system have no alternative but to strive for its destruction.* [25]

Striving for the destruction of totalitarianism meant consideration of the role of weapons systems; because weapons systems were thermonuclear and hence global, however, "thinking about the unthinkable" required a careful reevaluation of fundamental goals. Theories of totalitarianism, and the counter-ideologies they produced, provided the necessary value hierarchy.

4. JUSTIFICATION OF THE USE OF NUCLEAR WEAPONS

With the possible exception of the period preceding the Civil War, Americans have not since Revolutionary times felt the need to philosophize about fundamental questions of ultimate national purpose or to consider basic value priorities in the pursuit and defense of their politics. This comparative absence of philosophizing about basic questions is what commentators like Daniel Boorstin have in mind when they describe American politics and political thought as pragmatic, or practical, or realist, in nature.

With the end of World War II, the international environment and the resources of American national power were transformed in a manner that made confrontation of value questions existentially unavoidable: In the defense of which values would the United States risk the destruction of whole nations

---

24. Arendt, *op. cit.,* p. 504.
25. Friedrich and Brzezinski, *op. cit.,* p. 68. Emphasis added.

(including its own), the possible devastation of civilization, and even the potential annihilation of all human life? In what circumstances, and on behalf of which goals, could the United States justify to itself and to others the permanent and escalating risks of nuclear "brinkmanship"? Which were to be chosen and which spurned of the multiple values competing for American support? Peace or freedom? Liberty or security? Independence or survival? For most of American history, a combination of national abundance and international isolation had obviated the need for such choices; with the advent of nuclear weapons and the international involvement which arose out of the war, the making of moral choices became an imperative of national survival.

Once again, the concept of totalitarianism provided criteria for these difficult and unprecedented decisions — a perspective within which the new order of questions could be answered, or at least within which answers ascertained by other means could be justified. Characteristically, these justifications were couched in a language which radiated virtue without eschewing the requirements of pragmatism and national interest. The fundamental question of the ordering of values into a hierarchy which could be strategically implemented was most easily answered by theories of totalitarianism. If, as Hannah Arendt avows, "in the final stages of totalitarianism an absolute evil appears,"[26] some men may be led to believe that it becomes a correspondingly absolute moral imperative to contain, roll back, and eventually destroy the source of radical evil by all available means.

This is especially true in light of two of totalitarianism's allegedly most nefarious traits: its tendency to become increasingly total in scope and intensity, which is supposedly translated, in the international sphere, into a strategy of imperialistic expansion and permanent aggression; and its intrinsic invulnerability to revolution from within. The trait of aggressive imperialism, arising out of the functional requirements of the expanding domestic regime, and out of an ideology making "chiliastic claims as to the 'perfect' final society for mankind,"[27] makes a global stance by the United States a moral necessity as well as a moral duty. For the theory of totalitarianism makes clear that totalitarian regimes will not remain content with absolute control of their own helpless regions of the world, but must, in accordance with their development laws, seek to remake all humanity in their own image. Whereas it is a duty of only secondary importance to root out social disease wherever it appears even if it is not contagious, it becomes a moral imperative of the first magnitude to stymie the spread of a political malaise capable of and striving to infect all mankind.

At the same time, totalitarianism's own immunity to internal remedies — discussed in some detail above — lends still greater urgency to the external

26. Arendt, *op. cit.,* pp. viii – ix.
27. Friedrich, *Totalitarianism, loc. cit.*

struggle against it. To Friedrich and Brzezinski it "appears quite preposterous" that those who live in freedom and security should demand "that the subjects of totalitarian rule rise and overthrow their tormentors . . ."[28] If those who live under its terror cannot take on the burdens of opposition, those who live in "freedom and security" may feel justified in shouldering those burdens themselves. It can be convenient to believe that it is as much our duty today to uproot communist totalitarianism as it was, thirty years ago, to destroy fascist totalitarianism. We too are potential subjects of the totalitarian monolith; should communist totalitarianism ever succeed in imposing itself upon the whole earth through lack of effective opposition by those still capable of it, then all hope would be lost. Absolute evil of the type for which the Nazi concentration and extermination camps stood would exercise total control over mankind, probably for the rest of human history. This is an evil so great that any risk can be justified by those seeking to avert it.

The initial concrete threat that must be countered is the threat of nuclear blackmail by the totalitarians. The obvious and relatively safest strategy is to fight fire with fire — that is, to deter nuclear blackmail by resort to nuclear counter-blackmail. This presents few immediate moral problems because the United States only threatens to use (but does not, assuming that deterrence "works," actually use) nuclear weapons in response to any nuclear thrust by the totalitarians — primarily in the hope of precluding the use of such weapons altogether and thus neutralizing one of totalitarianism's more potent tactics.

But theories of totalitarianism have also led American strategic policy onto more precarious ground. There have been policy-makers both inside and outside the defense establishment who have urged that the United States consider a first-nuclear-strike policy — as a trip wire in Europe, to prevent aggression against Berlin or a conventional onslaught along the entire European front, as a logical step in escalating an unsuccessful "limited war" (MacArthur in Korea), or simply as part of a "preemptive" or "preventive war" tactic to get in the first licks in an "inevitable" world conflagration. In each of these cases, to the extent that something other than gaming models were at stake, the pertinent moral consideration seems to have been a weighing — in favor of the risks of nuclear war — of the damage which might be done by totalitarianism if not countered, and the destruction that would be wrought by nuclear war should threats not be sufficient to deter aggression. In the crudest terms, this choice of the lesser of two evils has been expressed in the slogan, "better dead than red." However, because totalitarianism is global in its aspirations, America has in effect elevated this slogan into a categorical imperative for all mankind. The evils of totalitarianism are such that the choice between

---

28. Friedrich and Brzezinski, *op. cit.,* p. 289. Friedrich and Brzezinski do not themselves draw from this assertion the inferences elaborated upon in the following paragraph and are obviously not responsible for them; but such inferences are not only possible, but in the urgent setting of policy rationalization, quite probable.

totalitarianism and the risk of physical oblivion must be made not only for America and its allies but for (though *not by*) all men in every nation. Thus, many Americans see nothing amiss in the fact that their country has, in effect, decided *for* the Vietnamese and the Cambodian people that they are better off dead than red — that, to keep them "free" (i.e, out of the clutches of communist totalitarianism) we may have to destroy them, just as we quite literally destroyed Ben Tre and Snoul in order to "save" them. So important a decision as the choice between radical evil and its opposite simply cannot be left to the whims of peoples who may not understand the portentousness of the issue facing them, nor possess the moral fiber and physical wherewithal to implement their choice.

In this manner, then, theories of totalitarianism performed their most important service by enabling hitherto and otherwise pragmatic Americans to "solve" for mankind the most profound and consequential practical and moral problem ever faced by Americans themselves. The shortcomings of this solution — evident both in the lack of success of the policies it has inspired and in the contempt it has bred for the peaceful resolution of issues — may be in part due to deficiencies in the concept of totalitarianism. Rhetoric has been known to mislead its promoters.

III

If ideologies are, as Hannah Arendt proposes, "isms — which to the satisfaction of their adherents can explain everything and every occurrence . . . ,"[29] then many of the manifold deficiencies of "totalitarianism" as a concept can probably be traced to the ideological character of the counter-totalitarianism that it has engendered; for despite the pragmatic and counter-ideological side of anti-totalitarianism, its primary impact on policy-making has been moral, and hence as ideological as the system it purports to oppose. Theories of totalitarianism have been used to explain "everything and every occurrence" in the international environment; they have reduced world politics to a simplistic duel between the forces of light and the powers of darkness; and they have subordinated means to a set of abstract ends far removed from reality and of dubious validity in any case. The attitudes and policies which have arisen out of anti-totalitarianism have, moreover, in the typical style of self-fulfilling prophecies, brought the world closer to the condition it was in — according to theories of totalitarianism — to begin with.

Nonetheless, a significant tension has persisted between the monolithic moral reality *postulated* by the counter-totalitarian ideology, and the much more diversified and pluralistic reality *observed* by those viewing the world from other perspectives. Without entering into epistemological quarrels about the "objectivity" of different perceptions, most disinterested observers would

29. Arendt, *op. cit.,* p. 268.

probably agree that the world is at least somewhat less rational, less predictable, more diversified, less polarized, more varied, less monolithic — in
short, less susceptible to simplistic moral analysis — than theories of totalitarianism are inclined to allow. This refusal of reality to accommodate itself to
theory has vexed many theorists of totalitarianism, and has been responsible
for certain modifications in and reservations about "laws" initially deemed to
be immutable. The "liberalization" of the Soviet Union following Khrushchev's Twentieth Congress speech, the new emphasis on socialist legality,
and the gradual transformation of Russia into a *status quo* power with interests which, compared to China's or those of many new nations, can only be
described as conservative, present difficulties for the notion that totalitarianism
"requires," as a function of its nature or essence, increasing totality, institutionalized and incessant terror, and permanent world revolution. Hence, in the
second edition of their influential work on *Totalitarian Dictatorship and Autocracy,* Friedrich and Brzezinski concede that "the notion that this evolution
means that totalitarian regimes will become more and more total (that was our
view expressed in the first edition, p. 300) is not tenable."[30] Adam B. Ulam
tries to rationalize the obvious waning of terror in post-Stalinist Russia with
the argument that terror was "interfering with the objectives of totalitarianism
itself" — a perplexing explanation in view of the fact that terror is generally
regarded as one of the defining characteristics of "totalitarianism itself."[31] In
the Epilogue to the second edition of her study, Arendt also essays to salvage
the concept of totalitarianism from the sinking ship of its defining characteristics: "neither the failures of 1956 nor the success of 1957 indicate a new
development of this form of government from within, either in the form of
enlightened despotism or some other form of dictatorship."[32] Rather we must
consider the possibility that this entire period is but a "repetition of the
relatively bloodless twenties," which could "again be followed by a full-fledged
terror like that of the thirties."[33] But on the whole such hypothetical and self-
contradictory explanations are less telling than the admission which they are
meant to rationalize.

30. Friedrich and Brzezinski, *Totalitarian Dictatorship and Autocracy* (New York: Praeger,
2d rev. ed. by C. J. Friedrich, 1966), pp. 375ff.
31. Ulam, *op. cit.,* p. 646. In the same vein, Ulam makes the assertion that the Russians have
of late been trying "to impose a sane pattern of totalitarianism, in contrast to the extreme of
Stalin's despotism. . . ." This hardly clarifies the issue, since Stalin's despotism is generally taken
to be archetypically totalitarian; to speak of a "sane totalitarianism" would, one imagines, be as
senseless as to postulate a "healthy leper."
32. Arendt, *op. cit.,* p. 509. No doubt some theorists of totalitarianism will find in the Soviet
occupation of Czechoslovakia a source of support for the totalitarian reading of Soviet foreign
policy; but — quite aside from the adequacy of theories of national interest or self-fulfilling
prophecy in explaining what has tragically transpired — the fact that internal liberalization in a
supposedly totalitarian country provoked the intervention to begin with makes the Czechoslovakian case a very ambiguous avenue of appeal.
33. *Ibid.,* pp. 509 – 510.

Yet despite the increasingly patent tension between theories of totalitarianism and the reality they pretend to describe, many theorists and politicians — liberals as well as conservatives — continue to accept the analogy between Nazi Germany and Soviet Russia suggested by totalitarian theory. Although the concept clearly lacks the conviction in the seventies that it carried in the fifties (see President Nixon's February 19, 1970 speech, "U.S. Foreign Policy for the 1970's: A New Strategy for Peace"), its spirit continues to inform attitudes toward China and the Soviet Union and debate about national defense and the ABM. Of course, liberals who retain the concept are somewhat more ready than others to apply it to "traditional dictatorships" in Spain, Portugal, or Greece, but the belief many hold that politics is a choice between evils leads most to condone alliances with these quasi-totalitarian traditionals in the common struggle against the much greater threat of "total" totalitarianism represented by aggressive international communism, even in its present bifurcated condition.[34]

Acceptance by the liberals is an indication of how pervasive theories of totalitarianism have been. Yet it obviously does not justify them. Whether the vision of a universal moral struggle between Right and Wrong is the product of any honest attempt to understand the world, or simply a cynical disguise for the aggressive designs of some Americans for America world hegemony,[35] it remains a vision rooted in the kind of fundamental distortions peculiar to ideologies (and ideological counter-ideologies). For the ideologue, when the simplistic sterotypes posited by theory are contravened by reality, it is not theory that is to blame. What Borkenau remarked about communism

34. This belief helps explain the feebleness of liberal criticism of American anti-totalitarianism; the view is also related to Neo-Orthodox Protestant social theory of the kind identified with Reinhold Niebuhr. The "dilemmas of power" naturally afflict the most powerful nation which, hence, must do wrong whatever it does. There is a profound affinity between this school of thought and those, who like Professor Epstein, worry about the "Hitler in ourselves." Liberals confront a similar difficulty when the assess the political role of the Roman Catholic Church, at least before Pope John XXIII. In *The Catholic Church and Nazi Germany* (New York: McGraw-Hill, 1964), for example, Guenter Lewy quotes the program of a Catholic youth organization as calling "for the full and close cooperation between totalitarian state and the totalitarian church," in what is partly a mistranslation from the German word "Totalität" (p. 106 and note 47, pp. 364ff.).

35. E. H. Carr's thirty-year-old portrayal of the cynical view remains compelling: "Theories of international morality are . . . the product of dominant nations or groups of nations. For the past hundred years . . . the English-speaking peoples have formed the dominant group in the world; and current theories of international morality have been designed to perpetuate their supremacy . . ." (*The Twenty Years' Crisis,* pp. 79 – 80). As one would expect, the Soviets have treated the theory of totalitarianism as a mask for American imperialism; see, for example, Y. Chekharin, "The Theoretical Speculations of the Ideologists of Anti-Communism," *Kommunist,* Moscow: No. 10, July, 1969 (available in English in the series, "Translations from *Kommunist,*" by the Department of Commerce Joint Publications Service). An earlier version of this essay is among the American studies discussed by Chekharin; readers will be pleased to know that Chekharin treats the authors of this essay as "perfectly authoritative representatives of the bourgeois social sciences . . ." who, however, "voluntarily or involuntarily expose . . . the bankruptcy of the entire concept of 'totalitarianism' [sic] . . ."

seems equally applicable to anti-communism: "every failure — not objective failure, but the failure of the reality to comply with the utopia — supposes a traitor."[36] Thus, some of the more committed counter-totalitarian ideologies in the United States have seen, in America's failure to roll back communism, not a failure of theory to predict adequately the tenor and direction of international life, but an act of treason by fellow Americans operating on behalf of the enemy in the higher reaches of the federal government — or for that matter, the colleges, universities, and learned journals.[37]

As an essentialist concept serving as a cornerstone of American counter-ideology in the Cold War, totalitarianism has nullified whatever utility it might have had — forgetting for the moment the conceptual objections that can be made to its analytic use — as an explanatory category in modern political science. On a more practical and perhaps more crucial level, the failures of the United States to cope with the difficult and diversified problems thrown up by the postwar international environment may be attributed at least in part to the role played by "totalitarianism" in the cognitive tool kit of scholars, politicians, and the public. As long as this condition persists, these failures are likely not only to multiply, but to become more and more disastrous for America and mankind.[38]

36. Franz Borkenau, *World Communism: A History of the Communist International* (Ann Arbor: University of Michigan Press, 1962), p. 179.

37. That was the reaction of a few learned critics to an earlier version of the present article. The authors were accused of trying to demonstrate that the United States had fought World War II in vain, and of letting their opposition to American policy in Vietnam blind them to the global threat of totalitarianism.

38. Theories of totalitarianism may have even served to intensify and exacerbate the internal cleavages which have racked our society in recent years; for the Manichean aura which has surrounded the world context for hegemony against the forces of totalitarianism abroad has infused the critics of dissent at home with a spirit of blind, chauvinistic self-righteousness whose ultimate cost one can only begin to measure by the dead at Kent State University.

The Cuban Missile Crisis: An Analysis of Soviet Calculations and Behavior*

In a television interview not long after the Cuban missile crisis of October 1962, President Kennedy observed that both the United States and the Soviet Union had made serious miscalculations in the Cuban affair. "I don't think we expected that he [Khrushchev] would put the missiles in Cuba," he said, "because it would have seemed such an imprudent action for him to take. . . . He obviously thought he could do it in secret and that the United States would accept it."[1]

As it turned out, of course, deploying strategic missiles in Cuba *was* an imprudent thing for Khrushchev to do, and his expectation that the United States would accept it proved to be mistaken. In the first few weeks after the immediate crisis was resolved by Khrushchev's withdrawal of the Soviet missiles, Soviet affairs specialists turned their attention to the puzzling questions raised by his behavior: (1) Why did Khrushchev deploy strategic weapons in

*Reprinted from *World Politics,* XVI, 3 (April, 1964), pp. 363–389, by permission of the author, RAND Corporation, and Princeton University Press. Copyright 1964 by RAND Corporation, published by Princeton University Press. This article is an abridgment of a RAND Corporation Memorandum written by the author as part of the research program sponsored by the United States Air Force under Project RAND. However, views or conclusions contained in this article are those of the author and should not be interpreted as representing the official opinion or policy of the United States Air Force.

1. *Washington Post,* December 18, 1962.

Cuba? (2) What led him to believe he could succeed? (3) Why did he withdraw the weapons so precipitately?

In the months that have elapsed since the first post-crisis flurry of speculation and analysis, a great deal of valuable new information has come to light, particularly in testimony before Congressional committees by high Administration officials. In mid-December 1962, Khrushchev broke the silence he had maintained for some six weeks and presented before the USSR Supreme Soviet the first in a series of detailed explanations of his actions.[2]

Although the new American and Soviet materials for the most part bear only indirectly on the questions posed above, they provide an improved basis for attempting to answer them. One minor participant in the events of October 1962, Fidel Castro, reportedly told a friendly French correspondent that the answers to these questions are "a mystery" which may perhaps be unraveled by historians "in 20 or 30 years."[3] Yet if we are to derive any useful foreign policy and defense lessons from the Cuban missile crisis, we can hardly wait that long. Though these questions cannot now be resolved definitively, we must at least arrive at some provisional answers that can be tested against Soviet behavior in the coming months and years. If we fail to do this, we reduce the momentous U.S.-Soviet Caribbean confrontation of October 1962 to mere episodic proportions.

I. Soviet Objectives

Unfortunately, much of the early post-crisis discussion of Soviet objectives was strongly conditioned by observers' attitudes toward the policy pursued by the U.S. Government in dealing with the crisis and by their appraisals of the probable consequences of its outcome. Among those who criticized the Administration for acting recklessly, as well as among those who regarded its policy as too cautious, the argument was encountered that the Soviet Union, directly or indirectly, had achieved much of what it intended.[4] In part, per-

---

2. *Pravda,* December 13, 1962. The continuing drumfire of Albanian and Chinese criticism obliged Khrushchev to return to the subject repeatedly, particularly in his East German SED Congress speech (*Pravda,* January 17, 1963) and his Supreme Soviet election speech (*Pravda,* February 28, 1963).

3. Conversation with Claude Julien, *Le Monde,* March 22, 1963.

4. Professor Leslie Dewart, who argued that the President played into Khrushchev's hands by *over*reacting, wrote that "yielding was the essence of the [Soviet] scheme." "The conclusion appears reasonable that Russia set up missile bases in Cuba in full knowledge or expectation of the consequences. It is those very consequences [to compel a shift from "rigidity to negotiableness" in U.S. foreign policy] which she can be presumed to have sought" ("Russia's Cuban Policy and the Prospects of Peace," *Council for Correspondence Newsletter,* No. 21 [October 1962], pp. 17, 21).

Stuart Chase has similarly suggested that "it is not impossible" that the withdrawal of Soviet strategic weapons from Cuba "was part of a plan, more political than military, to secure a pledge against invasion" ("Two Worlds," *Bulletin of the Atomic Scientists,* XIX [June 1963], p. 20).

Those who criticized the Administration for reacting too cautiously tended to regard the

haps, what brought critics of widely divergent political persuasions to similar conclusions was a shared image, born of Sputnik, of the ten-foot-tall Russians who rarely do anything wrong, and a complementary, equally erroneous image, fostered by the U-2 and the Bay of Pigs debacles, of U.S. Administrations that rarely do anything right. But to regard the outcome of the Cuban missile crisis as coinciding in any substantial way with Soviet intentions or interests is to mistake skillful salvage of a shipwreck for brilliant navigation. If the success achieved by the United States in October 1962 proved to be more limited in scope than many believed it would be or had to be, the outcome hardly constituted a net gain for the Soviet Union.

Some observers have imputed to the Soviet Union precisely those objectives they believe that Khrushchev achieved: the securing of desired political concessions from the United States, such as a public pledge by the President not to invade Cuba; or more generalized political gains, including credit for having saved the peace. Even if they had been fully achieved, these objectives would have been blatantly disproportionate to the means expended, and to the costs and risks incurred by the Soviet Union in the undertaking. The Chinese and Albanian Communists, and Castro, too, have correctly — from the Communist point of view — drawn attention to the emptiness of mere verbal pledges by the enemy.[5] Moreover, the U.S. Government has withheld a formal pledge, since one of the conditions for it set forth in the Kennedy-Khrushchev correspondence, on-site verification, has not been satisfied. Khrushchev has publicly treated the President's conditional pledge as if it were in full force because he has little else to show for his efforts. While Castro has complained formally to U.N. Secretary-General U Thant that "officials of the U.S. Govern-

---

outcome of the crisis as coinciding less with specific Soviet intentions than with general Soviet interests. For example, David Lowenthal wrote: "It is what he [the President] could have done but did *not* do that will most strongly impress our Communist foes. He forced them to retract the move, and for a brief while aired their malice before the world. But he did nothing to penalize an action aimed at inflicting an almost mortal wound on us, and he even made a noninvasion pledge that had never been given before. . . . We did not even get the *status quo ante*" ("U.S. Cuban Policy: Illusion and Reality," *National Review,* January 29, 1963, p. 63).

Along related lines, Robert D. Crane wrote: "The USSR might conclude that the United States was content with a vague promise of the verified removal of an indefensible Communist military gain. The Soviets on the other hand demanded — and apparently believed they had received — an assurance against an invasion of Cuba by any country in the Western Hemisphere, which under the circumstances could amount to the creation of a new doctrine strongly resembling a Monroe-Doctrine-in-reverse" ("The Cuban Crisis: A Strategic Analysis of American and Soviet Policy," *Orbis,* VI [Winter 1963], pp. 547–48).

5. "In no circumstances," the Peking *People's Daily* editorialized on October 31, 1962, can the people of the world trust "the empty promises of the U.S. aggressor." Tirana Radio chimed in the following day: "The Cuban people know from their own experience — the experience of the Bay of Pigs and of all that is happening around them — that Kennedy and the imperialist monopolies represented by Kennedy cannot be trusted." And Castro has said: "We do not believe in the words of Kennedy; but, moreover, Kennedy has not given any word. And if he gave it, he has already retracted it" (Havana Radio, January 16, 1963).

ment declare that they do not consider themselves bound by any promise,"[6] Khrushchev has prudently chosen to ignore these statements.

As to any credit Khrushchev may have gained for saving the peace, it is doubtful whether his "reasonableness" persuaded many observers of his dedication to peace who were not so persuaded before the crisis. It is more likely that his decision to withdraw the weapons served only to restore the confidence in him of those whose faith was shaken by the disclosure — or rather by Khrushchev's belated acknowledgment — that the Soviet Union had deployed strategic missiles and bombers in Cuba. On the other hand, the ranks of those, both in the Communist camp and outside of it, who regard Khrushchev as an "adventurer" or "capitulator" have certainly been augmented.[7] The growth of such beliefs about Khrushchev is not likely to enhance his future political effectiveness.

Finally, to achieve the limited political objectives imputed to them by those who contend that the outcome of the crisis was the one intended by the USSR, the Soviet leaders need not have invested so heavily or risked so much. At least 42 IL-28 bombers and an equal number of strategic missiles were brought into Cuba by Soviet ships; nine missile sites were established, six of them with four launchers each for the MRBM's, and three of them, fixed sites for the IRBM's, each designed to include four launching positions.[8] Yet a token force of a few conspicuously deployed MRBM's would alone doubtless have sufficed to provoke a U.S. demand that the Soviet Union remove them from Cuba.

The magnitude and character of the Soviet strategic weapon deployment in Cuba cast doubt also on a related hypothesis — namely, that the Soviet Union sought merely to compel the United States to withdraw its missiles from Turkey in exchange for the withdrawal of Soviet missiles from Cuba. Since the United States had only one squadron (15 missiles) of Jupiters deployed in Turkey,[9] only a third the number of MRBM's with a 1,100-mile range known to have been shipped to Cuba would have sufficed to make such a trade seem quantitatively plausible. The costly and essentially unsalvageable fixed sites that were being prepared to receive IRBM's with a 2,200-mile range were altogether superfluous to any intended Cuba-Turkey missile-base exchange since the United States had no equivalent missiles in Turkey, or anywhere else for that matter.

Of course, a mutual withdrawal of missiles from Cuba and Turkey was explicitly proposed by Khrushchev in his October 27 letter to President

6. *New York Times,* November 17, 1962.
7. The Chinese Communists have accused him of being both.
8. Briefing by John Hughes, Defense Intelligence Agency, *Department of Defense Appropriations for 1964,* Hearings Before a Subcommittee of the Committee on Appropriations, House of Representatives, 88th Congress, 1st Session (Washington 1963), Part I, p. 7; hereinafter cited as *Hearings.*
9. *Missiles and Rockets*, January 7, 1963, p. 26.

Kennedy. But the mere fact that Khrushchev proposed such an exchange at one point during the crisis, after the United States had demanded the withdrawal of Soviet strategic weapons, no more proves that this was his objective from the start than his subsequent withdrawal of the missiles without such a *quid pro quo* proves that his ultimate objective was simply to get President Kennedy to promise not to invade Cuba. It is true that the withdrawal of U.S. strategic weapons from Turkey, under apparent Soviet duress, would have given Khrushchev a more tangible return for his trouble than a conditional verbal pledge by the United States not to invade Cuba.[10] It is one thing for the United States and an allied host country to decide jointly to substitute for some bases other means of defense, such as Polaris submarines in adjacent waters; it is quite another for the United States, under Soviet duress, to withdraw from its bases, regardless of the wishes of its allies.

It seems questionable, however, that the Soviets would accept the costs and risks of deploying missiles in Cuba merely in order to remove them in return for the withdrawal of U.S. missiles from Turkey. The phasing out of U.S. missiles deployed overseas, without a Soviet *quid pro quo*, was already known to have been under consideration long before the October 1962 crisis,[11] though the Soviet leaders may not have been certain regarding U.S. intentions. Moreover, because of geographic considerations and the large U.S. advantage in intercontinental nuclear delivery capabilities, a strategic missile base in Cuba was a far more valuable military asset to the Soviet Union than a comparable base in Turkey to the United States. Finally, as pointed out earlier, if the Soviet leaders intended no more than to lay the groundwork for an agreement on the mutual withdrawal of U.S. and Soviet strategic missiles from Turkey and Cuba, they need not have deployed more than a token force of MRBM's and need not have constructed installations for IRBM's at all. It is more likely that the base-exchange proposal was an improvised or perhaps even a prepared fall-back position to cover unfavorable contingencies, but not the Soviet-preferred culmination of the Cuban venture.[12]

Khrushchev's official rationale is that Soviet strategic weapons were deployed in Cuba solely to defend the island against U.S. attack; and that once

10. Had the United States accepted the Soviet base-exchange proposal of October 27, Khrushchev would also have received such a U.S. pledge, since a reciprocal exchange of no-invasion pledges was part of the proposed bargain.

11. Secretary McNamara has testified that the long-standing program to replace the obsolete Thor and Jupiter missiles dated from early 1961 (*Hearings,* p. 57).

12. If the base-exchange proposal was a *prepared* fall-back position, the Soviet leaders failed to prepare their propagandists for it. On the same day (October 28, 1962) that it front-paged Khrushchev's base-exchange proposal letter to the President, the Soviet Government newspaper, *Izvestiia*, printed on an inside page a commentary which stated: "There are those in the U.S.A. who speculate that in exchange for denying Cuba the ability to repel American aggression, one might 'give up' some American base close to Soviet territory. . . . Such 'proposals,' if you can call them that, merely serve to betray the unclean conscience of the authors." The editor of *Izvestiia* is Alexei Adzhubei, Khrushchev's son-in-law.

the threat of such an attack was removed (by the President's conditional undertaking not to launch one), the Soviet weapons having served their purpose, were withdrawn and peace was preserved. Of course, even on its own terms this rationale is deficient, for Khrushchev also acknowledged, presumably to demonstrate that his decision to withdraw the missiles was not a needless concession, that he took that decisive step only when urgent word reached him that a U.S. attack on Cuba appeared imminent.

Far from deterring the "imperialists," by giving them, in Khrushchev's words, "a more realistic idea of the danger of thermonuclear war," the discovery of Soviet strategic missiles in Cuba provoked a U.S. naval quarantine, a rapid buildup of U.S. Army and Tactical Air Forces in the southeastern part of the country, and a worldwide alert of the Strategic Air Command. Thus, it would seem, the deployment of Soviet strategic weapons in Cuba did not succeed, as Khrushchev said he had anticipated, "in bringing the aggressors to their senses." In his words: "In the morning of October 27 we received information from our Cuban comrades *and from other sources* which directly stated that this [U.S.] attack would be carried out within the next two or three days. We regarded the telegrams received as a signal of *utmost alarm,* and this alarm was justified. Immediate actions were required in order to prevent an attack against Cuba and preserve peace."[13]

The action, of course, was Khrushchev's proposal to the President to withdraw from Cuba all the weapons "which you regard as offensive" in exchange for cessation of the quarantine and a pledge by the President not to invade Cuba. It must have appeared to Khrushchev, then, that the United States had not only been prepared to attack Cuba *despite* the presence of Soviet weapons, but precisely *because* the weapons had been brought in, since evidently only by agreeing to withdraw them did Khrushchev believe he could secure from the President assurances that the United States would not attack. Presidential statements, made repeatedly in the months preceding the deployment of Soviet missiles in Cuba, that the United States did not intend to invade if offensive weapons were *not* deployed in Cuba, had apparently not been deemed sufficient; only when such an assurance was made conditional on the removal of Soviet strategic weapons from Cuba with appropriate international verification, did it become acceptable.

The strange logic of Khrushchev's face-saving explanation of Soviet motives and behavior does not in itself disprove his contention that Soviet missiles were deployed in Cuba solely to deter a U.S. attack; it only indicates that if deterrence of a U.S. attack on Cuba was the sole Soviet objective, the plan backfired: the Soviet weapons provoked rather than deterred.[14]

13. *Pravda*, December 13, 1962; emphasis supplied. The "other sources" may have included the U.S. Government.
14. Khrushchev referred obliquely to this miscalculation in his speech at the 6th Congress of the SED (East German Party) in Berlin on January 16, 1963, when he acknowledged that "this

But there are other reasons for doubting Khrushchev's account of Soviet objectives. These have to do with the appropriateness of the weapons selected to be deployed in Cuba for the ostensible purpose of deterring a U.S. attack on that country. Surely a threat to destroy several southeastern U.S. cities, or even Miami alone, *if credible,* would have been adequate to deter such an attack. For this, tactical missiles with a range of several hundred miles would have sufficed. It could have been claimed that such weapons were designed to strike at airfields and marshaling and embarkation points in the Florida area from which a U.S. invasion might be mounted. Perhaps by employing a high lofting technique, the MRBM's that were deployed and the IRBM's that were being prepared could have been used to strike close-in targets, but such long-range missiles are not designed for that purpose. Whatever marginal incremental value for local deterrence (of an attack on Cuba) might have been obtained by deploying missiles with ranges in excess of several hundred miles was more than outweighed by the added provocation they offered.

Had the Soviet missiles remained in Cuba, declarations regarding the control arrangements established for them would have been important indicators of the objectives the Soviet Union sought to pursue. To maximize the effectiveness of Soviet missiles deployed in Cuba as a deterrent against a U.S. attack on Cuba and to reduce the risk that their employment, in the event of such an attack, would bring down U.S. nuclear retaliation against the USSR, it might have been desirable for Khrushchev to have the U.S. Government believe that the Soviet missiles were at Castro's disposal and under his control.

In the United States Castro had gained a reputation for impulsive, irresponsible behavior. Whether authentic or not, the post-crisis remarks attributed to Che Guevara, that the Cubans were prepared, in the event of a U.S. attack, to strike "the very heart of the United States, including New York,"[15] conformed to the image of the Cuban leadership that was widely held in the United States. Once an operational missile capability was established in Cuba, such beliefs on the part of Americans might have lent substantial deterrent value to the missiles deployed in Cuba.

On the other hand, to bring Cuba-based missiles to bear in support of Soviet interests in confrontations with the United States (for example in Berlin), belief that the missiles were at the disposal of the *Soviet* leaders would have been essential. Until such time as the Soviet Union might wish to bring the missiles so to bear, however, the Soviet leaders probably would have preferred to keep

---

enforced measure [stationing Soviet missiles in Cuba] had the effect of a shock *(shok)* on the imperialists," but argued that only such measures were capable of inducing U.S. statesmen "to make a more sober assessment of the objective reality" (*Pravda,* January 17, 1963).

15. According to Theodore Draper, these remarks were reportedly made by Guevara in an interview with a London *Daily Worker* correspondent, but did not appear in the version published on December 4, 1962 ("Castro and Communism," *The Reporter,* January 17, 1963, p. 44).

the question of control in an ambiguous state. Vague, generalized statements, such as characterize most Soviet strategic threats, might have been employed.

A consideration of probably lesser importance may have been that a premature explicit announcement on control would have obliged Khrushchev to accept certain political liabilities, regardless of whether he claimed that the Soviet Union retained control over the missiles or not. In either case, Khrushchev would have had to acknowledge that the Soviet Union was engaging in a military practice that he had repeatedly denounced: establishing a strategic base on foreign territory, if he claimed control for the Soviet Union; proliferation of nuclear strategic weapons, if he announced that the missiles had been turned over to Cuba.

On October 22, 1962, President Kennedy impaled Khrushchev on one of the horns of this dilemma by unilaterally resolving the ambiguity: ". . . it shall be the policy of this nation to regard any nuclear missile launched from Cuba against any nation in the Western Hemisphere as an attack by the Soviet Union on the United States requiring a full retaliatory response upon the Soviet Union."[16]

Initially, the Soviet Union attempted to evade the issue by refusing to acknowledge that it had emplaced strategic weapons in Cuba, while affirming in its first official statement on the crisis (October 23) that Cuba alone had the right to decide what kinds of weapons were appropriate for the defense of Cuba.[17] But the same statement, without acknowledging that the military equipment provided to Cuba by the USSR included strategic weapons, also reflected Soviet concern that the U.S. Government might feel impelled to strike quickly to prevent operational missiles from falling into Castro's hands. Thus, the following oblique reassurance was offered: "Nuclear weapons, which have been *created by the Soviet people and which are in the hands of the people*, will never be used for the purpose of aggression."[18]

On the same day, privately, Khrushchev made this reassurance explicit during a three-hour conversation in Moscow with Westinghouse Electric Vice-President William E. Knox, through whom he presumably wished to communicate informally with the U. S. Government. According to Knox, Khrushchev acknowledged that Soviet ballistic missiles had been furnished to Cuba, but were completely controlled by Soviet officers. "But the Cubans were very volatile people, Mr. Khrushchev said, and all of the sophisticated hardware furnished for their defense was entirely under the control of Soviet officers; it would be used only in the event that Cuba was attacked, and it

16. *New York Times,* October 23, 1962. The phrase "*full* retaliatory response upon the Soviet Union" may have implied to the Soviet leaders not only that the United States would not treat the Soviet Union as a sanctuary area if the Cuba-based missiles were fired, but that it did not intend to restrict itself to a limited strategic response ("tit for tat" retaliation).

17. *Pravda,* October 24, 1962.

18. *Ibid.,* emphasis supplied.

would never be fired except on his orders as Commander-in-Chief of all of the Soviet Union."[19]

Finally, in his October 27 letter to President Kennedy, the first published Khrushchev letter during the crisis, the Soviet Premier informed the President that "the weapons in Cuba that you have mentioned and which you say alarm you are in the hands of Soviet officers." "Therefore," he went on, "any accidental use of them whatsoever to the detriment of the United States is excluded."[20]

It thus seems clear that despite the advantages to be gained from ambiguity regarding control of the missiles in Cuba, Khrushchev felt compelled to reassure the President explicitly that Castro could not order the missiles to be fired and that there was therefore no need for the United States to make an immediate attack before the missiles became operational[21] in order to forestall a possible irrational act by the "volatile" Cubans. Whatever value the Soviet weapons may have been intended to have as a deterrent of a local U.S. attack on Cuba was seriously diminished by this reassurance.

It is questionable, however, whether deterrence of a local U.S. attack on Cuba was ever regarded by the Soviet leaders as more than a subsidiary and derivative effect of a venture intended primarily to serve other ends. Certainly the size and character of the intended deployment indicate that it was meant to achieve some broader purpose.[22] Castro has been quoted by a friendly source, the correspondent for *Le Monde*, Claude Julien, as having said that the Cuban leaders had considered among themselves the possibility of requesting that the USSR furnish Cuba missiles, but had not come to any decision when Moscow proposed to emplace them: "They explained to us that in accepting them we would be reinforcing the socialist camp the world over, and because we had received important aid from the socialist camp we estimated that we could not decline. This is why we accepted them. It was not in order to assure our own defense, but first of all to reinforce socialism on the international scale. Such is the truth even if other explanations are furnished elsewhere."[23]

Although Castro subsequently issued a refutation of an American press agency version of the Julien interview (not of the original *Le Monde* article),[24] this quotation has the ring of truth. Of course, the deployment of Soviet

19. *New York Times,* November 18, 1962.

20. *Pravda,* October 28, 1962. The implication is that if the weapons had been under Cuban control, the possibility that they might be "accidentally used" could *not* be excluded.

21. This did not occur for all MRBM systems until October 28; the IRBM's never achieved operational status, nor, apparently, did the IL-28 bombers (*Hearings,* pp. 12, 16).

22. For example, while the threat posed by MRBM's to cities, including Washington, D.C., in the southeastern part of the United States would, if credible, have been adequate to deter a U.S. attack on Cuba, most U.S. strategic bomber and missile bases would have been beyond the range of those weapons. These bases could have been covered by IRBM's.

23. *Le Monde,* March 22, 1963.

24. Havana, *Prensa Latina,* March 22, 1963. Specifically, Castro denied only that "I ex-

missiles in Cuba, to the extent that it would have strengthened the Soviet position in its "worldwide" confrontation with the United States, would also have added credibility to Soviet strategic threats, including the threat to defend Cuba against U.S. attack. In fact, the implication of the official Soviet rationale for deploying strategic weapons in Cuba — namely, that the threat posed to the United States by Soviet weapons *based in the USSR* lacked sufficient credibility to deter a U.S. attack on "socialist" Cuba — is one of the troublesome embarrassments with which Khrushchev has had to deal since the Cuban missile crisis.[25]

Before the crisis, Khrushchev's expressions of strategic support for Cuba were framed in notably cautious and equivocal terms: The USSR's capability to defend Cuba with Soviet-based missiles was affirmed, but a commitment to do so was carefully avoided.[26] Cuban leaders, however, consistently interpreted Khrushchev's words as if they represented a firm, though tacit, commitment. For example, according to Guevara, in January 1961 it was already

---

pressed myself in an unfriendly way at any time about Soviet Prime Minister Nikita Khrushchev." Castro's general refutation pointedly referred only to the UPI version of *Le Monde's* article: "I do not believe that Julien, whom we consider a friend of Cuba, can be guilty of untruths like *some* of the statements the UPI attributes to him" (emphasis supplied). The March 22 TASS version of Castro's denial *omitted* both of the statements quoted above.

After this article was written, Castro was questioned by two other journalists regarding the origination of the plan to deploy Soviet missiles in Cuba. According to Herbert L. Matthews (*Return to Cuba*, Stanford University *Hispanic American Report* series [1964], p. 16), Castro stated flatly on October 23, 1963, that "the idea of installing the nuclear weapons was his, not the Russians'." However, three weeks later, according to Jean Daniel's account of his interview with the Cuban Premier, Castro appeared to confirm the account given earlier in the Julien interview: "We thought of a proclamation, an alliance, conventional military aid. . . . They [the Russians] reasoned that if conventional military assistance was the extent of their assistance, the United States might not hesitate to instigate an invasion, in which case Russia would retaliate and this would inevitably touch off a world war. . . . Under these circumstances, how could we Cubans refuse to share the risks taken to save us?" (Jean Daniel, "Unofficial Envoy: An Historic Report from Two Capitals," *New Republic*, December 14, 1963, pp. 18–19). Matthews writes that he telephoned Castro after Daniel's account was published and was again told: "We were the ones who put forward the idea of the missiles" (*Return to Cuba*, p. 16).

25. Khrushchev handled this question gingerly in defending his Cuban policy against Chinese and Albanian criticism in his speech at the Congress of the SED in Berlin on January 16, 1963: "One may object that, under the influence of the most unrestrained incitement, the U.S. imperialists will not keep their promise and will again turn their arms against Cuba. But the forces which protected Cuba now exist and are *growing in strength every day*. It does not matter where the rockets are located, in Cuba, or elsewhere. They can be used with equal success against any particular aggression" (*Pravda*, January 17, 1963; emphasis supplied). The implicit question is: If so, why were Soviet missiles deployed in Cuba in the first place? The implicit answer is: Soviet-based strategic power was not *then* great enough to deter a U.S. attack, but it is "growing in strength every day" and soon will be (or will appear to be).

26. In July, 1960, Khrushchev said that "figuratively speaking, in case of need, Soviet artillerymen can support the Cuban people with their rocket fire. . . ." (*Pravda*, July 9, 1960). The conditional form of this threat ("can," not "will," support) was retained in the Soviet Government's statement on Cuba on September 11, 1962, which asserted that the USSR *"has the capability* from its own territory to render assistance to any peace-loving state" (*Pravda*, September 11, 1962).

"well known that the Soviet Union and all the socialist states *are ready to go to war* to defend our sovereignty and that *a tacit agreement* has been reached between our peoples."[27]

It may be assumed that the Cuban leaders had pressed Khrushchev for an explicit and unequivocal commitment to defend Cuba with Soviet-based weapons in the event of a U.S. attack. It was presumably to secure such a commitment, which the Soviet Union was evidently reluctant to give, that Castro in effect volunteered Cuba for membership in the "socialist camp" in 1961. As between an explicit and unequivocal Soviet guarantee, on the one hand, and the stationing of Soviet strategic weapons on Cuban soil, on the other, Castro might well have preferred the former under certain circumstances. To the extent that Castro (1) could have had confidence that the Soviet Union would honor such a commitment; or (2) believed that it would be credited to some serious extent in the United States; or (3) believed that a U.S. attack was unlikely in any case, he might not have deemed it necessary to request the Soviet Union to establish strategic missile bases in Cuba and might have been wary of the political consequences of such a move at home, throughout Latin America, and in the United States.

For the *Soviet Union* to propose that its strategic weapons be deployed in Cuba, however, may have been another matter. Let us assume that, regardless of the real intentions of the U.S. Government, Castro believed the probability of a U.S. attack was not negligible. He may have agreed to the Soviet proposal not only because of his dependence on the Soviet Union, but also because, from the Cuban point of view, if the Soviet leaders believed their "worldwide" position vis-à-vis the United States was such that it required reinforcement by drastic means, the reliability of Soviet pledges to defend Cuba with Soviet-based weapons — equivocal pledges to begin with — must have seemed seriously compromised.[28]

What was the "worldwide" position of the Soviet Union that needed to be reinforced by the emplacement of strategic weapons in Cuba? Despite boastful Soviet efforts to conceal it, the fact is that throughout the cold war the Soviet Union's capacity to strike the United States with nuclear weapons has been very much smaller than the U.S. capacity to strike the USSR. From the start, the bulk of the USSR's strategic nuclear capability has been effective only out to ranges of about 2,000 – 2,500 miles. The Soviet Union acquired a very potent nuclear capability against Western Europe, first with medium bombers and

---

27. *Obra Revolucionaria,* January 25, 1961, quoted by Draper, "Castro and Communism," p. 39 (emphasis supplied).

28. In the immediate aftermath of the crisis, the pre-crisis positions of the Soviet Union and Cuba on the firmness of Soviet pledges to defend Cuba were sharply reversed. Whereas the Soviet leaders, presumably to placate Castro, offered increasingly strong pledges to defend Cuba, Cuban leaders ignored them and vowed to resist any U.S. attack with their own resources. Later, however, as Soviet-Cuban relations recovered from the estrangement of the fall of 1962, Cuban leaders began to welcome Soviet pledges with great public enthusiasm.

then with medium- and intermediate-range ballistic missiles of the type it tried to emplace in Cuba. But the Soviet heavy bomber and ICBM forces — that is, the long-range weapons required to reach the United States — did not attain the strength levels that Western observers anticipated they would reach in the 1960's. Inflated beliefs in the West, actively promoted by misleading and deceptive Soviet claims, that the Soviet Union was rapidly acquiring a large intercontinental strike force tended, until the fall of 1961, to deprive continued and even growing U.S. strategic superiority of much of its *political* value. But, in the second half of 1961, the "missile gap" was found, in Secretary Mc-Namara's words, to be "a myth."[29] Confidence in U.S. strategic superiority was restored in the West; moreover, it became apparent, both from Soviet behavior and from the modification of Soviet strategic claims, that the Soviet leaders knew that the West had been undeceived about the strategic balance.[30]

The deployment of strategic weapons in Cuba may have recommended itself to the Soviet leaders as a "quick fix" measure to achieve a substantial, though far from optimal, improvement in Soviet strike capabilities against the United States. Of course, a large increase in the programmed Soviet-based ICBM force would have provided the Soviet leaders with a military capability far more effective (certainly for second-strike purposes) than could be achieved by the emplacement of highly vulnerable MRBM's, IRBM's, and light bombers in Cuba. But such an expansion of the ICBM (and missile-launching nuclear submarine) force could be achieved only gradually and at far greater cost. The Cuban deployment may not have been undertaken as a substitute for such a buildup, but as a stopgap measure, pending its completion.

Certainly the deployment of limited numbers of MRBM's and IRBM's in Cuba would not have solved the Soviet Union's strategic problem. The evident deficiencies of such a force have led some observers to conclude that military considerations were of little importance in the Soviet decision to emplace strategic weapons in Cuba. It is true that the missile sites were soft, very close to the United States, and, after detection, under close and constant surveillance. They would presumably have been highly vulnerable to a U.S. first strike, even with conventional bombs. As a Soviet first-strike force, the Cuba-based force deployed or being readied as of October 1962 was in itself too small to destroy the U.S. strategic nuclear strike force. Even together with the larger long-range strategic force based in the USSR, it seems most unlikely that the

---

29. Quoted in an interview by Stewart Alsop, "Our New Strategy: The Alternatives to Total War," *Saturday Evening Post,* December 1, 1962, p. 18.

30. Soviet strategic pronouncements after the fall of 1961 shifted from claims of superiority to efforts to deprive American claims to superiority of political value by emphasizing the adequacy of Soviet retaliatory capability. Soviet leaders began explicitly to declare their readiness to accept strategic parity as the basic assumption from which political settlements should proceed (e.g., Marshal Malinovsky's *Pravda* interview, January 25, 1962). The emphasis in claims regarding the USSR's strike capability against the United States shifted from the *high level* of destruction that could be inflicted to the *certainty* that some unspecified level of retaliation would occur.

force would have been adequate in the fall of 1962; moreover, there would have been a problem, though perhaps not an insurmountable one, of coordinating salvoes from close-in and distant bases so as to avoid a ragged attack. By the same token, however, the installation of Soviet strategic missiles in Cuba would have complicated a U.S. first strike, improved Soviet capabilities to launch a preemptive attack, and hence reduced the credibility of U.S. strategic deterrence of local Soviet aggression, say, in Europe. As to the first-strike potential of Cuba-based Soviet missiles, they could have brought a substantial portion of U.S. nuclear striking power under an attack essentially without warning; moreover, there is no assurance that the buildup would have stopped with the sites already completed or under construction when the Soviets were compelled to abandon the operation.

Whatever their strategic shortcomings, the additional capabilities with which Cuba-based missiles would have provided the Soviet leaders were not insignificant. It is difficult to conceive of any other measure that promised to produce so large an improvement in the Soviet strategic position as quickly or as cheaply. That the Cuban missile deployment would not in itself have provided the Soviet Union with a retaliation-proof first-strike capability against the United States is hardly a reason for dismissing it as of limited strategic importance, as some observers have attempted to do. As the President subsequently said, the Soviet leaders tried materially to change the balance of power. Certainly, the deployment of Soviet missiles in Cuba, in his words, "would have politically changed the balance of power; it would have appeared to [change it] and appearances contribute to reality."[31]

The "worldwide" position of the Soviet Union that needed to be reinforced in the fall of 1962 was not only its strategic position vis-à-vis the United States, but also its position in a range of political issues upon which the strategic imbalance in favor of the United States was having some important bearing. It had become evident, since at least the second half of 1961, that the forward momentum of the Soviet Union in international affairs had largely exhausted itself without yielding the gains which the Soviet leaders had anticipated and the West had feared since the mid-1950's.

These expectations had been fed by mounting evidence of the growing military, scientific, technological, and economic power of the Soviet Union vis-à-vis the West. Some of this evidence was real enough, but much of it, particularly in the realm of strategic power, was illusory. In the framework of the cold war, precisely this realm was central. The effects of other striking achievements, as, for example, in space exploration, were amplified, sometimes out of all proportion to their intrinsic political and military worth, by their presumed bearing on the strategic balance. With the discovery that the "missile gap" had failed to materialize, or had actually materialized in reverse,

31. *Washington Post,* December 18, 1962.

there was a perceptible change in the world political climate. Western self-confidence was restored and Soviet anxieties must have grown.

Moreover, confident Soviet expectations of a few years earlier in regard to dividends from Soviet military and economic aid to the underdeveloped countries failed to materialize. Western European prosperity had reached a new peak, and despite de Gaulle's intransigence the prospects for growing European economic and political unity must (then, at least) have looked distressingly good to Moscow. At the same time, the unity of the Communist camp was being shattered by the escalating conflict between its two most powerful members. Indeed, the Chinese Communist attack on Khrushchev centered precisely on the unfavorable trend in the cold war which the Chinese attributed to Khrushchev's faulty and overcautious leadership.

Finally, there was the long-smoldering, still unresolved problem of Berlin. After almost four years of threats and retreats, Khrushchev had still not succeeded in compelling the West to accept a Berlin settlement on Soviet terms. Khrushchev may therefore have sought some quick and dramatic means of achieving a breakthrough that would strengthen the USSR's position — militarily, diplomatically, and psychologically — on a whole range of outstanding issues, and particularly on Berlin.[32]

Rarely, if ever, are such fateful ventures as the Soviet strategic deployment in Cuba undertaken to achieve narrow or isolated objectives. Where nuclear weapons are involved, even small risks are acceptable only if important interests can be advanced by assuming them. It is most unlikely that the Soviet leaders drew up a precise blueprint or detailed timetable for exploitation of the improved military-political position they would have attained had the Cuban venture been successful. But they probably anticipated that the emplacement of strategic missiles in Cuba and their acceptance by the United States would contribute in some degree to the solution of a whole range of military-political problems confronting the Soviet Union and would alter the environment of the cold war in such a manner as to promote new opportunities for political gain whose nature could not be precisely foreseen.

II. Soviet Pre-crisis Calculations

Granted that the stationing of strategic missiles in Cuba promised to be advan-

32. A link between the Cuban missile deployment and Khrushchev's Berlin strategy was suggested by the Soviet Government's statement of September 11, 1962, in which the USSR acknowledged that it was providing military assistance — though of a strictly defensive type — to Cuba, and warned that a U.S. attack on Cuba might unleash the beginning of a thermonuclear war, but at the same time declared a moratorium on new moves in Berlin until after the U.S. Congressional elections *(Pravda,* September 11, 1962). Khrushchev may have hoped to discourage any new U.S. action in regard to Cuba until after the elections (i.e., until after the MRBM's, at least, became operational), by offering, in return, to desist from fomenting a new crisis in Berlin, and then, after establishing a strategic base in Cuba, to use this new leverage to press for a favorable settlement in Berlin.

tageous to the Soviet leaders for a variety of reasons; granted even that the pay-offs seemed so alluring as to justify the assumption of greater risks than they had taken in previous cold war maneuvers, still the question remains: What led the Soviet leaders to believe they could succeed?

With the benefit of hindsight, many Western observers have concluded that Khrushchev's bold move in Cuba was doomed to failure from the start. This in turn has led to the conjecture that Khrushchev never intended to leave the missiles in Cuba, but wished merely to exact political concessions from the United States in return for their withdrawal. This supposition has already been examined and rejected. Others, who also believed the odds against success for the Soviets were very high, concluded that Khrushchev's Cuban gamble explodes one of the articles of faith of Kremlinologists about Bolshevik behavior — namely, the tenet that holds that good Bolsheviks will not engage in adventurism, adventurism being defined as the taking of even small risks of large catastrophes, such as the destruction of the citadel of communism, the Soviet Union. Certainly if it were true that Khrushchev, in undertaking to deploy strategic missiles in Cuba, consciously and deliberately accepted the risk that by this action alone he might bring down a thermonuclear attack upon the Soviet Union, this indeed would have signified a sharp and very dangerous break with past Soviet practice, perhaps the initiation of a new and more ominous phase of the cold war.

But while the Soviet leaders evidently did accept some unusually high military and political risks in embarking on the Cuban venture, the risk of an immediate U.S. thermonuclear response against the Soviet Union was almost certainly not one of them. Moreover, whatever errors they may have made in anticipating the character and intensity of the U.S. response, they were doubtless correct in excluding that one. This established a very crucial upper limit on the risks they did willingly accept.

Given the considerable margin of American strategic superiority which the emplacement of Soviet missiles in Cuba was intended to reduce, on what grounds could the Soviet leaders be confident that the United States would not launch a first strike against the USSR in order to forestall an unfavorable change in the strategic balance? Throughout the cold war, Soviet leaders have demonstrated great confidence in their ability to control the danger of thermonuclear war by means other than the possession of very large intercontinental strategic capabilities. This was true when the strategic balance was far more unfavorable to the Soviet Union than it was in October 1962.

In part this confidence has been based on the powerful indirect deterrent threat of Soviet military power, at first only conventional, and then nuclear, poised to strike Western Europe, the hostage. Later it was reinforced by the threat of even a quantitatively modest intercontinental strike force and of growing U.S. uncertainty regarding the size of that force and the possible upper limits of damage that it could inflict upon the United States. But chiefly the grounds for this confidence have been political. Even when the United States enjoyed decisive strategic superiority, its leaders showed themselves to be strongly disinclined to initiate general war so long as the Soviet Union avoided extreme measures of provocation that could not be dealt with by other means. Increasingly it must have appeared to the Soviet leaders that nothing short of the actual *application* of violence against the United States or an important U.S. ally would risk a U.S. nuclear attack on the Soviet Union. Of course, lesser forms of provocation might create a situation in which the danger of thermonuclear war might be raised to higher levels, but in such cases the Soviet leaders have always allowed themselves ample room for maneuver, and, if necessary, retreat (as in Berlin). They have evidently estimated that sufficient *time* would be available to permit them to extricate themselves from a dangerous situation before it could become uncontrollably dangerous.

The history of the cold war demonstrates that the Soviet leaders have sufficient reason for such an estimate. This estimate is crucial for assessing Soviet risk calculations in Cuba. If one excludes from Soviet pre-crisis calculations serious concern that the United States, even if it detected the missile buildup before completion, would launch a thermonuclear attack against the Soviet Union, then the venture no longer appears to have been a reckless long-shot gamble, but a more familiar calculated and limited risk accepted for sufficiently weighty stakes. This does not mean that as the crisis unfolded the Soviet leaders did not become concerned that a situation might be arising in which a real danger of nuclear war might be created. In fact, the quick withdrawal of their missiles, as we shall see, may be interpreted as a decision to end the crisis quickly before it became necessary to accept even greater losses which could be avoided, if at all, only at the cost of facing serious risk of nuclear war.

Confidence that their action would not directly provoke nuclear war was a prerequisite for embarking on the Cuban missile venture, but it could not be a sufficient condition for success. What then, aside from their belief that the United States would not respond by striking the Soviet Union, were the calculations that led the Soviet leaders to believe their venture could succeed?

Undoubtedly, the Soviet leaders' understanding (or misunderstanding) of U.S. Cuban policy was a major factor in their decision. The ill-fated Bay of Pigs invasion attempt of April 1961, while it may have demonstrated the depths of U.S. hostility toward Castro, may have also suggested to the Soviet leaders that U.S. reluctance to engage its own forces directly in military action against Cuba was so great that even the emplacement of Soviet strategic weapons on the island would be tolerated, or at least resisted by means short of the direct use of U.S. armed forces. At the same time, the fact that the United States had attempted, even though ineffectually, through the use of Cuban exile proxies, to overthrow Castro, both increased Castro's desire for

Soviet military assistance and made such assistance seem legitimate to many third countries.

The U.S. Government's apparent acceptance of increasingly open Soviet involvement in Cuban affairs after the Bay of Pigs incident, including particularly the Soviet military involvement, may have strengthened the belief of the Soviet leaders that the United States would engage in armed intervention only in response to the actual use of Cuba-based weapons against some Western Hemisphere country.

The Soviet arms buildup in Cuba was conducted in fairly distinct phases, beginning with the delivery of basic conventional weapons, then working up to more sophisticated weapon systems of a tactical type, and finally to advanced SA-2 surface-to-air missiles, which had been at least partially deployed before strategic missiles were introduced into the island in September 1962. Doubtless the U.S. reaction to the arrival of each new type of weapon was closely observed in Moscow. However, the problem of interpretation must have become increasingly difficult over time, because as the character of the weapons shipped to Cuba grew more complex, their delivery and deployment became increasingly covert; hence, there must have been some uncertainty as to whether the U.S. Government was tacitly accepting the presence of new Soviet weapons or had not yet learned of their arrival. If so, the Soviet leaders evidently resolved these uncertainties in favor of assuming U.S. toleration.

However, if the Soviet leaders had placed a permissive interpretation on generalized statements by U.S. leaders during July and August 1962, regarding "defensive" (acceptable) and "offensive" (unacceptable) Soviet weapons in Cuba, the President on September 4 and again on September 13 explicitly placed surface-to-surface missiles in a category which the U.S. Government considered "offensive," and, hence, unacceptable.[33] Moreover, the President stated specifically on the second occasion that U.S. action would not have to await some overt act, but would occur "if Cuba should possess a capacity to carry out offensive actions against the United States."

The President's first explicit statement on surface-to-surface missiles came several days before the earliest date that the first Soviet missiles and associated equipment, clandestinely transported to Cuba in the holds of large-hatch Soviet ships, are estimated to have reached Cuban ports — around September 8.[34] The second statement, which warned that the mere presence of such weapons, even without any overt act, would require the U.S. Government to act, was made before the earliest estimated date for the initiation of site construction and deployment activity, between September 15 and 20.[35] Thus, the Soviets had two opportunities, shortly before their plan to emplace strate-

33. *New York Times,* September 5 and 14, 1962.
34. *Hearings,* p. 25.
35. *Ibid.*

gic missiles in Cuba entered its final and decisive phases, to reconsider their decision in the light of evidence of a U.S. commitment to oppose. The President's warnings may have raised anxiety in Moscow, but they clearly did not deter the Soviet leaders. Why?

Assuming that the Soviet leaders regarded the President's statements as a commitment by the U.S. Government to take some kind of action to oppose the emplacement of Soviet strategic weapons in Cuba, they may have believed that, at least initially, the United States would restrict itself to diplomatic means. They may further have relied on their ability to achieve an operational capability with the missiles quickly enough to ensure the success of the venture. The deployment was carried out with a rapidity that the U.S. intelligence community found "remarkable."[36] Had the Soviets succeeded in achieving their evident objectives of attaining an operational capability clandestinely and then confronting the United States with a *fait accompli*, the outcome *might* have been different. (However, the difference that a *fait accompli* need have made should not be exaggerated.)[37] Speaking of the week-long deliberations that preceded the President's crucial decision in October, Theodore C. Sorensen, special counsel to the President, said that the pressure of time was keenly felt· "For all of us knew that, once the missile sites under construction became operational, and capable of responding to any apparent threat or command with a nuclear volley, the President's options would be drastically changed."[38]

However, the Soviet leaders may not have relied entirely on avoiding detection before completion of the missile deployment, although this was doubtless their preference. Given the difficulties involved in maintaining complete secrecy and the apparent willingness of the Soviets to trade off some possible measures of concealment for greater speed, they could not exclude the possibility that some evidence of the deployment would be at the disposal of the U.S. Government before it could be completed. Allegations, sometimes attributed to Cuban refugees and sometimes even to unnamed members of the intelligence community, that Soviet strategic missiles were present in Cuba had been publicized in the United States even before the first shipment of these weapons is believed to have arrived in Cuba. From the Soviet point of view, the airing of these charges may not have been harmful. Since the Administra-

36. Testimony of John Hughes, Defense Intelligence Agency, *ibid.,* p. 6.
37. Actually, if the same U.S. policy had been adopted for dealing with the situation, the outcome need not have been different even if the Soviet missiles had been operational at the time of their detection. The missile sites would still have been highly vulnerable to attack and Soviet reluctance to initiate a U.S.-Soviet nuclear exchange would presumably still have been sufficiently great to make the threat of a U.S. attack on Cuban bases highly credible. However, sufficient doubt might have arisen on the U.S. side so as to cause a different U.S. policy to be adopted for dealing with the crisis.
38. Theodore C. Sorensen, *Decision-Making in the White House: The Olive Branch or the Arrows* (New York 1963), p. 31.

tion was obliged publicly to deny these allegations and to insist repeatedly that the Soviet arms buildup in Cuba posed no threat to U.S. security, the Soviet leaders might have calculated that the President and his advisers, having thus gone on record, would hesitate to charge the Soviet Union with installing offensive weapons in Cuba so long as the evidence placed before them was ambiguous. Moreover, the Soviet leaders may also have believed that the Administration would be reluctant to expose the Soviet Union publicly on the eve of national elections out of concern for unfavorable domestic political repercussions that might be expected if the elections were held with the missiles still in Cuba and no Soviet commitment to withdraw them.

In general, the Soviet leaders probably believed that time worked in their favor and that it was therefore necessary to utilize deception and diplomacy to gain it. They could hardly have expected to be able to maintain their deception indefinitely; indeed, the objectives they pursued required at some point that the new Soviet military capabilities be discovered or revealed. In the event of premature detection, the Soviet leaders may have relied on diplomacy to take over from deception. They probably viewed the likelihood of a strong U.S. reaction as declining over time as numbers of Soviet strategic missiles became operational and the American people and their government grew "accustomed" to the fact of their presence in Cuba.

The Soviet leaders may have come to the conclusion, based on their past experiences with and understanding of the U.S. decision-making process, that the ability of the U.S. Government to assess the situation rapidly and to plan and implement a policy for dealing with it quickly was severely constrained. They may also have counted for time on the likelihood that the U.S. Government would first have to consult with its NATO allies, who could be expected, at the least, to take a less urgent view of the situation than the U.S. Government. They may also have expected that there would be some significant opposition in the Organization of American States to any U.S. proposals for immediate joint action requiring the use of military forces. In short, the Soviet leaders probably estimated that the likelihood of prompt unilateral action by the United States was small. Moreover, they may have reckoned on reducing this probability even more by presenting the United States with a *fait accompli* of such a nature that the prompt unilateral action to reverse it would appear to the U.S. Government to require the initiation of violence.

If these were some of the calculations of the Soviet leaders, events proved them to be wrong on almost every point. This must have come as a great shock to them. The collapse of confidence which evidently caused Khrushchev on October 26 to send off to President Kennedy a private communication in which he reportedly indicated that he was prepared to yield may have been the culminating point of a whole series of disappointed expectations.[39] Because

39. Apparent inconsistencies and contradictions in communications received in Washington

these expectations were not realized, however, does not necessarily mean they were without reasonable bases. Many observers in the West, too, were surprised — though pleasantly — at the speed and efficiency with which the U.S. Government moved, once reliable evidence of the Soviet strategic weapon buildup in Cuba became available.

One other consideration that may have weighed heavily in Soviet planning must be mentioned here — Berlin. If, contrary to probable Soviet expectations, the U.S. Government deemed military action to be an appropriate response, and if the presence of Soviet missiles in Cuba, even supposing them to be operational, proved in itself insufficient to deter such action, the Soviet leaders may still have hoped that the United States would be restrained by fear of possible Soviet retaliation in Berlin. Eighteen months earlier, at the time of the landings in the Bay of Pigs, Khrushchev had in his first letter to President Kennedy obliquely invoked the threat of Soviet retaliation in another part of the world in response to U.S. intervention in Cuba: "We are sincerely interested in a relaxation of international tension, but if others choose to aggravate it, we shall reply in full measure. And in general, it is hardly possible to handle matters in such a way as to settle the situation and put the fire out in one area while kindling a new conflagration in another area."[40]

Whether the Soviet leaders were actually prepared to retaliate in Berlin in October 1962 is another matter, which we shall later consider. But there was no lack of evidence available to the Soviet leaders to make it appear plausible to them that U.S. policy on Cuba might be influenced critically by U.S. concern over the threat to West Berlin.

For example, in his press conference of August 29, 1962, President Kennedy directly linked U.S. policy on Cuba with U.S. obligations in West Berlin: "The U.S. has obligations all around the world, including West Berlin . . . , and therefore I think that in considering what appropriate action we should take we have to consider the totality of our obligations and also the responsibilities we bear in so many different parts of the world."[41]

That U.S. planners were concerned during the Cuban crisis about possible Soviet counteraction in Berlin has been widely reported.[42] In his October 22 speech, the President made a special point of warning the Soviet leaders against such a course of action: "This latest Soviet threat or any other threat which is made either independently or in response to our actions this week must and will be met with determination. Any hostile move anywhere in the world

---

from Moscow and in Soviet press treatment of the crisis suggest that Soviet decision-making was being conducted in an environment of considerable uncertainty and perhaps even sharp controversy among political and military elite groups. (See Roman Kolkowicz, *Conflicts in Soviet Party-Military Relations: 1962–1963.* The RAND Corporation, RM-3760-PR, August 1963.)

40. *Pravda,* April 19, 1961. The reference at that time was presumably to Laos.

41. *New York Times,* August 30, 1962.

42. See, for example, the chronological account of the Cuban crisis published in *ibid.,* November 3, 1962.

against the safety and freedom of peoples to whom we are committed, including in particular the brave people of West Berlin, will be met by whatever action is needed."[43]

If the Soviet leaders had hoped that such concerns would inhibit a strong U.S. reaction to their deployment of strategic weapons in Cuba, events, of course, proved them to be mistaken. But, again in this regard, their expectations were not entirely without foundation.

III. Soviet Crisis Calculations

We have now arrived at the third of the three questions posed at the beginning of this paper: Why did Khrushchev change course so precipitately and withdraw his strategic missiles and bombers from Cuba? Implicitly, some reasons have been adduced in the preceding discussion of probable Soviet pre-crisis miscalculations. It remains to make these points explicit and to amplify them.

(1) The Soviet leaders had evidently hoped to present the United States with a *fait accompli* in Cuba (like the hastily erected Berlin wall in August 1961). As it turned out, however, the Soviet deployment was not yet completed when the President instituted the quarantine and demanded the withdrawal of Soviet strategic weapons. The U.S. Government had more freedom of choice and action than the Soviet leaders probably foresaw.

(2) By effectively preserving secrecy regarding the response it had chosen to make, the U.S. Government, on October 22, was able to present the Soviet Union with what was, in some sense, an American *fait accompli*: the quarantine.[44]

(3) The character of the U.S. response, as set forth by the President on October 22, apparently confounded the Soviet leaders. By imposing a quarantine on strategic arms shipments to Cuba as the first in a series of measures designed not only to prevent a further buildup, but to secure the removal of weapons already on the island — the other measures remained deliberately unspecified — the United States in some sense shifted onto the Soviet side the immediate burden of decision regarding the precipitation of violence. As an initial response the quarantine was considerably less than a direct application of violence, but considerably more than a mere protest or verbal threat. The U.S. Navy placed itself physically between Cuba and Soviet ships bound for Cuban ports. Technically, it might still have been necessary for the United States to fire the first shot had Khrushchev chosen to defy the quarantine, though other means of preventing Soviet penetration might have been employed. But once the quarantine was effectively established — which was done

43. *Ibid.,* October 23, 1962.
44. Speaking of the deliberations which led up to the President's October 22 speech, Theodore Sorensen said that "all of us knew that, once the Soviets learned of our information and planning, our prospects for surprise and initiative would be greatly lessened" (*Decision-Making in the White House,* p. 31).

with great speed — it was Khrushchev who had to make the next key decision: whether or not to risk releasing the trip wire.

In dealing with the quarantine itself, the Soviet leaders essentially had three choices, all of them unpleasant, and one of them quite dangerous: (1) They could submit to the quarantine by permitting their vessels to be stopped, searched, and, if they carried contraband, to be seized; or (2) they could avoid a showdown by keeping their ships out of the quarantine area — which, with the exception of an oil tanker clearly identifiable as such, is what they actually did;[45] or (3) they could precipitate the use of violence by attempting to violate the quarantine, perhaps with the aid of submarines. Soviet prospects for success in such an undertaking were very poor; and the outlook could not have appeared any brighter to them at any of the successively higher local levels of violence that could be contemplated.

(4) U.S. success in securing prompt and unanimous support for the quarantine in the OAS and the active participation of naval elements from some Latin American countries in the operation must have made the Soviet leaders pessimistic about the chances of bringing diplomatic pressure effectively to bear on the United States to lift the quarantine.[46] This may have caused the Soviet leaders to regard a "waiting strategy" as less promising diplomatically than they had anticipated, while the U.S. military preparations also made such a strategy appear increasingly risky.

(5) The President's decision to confront the Soviet Union directly and to ignore Castro also compelled the Soviet leaders to determine their course of action quickly. It removed the ground from under any Soviet effort to involve the United States in negotiations with the Cuban Government, as the Soviet leaders subsequently attempted unsuccessfully to do in connection with the IL-28 bombers. Diplomatically and morally, the U.S. decision to confront the Soviet Union directly made it possible to separate the specific issue of the menacing Soviet weapon deployment in Cuba from the broad and controversial issue of U.S.-Cuban relations.

(6) Finally, there was the speed and evident resolution with which the U.S. Government acted in the Cuban missile crisis. This refers not only to the prompt and successful implementation of the quarantine, the rapid securing of OAS cooperation and NATO support, but above all to the speed and impressiveness of the U.S. conventional military buildup in the southeastern states and of the alert measures taken by U.S. strategic forces around the

45. Sixteen out of 18 Soviet dry-cargo ships en route to Cuba, presumably those containing quarantined items, reversed course and returned to the Soviet Union (*Hearings,* p. 13).

46. Theodore Sorensen has suggested that if the OAS had failed to provide the necessary vote authorizing a Cuban quarantine, "the Soviets and possibly others might have been emboldened to challenge the legality of our action, creating confusion and irresolution in the Western camp and giving rise to all kinds of cargo insurance and admiralty questions that this nation would not enjoy untangling" (*Decision-Making in the White House,* pp. 24–25).

world. There is no doubt that these preparations were carefully noted by Moscow, and we can probably take at face value Khrushchev's statement of December 12, 1962, that he took his decision to withdraw Soviet missiles from Cuba after receiving urgent word that a U.S. attack was imminent. These preparations must have persuaded him that he had to act quickly in order to limit his losses. Evidently Khrushchev was unwilling to gamble further on the possibility that the U.S. Government would ultimately stop short of direct military action, for losing such a gamble would have meant accepting far greater local losses, and perhaps even risking general war.[47]

Whether it was mainly conventional U.S. military superiority in the Caribbean area or overall U.S. strategic nuclear superiority that won the day — a hotly debated question in the aftermath of the crisis — does not strike this writer as a useful way to pose the problem. The United States possessed superiority of both types and brought both to bear in the crisis: the presence of one reinforced the effectiveness of the other. The *immediate* military threat confronting the Soviet leaders was, of course, that posed locally to Soviet forces in Cuba and to the Castro regime. But this threat was amplified by U.S. strategic superiority, which made credible the announced determination of the U.S. Government to employ force locally if other measures, such as the quarantine, proved inadequate, and to retaliate against the Soviet Union if Cuba-based weapons were launched against targets anywhere in the Western Hemisphere. Extraordinary alert measures taken by the Strategic Air Command, including such conspicuous ones as the dispersal of B-47's to auxiliary civilian airfields, underscored this determination. Manifest U.S. strategic superiority rendered Soviet strategic deterrence of a local U.S. attack on Cuba inoperable.

It may be true that even a strategic balance less favorable to the United States — say, one of acknowledged parity — would have been sufficient to support the policy implemented by the U.S. Government in October 1962; that is, the Soviet leaders would still have been unable to deter a U.S. attack on Cuba by credibly threatening strategic retaliation against the United States. But U.S. strategic superiority also made it too risky for the Soviet Union to play or, under the circumstances, even threaten to play the Berlin trump card.

47. In regard to the role played by the danger of general war in Khrushchev's decision to withdraw Soviet strategic weapons from Cuba, Secretary McNamara testified before a Subcommittee of the House Committee on Appropriations in February 1963: ". . . we had a force of several hundred thousand men ready to invade Cuba . . . had we invaded Cuba, we would have been confronted with the Soviets . . . had we been confronted with the Soviets we would have killed thousands of them . . . had we killed thousands of them the Soviets would probably have had to respond . . . they might have had nuclear delivery weapons there [that] might have been operational and they might have been launched . . . in any event, Khrushchev knew without any question whatever that he faced the full military power of the United States, including its nuclear weapons . . . we faced that night the possibility of launching nuclear weapons and Khrushchev knew it, and that is the reason, and the only reason, why he withdrew those weapons" (*Hearings,* p. 31).

While some Western observers feared that the Soviet Union might attempt to dissuade the United States from calling the Soviet hand in Cuba by threatening to retaliate in Berlin, the Soviet leaders apparently feared that a threatening Soviet move in that city, *particularly* in the midst of a crisis in the Caribbean, would be dangerously provocative. Emphasizing that the Cuban crisis "had brought the world one step, perhaps only half a step, from an abyss," Foreign Minister Gromyko told the Supreme Soviet in December 1962: "This [Cuban] crisis . . . made many people think how the whole matter might have developed if yet another crisis in Central Europe had been added to the critical events around Cuba."[48] Indeed, Soviet quiescence in Berlin during and immediately after the Cuban missile crisis demonstrates the severe limitations of even overwhelming local military superiority in the hands of a strategically inferior power when the issue at stake is of central, not peripheral, importance to the opponent.[49]

The role played by Berlin in the Cuban crisis during the fall of 1962 dramatizes the curious role that threats, expectations, fears and hopes regarding that city have played in the cold war since Khrushchev in November 1958 opened the long second round of the East-West struggle over the divided city. Much of Soviet foreign policy behavior since that time has been interpreted as maneuvering to secure a stronger position from which to impose on the West a Soviet-preferred solution of the Berlin "problem." Many regarded the Cuban missile deployment as designed chiefly to improve the Soviet bargaining position in the renewed crisis that was expected to be raised by the Russians after the U.S. elections in 1962. Since the Soviets appeared to be so intent on securing better leverage in Berlin, it would seem that they regarded it as too risky to proceed there without such leverage. Yet many who believed that Berlin was the real objective of the Soviet missile deployment also believed there was great danger that the Soviet leaders would retaliate in Berlin for any local defeat inflicted upon them in Cuba by the United States. The logic is strange: U.S. strategic superiority and the Western Allies' determination to preserve their rights in West Berlin made it too risky for the Soviets to employ their local military superiority in order to impose a settlement; yet the West must proceed with great caution elsewhere lest it provide the Soviet Union with a pretext for imposing its will in Berlin, or compel the Soviet leaders to do so, even against their better judgment, in order to "save face" for a defeat in some other part of the world.[50]

48. *Pravda,* December 14, 1962.

49. For an illuminating discussion of this point and its relevance for decisions regarding the extent to which NATO should rely on conventional weapons for the tactical defense of Europe, see Bernard Brodie, "What Price Conventional Capabilities in Europe?" *The Reporter,* May 23, 1963, pp. 25–33.

50. Walter Lippmann continued to argue after the crisis that "it would have been an incalculable risk to invade and occupy Cuba at the risk of retaliatory military action against Berlin, action which could have escalated into nuclear war." Yet the Soviet Union evidently yielded

However, the Soviet leaders have never needed pretexts for plucking ripe fruits from the vine. The foreseeable consequences of a Western defeat in Berlin provide more than enough incentive for the Soviet leaders to administer it if they think they can do so safely. Khrushchev's need to "save face" has, in this writer's opinion, been grossly exaggerated; in any case, the Cuban missile crisis was not the first occasion on which Khrushchev seemed to be in need of "face-saving." The four preceding years of bluster and retreat in Berlin had certainly been "humiliating" enough.

Hopefully, one lesson that both sides have learned from the Cuban experience is that, so long as the West maintains a favorable strategic balance, the Soviet Union cannot use West Berlin as a hostage to cover Soviet offensive moves and probes in other parts of the world against strong Western countermeasures. "Hostage Western Berlin" should not be confused with "Hostage Western Europe." The Soviet threat to strike Western Europe in the event of a U.S. attack on the Soviet Union is highly credible because the ultimate catastrophe to the USSR would have already occurred when the threat would have to be executed; but to retaliate in West Berlin for some lesser Western "provocation" might cause that very catastrophe to be brought down upon the Soviet Union when it could otherwise be avoided.

---

because its leaders found it highly credible that the United States would assume this "incalculable risk." According to Lippmann, "the United States prevailed in Cuba because, after nuclear power had been neutralized, it had powerful conventional weapons" ("Cuba and the Nuclear Risk," *The Atlantic*, February 1963, pp. 56, 58). But if U.S. nuclear power served no function other than to neutralize that of the Soviet Union, it is difficult to understand why preponderant Soviet conventional military power has not enabled the USSR to prevail in Berlin.

The Limitation of Strategic Arms*

The preliminary phase of the strategic-arms-limitation talks ("SALT") be-tween the U.S. and the USSR was conducted in a convivial atmosphere and with a refreshing lack of familiar rhetoric. The road ahead for the negotiations nonetheless remains a steep and slippery one. The fact that the talks were delayed for as long as they were by both sides is not an encouraging sign. The initial unwillingness of the Russian leadership to negotiate because of the American involvement in Vietnam and the subsequent unwillingness of the American leadership to negotiate because of the Russian intervention in Czechoslovakia both reflect a failure to perceive the extraordinary and possibly fleeting nature of the opportunity presented at this particular juncture in the arms race and a failure to recognize that the strategic-arms confrontation can and should be largely decoupled from other sources of conflict between the two superpowers. More recent delays, first by the U.S. and then by the USSR, reinforce the view that on both sides there has been a fundamental failure in the ordering of priorities — a failure to recognize that the dangers to national security associated with arms-control agreements can be far less than those inherent in the ongoing arms race.

As the substantive phase of the arms talks is about to begin, it is still not

*Reprinted from *Scientific American*, CCXXII, 1 (January, 1970), pp. 19 – 29, by permis-sion of the authors and the publisher. Copyright 1970 by Scientific American, Inc. All rights reserved.

obvious that policy-making circles of the two superpowers have consonant views about such basic questions as what objectives strategic forces serve, what relative roles offensive and defensive strategic forces play, and what the desired effects of limitations on such forces are. If it should develop that there is no agreement on these points, it may not be possible to negotiate any meaningful limitation on strategic forces.

This article is written in the hope that by stimulating discussion of these questions the differences between the two powers may become more clearly understood and in time narrowed. Even if the talks fail to produce significant agreement, a better grasp of the issues involved will be in the ultimate interest of everyone.

A number of recent developments make the prospects for successful negotiations seem to be more favorable now than they might have been some years ago. Advances in the strategic reconnaissance capabilities of the super-powers (chiefly in the area of surveillance by artificial satellites) are steadily reducing the need for intrusive inspection to establish the degree of compliance with possible future agreements. Thus the thorny issue of verification may be less of a barrier to agreed arms limitation than it has been in the past. In addition the rapid growth of Russian offensive-missile forces has effectively erased a disparity with the U.S. that existed in the past, thereby making an arms-limitation agreement a more realistic possibility. Finally, there is the growing popular realization — at least in the U.S. and presumably also in the USSR — that each side already has an enormous "overkill" capacity with respect to the other, and that further escalation in strategic-force levels would entail tremendous costs and new dangers at a time when both countries are confronted with a host of other pressing demands on their resources.

Although these developments would seem to favor successful negotiations, they are possibly outweighed by developments on the other side of the ledger. The most troublesome items are two emerging technical capabilities: multiple independently targeted reentry vehicles (MIRV's) and anti-ballistic-missile (ABM) defenses. It is frequently argued that the development and deployment of either (or particularly both) of these systems by one superpower could lead to a situation in which a decision to attempt a preemptive attack against the other's strategic forces might be considered rational. Indeed, some strategic planners contend that the threat is so great that offsetting actions must be started even before it is clear whether or not the adversary intends to acquire either a MIRV or an ABM capability. It is our belief that such arguments are largely fallacious and are made without real appreciation of the fact that a thermonuclear war between the superpowers, considering the vulnerability of the two societies, is a totally irrational policy choice. No combination of tactics and weapons, offensive and defensive, could provide either power with suffi-cient assurance that at least a small fraction of its adversary's weapons would

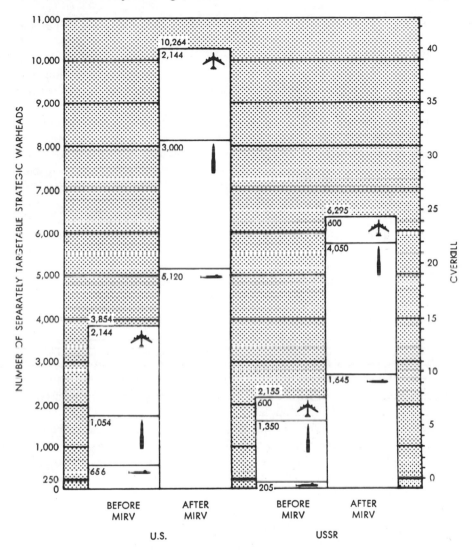

*Table 1. STRATEGIC BALANCE between the U.S. and the USSR is shown at left in
terms of the numbers of separately targetable strategic nuclear warheads already deployed and the numbers projected for 1975 if present plans to deploy
multiple independently targeted reentry vehicles (MIRV's) go into effect. The
symbols indicate the means of delivery; the numbers give the actual total of
deliverable warheads in each category. The scale at right suggests the enormous
"overkill" capacity possessed by each side in either circumstance; it is calibrated
in units of 250 — a highly conservative estimate of the number of nuclear
warheads required to devastate the 50 largest cities on each side. The chart
includes only strategic (that is, intercontinental) nuclear warheads, not tactical
or intermediate-range nuclear weapons.*

not be successfully delivered, thus inflicting in retaliation damage that would be clearly unacceptable.

We are confronted here, however, with a paradox that will haunt the rest of this discussion. Unilateral decisions regarding the development and procurement of strategic-weapons systems, and hence planning for arms-control negotiations, have been and will continue to be greatly influenced by a fundamentally simpleminded, although often exceedingly refined, form of military analysis. This approach, sometimes characterized as "worst-case analysis," invariably ascribes to one's adversary not only capabilities that one would not count on for one's own forces but also imputes to him a willingness to take risks that would seem insane if imputed to one's own political leadership. Thus the U.S. will react to Russian MIRV and ABM programs, and vice versa, whether or not national security demands it. Even if the reaction is totally irrational, it nonetheless becomes as much a part of reality as if the decision were genuinely required to preserve a stable strategic balance. We reluctantly accept the fact that in both the U.S. and the USSR policy will be influenced excessively by those military planners and their civilian allies who persist in behaving as if a thermonuclear war could be "won," and in asserting that responsible political leaders on the other side may initiate it on that assumption.

The development of a strategic nuclear capability by lesser powers, particularly China, seems also destined to complicate efforts to curtail the strategic-arms race between the superpowers. Here there are essentially two problems. First, what was said earlier about the unacceptability of nuclear war between the superpowers may be less applicable to conflicts between emerging nuclear powers, because their political leadership will be less knowledgeable about the effects of nuclear warfare and because the nuclear stockpiles involved will, at least initially, not be large enough to ensure the destruction of entire societies. Thus, with proliferation, the probability of thermonuclear war is likely to increase, and the superpowers will have a real basis for concern about their becoming involved. Second, a phenomenon not unlike the much discussed action-reaction effects of ABM defenses and MIRV's is likely to come into play. Nuclear proliferation may complicate Russian-American efforts to curtail the strategic-arms race even more than the objective facts warrant, as each superpower overreacts not only to the development of new centers of nuclear power but also to the other's reaction to them.

In fact, the rising threat of nuclear proliferation is already increasing the pressure in the U.S. (and probably in the USSR) to develop defenses that might be effective at least for a few years against emergent nuclear powers. The enthusiasts talk about neutralizing completely the effects of such developments; the realists propose measures aimed at reducing the damage that might be inflicted in the unlikely event of a nuclear attack by a smaller power. Unfortunately the capabilities that might prove effective, for instance an ABM system adequate to cope with first-generation Chinese missiles, would probably lead the other superpower to expand or qualitatively improve its strategic forces.

The other major considerations that will have a bearing on the prospects for SALT are domestic. As the failure of American policy in Southeast Asia and its implications become apparent, it seems likely that there will be a sharp reaction in an important segment of American society, with the polarization of attitudes proceeding even further than it has in the past year or two. It will be a difficult time for arms-control negotiations. Indeed, the strategic-arms-limitation talks are likely to be a divisive factor in the same way that the recent debate on the Safeguard ABM system was.

The situation in the USSR, although less clear, seems no more promising. The controversy between China and the USSR might lead one to expect that accommodation and cooperation with the West would be increasingly attractive to the Russian leadership. But that controversy, like the recent Russian difficulties in Eastern Europe, is also likely to be a factor in reinforcing the trend toward orthodoxy and conservatism within the USSR, which is hardly a favorable augury for an arms-control agreement.

Thus for SALT to be successful will require not only that the two governments be sincere in approaching the talks but also that they be prepared to display leadership and steadfastness of purpose in dealing with domestic opposition. On both sides there will have to be a rejection of many of the premises on which military policy has been at least partially based for two decades, for example the importance of "superiority" in strategic strength, the concept of "winning" a thermonuclear war, and the view that one can build meaningful defenses against a thermonuclear attack. The leadership in each nation will be confronted with arguments about the great risks inherent in various kinds of agreement — barely feasible (or at least not provably unfeasible) developments that might be taken advantage of by an adversary. Such arguments will undoubtedly resemble those to which the Kennedy Administration had to respond, when in connection with the nuclear test-ban treaty it was asserted that the USSR might conduct nuclear tests behind the moon or behind the sun to our great disadvantage. If agreement is to be reached, such arguments will have to be judged for what they are: nightmares of people who have focused so narrowly on such problems that they simply lack the perspective for weighing the risks of agreement against the risks implicit in continuing the arms race without any agreed constraints.

In the case of the U.S. the President will have a special problem and a formidable challenge, perhaps the greatest faced by any American leader since President Wilson's effort at the end of World War I to gain acceptance for his views regarding the Treaty of Versailles and the League of Nations. Although most Americans, including probably a majority of those who supported President Nixon in his campaign for the Presidency, would support him in his efforts to reach an arms-control agreement, almost certainly the conservative wing of the President's political supporters will counsel him to exercise extreme caution in approaching SALT. In so doing this latter group will give unwarranted weight to the technical and military risks that might be involved in any agreement under consideration. It is equally certain that the military will attempt to influence him with similar arguments, both through its direct channels and through its Congressional allies.

It is inconceivable that any meaningful agreement can be reached if the views of these groups should prevail. They need not, of course. Exercising broader judgment, the President can reject such advice and, as suggested above, draw on very substantial nationwide support for an agreement. Should he choose to do so, he will be in a better position to make his decision politically acceptable than would have been the case for any of his recent predecessors, or for that matter for his opponent in the last election. There is almost certainly a sizable segment of the American body politic that could accept a decision by President Nixon to conclude a very far-reaching agreement as a result of SALT that would not accept a similar position were it offered by, say, a liberal Democratic president.

President Nixon's prospects for such an achievement will be enhanced if the SALT negotiators make substantial progress in the next few months. With momentum established as a result of some limited agreement, and with the prospects of broader agreements before them, both the American and the Russian leadership might well make the judgment that it would be worthwhile to expend the political capital that might be required to effect broader agreements. If, on the other hand, the talks bog down in procedural discussions or in defense of obviously non-negotiable positions, the political leadership in both the U.S. and the USSR will be in a weakened position in dealing with those who are most skeptical and fearful of an agreement. Thus the importance of early limited agreement in connection with SALT cannot be overestimated.

In what areas might such limited agreement be immediately feasible? In order to answer this question we must first examine some of the technical realities of the present strategic balance. We believe that for the foreseeable future technological considerations will continue to make nuclear offensive forces dominant over nuclear defensive forces. In other words, we assert that, as has been the case since the initial deployment of thermonuclear weapons, it will be easier to destroy a technologically advanced society than to defend one. What can and should be done both in structuring strategic forces in the absence of agreement and in agreeing to limitations is critically dependent on whether or not this judgment is correct. There is some dispute about its correctness in the U.S. For example, some assert that with recent developments in ABM technology it may be possible to offset the effects of an incremental expenditure on offensive capabilities by a similar or even lesser expenditure on defenses. Nonetheless, we share the prevailing view that defense of population, at least against a determined adversary with comparable resources, is essentially hopeless.

To facilitate discussion we shall now define two terms that have come to be applied to strategic forces and to their uses. By "damage limitation" we mean the prevention of damage to industry and population in a nuclear war or the reduction of such damage to below the levels that might be expected without the use of certain damage-limiting measures or systems. Antiaircraft or ABM defenses of cities would be categorized as being damage-limiting systems. The use of civil defense measures such as population shelters or evacuation of threatened cities would be regarded as damage-limiting measures. So would be attempts to limit the adversary's ability to inflict damage by preemptively attacking any component of his offensive strategic forces. By "assured destruction" we mean the destruction with high confidence of the adversary's society. Measures to achieve such destruction, or systems that might be used for the purpose, would be characterized as assured-destruction measures or systems. They include the use of offensive missiles and bombers against civilian targets, as distinguished from strictly military targets.

With these definitions we recast our earlier statement about the relative roles of offensive and defensive strategic weapons to assert: *In the superpower confrontation any attempt to build significant damage-limiting capabilities can be offset by changes in the adversary's assured-destruction capabilities.* To take a specific example, attempts to limit and reduce the damage to American society by deploying ABM defenses (including appropriate civil defense measures) can be offset by qualitative and quantitative improvements in the adversary's offensive capabilities at a cost to him certainly no greater than the cost of the damage-limiting measures taken. What is more, we believe that by and large such responses will occur, in spite of the fact that realistic security considerations do not necessarily require a response. Even a very large-scale and technically sophisticated American ABM system could not be counted on to prevent totally unacceptable destruction in the U.S. by a Russian attack — even by an attack launched in retaliation after the Russian forces had already been preemptively struck. Such an American ABM system would in no way make our strategic forces more useful as political instruments, and hence no Russian response would really be required to preserve the effectiveness of the USSR's assured-destruction forces. Because of fear, conservatism, and uncertainty, however, it seems a foregone conclusion that a fully compensating buildup in Russian strength would follow.

There may, of course, be circumstances in which damage-limiting efforts will be effective. Each of the superpowers would temporarily be able to maintain a strategic posture that might greatly limit the damage to it in a conflict with a lesser nuclear power such as China. This will be particularly true if a preemptive, or "counterforce," attack against the lesser power's strategic nuclear forces is not excluded.

Moreover, if a nuclear exchange between the two superpowers should ever occur, parts of the strategic forces in being at that time probably would be used for active defense or in attacks on the strategic forces of the opponent. Thus they would be used in a damage-limiting role. Their effect would not be great, however, simply because the overkill capacity of each superpower's assured-destruction capabilities is so enormous. Both superpowers almost certainly now have the ability to destroy at least half of the adversary's population and three-quarters of his industrial capacity in spite of any damage-limiting measures that might be undertaken by the other. This situation has come about as a result of two factors. A strategic doctrine has developed, at least in the U.S., that has called for the maintenance of a very great assured-destruction capability under all conceivable circumstances. The doctrine has been one that could be easily implemented simply because thermonuclear weapons and strategic delivery systems are cheap in terms of the damage they can inflict on civilian targets.

This tremendous buildup of offensive forces means that the effectiveness of the last weapons used in destroying another society (in fact, the effectiveness of something like the last 90 percent of all weapons used) would be relatively small, since those already expended would have left so little to destroy. The amount of life and property saved by damage-limiting efforts would be dwarfed by the amount destroyed by weapons whose delivery could not be prevented.

We believe this situation will not change significantly in the near future. Any realistic approach to limitations on strategic armaments in the near future must almost certainly be in the context of the maintenance of very great assured-destruction capabilities. Agreements that would embody quite different strategic balances might result if any of several changes were to occur: technological breakthroughs that would lead to the dominance of the defense over the offense, the development of a high degree of trust between the U.S. and the USSR, the willingness of both nations to accept intrusive inspection, or an increased appreciation that strategic forces designed to inflict much lower damage levels would also serve effectively as a deterrent. We do not see any of these changes as short-term possibilities.

Because the assured-destruction, or damage-inflicting, capabilities of the two superpowers are so large and so varied, the present strategic balance is remarkably insensitive to either qualitative or quantitative changes in strategic forces. Even major changes in force levels, including the neutralization of entire systems (for example all bomber aircraft), would not be likely to have major effects on the damage levels one would expect each of the superpowers to suffer in a nuclear war. Worldwide radioactive fallout might be reduced significantly, but as far as the superpowers are concerned, cross-targeting with other systems would ensure that all major population and industrial centers would continue to be in jeopardy. When considered in the framework of the virtually certain collapse of an entire society, changes of a few percent in

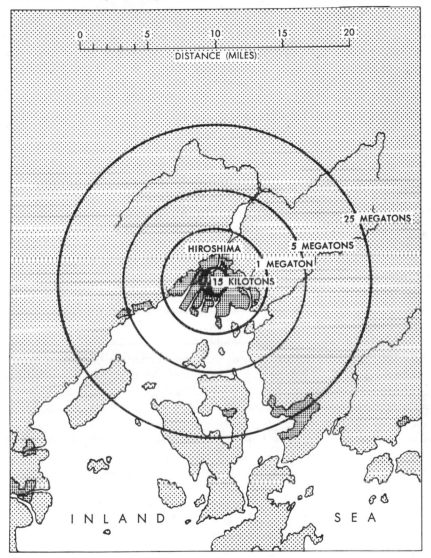

*Table 2. RELATIVE DESTRUCTIVENESS of several currently deployed thermonu-
clear weapons is illustrated here in relation to the damage caused by the nuclear
bomb that was exploded over Hiroshima on May 8, 1945. The circles super-
posed on the map denote each weapon's "lethal area": the area within which
the number of survivors equals the number of fatalities outside the circle. For
a perfectly uniform population distribution the lethal area times the population
density gives the total number of people killed in the explosion. At present most
of the strategic warheads deployed by the U.S. and the USSR are in the
megaton range or larger. Even after MIRVing all the strategic warheads on
both sides will exceed the estimated 15-kiloton explosive yield of the Hiroshima
bomb.*

fatalities, which is all one might expect with foreseeable changes in strategic-force levels, are not likely to affect political decisions. Although it may have been correct some years ago to characterize the balance of terror as a "delicate" one, it is not so today, nor is it likely to be so in the foreseeable future. It will not be easily upset. Opponents of the Safeguard ABM decision have argued with some effect (although obviously not with complete success) that the U.S. deterrent was most unlikely to be in jeopardy at any time in the near future simply because of its diversity and because of the improbability of the USSR's being able to develop damage-limiting capabilities and tactics that would effectively neutralize all the deterrent's components.

We have argued so far that one general premise on whose acceptance a successful SALT outcome depends is that the offense will continue to dominate the defense for the foreseeable future. A second technical generalization that may be equally important is: *The uncertainty about the effectiveness of damage-limiting capabilities will be considerably greater than about assured-destruction capabilities.* This statement can be supported by a number of arguments. First, the characteristics of the target against which assured-destruction capabilities would be used (population and industry) will be known with some precision and will change only slowly with time. On the other hand, the characteristics of the systems (and the environment) against which damage-limiting capabilities must operate (adversary's warheads, delivery vehicles, and launch facilities) will be generally less well known and more susceptible to rapid variation, both in quality and in number, at the option of the adversary. Second, some of the damage-limiting systems (such as ABM defenses, antiaircraft defenses, and under some circumstances antisubmarine warfare, or ASW, systems) must function at the time chosen by the adversary for his offensive, whereas for assured destruction there is a much bigger "time window" during which performance will be acceptable. The effectiveness of submarine-launched missiles in destroying cities will not depend much on the instant of launch. Third, damage limitation generally will involve the use of more intimately coupled systems (for example the radars, computers, and missiles of an ABM system), inviting the possibility of "catastrophic" technical failures. All these factors tend to make the advance estimates of the effectiveness of assured-destruction systems far more reliable than estimates of damage-limiting systems.

The inherent uncertainty in effectiveness that characterizes the performance of damage-limiting systems has been of profound importance in the Russian-American strategic-arms race. Each side has reacted to the development, or even the possible development, by the other of damage-limiting capabilities by greatly strengthening its offensive forces — to the point of overreaction because of the conservative assumption that the adversary's damage-limiting forces will be far more effective than they are in fact likely to be. For example, the uncertainty about the possible deployment and effectiveness of a large-scale Russian ABM defense has provided the primary rationale for the U.S. decision

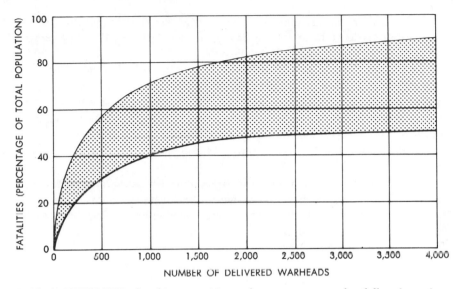

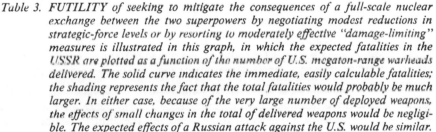

Table 3. FUTILITY *of seeking to mitigate the consequences of a full-scale nuclear exchange between the two superpowers by negotiating modest reductions in strategic-force levels or by resorting to moderately effective "damage-limiting" measures is illustrated in this graph, in which the expected fatalities in the USSR are plotted as a function of the number of U.S. megaton-range warheads delivered. The solid curve indicates the immediate, easily calculable fatalities; the shading represents the fact that the total fatalities would probably be much larger. In either case, because of the very large number of deployed weapons, the effects of small changes in the total of delivered weapons would be negligible. The expected effects of a Russian attack against the U.S. would be similar.*

to introduce MIRV's into both land-based and sea-based missile forces, the net effect being a severalfold increase in the number of warheads these forces will be able to deliver. Barring unforeseeable technical developments, we must expect that the great uncertainty that characterizes the performance of damage-limiting systems will continue, and we must base our approach to SALT on that assumption.

If one accepts the judgments we have made about the relative effectiveness of defense and offense, about the insensitivity of assured-destruction capability to changes in force levels and about the uncertainty that characterizes damage-limiting efforts, one is led to some possibly useful generalizations about the forthcoming substantive phase of SALT.

First, the level of damage that each of the superpowers can inflict on the other is not likely to be altered significantly in the near future. Measures that might possibly be agreed on could change the level of damage that each side could inflict on the other by at most a few percent. Therefore the problem of the reduction in damage in the event of war should probably be given low priority as a short-term negotiation objective. More realistic objectives of the negotiations could be to lower the level of tension between the superpowers and so reduce the probability of nuclear war.

Second, apart from possible worldwide fallout effects and domestic political considerations, neither side need be much concerned about the possibility of modest, or even substantial, expansions in the strategic offensive forces of the other side, nor about precise limitations on those forces, as long as the other side does not have a damage-limiting capability. Because of the large overkill capacities discussed above, even large increases in strategic forces will have little military effect.

Third, measures to constrain the introduction or improvement of damage-limiting systems, particularly those whose performance is expected to be highly uncertain, merit high priority. The introduction or improvement of damage-limiting capabilities by either side is likely to result, as we have noted, in an excessive reaction by the other. Because of the insensitivity of the strategic balance to modest changes in force levels, a move toward the development of a narrowly circumscribed damage-limiting capability by one side could in principle be tolerated without undue concern by the other. Such a move might be perceived, however, as an indicator of the adversary's intent to develop an across-the-board damage-limiting capability. (Witness Secretary of Defense Laird's public reaction to a possible Soviet SS-9 MIRV capability.) This, coupled with the fact that a development of damage-limiting capabilities can be offset rather quickly and cheaply, virtually ensures a reaction. The overall effect of such an action-reaction cycle on the ability of each side to inflict damage on the other is likely to be small, but the expenditures of both sides on strategic armaments are likely to be much increased, as will be the tensions between them.

Fourth, owing to the large uncertainty that characterizes the effectiveness of damage-limiting systems and tactics, the two superpowers will face a very troublesome dilemma if, on the one hand, they try to develop effective damage-limiting capabilities with respect to emerging nuclear powers and, on the other, they attempt to limit the strategic-arms race between themselves. With a few exceptions, such as a deployment of Russian intermediate-range ballistic missiles (IRBM's) in Siberia, the measures that could have long-term effectiveness against a third country's nuclear strength would appear to the other superpower to foreshadow an erosion in its own assured-destruction, or deterrent, capability. This creates an authentic problem of conflicting desires. We would hope that in efforts to deal with this problem the usefulness of damage-limiting capabilities with respect to the lesser nuclear powers would not be overrated. Although such damage-limiting capabilities probably would be effective in reducing damage in the event that a lesser power attempted a nuclear attack against one of the superpowers, we question whether either superpower would ever be willing to take action against a lesser power on the assumption that damage-limiting efforts would be 100 percent effective, that is, on the assumption that "damage denial" with respect to a lesser power could be achieved. Considering one's inability to have high confidence in the effectiveness of damage-limiting measures, and considering the effects of even a single thermonuclear weapon on a large American or Russian city, we doubt that efforts to develop damage-limiting capabilities with respect to the smaller powers would materially increase the options the superpowers would have available for dealing with these powers.

With this background in mind one would be in a good position to evaluate the relative desirability of limiting various strategic systems if each were unambiguously useful only for damage limitation or assured destruction. Unfortunately many existing or prospective strategic systems may play several roles, a factor that greatly complicates the problem.

Of all the ambiguous developments now under way none is more troublesome than MIRV. The development of a MIRV capability may facilitate the maintenance of an assured-destruction capability by providing high assurance that ABM defenses of industry and population can be penetrated. Given sufficient accuracy, reliability and yield, however, MIRV's may also make it possible for a small number of missiles to destroy a larger number of fixed offensive facilities, even if they are "hardened" against the effects of nuclear weapons.

Although the effectiveness of a given missile force in a damage-limiting preemptive attack against an adversary's intercontinental ballistic missile (ICBM) force might be much increased through the use of such MIRV's, it does not necessarily follow that the deployment of the MIRV's would make such a strike more likely. As we have noted, in the context of a confrontation between superpowers such an attack would surely be irrational, no matter how severe the crisis, simply because no responsible political leader could ever have high confidence in the effectiveness of the attack and in the effectiveness of the other damage-limiting measures that would be required to keep the damage from a retaliatory response down to acceptable levels. Although MIRV's are not likely to have much actual effect on the willingness or ability of nations to use strategic nuclear forces to attain political objectives, we must accept the fact that arms policies will, to a substantial degree, be based on the assumption that they might be so used.

Beyond that, there is the problem of the impact of MIRV's on events if a crisis should ever escalate to the point where limited numbers of nuclear weapons will have been employed by the superpowers against each other. At some point in the process of escalation it is likely that one or both powers would initiate counterforce attacks against the other's remaining offensive forces. Such an attack would probably come earlier if one or both sides had counterforce-effective MIRV's than if neither did.

Because of what we regard as unwarranted, but nevertheless real, concern about MIRV's being used in a preemptive counterforce attack, and because of more legitimate concern that once a thermonuclear exchange has begun

MIRV's may make further escalation more likely, MIRV development may well have a critical impact on the outcome of SALT, and for that matter on the force levels of the two sides independent of the talks. It is generally, although not universally, accepted that the tests of MIRV's have not yet gone far enough for one to have confidence that their reliability and accuracy would be sufficient to assure their effectiveness in a counterforce role against hardened ICBM's. On the other hand, the MIRV principle is now demonstrated, and the expectation is common that with perhaps the second generation of such systems, if not with the first, MIRV's will be effective as counterforce weapons.

If no constraints are put on the development of MIRV's, it is likely that each superpower will go ahead with such development and (in the case of the U.S. at least) an early deployment program. This will be regarded as particularly urgent if ABM deployment continues, or even if there continues to be evidence of significant research and development that might later lead to ABM deployment. Assuming that MIRV programs do continue, each superpower will perceive in the other's deployment a possible threat to its fixed-base ICBM's and will react to counter that threat. The U.S. has already begun to do so in deciding to go ahead with an active ABM defense of Minuteman sites: the Safeguard program. Acceleration in the USSR's missile-launching submarine program and a possible mobile-ICBM program are plausible reactions to the U.S. MIRV programs.

We anticipate that in the absence of agreements the technological race will go much further. It seems likely that the arguments to "do something" about the vulnerability of fixed ICBM's will increase in tempo and will carry the day in both the U.S. and the USSR. Super-hardening alone will be perceived to be a losing game, considering how easily any moves in that direction could be offset by further improvements in missile accuracy. A defense of the Safeguard type will probably also be judged to be a losing proposition. A very heavy defense with components specifically optimized for the defense of hardened ICBM's might be one response. There is likely to be even further reliance on mobile systems: missile-launching submarines, new strategic bombers, and, in the case of the USSR, probably mobile ICBM's. It is conceivable that fixed ICBM's may be given up altogether, although the arguments we have advanced against the acceptability of attacking them preemptively would still be valid.

It is also likely in the absence of agreements that one or the other of the superpowers will deploy ABM systems that will provide more extensive and effective defense of population and industry than either the present Russian defenses around Moscow or the projected Phase II of Safeguard. Defense against a Chinese missile capability may be the rationale, but it is to be expected that the other superpower will respond to any such deployment both by emulation and by increasing its strategic offensive capabilities.

Whereas the strategic-forces budget of the U.S. now amounts to about $9 billion per year (excluding some rather large items for nuclear warheads, research and development, command and control, communications, and intelligence activities), outlays for strategic systems could well double by the mid-1970's. Continuing large expenditures on strategic systems are probably also to be expected in the USSR.

As we have stated, there appears to be no basis for expecting SALT to lead to significant reductions in the assured-destruction capabilities of the superpowers. Therefore other objectives must command our attention. The most important objective is, of course, to reduce the probability that a thermonuclear exchange will ever take place.

The major factors affecting that probability are likely not to be simply technical but to be largely political. They involve the degree of tension that will exist between the superpowers based on international political considerations, on domestic politics in each country and in an important sense on the strategic-arms race itself. We believe that in contrast to some previous eras, when the motivations for continuing arms races were largely political and economic conflicts, the strategic-arms race now has a life of its own. For instance, the strategic-weapons programs of each superpower are more dependent on the programs of the other than on the levels of tension between the two countries. If this race can be attenuated, it would have a number of effects that would result in a diminution of tensions and hence in a reduction in the risk of war. That is perhaps the major reason for the urgency of a serious SALT effort. Keeping budgets for strategic forces at low levels is desirable in its own right in that significant resources, both financial and intellectual, will be freed for more constructive purposes. More important, in the U.S. lower military budgets will diminish the role of what President Eisenhower termed the military-industrial complex: those who have a propensity for, and in some cases obviously a vested interest in, the acquisition of more armaments and in exciting and maintaining an often unwarranted attitude of alarm and suspicion regarding an adversary's intentions. Lower military budgets in the USSR would almost certainly have a similar desirable effect.

A poorly designed agreement could, of course, prove to be a vehicle for increasing suspicion and tension. Venturing into the realm of unprovable value-judgments, however, we assert that it is not beyond the wit of man to design agreements that would result in there being less objective cause for concern than if the strategic-arms race continues unabated. In general, it would seem that any understanding that slowed the rate of development and change of strategic systems would have an effect in the right direction.

Beyond affecting the probability of a nuclear exchange's beginning, one would like to see strategic forces structured so that there would be at least some possibility that, if an exchange started, it would not have to run its course. A necessary but, of course, not sufficient condition for this is that there be no particular advantage to be gained from precipitate launch of more nuclear

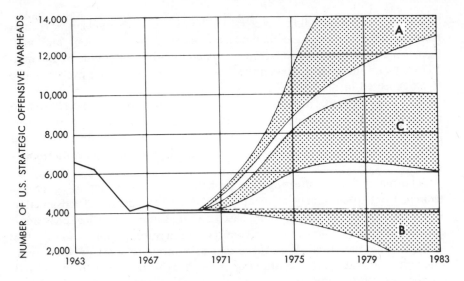

Tables 4 and 5.   **PROJECTED EFFECTS** *associated with three possible outcomes of the strategic-arms-limitation talks are expressed in the graphs on these two pages in terms of the number of U.S. strategic offensive warheads (left) and the U.S. budget for strategic forces (right). With no agreement (A) the number of weapons and the strategic-forces budget are likely to grow with no obvious limit. A SALT agreement that included a prohibition on the development and deployment of MIRV's (B) could lead to stability in strategic forces and a reduction in the budget to a level required to maintain them. With an agreement that did not constrain MIRV's (C) there would certainly be an increase in the strategic-forces budget for a few years as the composition of these forces changed, probably accompanied by the replacement of some fixed-base offensive missiles by mobile systems (either land-based or sea-based) or possibly by "super-hardening"*

weapons after a few have been dispatched. By this criterion vulnerable ICBM's would seem to be the quintessence of undesirability. If both sides have them, each will recognize that if they are withheld, they may be destroyed.

Whether or not MIRV development and deployment will be controlled may not be a question for the SALT negotiators to consider, because of the inability of one side or the other to decide in a timely fashion the position it wishes to take on the issue. The rate of MIRV development is so rapid that the question may thus be settled before the substantive phase of the talks is well advanced. If such development is still in doubt, however, either because the talks get to such substantive issues very quickly or because of a moratorium on MIRV testing, MIRV limitation should be an issue of the highest priority.

The arguments for preventing deployment of MIRV's advanced enough to be effective counterforce weapons are persuasive. They have been made at great length elsewhere (for example in public hearings before committees of

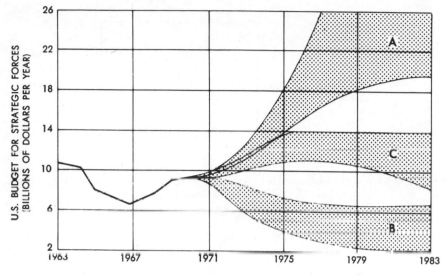

and heavy specialized ABM defense of missile sites. Assuming under case C that a large-scale ABM defense of population is prohibited, there would be little military rationale for either side to acquire large additional numbers of offensive warheads. Nonetheless, the numbers might increase significantly with the implementation of present plans to deploy MIRV's. Future Russian strategic-forces levels would probably display similar trends, but budget projections would differ somewhat. The Russian budget for strategic weapons is possibly at an unprecedentedly high level now, considering the present rapid rate of growth in their strategic systems. Thus in case B the drop in the strategic-forces budget for the USSR might be sharper than for the U.S., and in the two other cases there would be a less pronounced increase. Estimates are in constant-value 1969 dollars.

the Senate and the House of Representatives). We simply summarize here by pointing out that if MIRV deployment is prevented, it may be possible to freeze the strategic balance at something approximating its present level. Most of the incentive to defend hardened ICBM's or to replace them with mobile systems will have been reduced, if not eliminated.

The arguments for continuing MIRV testing and then deployment because MIRV's may someday be required to penetrate an adversary's ABM defenses are not convincing. There is little doubt that currently designed U.S. MIRV's could be deployed on a time scale short compared with that required for deployment of any significant Russian ABM defenses. Accordingly there is no need for any MIRV deployment pending firm evidence that the USSR is beginning the construction of such defenses. And there is no need for further research and development tests unless a counterforce capability is intended.

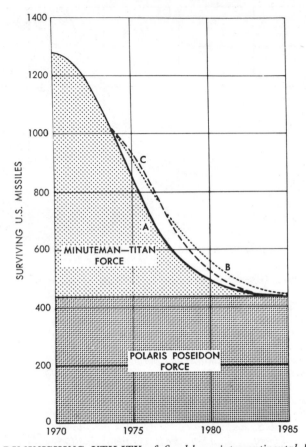

Table 6. DIMINISHING UTILITY of fixed-base intercontinental ballistic missiles (ICBM's) as a component of the U.S. "assured-destruction" forces would result from further development and deployment of MIRV's, even in the event of a SALT agreement that freezes the number of missiles on both sides. In preparing this graph we assumed that in a preemptive, or counterforce, strike against the U.S. the USSR would target its SS-9 missile force (estimated to be frozen at 280 missiles) at the U.S. Minuteman-Titan force. The numbers of surviving U.S. ICBM's are based on the assumption that each SS-9 will carry one 25-megaton warhead in 1970, three five-megaton warheads in 1975, nine 500-kiloton warheads in 1980, and 25 50-kiloton warheads in 1985; delivery accuracies are assumed to improve by a factor of two every five years. Curve A assumes that no additional measures are taken to protect the already "hardened" U.S. ICBM force. Curve B assumes that the blast resistance of the ICBM sites is improved by "superhardening" so that by 1972 they can withstand three times the overpressure sustainable in 1970. Curve C assumes full operational capability (and a generous estimate of performance) of the Safeguard ABM system by 1978. It is apparent that neither super-hardening nor active defense (unless many times more effective than Safeguard) is likely to extend the period of invulnerability for U.S. ICBM's by very much. (The number of surviving submarine-launched missiles is based on the assumption that a third of the Polaris-Poseidon force is destroyed in part by the Russian preemptive attack.)

For similar reasons the USSR should also abstain from further multiple-warhead tests and deployment, which it can do at no great risk to its security.

Essential to the survival of an agreement not to test MIRV's would be a prohibition of large-scale ABM deployment. If ABM systems were deployed, the pressures to deploy MIRV's and to test them frequently in order to maintain confidence in their reliability would be overwhelming. Furthermore, there would undoubtedly be great domestic pressure to develop and test more sophisticated penetration aids. Under such circumstances neither side could have any confidence that the other was not developing counterforce-effective MIRV's. An ABM freeze would be a logically required companion measure to any agreement prohibiting MIRV's.

Assuming that ABM deployment and MIRV testing are both frozen, the other important component of a strategic-arms-limitation agreement would be an understanding to maintain something like parity in ICBM-force levels by freezing these levels or preferably reducing them, and if necessary permitting replacement of fixed-base ICBM's by mobile systems whose levels could be verified by unilateral means. In the absence of such a measure there would be the possibility of one side's gaining such a superiority in missle strength that, with improved accuracies and even without MIRV's, would enable it to knock out a large fraction of its adversary's forces by delivering a counterforce attack against them. The reasons for concern about such a possibility have been identified above: the probability of arms-race escalation and the reduction in whatever small chance there may be of a nuclear exchange's being terminated short of running its suicidal course.

If the development of MIRV's that are perceived by the adversary to have counterforce capability cannot be prevented (and we are pessimistic about preventing it), the relative importance of some of the measures discussed above will be changed materially. A prohibition on large-scale ABM deployment would still be desirable, but it would be less important; it would not in this case prevent the MIRV genie from escaping the bottle. Moreover, continuing development and deployment of MIRV's would make a large-scale ABM defense unattractive simply on cost-effectiveness grounds.

A provision permitting the replacement of fixed ICBM's by mobile systems would seem virtually unavoidable because of concern about the vulnerability of the ICBM's to counterforce attack. Indeed, in the interest of stabilizing arms at low levels, and to minimize concern about damage-limiting strikes, agreements could probably include measures that would enhance the viability of mobile systems. An area of agreement that would seem to merit most serious consideration would be prohibition on certain improvements in antisubmarine-warfare capabilities. Actually the possibility of breakthoughs in antisubmarine warfare is extremely remote. It is probable that through noise reduction, extension of missile range, and other techniques the gap between ASW capability and the capability of the missile-launching submarine to escape detection and destruction will widen rather than narrow. Yet it seems likely from recent debate in the U.S. that the present American leadership, and presumably the leadership of the USSR as well, would be reluctant to rely solely on a missile-launching submarine force for deterrence, given the possibility of further ASW development by its adversary. Constraints on ASW such as a limitation on the number of hunter-killer submarines would increase the acceptability to both sides of relying more heavily on missile-launching submarines for deterrence.

Similar arguments might be made for limitations on or curtailment of air defense. Such moves would seem less realistic on three counts. First, compliance with limitation on air-defense capabilities could probably not be verified with unilateral procedures as well as could limitations on ASW systems, or for that matter on ABM systems. Intelligence on short-range antiaircraft systems is likely to be poorer than on hunter-killer submarines, specialized ASW aircraft or large-sized components of ABM systems. Second, the overlap between tactical and strategic antiaircraft capabilities is considerable, and neither superpower is likely to be willing to greatly reduce tactical antiaircraft capabilities in the context of SALT. ASW capabilities (except for destroyers) would, on the other hand, have little role other than attack against an adversary's missile-launching submarines. This is far truer now than it was a few years ago because the realization is more widespread that a major war involving large antishipping campaigns is extremely unlikely. Third, neither the U.S. nor the USSR is likely to have enough confidence in bombers to rely much on them in a missile age even if air defenses are constrained, whereas both superpowers obviously are prepared to rely heavily on submarine-launched missiles.

Finally, if counterforce-effective MIRV's were a reality, and if as a consequence both sides were to place reliance very largely on mobile systems, additional offensive weapons on one side could not be used effectively to limit the other side's ability to retaliate. Considering this fact and the fact that since strategic-force levels are already at least an order of magnitude larger than is rationally required for deterrence, there would be little incentive for either side to acquire additional offensive capabilities. Also in this situation it would hardly matter if either side were to introduce new assured-destruction systems such as, for example, small mobile ICBM's that could not be easily counted.

Even this incomplete discussion shows that the strategic balance between the superpowers is likely to be very different depending on whether or not MIRV development and ABM deployment are allowed to continue. Both possibilities will have a serious impact on future strategic postures, but with respect to ABM deployment nothing much is going to happen overnight. Dealing with the issue of MIRV development, although perhaps no more important, is far more urgent. That is why it is the watershed issue for SALT. If counterforce-effective MIRV's (and large-scale ABM deployment) can be stopped, the present strategic balance of force levels may endure for some time. If such MIRV's are deployed, the balance will unavoidably change in qualitative ways. How large an escalation in the arms race will result will depend on whether agreement to constrain or cut back other strategic systems could still be negotiated.

We have attempted here to present an objective analysis of the prospects for various agreements to limit strategic armaments. In so doing we are aware that many of our readers will be dismayed that our discussion has been in the context of each superpower's preserving the capability of destroying the other. This has been so not because we ourselves favor the continuing retention of huge stocks of thermonuclear weapons but because we have tried to be realistic. The distrust that exists between the U.S. and the USSR will induce both to preserve the capability of destroying the other; such a capability, as we have noted, is unfortunately easier to attain than an effective defense of one's own society, whether or not there are agreements on strategic armaments. Both superpowers will preserve this capability because they see it as the only effective deterrent to the war that neither wants or could win.

The most that can reasonably be expected of the forthcoming talks is a move toward a strategic balance where (1) uncertainties about the adversary are reduced and with them some of the tensions; (2) each side can inflict a level of damage on the other sufficient to destroy its society but neither feels a need to maintain a great overkill capability as a hedge against possible damage-limiting efforts by the other; (3) there will be an improved chance that a thermonuclear exchange, should one begin, would be terminated short of running its course; and (4) the levels of expenditure on strategic armaments are lower, so that larger fractions of the resources available to each society can be used for more constructive endeavors.

We believe that the realization of these objectives would be a tremendous accomplishment and one that is possible without the solution of the deep-seated political problems of the Russian-American confrontation. To go further will require dealing with those problems. We do not believe, however, that the superpowers can afford to delay attacking the strategic-arms race while trying to solve political differences. Regrettably the situation with respect to technical developments (MIRV's, ABM defenses, and nuclear proliferation), and quite possibly with respect to domestic politics as well, will probably make strategic-arms limitation negotiations less likely to be successful several years hence than now. Time is of the essence, and we write with a feeling of urgency. Although our tone is pessimistic, we do not despair. We are convinced that latent public support for an agreement could be exploited by effective political leadership on both sides to reverse the trends we have lived with for two decades.

PART VI

The Third World and Soviet Foreign Policy

Soviet policy toward the Third World has been one of "constant reassessment and revision" since the death of Stalin, Professor Kanet concludes. Momentous changes were initiated by Khrushchev between 1954 and 1956, the first years of rapprochement with the neutral developing nations (see Pendill, Chapter 5 above). Flexibility in Soviet policy was further encouraged and legitimized in the early 1960's by doctrinal pronouncements concerning "the new, third stage of capitalism's general crisis." These innovative assertions by Khrushchev and others clearly implied that Lenin's *Imperialism* was no longer directly relevant to contemporary international conditions. Thus, Soviet foreign policy-makers and analysts were tacitly encouraged to avoid excessive reliance on Leninist assumptions and categories of analysis. This "collapse of general theory," as it has been called,[1] may have significantly affected Soviet perspectives on the countries of the Third World. For in contemporary Soviet research on developing areas, "the trend is away from the deductive assignment of definite political behavior to 'peasants,' 'workers,' and 'national' and 'compradore' bourgeoisie and toward detailed studies of the actual social composition of a country or of a social stratum peculiar to the third world."[2]

Stalin, it has been suggested, would probably have regarded Soviet eco-

1. See William Zimmerman, *Soviet Perspectives on International Relations, 1956–1967* (Princeton: Princeton University Press, 1969), pp. 131–157, 259.
2. Elizabeth Kridl Valkenier, "Recent Trends in Soviet Research on the Developing Coun-

nomic and military aid to developing non-Communist countries as "ideologically unsound and counterrevolutionary."[3] At the heart of the Stalinist "two-camp" view of the world was the idea that "he who is not with us is against us." To have considered all nonsocialist countries "capitalist" may seem ludicrous in retrospect. But the fact remains that this idea reflected official Soviet thinking and, to a large extent, actual Soviet behavior until 1954 – 1955. "Drift and indecision . . . characterize Soviet Eastern policy during most of Stalin's rule," Professor McLane concludes.[4] Sporadic efforts were made to support local Communist parties, subvert established governments, and support or subvert "bourgeois" national liberation movements (e.g., the Kuomintang). Not until the mid-1950's, however, did the USSR launch a sustained campaign to increase its contacts with and influence over established Third World governments. Despite a persistent doctrinal interest in developing countries, Lenin and Stalin assigned a low priority to Soviet activities there. McLane observes that "Soviet efforts in the colonies, despite repeated reminders to the international movement that more vigorous activity was needed there, were on the whole parsimonious . . . and one might well ask what purpose a *doctrinal* interest in the East served if so little thought was given to an *operational* program supporting it." Somehow, Third World Communism survived Moscow's neglect.[5]

Let us briefly examine the "reassessment and revision" of Soviet policy since Stalin's death. In most general terms, the USSR has sought to increase its influence over Third World nations and regions, and to reduce the influence of Western nations and of Communist China. In pursuit of these goals, the Soviet Union has utilized economic, military, ideological, and diplomatic means.[6] Increasingly, the USSR has provided economic and military assistance to selected non-Communist countries regardless of their social structure, treatment of local Communists, or economic and even military ties with the West. Furthermore, Soviet policy has been periodically revised in light of changing international developments and the results of previous policies, foreign and domestic. In the early 1960's, for example, Soviet activities in the Third World were significantly affected by the USSR's domestic economic problems, the Sino-Soviet dispute, and the Soviet Presidium's increasing awareness that "a developing country's 'progressive' political orientation was not by itself a suitable yardstick for choosing it as a recipient of aid."[7]

tries," *World Politics,* XX, 4 (July, 1968), p. 656.

    3. Wynfred Joshua and Stephen Gibert, *Arms for the Third World: Soviet Military Aid Diplomacy* (Baltimore: The Johns Hopkins Press, 1969), p. 1.

    4. See Charles McLane, *Soviet Strategies in Southeast Asia: An Exploration of Eastern Policy under Lenin and Stalin* (Princeton: Princeton University Press, 1966), p. 480.

    5. *Ibid.,* pp. 248, 479 – 480.

    6. See Michael Gehlen, *The Politics of Coexistence* (Bloomington: Indiana University Press, 1967).

    7. R. A. Yellon, "Shifts in Soviet Policies towards Developing Areas 1964 – 1968," in W.

In response to these and other factors, Soviet decision-makers reevaluated and rearranged policy priorities. Between 1961 and 1963, the USSR's increasingly scarce economic resources were used to meet domestic economic needs rather than to expand foreign aid commitments. In the following years, substantial foreign assistance was again forthcoming, and many new projects were funded. But more and more Soviet assistance was proffered to "moderate" and "conservative" Third World countries which had the capacity effectively to absorb and utilize this aid, and thus indirectly to assist in the Soviet military, economic, and ideological "containment" of Communist China. Ties with Turkey, Iran, Afghanistan, Pakistan, and India were considerably broadened, whereas aid to other Asian, African, Middle Eastern, and Latin American countries, "revolutionary" or not, was highly selective.[8]

Elizabeth Valkenier, in her article below, carefully examines the economic aspects of Soviet policy. She notes a recent tendency to link "the allocation of aid with the expansion of trade." An increasing number of Soviet officials seem to view foreign aid as "an alternative to domestic investment," and they argue that "it would be cheaper for the USSR to import certain goods and materials than to produce them at home, as well as to have the East European states replace some of the raw materials they obtained from the Soviet Union by imports from Africa or Asia." Consequently, Soviet efforts to develop profitable relations with Third World countries involve "a certain amount of economic integration, based on coordinating relevant aspects of the Soviet plan with those of the recipient," especially in the extraction and joint production of raw materials. Significantly, new Soviet thinking on development economics (for example, the role of planning, private enterprise, Western capital) seems to be increasingly reflected in Soviet policy and behavior. Valkenier concludes that economic cooperation may well provide a durable source of Soviet influence in developing countries.[9]

Military aid is another important instrument of Soviet policy in the Third World. Since almost all Soviet military assistance must be repaid with interest over long periods of time, it is technically more accurate to speak of "military loans" than "military aid."[10] By conducting arms diplomacy with developing nations, the USSR is again attempting to increase its influence relative to that of major Western, unaligned, and other Communist powers. Decisions to

Raymond Duncan (ed.), *Soviet Policy in Developing Countries* (Waltham, Mass.: Ginn-Blaisdell, 1970), p. 242. See also pp. 242–246 ff.

8. See Yellon, *op. cit.,* pp. 242–286 ff. Also see the six-fold typology of Third World states presented in Kanet's essay below.

9. See also Valkenier, *op. cit.,* pp. 644–659; Charles Wilber, *The Soviet Model and Underdeveloped Countries* (Chapel Hill: University of North Carolina Press, 1969); Marshall Goldman, *Soviet Foreign Aid* (New York: Praeger, 1967); Joseph Berliner, *Soviet Economic Aid* (New York: Praeger, 1958).

10. Joshua and Gibert, *op. cit.,* p. 6. See also Uri Ra'anan, *The USSR Arms the Third World* (Cambridge, Mass.: MIT Press, 1969).

supply arms to specific governments have probably been based on careful calculations concerning Soviet strategic and economic interests, the probable willingness of the recipient to use the arms only when Soviet leaders consider it in the USSR's interest to do so, the likely political impact of the assistance on the recipient country and its region, and the technological capability of the recipient to utilize this aid. The present Soviet leaders are surely under no illusions that military assistance can be easily transformed into political influence, or that the aims of the recipient country are identical with or even similar to those of the Soviet Union. For example, CPSU leaders have been particularly cautious about providing military support for "wars of national liberation." A recent study concludes that although the Soviet Union "proclaims its support in theory for all wars of liberation, in practice each individual case is judged on its own merits. . . . The dangers of war escalation . . . are of prime concern. The USSR is careful not to contribute toward escalating conflicts and is not apt to embark on reckless adventures."[11]

The impact of Soviet economic and military aid is exceedingly difficult to measure. But the important fact remains that Soviet influence in the Third World has significantly increased over the past two decades, and it is probably greater now than ever before. In the 1950's, the leaders of many developing countries feared Soviet military, economic, and ideological penetration, and they felt dependent on United States' military and economic assistance to preserve their country's newfound independence and/or their own positions. In the 1960's, however, fear of the Soviet Union considerably diminished, and resentment of American economic and military activities abroad greatly increased. In many countries, American or Chinese penetration is now considered a greater threat than Soviet penetration. In sum, the power and prestige of the United States, Great Britain, and France are in serious, perhaps precipitous decline, in numerous Third World countries, and Soviet influence, in absolute and relative terms, is growing. These trends are unmistakable but not irreversible.

Long-range Soviet goals in the emerging nations are difficult to discern. To say that the USSR seeks "to extend its influence" is an important but very general assertion. It is much more difficult to explain *why* the Soviet Union seeks to increase its influence and to cite specific instances when its representatives have done so. Evaluating past activities, many Soviet officials have probably recognized that "To the extent that Soviet foreign aid did in fact facilitate the industrialization of developing countries, and to the extent that these countries became economically viable, a Communist revolution became less likely."[12] But Soviet leaders may feel that only in the short run will the enhancement of Russian national prestige occasionally run counter to the goals

11. Joshua and Gibert, *op. cit.,* pp. 125 – 126.
12. Goldman, *op. cit.,* p. 188.

of disseminating Soviet Communist ideas and of creating additional Soviet-dominated Communist states. Given the difficulty of the tasks, the availability of Soviet resources, and the higher priority of other goals (e.g., national defense, strategic interests), one might well conclude that Soviet efforts to create a Communist world have been realistic, rational, and responsive to the present "correlation of world forces."

Whether the pursuit of influence and prestige in the Third World is a means of bringing into existence a worldwide Communist system, or an impediment to world revolution, is a crucial question to which Soviet policy-makers would surely like to know the answer.[13] Whether it would affect their present policies is a moot question. In any case, the purposes and effects of Soviet economic and military aid have varied considerably in the past and are likely to do so again in the future.

In his article below, Professor Clemens forecasts the probable course of Soviet Third World policy in the 1970's. He see five alternatives: (1) the continuation of present policies ("the standard model"); (2) a forward strategy, (3) a stability or status quo orientation; (4) a development or aid orientation; and (5) isolationism. The first alternative he considers the most likely, and, interestingly enough, it is essentially a combination of the last four. One may protest that these goals are logically incompatible, and that progress toward one impedes progress toward the others. But that is precisely Clemens' point. Conflicting goals and priorities, contradictory commitments, cross-pressures, compromise policies on some issues and in some geographical areas, clear-cut but different policies pursued in other areas — all of these "conflicting impulses" are in fact Soviet foreign policy and will probably remain so, Clemens believes. "Precisely because the standard model is a response to many factors — all pushing and pulling in different directions — it seems unlikely that any of these conflicting impulses will increase so greatly as to bring about a clear-cut trend in Soviet policy, a trend that would override the ambivalence inherent in a strategy seeking to obtain the best of several possible worlds."

13. See John Kautsky, *Communism and the Politics of Development* (New York: Wiley, 1968); John Kautsky (ed.), *Political Change in Underdeveloped Countries* (New York: Wiley, 1962); Cyril Black and Thomas Thornton (eds.), *Communism and Revolution* (Princeton: Princeton University Press, 1964); Adam Ulam, *The Unfinished Revolution* (New York: Random House, 1960).

TWENTY-THREE

The Recent Soviet Reassessment of Developments in the Third World*

In the past three years a number of very important changes have occurred in the countries of the Third World. Ben Bella, Nkrumah, and Sukarno — all of whom had been praised by the Soviets — have been overthrown; military regimes have come to power in much of Africa; Pakistan's relations with the United States have cooled appreciably; a number of African and Asian governments have nationalized large portions of their economies. All of these developments have had their repercussions on Soviet attitudes toward the Third World. The Soviets have expanded their contacts with developing countries to include such conservative African regimes as those of Senegal and the Ivory Coast and members of the Western alliance system, such as Turkey, Iran, and Pakistan. The Soviets have also recognized that the national revolutionary movement has not progressed so smoothly and rapidly as they had hoped it would. One writer, for example, has emphasized the difficulties encountered in attempting to explain developments in the Third World:

> The only general conclusion that can be drawn is that there is no peace in the Third World, nor political stability, nor smooth political, economic and social development. . . .

*Reprinted from *The Russian Review,* XXVII, 1 (January, 1968), pp. 27–41, by permission of the author and the publisher. Copyright 1968 by *The Russian Review.* The author is grateful for financial support from the University of Kansas and the Social Science Foundation and Graduate School of International Studies of the University of Denver.

All the storm and stress in the Third World is but a manifestation of social and other antagonisms which inevitably become more acute as the national liberation movement spreads and develops.[1]

However, all is not bleak for, even though there might be temporary setbacks in the movement, in the long run things will work out well.[2]

During the first years of the present decade, Soviet theoreticians developed a model for the newly independent countries to follow in order to make the transition from the stage of underdeveloped, agricultural ex-colonies to that of socialist states. This model of a state of "national democracy" represented an interim goal — the completion of the tasks of the nationalist stage of the colonial revolution, which was still necessary because most of the former colonial countries had achieved independence without acquiring the prerequisites for the socialist stage of the revolution.[3]

The major characteristics of this new type of state, according to the Soviet writers, included: (1) the refusal to join military blocs or to permit foreign military bases on its territory; (2) a major effort to decrease Western economic influence in its economy; (3) the granting of democratic rights and freedoms to progressive political parties, including the Communist Party, to labor unions and to other social organizations; and (4) the introduction of major social changes, especially agrarian reforms, in the interests of the people.[4] The "national democratic" state was not viewed as a state of one class, but as one of the whole patriotic section of the nation which was to eliminate the reactionary elements which still existed.[5] The progressive forces, which were to come to power, were composed of a united front of workers, peasants, the democratic intelligentsia, and a segment of the national bourgeoisie. However, in the state of "national democracy" it was not necessary for the proletariat to play the leading role, according to Soviet theory, for any progressive class could initiate the necessary reforms. Actually the whole doctrine represented an attempt to pave the way for the gradual development of the necessary prerequisites for a socialist society in countries in which the working class was extremely weak. Although any class could fulfill the tasks of national liberation

---

1. Lev Stepanov, "Troubled Year in the Third World," *New Times,* No. 1 (1967), p. 13. See also the earlier admission of G. Mirsky, at a discussion held in Moscow, that there may be a swing to the right in some developing countries. "Metropolii bez kolonii," *Mirovaia ekonomika i mezhdunarodnye otnosheniia,* No. 10 (1965), p. 107.

2. See O. Tuganova, "Co-operation for Peace and Progress," *International Affairs* (Moscow), No. 9 (1966), p. 38.

3. The most complete and detailed study of the "national democracy" doctrine has been written by Leland G. Stauber, "Recent Soviet Policy in the Underdeveloped Countries: The Significance of the 'National Democracy' Doctrine," unpublished doctoral dissertation, Harvard University, 1964.

4. B. Ponomarev, "O gosudarstve natsionalnoi demokratii," *Kommunist,* No. 8 (1961), pp. 43 – 45. See also G. Skorov, "Krushenie kolonialnoi sistemy," *Mirovaia ekonomika i mezhdunarodnye otnosheniia,* No. 3 (1961), pp. 17 – 18.

5. Ponomarev, *op. cit.,* p. 41.

and begin the work of the state of "national democracy," only the proletariat was considered capable of completing the tasks and bringing the country to full socialism.[6]

Although the Soviets were willing to proclaim that a number of countries — especially Ghana, Guinea, and Mali — were approaching the goal of a state of "national democracy," none of these countries was willing to permit the development of local Communist parties in accordance with one of the requirements of the state of "national democracy." In all three of these "progressive" countries, single-party systems were established which precluded the existence of independent Communist parties or independent labor unions, youth organizations, and so forth. In the United Arab Republic, Algeria, and other "progressive" countries, local Communists were arrested and thrown into jail. With the sole exception of Indonesia, none of the revolutionary states of the Third World permitted the development of strong Communist parties. The policy of "national democracy" seemed to be a failure.[7]

Beginning in 1963, the Soviets revised their attitudes toward non-Communist, one-party regimes in the Third World, as well as toward the socialism advocated by the nationalist leaders of Africa and Asia. In an article published in 1962, Professor Ivan Potekhin, the dean of Soviet African scholars until his death two years later, had condemned the negative aspects of attempts on the part of African and Asian leaders to seek a "third way." According to him, "African Socialism," although it contained "sincere efforts of progressive individuals to find the transition to socialism which fits in with the special conditions of African reality," was also "used as a means to deceive the working masses in the interests of capitalist development."[8] Another Soviet specialist on developing countries was more blunt in his denunciation of ideas of a "third way": "There is not and cannot be any 'third path' and experience shows that the African peoples are not looking for one."[9] In this period, although the Soviets were willing to develop economic and political ties with one-party regimes, they were extremely critical of their political and ideological positions.[10] More recently, however, they have been much more lenient in

6. See N. S. Khrushchev, "For New Victories for the World Communist Movement," *World Marxist Review,* IV, No. 1 (1961), p. 21.

7. John Kautsky argues that the doctrine of "national democracy" represented merely a verbal change and that even during the early 1960's the Soviets made no efforts to encourage the independent action on the part of local Communists. During this period, he maintains, the Soviets continued to support all types of regimes, including those which did not permit the development of local Communist parties. John H. Kautsky, "Soviet Policy in the Underdeveloped Countries: Changing Behavior and Persistent Symbols," in Adam Bromke and Philip E. Uren, eds., *The Communist States and the West* (New York, 1967), pp. 19–20, especially footnote 5.

8. Ivan I. Potekhin, "Nekotorye problemy Afrikanistiki v svete reshenii XXII s'ezda KPSS," *Narody Azii i Afriki,* No. 1 (1962), p. 15.

9. G. Mirsky, "Whither the Newly Independent Countries," *International Affairs* (Moscow), No. 12 (1962), p. 25.

10. See, for example, Khrushchev's statement at the Twenty-First CPSU Congress in 1959,

their evaluation of these regimes. The reasons for this change in attitude seem to be easy to find. According to the "national democracy" doctrine, only the working class and its vanguard were considered capable of initiating the social revolution which was required for the development of truly independent states. However, some of the very regimes which banned the activities of local Communist parties also initiated radical measures of nationalization of "both domestic and foreign capital and were willing to rely on the support of the Soviet bloc in any ensuing conflict with the Western powers."[11] The question which the Soviet leadership must have asked itself was: "Why wait for the development of strong local Communist parties, if non-Communist nationalist governments were willing to carry out much of the program advocated by the Soviets?"

In an article published in *Kommunist,* the theoretical organ of the CPSU, R. Ulianovsky has outlined the new policy which is to be followed by local Communist parties. Rather than calling for the formation of strong Communist organizations, the Soviets now argue that "the most consistent and best trained Marxist-Leninist elements should play the role of friend and assistant" of the nationalist leaders:

> Upholding the principles of Marxist-Leninist doctrine, Marxists must be flexible and shrewd, in order not to antagonize the masses. They must constantly seek to find their allies among those social strata and groups which at the moment do not fully accept the theory of scientific socialism, but who today make partial use of it and may fully arm themselves with it tomorrow.

Ulianovsky adds that the question concerns the initial approach to the building of socialism and not its detailed construction or completion:

> If the working people of an economically underdeveloped country, without a formed working class, had to wait for the possibility of forming a national proletarian dictatorship in order to begin the transition to socialist development, this would mean that it was necessary to develop capitalism rapidly in order that a working class might be created on the basis of capitalist industrialization and, subsequently, a Marxist-Leninist party might be formed on this base.[12]

in Leo Gruliow, ed., *Current Soviet Policies III: The Documentary Record of the Extraordinary 21st Communist Party Congress* (New York, 1960), p. 60. Three years later Khrushchev voiced a strong Soviet complaint about the treatment of Communists in developing countries: "Unfortunately, truths which are fully obvious to us Communists are not always acceptable to many leaders of the national-liberation movement. . . .Under contemporary conditions the national bourgeoisie has not yet exhausted its progressive role. However, as contradictions between the workers and other classes accumulate, it reveals more and more an inclination for agreement with reaction.

"Leaders who really hold dear the interests of the people and of the toiling masses will have to understand sooner or later that only by relying on the working class . . . can victory be achieved. . . . Either they will understand this, or other people will come after them who will understand better the demands of life." *Pravda,* May 19, 1962, pp. 2–3.

11. Richard Lowenthal, "Russia, the One-Party Systems, and the Third World," *Survey,* No. 58 (January, 1966), pp. 46–47. In this article Lowenthal gives an excellent analysis of the recent shifts in Soviet doctrine.

12. R. Ulianovsky, "Nekotorye voprosy nekapitalisticheskogo razvitiia osvobodivshikhsia stran," *Kommunist,* No. 1 (1966), pp. 113–114.

Actually, before the shift in Soviet attitudes and policies toward the nationalist, one-party regimes in Africa and Asia had occurred, Soviet scholars were already questioning the foundations of the "national democracy" doctrine. First of all, the question of class structure in the developing countries was raised. Already in 1958 and again in the early sixties, Professor Potekhin admitted that classes, as defined in Marxism-Leninism, did not exist in Africa.[13] Two young Soviet economists, Gordon and Fridman, published studies of the class structure in the Middle East and North Africa in which they argued:

> An underestimation of the depths of the real socio-political differences between the modern proletariat, which is connected with large-scale capitalistic ownership on the one hand, and the majority of agricultural and artisan-handcraft workers on the other, will lead to an oversimplified understanding of the problems of the formation of the working class in Asia and Africa. An unconditional unification of all elements of the army of hired labor into an entity embracing almost one-half of the gainfully employed population would in reality be an admission that the proletariat has already become the most numerous class of society. Such an approach could produce an incorrect evaluation of the degree of capitalist development and arrangement of the class forces.[14]

Besides reevaluating the position of the workers, Soviet writers began to take a closer look at the role of the military and the intellectuals in the developing countries. Georgy Mirsky, a scholar at the Institute of World Economics and International Relations called for more detailed study of the intelligentsia and the army, from whose ranks have come the "revolutionary and national democrats" in the developing areas. Mirsky argued that the group of revolutionary leaders who were ruling in such countries as the U.A.R., Ghana, Guinea, and Mali could not be called members of the bourgeoisie, but were composed of progressive elements of the intelligentsia and the army, and the men who make up the class were truly striving to build the foundations for future socialism.[15]

In addition to reconsidering their views of the class structure and leadership of the nationalist regimes in the Third World, Soviet theoreticians began to analyze the economic policies of these leaders. According to the "national

13. See, for example, I. I. Potekhin, *Afrika smotrit v budushchee* (Moscow, 1960), pp. 18 – 19. For discussion of Soviet views of the class structure in Africa see Roger E. Kanet, "The Soviet Union and Sub-Saharan Africa: Communist Policy toward Africa, 1917 – 1965," unpublished doctoral dissertation, Princeton University, 1966, pp. 247 ff.

14. L. Gordon and L. Fridman, "Osobennosti sostava i struktury rabochego klassa v ekonomicheski slaborazvitykh stran Azii i Afriki (na primere Indii i OAR)," *Narody Azii i Afriki*, No. 2 (1963), pp. 3 – 22. Translated in Thomas Thorton, ed., *The Third World in Soviet Perspective: Studies by Soviet Writers on Developing Areas* (Princeton, 1964), pp. 180 – 181. For a later study by the same authors see "Rabochii klass osvobodivshikhsia stran," *Mirovaia ekonomika i mezhdunarodnye otnosheniia*, No. 12 (1965), pp. 75 – 87 and No. 1 (1966), pp. 27 – 39.

15. G. I. Mirsky, "Tvorcheskii marksizm i problemy natsionalno-osvoboditelnykh revoliutsii," *Mirovaia ekonomika i mezhdunarodnye otnosheniia*, No. 2 (1963), p. 65. More recent Com-

democracy" doctrine, only the active influence of the Communists would lead to the introduction of socialist programs in the developing countries. Domestic "progressive" forces were urged to bring pressure on their governments to initiate radical internal reforms. However, even without the existence of legal Communist parties, a number of African and Asian regimes did decide to select the non-capitalist path of development. For example, in discussions held in Moscow by the Institute of World Economics and International Relations and published in its journal in 1964, Soviet scholars admitted that some developing countries had begun economic reforms which were aimed at both foreign and domestic capital. In these countries — especially Burma, the U.A.R., and some African countries — the state sector was growing at the expense of the private sector of the economy. According to G. Akopian, one of the participants at the discussion, "in a number of liberated countries of Asia and Africa not only have the principles of socialism been proclaimed, but the first practical steps to the realization of these principles have been made."[16] One Soviet writer went so far as to say: "If the conditions for proletarian leadership have not yet matured, the historic mission of breaking with capitalism can be carried out by elements close to the working class."[17]

Not only did the Soviets reassess the class structures of the developing countries and the role of the nationalist leaders in economic and political development, but they also shifted their attitudes toward the nationalist versions of socialism which have been expounded throughout Africa and Asia. As noted above, as late as 1962, Professor Ivan Potekhin had strongly condemned those who proposed a "third path" for the new states. However, more recent Soviet writing on the non-capitalist path of development has emphasized the progressive influence of such doctrines. After speaking of the great differences between scientific socialism and the various forms of national socialism, R. Avakov noted:

> However, all this cannot hide the fact that in the socialist doctrines of a nationalist type there are definite revolutionary and progressive beginnings. The existence of principles found at the heart of these doctrines can assist national progress, the

munist writings have reemphasized the potentially progressive nature of the military in developing countries. See, for example, A. Iskenderov, "Problems and Judgments: The Army, Politics, and the People," *Izvestiia,* January 17, 1967, p. 2, translated in *Current Digest of the Soviet Press,* XIX, No. 3 (February 6, 1967), pp. 9 – 10. Tigani Babiker, a Sudanese journalist on the staff of *Problems of Peace and Socialism,* has argued that the new generation of African military officers is drawn from the petty bourgeoisie and workers and peasants, has fought against colonialism, and is, therefore, "more likely to be imbued with hatred of imperialism, to find friends among the younger people, presently active in the revolutionary struggle, and to be more amenable to revolutionary ideas." "At the Cairo Seminar," *World Marxist Review,* X, No. 1 (1967), p. 54.

16. "Sotsializm, kapitalizm, slaborazvitye strany," *Mirovaia ekonomika i mezhdunarodnye otnosheniia,* No. 4 (1964), pp. 117, 119, and No. 6 (1966), p. 75. See also K. Ivanov, "National-Liberation Movement and Non-Capitalist Path of Development," *International Affairs* (Moscow), No. 5 (1965), p. 61.

17. G. Mirsky, "The Proletariat and National Liberation," *New Times,* No. 18 (1964), pp. 8 – 9.

development of revolutions of liberation, and their transition to the stage of national democracy.[18]

Another Soviet writer argued that the ideologies of the developing states are not the most important factor in evaluating their progressive nature. "Actually the real content of any revolution is determined . . . solely by the objective socio-economic content of the changes (chiefly in settling the question of ownership of the means of production) which the revolution brings about."[19] Revolutionary practice in such countries as the U.A.R., Burma, and Mali is said to be ahead of the development of ideological doctrine: "Social and economic reforms in these countries are often deeper and more radical than the theories 'elucidating' them. . . ."[20]

Since the Soviet reassessment of the nationalist regimes has led to the conclusion that these regimes are truly progressive, even though they have banned local Communist organizations, the Soviets have decided that their interests would be better served by not calling for independent Communist movements, but rather by having local Communists operate inside the single-party regimes. In late 1963 and early 1964, even before the new doctrines had been fully enunciated, the Algerian Communists supported the establishment of a non-Communist, one-party state in Algeria. Ben Bella was declared a "hero of the Soviet Union" and the local Communists accepted positions within the nationalist government.[21] In April 1965, the Egyptian Communist Party officially dissolved itself and declared that Nasser's single party was the only organization capable of carrying out the revolution in the U.A.R.[22] Obviously the Communist leaders in Moscow had decided that the best means to maintain and increase Soviet influence in the Third World — at least in the "revolutionary" countries — was by infiltrating nationalist parties with individual Communists. This course has been followed in Algeria and the U.A.R., as well as in Mali, Guinea, and Ghana (until the 1966 overthrow of Nkrumah). European and African Communists have been sent to man training schools for party and labor leaders which have been constructed with Soviet aid. Soviet and East European economic and technical advisors have played important roles in economic planning in these countries.

However, even though the Soviets have been relatively successful in implementing this new program, they have found that the instability of the domestic political situation in many developing countries is a threat to the continued

18. "Sotsializm, kapitalizm, slaborazvitye strany," *Mirovaia ekonomika i mezhdunarodnye otnosheniia,* No. 6, p. 66.

19. Ivanov, "National-Liberation Movement," p. 65.

20. V. Tiagunenko, "Sotsialisticheskie doktriny obshchestvennogo razvitiia osvobodiv-shikhsia stran," *Mirovaia ekonomika i mezhdunarodnye otnosheniia,* No. 8 (1965), p. 85. See also Iskenderov, "Problems and Judgments," p. 9.

21. See Lowenthal, "Russia," pp. 50–52, and V. Kaboshkin and Iu. Shchepovsky, "Alzhir: ot natsionalnogo osvobozhdeniia k sotsialnomy," *Kommunist,* No. 16 (1963), pp. 115–119.

22. "Party Dissolved by Reds in Cairo," *The New York Times,* April 26, 1965, p. 16.

success of their policy. In the past two years three of the leaders to whom the Soviets had given the most economic and political support were overthrown by military coups — Ben Bella, Nkrumah, and Sukarno. The Soviets now realize the weakness of a policy which is based largely on favorable relations with a single charismatic leader and are now encouraging the development of "vanguard" parties which would be able to institutionalize the revolutionary policies of individual leaders, even if the leader himself were to disappear. The Communist interpretation of Nkrumah's overthrow emphasizes the "absence of a well-organized vanguard party capable of rallying the masses to the defense of their gains."[23] George Mirsky has written of the necessity for the Egyptian leaders "to train a new cadre of officials and extend the political education of the masses." He argues that a mass party like the Arab Socialist Union, although it has played a positive role in Egyptian life, "cannot act as a politically conscious vanguard. Socialist development is inconceivable without a party, without ideological work among the masses. That is precisely what the Egyptian revolution lacks, for from the very outset its leaders came from the middle strata, which had no social platform, and were inspired solely by the ideals of 'pure' nationalism."[24]

Since the proletariat is extremely weak in most African and Asian countries, "socialist consciousness" must be stimulated from the outside, with the cooperation of the international proletariat — that is, of the Soviet Union and other Communist countries. Developing countries should look to the example of other backward regions which have made the transition from feudalism to socialism, such as Soviet Central Asia and Mongolia.[25] The major thrust of Soviet policy in the "progressive" states of the Third World is now support for revolutionary regimes. No longer do the Soviets call for freedom for Communist party activities as a sign of a progressive regime, as they did when the doctrine of "national democracy" was in vogue.[26] According to the more recent view, the only political prerequisites for progressive regimes are internal democracy for progressive elements, not necessarily Communists, and a strengthening of ties with the socialist countries.[27]

The Soviets have implemented their policy by granting large amounts of economic and military assistance to such countries as Algeria and the U.A.R.

---

23. Thierno Amath, "Some Problems of Tropical Africa," *World Marxist Review,* IX, No. 8 (1966), p. 33. One Soviet writer points to the examples of Mali and the U.A.R., which are attempting to create vanguard parties inside the mass parties that have existed for a number of years. N. Gavrilov, "Africa: Classes, Parties and Politics," *International Affairs* (Moscow), No. 7 (1966), pp. 43 – 44.

24. Georgy Mirsky, "United Arab Republic: New Stage," *New Times,* No. 48 (1965), p. 4.

25. G. Kim and P. Shastiko, "Proletarskii internatsionalizm i natsionalno osvoboditelnye revoliutsii," *Pravda,* September 14, 1966, p. 4.

26. See Khrushchev, "For New Victories," p. 21 and A. Sobolev, "National Democracy — The Way to Social Progress," *World Marxist Review,* VI, No. 2 (1963), p. 45.

27. I. Pronichev, "Nekapitalisticheskii put' razvitiia i ego mesto v istoricheskom protsesse,"

Through 1965, Soviet economic aid to Algeria totaled $230 million and the U.A.R. had received more than one billion dollars in assistance. Indonesia was also a major recipient of Soviet largesse before the recent turmoil there removed Sukarno from power — approximately $740 million in aid was sent by the Soviet Union.[28] Developments in the Middle East since the June War of 1967 indicate that the Soviets, although they speak of undying support for the Arabs in their struggle with Israel, are not willing to take any action that might bring them into military conflict with the United States. They are willing to supply arms and grant diplomatic support, as they are doing at the United Nations, but they are not willing to risk military confrontation with the West. Such an attitude has also been evident in Africa, where they refused to take concrete measures to return Nkrumah to power.[29] In spite of an initial loss of prestige because of their refusal to take concrete steps to support the Arabs, the Soviets have been able to expand their influence in the Arab world far beyond the pre – 1967 level. Elsewhere, also, the Soviet leadership has been successful, to the present time, in increasing its influence among the leaders of the revolutionary states of the Third World. On most international issues of importance to the Soviets, such as the war in Vietnam, they have had the diplomatic support of these countries. In domestic developments, these nationalist regimes are carrying out much of the program that the Soviets have proposed.

So far we have spoken only of Soviet views toward the "revolutionary" regimes in the developing world. What of their attitude toward the much larger number of countries whose leaders must be classified as moderate or conservative? In 1962, two Soviet writers presented a classification of developing countries based on the class or classes in power, the type of foreign policy pursued, and the nature of the domestic policies implemented in these countries. According to them, the developing countries could be divided into six different categories of states:

Mirovaia ekonomika i mezhdunarodnye otnosheniia, No. 12 (1966), pp. 7 – 8.

28. U. S. Department of State, Bureau of Intelligence and Research, *Communist Governments and Developing Nations: Aid and Trade in 1965.* Research Memorandum, RSB-50, June 17, 1966, p. 2.

29. In a *Pravda* editorial of October 1965, it was argued that the best assistance which the Soviet Union could render the new states was the strengthening of its own economy: "In building socialism and Communism, the socialist countries make the most important and decisive contribution to the world revolutionary movement. This is what determines their vanguard role in the contemporary revolutionary struggle." The primary role in ending all forms of colonialism and neo-colonialism must be taken by the peoples of Asia and Africa. The Soviet Union and the other socialist countries "cannot take the place of the peoples of the young national states in the solution of the tasks of the national liberation movement," for this would result in forcing one's own will on these peoples. Besides, such assistance might lead to the unleashing of a worldwide nuclear war. "Vyshnii internatsionalnyi dolg stran sotsializma," *Pravda,* October 27, 1965, pp. 3, 4.

1) National bourgeois regimes, seeking independent economic development and non-aligned foreign policies;
2) Alliances of the national bourgeoisie with feudal elements, seeking
   independent economic development and non-aligned foreign policies;
3) Regimes composed of pro-imperialist bourgeoisie, either alone or in
   alliance with feudal landowners, which do not seek real political or
   economic independence;
4) Regimes in which neither the national bourgeoisie nor the feudal class
   is strong enough to dominate and which favor a non-capitalist path of
   development and non-alignment;
5) Regimes in which the class structure is similar to that in the fourth
   category, but which are strongly influenced by the imperialists; and
6) Feudal regimes which follow a neutralist policy in foreign affairs.[30]

The countries about which we have spoken so far have been mainly those
which are in the fourth group. The Soviets have maintained friendly relations
with countries which were listed in some of the other groups: India, Mexico,
Syria (group 1); Somalia, Nigeria (group 2); and Ethiopia, Afghanistan, and
Nepal (group 6). However, it has only been recently that they have developed
contacts with countries in the other two categories — pro-imperialist bourgeois regimes and countries, mainly in Africa, which are still strongly influenced by the West. Now Turkey, Iran, and Pakistan, which were classified
as countries ruled by the pro-imperialist bourgeoisie, receive large amounts of
Soviet economic and military aid.[31] Senegal, the Ivory Coast, and Cameroon,
which were strongly condemned by Soviet writers in the early sixties, now have
diplomatic relations with the Soviet government and have received Soviet
economic and technical assistance.[32] The Soviets have even continued to maintain diplomatic relations with the new anti-Communist governments of Ghana
and Indonesia, although they have strongly criticized developments in these
two countries.

Whereas the Soviet goal in the more radical countries is aimed at support
for anti-Western policies and the promotion of the transition to socialism, even

---

30. R. Avakov and G. Mirsky, "O klassovoi strukture v slaborazvitykh stranakh," *Mirovaia
ekonomika i mezhdunarodnye otnosheniia,* No. 4 (1962), pp. 76–77.

31. For a recent Soviet evaluation of developments in Turkey, see I. Shatalov, "Ankara: New
Climate," *International Affairs* (Moscow), No. 3 (1967), pp. 71–75.

32. The government of Cameroon was called a group of marionettes; the politicians of the
moderate African countries were termed propagandists for imperialism; Khrushchev himself
spoke of those African leaders whose "skin is the same color as that of their countrymen, but
[whose] morals and habits have been acquired in the service of the colonialists." See V. G.
Trukhanovsky, *Istoriia mezhdunarodnykh otnoshenii i vneshnei politiki SSSR 1917–1963* (Moscow, 1964), III, p. 639; S. Volk, "Sudilishche v Senegale," *Aziia i Afrika segodnia,* No. 8 (1961),
p. 54; N. S. Khrushchev at a meeting of the Mali-Soviet Friendship Association in Moscow,
Pravda, June 1, 1962. p. 2.

if this is not scientific socialism, the goal in less revolutionary countries is one of denial of these areas to the West or intrusion into areas of Western control. In some areas of Latin America, in Turkey and Iran, the Soviets are attempting to weaken the ties to and dependence on the West. By offering alternative markets for the products of these countries, as well as new sources of economic and military assistance, the Soviets hope to be able to break the monopoly of contacts which the West has been able to maintain ever since World War II. [33] Rather than relying on military threats and subversion, as they did for many years, the Soviets have renounced all territorial claims on their neighbors and have offered, instead, the means for economic development.

If one were to characterize the policy of the Soviet Union in the Third World during the fourteen years since Stalin's death, one would have to say that this policy has been one of constant reassessment and revision. When it became clear that a policy of isolation was unsuccessful, the Soviets developed economic and political contacts with the Third World; when it became evident that neutralism was the basis of the foreign relations of many of the new states, Soviet leaders came out in favor of non-alignment; when the weakness of the proletariat and local Communist parties was recognized, the Soviets intro-duced the doctrine of "national democracy." Most recently, they have once again revamped their doctrine in order to fit it more closely to reality. The goal of scientific socialism and workers' states has been pushed far into the future. The major immediate task is the increase of Soviet influence in the developing countries. This, it is felt, can best be accomplished by supporting the existing nationalist governments, by granting military and economic assistance, and by developing political, economic, and cultural ties with the peoples of these countries.

33. See Shatalov, "Ankara," pp. 72 – 75.

New Trends in Soviet Economic Relations
with the Third World*

The trend toward economic rationality in the USSR has not been confined to domestic issues alone. It is also manifest in the search for more advantageous and efficient procedures in foreign economic relations, specifically aid and trade with the Third World. In this search for ways to secure tangible gains, Soviet relations with the developing countries are entering a new phase, in which economic considerations of profit are challenging the hitherto dominant political motivations.

Change in this area has not been so dramatic as in domestic economic policies. A critical reevaluation began in late 1961, but it has not been capped with any announcement of sweeping reforms. It has, however, brought some new policies and much discussion that presses with mounting intensity for further innovations.

I. Reevaluation

At the same time that the Russians began to discuss publicly the ways of reviving their lagging economy, the disastrous failures of two large-scale aid programs — those in Cuba and Indonesia — became evident. Whatever the

*Reprinted from *World Politics,* XXII, 3 (April, 1970), pp. 415–432, by permission of the author and Princeton University Press. Copyright 1970 by Princeton University Press.

causes and confluences, the regime reduced aid commitments to a bare minimum during 1961 – 1962 and started looking for better ways to realize returns on its investment.

Speaking before the 22nd CPSU Congress in October, 1961, Anastas Mikoyan informed his audience that "it will be necessary to make wide use of foreign trade as a factor for economizing in current production expenditures and in capital investment."[1] Even though he did not specifically refer to it, trade with the Third World was of concern to the government. At about this time the Presidium of the Academy of Sciences set up a research group in the Institute of the Economy of the World Socialist System to devise indices of the effectiveness of economic relations with the newly independent countries.

Very little of the ongoing reevaluation leaked into the open at first. There were general criticisms of autarky and equally general proposals to "utilize the advantages of international division of labor" to speed up domestic development.[2] Although this indicated concern over the economic costs that the policy of limited dependence on foreign trade entailed and an acceptance of the principle of comparative advantage, the time did not seem ripe for new policy moves. At the first UNCTAD in 1964, the Soviet delegates mentioned only in passing their country's readiness to conclude long-term agreements and contracts with the developing countries for specialization in different types of production. But neither they nor the documents they submitted to the Conference came up with any specific proposals to bring this about.

A possible explanation for Soviet vagueness at Geneva may have been Khrushchev's opposition to any public airing of the USSR's interest in a fair return on all the money and resources it poured into the Third World. He never tired of boasting that the Kremlin valued trade with the former colonies primarily for political reasons and found it burdensome to give them economic aid. Understandably, then, it was only after his fall in October, 1964, that detailed, practical policy proposals appeared.

The first article, based on the findings of the research group working on the effectiveness of Soviet economic relations with the developing countries, was published in February, 1965;[3] it was followed by several articles and at least two studies in the next eighteen months. One book discussed the planning of foreign trade and the profitability of such operations financed through long-term credits.[4] The other, written by the researchers at the Institute of the

1. *Pravda,* October 22, 1961, p. 8.
2. V. Sergeev, "K voprosu kategorii vsemirnyi rynok" [On the problem of the world market], *Vneshniaya torgovlia,* No. 4 (April, 1963), pp. 17 – 24. S. Stepanov, "Sotsialisticheskoe vosproizvodstvo i vneshniaya torgovlia" [Socialist production and foreign trade], *ibid.,* I (January, 1962), pp. 3 – 10.
3. L. Zevin, "Vzaimnaya vygoda ekonomicheskogo sotrudnichestva sotsialisticheskikh i razvivayushchikhsia stran" [Mutual benefits in the cooperation between the socialist and the developing countries], *Voprosy ekonomiki,* II (February, 1965), pp. 72 – 83.
4. B. S. Baranov, ed., *Vneshniaya torgovlia sotsialisticheskikh stran* [Foreign trade of the

Economy of the World Socialist System, offered recommendations for stabilizing and expanding ties with the developing countries through closer economic integration.[5]

Basically these works proposed a precise economic rationale for Soviet dealings with the developing countries through integrating the allocation of aid with the expansion of trade. They viewed aid-giving primarily as an alternative to domestic investment and argued that it would be cheaper for the USSR to import certain goods and materials than to produce them at home, as well as to have the East European states replace some of the raw materials they obtained from the Soviet Union by imports from Africa or Asia.

Rendering aid on such principles would involve the USSR in planning with the developing countries the joint extraction or processing of various natural resources and the joint production of some goods, based on long-term aid and trade commitments. The list of suitable raw materials most frequently included iron ore, lead, copper, zinc, aluminum, and petroleum. The list of manufactures has been much shorter and less explicit, usually starting with cotton fibers and textiles and quickly trailing off into unspecified consumer products and processed goods.

Pronouncements by top government figures indicated that new relations were actually being established. Reporting to the 23rd CPSU Congress in April, 1966, Kosygin claimed that cooperation with the developing countries enabled the USSR to "make better use of the international division of labor."[6] Although this may not have been so readily apparent at the time, there is enough evidence four years later to show that the Soviets are seriously working out a long-range policy based increasingly on projects that intermesh with the needs of their economy and transcend the traditional approach based on barter.

II. New Forms and Methods in Aid and Trade

Planning is visible on various levels. At the first UNCTAD, Nikolai Patolichev, the Soviet Foreign Trade Minister, did not mention planning at all. At the second, however, he not only repeated that the Soviet Union would increase its imports from the developing countries through the conclusion of long-term trade agreements and through specialization and coordination arrangements in various industries, but also added that it would take these matters into consideration in drawing up its own plans.[7]

There is no evidence of any overall coordination of production and trade,

---

socialist countries] (Moscow 1966).

5. G. M. Prokhorov, *Problemy sotrudnichestva sotsialisticheskikh i razvivayushchikhsia stran* [Problems of cooperation between the socialist and the developing countries] (Moscow 1966).

6. *Pravda,* April 6, 1966, p. 6.

7. Interview, *New Times,* XV (April 17, 1968), p. 9.

but extensive long-range planning is being introduced in Soviet relations with individual countries.[8] In October, 1968, Moscow and Teheran agreed to work out twelve- to fifteen-year projections for increased economic collaboration and trade based on their natural resources as well as other economic and technical potentials. Similarly, a year earlier, Pakistan and Russia had decided to "draft a plan on a further substantial increase in economic cooperation and trade" extending to 1975. In India the 1968 talks on cooperation in industrial production and dovetailing these projects with a long-term trade agreement and the plans of the two countries have faltered because of the poor production record of Soviet-aided projects in the public sector. The agreement that was finally concluded in December, 1968, committed the USSR to buying certain Indian products more to pull India out of economic difficulties than to provide the Soviet Union with vitally needed goods.[9]

Such arrangements go far beyond the simple Soviet commitment to provide aid for constructing a given number of projects in a country's forthcoming plan, as had been the case hitherto. They involve a certain amount of economic integration, based on coordinating relevant aspects of the Soviet plan with those of the recipient. Increasingly, Soviet experts helping the developing countries in drawing up their plans or concluding aid agreements with them will be seeking areas open to closer coordination, such as the joint production of raw materials and manufactures and the setting up of mixed companies and assembly plants. Permanent administrative machinery to institute and supervise closer economic relations between the USSR and other countries is being created. Joint permanent commissions, composed of high-level officials and experts, have recently been set up with India, the U.A.R., Iran, Algeria, Morocco, and Afghanistan to facilitate consultations and planning. For example, it is the Soviet-Iranian commission that is working out, together with the planners of both countries, the prospects for long-range collaboration men-

8. The East European, not the Soviet, economists have been the persistent advocates of the need to coordinate and integrate the Bloc's economic relations with the Third World. Cf. L. Dvorzhak, "Glavnye tendentsii v ekonomicheskom sotrudnichestve sotsialisticheskikh i slaborazvitykh stran" [Main tendencies in economic cooperation between the socialist and the underdeveloped countries], *Novye yavleniya v ekonomike sovremennogo imperializma* [New phenomena in the economy of present-day imperialism] (Moscow 1963), pp. 90 – 104. Even though the USSR and the East European states have been participating in the construction of a number of large aid projects, collaboration seems to be limited to subcontracting, and there has been no mention of any office within CEMA that might work on or administer a multilateral approach. However, the East European states are beginning to innovate on their own. Poland, Hungary, and Rumania have committed themselves in their 1969 trade plans with India to trilateral import arrangements and have agreed to consider transferability of funds. *Weekly India News,* No. 36 (November 22, 1968), p. 3. At present the Soviets are only discussing the desirability of departing from bilateralism in trade with the developing countries and of setting up multilateral clearing accounts within the Bloc. V. Savelev, "Obmen mezhdu razvivayushchimisia i sotsialisticheskimi stranami" [Exchanges between the developing and the socialist countries], *Ekonomicheskie nauki,* I (January, 1968), pp. 58 – 64.

9. I. Temirskii, "Moscow and Delhi," *New Times,* V (Feb. 5, 1969), pp. 10 – 11.

tioned above. The meetings of these joint commissions are no *pro forma* gatherings. They are hard-working sessions, lasting as long as two weeks, at which supplementary agreements are signed.[10]

Thus far, the Soviets have been mainly active in the *joint production of raw materials.* Geological prospecting figures very prominently in Soviet aid. In some cases, Syria and India for example, the discovery of oil deposits has been followed up with additional aid for its extraction and commercial exploitation. Increasingly, a third step provides for direct Soviet utilization of the raw material and even for Soviet marketing of the product. After Soviet geologists discovered rich natural-gas deposits in Afghanistan, an agreement was signed in October, 1963, to deliver a large part of the output to the Soviet Union in repayment for aid in extracting the gas and constructing a pipeline to the Soviet border. (In May, 1967 just before the pipeline was opened, Afghanistan agreed to supply 58 billion cubic meters through 1985, not only to repay the debts incurred in this venture but also to finance additional trade.)

In cases where the USSR has not helped to locate natural resources, Moscow is willing to accept raw materials in exchange for aid. Under the terms of the January, 1966, agreement, Iran pays with natural gas for Soviet aid in the construction of a steel mill, a machine-tool plant, and part of the pipeline to the Soviet border. (Shipments are to start in 1970, and by 1975 the annual volume is to amount to 15 billion cubic meters.) Under the terms of the June, 1969, agreement with the Iraqi National Oil Company, the USSR will provide equipment and technicians to develop the oil fields, as well as help in marketing, in return for Iraqi oil.

By the Soviets' own admission, the additional supply of natural gas enables them to alleviate the fuel shortage in the Central Asian republics.[11] But what remains unmentioned is that it also frees considerable amounts of natural gas produced in European Russia for export to the West in exchange for scarce industrial products. In June, 1968, Moscow contracted to export natural gas to Austria in exchange for large-diameter pipes. As for the Iraqi oil, it might either be sold through the refining and marketing companies the Soviets are setting up in Western Europe or be diverted to East Europe in order to free Soviet oil for Western transactions.

Cooperation in manufacturing has not been so much in evidence as has cooperation in the development of extractive industries. Thus far, several aid agreements have provided for the repayment of credit with the finished product. The Soviet Union is already getting high-quality cotton yarn from textile mills it helped set up in the U.A.R. A similar agreement was concluded in March, 1968, with Uganda. Since late 1965, Guinea has been shipping canned foods to repay part of the loan for a food-processing plant.

10. Results of an Algerian-Soviet commission's meeting are reported in *Pravda,* October 27, 1969, p. 5.
11. *Kommunist* (Erevan), September 8, 1968, p. 3.

Recently the Soviet Union has been negotiating with India on specialization and coordination in the more complex branches of industry, such as petro-chemicals and fertilizers. This calls for a much more intricate and closer relation between the contracting parties than, say, that in the food and textile industries, which merely involves exporting part of the production to Russia. As of late 1969, no definite plans have emerged for the heavy-industry ventures. But India has agreed to set up a shoe factory specifically catering to Russian needs.[12] Although this falls within the light-industry category, it is nevertheless a new departure involving a higher degree of coordination, with production specifications geared to Soviet standards and needs. Soviet assistance to Algeria in the production of brandy, most of which is to be shipped to the USSR, is another instance of integration. At first, after Algeria lost much of its French market, the Russians merely offered to import increased quantities of wine.

There is much talk about getting better returns on aid and trade through new forms of partnership. Economists urge the formation of *mixed companies* as an advantageous type of investment that would also assure the USSR a steady supply of needed raw materials and industrial goods.[13] But the practical and legal aspects of partnership have hardly been discussed in print. One recent article indicated that the Soviet Union should take less profit for its share in a joint enterprise than would a Western partner, but at the same time it should obtain an unspecified but "fair" return on its investment. Moreover, the author envisaged a partnership of limited duration, with the Soviet share being gradually bought up by the assisted country.[14]

Highly placed aid officials are considered to be hostile to this administrative and ideological innovation. The statement that, unlike the West, the USSR renders "disinterested" aid and does not seek any assets on the territory of other countries to derive profit at their expense has been such a cardinal principle in the Soviet aid program that it seems hard to compromise. Thus far, the Soviets have established joint trading companies with only Ethiopia, Nigeria, and Morocco, and a joint shipping line with Singapore.[15] By contrast, the East European states have no reservations and have been busy in Africa and Asia setting up joint ventures ranging from sugar refineries to copper mines.

12. *The Times of India,* October 5, 1968, p. 1.
13. L. Zevin, N. Ushakova, M. Strepetova, "Ekonomicheskoe sotrudnichestvo sotsialisticheskikh gosudarstv s razvivayushchimisia stranami" [Economic cooperation of the socialist states with the developing countries], *Nova i noveishaya istoriya,* II (February, 1966), p. 12.
14. Yu. Shamrai, "Problemy sovershenstvovaniya ekonomicheskogo sotrudnichestva sotsialisticheskikh i razvivayushchikhsia stran" [Problems of perfecting economic cooperation of the socialist and developing countries], *Narody Azii i Afriki,* IV (August, 1968), pp. 10–13.
15. In the case of the trading company in Ethiopia, the USSR supplied 51% of capital and the local entrepreneurs the rest. *Za Rubezhom,* XXIII (June 2–8, 1967), p. 27.

Soviet economists believe that practical considerations will force the aid officials to look with a more tolerant eye on their proposals and to accept mixed companies for the sake of efficiency, if not of profit. Often enough in the past, a completed aid project handed over to the recipient government was either bankrupted by maladministration or offered to a Western company for management. Because of such miscarriages of Moscow's expectations, the Deputy Director of the Soviet aid agency now concedes the need for joint management as a possible form of control preferable to sending emergency teams to reorganize administration, production, and marketing.[16]

In the case of *assembly plants* there seems to be a comparable reluctance to venture into a new field. For several years, specialists have been pointing out that the shipment of unassembled machinery to the countries of the Third World would make exports much more profitable, reduce transportation costs, and enable the recipients to go through an intermediate stage of industrialization.[17] But there is scarcely any mention of such projects. There is a plant in India assembling Soviet watches; negotiations are under way on assembling tractors in Morocco and in Pakistan; and an unconfirmed Western report states that the Soviet Union plans to assemble cars in Australia for reexport to Asia.[18]

Despite the obvious timidity of the Soviet trade and aid officials, it seems very likely that more assembly plants will be set up in the future. Such projects will promote the current drive to raise the ratio of machinery in Soviet exports. Since the Russians believe that they enjoy an advantage in the production and export of machinery, the economic directives prepared for the 23rd CPSU Congress, as well as Kosygin's speech at the Congress, called for structural changes in trade with the developing countries through expanded exports of machinery and equipment.[19]

16. D. Degtiar, "Ekonomicheskoe i tekhnicheskoe sotrudnichestvo SSSR so stranami Afriki" [Economic and technical cooperation of the USSR with African countries], *Vneshniaya torgovlia*, IX (September, 1968), pp. 2 – 5. For the story of how additional Soviet technicians revived the milk processing plant in Somalia, see V. Bulimov, "Pervyi v Somali" [The first in Somalia], *Ekonomicheskaya gazeta*, XXXII (August, 1968), p. 46.

17. I. F. Andreev, "SSSR — krupneishii eksporter mashin i oborudovaniya" [USSR — the biggest exporter of machinery and equipment], *Vneshniaya torgovlia*, VI (June, 1966), pp. 3 – 9. I. F. Andreev, "Sovetskie mashiny na mirovom rynke" [Soviet machinery in the world market] *Mashinostroitel'*, IV (April, 1968), pp. 4 – 6. Yu. Shamrai, "Nekotorye voprosy rynochnykh otnoshenii mezhdu sotsialisticheskimi i razvivayushchimisia stranami" [Some problems in market relations between the socialist and the developing countries], *Narody Azii i Afriki*, II (April 1969), p. 22.

18. "Soviet Planning Production of Its Cars in Australia," *The New York Times*, July 4, 1965.

19. *Pravda*, February 20, 1966, p. 5, and April 6, 1966, p. 6. In 1960, the share of the developing countries in the total value of Soviet machinery exports was 11%; by 1966, it had doubled to 22.4%. Capital goods constitute a very high proportion of Soviet exports to many countries: in 1966, they accounted for 52% of exports to India, 60% to Pakistan, 39% to Iran,

At present complete plants account for more than 60 percent of Soviet exports of machinery to the Third World.[20] However, the major importers of Soviet equipment have reached levels of industrialization that enable them to contribute substantially to plant construction on their own. India has already indicated that she is no longer interested in being presented with completed projects on a turn-key basis, as was the case with the Bhilai steel plant. Because much equipment and technical skill are now available indigenously, and will be increasingly available in the future, additional pressures are created for new forms of partnership.

Marked interest in *commercial contracts* is another aspect of the Soviet drive for more profitable relations with the developing countries. When asked about new forms of economic cooperation in the next Five-Year Plan, the Soviet aid administrator, S. Skachkov, answered that "as an independent national economy was being set up and developed in the former colonies, it was becoming increasingly possible for the USSR to establish business relations with them on a commercial basis." He cited several such contracts previously concluded: with Iran for equipping a thermoelectric station, and with the U.A.R. for geological surveying and for the construction of vocational schools.[21]

Much has been made of the commercial loans that were granted in 1967 to Brazil and Chile to promote exports of machinery. (The four-year $100-million loan to Brazil carried a 4 percent interest; the $15-million loan to Chile was repayable over 8 years at 3 percent interest. The customary terms of the ordinary "aid" credits are 2 1/2 percent repayable in 10–12 years after the completion of the project.) Articles and comments single out these agreements as examples of new, purely commercial contracts that should be concluded more frequently. Moreover, because the Russians are now willing to collaborate with India in setting up projects in third countries[22] and to sell technical assistance to private firms,[23] new opportunities for other commercial ventures are opening up.

At present, the cumbersome state monopoly over all foreign economic transactions hinders the search for business deals abroad. Trade and aid agreements are negotiated by the representatives of the Foreign Trade Ministry and the State Committee on Foreign Economic Relations. Actual work on trade orders and aid projects, ranging from surveys and designs to personnel training, is entrusted to All-Union Associations, which in turn subcontract specific

and 67% to the U.A.R. I. F. Andreev, p. 5.

    20. *Vneshniaya torgovlia,* VII (July, 1967), p. 12.

    21. *Ibid.,* I (January, 1966), p. 6.

    22. *The Times of India,* October 5, 1968, p. 1.

    23. I. Kapranov, "The U.S.S.R. and the Industrial Development of the Newly Free States," *International Affairs,* VI (June, 1966), pp. 33–36.

jobs within the industry they represent. However, Soviet economists have been discussing the fact that in Hungary, East Germany, Poland, and Czechoslovakia large individual enterprises are now permitted to engage in direct bids and negotiations with foreign clients, hinting thereby that similar reforms could be introduced at home.[24] However, high officials are outspokenly opposed to these proposals. The Foreign Trade Minister, N. S. Patolichev, has indicated that the regime intends to continue the central control of aid and trade transactions, having them conducted by juridically and economically independent state organizations.[25]

So far, the only concession the regime has made in the direction of involving enterprises more directly in foreign transactions was to set up, in the All-Union Associations, special advisory councils in which representatives of industry participate. Conceivably, it may not be very long before decentralization and plant autonomy reach the point where it will become possible for larger plants to bid for foreign contracts directly

III. New Thoughts on Development

A review of new trends in Soviet economic relations with the Third World would be incomplete without mentioning new views on problems of development. It is not coincidental that at the same time as the officials began to grope for more advantageous and economically viable forms of aid and trade, economists began to alter their dogmatic views on underdevelopment. Since theoretical writings produced by the various research institutes of the Academy of Sciences are far from being purely academic exercises and are often the basis for policy-making, the timing of the change indicated that the search for new forms in economic relations was supported by serious work in development economics.

The Soviet approach to the economic problems of the former colonies was unrealistically simple in the late 1950's and early 1960's. Backwardness, it was alleged, was caused by colonial rule and persisted because of unequal relations with the former metropoles. Therefore, curtailing relations with the West through nationalization, industrialization, and extensive dealings with the Socialist bloc would produce rapid growth. This political approach to development, based on the theory of "economic liberation," was pointed up by a Soviet

24. G. Gertsovich, Yu. Shamrai, "Vneshneekonomicheskii aspekt khoziaistvennoi reformy v stranakh SEV" [The external economic aspects of economic reforms in the CEMA countries], *Voprosy ekonomiki,* IV (April, 1968), pp. 58–70.

25. Speech in commemoration of the 50th anniversary of Soviet trade. *Vneshniaya torgovlia,* VI (June, 1968), p. 8. Similarly, the Rector of the Foreign Trade Academy, B. Vaganov, favors continuing state monopoly of foreign trade in its traditional form to avoid competition between Soviet organizations and to save money on maintaining trade agencies abroad. *Ekonomicheskaya gazeta,* XXIII (June, 1968), p. 42.

readiness to grant aid for prestige projects or for almost any ventures proposed by a newly independent country without a prior investigation of their economic viability and overall effects.

A new look at the process of economic growth was heralded by the publication in the September, 1962, issue of *Kommunist,* the theoretical organ of the CPSU, of several articles on the current stage of the national liberation movement. They all eschewed radicalism for a moderate, gradual approach that recognized the usefulness of light industry, of private local and foreign capital, and of noncomprehensive planning.

Since then numerous articles, symposia, and books on economic growth, on industrialization and agrarian problems, on the prospects of individual countries and continents, have broadened and refined Soviet views almost beyond recognition.[26] It is now generally accepted that economic growth involves prerequisites, stages, diversification, and interrelations among the various branches of the national economy. Considerably more attention is being paid to the internal retarding factors than to the adverse effects of Western domination and other external influences. In short, analysis and evaluation are based more on economic facts than on political dogma.

A good illustration of advanced thinking on the subject is a statement by one expert on development: the more backward an economy, the wider the circle of concrete problems that will have nothing to do with either socialism or capitalism but will have to be solved through certain basic, essential steps.[27]

To what extent are these trends in development economics reflected in actual policies? From scattered sources and comments we get the impression that the Russians are guided these days by pragmatic economic considerations, particularly since they give less and less of their aid for individual projects and are increasingly becoming involved in a plethora of interlocking economic activities.

Current Soviet views on *planning* can give an indication of the policy suggestions offered in the Third World by Soviet experts when they help in drawing up a national development plan.[28] It used to be argued only a few years ago that effective long-range national development plans could be constructed only after the nationalization of production and the neutralization of market forces and the price system, and within the socio-political framework of a proto-socialist state. Nowadays such sweeping steps are frowned upon as "voluntaristic," for they ignore the actual costs and other economic realities.

26. Elizabeth K. Valkenier, "Recent Trends in Soviet Research on the Developing Countries," *World Politics,* XX (July, 1968), pp. 644–59.

27. V. M. Kollontai, *Puti preodoleniya ekonomicheskoi otstalosti* [Ways of overcoming economic backwardness] (Moscow 1967), p. 206.

28. The Soviets have had a hand in the plans of India, the U.A.R., Uganda, Afghanistan, Iran, and Algeria.

The Soviet NEP experience is now discussed as a possible model for Africa and Asia, and it is broadly hinted that the Soviet policies following upon that period should not be copied blindly.[29] There is serious research on the planning carried out by "capitalist-oriented states," such as Iran,[30] and it is acknowledged that they have pioneered some successful policies.[31]

Although a command economy is no longer advocated, there is quite a variety of views on the extent of central direction. Some economists still feel it necessary to stress the advantages of central controls over the market.[32] Others opt for more indirect methods and speak in terms of the state's "influence."[33] Still others argue outright that the market should not be supplanted altogether by detailed central controls.[34]

With this background of recent economic literature, we can assume that Soviet experts no longer urge upon Afro-Asian countries a crude and stereotyped imitation of the Soviet experience of the 1930's, as they did for the Second Indian Five-Year Plan. After Zanzibar rejected realistic Soviet and East German advice in favor of radical Chinese proposals, the Russians must have felt vindicated when they broadcast Vice President Hangu's attribution of the failure of the plan to the "lack of proper economic justification and insufficient study of profitability."[35]

It should not be assumed that every aid decision or counsel on planning will be offered with only cost and profit considerations in mind. Soviet development literature recognizes that, especially on the macro-level, profit cannot be the only criterion for investment, since social gains and future goals are often of overriding importance. But there is no doubt that Soviet experts recognize now the organizational role of costs as well as the dynamic factor of the profit motive and will try to prevail on African and Asian regimes to take them into consideration in national development plans.

Current Soviet views on the role of the state and private sectors are closely related to the changed outlook on planning. As recently as 1965, economists

29. N. Shmelev, "Stoimostnye kriterii i ikh rol' v ekonomike razvivayushchikhsia stran" [Cost criteria and their role in the economy of the developing countries], *Mirovaya ekonomika i mezhdunarodnye otnosheniye* (hereafter cited as MEMO), VI (June, 1968), p. 51.

30. A. Z. Arabadzhian, A. I. Medovoi, eds., *Plany-programmy ekonomicheskogo razvitiya stran Azii* [Plans-programs of economic development in Asian countries] (Moscow 1966).

31. R. Andreasyan, "New Aspects of Middle East Countries' Oil Policies," *International Affairs,* IX (September, 1968), p. 30.

32. *Stroitel'stvo natsional'noi ekonomiki v stranakh Afriki* [The building of a national economy in the countries of Africa] (Moscow 1968), pp. 36–59.

33. "Finansirovanie ekonomiki razvivayushchikhsia stran" [Financing the economy of the developing countries], *Narody Azii i Afriki,* I (January, 1968), pp. 3–20.

34. N. Shmelev, "Razvivayushchiesia strany: formirovanie khoziaistvennogo mekhanizma" [The developing countries: formation of economic mechanism], MEMO, VIII (August, 1968), pp. 52–62.

35. Quoted in *Mizan,* IX, 5 (September–October, 1967), p. 199.

still argued that the larger the *state sector,* the faster and better an economy would grow. This is now definitely an outdated view. What interests specialists is the performance, not the size.

There is a frank discussion of the ills that afflict the state sector: overextension, burdensome bureaucracy, corruption, and deficit operations. However, we should not conclude that the Soviets are going to turn their backs on public ownership, which remains a cardinal tenet in Communist development theory as the proper organizational moving force. The recent criticism does not mean that the Russians will ever advise countries like India and the U.A.R. to dismantle the public sector — merely that they are now searching for ways to make it function efficiently.

Thus far, two approaches are apparent. One method is to make careful preparations so that the state sector is not hampered by limited administrative resources. The other is to extend additional aid and technical services to existing state enterprises. In Algeria, for example, the Soviets have nothing against the eventual nationalization of the oil industry. In the meantime they are helping to prepare the ground by setting up a large Petroleum Training Institute in that country and by training many Algerian oil engineers in the USSR.

The September, 1967, aid agreement with Guinea specifically allocated funds only for projects meant to improve the functioning of those already built.[36] Thus, the food-canning factory that had been plagued by short supplies is going to be backed up by large tomato plantations. Similarly, in the U.A.R., the Russians have been advising the Egyptians to raise productivity through better use of the existing industrial capacity as well as through higher material incentives and a smaller labor force rather than undertake new construction.[37] During his January, 1968, visit to India, Kosygin was so upset by the poor performance of the Soviet-aided projects in the public sector that he promptly dispatched teams of experts to the scene. One team blamed the deficit operations and below-capacity production on inexperienced management and the lack of labor discipline and of proper material incentives.[38] As a result of several inspecting missions, the 1966 credit agreement was revised in December, 1968, and some of the Soviet funds were earmarked for "raising the efficiency" of large industrial projects.[39]

The other side to recognition of the pitfalls of excessive and premature public ownership is an appreciation of the contribution that *private business* makes to the economic well-being of the new nations, provided that it does not assume the predominant position. Economists, who are now eager to draw attention to this fact, back their arguments with appropriate quotations from

---

36. *Vneshniaya torgovlia,* IX (September, 1968), p. 20.
37. Hendrick Smith, "Russians Suggest Reform in the UAR," *The New York Times,* October 24, 1966. E. Primakov, "Segodnia v Kaire," [Today in Cairo], *Pravda,* April 26, 1968, p. 4.
38. *The Hindu Weekly Review,* March 25, 1968, p. 10.
39. I. Temirskii, p. 10.

Lenin, who held in the early 1920's that, during the transition from small production to socialism, capitalist relations could and should play a role in increasing output.[40]

The new look at the small entrepreneur extends even further. There have been Western reports from Kabul that Russian advisers told the Afghan government to expand private enterprise.[41] Even the Communist parties of Asia and Africa are beginning to display changed attitudes, and a number of recently adopted programs urge that the climate be hospitable for small businessmen.[42]

In the last two years there has been increasingly outspoken criticism of excessive nationalization of small business carried out by the radical nationalist leaders, like Ne Win or Modibo Keita. The CPSU has singled them out as "national democrats" who are the moving force of the national liberation revolution and has sought to draw them closer into the Soviet orbit by establishing official relations with their parties. Though still held up as examples for the rest of the Third World to follow, the national democrats are now often criticized for resorting to "economically unsound" reforms. R. A. Ulianovskii, who heads the Central Committee department that deals with these radicals, does not approve of nationalizing domestic trade and services, or small and medium-size industry, since most newly independent countries are neither administratively nor economically ready for these steps. Such measures only contribute to the deterioration of an already difficult economic situation.[43] Given Ulianovskii's position and training as an economist specializing in Asia, similar criticism is undoubtedly meted out in personal encounters with the government figures of the radical states.

Despite occasional thundering about the need to oust "monopoly capital," the Soviets recognize now the contribution of *Western capital* to the development of the Third World, as well as the unreadiness of the new states to dispense with the Western presence altogether. What the Soviets favor is not wholesale expulsion but arrangements that recognize the sovereignty of each nation over its natural resources and leave as large as possible a share of profits at home.

In this field too, the Russians are likely to advise against hasty nationalization. Speaking before an international audience in Dakar, V. G. Solodovnikov, a prominent economist specializing in the developing countries, recalled how at the January, 1967, ECA conference he advised changing the conditions under which foreign capital was invested — mainly reinvestment or limitations

40. V. M. Kollontai, pp. 184–95.
41. Drew Middleton, "East Meets West in Afghanistan," *The New York Times,* May 28, 1967.
42. See, for example, the program of the Sudanese party, *Pravda,* December 16, 1967, p. 4, and a statement of the Iraqi party, *The World Marxist Review Information Bulletin,* XIX (November 7, 1968), pp. 16–19.
43. "Nauchnyi sotsializm i osvobodivshiesia strany" [Scientific socialism and the liberated countries], *Kommunist,* IV (March, 1968), p. 104.

on profit — in the hope that such modifications "would considerably weaken the tendency toward nationalizing foreign private property."[44]

It is instructive to look at the treatment accorded in the Soviet press to the Congo-Union Minière copper agreement. It was defended in *New Times* as a "reasonable compromise" in which both sides made concessions. A reader, who termed the settlement with Union Minière a complete capitulation, was told that since the Congolese were incapable of processing and selling copper on their own, they had no other way out but to enter into a compromise agreement with foreign capital. "There is no reason to assume that such agreements are . . . instances of capitulation. Such an approach bears a strong imprint of dogmatism. In the present situation, the newly independent countries can benefit by making use of foreign capital, provided . . . that [it] is placed under strict local control and the over-all economic interests of the given country are safeguarded."[45]

Two other issues of development economics — *agriculture* and *industry* — have been liberated from the doctrinal approach. And Soviet aid programs reflect the change.

Since the agrarian problem is now seen in terms of output, and not in terms of ownership or management, radical land reform is no longer advocated in theoretical writings. There is now open and frank discussion of the fact that expropriation of large landowners is likely to have disastrous economic effects. R. Andreasyan, a frequent contributor to the academic journals and a member of the staff of the Foreign Trade Ministry, noting that reforms could reduce farm output, has cautioned that "carrying out land reform requires a careful preliminary analysis and weighing of all the possible economic factors." He is against the subdivision of large estates farmed by extensive methods, for their "fragmentation would impair the organization of labor which has been established and the settled crop rotation. Their profitability would decrease."[46]

Other specialists have stressed assistance to the small peasant farmers and approve the setting up of cooperative and state farms only when adequate administrative personnel and machinery are available to assure full production.[47] Since state management is no longer regarded as an answer to productivity, the report that the Soviet planning experts have suggested that their

44. V. G. Solodovnikov, "Some problems of economic and social development of independent African nations," *II International Congress of Africanists*. Papers presented by the USSR delegation (Moscow 1967), pp. 5, 8 – 9.

45. Y. Bochkarev, "Letter to the Editor," *New Times*, XXIX (July 19, 1967), pp. 13 – 14. There was a similar defense of the July 1965 Algerian-French agreement on the Sahara oil. N. Prozhogin, "Neft Sakhary" [Sahara oil], *Pravda*, November 14, 1967, p. 4.

46. R. Andreasyan, A. Elianov, "Razvivayushiesia strany: diversifikatsiya ekonomiki i strategiya promyshlennogo razvitiya" [The developing countries: diversification of the economy and the strategy of industrial development], MEMO, I (January, 1968), p. 32.

47. V. G. Rastiannikov, "Prodovol'stvennaya problema v razvivayushchikhsia stranakh" [The food problem in the developing countries], *Narody Azii i Afriki*, I (January, 1967), pp. 41 – 42.

Algerian counterparts decentralize the state management of agriculture is not at all surprising. [48] For similar reasons, the Soviets no longer seem to set up state farms in order to introduce radical organizational concepts. Economists refer nowadays to research and experimental stations working to improve and increase yields.[49]

This concern for farm output has been accompanied by an entirely new attitude toward aid to expand agriculture. It used to be passed over in silence, and only recently have aid officials begun to speak of it as an important contribution to development. The fact that the USSR has built and is committed to construct over one hundred projects in irrigation, land reclamation, etc. (i.e., one-sixth of all the aid projects), is often mentioned nowadays and is publicized almost as much as is aid to industry. Without doubt, Soviet advisers no longer think of progress primarily in terms of rapid industrialization. When asked about favoring either the agricultural or the industrial sector while collaborating with Algerian planners, M. Misnik, the Deputy Chairman of Gosplan, stressed their interdependence: industry was essential to modernize and to mechanize agriculture, for without adequate food production "economic independence was unrealizable."[50]

The days of one-sided preference for *industry* are over. Strange as it may sound, Russians now inveigh against an excessive buildup of heavy industry in countries like India and the U.A.R., which used to be, and at times still are, cited as examples of the efficacy of Soviet aid policies, whose distinguishing feature was generous credit for large industrial projects.

In discussing the strategy of development many specialists warn that impairment of the proper balance between industry and agriculture "creates bottlenecks in the economy, causes excessive stress, and in the long run leads to worsening of the general condition of economic growth." The U.A.R. is blamed for "overstepping in the direction of industrialization." India's troubles are diagnosed as due to "inadequate attention to agriculture" and "faulty industrialization policy."[51]

It should not be concluded, however, that the Soviets have become disillusioned with industrialization. In general, Soviet economists are convinced that production of capital goods is *the* dynamic factor in development. They have merely become aware through costly experience that industries have to be carefully adapted not only to the availability of raw materials but also to the potentials of the domestic and the trends in the international market. Having assisted India to build up its steel industry, Moscow has had to bail it out of

48. Henry Tanner, "Algeria under Boumedienne Struggles for Stability," *The New York Times,* January 16, 1967.

49. G. M. Prokhorov, "Druzhba, vzaimoponimanie" [Friendship, mutual understanding], *Ekonomicheskaya gazeta,* XVIII (April, 1968), p. 46.

50. *Révolution Africaine,* CIV (January 9-15, 1967), p. 18.

51. R. Andreasyan, E. Elianov, pp. 30–31.

difficulties by agreeing in 1968 to purchase considerable quantities of steel and railway cars to dispose of unsold production and assure fuller operations in the future.

To judge from recent aid agreements, we may expect that there will be a more cautious, as well as a broader, approach toward industrialization. The marked preference for steel and metal-working over other types of heavy industry is undergoing modification. In the October, 1968, agreement with India, the USSR has undertaken to assist in a range of industrial ventures ranging from petrochemicals to cellulose. Eager now to avoid excessive and prolonged subsidization, the Soviets favor projects that are quickly self-liquidating, even though they may be less spectacular and prestigious than large complexes. The Afghan king made it a point to stress, after obtaining Soviet commitment for the Third Five-Year Plan, that the USSR had shown understanding for his country's problems and had agreed to supply aid for consumer-goods industries that quickly repay for themselves.[52]

IV. Conclusion

Though the main direction of new trends in Soviet aid and trade policies with the Third World is readily apparent, its consequences are not so clear.

First of all, the new types of relations form as yet a very small part of the overall pattern of economic dealings with the developing countries. In the case of mixed companies, after four years of study and discussion, they still remain paper proposals. There is an obvious reluctance in many circles to reallocate resources in the USSR to make a fuller international division of labor possible. Moreover, the new states conduct only about 2.5 percent of their trade with the USSR, and their share in total Soviet trade is 12 percent. Therefore, neither Soviet economic relations with the new states nor the new patterns in these relations can as yet be of decisive importance.[53]

However, the portents for the future are by no means minimal. We should not jump to the conclusion that since the USSR is beginning to treat aid and trade as a form of investment there is another field of convergence and another reason to feel relaxed about the Soviet challenge. Even when the Soviet Union enters into profitable ventures in the Third World, it does so on terms different from those of the West. And the difference is not lost on the developing countries. As an example we may cite their demand that Western companies enter into "Soviet-type" agreements in petroleum explorations wherein the

---

52. *Pravda,* June 3, 1968, p. 4.
53. Although the degree of dependence of most developing countries on trade with the USSR and its allies has not reached a high level, it should be noted that some, i.e., Afghanistan, India, Syria, and the U.A.R., conduct over 20% of their trade with the Soviet Bloc and have obtained even larger percentages of foreign aid component of their development plans from the Communist states.

companies must rest satisfied with mere service contracts rather than with concessions on oil lands or with the offer of crude oil, instead of cash, for their services.

Many other aspects of the new Soviet policy fit the needs and aspirations of the developing countries. Soviet willingness and ability to extend long-term aid, to correlate aid with trade, to intermesh planning, as well as to import manufactured goods, respond to the needs of new nations for long-range-program aid on a continuing basis and for expanded markets for their new industries.

The closer economic cooperation, involving as it does integration, is bound to bring the developing countries closer into the Soviet orbit. The case of Algeria illustrates that where extensive economic aid has been sensibly planned and implemented, the overthrow of a pro-Soviet regime does not lead to a collapse of an alliance. Even though the pro-Communist ideologists no longer have a say in Algerian politics, Soviet planners and experts continue to be active in Algerian economic life, and Algeria has not become noticeably more pro-Western. It seems that a well-coordinated and well-executed economic penetration may produce more durable sources of influence in the unstable Third World than does political infiltration.

Soviet Policy in the Third World
in the 1970's*

The approach of this essay represents an adaptation of methods employed by Herman Kahn, Lincoln P. Bloomfield, and others who have sought to outline the likely contours of political, technological, and cultural change in decades to come.[1] It seeks first to outline a finite number of alternative worlds which are both conceivable and reasonably likely for a given time frame — the 1970's. The pictures presented will resemble a series of still shots rather than dynamic scenarios. We shall analyze what appear to be the decisive factors that will determine which alternative model comes to the fore, and try to suggest what changes in each of these parameters will produce what results. We will then attempt to rank-order the likelihood of the alternative futures, based on the probability of change in each of the controlling factors studied. This approach will also suggest implications for U.S. policy, on the assumption that American

*Reprinted from *Orbis,* XIII, 2 (Summer, 1969), pp. 476–501, by permission of the author and *Orbis,* a quarterly journal of world affairs published by the Foreign Policy Research Institute. A longer version of this article, with further methodological discussion and bibliographical reference to the content of Soviet policy, appears in W. Raymond Duncan (ed.), *Soviet Policy in Developing Countries* (Waltham, Mass.: Ginn-Blaisdell, 1970).

1. Herman Kahn and Anthony J. Wiener, *The Year 2000: A Framework for Speculation on the Next Thirty-three Years* (New York: Macmillan, 1967); Lincoln P. Bloomfield, *Western Europe to the Mid-Seventies: Five Scenarios* (Cambridge: M.I.T. Center for International Studies, 1968). For a Soviet criticism of the Kahn-Wiener book, see Gregory Ratiani,"The Futurology of Mr. Herman Kahn," *Soviet Military Review,* No. 7 (1968), pp. 49–51.

action would influence the nature of change in at least some of these parameters.

The crucial factors likely to shape the future of Soviet policy in the Third World may be analyzed under three main categories: (1) military — strategic and technological; (2) external political; and (3) domestic — economic and social. The particular Gestalt and intensity of these factors are important variables. We shall see that certain trends may function to strengthen contradictory models, or that a factor such as the level of Soviet consumer goods may work to support a particular model — no matter whether the level of intensity is high or low. On the one hand, this illustrates that some factors are more important than others in shaping certain models. But it also shows how crucial are variables such as the rate and intensity of the salience of a particular factor. Most important, it underlines the importance of the total configuration of these factors: given one context, a factor such as Soviet affluence may support an inward-looking isolationism; in another it may further a development orientation; in still another, a hard-hitting forward strategy.

Five alternative futures will be examined. The first — what we call the "standard" world — amounts to a continuation of patterns that have characterized Soviet policy for almost two decades. The other four models are defined as "canonical" variations of the first.[2] The main characteristics of each variation have already appeared in Soviet policy — indeed, they have constituted its basic content — but none of them has achieved predominance except perhaps for a short time, for example, during or immediately following a crisis. But if one of these characteristics were to emerge as the main theme of Soviet policy, a significantly different situation from the standard world would result. These canonical variations may be defined as: (1) a forward strategy, (2) a stability or status quo orientation, (3) a development or aid orientation, and (4) isolationism.

Each of the five models can be broken down into various submodels and variations, depending, for example, on the admixture of competition and cooperation with other powers involved. We should be clear that each model could express itself primarily in military, political, economic, or cultural dimensions — or in all these senses. Geographical extension is another important variable: Does a particular model apply to all Third World regions and countries or only to some?

Considering these and other possible variables, we should be aware that there may be no uniform Soviet policy throughout the Third World. Nevertheless, it is theoretically possible that some major theme may surge ahead to characterize Soviet policy. Even if a theme such as forward strategy prevails in one region but not in others, the general principles suggested in this essay

2. These terms are used in a slightly different sense from that developed by Kahn and Wiener, *op. cit.*

can be adopted and made relevant in a more limited context, although East-West cooperation in one area will be less feasible if a tense confrontation persists in another.

The five models are presented in terms of their relative probability. Virtually by definition, the standard model appears most likely for the near and even the middle-range future. On the other hand, as Bloomfield has warned, to expect "more of the same" may turn out to be the least realistic approach, because of the contingent nature of history.[3]

The Standard Model

The standard model of which the other scenarios suggest significant variations is one that has existed throughout the 1960's, going back even to several years before Stalin's death when Moscow moved toward a more flexible line. It is a world that embodies what a dialectician would immediately recognize as a unity of opposites or, to be more precise, many unities of opposites. It is a world of contradictory impulses, cross-pressures, conflicting goals and restraints, where progress toward one objective undermines movement toward another desideratum.

The term "standard" applies in three senses. First, it suggests patterns that extend back a decade or more. Second, the existing model provides a norm by which future change may be considered and evaluated. Third, this model is the one deemed most likely to characterize Soviet policy for the next five or ten years. Precisely because the standard model is a response to many factors — all pushing and pulling in different directions — it seems unlikely that any of these conflicting impulses will increase so greatly as to bring about a clear-cut trend in Soviet policy, a trend that would override the ambivalence inherent in a strategy seeking to obtain the best of several possible worlds.

The forward strategy theme in Soviet policy toward the Third World combines both revolutionary and anti-imperialist motives, deriving from *Realpolitik* as well as ideology. The meshing of the two objectives was seen in the early 1920's when Moscow supported Kemal Ataturk's military and diplomatic campaign against Greece, France, and Britain. The Kremlin's policy reflected security concerns like those that inspired centuries of Tsarist policy, but now it was rationalized as support of a nationalist, anti-imperialist regime which could be transformed into a socialist government at a later stage.

Following the 1927 debacle of Stalin's support for another national bourgeois leader, Chiang Kai-shek, Soviet policy in the Third World became less forward and more isolationist. After World War II, Moscow even applied the two-camp doctrine to such Third World leaders as Nehru and dubbed them capitalist lackeys. In 1954 – 1955, however, the pendulum of Soviet policy

3. Bloomfield, *op. cit,* p. 1.

swung away from frontal pressure on the West to exploit once again what Moscow perceived as a vacuum in the developing world. From the beginning of the Khrushchev decade through the first years of the Brezhnev-Kosygin regime, elements of a forward strategy have again influenced Soviet policy. These have been manifest most troublesomely in Soviet-bloc military assistance to President Nasser and in vastly increased military aid to Hanoi since late 1964 (Khrushchev's successors apparently having reversed his general hands-off policy). But there have also been sharp limits to Soviet military involvement in the Third World, as we saw, for example, in the departure of Soviet planes from Egypt as soon as the 1956 war began, and in the contrast between Moscow's and Peking's views of U.S.-Hanoi negotiations to end the Vietnamese war. In general, Moscow's support for wars of national liberation has been more vocal than actual, inspired no doubt by a concern not to be outdone by Peking.

The Kremlin's forward strategy since 1954 has not been limited to military programs. For purposes of this analysis, any Soviet policy aimed at winning over leaders or peoples in the Third World and turning them against the West (or Peking) falls under the rubric of "forward strategy." Thus, economic assistance as well as cultural and propaganda programs could serve these objectives. In some cases, of course, the motivation behind a particular program is not clear — perhaps even in Moscow — for economic aid might help to influence an emerging nation toward the USSR, but it might also contribute to stability or development that would be welcomed by the West. Similarly, the training of African students at Lumumba University in Moscow might be conceived as a way to turn them into revolutionary or at least anti-Western elites, but in practice could prepare them for a status quo or even anti-Soviet orientation. Thus, the results of a program may not square with its supposed objectives.

In the last decade, a tendency to cooperate with the West in maintaining order in the Third World has been threaded into Soviet policy, though it has played a subordinate role. This tendency rests on parallel if not precisely mutual interests in maintaining peace, thwarting Chinese inroads, and — to a degree — preserving agreed spheres of influence. U.S. and Soviet policy in the 1956 Suez crisis functioned to curtail the hostilities and protect Egypt from further advances by Israel, France, and Great Britain. Subsequently, Washington and Moscow found themselves on India's side in her frontier conflicts with China, not only in 1962 but even as early as 1959, despite Moscow's neutrality proclaimed at that time. While these instances of parallel action were probably not consciously coordinated, Washington appeared content to support Premier Kosygin's good offices in arranging the Tashkent settlement of Pakistan-Indian differences over Kashmir. More dramatically, the superpowers have clearly formed a common front to prevent nuclear proliferation in the Third World.

Against this common front to uphold the status quo there are profound counter-tendencies, deriving from Moscow's desire to appear as the leader of the revolutionary movement and its reluctance to pass up an opportunity to gain influence at the expense of the United States or other Western countries. The main indicator of Moscow's reservations about collaboration with the West has been the Kremlin's policy toward United Nations peacekeeping operations. Only in the initial stages of the Congo operation, when the Soviets expected that UN activity would help to expel Western economic interests, have UN peacekeeping actions received Soviet support. Otherwise Moscow has seen them as instruments of U.S. foreign policy, thanks to Washington's influence on the votes of UN member nations. The Kremlin's response has been logical in terms of its interests, but deleterious for the cause of peacekeeping: a demand that no UN operation be launched without Soviet permission. Paradoxically, Moscow's crippling of UN peacekeeping activities may have contributed in the early and mid-1960's to a U.S. determination to intervene unilaterally where necessary to uphold the interests of law and order (and of the United States).

A third theme in Soviet policy, parallel or joint action with the West to promote economic and political development in the Third World, has operated to date, unfortunately, only in low key. The major manifestations of this theme — like parallel efforts to maintain the status quo — have not been coordinated by Moscow and Washington. To the contrary, most of their aid programs have been inspired more by competition than by cooperation. Each has conceived of its economic aid as, *inter alia,* an instrument for winning over the new nations to its foreign and domestic policy orientation or, at a minimum, denying these countries to the sphere of the other side. As a result, the action (or inaction) of each superpower has helped to promote similar policies by the other. In fact, the amounts (and rates) of economic assistance from Moscow and Washington to the Third World have declined in the mid- and late-1960's. Even in the few instances where Washington and Moscow have contributed, with other nations, to joint ventures — as in the space research program at Thumba, India, or in the UN Institute for Training and Research (which offers professional training for Third World students) — U.S. and Soviet motivation has been in large part competitive.

Nevertheless, even though Soviet aid programs may have been partly inspired by a forward strategy, their net impact may be, as in India, to strengthen the forces of progress and evolution rather than those favoring chaos and revolution. To this extent, Soviet contributions to the economic, cultural and political development of emerging nations may coincide with the true interests of the United States. As Millikan and Blackmer have pointed out, the goal of U.S. policy should not be to make the new nations capitalistic or to ally them with the United States, but to put them on the road to development so that they will have the inner resources for political self-determination and self-perpetuating economic growth.[4]

Implicit in the foregoing is the fact that Soviet policy, despite its activist leanings, has also displayed inward-looking, cautious, even isolationist tendencies. The term isolationist fits the withdrawn, xenophobic posture of Stalin's policies toward the Third World. But it likewise fits the Kremlin's reluctance since 1953 to commit Soviet troops to the Third World; Moscow's disillusionment in the early 1960's about the prospects of winning over the emerging nations of Africa and Asia; Soviet reserve deriving in part from doubts about the reliability of a Latin temperament such as Castro's, and anxiety lest an engagement such as Vietnam escalate to catastrophic proportions. Although "wars of national liberation" are termed "unavoidable," Soviet spokesmen have cautioned about the great dangers of escalation. Unlike the Chinese, who tend to extol the merits of purgation by fire, Soviet ideologues have tended in the 1950's and 1960's to treat violence as at best a necessary evil. While Moscow grants that "national liberation" must be achieved by force of arms, the Soviet line is that the transition from a bourgeois to a socialist regime can be achieved by nonviolent as well as by violent means. Such revolutions, both Moscow and Peking agree, cannot be "exported," but depend on internal forces within the country in question.

"Standard" Soviet policy in the Third World, then, has reflected contradictory commitments. Ideology and power politics point to a forward strategy, but this is curtailed by the dangers of war, limitations on Soviet economic and military power, disappointments in the Third World, and lack of enthusiasm for overseas ventures among the Soviet people. By the same token, however, a strictly isolationist posture has been untenable because challenges as well as opportunities have been present. Moscow has sought to handle some of these problems by parallel or even coordinated policies with the United States, but continued competition between the superpowers and continued Soviet aspirations to the mantle of revolutionary leadership have severely inhibited this relationship. Moscow has engaged in relatively large aid programs, chiefly in competition with the United States, but the Kremlin has tempered these not only because its resources are limited but because the political payoffs have not been sufficiently rewarding — most of the emerging nations have demonstrated their ability as well as their desire to play off the great powers to local advantage.

The standard model of Soviet involvement in the Third World, as suggested at the outset, seems likely to endure, at least into the mid-1970's, if only because Moscow will continue to ride several horses in different directions at the same time. Although expecting "more of the same" may prove to be

---

4. Max F. Millikan and Donald L. M. Blackmer, *The Emerging Nations: Their Growth and United States Policy* (Boston: Little, Brown, 1961).

unrealistic, it nevertheless appears — if we analyze the key determinants of Soviet policy — that the standard model will prevail for the next five to ten years, if not longer. Militarily, the present strategic balance of power seems likely to persist, at least to the degree that neither superpower gains a usable advantage over the other. Neither Washington nor Moscow is apt to obtain the kind of leverage that would lead one to attempt nuclear blackmail against the other, or to take great risks (such as Khrushchev's Cuban missile venture) to redress its bargaining position. While Moscow's air- and sea-lift capability for military intervention abroad will continue to grow, the extent of this growth is uncertain. In any event, Soviet practice is likely to be conservative, due to continued fears about escalation, even if Soviet theorists talk increasingly about the need for an ability to fight limited wars. An adventurist spirit arising from improvements in Soviet conventional forces would also be tempered by the growing pragmatism of Soviet decision-makers, in contrast to the more "subjective" behavior of Chairman Khrushchev. Equally important, the growing threat posed by Communist China's strategic and conventional force would tend to rein in Moscow's involvements in the Third World.

Contributing to this standard world will be a persistence of conflicting foreign policy priorities: on the one hand, a desire to drive the West (and China) from the Third World and to uphold Moscow's claim to lead the revolutionary movement; on the other hand, a desire to live in peace and to improve relations with the West for economic and other reasons. Furthermore, while soft spots in the Third World will present tempting power vacuums to the Kremlin, the new nations on the whole will seek to resist domination by any foreign power.

Economic developments in the Soviet Union will permit Moscow to maintain or even increase assistance programs, but a substantial accretion will be ruled out, not only by the objective limits to Soviet growth, but by mounting consumer demands in the USSR for something more than "goulash communism." Moscow will see no clear economic reason to alter the current patterns of trade and investment in the Third World, for the incentives to increase these activities will be neutralized by other reasons to curtail them.

The orientation of Soviet political elites and the public at large will be to build a great society at home rather than abroad. Now that the USSR has approached the threshold of consumer affluence, the pressures of rising expectations, coupled with democratic stirrings across the society, will direct attention toward internal construction rather than external adventures. Whether or not the Kremlin leadership remains basically unified, there will be no powerful constituency for political or economic activism in the Third World. Nevertheless, since the costs of maintaining the current levels of involvement are not high, there will be few overriding domestic pressures — elite or mass — to alter these levels. To the extent that the Soviet military gains a stronger hand over decision-making, their attention would probably be aimed more at changing

Soviet policy toward China or toward the West than toward the Third World. Assuming that the strategic balance remains roughly similar to that of the mid-1960's, there will be little pressure to use some point in the Third World as a bridgehead to improve the USSR's position vis-à-vis the West.

The standard model of Soviet policy has become familiar. In a sense we can abide it, for the problems it raises have to date been managed without approaching the brink of major war. To be sure, the Cuban missile crisis arose in part from Moscow's activities in the Third World, including a commitment to protect Havana against a putative threat from the United States, but the main cause of that confrontation probably derived from Moscow's desire to alter the strategic balance of power quickly and inexpensively — an aim which a Cuban missile base would conveniently serve. Other superpower engagements in the Third World have been limited to date because only one side (usually the United States) has entered in force. Clearly, however, the standard model has many shortcomings. It might easily give rise to pressures that could lead U.S. and Soviet forces to join combat in some trouble spot, perhaps catalyzed by protégés in Tel Aviv and Cairo. Further, the standard model is not adequate for coping with such problems as (1) the rise of a nuclear-armed and possibly territorially revisionist government in Peking; (2) nuclear spread to other powers, many of them capable of precipitating a conflict between the larger powers; and (3) the widening gap between the have and have-not nations.

The Forward Strategy Model

The next most likely scenario is also the most undesirable from the standpoint of world peace. If the variables that account for a "standard world" are modified but slightly, a Soviet forward strategy seems highly plausible. Several Soviet scholars have commented that this scenario seems the least likely of those presented here, yet its probability derives largely from a kind of materialist argument Soviet spokesmen have sometimes used to portray the dangers of the arms race.[5] The main assumption of this argument is that, if means exist, it is only a question of time until they will be used, particularly in the volatile political climate foreseen in the Third World for years to come.

This assumption is then linked with what intelligence analysts deem to be an incontrovertible fact: the growth in Moscow's capability to initiate and sustain military and economic intervention in far-flung parts of the globe. Even if the USSR seeks only parity and not superiority in such forces, the result may be that, for the first time in history, two superpowers will possess overlapping capabilities for intervention on a global scale. U.S. interventions from Greece

---

5. See N. M. Nikol'skii, *Osnovi vopros sovremennosti* (Moscow: *Mezhdunarodnye otnosheniia*, 1964), pp. 318–383.

(1947) to Lebanon (1958) to Vietnam (1960's) were facilitated because Moscow had no comparable capability that might be used to preempt or engage American forces. Moreover, for much of this period U.S. strategic superiority provided a shield which added to Washington's confidence that its intervention would go unchallenged.

Today, however, both Washington and Moscow are cognizant that neither side can mount a first strike capable of destroying the other's retaliatory forces. Anti-ballistic missile defenses, whether "thick" or "thin," will not alter this picture. The result is that Moscow, like Washington in the past, can intervene in the Third World with little fear of a U.S. strategic attack, since the stakes would hardly justify the risk of a retaliatory strike against the United States. Rather than being sobered by the brinkmanship already experienced in Vietnam, the Middle East, and elsewhere, strategists of both sides may come to believe that the record since 1945 indicates that war in the Third World can be localized and limited — despite involvement by one or more great powers. If nuclear weapons do not spread to many additional states, and if China remains a clearly second-rate nuclear power, the superpowers may feel still fewer inhibitions about carrying out limited combat in the dueling grounds of the Third World.

The next most important ingredient for the development of this scenario is chaos in the Third World itself. Moscow may believe that the outcome of a crisis can be favorably directed by the injection of Soviet military, economic or political force. The Kremlin might decide that, even though the new nations generally resist foreign domination, several key areas would serve as useful footholds, in the manner of Cuba or Egypt. The area might be particularly attractive for its economic, political, strategic, or other assets. Moscow might devise some pretext for intervention, or its involvement might be invited by indigenous forces.

A Soviet forward strategy is compatible with wide fluctuations among other key variables. It could be motivated by ideological renaissance in Moscow and/or by power politics. It is compatible with a high degree of U.S.-Soviet-Chinese competition in the Third World or with the withdrawal of other major competitors so that the area was left without external defenses. All might be quiet on the Western front, or there could be tension in Europe which Moscow would somehow exploit to carry out decisive actions in another arena. China might be allied with a Soviet forward strategy or constitute one of its targets.

True, economic and political developments at home place limits on the extent to which Moscow can mount a forward strategy. If interventions are surgically quick and precise, their economic and political costs may not be prohibitive. As Moscow has already learned in Cuba, the long-term expense of subsidizing the economy as well as shoring up the defenses of a client state can be gigantic. Cost factors such as these, however, manifest themselves over a medium- or long-range time span, and might not be decisive, given the perceived threat or gain of a particular moment.

A forward strategy is also compatible with a variety of political developments within the Soviet Union. Assuming few serious internal challenges, the Kremlin leaders will retain a relatively free hand to decide the basic thrust of foreign policy. But should internal rivalries or domestic pressures increase, and key leaders seek to override opposition and build cohesion by mounting a bold policy abroad, the area of the Third World would present the fewest dangers and the greatest opportunities. Problems with minority nationalities within the USSR, for example, might be manipulated by selective applications of a forward strategy abroad, particularly in the Middle East.

The forward strategy model clearly presents the greatest dangers to world peace of all the scenarios envisaged here. Soviet penetration of the Third World is likely to generate counteractions by other interested nations. It is not clear how to avert the rise of such a strategy. Third World chaos that breeds temptation is beyond the control of great powers standing outside it, at least in the short run. The development of a powerful Soviet capability for intervention is also beyond the control of other governments, except to the degree that Moscow may be trying to emulate U.S. successes or to constrain Washington's future activities. On the other hand, for Washington to stand by while Moscow adopts an interventionist policy might only lead to an increase in Soviet intervention.

Three policy guidelines may be suggested: First, Washington should refrain from challenging the Soviet Union by unilateral U.S. interventions in civil strife (as opposed to cases of aggression across frontiers). Second, programs should be carried out to promote the kind of stability that will reduce chaos in the Third World. Third, UN machinery for peacemaking as well as peacekeeping should be strengthened, and in a manner that elicits Soviet (and if possible, Chinese) support.

A Status Quo Orientation

The third-ranked model for Soviet policy in the developing world is an orientation toward maintenance of the status quo, probably by parallel or joint actions with the United States and other like-minded powers. To take in the broad spectrum of possibilities, however, we should note that a preference for the status quo could conceivably have several important variations. Like all the alternatives presented, a status quo approach could be of long or short duration; it might be a tactic or a strategy. It could be directed toward *(a)* limiting violence across national frontiers; *(b)* limiting violence within Third World states; *(c)* containing a military threat by the Third World against the industrialized nations; *(d)* limiting the influence of other external powers, such as China, within the Third World; *(e)* limiting social and economic change in the

Third World, even though it is pursued by nonviolent means; (*f*) thwarting attempts by the Third World to make inroads on the political or economic advantages of the northern "have" nations.

What conditions would favor an accentuation of the status quo orientation so that it became the predominant theme in Soviet policy? Such an orientation requires not only a basic satisfaction with the present order, but a concern lest it be upset by unwelcome developments. Fear of nuclear proliferation has already provided a strong incentive to support the status quo. If the Nonproliferation Treaty is generally successful, the Soviet commitment to help secure the nonnuclear nations against nuclear threats may generate a series of behavior patterns entailing U.S.-Soviet collaboration that could form an important component in a status quo orientation. Even if the treaty fails and nuclear proliferation does occur, the Soviet Union may still find itself leagued with Washington in an attempt to cope with actual threats of nuclear wars initiated by smaller powers rather than with merely the potential threat of such wars.

Regardless of what happens with respect to India and other potential nuclear-weapon countries, however, a growing Chinese threat — conventional as well as nuclear — would probably serve to strengthen U.S.-Soviet cooperation, unless one of the superpowers teamed up with Communist China against the other superpower. For Moscow to cooperate with Washington in such a manner would probably imply Soviet acceptance of either nuclear parity or inferiority vis-à-vis the United States. Were the Soviet Union to entertain a hope of nuclear superiority over the United States, relations between them would doubtless be too strained and laden with distrust to make duopoly work. On balance, it might be useful for neither side to feel that it was protected against smaller nuclear powers by an anti-ballistic missile system, for without an ABM defense the superpowers' interest in preventing catalytic wars would be higher. On the other hand, an ABM defense would give them a stronger bargaining hand in case they did have to deal with a series of smaller nuclear powers.

Apart from a nuclear threat, it is possible that a growing division of the world into haves and have-nots might force the superpowers into collaboration to defend the status quo. Already Peking claims that the focus of revolutionary struggle lies in the conflict between the oppressed peoples of Asia, Africa, and Latin America and the traditional centers of White Man's imperialism, with which the USSR is associated. The Soviet Union refutes this, maintaining that the revolutionary struggle is primarily between the socialist camp (which Moscow still claims to lead) and the capitalist camp. For the present, the nations of the Third World do not pose a serious, active danger to Soviet interests. Yet, if Peking does succeed in mobilizing these nations against the superpowers, the Soviet Union might fear that the general threat to the security and stability of the present order was undermining her own position.

The condition that would do most to produce a status quo orientation in

Moscow would be a growing indifference to the Soviet Union's image as leader of the Communist movement and the revolutionary peoples of the world. In the mid-1960's the maintenance of this image has apparently been an important policy priority, as witnessed by the Kremlin's concern over the "bombing of a sister socialist state, North Vietnam" and more to the point — Moscow's recurrent efforts to hold a "unity" meeting of the Communist movement. Nevertheless, the Soviets have for decades taken action to promote the interests of Soviet security at the expense of local Communist parties, ranging from France to India. Given a sufficient security threat, Moscow's political and ideological aspirations might again be shunted to one side. A downgrading of revolutionary aspirations could be considered appropriate if events in the Third World continue to indicate that this area is not amenable to a high degree of Soviet influence. Thus, if events in the Third World seem to threaten the Soviet Union or if the area appears to be unripe for the advance of Soviet interests directly, Moscow is more likely to adopt a status quo policy.

The prospects for a status quo orientation would seem to improve as Soviet-U.S. relations improve. Continued competition in some domains such as outer space, or even in key geographical regions such as Western Europe, might be consonant with U.S.-Soviet collaboration to maintain the existing order in the Third World. Certainly, positive ties between the superpowers, including economic and technological interdependence, would favor their taking a common front against Third World threats. If Soviet security interests in Eastern Europe seem to be threatened by policies of the United States, it might be more difficult to achieve a common front in dealing with geographical regions more remote to Soviet interests.

At home the status quo orientation would be favored by a growing sense of economic and political satisfaction, although it might also be strengthened by a sharp preference for radical improvements in Soviet living conditions. The tighter Soviet resources become, due either to a slow growth rate or mounting consumer demands or both within the country, the more reactionary and rigidly status quo might be Moscow's orientation to the Third World. Moreover, the more meager the Soviet resources for coping with Third World problems, the more the Soviet leadership would disregard ideological considerations in favor of cooperation with the United States. If Soviet resources did appear meager, the model of Soviet development would be less appealing to leaders of the Third World, and Soviet leaders would be more inclined to view the area as unreceptive to Soviet influence.

A domestic political situation in which the power of public opinion was growing simultaneously with mounting consumer demands might be the most favorable to a status quo policy. If consumer demands rose, but mass influence on the decision-making process remained weak, a more activist orientation might be possible. Nevertheless, a degree of stability in the Soviet state would be useful in promoting a status quo outlook insofar as this encouraged the government to concentrate on its own internal development, while trying to hold the line on challenges from the Third World.

We must, as suggested earlier, distinguish a status quo orientation with respect to economic development in the Third World from an orientation concerned primarily with maintaining the existing political-territorial system free from international violence. But the two may be coupled. Thus there have been signs that Moscow has pressed the U.A.R. to negotiate a reasonable settlement with Israel, and that the Kremlin has used economic as well as other influences to this end.

A Development or Aid Orientation

By definition, a development orientation could not go hand-in-hand with a strategy aimed at preventing economic and social change, even if the rationale for the former was to thwart disruptions that could lead to cross-national aggression and external intervention. But an orientation in Soviet policy toward development is not incompatible with a strategy of maintaining international peace. Indeed, it may be that in the most profound sense the best way to maintain "stability" is by "development," in the Third World as elsewhere. If positive adjustments to changing technological, psychological, and other patterns are not made, the pull is toward revolution and chaos rather than orderly progress. Thus, from a practical as well as a moral standpoint, a development orientation in Soviet policy to the Third World — particularly if parallel policies are pursued by the other major powers — is the most desirable of the five scenarios.

This canonical variation itself has two important variations: a development orientation could take place either in competition or — less likely — in coordination with the West. The first variation might resemble the "peace race" urged, for example, by Seymour Melman as an alternative to the arms race. [6] Soviet leaders such as Khrushchev have also urged that the struggle between the "socialist" and "capitalist" systems be waged in a nonmilitary arena, in a competition to demonstrate which system is superior, both in the developed and in the developing countries. The outcome of this competition presumably would be determined by the appeal of each system. Other authors — not so concerned with gaining points for either system — favor competition between the two on the ground that it would be more conducive than East-West cooperation to *(a)* the generation of large resources for development and *(b)* strengthening the independence and self-determination of Third World countries.

If pushed with great vigor, a development orientation could be a major aspect in a Soviet "forward strategy," particularly if Moscow sought to exploit

6. *The Peace Race* (New York: George Braziller, 1962).

primarily nonmilitary instruments of foreign policy. This approach, however, might not prove to be long-lived, or, more generally, conducive to superpower allocation of significant aid resources to the Third World. If Moscow and Washington envisaged a "peace race" mainly as a way of defeating one another, the accompanying tensions would probably lead each to place a high premium on a powerful military posture as well — both in the Third World and in the bipolar confrontation. If these assumptions are correct, it may be that in the longer run the best prospect for a powerful aid orientation on the part of the major powers would derive from a basically cooperative rather than a competitive approach.

A cooperative approach to development of the Third World could be carried on by parallel courses of action, by multilateral actions (e.g., through United Nations agencies), or — most awkward politically — joint programs. Elements of competition could continue, of course, for there is a theoretical spectrum ranging from pure competition at one extreme (the notion of a zero-sum game) to pure cooperation and harmony at the other, with various mixes in between.[7]

For either a competitive or a cooperative strategy to prevail, the strategic military balance would probably need to rest at a relative equilibrium, at a level where each superpower perceived that neither could easily achieve a meaningful advantage over the other. Under these circumstances there would be something to gain and little to lose from directing more resources toward aiding the Third World. An aid orientation could conceivably persist even though Moscow and Washington maintained powerful conventional forces for intervention, assuming that these were not actively engaged but were kept mainly as a form of mutual deterrence. But it would be helpful if United Nations forces could be built up so as to prevent cross-national violence in the Third World and hence discourage intervention.

As regards the external political climate, tension between the superpowers might be conducive to a competitive aid strategy if the two were checkmated elsewhere, while a cooperative orientation would profit more from a broad sense of *détente*. Before the United States and the USSR would divert large resources to the Third World either competitively or cooperatively, however, they would have to feel that no serious threat to the peace was likely to arise in Europe. A dynamic and united Europe could contribute to a Soviet aid orientation by sparking a competitive effort or by joining in a grand coordinated design on the part of the industrialized, northern states to assist those of the southern hemisphere. A widely perceived threat from China could also spur efforts to make the Third World more "satisfied." Japan is already in a

7. Such an approach has been formulated, e.g., by A. D. Sakharov, whose manuscript appeared in *The New York Times,* July 22, 1968 and, with commentary by Harrison E. Salisbury, as *Progress, Coexistence and Intellectual Freedom* (New York: W. W. Norton, 1968).

strong position to assist other nations' development, and has been making useful contributions for some time, as has Taiwan. In time, other developing nations such as India and Argentina might — like China — be able to contribute to, as well as profit from, a wide-scale development orientation.

A cooperative orientation would be favored by an increase in Soviet trade with the West, while the prevalence of restrictions on such transactions might lead to more competitive relations in the Third World where trade as well as aid might be employed as an instrument for winning over potential allies. To the degree that important Third World countries appear vulnerable to domination by external powers politically or economically, the chances of competitive aid programs gain. Competition could also be spurred by the developing countries playing off one major power (or bloc) against the other. In contrast, cooperative programs would be more likely if the superpowers see that they cannot dominate key parts of Asia, Africa, or Latin America. Indeed, a threat from the have-nots of the south against the haves of the north might be useful in compelling the latter to adopt a significant cooperative aid program.

Massive assistance to the Third World would require continued and even increased economic growth in the USSR (and in other developed nations), since domestic requirements would limit the resources available to the Kremlin if it decided to embark on a development strategy. In any case, even though Soviet living standards lagged behind those in many Western countries, the USSR would have available certain types of surpluses — perhaps, for example, trained technicians who could contribute to development programs.

Sociological change in the Soviet Union may also favor an interest in foreign aid, comparable to developments in the United States stimulating many young people to seek a creative outlet in the Peace Corps and other service programs. A sense of security and relative affluence at home — in contrast to the "depression" mentality of their elders — may spark in the young a wider interest in humanities and social service instead of more practical careers such as engineering. The milieu may induce a cosmopolitan instead of a chauvinistic outlook, beginning with a deeper interest in and greater opportunity for foreign travel.

Either an authoritarian or a more democratic government could preside over an aid orientation in Soviet policy. An authoritarian regime might wield the necessary resources for competition or even — presuming a kind of enlightened despotism — at least tacit cooperation with the West. Greater public influence over foreign policy could — as in the United States — make it more stingy and inward-looking. Between these two extremes, however, is a plausible development that could improve foreign aid prospects: more power over government decisions by technocratic elites who are better educated, more affluent, and (except for the military) more internationalist than traditional party *apparatchiki* or the population at large.

To summarize, it appears that a competitive orientation to development is more likely than a cooperative one — at least by the familiar logic of the Cold War. A competitive development strategy can merge with a forward strategy generally. This could make the Third World more an object than a subject for development, and limit the degree of great-power economic aid to the area, because each power would seek to maintain high levels of military capability as well. To be sure, there is a danger that, if Soviet tensions with the West should diminish, the superpowers might turn inward and tend to neglect the Third World, dealing with it mainly through the apparently cheaper route of a status quo orientation or by strategic withdrawal.

Isolationism

The Soviet posture deemed least likely is an accentuation of inward-looking tendencies in the direction of isolation and withdrawal from economic and political involvement in the Third World. This orientation resembles a status quo strategy in some respects, and could follow from some of the same underlying factors, but it differs in being more passive in regard to the developing countries. Whereas a status quo policy would intervene to prevent cross-national aggression and perhaps even to throttle social and economic change, an isolationist tack would allow the emerging nations to fight out their own battles and organize common if ineffectual fronts against the northern tier. Despite these conditions, Moscow — joined perhaps by other great powers — would rest content behind an overwhelming military superiority vis-à-vis the Third World and an economic strategy that ensured satisfactory growth for the USSR without involvement in the problems of the new nations.

The strategic bedrock for isolationism would be a Fortress Russia mentality. This attitude could flourish whether the strategic military balance registered parity or a slight Soviet disadvantage. If Moscow possessed a massive superiority over the West, it might well be reluctant to pass over an opportunity for global penetration; if it felt significantly inferior to the West, compensating actions might be attempted in the Third World. A Soviet ballistic missile defense would probably facilitate an isolationist attitude, although the existence of such a system could also encourage a forward strategy on the premise that a counterblow from the West or from China would not be fatal. An isolationist posture would be favored if Moscow did not possess a powerful conventional force, although frequent military interventions in the Third World by other external powers would tend to provoke Soviet countermeasures. Isolationist tendencies would also be strengthened if Soviet experiences and doctrine warned of the dangers of local war and set forth reasons why active Soviet support for such conflicts was neither necessary nor desirable.

Withdrawal from deep involvement in the Third World would be facilitated if Moscow felt that this would not leave the area ripe for takeover by hostile great powers which would exploit it to Soviet disadvantage. A sharp decline in Moscow's resolve to pose as leader of revolutionary forces would not necessarily lead to a decrease in Soviet involvement in Asia, Africa, and Latin America, for Kremlin policies in these areas are probably dictated by *raison d'état* as well as by ideology.

Thus, if great-power competition ceased almost entirely, Moscow could afford to consider withdrawal from this one possible arena. But, if competition between Moscow and either Peking or Washington continued rather intensively across the board, this rivalry would probably spill over into the Third World. Only if tensions crossed a high threshold (e.g., in Europe or along the Sino-Soviet frontier) would the Kremlin feel compelled to withdraw from peripheral areas of interest, as in Africa, to defend vital interests closer to home.

Withdrawal would also be facilitated if the Third World proved itself highly resistant to domination — political, economic, or other — by outside powers. If the area presented few opportunities to the USSR and little threat either from within or from external sources, Moscow would be more inclined to ignore the emerging nations. They might show economic stagnation or a capacity for take-off and growth, but if Soviet interests were not affected, the Kremlin might focus its attentions elsewhere.

Clearly, one variant of the isolationist model would be to withdraw from some areas but not from others. The Kremlin might attempt to dominate (and/or develop) a few key areas, such as the Middle East, while leaving others to work out their own destinies, e.g., Black Africa. Such a policy would make sense in that some areas are geographically more convenient, richer in resources, more significant strategically, and more amenable to Soviet influence than others. But it is extremely difficult to draw and maintain such a line, because the USSR as a superpower with interests to the east, to the west, and to the south, can hardly disregard political and economic trends in any part of the world. And if she should succeed in dominating one area, such as the Middle East, this would encourage her appetites elsewhere and, at the same time, generate competitive strategies on the part of other great powers.

Paradoxically, either failures or successes on the domestic economic front could strengthen isolationist trends. Failures would limit resources available for aid. Difficulties in foreign trade, with either the developed or the developing countries, might lead to a heightened priority on self-sufficiency. If other developed countries' economies moved ahead while the Soviet Union (and perhaps her East European allies) experienced difficulties, pressures would mount for channeling marginal gains to domestic consumption rather than to Third World development. Further, if East-West competition became intense, and assuming that America cut her involvement in Southeast Asian conflicts, a U.S. decision to seek clear-cut superiority in defensive and offensive missile systems could put tremendous pressures on Soviet economic resources available to the developing nations.

On the other hand, if the Soviet economy continued to expand and was accompanied by *détente* on the external scene, Soviet society might become fixed on its internal problems. The USSR might become one of the "increasingly Sensate (empirical, this-worldly, secular, humanistic, pragmatic, utilitarian, contractual, epicurean or hedonistic, and the like) cultures" anticipated in the "standard world" of Herman Kahn and Anthony Wiener.[8] There would be increasing affluence and leisure. "National interest" values might erode, but the humanistic and hence cosmopolitan influences would be countervailed by self-indulgence tendencies.

The stronger the popular influence over government policy, the greater the chances may be for an inward orientation. This tendency follows from the expectation that the Soviet people will be more interested in building a good life and catching up with living standards elsewhere, than in nationalist or internationalist adventures. A high degree of participatory democracy is unlikely to develop in the USSR, at least for a decade to come, but the government may have to reckon increasingly with popular sentiments, and hence reduce the resources devoted to competition in, or assistance to, the Third World.

Although isolationism has fairly strong prospects conditioned by the USSR's economic or political situation, the domestic forces inclining toward it will probably be neutralized by military and general foreign policy pressures to maintain the present level of involvement in the Third World. Hence, "more of the same" has a sounder basis than a distinct trend toward isolationism. Whether Soviet economic growth continues at a low or a high rate, and whether popular opinion comes to affect Soviet policy-making in a more direct or indirect manner, the costs of continuing the present level of involvement will not be painfully high. Indeed these expenditures will probably decrease relative to the present allocation of resources, because the Soviet economy can easily grow at a faster rate than the volume of resources required for military and economic penetration in Asia, Africa, and Latin America (which can be accomplished in part by dumping surplus material not needed domestically).

Implications for United States Policy

If we examine the ways the standard model might be most easily altered so that one of its present components came to the fore, the forward strategy seems the most likely variation to emerge. This change in existing patterns might come by the early 1970's, assuming that Moscow has by then persisted in expanding its conventional air, sea, and land forces for intervention in remote areas.

A status quo orientation might also come about more readily than some observers would anticipate, perhaps in response to such factors as a broad

8. Kahn and Wiener, *op. cit.*, p. 186.

threat from China; a superpower accord to halt nuclear spread and to prevent disruption of the Nonproliferation Treaty; the removal of an interventionist challenge to Moscow by U.S. policies which aim at ending the U.S. influence in Vietnam and elsewhere; or a diminution of Soviet concern about the USSR's image as leader of revolutionary peoples.

A development orientation might take longer to emerge, since it would require a much larger commitment of human and material resources — vast surpluses of which do not appear imminent in the USSR (or even in the United States) — although selective use of Soviet assets might make an aid orientation feasible immediately on a somewhat restricted scale. But there are also political obstacles that would need to be overcome, e.g., internal resistance as well as concern about tense Soviet relationships with Washington, Bonn, Peking, and other powers.

An isolationist trend seems still less likely. The economizing advantages would probably be insufficient to make Moscow depart from the familiar standard model. After all, the present posture is maintained by virtue of the military-strategic and external political concerns of the largest country on earth, stretching across the Eurasian land mass as a key part of the "world island."

The five models outlined here vary considerably in their effect on the basic objectives of U.S. foreign policy. The model of Soviet policy least consonant with U.S. objectives is the forward strategy. The most desirable is a development orientation, particularly if carried out in coordination with other industrialized nations. The other three models have advantages and disadvantages, making it difficult to assign them a clear rank order.

The forward strategy is undesirable because it presents the clearest threat to peace; if it is not matched by effective countermoves, Soviet influence will probably spread and that of the United States diminish, weakening the economic and political independence of the Third World. It may be argued that in the long run Moscow would find that a forward strategy achieved little real or worthwhile influence abroad. Even if this is true, however, such a strategy still poses a strong immediate danger. The United States is not apt to sit back and take a philosophical view of unrestrained Soviet advance into regions with important economic, political, and military assets which could strengthen the Soviet global position — particularly if Soviet successes should also revitalize the Communist movement and even induce China to link forces with the Kremlin juggernaut. Since resistance from the United States (and possibly from Europe, China, and Japan) is likely, there is a good chance of a confrontation with an explosive potential for escalation.

A Soviet orientation toward aid and development, however, would square with U.S. interests in stable economic growth and self-determination for the Third World. Even if the admixture of competition outweighed elements of cooperation in a Soviet policy of aid and development, the gains for the developing world and for international peace and security would be high — provided the competition did not take on a predominantly forward strategy aspect. The neuroses of the excessively hedonistic and self-indulgent societies might be partially cured by the same actions that helped the poorer nations to lift themselves and, in so doing, alleviated their tendencies toward self-pity, hate, and fatalistic despair.

Either the isolationist model or the status quo orientation seems safer from the standpoint of U.S. interests than the "standard" (more of the same) model or, *a fortiori,* the forward strategy. If the isolationist model also permitted the United States to pursue her interest in the Third World, including aid and development, this approach need not exert a negative impact on economic and political development, except to the extent that Soviet contributions would be lacking. As we have seen, however, it is improbable that Moscow would elect to leave the field to the United States — and unfortunately it is just as doubtful that Washington would enter the field more vigorously for purely altruistic reasons.

These same considerations hold for the status quo model. While it presents little danger of U.S.-Soviet military confrontation, it implies little external aid for the new nations. By comparison, the standard world has the advantage that it calls forth some aid for development purposes (mainly by superpower competition), but it has the serious liability that it can easily shade into an aggressive policy leading to a superpower crunch, as one or the other moves to exploit an opportunity in the Third World.

The problem, then, is to encourage Moscow toward policies that minimize competition, particularly in the military realm, while enhancing its interest in promoting economic stability and growth in the developing areas. It would be to the advantage of all concerned if local arms races could be avoided, for they waste local resources while stimulating competition, regionally and globally, in unproductive ways. As noted earlier, a development orientation based on Cold War competition promises a bigger outlay by the superpowers in the immediate future than a cooperative effort, but such competition has important liabilities — mainly its impetus for forward strategy postures by both sides. Coordinated aid programs, whether bilateral or multilateral, have fewer undesirable side effects and greater potential for orderly development over the long haul.

If we review the range of factors on which alternative Soviet strategies may rest, some guidelines emerge as to the kinds of U.S. policies most conducive to favorable rather than dysfunctional trends in Moscow's orientation to the Third World. In the realm of strategic weaponry, it seems clear that neither U.S. inferiority nor superiority will be functional, for either may encourage Soviet activism — whether out of overconfidence or from anxiety. A stable strategic balance ensuring that neither side can gain a commanding advantage will help to deter Soviet adventures while at the same time reducing incentives for quick fixes to compensate for strategic vulnerabilities. A freeze or a turning down in the levels of Soviet and U.S. armaments might not only free resources for development programs but contribute to an atmosphere in which smaller nations perceive reasons to diminish local arms races and concentrate on development. An effective Nonproliferation Treaty and an effective system of guarantees for the nonnuclear nations will also promote both development and security.

The United States should seek to build up United Nations capabilities for peacemaking and peacekeeping and to do so in ways that elicit Soviet (and Chinese) support rather than opposition. In the meantime, until such machinery exists, Washington should try to work in concert with Moscow to maintain law and order as *between* states in the Third World, while avoiding intervention in basically internal disputes. Apparently the United States will have to maintain a conventional force capable of deterring Soviet (or Chinese) intervention, but this power should not be used loosely (as it may have been, for example, in the Dominican Republic) because this will tend to provoke Soviet actions of a similar nature.

In several of the scenarios it has been noted that vulnerabilities in the Third World may tempt Soviet intervention. It is in the U.S. interest, therefore, as well as in the interest of the countries concerned, for economic and political development to be of a kind that discourages attempts at domination by foreign powers. To the extent that the new nations are strong, Moscow should see that it cannot dominate them but that it should — for its own reasons — aid them.

The better the Kremlin's relations with the West, the more it can afford to take a positive attitude toward peaceful and prosperous development in the Third World. East-West trade and a reduction of trade barriers globally will be conducive to such an attitude. Soviet economic growth is welcome, not only because of its potential for Soviet living standards, but because it provides a margin of strength for aiding the new nations. While the emergence of an overly complacent and self-indulgent populace in the USSR is a possibility, it is also likely that some of the technocratic elite and intelligentsia will see both moral and practical reasons for assisting the developing areas.

This perception will be strengthened if the United States shows by her own example that it is feasible and worthwhile to channel resources to the Third World. We have already seen, for example, the galvanizing effect of the U.S. Peace Corps on West European and Japanese youth, many of whom have been influenced to carry out similar programs for their countries. Before the arrival of that better world in which cooperation outweighs competition, a U.S. lead in allocating much greater resources to aid and development will challenge

Moscow — out of competitive instincts — not to leave the field to a major adversary. At the same time, while cultivating the habit of greater contribution to Third World development, the two superpowers as well as other industrialized nations may grope toward patterns which involve more coordination and less rivalry.

PART VII

Retrospect and Prospect

What distinguishes Professor Shulman's review of recent Soviet foreign policy is his identification of many important factors — calculations of Soviet leaders, domestic developments, technological changes, events in Western, Third World, and other Communist countries — that have significantly influenced Soviet behavior in the past and will probably do so in the future. Moreover, Shulman evaluates the relative importance of different factors at various important stages of Soviet history between 1961 and 1966. For example, he argues that the transition from "a relationship of low tension and even tacit restraint between the Soviet Union and the United States" in the fall of 1964 to a more hostile and noncooperative relationship by mid-1966 "mainly resulted from the interaction of three factors: the intensification of the Vietnam conflict, a further heightening of Chinese power and militancy, and changes in the substance and the style of decision-making under the new Soviet leadership." Furthermore, Shulman assesses the responses of Soviet leaders to changing conditions, internal and external, and he identifies some general patterns or trends in recent Soviet international behavior.

Other Western overviews of contemporary Soviet foreign policy include: Vernon Aspaturian, "Soviet Foreign Policy at the Crossroads: Conflict and/or Collaboration?" *International Organization,* XXIII (Summer, 1969), pp. 589 – 620; John C. Campbell, "The Soviet Union in the International Environment," in Allen Kassof (ed.), *Prospects for Soviet Society* (New York: Praeger,

1968), pp. 473 – 496; and Robert Slusser, "America, China, and the Hydra-Headed Opposition: The Dynamics of Soviet Foreign Policy," in Peter Juviler and Henry Morton (eds.), *Soviet Policy-Making* (New York: Praeger, 1967), pp. 183 – 269.

Recent Soviet Foreign Policy:
Some Patterns in Retrospect*

The law of life is change, but rarely it seems, has the life of international politics changed in so many of its dimensions and with such accelerating speed as in the present. Continents seethe with change and conflict; nations form, unite, and disunite; the guerrilla and the missile transform the art of war. In the words of Leonid Brezhnev: "Foreign political tasks have become more complex."

Indeed, the impression is inescapable that the leadership of the Soviet Union has been groping for the most effective way to deal with some complex and unanticipated problems, and that it may now be poised at a fork in the road. It is evident that the Vietnam issue, only recently a small cloud on the horizon, now darkens the skies over every continent; but the question it poses is whether this issue will prove to be but a transient interruption in the long-term evolutionary trends in Soviet policy, or whether this conflict, and the complications flowing from it, will mark a significant turn in the direction of Soviet policy.

Over the postwar period as a whole, and especially after the death of Stalin, it has appeared that the long-term trends in Soviet policy were moving in the

*Copyright by the Board of Editors of the *Journal of International Affairs,* reprinted from XXII, Number 1, 1968, pp. 26 – 47. Permission to reprint is gratefully acknowledged to the Editors of the *Journal.* This study was originally prepared in the summer of 1966 under the auspices of the Brookings Institution.

direction of traditional power-bloc politics based on nation-state interests, with increasing reliance upon the indirect strategy of "peaceful coexistence." Within this formulation, significant fluctuations have been marked, particularly in response to changing perceptions of the power balance. What is in question now is whether the efforts to deal with the events of the last few years, and in particular those growing out of the Vietnam conflict, are to be regarded as fluctuations within this evolutionary pattern, or whether some new departures may be in the making.

It is not the Vietnam issue alone which creates this necessity for choice, but the many underlying factors in international politics which are sharply highlighted by this conflict: the potentialities for revolutionary upheavals elsewhere in the underdeveloped areas; the continued militancy of the Chinese Communist regime; the diplomatic isolation of the United States on the Vietnam issue; the widening of divisive trends in the non-Communist world, including Europe; the rise in United States military capabilities; and the smarting inferiority of Soviet strategic and local military power, pressing against other claims on Soviet resources. It has been the interplay of such considerations as these that has posed the alternatives confronting the Soviet leaders in their recent deliberations on foreign policy.

A brief review of certain main trends in Soviet foreign policy between the Twenty-Second Congress of the Communist Party of the Soviet Union (October 17 – 31, 1961) and the Twenty-Third Congress (March 29 – April 8, 1966) offers an illuminating impression of the mounting claim these issues have made upon the attention of the Soviet leadership, and of the evolution of Soviet responses to them.

I

In the fall of 1961 when the Twenty-Second Congress assembled, Soviet policy was suffering from a hangover as an aftermath of Khrushchev's inflated claims to a "shift in the balance of power" during the post-Sputnik euphoria. From 1958 until mid – 1960, the main thrust of Soviet policy had been an effort to translate into political advantage the general impression that the achievements of Soviet science and technology in orbiting the first artificial space satellite and in testing the first intercontinental ballistic missile in late 1957 signified at least a potential gain for Soviet power. This effort proceeded along three main lines: (1) pressure for political concessions from the West (in particular, on Berlin in 1958); (2) a damping-down of international tension to restrain Western overreaction to Soviet achievements (the Khrushchev visit to America in 1959, from which emerged the "spirit of Camp David"); and (3) an intensified cultivation of Soviet influence among the new nations of Africa and Asia. By the time of the U-2 episode in May of 1960 and the subsequent disintegration of the Summit Conference, it had already become apparent that the symbolic effect of Soviet space and missile demonstrations had not produced Western concessions on Berlin or on Eastern Germany. Moreover, the atmosphere of *détente* had not headed off an intensified United States effort to close the presumed "missile gap" — as evidenced by the testing of the first Atlas intercontinental missile and the launching of the first Polaris submarine. In fact, it became evident that Khrushchev's effort to squeeze maximum advantage out of the Soviet test demonstrations had so galvanized the American missile production effort that the strategic balance in the coming missile period favored the United States even more than it had in the preceding period of the strategic bomber, and the Soviet Union became the "Avis" of international politics. As a result of information from overflights and other intelligence sources, it became clear that Khrushchev had not backed up his claims by going into large-scale production of intercontinental missiles (as the Soviet Union had done in missiles of shorter range). The net effect of his effort to capitalize on purely symbolic demonstrations was therefore massively adverse to the Soviet power position.

Nevertheless, Khrushchev's impulse was to respond to the puncturing of the "missile gap" by going over to the attack. Influenced perhaps by his reading of President Kennedy's susceptibilities, and by the weakening of the American position as a result of the Bay of Pigs disaster, Khrushchev reopened the Berlin crisis in the spring of 1961. Thus the international climate in the background as the Twenty-Second Party Congress opened that fall was one of tension. There had been a confrontation of Soviet and American tanks in Berlin; the exodus from East Germany had reached such flood proportions that a Berlin Wall was required to staunch it; and the three-year moratorium on nuclear testing was ended as first the Soviet Union and then the United States began a new round in the development of more advanced missiles and nuclear warheads. Khrushchev did his best to wring maximum political advantage out of the test explosion of a weapon in the 55 to 60-megaton range, and spoke of the possibility of a 100-megaton weapon.

What is interesting about this brief recapitulation of the events prior to the Twenty-Second Congress is the way they illustrate several persistent elements in the Soviet experience:

1) A major determinant of the policy emphasis in this period appears to have been an essentially political calculation of the effect of present and future power upon political behavior.

2) Related to this was a (perhaps distinctively Khrushchevian) tendency to give great weight to the anticipated political effect of demonstrations of token military capability, rather than to actual military capability.

3) The dampening of the atmosphere of tension to restrain Western policy and military preparations was carried forward at the same time as pressure was

applied to gain advantages, and resources were concentrated on building the Soviet power base, notwithstanding the contradictory effect of those policies.

4) In this period, as has so often been the case in the Soviet experience, the effort to apply pressure to gain political advantages tended to have counterproductive results, stimulating the cohesion and mobilization of the Western powers.

II

The central strategic conception of the Soviet leadership, as it emerged from the proceedings of the Twenty-Second Congress, appeared to have been that the urgent immediate task was the strengthening of the Soviet economic base as the source of future power in its multiple aspects, meanwhile relying upon an easement of international tension to prevent further disadvantageous trends in the Soviet power position. The main business of the Congress was intended to center around a twenty-year economic plan, but foreign policy questions would not remain in the background, particularly because of the Albanian-Chinese attack upon the fundamental direction of Soviet policy. Against this attack, Khrushchev elaborated and defended "peaceful coexistence" as a strategy which was both prudent and effective, emphasizing the following three considerations:

1) The development of thermonuclear weapons is a qualitative change in the international situation which requires the avoidance of a general nuclear war.

2) The advanced industrial countries, while showing no signs of imminent revolutionary potentialities, are vulnerable to internal and external pressures that can weaken their international power position, and are susceptible to a policy of division and détente.

3) The newly independent nations, following a more-or-less "neutral" course, have become a favorable factor in international politics, which can be brought by a "peaceful coexistence" policy to augment the influence of the Soviet bloc.

While it was clear that the absorption of the significance of thermonuclear destructiveness into Soviet thought was resulting in an increasing conservatism in regard to general war, this did not remove the military plane of conflict from a significant place in the struggle, even under the strategy of "peaceful coexistence." This is reflected in continuing efforts to find ways to make effective political use of military capabilities, thereby achieving gains without general war. This may be observed in the intimidatory pressure of Soviet military capabilities upon Western public opinion to produce a spirit of accommodation. Examples are Khrushchev's reminder to the countries of Western Europe that they are "hostages" to Soviet medium-range rockets, and Gromyko's enjoinder to the Western powers to be "realistic" in the spirit of Franklin Roosevelt and accommodate themselves peacefully to the changes which the growing power of the Soviet Union necessitates. This effort may be seen also in the Khrushchev speech of January, 1961, and in the declarations at the Congress regarding the necessity of Soviet military aid for those local conflicts described as "wars of national liberation." The declarations were nevertheless tempered by some ambiguous recognition of the danger that limited conflicts might enlarge into general war.

What was not expressed at the Congress, but what, in the light of subsequent actions, must have been in the forefront of the consciousness of the Soviet leaders and an active issue in behind-the-scenes debates, was the conviction that the strategic military superiority of the United States must be overcome as soon as possible. This lesson had been dramatized during the Berlin crisis of 1961, when the confrontation of tanks at "Checkpoint Charlie" made it clear that however great might have been the advantage of the Soviet Union in local forces, the risk of escalation would have carried the encounter to a strategic plane at which the comparative advantage of the United States would have been decisive. The anticipatory awareness of this disadvantage necessarily narrowed the limits beyond which Soviet diplomacy could press the issue. But the question was how, given the limitations of Soviet resources, the American lead could best be overcome? With a gross national product roughly half that of the United States, with serious problems in the administration of the Soviet economy reflected in a slowing-down of the rate of growth, and with political considerations limiting the capacity of the leadership to deflect resources into the military sector at the enormous levels required, the choices were obviously difficult.

It is now apparent, in the light of Soviet behavior in the course of the following year, that three lines of action were followed to try to narrow the gap of Soviet strategic inferiority:

1) Efforts were made to slow down the American strategic advance (still accelerating in response to the crisis of the previous year) by re-creating a climate of reduced tension. The Berlin issue was cooled by a private message from Khrushchev to Kennedy in September 1961, and more specifically in March, 1962, at a meeting of the Foreign Ministers of the Soviet Union, the United States, and the United Kingdom. Significantly, that meeting took place at the reopening of disarmament negotiations, which had been broken off by a Soviet walkout from the ten-nation disarmament conference two years earlier. A conference on Laos successfully reached agreement on the neutral status of that trouble-spot. Agreements were reached with the United States on the extension of cultural exchanges and for technical cooperation in the peaceful uses of outer space. An exchange of private correspondence with Kennedy was opened by Khrushchev in this period. It was evident that Khrushchev had hoped his improvement of relations with Kennedy would

head off the resumption of atmospheric testing by the U.S. in response to the Soviet tests in the fall of 1961, and he was angered when the American tests were announced in March, 1962.

2) Some additional resources were transferred to the military sector. It was explained that the rise in the retail price of butter and meat by 25 and 30 percent, and the postponement of the scheduled reduction in income tax, were made necessary by increased defense expenditures. Some of these expenditures were clearly absorbed by the development of nuclear weapons tested in a series beginning in September, 1961, and in a new series of tests which lasted from August until November of 1962; some by the large number of space experiments, including a number identified as "cosmic satellites," and one referred to by Khrushchev as a "global rocket"; and some, to judge by the lead-times involved, must have gone toward the increase in the Soviet stockpile of intercontinental missiles which began to make its appearance in the following years.

3) The most daring effort to find a short-cut toward strategic parity was of course the abortive emplacement of medium and intermediate-range missiles (of which the Soviet Union had an abundance) in Cuba. The targetting of the United States from Cuba would have enabled the Soviets to perform a strategic function, substituting for their deficiency in intercontinental missiles.

The failure of this third action produced such a spectacular crisis that all parties concerned and most spectator nations seem to have experienced something of a catharsis. Largely because of this experience, but also because of several coincidental factors to which we will turn in a moment, Soviet foreign policy reflected a marked shift of emphasis during the two years which followed, from the end of 1962 until the last months of 1964.

The most striking feature of this period is that it marked the lowest level of tension between the Soviet Union and the United States of the entire postwar period. For a brief period at least, while the memory of the Cuban missile crisis was fresh in mind, the function of *détente* measures qualitatively deepened. In the previous periods, intermittent efforts to damp down the atmosphere of tension seemed specifically intended to reduce the United States military effort and the cohesion of the Western alliance. Now, although these purposes were also served, the measures involved had a somewhat more substantive character, and appeared intended to defuse the conflict relationship with the United States to some degree in order to reduce the risk of general war and bring down the level of military expenditures required.

III

In the post-crisis atmosphere, the Soviet Union moved with relative speed toward a number of arms control measures. In December 1962, Khrushchev indicated to Kennedy his willingness to accept two or three on-site inspections, plus three "black boxes," in verification of a ban on underground testing; since the United States position at that time was that a minimum of eight inspections were required, no agreement resulted. The following July, Khrushchev accepted an earlier American proposal for a test ban in the three environments in which no on-site inspection was required: outer space, the atmosphere, and underwater — with an ambiguous suggestion that this agreement be tied to a non-aggression treaty between the Warsaw Pact and NATO powers. Although the latter proposal was not realized, the Partial Test-Ban Treaty was quickly negotiated within a month. The fact that the United States and the Soviet Union had both completed a series of atmospheric tests the previous summer and fall was doubtless a contributory circumstance. Among other measures taken in this period was an agreement for a "hot line" of immediate communications between the Soviet and American leaderships, acceptance by both powers of a resolution in the General Assembly of the United Nations prohibiting the orbiting of nuclear weapons, and a reciprocal exchange of unilateral pledges by the Soviet Union and the United States to reduce the production of fissionable materials for weapons purposes. The Soviet Union also announced a reduction in its military budget, although the impression prevailed in the West that Soviet production of intercontinental missiles in this period was intensified following the Cuban crisis. Foreign Minister Gromyko also announced that the Soviet Union was now prepared to accept the Western proposal for a "nuclear umbrella" — a certain residual number of missiles to remain in the hands of the Soviet Union and the United States in the earlier stages of the disarmament process, but the proposal remained tied to the Soviet plan for "general and complete disarmament," and came to naught.

A number of actions by the Soviet Union in other fields during this period strengthened the impression that it was seeking to improve relations, such as the cessation of jamming the Voice of America and the British Broadcasting Corporation programs, and the agreement on the designation of U Thant as Secretary-General of the United Nations without any further pressure that the UN Secretariat be reorganized along "troika" lines. The period was not without incidents that might under other circumstances have given rise to considerable tension: some interference with American and British convoys on the road to Berlin, the arrest of Professor Frederick C. Barghoorn, and a dispute over the financing of UN peacekeeping operations, but these were handled by the Soviet Union with an evident desire to minimize the disturbance to the overall relationship of diminished tension.

Although the Cuban missile crisis was the most dramatic cause of the turn toward low-tension policies in this period, there were a number of other factors present which operated in the same direction, and may have played important contributory roles. Among these factors was Khrushchev's impression of current American politics and policies. Once Kennedy's firmness in the Berlin and Cuba crises had dispelled Khrushchev's earlier impressions of Kennedy's vulnerability to pressure, there developed an obvious interest in the Kremlin in cultivating a private relationship of confidence with the American President. Kennedy's appeal for an end to the Cold War in his commencement address at The American University on June 10, 1963, had a powerful public impact in the Soviet Union (many Russians carried the clipping of the speech in their wallets) and made an obvious impression on Khrushchev. The sale of wheat to the Soviet Union and the tone of confidence and candor in the private communications between the two leaders strengthened the Soviet impression that some collaboration was possible between adversaries. After the death of the President, and particularly during the election campaign between Johnson and Goldwater in the autumn of 1964, the Soviet leadership exercised great care that no action on its part should strengthen any potential "hard-line" tendencies in American politics.

In other parts of the world, political trends also argued for the advantage of a low-tension policy. In Western Europe, although the Bonn-Paris Treaty evoked some harsh and anxious reactions from the Soviet Union, the famous press conference of General de Gaulle in January, 1963 was regarded in Moscow for the most part as a positive development. Prospects for the continued momentum of the European Common Market, which had been a source of mounting concern in the Soviet Union and in Eastern Europe, now appeared diminished. Moreover, the influence of the United States and the effectiveness of NATO were both diminished by the French line of sovereign independence, and Soviet diplomacy, despite some sensitivity about the General's conception of "Europe from the Atlantic to the Urals," accepted his thrust toward national independence as an "objectively progressive" development. During the last months of the Khrushchev regime, Soviet diplomacy also began to explore the possibility of influencing the orientation of the Federal Republic in a more favorable direction, notwithstanding the continuous drumfire of Soviet propaganda on the themes of German "militarism and revanchism." These divisive trends clearly depended upon a Western European perception of a diminished Soviet threat, and therefore added further weight to the argument for a low-tension policy.

Meanwhile, acute problems within the Communist bloc became a major preoccupation. The Sino-Soviet dispute had by now burst into an open exchange of polemics; Chinese incursions into Africa and Chinese encouragement of an independent line on the part of the Eastern European states, Rumania in particular, occupied the attention and energies of the Soviet leadership. At home, the declining growth rate of the Soviet economy was dealt with by a succession of administrative and political reorganizations, piling one improvisation upon another, the effect of which was to strengthen Soviet requirements for trade and credits from the West and to create stringent claims upon Soviet resources and dissatisfactions within the Party that were to lead to the ouster of Khrushchev in October, 1964.

One other important contributory factor in the background during this period was the effect of changing military technology. A significant revolution had been taking place in the qualitative character of the strategic weapons systems on both sides during the four or five years preceding, and it was to have important political consequences. Both the Soviet Union and the United States had been moving away from reliance upon vulnerable "first-strike" weapons systems. The advent of "hardened" intercontinental missile systems and missile-bearing nuclear submarines encouraged the evolution of "second-strike" retaliatory strategic doctrines and diminished the fear of surprise attack. The prevailing conception of a balance of mutual deterrence, insensitive to substantial inequalities in the number of weapons in any particular category available to either side, encouraged a certain sense of stability in the strategic military confrontation. Although military strategists on both sides continued to be concerned about the requirements for a war-fighting capability in the event that deterrence should break down, the political climate during this period encouraged a relatively low expectation of general war.

IV

As of the fall of 1964, therefore, it appeared that a combination of circumstances tended to push the Cold War into the background. Domestic preoccupations, fragmenting alliances, and a certain strategic stabilization all added encouragement to a relationship of low tension and even tacit restraint between the Soviet Union and the United States. It is of course difficult to document the presence and the growth of this tacit restraint; perhaps the most that can be recorded now is the impression that the political and military decision-makers on both sides had begun to take into account the interacting processes in the defense field, and that certain decisions regarding procurement, deployment, the staging of maneuvers, etc., were affected by the desire to avoid stimulating undesired reactions from the other side.

The transition to a new inflection of policy during the year and a half which followed, from the fall of Khrushchev to the Twenty-Third Party Congress in March-April of 1966, mainly resulted from the interaction of three factors: the intensification of the Vietnam conflict, a further heightening of Chinese power and militancy, and changes in the substance and the style of decision-making under the new Soviet leadership.

Toward the latter part of 1964, the tide of battle and politics in Vietnam appeared to be moving toward an early Communist victory. One clear departure in policy by the new Soviet leadership, in contrast to the contraction of Soviet commitments to Southeast Asia in the latter Khrushchev period, was to reassert Soviet interests in the area. A major motivation for this decision may have been the desire to limit the extension of Chinese Communist influence, advanced by the apparent validation of militant Chinese support for the Viet Cong and the North Vietnamese regime. The reassertion of Soviet interests was dramatized by the visit of Premier Kosygin to Hanoi and North Korea in February, 1965. Stopping in Peking en route, Kosygin continued the effort of the new leadership to effect a *modus vivendi* with the Chinese. From later exchanges of recriminations, it appeared that Kosygin may have been urging Hanoi and Peking to encourage a graceful withdrawal of the United States from the area by allowing negotiations to begin. The Chinese Communist regime, however, was adamant. Fortified by the recent explosion of the first Chinese nuclear device and by the favorable course of events in Vietnam, the Peking leadership refused to support any moves toward negotiation, and offered no terms of reconciliation short of Soviet surrender. Moreover, during the ensuing period the Chinese intensified their attack, accusing the new Soviet leadership of continuing the policy of Khrushchev "revisionism," of sacrificing the interests of the world revolutionary movement to Soviet national interests, and — worst of all — of entering into a collaboration with the American imperialists.

Meanwhile, the United States opted for a heightened commitment in Vietnam to try to stem the deterioration of the position of the Saigon government. American forces were now frankly committed to a combat role, and American military power began to flow into the area in greatly increased volume. The attack by United States planes upon North Vietnam territory, coincident with the visit of Kosygin to Hanoi, dramatically engaged Soviet prestige in the conflict. By the late spring of 1965, Soviet planes and surface-to-air missiles were engaged in unacknowledged combat with American airpower and the Soviet leaders were beginning to talk of the possibility of sending Soviet "volunteers" to support the allied government of North Vietnam. After a declining interest in accepting the hazards of mediation following the spring of 1965, Soviet diplomacy appears to have been temporarily active in encouraging a reliance upon negotiations during the United States bombing lull and "peace offensive" of December, 1965 – January, 1966, but without success. In the period following, particularly after the bombing of oil installations in the vicinity of Hanoi and Haiphong, the Soviet Union turned determinedly away from any role as mediator.

By the time of the Twenty-Third Party Congress, Soviet pronouncements and actions made it clear that there was now little expectation of a return to the kind of *détente* that had prevailed two years earlier; instead, the conviction seems to have taken root that a qualitative change was beginning to alter the international picture. Among the elements associated with the Vietnamese conflict which are cited or implied in the Soviet analysis as signifying a change in the international situation are the following:

1) The increase in military expenditures by the United States, not only for Vietnam, but to raise its military capabilities generally. The United States, said Kosygin at the Congress, "has used the war in Vietnam to begin a new stage in the arms race." He went on to cite the supplementary defense appro-

priations requested by the Administration, and the increased military budget for the next fiscal year. The possibility that the war may continue to expand leads to an expansion of military effort in all categories, and in research and development of new weapons systems; moreover, as it appears to Moscow, the United States is building up mobile forces and acquiring valuable training experience in local and guerilla combat as a result of the conflict in Vietnam, thereby adding to its military capabilities.

2) American policy appears to have taken a turn toward greater militancy. From the Soviet point of view, this seems indicated by the United States effort to use force to reverse the course of a local revolutionary trend. The impression is strengthened by the action of the United States in the Dominican crisis, in the Congo airlift, and by the bombing of North Vietnam. (Purely as a conjecture, it may be added that the frontal challenge to Soviet prestige and influence in Hanoi presented by the bombing of the North, particularly of the Hanoi and Haiphong areas, may have appeared to Moscow as violative of the tacit restraints assumed to exist between the United States and the Soviet Union during the 1963 – 64 period.) Gromyko's references at the Congress to American "preachings of *diktat* and arbitrariness," "glorifying the policy of strength in international relations," and the frequent references to American "violations of international law" and of "norms of international conduct," obviously have a propaganda function but also reflect a Soviet assessment of a change in American policy.

3) The possibility of general war appears greater now than it did two years ago. While the balance of mutual deterrence may still be operative as a restraint against deliberate attack, the risk of escalation out of the Vietnamese conflict, even though unintended, now appears to be given increasing weight in the Soviet outlook. At least, policy no longer proceeds on the assumption that a larger war is out of the question in the foreseeable future.

4) There may be other Vietnams. That is to say, this war may be a forerunner of a whole category of conflicts, arising out of the political turbulence to be seen in Asia, Africa, and Latin America. Some of these conflicts may be in situations which the Soviet Union identifies as "struggles for national liberation," and are more likely now to result in violence than was formerly thought because of the general heightening of the propensity for violence in the underdeveloped world in recent years, and because of the assumed disposition of the United States to interfere in these transitions with force, as the "gendarme of the world."

5) The United States is growing more isolated in the world, and there is a tempting opportunity to derive advantage from furthering this isolation by unifying opposition to the United States under the theme of "anti-imperialism." The slogan of "anti-imperialism" is evidently regarded in the Soviet analysis as an increasingly successful rallying-cry in Europe as well as in the underdeveloped areas.

6) The exploitation of this theme against the United States has also been regarded as advantageous in the context of the Sino-Soviet competition. The Chinese are thereby deprived of an opportunity to capitalize on potent "anti-imperialist" attitudes around the world, and they are also given less grounds for a plausible charge of Soviet-American collusion.

These elements of the international situation growing out of the Vietnamese war as seen from Moscow deeply influenced the whole range of foreign policy projected at the Twenty-Third Congress, although the impression suggested is one of tentativeness, of uncertainty, of changes in degree. The feeling that seems most marked in the discussion is that events have taken over, that the initiative is in the hands of external forces whose shape is not yet clear, and that the main business at hand is not in foreign policy but at home, in the repair of the economy. Also implicit, particularly in the "consensus" tone of Brezhnev's report on behalf of the Central Committee, is the suggestion that events have released many voices from among contending interests in the Soviet bureaucracy, and that many decisions remain to be made, particularly in regard to the allocations of resources and the administration of the economy.

V

One area in which fundamental policy alternatives have been opened up for discussion is that of military doctrine and the nature of military forces to be built. Since early 1965, as a consequence of the change in leadership in the Soviet Union and the intensification of the fighting in Vietnam, arguments have been more widely aired concerning the need for the diversion of additional resources to military purposes in the light of the perceived "dangerous trends" in American policy, although, as might be expected, there have been sharp differences about which services should be the beneficiaries. On the whole, the Soviet leadership appears to have followed a middle course in meeting these pressures. The military budget for 1966 reflected a five percent increase in acknowledged military expenditures, and the new Five-Year Plan allows for some substantial military increases — just how much, it is difficult to say.

Notably, the ground forces, economized upon in favor of the rocket forces since the decline of Zhukov in October, 1957, have tended to come back into their own, along with other theater forces required to strengthen the Soviet capacity to deal with local wars, including nonnuclear wars and, if need be, in distant places. This has meant increases in merchant shipping, amphibious and air-lift capacity, naval infantry, and conventional weapons.

Soviet strategic capabilities, however, are not neglected. From about midsummer, 1965, claims of Soviet advances in this area began to be asserted and demonstrated. At the Congress, the Soviet Defense Minister spoke of new

Soviet capabilities in mobile rocket launchers and of a missile-equipped nuclear submarine which had just completed a trip around the world under water. Implicit in the military discussion is the question whether enlarged research and development expenditures can lead to a technological breakthrough that might make it possible for the Soviet Union to overcome its situation of strategic inferiority. The question appears to be posed with more urgency than in recent years, and the amounts budgeted for scientific research have risen substantially, but no signs of such a potential breakthrough are in sight. Neither an anti-missile deployment nor an orbital missile system holds the promise of a drastic shift in the strategic balance. The deployment of an anti-missile system risks precipitating another upward spiral in the arms race that would greatly increase military expenditures on both sides without any substantial increase in security. On an *a priori* basis, one would surmise that the Soviet leadership is carefully weighing the stimulation of a higher arms race against such disadvantageous economic odds, but the question of anti-missile deployment is complicated on both sides by the existence of smaller nuclear powers, China in particular.

In sum, the partial stabilization in the strategic military field is reduced; the previously accepted assumption that the likelihood of general war was extremely remote is weakened; and the trend toward tacit restraints in the U.S.-Soviet inter-adversary relationship, although still apparent in the Vietnamese conflict, commands less confidence than in the recent past.

The tone of the discussion at the Twenty-Third Congress regarding military preparations is conveyed in the following minatory paragraph from Brezhnev's report:

> We must never forget about the possibility of future trials which can again fall on the shoulders of the Soviet people. In the complex and tense international situation of today, our duty is to display unremitting vigilance. The Party considers it necessary to insure the further development of the defense industry, the perfection of rocket-nuclear weapons, and all other types of equipment. Such are the demands of our homeland's security.

Brezhnev also called for the perfection of civil defense preparations, for the further extension of the current Soviet practice of equipping the Warsaw Pact forces with "the most modern weapons," and for joint training maneuvers with those forces "in the face of the intensified aggressive actions of the imperialist forces headed by the United States of America."

VI

On the political side of Soviet foreign policy, the broad strategy of "peaceful coexistence" is reaffirmed, although in somewhat harder terms and with some new differentiations in political strategy toward the advanced industrial countries and the underdeveloped areas.

Brezhnev's formulation of "peaceful coexistence" at the Congress illustrates the difficulty of reconciling its various aspects:

At the same time that we expose the aggressive policy of imperialism, we consistently and unswervingly pursue a policy of peaceful coexistence of states with different social systems. This means that while regarding the coexistence of states with different social systems as a form of the class struggle between socialism and capitalism, the Soviet Union at the same time consistently advocates normal, peaceful relations with capitalist countries and a settlement of controversial issues between states by negotiation and not by war. . . . Naturally, there can be no peaceful coexistence when it comes to internal processes of the class and national-liberation struggle in the capitalist countries between oppressors and the oppressed, between colonialists and victims of colonial oppression.

Although the various elements involved in this formulation have all been expressed before, this combination of them has an unmistakable unsmiling emphasis upon the "struggle" side of the "peaceful coexistence" strategy. What this means in operational terms becomes clearer from an examination of the policies projected for the industrialized and the underdeveloped areas of the world.

One of the active fronts in recent Soviet diplomacy has been Western Europe and the cultivation of the Pan-European idea. In contrast to the freeze on Soviet relations with the United States and efforts to isolate the United States by an intensive "anti-imperialism" campaign, the Soviet *détente* policy has flowered in relation to Western Europe.

The notion of an "All-European Conference" to discuss European security problems "without outside interference" has been advanced by the Soviet Union and the Warsaw Pact powers without actually pushing for an early convocation of such a meeting. For the time being, the Soviet Union seems content to have the idea in circulation, and perhaps, it has suggested, the convocation might better come, when the time seems ripe, from the neutral nations of Europe, or possibly from Rome, where Foreign Minister Gromyko publicly restated the proposal.

The fullest expression of the idea has come from a statement issued at Bucharest on July 5, 1966, by the Warsaw Treaty members. This makes it clear that the Pan-European proposal has a broader political sweep than the Rapacki or Gomulka proposals, which it may be intended to supplant. Among other things, the measures proposed would liquidate NATO and the Warsaw Pact organization, eliminate United States troops and bases from Europe, bring about recognition of the German Democratic Republic, commit the Federal Republic of Germany not to have access to nuclear weapons in any way, and substitute an all-European trade arrangement for the European Common Market.

The Soviet Union clearly sees the reduction of United States influence in Western Europe as a favorable development, and it has cultivated General de Gaulle with this thought in mind. However, it is not yet clear whether the

Soviet leadership has decided how far it would like to see this political strategy pushed. A central theme in current Soviet propaganda is the liquidation of all foreign military bases and the withdrawal of all foreign troops. At the Party Congress, Gromyko quoted Roosevelt as saying at Yalta that American troops would be out of Europe two years after the war. "Ten times two years has passed," he went on, "but the American Army is still in Europe and by every indication claims a permanent status here. But the peoples of Europe are saying and will yet say their word on this score." In his discussion of the German problem, however, Gromyko evokes the principle of the Potsdam agreement that would imply a continued American presence in Germany.

This is perhaps the heart of the dilemma for the Soviet Union. Under present circumstances, the most obvious immediate effect of the reduction or elimination of American influence from Europe is to strengthen the possibility of the Federal Republic of Germany's becoming the dominant power on the continent, economically, militarily, and politically. This prospect may account for the increasing intensity of the Soviet concentration on the themes of German "militarism and revanchism." Soviet commentators on international affairs have made clear their awareness that the de Gaulle withdrawal from NATO is a mixed blessing. In their opinion, it is leading into a situation in which the Federal Republic now becomes the principal partner of the United States and later, with the decline of American influence, may stand in decisive control of Western Europe and whatever may remain of the Western Alliance.

The Soviet diplomatic response to this problem is by no means fully resolved, but it has begun to move along the following lines, not altogether consistent with each other:

1) A continued campaign to isolate the Federal Republic by hammering away at the themes of "militarism and revanchism."

2) A strong effort to inhibit the military strengthening of the Federal Republic by advancing the nuclear-free zone proposal for Central Europe, and by making the renunciation of access to nuclear weapons by the FRG a condition for West German participation in Pan-European discussions. The Soviet insistence on the exclusion of West German participation in a Multilateral Force, an Atlantic Nuclear Force, or a European Nuclear Force, as a prior condition for a treaty on non-proliferation, is a further effort in this direction; so also is its pressure for the withdrawal of American tactical nuclear weapons under the present "two-key" arrangement from West German territory.

3) An effort to encourage other West European countries — particularly France, Italy, Britain, and the Scandinavian countries — to take the lead in European affairs.

4) The cultivation of political elements within the Federal Republic that seem disposed to improve relations with Eastern Europe and the German Democratic Republic. This, it is believed, is best achieved by dangling the possibility of German unification. Gromyko, at the Party Congress, declared:

"We stand for the normalization and improvement of relations with the Federal German Republic on the basis of its turning to the policy of peaceful cooperation and realism." The Bucharest communique was even more specific:

> As for the unification of the two German states, the road to this goal lies through a relaxation of tension, a gradual rapprochement of the two sovereign German states and agreement between them, through agreements on disarmament in Germany and Europe, and on the basis of the principle that once the unification of Germany is achieved, the united German state will be genuinely peace-loving and democratic. . . .

5) At the same time, the Soviet Union continues to consolidate its position in Eastern Germany, and effectively deepens its commitment to the continued division of Germany. A major theme of Soviet diplomacy and a fundamental Soviet condition for the improvement of relations between Eastern and Western Europe is the recognition of the sovereignty of the German Democratic Republic and the acceptance by the Federal Republic of existing borders.

While the German issue is far and away the central pillar of Soviet policy toward the advanced industrial countries, there are a number of other continuing lines of action in this area which require at least brief mention. The central theme of this part of Soviet policy draws its sanction from Lenin's injunction to play upon differences within the capitalist camp. Gromyko sounds the note in these terms: "Weighing the facts of modern international life, analyzing the differences and shades in the foreign political platforms of bourgeois parties, tendencies, and groupings, one should say that the conclusions drawn by the founder of the Soviet state in the first years of Soviet power are as topical today as then." In practice, this means an increasing effort to differentiate policy in order to take advantage of conflicting interests between and within the Western countries, and to cooperate "with those forces in the bourgeois camp that understand the need to improve international relations."

While accepting the high level of economic growth in Western Europe and the progress of the European Economic Community as a fact of life, Western Communists are enjoined to work within the framework of the Common Market to "democratize" it by using the "anti-monopoly" theme. The French Communist Party is encouraged to increase its political effectiveness by working with "the working class and all the left-wing forces of France." The Italian Party is given encouragement to proceed with its efforts to form a "broad progressive front," and Gromyko's visit to the Vatican was a sign that religious differences should be no ideological barrier to this effort. Kosygin emphasizes that a further expansion of trade with the capitalist countries would be welcomed, and visits by Soviet officials to Canada and Japan have translated this desire into specific terms.

Meanwhile, the Soviet Union has not allowed the Vietnam issue to be compartmentalized in its relations with the U.S., and has thereby sought to exercise some direct pressure by generalizing the tensions of that issue into the fields of cultural exchanges, arms control discussions, and many other forms of overt contact. But the level of tension has been carefully modulated by the continuation of negotiations toward a treaty regarding celestial bodies, by negotiations at the Eighteen-Nation Disarmament Committee in Geneva, and by the preservation of a certain decorum in the everyday business of international life. As noted earlier, Soviet diplomacy seeks to exert indirect pressure upon the United States and a weakening of its international influence by a broad political coalition organized around the twin themes of opposition to imperialism and to war.

VII

While the industrialized areas have always occupied the forefront of Soviet attention because of their capacity to influence the balance of power even by small shifts in orientation, the underdeveloped world has been claiming an increasing share of Soviet attention in recent years for two principal reasons:

1) The dynamism of political life in Asia, Africa, and Latin America, seized by the travails of nation-building, susceptible to sudden violent changes, constantly presents new problems, dangers, and opportunities to which the Soviet leadership finds itself obliged to respond.

2) This area is an important locus of the Sino-Soviet competition, with the consequence that Soviet policy finds itself operating in a triangular configuration, against the West on one side and the Chinese on the other, requiring innovative responses to particular situations according to the strength of interests engaged on each side of the triangle.

As a consequence, both Soviet theory and policy have a particularly tentative character in this sector. In broad terms, Soviet doctrine as reflected in the Brezhnev report to the Twenty-Third Congress tends to distinguish between four categories within the underdeveloped world:

1) "Neo-colonialist" states, which may have achieved political independence, but are dominated by pro-Western regimes;

2) States which are following the "road of progressive social development," or, to use a particular term of art, are moving along the path of "non-capitalist development";

3) Countries which are "building socialism"; and

4) States or political forces which are "fighting for national liberation."

Tactics vary accordingly. Principal attention is focused on the second and fourth categories. In the case of the "neo-colonialist" countries (Saudi Arabia and the Portuguese colonies are mentioned), relations are minimal and the struggles are not in an active phase. As regards the third category, no countries are mentioned by name, reflecting some disappointments in the recent past. At the time of the Twenty-Second Congress, a corresponding category of present or potential "national democracies" included, in addition to Cuba, the names of Indonesia, Ghana, Guinea, and Mali. The whole discussion of how states might evolve from "national democracy" to "socialism" (in the Soviet sense) received minimal attention at the 1966 Congress.

Instead, the second category has been enlarged, to embrace countries that are not pro-Western in orientation, and that are engaged in processes of social change which are accepted as "progressive," even though they may not correspond with the Soviet conception of socialism. A great deal of sad experience in the recent past has moved the Soviet Union to take a much less doctrinaire view of indigenous forms of socialism. In his report, Brezhnev indicates an attitude of broad tolerance toward the states that are following the "non-capitalist path of development":

> Major social reforms have been carried out in such countries as the United Arab
> Republic, Algeria, Mali, Guinea, Congo Brazzaville, and Burma. . . .It goes without
> saying that the form and scale of these processes vary in different countries. The
> revolutionary creative work of the people who have proclaimed the construction of
> socialism as their objective introduces distinctive features into the forms of move-
> ment along the road of social progress.

Brezhnev indicates a willingness to continue collaboration with nationalist leaders in these areas, but he goes on to say that the closer these countries come to socialism, the better their relations are likely to be with the Soviet Union.

The developments in Algeria, Ghana, and Indonesia posed especially painful problems for the Soviet Union. For a while, Soviet analysts toyed with the conception of "proletarian democratic dictatorships" to deal with the phenomenon of military dictatorships potentially anti-Western in outlook, but this formulation did not make its appearance at the Congress. Brezhnev confined himself to a modest hope for an improvement of relations with Indonesia, and a plea for an end to the mass slaughter of Communists in that country.

Category four, however, is where the action is. Here are the liveliest questions about future decisions to be made in Soviet foreign policy. In those conflict situations defined as "struggles for national liberation," Soviet leaders have already made it plain that the strategy of "peaceful coexistence" does not apply. However, the questions remain — how active Soviet intervention should be, whether it should operate directly or only through intermediaries, how great a risk of general war this might entail and what enlargement of Soviet capabilities would be required to intervene effectively in a number of such local conflict situations? The last question particularly depends upon the Soviet assessment of whether United States policy in Vietnam and in the Dominican Republic reflects a general American intention to intervene actively and with force wherever pro-Communist movements are successful.

The other side of Soviet policy is illustrated by its response to the fighting between India and Pakistan over Kashmir, a conflict which was not regarded as a "struggle for national liberation." The success of Soviet mediation at Tashkent was hailed as a victory for "socialist diplomacy . . . something completely new in the practice of international relations," and Gromyko spoke proudly at the Congress of the widespread recognition and respect gained for the Soviet Union as a result of this act of statesmanship.

These two experiences, Tashkent and Vietnam, open up and define a spectrum of possible responses to local conflict situations. In each case, Soviet policy was directed toward containing the expansion of Chinese influence, and in the former case, the Soviet and Western interests were not in sharp opposition.

Several other aspects of Soviet policy toward the underdeveloped areas require at least passing mention. Relatively little attention is given to Latin America in current Soviet discussions; the prospects there are clearly for the future rather than for the immediate present, and little encouragement is given to Cuban efforts to stimulate an active revolutionary front on that continent. Soviet representatives at the Tri-Continental Conference in Havana during January, 1966, did sound like revolutionary enthusiasts, but Moscow took pains afterwards through diplomatic channels to disassociate itself from these sentiments. At the Twenty-Third Party Congress, the Cuban spokesman was alone in trying to drum up enthusiasm for a policy of revolutionary militancy.

Soviet economic aid programs have shown some modest increases, after declining in recent years. Most of these programs take the form of long-term, low-interest credits, and are concentrated in relatively few countries. The largest recipients by far are India and Egypt, and recently Soviet and Eastern European economic aid programs have been extended into Africa.

Finally, in this connection, it should be noted that Brezhnev implied a possibly greater interest in the United Nations, anticipating that the great increase in the number of new nations admitted to that organization might operate, if not in the Soviet favor, at least against the interests of the United States. The context of his remarks, however, emphasized the potentialities of the organization "as an arena of active political struggle," rather than as an instrument of conciliation and collaboration.

Conclusions

It is manifest, even in so brief a review of the principal trends in recent Soviet foreign policy, that the area of choice is severely constricted in comparison to the complexity of the environment in which this policy must operate. The possibility of further violence in the underdeveloped areas; the rise of nationalism in the world, with its prospects of further fragmentation and disorder; possibilities for upsetting technological developments in weapons; uncertainties regarding the future unfolding of Chinese behavior in the world — those are but a few of the determinants to which the Soviet leaders will find themselves obliged to respond in the period ahead.

And yet the area of choice, though limited, remains decisive.

The Soviet leadership can decide whether the most effective response to the Chinese challenge is by proving its revolutionary militancy, or by championing the issue of peace.

The Soviet leadership can decide whether to try for short-term advantages in a political campaign against the United States, or to make the effort to restore some measure of restraint in their competitive relationship — provided, of course, the United States makes a reciprocal effort in this direction.

The Soviet leadership can decide whether to ride the crest of a wave of revolutionary violence in the former colonial territories, or to make an effort toward collaboration in international procedures to contain and pacify these conflicts.

Most important of all, it will be for the Soviet leadership to decide whether a competition for military advantage under conditions of an uncontrolled arms race better serves Soviet long-term interests than the compromises that would be required (and not from the Soviet Union alone) to allow for some safeguards against the increasing risk of war.

Index

471